the ULTIMATE
ENCYCLOPEDIA *of*
WINE, BEER,
SPIRITS *&* LIQUEURS

the ULTIMATE
ENCYCLOPEDIA *of*
WINE, BEER,
SPIRITS *&* LIQUEURS

STUART WALTON AND BRIAN GLOVER

HH
HERMES
HOUSE

This edition is published by Hermes House, an imprint of Anness Publishing Ltd
Hermes House, 88–89 Blackfriars Road, London SE1 8HA
tel. 020 7401 2077; fax 020 7633 9499
www.hermeshouse.com; www.annesspublishing.com

If you like the images in this book and would like to investigate using them for publishing, promotions
or advertising, please visit our website www.practicalpictures.com for more information.

Publisher: Joanna Lorenz
Senior Editor: Linda Fraser
Illustrations: Madeleine David
Maps: Steven Sweet
Designers: Siân Keogh, Sheila Volpe and Sara Kidd
Cover Design: Claire Baggaley

A CIP catalogue record for this book is available from the British Library.

ETHICAL TRADING POLICY
Because of our ongoing ecological investment programme, you, as our customer, can have the
pleasure and reassurance of knowing that a tree is being cultivated on your behalf to naturally replace
the materials used to make the book you are holding. For further information about this scheme,
go to www.annesspublishing.com/trees

PUBLISHER'S NOTE
Although the advice and information in this book are believed to be accurate and true at the time of going to press, neither the
authors nor the publisher can accept any legal responsibility or liability for any errors or omissions that may be made.

CONTENTS

Introduction 6

Wine 10

Principles of Tasting 12

Storing and Serving 14

Glasses 18

Drinking Wine with Food 20

Labelling 24

France 26

Europe, Africa and the East 80

Rest of the World 132

Beer 184

Ingredients 186

Styles of Beer 202

A World Tour 214

Spirits 392

Liqueurs 438

Fortified Wines 484

Non-Alcoholic Mixers 500

Index 502

INTRODUCTION

Alcoholic drinks have been inextricably bound up with man's history since time immemorial. Precisely when grain and grape were first deliberately fermented is not known, but it is certain that by the time of the Pharaohs, both brewing and wine-making were well established. Archeologists excavating ancient tombs have found the remains of beer, while on the walls were paintings of grapes being harvested and crushed, and wine being stored in clay vessels.

The first documentary evidence of beer-making was discovered on clay tablets dating from the Sumerian or Mesopotamian civilization, which flourished over 5,000 years ago in the fertile lands between the Tigris and the Euphrates rivers, in what is now Iraq. Inscriptions on tablets described more than twenty different varieties of beer, and even included recipes based on beer.

The making of intoxicating drinks probably developed independently more or less the world over. In Africa, sorghum and millet were the preferred grains, while the ancient Chinese used millet and rice. In Latin America, the Aztecs had their own beer gods, while Brazilian Indians produced dark, smoky-tasting brews from manioc roots and grain roasted over hardwood fires. South American Indian women made a drink called chicha by chewing maize kernels, spitting them out into pots, mixing the mush with water and leaving it to ferment.

Wine played a central role in the lives of ancient Greeks and Romans, as evidenced by their paintings and writings, and the beautiful vessels they made for storing and drinking the beverage. The ancient Greeks liked their wine strong and heavy. They spread grapes on wicker trays and dried them in the sun before

Right: Turning the drying germinated barley in the peat kiln at Glendronach Distillery near Huntly, Banffshire, Scotland.

making them into wine. The Romans had similar tastes, and concentrated their wines by pouring them into amphorae and exposing them to heat. Wine was traditionally diluted with water before being served.

In classical Greece and later Rome, wine was also used in cooking, not initially as a means of adding flavour, but as a marinade. The discovery that the acids in wine could be used as a tenderizer proved a boon, especially as meat often came from older animals and could prove extremely tough. As well as making tough meat more supple, marinating removed excess salt from meats that had been encrusted with it, or soaked in brine, for preservation. Wine vinegar, its alcohol lost to acetic acid, may have been used initially, but wine itself appears in sauce recipes in the historically important late Roman cookery book of Apicus (3rd century AD). The wine itself was commonly infused with spices to mask the rank flavours of oxidation or acetification.

The Romans were great ambassadors for wine. They planted vines in many of the countries they conquered, including modern-day Germany, Austria and France, all of which had hitherto been home to beer-drinkers. In the 1st century AD, the Roman historian Tacitus stated that beer was the usual drink of Germans and Gauls, while Pliny the Elder wrote in AD77 that the tribes of Western Europe made "an intoxicating drink from corn steeped in water".

In medieval times, beer continued to be the principal drink of the cooler climes of northern Europe, although the spread of Christianity meant that some grapes were cultivated so that wine could be made for religious ceremonies. In southern Europe, wine reigned supreme.

Beer-making on a substantial scale was the preserve of the religious orders. Many of the monastic settlements that sprang up across Europe from the 5th century onwards had large breweries. The monasteries supplied not only their

Right: This burbling stream provides one of the essential ingredients for whisky distillation – clear spring water.

own needs, but also those of thirsty travellers and pilgrims.

Beer was also brewed at home, where it was viewed as a domestic score, on a par with cooking and cleaning. In medieval Britain, most ale was produced by women known as "ale wives". The most successful of these early home brewers attracted people to their houses, which became the social centres (public houses) of the community.

Spirits, liqueurs and fortified wines differ from wine and beer in that they all depend to some degree on distillation. Even the fortified wines – sherry, port, Madeira and the like – are made stronger (and in some cases naturally sweeter) than ordinary wine by the addition of a distillate.

Distillation (from the Latin *destillare*, to drip) is the process of evaporating or boiling a liquid and condensing its vapour. Alcohol has a lower boiling point than water (about 78˚C compared to 100˚C) so when a fermented drink is heated, the alcohol vaporizes some time before the water is driven off as steam. When the alcohol vapour hits a cool surface, it condenses and reverts to a liquid with a much higher percentage of alcohol than the original drink. If the condensed liquid is boiled up again, and the procedure repeated, the alcohol content in the condensed liquid will be even higher.

Much academic debate has been generated in the last 30 years or so as to when and where distillation was first discovered. The Greek philosopher Aristotle, who lived in the 4th century BC, writes of distillation as a means of purifying seawater to make it drinkable. He comments in passing that the same treatment can be given to wine, which is reduced thereby to a sort of "water". He was tantalizingly close to the breakthrough, but the experiment did no more than prove for him that wine is just a form of modified water, and that a liquid can only derive flavour from whatever happens to be mixed with the water that forms its base.

The documented beginnings of systematic and scientifically founded distillation, at least in Europe, come from the celebrated medical school at Salerno around AD1100. Wine had long been regarded as having a range of medicinal properties (a view that has once again found favour in the 1990s), and alcohol was believed to be the active ingredient that gave wine its healing powers. The extraction of what was held to be the soul or spirit of the wine (the alcohol), through distillation, is what led to the naming of distillates as "spirits".

"Alcohol" was originally a generic term applied to any product arrived at by a process of vaporizing and condensation. The word owes its origin to al-kuhl, an Arabic term describing the practice of producing a black powder by condensing a vapour of the metal antimony. The powder was used cosmetically, and the name survives as kohl, a black eye-liner used primarily in India.

It was not until the 16th century that "alcohol" was used specifically with reference to distilled spirits.

The medicinal uses of spirits were to endure for hundreds of years. It was Arnaldo de Villanova, a Catalan physician of the 13th century, who first coined the Latin term *aqua vitae*, "water of life", for distilled spirits, indicating that they were still held to be associated with the promotion of vitality and health. (That term lives on in the Scandinavian aquavit, the French eau de vie and similar spirituous names.)

The earliest distillates were almost certainly derived from wine, since it had a more salubrious and exalted image than did beer, but grain distillation to produce the first whiskies and neutral spirits followed, in the Middle Ages. Many of these prototypes contained herb and spice extracts, or were flavoured with fruit, in order to enhance their medicinal properties. The additives also conveniently masked what must have been the fairly raw taste and off-putting aroma of the unadulterated liquor. Anyone who has smelt and tasted clear spirit dribbling off the still in a brandy distillery (or, for that matter, has had a brush with illicit Irish poteen or American moonshine) will know how far such untreated spirit is from the welcoming smoothness of five-star cognac or single malt Scotch. The infused distillates were the antecedents of many of the

Right: An original pot still has become a museum piece at the Jameson Heritage Centre, Midleton, County Cork.

traditional aromatic liqueurs and flavoured vodkas of today.

That, for centuries, was the official account of the birth of distilled spirits. In 1961, however, an Indian food historian, O. Prakash, argued that there was evidence that distillation of rice and barley beer was practised in India around 800 BC. If so, it probably arrived there from China even earlier. The current theory cautiously credits the Chinese as the discoverers of the art.

It seems strange that soldiers of Alexander the Great failed to encounter distilled alcohol when they invaded India in 327BC. The campaign is credited with having brought back rice itself to Europe, but rice spirit appears to have been overlooked. Perhaps, if it was drunk at all by the invaders, it was diluted, and was not therefore perceived to be any higher in alcohol than the grape wine with which they were familiar.

The original and still widespread distillation vessel, used in the Cognac region of France, as well as by the whisky distillers of Scotland, is the pot still. It consists of the only three elements absolutely essential to the process: a pot in which the fermented product (malted grains, wine, cider etc.) is heated; the alembic, or tube, through which the alcohol vapour driven off is sucked; and the condenser where the steam is cooled and reliquified. To obtain a better quality product, spirits are generally distilled at least twice for greater refinement, so the still has to be started up again. Moreover, not all of the condensed vapour is suitable for use in fine liquor. The first and last portions of it to pass through (known as the "heads" and "tails") are generally discarded due to the relatively high level of impurities they contain. The invention of the continuous still in the early 19th century, in which the process carries on to a second distillation uninterrupted, made spirit production more economical and easier to control. This is the method used to produce France's other classic brandy, armagnac, and the continuous still is now the preferred apparatus for most spirits production worldwide.

Probably the first spirit to be taken seriously as an object of connoisseurship, as distinct from being purely medicinal (or just a method of using surplus grapes or grain), was the brandy of the Cognac region of western France. It was noticed that the superior, mellower

Above: The final character, precise colour, and the richness and roundness of flavour of both cognac and whisky are derived from the final maturation period in wood.

Left: Copper pot stills – the original distillation vessel – are widely used in the Cognac region of France as well as by the whisky distillers of Scotland.

spirit produced by the light wines of Cognac responded particularly well to ageing in oak casks. The casks were traditionally fashioned out of wood from the Limousin forests of the region. Cask-aged spirits derive every bit of their final character from the precise shade of tawny in the colour to their richness and round-ness of flavour, from the maturation period they undergo in wood. They will not continue to develop in the bottle. The complex classification system for cognac in operation today is based on the length of time the spirit has been aged. It is testimony to a reputation for painstaking quality that dates back to around the end of the 1600s.

Scottish and Irish whiskies rose to similar prominence not long after. Their differing production processes result in distinct regional styles, depending on the quantities of peat used in the kilns where the malted grain is dried, the quality of the spring water used in the mash, and, some have claimed, the shape of the still.

Varieties of whisky are made across the world these days, from North America to Japan, but all attempts to replicate the precise taste of great Scotch - for all that the ingredients and procedures may be almost exactly identical - have inexplicably foundered.

Where a distilled drink stops being a spirit and turns into a liqueur is something of an elusive question. The one constant is that, to be a liqueur, a drink should have some obvious aromatizing element. This doesn't mean that all flavoured distillates are liqueurs – flavoured vodkas are still vodka – but there are no neutral liqueurs. Some of these products have histories at least as venerable as those of cognac and Scotch. The most notable are those produced by the old French monastic orders. Bénédictine, the herby, cognac-based potion that originated at the monastery in Fécamp, in Normandy, can convincingly lay claim to a lineage that rolls back to the beginning of the 16th century.

The first and greatest cocktail era, which arrived with the advent of the Jazz Age in the 1920s, rescued a lot of the traditional liqueurs from the niches of obscurity into which popular taste had relegated them. The Bénédictine monks may have been a little shocked to hear that their revered creation was being mixed with English gin, American applejack, apricot brandy and maple

Above: The all-important water that flows through an old-fashioned water wheel at a traditional distillery in Northern Ireland.

syrup, shaken to within an inch of its life and then rechristened the Mule's Hind Leg, but at least it was drunk - as were any giggling flappers unwise enough to knock back three of four of them.

Cocktails continue to prove popular, especially in the USA and the Caribbean, where clubs and dedicated bars promote new blends as well as old favourites, largely based on the "big five": whisky, gin, vodka, white rum and brandy.

The Ultimate Encyclopedia of Wine, Beer, Spirits and Liqueurs is the most comprehensive guide ever to alcohol-based drinks and mixers, providing worldwide information on styles, storing, serving and tasting, so whether you're a serious student of the subject, or merely a social drinker who's a bit of a thinker, this excellent volume will provide the perfect excuse for whiling away a happy hour or two in a comfortable armchair – with your favourite tipple, of course.

WINE

PRINCIPLES *of* TASTING

All that sniffing, swirling and spitting that the professional winetasters engage in is more than just a way of showing off; it really can immeasurably enhance the appreciation of any wine.

THE WINETASTER'S ritual of peering into a glass, swirling it around and sniffing suspiciously at it, before taking a mouthful only to spit it out again looks like a highly mysterious and technical procedure to the uninitiated. It is, however, a sequence of perfectly logical steps that can immeasurably enhance the enjoyment of good wine. Once learned, they become almost second nature to even the novice taster.

Don't pour a full glass for tasting because you're going to need room for swirling, but allow a little more than the wine waiter in a restaurant tends to offer. About a third full is the optimum amount.

When pouring a tasting sample, be sure to leave enough room in the glass for giving it a good swirl (below).

Firstly, have a good look at the wine by holding it up to the daylight or other light source. Is it clear or cloudy? Does it contain sediment or other solid matter? In the case of red wines, tilt the glass away from you against a white surface and look at the colour of the liquid at the far edge. Older wines start to fade at the rim, the deep red taking on an autumnal brownish or tawny hue.

Now swirl the glass gently. The point of this is to activate the aromatic compounds in the wine, so that when you come to stick your nose in, the bouquet can be fully appreciated. Swirling takes a bit of practice (start with a glass of water over the kitchen sink) but the aim is to get a fairly vigorous wave circulating in the liquid. If you are nervous about performing the swirl in mid-air, there is nothing wrong with doing it while the glass is still on the table and then bringing it to your nose, but beware of scraping your best crystal around on a rough wooden tabletop.

When sniffing, tilt the glass towards your face and get your nose slightly inside it, keeping it within the lower half of the opening of the glass. The head should be bent forward a little with the glass tipped at a 45° angle to meet it. Inhale gently (as if you were sniffing a flower, not filling your lungs on a blustery clifftop) and for a good three or four seconds. The scents a wine offers may change during the course of one sniff. Nosing a wine can reveal a great deal about its origins and the way it was made, but don't overdo it. The sense of smell is quickly neutralized. Two or three sniffs should tell you as much as you need to know.

Now comes the tricky part. The reason that wine experts pull those ridiculous faces when they take a mouthful is that they are trying to spread the wine around all the different taste-sensitive parts of the tongue. At its very tip are the receptors for sweetness. Just a little back from those, saltiness is registered. Acidity or sourness is tasted on the sides of the tongue, while bitterness is sensed at the very back. So roll the wine around your mouth as thoroughly as you can.

It helps to maximize the flavour of a wine if you take in air while it's in your mouth. To reduce the risk of dribbling, make sure the head is now back in an upright position. Using gentle suction with the lips pursed, draw in some breath. It will only be necessary to allow the tiniest opening – less than the width of a pencil – and to suck in immediately. Again, practise over the sink. Close the lips again, and breathe downwards through the nose. In this way, the taste of the wine is transmitted through the nasal passages as well as via the tongue, and the whole sensation is more intense. And *think* about the taste. What messages is the wine giving you? Do you like it or not?

When you have tasted the mouthful of wine, you can either swallow it – much the best thing in polite company – or, if you are tasting a number of wines at a time of day when you wouldn't normally be drinking, then spit it out. At public tastings, there will be buckets or lined boxes for spitting into, or else at an outdoor fair or in a marquee at a wine show, spit it out on the ground, taking care not to spray the shoes of unsuspecting passers-by. Spit confidently, with the tongue behind the ejected liquid, so as to avoid it trickling down your chin, but spit downwards. You are not aiming to extinguish a fire.

There are five principal elements to look for in the taste of a wine. Learn to concentrate on each one individually while tasting, and you will start to put together a set of analytical tools with which to evaluate the quality of any wine.

Dryness/Sweetness From bone-dry Chablis at one end of the spectrum to the most luscious Liqueur Muscats at the other, through a broad range of intermediary styles, the amount of natural sugar a wine contains is perhaps its most easily noted attribute.

Acidity There are many different types of acid in wine, the most important being tartaric, which is present in unfermented grape juice. How sharp does the wine feel at the edges of the tongue? Good acidity is necessary to contribute a feeling of freshness to a young wine, and to help the best wines to age. In a poor vintage though, when the grapes didn't ripen properly, an excessive sourness or even bitterness can spoil a wine. Don't confuse dryness with acidity. A very dry wine like fino sherry can actually be quite low in acid, while the sweetest Sauternes will contain sufficient acidity to offset its sugar.

Tannin Tannin is present in the stalks and pips (seeds) of fresh grapes, but also in the skins. Since the colour in red wine comes from the skins (the juice of even black grapes being colourless), some tannin is inevitably extracted along with it. In the mouth, it gives that furry, drying feeling that makes very young reds hard to drink, but it disappears gradually as they mature in the bottle.

Oak Many wines are matured in oak barrels, and may even have gone through their initial fermentation in oak, and the flavour imparted to them by contact with the wood is an easy one to appreciate, particularly in the case of whites. An aroma or taste of vanilla or other sweet spice such as nutmeg or cinnamon is a strong indicator of the presence of oak, as is an overall feeling of creamy smoothness on the palate in the case of the richer reds. If the barrels a wine was kept in were heavily charred (or "toasted") on the insides, the wine will display a pronounced smokiness like toast left under the grill a little too long or a match that has just been blown out.

Fruit Anybody who has read a newspaper or magazine wine column in which the writer describes wines as tasting of raspberries, passion fruit, melon and glacé (candied) cherries (often all at once) will have wondered if there isn't an element of kiddology in it all. In fact, there are sound biochemical reasons for the resemblance of wines to the flavours of other foods (and not just fruit, but vegetables, herbs and spices too). In the sections on the main grape varieties, I have suggested some of the flavours most commonly met with in the wines made from those grapes. Let your imagination run free when tasting. Bright fruit flavours are among the most charming features a wine can possess.

A gentle swirling action of the hand is sufficient to produce quite a vigorous wave in the glass (above).

Sniff lightly and long, with the nose slightly below the rim of the glass (above).

Take a good mouthful of the wine, in order to coat all surfaces of the mouth with it (above).

STORING *and* SERVING

Where is the best place to keep wine for maturation? Should it be allowed to breathe before being served? What does decanting an old wine involve? None of these questions is as technical as it seems.

NONE OF THE TECHNICALITIES involved in the storage and serving of wine needs to be too complicated. The following guidelines are aimed at keeping things simple. **Creating a cellar** Starting a wine collection requires a certain amount of ingenuity now that most of us live in flats or houses without cellars. If you have bought a large parcel of wine that you don't want to touch for years, you can pay a nominal fee to a wine merchant to cellar it for you, but the chances are that you may only have a couple of dozen bottles at any one time. Where to keep it?

The two main points to bear in mind are that bottles should be stored horizontally and away from sources of heat. You can pile them on top of each other if they are all the same shape, but it's safer and more convenient to invest in a simple wooden or plastic wine rack. Keeping the bottles on their sides means the wine is in constant contact with the corks, preventing them from drying out and imparting off-flavours to the wine.

Don't put your bottles in the cupboard next to the storage heater or near the cooker because heat is a menace to wine. Equally, don't leave it

A simple wine rack is much the best way of storing bottles (right). This one allows enough space to see the labels too, so that they don't have to be pulled out to identify them.

in the garden shed in sub-zero temperatures. Choose a cool cupboard that's not too high up (remember that heat rises) and where it can rest in peace in the dark.

Serving temperatures The conventional wisdom that white wine should be served chilled and red wine at room temperature is essentially correct, but it isn't the whole story.

Don't over-chill white wine or its flavours will be muted. Light, acidic whites, sparkling wines and very sweet wines (and rosés too for that matter) should be served at no higher than about 10°C (50°F) but the best Chardonnays, dry Semillons and Alsace wines can afford to be a little less cool than that.

Reds, on the other hand, generally benefit from being slightly cooler than the ambient temperature in a well-heated home. Never warm the bottle by a radiator as that will make the wine taste muddy. Some lighter, fruity reds such

as young Beaujolais, Dolcetto or the lighter Loire or New Zealand reds are best served lightly chilled – about an hour in the refrigerator.

Breathing Should red wine be allowed to breathe? In the case of matured reds that are intended to be drunk on release, like Rioja Reservas or the softer, barrel-aged Cabernet Sauvignons of Australia, the answer is that there is probably no point. Young reds with some tannin, or immature hard acidity, do round out with a bit of air contact, though. Either pour the wine into a decanter or jug (pitcher) half an hour or so before serving or, if you haven't anything suitable for the table, pour it into another container and then funnel it back into the bottle. Simply drawing the cork won't in itself make any difference because only the wine in the neck is in contact with the air. And remember the wine will develop in any case in the glass as you slowly sip it.

Here is an ingeniously designed winerack that ensures that the undersides of the corks are kept constantly in contact with the wine, thus preventing them from drying out.

Corkscrews The spin-handled corkscrew is undoubtedly the easiest to use because it involves one continuous motion and very little effort. The type with side-levers is less good because it often needs two or three attempts with longer corks. If you are good at displays of brute force, the Wine Waiter's Friend is the model for you, but a particularly obstinate cork can make you look very silly. The widely used synthetic corks with which many cheaper wines are sealed are far more likely to stick fast in the neck than real cork, and have become a bit of a bugbear in this regard. They can break a plastic corkscrew. By contrast, screwcaps – now being used by many Southern Hemisphere producers for all quality levels of wine – mean you can leave the corkscrew in the drawer. These too can be stubborn though, in which case, resort to that gadget for removing stiff lids from jars.

The Spin-handled Screwpull (above) was the corkscrew that revolutionized the business of bottle opening. Not only does it require very little in the way of brute force, but it virtually never breaks a cork in two. That is because the screw itself (or thread) is so long.

The most basic type of corkscrew (above left) involves simply tugging. The levered model (above right) can sometimes break a long or old cork. A bottle with a screwcap (right) avoids the need for any sort of special implement at all. There are now three kinds of bottle closure (far right): natural cork, synthetic cork and the Stelvin or screwcap.

Opening fizz Many people are still intimidated about opening sparkling wines. Remember that the longer a bottle of fizz has been able to rest before opening, the less lively it will be. If it has been very badly shaken up, it may need a week or more to settle. Also, the colder it is, the less likely it will be to go off like a firecracker.

Once the foil has been removed and the wire cage untwisted and taken off too, grasp the cork firmly and take hold of the lower half of the bottle. The advice generally given is to turn the bottle rather than the cork, but in practice most people probably do both (twisting in opposite directions, of course). Work very gently and, when you feel or see the cork beginning to rise, control it every millimetre of the way with your thumb over the top. It should be possible then to ease it out without it popping. If the wine does spurt, put a finger in the neck, but don't completely stopper it again.

When pouring, fill each glass to just under half-full, and then go round again to top them up once the initial fizz has subsided. Pour fairly slowly so that the wine doesn't foam over the sides. Do not pour into tilted glasses: you aren't serving lager.

Decanting Decanting can help to make a tough young wine a bit more supple, but it is only absolutely necessary if the wine being served is heavily sedimented. In that case, stand the bottle upright for the best part of the day you intend to serve it (from the night before is even better) so that the deposits settle to the bottom. After uncorking, pour the wine in a slow but continuous stream into the decanter, looking into the neck of the bottle. When the sediment starts working its way into the neck as you reach the end, stop pouring. The amount of wine you are left with should be negligible enough to throw away, but if there's more than half a glass, then strain the remainder through a clean muslin cloth. Do *not* use coffee filter-papers or tissue as they will alter the flavour of the wine.

When opening sparkling wines, it is important to restrain the release of the cork (left). Control it every millimetre of the way once it begins to push out.

The quicker you pour, the more vigorous will be the foaming of the wine in the glass (left). Pour carefully to avoid any wastage through overflowing.

The Champagne Saver is a good way of preserving the fizz in any unfinished bottles of sparkling wine (left). Some swear, quite unscientifically, by inserting a spoon-handle in the neck.

GLASSES

Wine doesn't have to be served in the most expensive glassware to show it to advantage, but there are a few basic principles to bear in mind when choosing glasses that will help you get the best from your bottle.

Glasses these days come in all shapes and sizes (below). From left to right in the foreground are: a good red or white wine glass; a technically correct champagne flute; the famous "Paris goblet" much beloved of wine-bars, not a bad shape but too small; an elegant-looking but inefficient sparkling wine glass with flared opening, causing greater dispersal of bubbles; a sherry copita, also useful for other fortified wines.

ALTHOUGH I CAN scarcely remember any champagne that tasted better than the stuff we poured into polystyrene cups huddled in my student quarters after the examination results went up, the truth is that, certainly when you're in the mood to concentrate, it does make a difference what you drink wine from. Not only the appearance but the smell and, yes, even the taste of a wine can be substantially enhanced by using the proper glasses.

They don't have to be prohibitively costly, although – as with everything else – the best doesn't come cheap. The celebrated Austrian glassmaker Georg Riedel has taken the science of wine glasses to its ultimate degree, working out what specific aromatic and flavour components in each type of wine need emphasizing, and designing his glasses accordingly. Some of

them are very peculiar shapes indeed, but they undeniably do the trick.

There are some broad guidelines that we can all follow, however, when choosing glasses. Firstly, always choose a plain glass to set off your best wines. Coloured ones, or even those that have just the stems and bases tinted, can distort the appearance of white wines particularly. And, although cut crystal can look very beautiful, I tend to avoid it for wines because it doesn't make for the clearest view of the liquid in the glass.

Look for a deep, wide bowl that tapers significantly towards the mouth. With glasses like that, the aromatic compounds in the wine can be released more generously, both because the deeper bowl allows for a more demonstrative swirling action than anything too small, and because the narrower opening channels the

scents of the wine to your nostrils more efficiently. A flared opening disperses much of the bouquet to the surrounding air.

Traditionally, red wine is served in bigger glasses than white. If you are serving both colours at a grand gastronomic evening, it helps to allot different wines their particular glasses, but the assumption is that reds, especially mature wines, need more space in which to breathe. More development of the wine will take place in the glass than in any decanter or jug the wine may have been poured into. If you are only buying one size, though, think big. A wine glass can never be too large.

Sparkling wines should be served in flutes, tall thin glasses with straight sides, so that the mousse or fizz is preserved. The old champagne

saucers familiar from the films (and originally modelled, as the legend has it, on the breast of Marie Antoinette) are inefficient because the larger surface area causes higher dispersal of bubbles and flattens the wine more quickly. Having said that, I have to confess a sneaking fondness for them myself, at least for a more riotous occasion.

Fortified wines should be served in smaller, narrower versions of the ordinary wine glass in recognition of their higher alcoholic strength. The *copita*, traditional glass of the sherry region, is a particularly elegant receptacle and will do quite well for the other fortifieds too. Don't use your tiniest liqueur glasses, though; apart from looking spectacularly mean, they allow no room for enjoying the wine's aromas.

These three glasses (left) are all perfectly shaped for tasting. The one on the right is the official international tasting-glass.

DRINKING WINE *with* FOOD

Matching the right wine to its appropriate dish may seem like a gastronomic assault course but there are broad principles that can be easily learned. And very few mistakes are complete failures.

A T ONE TIME, the rules on choosing wines to accompany food seemed hearteningly simple. It was just a matter of remembering: white wine with fish and poultry, red wine with red meats and cheese, with sherry to start and port to finish. In recent years, that picture has become much more complicated, although its essential principles were mostly fairly sound. Today, magazines frequently run tastings to find wines that match a variety of increasingly exotic dishes, often created specifically for the article in question. And there is a whole library of books devoted to advising you, often in maniacal detail, what to drink with what, with many suggestions seeming to strive after novelty for its own sake.

The exceptions to the original rules continue to multiply. Port is fashionable as an aperitif in France, the meatier types of fish, such as swordfish and tuna, are often found to go well with light reds, while it has now become almost a cliché to observe that most cheeses are happier with white wines than with reds.

What is clear is that this is one of those areas in which there are no fixed rules. Even though a particular dish may be a firm favourite, why drink the same type of wine with it every time?

The following are rough guidelines that incorporate some less obvious suggestions that you may not have thought of. At best, a particular partnership of wine and food adds up to something greater than the sum of its parts. At worst, a strongly flavoured food might strip the wine of some of its complexity, and make it taste rather ordinary – a phenomenon that becomes more distressing in direct proportion to the cost of the wine. But on the whole you can afford to be bold: very few combinations actually clash.

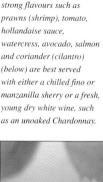

Pre-dinner nibbles with strong flavours such as prawns (shrimp), tomato, hollandaise sauce, watercress, avocado, salmon and coriander (cilantro) (below) are best served with either a chilled fino or manzanilla sherry or a fresh, young dry white wine, such as an unoaked Chardonnay.

APERITIFS

The two classic (and best) appetite-whetters are sparkling wine and dry sherry. Choose a light, non-vintage champagne (blanc de blancs is a particularly good style to start things off with) or one of the lighter California or New Zealand sparklers. If you are serving highly seasoned canapés, olives or nuts before the meal, dry sherry is better. Always serve a freshly opened bottle of good fino or manzanilla. Kir has become quite trendy again: add a dash of cassis or other blackcurrant liqueur to a glass of crisp dry white (classically Bourgogne Aligoté) or to bone-dry fizz for a Kir Royale.

FIRST COURSES

Soups In general, liquidized soups are happier without wine, although thickly textured versions containing cream can be successful with richer styles of fizz, such as blanc de noirs champagne. A small glass of one of the nuttier-tasting fortified wines such as amontillado sherry or Sercial madeira is a good friend to a meaty consommé. Bulky soups such as minestrone may benefit from a medium-textured Italian red (Chianti or Montepulciano d'Abruzzo) to kick off a winter dinner.

Fish pâtés Light, dry whites without overt fruit are best: Chablis, Alsace Pinot Blanc, Muscadet *sur lie*, German Riesling Kabinett, young Viura from Navarra. But serve something more robust such as young white Rioja or fino sherry with the oilier fish like mackerel.

Chicken or pork liver pâtés Go for a big, pungently flavoured white – Alsace Gewürztraminer, California Fumé Blanc, Hunter Valley Semillon – or a midweight, soft red such as Valpolicella, Valdepeñas, a light *cru* Beaujolais like Brouilly or Chiroubles with a couple of years' bottle-age or red Sancerre.

Smoked salmon Needs a hefty white such as Gewürztraminer or Pinot Gris from Alsace, or an oak-fermented Chardonnay from the Côte de Beaune or California.

Melon The sweeter-fleshed aromatic varieties require a wine with its own assertive sweetness. Try noble-rotted Muscat or Riesling from Washington or California, or even young Canadian Ice Wine.

Prawns, shrimp, langoustines, etc Almost any crisp dry white will work – Sauvignon Blanc is a good grape to choose – but avoid heavily oaked wines. Go for high acidity if you are serving mayonnaise.

Salt-cured salmon (above) needs a white wine with plenty of weight, such as an Alsace Gewürztraminer or a Pinot Gris.

Deep-fried mushrooms Best with a medium-bodied simple red such as Côtes du Rhône or one of the lighter Zinfandels.

Asparagus Richer styles of Sauvignon, such as those from New Zealand, are perfect. Subtler wines will suffer.

Pasta dishes These really are best with Italian wines. Choose a concentrated white such as Vernaccia, Arneis or good Soave for cream sauces or those using seafood. Light- to medium-bodied reds from indigenous grape varieties work best with tomato-based sauces. Or you could try a Barbera or Sangiovese from California.

FISH AND SHELLFISH

Oysters Classic partners are champagne, Muscadet or Chablis. Most unoaked Sauvignon also makes a suitably bracing match.

Scallops Simply poached or sautéed, this most delicate of shellfish needs a soft, light white – Côte Chalonnaise burgundy, medium-dry German or New Zealand Riesling, Chardonnay from Alto Adige – becoming correspondingly richer, the creamier the sauce.

Chardonnay, dry Rieslings from Alsace or Germany. Equally, it is capable of taking a lightish red such as *cru* Beaujolais or Pinot Noir.

Tuna Go for a fairly assertive red in preference to white: well-built Pinot Noir (California or Côte de Beaune), mature Loire red (Chinon or Bourgueil), Washington State Merlot, Australian Shiraz, Chilean Cabernet, even Zinfandel.

MEAT AND POULTRY

Chicken If the bird is roasted, go for a soft-edged quality red such as mature burgundy, Crianza or Reserva Rioja or California Merlot. Lighter cooking treatments may mandate one of the richer whites, depending on any sauce.

Turkey The Christmas or Thanksgiving turkey deserves a show-stopping red with a little more power than you would serve with chicken. St-Emilion or Pomerol claret, Châteauneuf-du-Pape, Cabernet-Merlot or Cabernet-Shiraz blends from the USA or Australia will all oblige.

Rabbit As for roast chicken.

Pork Roast pork or grilled chops are happiest with fairly full reds with a touch of spice: southern Rhône blends, Australian Shiraz, California Syrah or the bigger Tuscan reds such as Vino Nobile or Brunello.

Lamb The meat that Cabernet Sauvignon might have been invented for, so go for the ripest and best you can find – from Bordeaux to Bulgaria, New Zealand to Napa.

Lobster Thermidor (above) is best with a rich, ideally oak-aged white. Best white burgundy or hot-climate Chardonnay are ideal.

Lobster Cold in a salad, it needs a pungent white with some acidity, such as Pouilly-Fumé, dry Vouvray, Chablis, South African Chenin Blanc, Australian Riesling. Served hot as a main course (eg. Thermidor), it requires an opulent and heavier wine – Meursault, Chardonnay from California or South Australia, Alsace Pinot Gris, or perhaps one of the bigger Rhône whites like Hermitage.

Light-textured white fish Sole, trout, plaice and the like go well with any light, unoaked or very lightly oaked white from almost anywhere.

Firm-fleshed fish Fish like sea bass, brill, turbot or cod need full-bodied whites to match their texture. *Cru classé* white Bordeaux, white Rioja, Australian Semillon, California Fumé Blanc and most oaked Chardonnays will all fit the bill.

Monkfish Either a heavy, alcoholic white such as Hermitage or Condrieu or the biggest Australian Chardonnay, or – if cooked in red wine – something quite beefy such as Moulin-à-Vent, young St-Emilion, or even California Cabernet.

Salmon Goes well with elegant, midweight whites with some acidity such as *grand cru* Chablis, California, Oregon or New Zealand

Rabbit dishes (right) will take either red or white wines, depending on the treatment. A rich white would be good with mustard sauce, while Pinot Noir would work well alongside rabbit with red wine and prunes.

Beef A full-flavoured cut such as rump or sirloin can cope with the biggest and burliest reds from anywhere: Hermitage, Côte-Rôtie, the sturdiest Zinfandels, Barolo and Barbaresco, Coonawarra Shiraz. Fillet steak needs something a touch lighter such as Bordeaux or a midweight Châteauneuf. Peppered steak or sauces containing mustard or horseradish call for an appropriate bite in the wine, either from Syrah or Grenache varietals or from the high acidity of Italian blends.

Duck A midweight red with youthful acidity to cut any fattiness is best: Crozes-Hermitage, Chianti Classico, California or New Zealand Pinot.

Game birds Best of all with fully mature Pinot Noir from the Côte d'Or, Carneros or Oregon, or – at a pinch – an aged Morgon.

Venison Highly concentrated reds with some bottle-age are essential. *Cru classé* Bordeaux or northern Rhône are the reference points. Cabernet, Shiraz and Zinfandel from hotter climates work well.

Offal Liver and kidneys are good with vigorous young reds such as Chinon, Ribera del Duero, Barbera or New Zealand Cabernet. Sweetbreads are better with a high-powered white such as a mature Alsace varietal.

DESSERTS

Fresh fruit salads are best served on their own, as there is generally too much acidity in them to do wine any favours. Similarly, frozen desserts like ice-creams and sorbets tend to numb the palate's sensitivity to wine. Anything based on eggs and cream, such as baked custards, mousses and *crème brûlée,* deserves a noble-rotted wine, such as Sauternes, Barsac, Monbazillac, Coteaux du Layon, the sweetest Vouvrays, or equivalent wines from outside Europe. Chocolate, often thought to present problems, doesn't do much damage to botrytized wines, but think maximum richness and high alcohol above all. Fruit tarts are best with a late-picked rather than rotted style of dessert wine, such as one of the lighter German or Austrian Rieslings, Alsace Vendange Tardive or late-harvest Muscat or Riesling from North America or the Southern Hemisphere. Meringues and creamy gâteaux are good with the sweeter styles of sparkling wine, while Asti or Moscato d'Asti make refreshing counter-balances to Christmas pudding. Sweet oloroso sherry, Bual or Malmsey madeira and Liqueur Muscat from Victoria are all superb with rich, dark fruitcake or anything nutty such as pecan pie.

The classic partner for boeuf bourguinonne (left) is a soft, mature burgundy – the region from which the dish originated.

Mince pies with orange whisky butter (below) could be paired either with sparkling Italian Asti, or with a marmaladey Australian Liqueur Muscat.

LABELLING

Champagne labels are rarely complicated. The house name will always dominate, since it is a form of brand, in this case Billecart-Salmon at Mareuil-sur-Ay. Above is the style, Brut being virtually the driest, and this one is pink. Champagne is the only AC wine that doesn't require the words *appellation contrôlée* to appear. Beneath the alcohol, the reference number of this house denotes that it is an NM (*négociant-manipulant*), a producer that buys in grapes and makes its own wine.

The most prominent detail on a Bordeaux label is the property at which the wine was made. A classed growth always announces itself with the formula "*cru classé* en 1855". Lower down, the sub-region from which the wine hails is stated, in this case St-Julien, which also forms the name of the appellation.

Burgundy labelling can be a minefield. The merchant's name (Drouhin) is followed by the appellation. This label tells you this is a *grand cru* wine, but doesn't have to state which village it belongs to (Morey-St-Denis, in fact). Note that *mis en bouteille* is not followed by *au domaine*, because it has not been bottled on an individual estate, but by a négociant based elsewhere.

Reading down this Italian label, we have the name of the vineyard (Vigna del Sorbo), then the producer (Fontodi) and then the appellation or denominazione (Chianti Classico). Then comes the quality level – Italy's highest, DOCG. Riserva denotes a wine aged for at least three years before release. Below is the information that the wine was bottled at the estate by its producer.

La Rioja Alta, S.A.

VIÑA ARANA

RIOJA
DENOMINACION DE ORIGEN CALIFICADA

Embotellado en la propiedad
La Rioja Alta, S.A.
LABASTIDA - ESPAÑA

75 cl.
12,5% Vol.

RESERVA 1997

The practised eye begins to discern similarities between the labels of different European countries. On this Spanish label, we see the name of the producer (La Rioja Alta SA), then the brand name (Viña Arana), used to denote a particular blend in this case rather than an individual vineyard. The appellation is Rioja, below which appears the AC formula, DOC. *Embotellado en la propiedad* means "bottled on the estate". In the case of Rioja, Reserva denotes a wine that has been kept for three years before release, of which at least one must be spent in oak.

HAUS KLOSTERBERG

MARKUS MOLITOR

2003
Bernkasteler Badstube
Spätlese
Riesling Feinherb

MOSEL · SAAR · RUWER

Gutsabfüllung		Product of Germany
Weingut Markus Molitor		A.P.Nr. 2 576 609 55 04
D-54470 Bernkastel-Wehlen		Qualitätswein mit Prädikat

750 ml   ALC. 11,5 % BY VOL.

Above the vintage date on this German label, we see the name of the proprietor, and below it the vineyard the wine comes from: Badstube in the village of Bernkastel. The grapes were Spätlese (late-picked), the grape variety is Riesling and the style of this wine is Feinherb, literally "finely tart" or medium-dry. *Gutsabfüllung* means "bottled at the estate".

Tim Adams

2 0 0 1

SEMILLON

CLARE VALLEY

WINE MADE IN AUSTRALIA
750ml   12.5%VOL

In the sometimes complex world of bottle labelling, what could be simpler than the information on this varietal wine from an acclaimed South Australia producer? The proprietor has given his own name to the estate, which appears prominently at the top (Tim Adams), with the vintage (2001), grape variety (Semillon) and region (Clare Valley) following on below it. In essence, this is pretty much what that German label is also telling you, but notice how much more straightforward the Australian label looks.

THELEMA
1994
Chardonnay

WINE OF ORIGIN STELLENBOSCH
Grown, produced and bottled by
Thelema Mountain Vineyards, Helshoogte, Stellenbosch.
13,5% Alc. Vol.   Produce of South Africa   750 ml

This South African wine simply tells us the name of the estate (Thelema), the vintage year (1994), the grape variety (Chardonnay) and the region of the country in which it was grown and produced (Stellenbosch). "Wine of Origin" is the rough equivalent of the French *appellation contrôlée*.

FRANCE

1994
GALET
VINEYARDS
Merlot

PRODUIT DE FRANCE
VIN DE PAYS D'OC
VINIFIE ET MIS EN BOUTEILLE PAR
GABRIEL MEFFRE, 84190 FRANCE
75cl e

The Loire valley region is famed for its many riverside châteaux of great opulence, like this one (above) at Azay-le-Rideau, on the Indre tributary, southwest of Tours.

Why should we begin with France? Is it the world's largest producer of wine? No, that honour – if honour it is – usually goes to Italy, as it has done for a very long time. Does it still make the best wine then? Not in the opinion of increasing numbers of consumers who, in many parts of the Northern Hemisphere, have been turning away from French wines in droves, and embracing the produce of wine nations like Australia and South Africa as their export sectors have moved into top gear.

So what is it about France that makes it the logical starting-point?

The answer to that comes in two parts. One concerns historical pre-eminence, and the other – more controversially these days – is about quality control. The viticultural history of France is still, to a great extent, the template for premium wine production wherever in the world individual grapegrowers and winemakers are seeking to make great wines – wines that are expressions both of their environments and of the personal passions and philosophies of those who made them. And, in its formulation of the *appellation contrôlée* system, the first of its

kind in the world, France's wine industry established the concept of protecting the reputation of its best wines by circumscribing them within tightly drawn regulations.

To take the first of these two aspects, you may well ask – as many winemakers and consumers outside Europe do – why history should be so important. The fact that something was once great doesn't mean we should give it the benefit of the doubt forever more. That of course is true, but whatever individual attitudes people hold towards French winemaking, it is still a force to be reckoned with. And here's why.

With a couple of exceptions, all the major grape varieties we looked at in the preceding section of this book are French, but they are also grapes that are grown around the world. France has no particular monopoly on grape types – it has been estmated that commercially invisible Turkey, for example, has over 1100 indigenous varieties – but it is the Chardonnays, Cabernets, Sauvignons and Pinots that have travelled the world's vineyards most extensively. That isn't to say that every

France's appellation con-trôlée *regions (right), from the cool vineyards of Champagne to the hotter regions of the Midi in the south.*

1. BORDEAUX
2. LOIRE
3. CHAMPAGNE
4. ALSACE
5. BURGUNDY
6. RHÔNE
7. PROVENCE
8. LANGUEDOC-ROUSSILLON
9. GASCONY & SOUTHWEST
10. JURA
11. SAVOIE & BUGEY
12. CORSICA

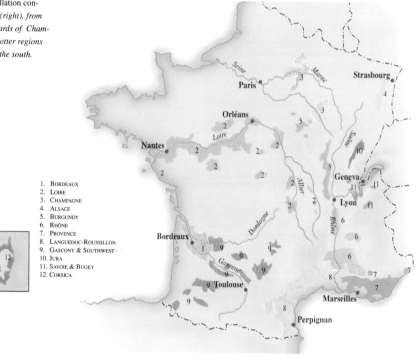

Australian winemaker with a cellarful of Chardie is trying to make white burgundy, but the presence of the grape in the vineyard indicates that the original model was French. Otherwise, why not transplant some Austrian Grüner Veltliner or Spanish Verdejo?

In time, that will change. The spread of Italian grape varieties into California is one of the most intriguing phenomena of recent years. In order to plant Sangiovese, Dolcetto and Nebbiolo, some of those old cash crops, Cabernet and Chardonnay, are having to come out.

Secondly, the question of *appellation contrôlée* arouses much vexatious debate around the world. Consumers in the USA, Australia and the UK have come gradually to the view that the appellation regulations are what have held France's wine industry back from competing in the modern world. If a grower in Beaujolais has to replant, he or she can only put in more Gamay. It might be fascinating to see how Italian Dolcetto or Austrian Blaufränkisch fared on the granite hills of the region but, however well it did, the wine it made could not be called Beaujolais.

The French counter this argument by saying that, far from holding them back, the restrictions are precisely what has made their greatest wines possible. The high-yielding, thin-tasting Muscadet grape Melon de Bourgogne is so named because it was once grown in Burgundy. As far back as the 17th century, though, there were official moves to kick it out of that region as not being worthy of the best wines. It now produces clean, zippy little whites at the western end of the Loire. It's refreshing enough in the right vintages, but Puligny-Montrachet it ain't. And the point is that Puligny-Montrachet itself would not have become what it has if it still contained Melon de Bourgogne. As consumers, we know what to expect from the wines because their names have been made to mean something legally.

What has undermined the image of French wines, however, in the last decade is that too much resting on laurels has occurred. Certain catchall appellations – AC Bordeaux springs readily to mind – still hide a multitude of vinous sins, with overcropped grapes and sloppy wine-making dragging down overall quality. In 2003, an initiative was announced to overhaul the whole system, creating a new super-category of

the best in each appellation, but at the time of writing, the proposals are still resting in the long grass into which they have been kicked.

It is more than ever necessary to ensure that everybody involved in French wine plays by the same rules for the greater glory of the industry, even though it is regrettably as impossible as ever to legislate for talent. Not only best practices in the vineyard and cellar are required from the producers, but a fully operational quality-control system based on random inspections to eliminate the dross before it gets to market is esssential. Otherwise, those blockading the *autoroutes* to protest about their plunging market share will have only themselves to blame for their decline.

The way ahead most definitely doesn't lie in trying to compete with the Southern Hemisphere countries on their own terms. Quite apart from the obvious difference in climate, there simply isn't any commercial mileage in imitating what can be done better elsewhere.

After all, when all is said and done, some rudimentary version of the controlled appellation concept is being introduced in every wine-producing country on earth. And it is for that reason, because rules are the only guarantor of quality, and because it is the French who invented them, that we turn our attention first to the wines of France.

Dusk descends over vineyards in Corbières, in the Languedoc (above).

Ancient presses in the underground cellars at Gaston Huët (above), producer of fine sparkling Saumur, Loire.

BORDEAUX-*Red*

Occupying a position at the pinnacle of world winemaking, the grand châteaux of Bordeaux produce fine clarets and sweet whites in a landscape that could not have been better designed for growing vines.

BORDEAUX-RED

GRAPES: Cabernet Sauvignon, Merlot, Cabernet Franc, Malbec, Petit Verdot

The Bordeaux region lies within the Gironde départe-ment. The Médoc is a narrow strip on the left bank of the Gironde estuary. Upstream, the river Garonne provides the damp climate so suitable for the botrytized wines of Sauternes.

THE RED WINES OF Bordeaux – or clarets, as the British have called them for at least the last four centuries – have long been synony-mous with the popular image of fine wine. Any major auction of vintage wines is likely to be dominated by old bottles and cases of Bor-deaux, since that is where most of the attention of investors in wine was, and largely still is, concentrated. In this respect, the profile of Bor-deaux has always been higher than that of France's other classic red wine region, Burgundy, partly because the most magisterial clarets are considerably longer-lived than most burgundy, and partly because the annual production of the Bordeaux region is incomparably larger.

Claret is not exclusively about well-heeled bidders with private cellars to stock. Its wines span the whole spectrum of status, from the humblest and most *ordinaire* to the kind that would require an uncommonly sympathetic bank manager to allow you the merest taste. The issue for the high-street consumer to confront is that most of the wines require some degree of ageing in the bottle, and most retail outlets only trade in immature bottles. So, either you keep them in your own cellar, or you go to an inde-pendent merchant who specializes in one-off purchases of good mature vintages.

During the economic boom-time of the 1980s, a trend for buying claret directly from the château in the spring following the vintage, for delivery at a later date – a deal known as buying *en primeur* – became the smart way to invest. It was certainly cheaper than waiting until the merchants had bought the wine them-selves and then paying their mark-ups. Everything went well until a run of mediocre to poor vintages in the region, starting in 1991, sent market values tumbling. Some investors who had bought those wines either lost money or else found themselves with rather a lot of thin, insipid wine to drink up.

The result was that, by the mid-1990s, Bor-deaux's cellars were awash with unsold wine. Some châteaux would only sell wines from the slightly better vintages on condition that their regular buyers bought some of the produce of the disaster years. As the chances for greatness in successive vintages were rained off at the last minute by inclement weather at harvest-time, Bordeaux experienced its worst commercial sticky patch since the early 1970s. Some relief was at hand in the form of decisive intervention by Japanese investors, as keen to buy a stake in the alcoholic pinnacles of Western culture as in its finest artistic achievements.

For all the torrid machinations of high finance, Bordeaux remains at its best one of the world's most irresistibly succulent red wines. Opened in its youth, a good claret is really wast-ed, for all that the French themselves have a taste for the juvenile article. They are tight and tough in texture, and rigid with tannin. After around five or six years, they can begin to soft-en up a bit and display some of the blackcurrant or plum fruit of the Cabernet Sauvignon or Mer-lot grapes more readily. Then, in a curious

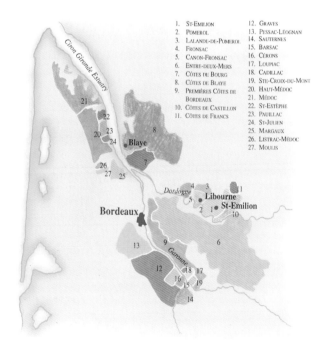

1.	ST-EMILION	12.	GRAVES
2.	POMEROL	13.	PESSAC-LÉOGNAN
3.	LALANDE-DE-POMEROL	14.	SAUTERNES
4.	FRONSAC	15.	BARSAC
5.	CANON-FRONSAC	16.	CÉRONS
6.	ENTRE-DEUX-MERS	17.	LOUPIAC
7.	CÔTES DE BOURG	18.	CADILLAC
8.	CÔTES DE BLAYE	19.	STE-CROIX-DU-MONT
9.	PREMIÈRES CÔTES DE BORDEAUX	20.	HAUT-MÉDOC
		21.	MÉDOC
10.	CÔTES DE CASTILLON	22.	ST-ESTÈPHE
11.	CÔTES DE FRANCS	23.	PAUILLAC
		24.	ST-JULIEN
		25.	MARGAUX
		26.	LISTRAC-MÉDOC
		27.	MOULIS

development that remains hard to account for, they seem to go into a sulky state of withdrawal, in which they taste rather flat and inert. You must now leave the rest of your bottles alone for perhaps three or four years, after which they will blossom again, still full of fruit hopefully, but with the scents and flavours now deepened into all sorts of seductive and complex modes. The infamous Bordeaux classification formulated for the Paris Exhibition of 1855 remains the principal determining factor in the pricing of these wines; the five-tier hierarchy is in fact based on the market values of the wines when the list was originally drawn up at the behest of Napoleon III. As we saw in the Merlot chapter, the league table for reds saw fit only to include the wines from the Haut-Médoc, plus Château Haut-Brion in the Graves. The Graves itself was then classified in the 1950s, along with St-Emilion. The other great red wine district, Pomerol, has never been classified.

Although much of the classification still holds good, properties do change hands, new winemakers are employed, different winemaking philosophies are explored, and the performances of individual châteaux inevitably fluctuate. Since the Bordelais themselves look likely never to amend the 1855 classification for fear of unleashing a vinous Armageddon, it is left to individuals to offer their own periodic reassessments. This is a practice positively encouraged by a past president of the regional organization for the top brass, the Syndicat des Crus Classés (what you might call Club 1855). Château names on the table below are followed by a star rating up to a maximum of five, based on the general consensus as to their performances over the last 20 years – a period that ranges in quality from the frost-devastated '91s, rain-soaked '87s and mediocre '99s to the out-and-out stunners of '89, '90 and 2000.

1855 AND ALL THAT

(Appellation shown in brackets – P = Pauillac, M = Margaux, P-L = Pessac-Léognan, *formerly Graves,* S-J = St-Julien, S-E = St-Estèphe, H-M = Haut-Médoc)

First Growth/1er cru
Lafite-Rothschild (P) ***** Margaux (M) ***** Latour (P) ***** Haut-Brion (P-L) ***** Mouton-Rothschild (P) *****

Second Growth/2ème cru
Rauzan-Ségla, *formerly Rausan-Ségla* (M)*****

Rauzan-Gassies (M) ** Léoville-Las Cases (S-J) ***** Léoville-Poyferré (S-J) *** Léoville-Barton (S-J) **** Durfort-Vivens (M) *** Lascombes (M) **** Brane-Cantenac (M) ** Pichon-Longueville, *formerly Pichon-Longueville Baron* (P) ***** Pichon-Longueville Comtesse de Lalande, *formerly Pichon-Lalande* (P) ***** Ducru-Beaucaillou (S-J) **** Cos d'Estournel (S-E) ***** Montrose (S-E) **** Gruaud-Larose (S-J) ****

Third Growth/3ème cru
Kirwan (M) ** d'Issan (M) *** Lagrange (S-J) **** Langoa-Barton (S-J) **** Giscours (M)*** Malescot St-Exupéry (M) *** Boyd-Cantenac (M) *** Cantenac-Brown (M) *** Palmer (M) **** La Lagune (H-M) **** Desmirail (M) *** Calon-Ségur (S-E) **** Ferrière, *not generally available outside France* (M) ** Marquis d'Alesme Becker (M) **

Fourth Growth/4ème cru
St-Pierre (S-J) *** Talbot (S-J) *** Branaire-Ducru (S-J) *** Duhart-Milon-Rothschild (P) *** Pouget (M) ** La Tour-Carnet (H-M) ** Lafon-Rochet (S-E) *** Beychevelle (S-J) **** Prieuré-Lichine (M) *** Marquis-de-Terme (M) ***

The hard way of transporting a barrel through the extensive chai, or cellar, of first-growth Château Margaux (above).

Ripe Cabernet Sauvignon grapes being harvested for first-growth Château Latour in Pauillac (below).

Fifth Growth/5ème cru

Pontet-Canet (P) ***   Batailley (P) ***   Haut-Batailley (P) ***   Grand-Puy-Lacoste (P) ****   Grand-Puy-Ducasse (P) ***   Lynch-Bages (P) *****   Lynch-Moussas (P) *   Dauzac (M) *   d'Armailhac, *formerly Mouton-Baronne-Philippe* (P) ***   du Tertre (M) ***   Haut-Bages-Libéral (P) ***   Pédesclaux (P) **   Belgrave (H-M) ***   de Camensac (H-M) **   Cos-Labory (S-E) ***   Clerc-Milon (P) ***   Croizet-Bages (P) *   Cantemerle (H-M) ***

GRAVES/ST-EMILION/POMEROL

Graves This extensive sub-region, lying mostly south of the city itself on the west bank of the river Garonne, is named after the gravelly soils that predominate there. Many tasters insist that there is a gravelly, earthy taste in the red wines themselves, and certainly they tend to come clothed in much more austere garb than the lavish finery of the Médoc wines. However, they are quite as capable of ageing, notwithstanding the fact that many châteaux are attempting to make a more easy-going, early-drinking style of red.

The Graves was finally classified in 1959, for both red and dry white wines. Either a château in Graves is *cru classé* or it isn't; it's as simple as that. A superior swathe of land at the northern end of the region was separately demarcated as Pessac-Léognan in 1987, all of the classed growths of 1959 falling within that appellation. (Château Haut-Brion is the only property that also appears in the 1855 classification.) For the reds, they are:

Bouscaut **   Haut-Bailly ****   Carbon-nieux ***   Domaine de Chevalier *****   de Fieuzal ***   d'Olivier **   Malartic-Lagravière **   La Tour-Martillac **   Smith-Haut-Lafitte ***   Haut-Brion *****   La Mission-Haut-Brion ****   Pape-Clément ****   La Tour-Haut-Brion ***

St-Emilion Situated on the right bank of the river Dordogne, this is predominantly Merlot country – although not quite to the same degree as Pomerol to the north. The reds are supplemented largely by Cabernet Franc, with only a soupçon of Cabernet Sauvignon. The style is consequently leaner than in the Cabernet-dominated Médoc, but sharpened with a slightly grassier feel from the Cabernet Franc. The generality of wines are not that distinguished – many properties are guilty of overproduction – but the top names are worth the premium.

The classification of St-Emilion's reds was drawn up in 1955, but it is subject to revision every decade, the latest having been announced in 1996. At the humblest level, *grand cru* is so inclusive as to be meaningless. A step up is *grand cru classé* with around five dozen properties (among which l'Angélus and Troplong-Mondot stand out as worthy of ****)

and at the top is *premier grand cru classé*, which is subdivided into A and B. Class A consists of just two properties:

Ausone **** Cheval Blanc *****

Class B contains nine:

Beauséjour (Duffau la Garrosse) ****
Belair *** Canon ***** Clos Fourtet ***
Figeac **** la Gaffelière **** Magdelaine
**** Pavie **** Trottevieille ***

Pomerol Immediately to the north of St-Emilion, and the only one of the top division of Bordeaux districts never to have been subjected to the indignity of classification, Pomerol's reds are as close to varietal Merlot as Bordeaux gets. Many have simply the merest seasoning of Cabernet Franc to add an edge of ageworthy sternness to what is essentially pure velvet-soft opulence, the sweetness of prunes coated in dark chocolate, and with a gorgeous creaminess that stays in the mouth for the longest time.

Anybody setting out to play the Pomerol classification parlour-game for themselves would have to start with the hyper-expensive Pétrus (*****) at the top, probably joined by Lafleur (*****). In the next rank (****) would come Bon Pasteur, Certan de May, Clinet, la Conseillante, la Croix de Gay, l'Eglise-Clinet, l'Evangile, la Fleur de Gay, la Fleur-Pétrus, le Gay, Latour à Pomerol, Petit-Village, le Pin, Trotanoy and Vieux-Château-Certan.

CRUS BOURGEOIS/PETITS CHATEAUX/SECOND WINES

Crus Bourgeois Immediately below the five layers of Médoc *crus classés* are a group of wines known, in an echo of 18th-century social stratification, as the *crus bourgeois*. For the purposes of this category, not only the Haut-Médoc but the bottom-line Médoc area to the north of St-Estèphe comes under consideration. Many of the properties would, if the 1855 document were to be redrafted, be included among the aristocracy, including a fair handful from the less well-known commune of Moulis.

Consistent reputations for reliably excellent wines over the last decade have been forged by the following (****): d'Angludet (M), Chasse-Spleen (Moulis), la Gurgue (M), Haut-Marbuzet (S-E), Gressier-Grand-Poujeaux (Moulis), Labégorce-Zédé (M), Lanessan (H-M), Maucaillou (Moulis), Meyney (S-E), Monbrison (M), de Pez (S-E), Potensac (Médoc), Poujeaux (Moulis) and Sociando-Mallet (H-M).

Next best (***) would be: Patache d'Aux (Médoc), Ramage-la-Batisse (H-M), Sénéjac (H-M), la Tour-de-By (Médoc) and la Tour-du-Haut-Moulin (H-M).

Petits châteaux and other districts Other important quality districts (with good unclassified properties known as *petits châteaux*) are Lalande-de-Pomerol, adjoining Pomerol to the northeast (Bel-Air, Bertineau-St-Vincent), Fronsac and Canon-Fronsac to the west of Pomerol (Canon-Moueix, Dalem, Mazeris, la Truffière) and the various satellite villages to the northeast of St-Emilion, such as Lussac (Lyonnat), Puisseguin and St-Georges.

Many of the châteaux of Bordeaux have idiosyncratic architectural features, such as the pointed turret (above) after which Château la Tour-de-By is named.

Looking over the medieval rooftops of the City of St-Emilion (below) out towards the vineyards.

The huge area of Entre-Deux-Mers between the Garonne and Dordogne rivers tends to produce pretty rough-and-ready reds, which are only entitled to the most basic appellations of Bordeaux and Bordeaux Supérieur. On the right bank of the Gironde, directly opposite the *cru classé* enclaves of the Haut-Médoc, are the Côtes de Blaye and Côtes de Bourg areas. The latter is much the smaller of the two and is home to some rapidly improving properties. The long strip on the right bank of the Garonne, the Premières Côtes de Bordeaux, makes a mixture of simple sweet whites and some increasingly satisfying, firm-textured reds.

To the east of St-Emilion are two areas that are among the most unsung (and therefore good-value) sources of classy wine in the whole region: the Côtes de Castillon and Côtes de Francs. The style is lightish, depending significantly on Cabernet Franc for its appeal, but some châteaux (***) are turning out wines of impressive concentration. From Castillon:

Belcier, Moulin-Rouge, Parenchère and Pitray. From Francs: Puygueraud.

Second wines When the prices of Bordeaux began seriously inflating in the 1980s, much commercial attention came to be focused on the second wines of the principal châteaux. Most properties make a subsidiary wine to their main wine, or *grand vin*, to use surplus grapes that were not thought quite good enough for the main *cuvée*, or came from vines that were just too young to produce thoroughly concentrated fruit. A ready market was found for those who may not have been able to afford Château Margaux, but were interested in acquiring a broad impression of its style.

The point to remember when considering buying a second wine is only to buy from the best vintages. Top châteaux may be able to make a silk purse out of the sow's ear of a vintage like 1999, and it should be correspondingly cheaper, so you don't need the second wine – indeed, they probably shouldn't have made one. In a super-vintage like 2000, however, when the *grand vin* prices soar into the stratosphere, the second wines make economic sense.

These are regularly some of the best. They are not rated, as their quality should be in proportion to the ratings for the *grands vins*. The main château name is shown in brackets.

Les Forts de Latour (Latour), Carruades de Lafite (Lafite-Rothschild), Pavillon Rouge du Château Margaux (Margaux), Bahans Haut-Brion (Haut-Brion), Clos du Marquis (Léoville-Las Cases), Réserve de la Comtesse (Pichon-Longueville Comtesse de Lalande), Marbuzet (Cos d'Estournel), La Dame de Montrose (Montrose), Sarget de Gruaud-Larose (Gruaud-Larose), Lady Langoa (Langoa-Barton), Réserve du Général (Palmer), Haut-Bages-Avérous (Lynch-Bages), La Parde de Haut-Bailly (Haut-Bailly), Grangeneuve de Figeac (Figeac), La Gravette de Certan (Vieux-Château-Certan), La Petite Eglise (l'Eglise-Clinet).

VINTAGE GUIDE

The following is a broad overview of the most recent vintages, as represented by the best wines of each year, plus some earlier stars.

2004 **** A very late but prolific vintage has produced reds with big tannins and whopping alcohol levels.

2003 ***** A long hot summer and more temperate picking conditions produced a humdinger. Best districts are Pomerol,

St-Emilion, St-Estèphe and Pessac-Léognan.
2002 *** A good showing on the left bank
(Pauillac, St-Julien, St-Estèphe, Margaux), but
much of the right bank Merlot failed to ripen well.
2001 *** Harvest rains spoiled the chances of
some, but this vintage has turned out better than
expected.
2000 ***** A fabulous vintage, the best since
1990, mostly now snapped up. Buy any you see.
1999 ** Very dull (although Mouton is good).
1998 *** Pretty good, though not outstanding.
St-Emilion and Pomerol are the safest bets.
1997 *** Much underrated at first, the '97s
have turned out to be midweight but reasonably
complex wines.
1996 **** Some classic, austere, ageworthy
wines from the Médoc make this a vintage
worth keeping.
1995 **** The first good one after 1990.
The Cabernet-based wines of the Médoc in
particular are very ripe and attractive.
1990 ***** Wonderful, superripe wines, full
of richness and power and enormous ageing
potential. Merlot was particularly good, so
Pomerols are superb, but all districts made fine
wine. Definitely one to keep.

1989 **** A long hot summer led to gloriously
ripe Cabernet and some rather overripe Merlot.
Most of the Médoc produced accessible wines
of great charm that began to open out
surprisingly quickly.
1988 **** Deeply classical wines with intensely ripe fruit and solid structure in pleasing
balance. Most of the Médoc, Graves and
St-Emilion produced fine wines.
1986 **** A good vintage all in all, but the
tannins in many wines were exceptionally
severe and, with some, the fruit has broken up
without the tannin having entirely dispersed.
1985 **** A warm year led to a large
production of charming, fruit-filled wines,
most now past their peak.
1983 **** Fine vintage of classically
proportioned wines.
1982 ***** One of the very greatest postwar
vintages. Powerful, exotically rich and deeply
beautiful wines by the score, some still needing
several more years to show their true colours.
PICK OF THE OLDER VINTAGES: *1978* ****
1970 **** *1966* **** *1961* ***** *1959* ****
1955 **** *1953* **** *1949* **** *1947* ****
1945 *****

*Despite its venerable history,
Domaine de Chevalier, one
of the Graves crus classés,
has always kept abreast of
the times, as witness its
state-of-the-art cellars at
Pessac-Léognan (above).*

BORDEAUX-*Dry White*

The dry white wines of Bordeaux have enjoyed a remarkable renaissance in recent years, shaking off their image of being poorly-made and dull, and emerging with the kinds of flavours normally only found in America's finest.

BORDEAUX-DRY WHITE

GRAPES: *Sémillon, Sauvignon Blanc, Muscadelle*

IT IS ONLY IN THE last 20 years that the reputation of the dry white wines of Bordeaux has come once more into the ascendancy. Certain properties, such as Domaine de Chevalier, have always been highly valued for their white wines, and some of the *crus classés* showed themselves adept in both colours, notably Haut-Brion. The generality for a long time, though, was fruitless, stale-tasting rubbish, often loaded with too much sulphur dioxide (an antioxidant that helps to keep wine fresh, but that, used in excess, gives off an acrid smell and leaves a catch in the throat). These were the least prepossessing dry whites produced in any of France's classic regions.

The upturn came about via a handful of winemakers who began, in the early 1980s, to incorporate Californian and Australian ways of doing things. Denis Dubourdieu at Château Reynon, André Lurton at La Louvière and Peter Vinding-Diers, who consulted at a number of properties in the Graves, were among the pioneers who returned to Bordeaux a sense of pride in their wines. They achieved this through such obvious means as ensuring only impeccably ripe grapes are picked, that they are fermented at controlled temperatures and often given some judicious maturation in new oak to add an extra dimension to their flavours.

The Graves, and in particular Pessac-Léognan, have been the principal beneficiaries of the quality movement. Where it was most needed, in Entre-Deux-Mers, progress has been slower, partly because the soil contains quite a lot of clay, which inhibits drainage. (If it rains heavily, the vines' roots can become waterlogged.) Widespread use of a vineyard technique which originated in Austria, involving training the vines on high trellises for maximum heat absorption and therefore optimum ripeness in the grapes, has undoubtedly proved helpful.

Only the Graves has a classification for dry white wines, drawn up in 1959, with the white wine of Haut-Brion added the following year. As with its red wines, all of the properties come within the Pessac-Léognan AC in the northern Graves; in fact, all but three of them are dual classifications for red as well as white. The whites are:

Bouscaut ** Carbonnieux *** Domaine de Chevalier ***** Olivier ** Malartic-Lagravière *** La Tour-Martillac **** Laville-Haut-Brion ***** Couhins-Lurton **** Couhins ** Haut-Brion *****

Unclassified fine dry whites from the Graves include de Fieuzal *****, Clos Floridène **** and La Louvière ****.

In the Entre-deux-Mers, the best property without a doubt is Thieuley (****). Elsewhere, the catch-all appellation of Bordeaux Blanc applies, and quality is all over the place. Some companies who make blended bottlings from all over the region can be reliable (for example, Coste, Dourthe, Mau and Sichel).

Down in the Sauternes region, the best makers of sweet wine make some dry white from the grapes that are not sufficiently shrivelled to be used for the Sauternes. Sometimes known as "dry Sauternes", they are in fact AC Bordeaux Blanc, and are named after the initial letter of the château – R from Rieussec, G from Guiraud and – best of all – Y from Yquem. Reputations make them expensive, but they are worth trying for some of the most majestically austere flavours in all dry white Bordeaux.

An ancient windmill presides over vineyards at Gornac, in the Entre-deux-Mers (above).

VINTAGE GUIDE

The simpler wines that use a high percentage of Sauvignon are best drunk on release. The top *crus classés* are intended for longer ageing.
2004 **** Crisp, taut wines but with good fruit.
2003 ***** Exotically perfumed, soft, generous wines of great charm. A vintage to keep.
2002 *** Similar style to 2004, but the acidity is more pronounced.
2001 **** Very attractive wines from the top châteaux that have a few years left to go.
2000 ***** Beautifully composed, concentrated wines for ageing.
1999 *** Initially underrated, but have turned out very attractive. Drink soon.
1996 **** Some lovely creamy, tropical-fruited wines worth trying.
1995 *** Fairly rich, full-bodied wines.
1990 *** Some stunning wines from the top properties, but others found the sun just too hot for the Sauvignon, and the wines lack acid grip.
1989 *** Again, a very hot ripening period meant critically low acidity levels in many wines, so a lot will have had difficulty lasting this long. Only the very best (Haut-Brion, Laville-Haut-Brion and the like) made out-and-out classics.
1988 **** A good vintage of generally well-balanced wines, with the Graves *crus classés* still improving.

The gently sloping vineyards of Château Benauge on the border between the Entre-deux-Mers and Premières Côtes de Bordeaux regions (left). Many of the dry whites made in these regions are now much improved.

BORDEAUX-*Sweet White*

Its lofty reputation founded on botrytis, a fungal disease that attacks ripened grapes in late summer and early autumn, the sweet wine of Bordeaux is the most celebrated of its kind in the world.

BORDEAUX-SWEET WHITE

GRAPES: Sémillon, Sauvignon Blanc, Muscadelle

The Sauternes region of Bordeaux contains some of the most valuable land in the world for producing sweet wines, none more so than at Château d'Yquem (below).

THE FINEST DESSERT wines in the world, whether in Bordeaux or elsewhere, are made from grapes infected by a strain of fungus called *Botrytis cinerea*, widely known as noble rot. Rot normally develops on grapes if the weather turns wet towards harvest time. This grey rot is the decidedly ignoble sort and, particularly with red grapes, can utterly shatter any hopes of making great wines. Botrytis, on the other hand, occurs in damp rather than drenching conditions.

Because of its proximity to the Atlantic Ocean, Bordeaux experiences increasingly humid, misty mornings as the autumn comes on, relieved by late sunshine during the day. This gentle process of dampening and drying off is the ideal climatic pattern for the encouragement of botrytis. (For an explanation of the vinification procedure, see the chapter on Sémillon.)

The most celebrated sweet wines on earth come from the southerly Bordeaux communes of Sauternes and Barsac. Although the technique was almost certainly discovered in Germany – by accident, of course, like many of the best inventions – it is here that it has been put to the most illustrious use. Not every vintage produces the right conditions, and the more quality-conscious châteaux simply don't bother making a wine in the off-years.

Quality depends on making painstaking selections of only the most thoroughly rotted grapes. In many cases, proprietors have decided the only way of doing that is by individual hand-sorting, picking only those berries that are completely shrivelled and leaving the others to moulder a little further on the vine before going through the vineyard again. Several such turns (or *tries*, as they are known in French) may be necessary to make the most concentrated wines possible. That, together with the long maturation in oak casks that the wines are generally given, explains the drop-dead prices that classic Sauternes sells for. It is an immensely labour-intensive wine.

A group of five villages in the southern Graves famous for their botrytized wines – Sauternes, Barsac, Bommes, Preignac and Fargues – was included in the 1855 classification. Together, they now constitute the Sauternes appellation, although Barsac is entitled to its own appellation as well, if an individual property so chooses. (Just for good measure, it can also be AC Sauternes-Barsac if it wants the best of both worlds.)

At the top of the classification, and with a category to itself like the duck-billed platypus, is the legendary Château d'Yquem, for many the supreme achievement in botrytized wine. Fantastically expensive and fabuously rich, its best vintages last literally for centuries.

Grand first growth/1er grand cru
Yquem *****

First growth/1er cru
La Tour Blanche ****   Lafaurie-Peyraguey ****
Clos Haut-Peyraguey **   Rayne-Vigneau ***
Suduiraut ****   Coutet ****   Climens *****
Guiraud ****   Rieussec *****   Rabaud-Promis
***   Sigalas-Rabaud ***

Second growth/2ème cru

de Myrat, *began replanting in 1988 after coming close to total extinction* Doisy-Daëne ***
Doisy-Dubroca **** Doisy-Védrines ***
d'Arche ** Filhot *** Broustet ***
Nairac ** Caillou *** Suau ** de Malle ***
Romer-du-Hayot ** Lamothe-Despujols *
Lamothe-Guignard ***

Other good properties in Sauternes-Barsac, but outside the classification, are Raymond-Lafon (****), Gilette (****) and Bastor-Lamontagne (***).

In the immediate vicinity of Sauternes are four less well-known ACs for botrytis-affected wines. When the vintage is propitious, they can produce wines that give something of the flavour of their more exalted neighbours, while lacking those final layers of richness that make Sauternes so fabled. Given that, they are much more humanely priced. They are Cérons, Loupiac, Cadillac and Ste-Croix-du-Mont. Of these, all but Cérons, to the northwest of Barsac, are on the opposite bank of the river Garonne. The best properties are Cérons and Archambeau in Cérons and Loupiac-Gaudiet in Loupiac.

Sweet wines from the Premières Côtes de Bordeaux region, along the eastern side of the Garonne, are not invariably fully botrytized. However, one exception in recent years that has provided excellent value for money is Château de Berbec.

VINTAGE GUIDE

If a sweet white Bordeaux has been conscientiously made, it can easily last a good 20-30 years, and the very top ones are virtually indestructible. They turn from rich yellow to burnished orange and then the distinguished deep brown of dark sherry as they age, and go on selling for phenomenal sums.

2004 **** A patchy vintage, but the best properties have managed wines of genuine concentration.
2003 ***** Get ready. A sensational vintage of fully rotted wines with long lives ahead of them. Another 2001.
2002 **** Fine rot development produced another elegant vintage.
2001 ***** Brilliant, complex, hauntingly beautiful wines, the best since 1990.
2000 ** Generally disappointing.
1999 **** Highly appealing wines that began to show their class quite early.
1998 *** Overshadowed by its predecessor, but still a fine, dependable vintage.

1997 **** Potentially exciting year for full-fledged, creamy Sauternes.
1996 *** Plenty of noble rot about, resulting in a fine, ageworthy vintage.
1995 *** Not bad, but many wines lack full richness.
1990 ***** Virtual perfection – some say the vintage of the century. Unbelievable levels of concentration and intensity.
1989 **** Generally ripe and rich, although some of the *crus classés* are unaccountably slender and haven't aged well.
1988 **** The first of the three fine vintages known in France as *les trois glorieuses*. Huge, hefty stunners in which the influence of botrytis ran rampant.
1986 **** Beautiful vintage of properly botrytized wines.
1983 **** The equal of '86, '88 and '89, these are memorable, succulent, full-on Sauternes.
PICK OF THE OLDER VINTAGES: *1976* ****
1975 **** *1971* **** *1970* *** *1967* *****
1962 **** *1959* ***** *1955* **** *1953* ****
1949 **** *1947* **** *1945* *****

Pre-war vintages worth ***** would be *1937*, *1929* and *1921*. I am told the *1899* and *1900* were rather good too.

Autumn vines resplendent beneath a clear blue sky at Château Rieussec (above), one of the best first-growth properties in Sauternes.

LOIRE

The river Loire flows through five wine-producing areas, from the Pays Nantais in the west, far inland to Sancerre in the east, each of them boasting very different styles of wine.

Château de Nozet (above) set in the upper Loire, where Pouilly-Fumé is produced.

PAYS NANTAIS

GRAPES: *Melon de Bourgogne (Muscadet), Folle Blanche (Gros Plant).*

The five wine regions of the Loire valley (below) lie along the banks of the river Loire.

WERE IT NOT FOR the unifying presence of the river itself, it would be difficult to see the various viticultural districts that the Loire valley encompasses as one single region. The Loire is the longest river in France, rising more or less in the centre of the country and flowing out into the Atlantic Ocean west of Nantes. To get a coherent view of it as a wine region, it makes sense to subdivide it into five areas. Running from west to east, these are: the Pays Nantais, Anjou, Saumur, Touraine and the Upper Loire (the last sometimes referred to as the Central Vineyards because they are in the centre of France).

Pays Nantais The main business of the area around the city of Nantes is Muscadet, France's most exported wine. The epitome of bone-dry, crisp, neutral-tasting white wine, Muscadet wouldn't seem to have a lot going for it in an era of oak-aged Chardonnay-mania, and yet it continues to find export customers for around half of what it produces each year.

There are four ACs. Muscadet de Sèvre-et-Maine, in the centre of the region, makes about 80 per cent of all Muscadet and is generally considered the best in terms of the character of its wines. Growers based in the villages of St-Fiacre and Vallet are particularly noteworthy. Muscadet Côtes de Grandlieu is the youngest appellation, created in 1994. Centred on a large

lake, the district contains a fair amount of the sandy soil thought to impart more personality to the wines. Corcoués/Logne and St. Philbert de Bouaine are a couple of addresses to look for in the fine print on the label.

The small district of Muscadet des Coteaux de la Loire turns out a negligible quantity of undistinguished wine, and the rest is basic AC Muscadet, not by and large worth dwelling on.

About half of all Muscadets include the words *sur lie* on the label. This refers to a vinification technique whereby the finished wine is left on its lees (the dead yeast cells left over from fermentation), from which it picks up a gently creamy, slightly fuller feel than the unadorned version, as well as a touch of spritz. It is always worth buying a *sur lie* wine in preference to the alternative. Some producers have resorted to maturing their wines in oak casks, a risky technique for such a light wine, but the best improbably succeed in achieving some genuine complexity.

A more "natural" way of making Muscadet complex, however, is to age it for yourself in the bottle. At about five years old, it takes on a vaguely cabbagey pungency that is admittedly an acquired taste, but makes the wine a lot less spiky than the more conventional way of drinking it hot off the press as it were, screaming with raw young acid.

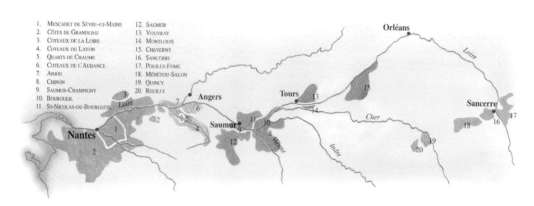

1. MUSCADET DE SÈVRE-ET-MAINE
2. CÔTES DE GRANDLIEU
3. COTEAUX DE LA LOIRE
4. COTEAUX DU LAYON
5. QUARTS DE CHAUME
6. COTEAUX DE L'AUBANCE
7. ANJOU
8. CHINON
9. SAUMUR-CHAMPIGNY
10. BOURGUEIL
11. ST-NICOLAS-DE-BOURGUEIL
12. SAUMUR
13. VOUVRAY
14. MONTLOUIS
15. CHEVERNY
16. SANCERRE
17. POUILLY-FUMÉ
18. MÉNÉTOU-SALON
19. QUINCY
20. REUILLY

PRODUCERS: Sauvion, Métaireau, Donatien Bahuaud, Luneau, Bossard, Guindon.

Talking of screaming acidity, there is a VDQS in this area (*vin délimité de qualité supérieure*, the intermediate quality stage between *appellation contrôlée* and *vin de pays*) called Gros Plant du Pays Nantais. This is the archetypal French "local wine", much beloved of the Nantais themselves, but not one they dare export to any great degree. It is so extraordinarily acidic that it can induce instant heartburn in the unwary. Served bone-chillingly cold with a platter of Atlantic shellfish, though – various species of prawn (shrimp), tiny winkles (periwinkles), and slatherings of mayonnaise – Gros Plant is a winner.

PRODUCERS: Sauvion, Métaireau, Bossard.

Anjou The area south of Angers is the start of Chenin Blanc country, and it is here that the great sweet wines of the Loire are made. As we saw in the chapter on Chenin, the variety submits to botrytis with obliging regularity in these districts, producing some of France's most finely balanced dessert wines – full of mouth-coating sticky marmalade, but thrown into a state of nervous excitement by that lemon streak of acidity.

Coteaux du Layon is the largest area for sweet wines, and regularly produces liquorous but refreshing examples. Even in years when there is a lower concentration of noble rot, and the resulting wines have much less intense sweetness, these are generally pretty reliable.

PRODUCERS: Ch. du Breuil, Ch. de la Roulerie, Dom. de la Soucherie, Dom. des Deux Arcs.

Within the Coteaux du Layon appellation is a small enclave answering to the name of Bonnezeaux, once neglected but now recovering its reputation for alcoholic, concentrated sweet wines of great class.

PRODUCERS: Ch. de Fesles, Angeli.

In the northwest of the Coteaux du Layon area, and likewise enclosed within it, is another small AC that scores highly for quality across the board – Quarts de Chaume. Growers here tend only to make wines when botrytis has been sufficiently widespread not to need to use non-rotted grapes. The result is almost unbearably intense sweet Chenin with all the majesty of top-flight Sauternes at considerably lower prices.

PRODUCERS: Baumard, Ch. de Bellerive.

Northeast of Chaume, the much larger Coteaux de l'Aubance makes medium-sweet, generally non-botrytized wines that offer a lighter option when full-blown rot is too daunting a proposition to accompany a lighter dessert.

Anjou is also the location of Savennières, the long-lived, brittle, bone-dry Chenin wine that achieves an impressive mineral purity in the best vintages and is always highly priced. Be warned that the wines positively command ageing, though, and should not be touched at less than seven or eight years old.

PRODUCERS: Dom. de la Bizolière, Baumard. Within the appellation, there are two superfine enclaves with their own ACs – La Roche-aux-Moines (Soulez makes a good wine) and Coulée de Serrant, which is wholly owned by one family. Here, Nicolas Joly makes his unearthly wine according to biodynamic principles, an abstruse practice involving much consulting of astrological star-charts.

Anjou Blanc Sec AC is the bottom line for everyday dry white. It is allowed to mix in some Chardonnay and/or Sauvignon with the Chenin, but producers such as Dom. Bablut make opulent straight Chenin by fermenting in oak.

For reds, the two Cabernets – Sauvignon and Franc – may be used in the passable appellation of Anjou-Villages that covers the better village sites. Basic Anjou Rouge can be sandy-dry and charmless when made from the Cabernets, or lightweight and simple produced from the Beaujolais grape Gamay. (Varieties will be indicated on the label.)

Much rosé wine is made throughout the Loire, its quality gradually improving. Rosé d'Anjou is made from a local grape called Grolleau (Ch. de Fesles makes a peachy, summery one with a typical hint of residual sugar). Cabernet d'Anjou is more acerbic.

Poplar trees break the skyline in vineyards near Vallet (above), Muscadet de Sèvre-et-Maine.

ANJOU
GRAPE: *Chenin Blanc (whites)*

Harvesting Muscadet grapes at Clisson (above), in the Sèvre-et-Maine AC.

SAUMUR
GRAPES: *Cabernet Franc*
(reds); Chenin Blanc
(whites)
SPARKLING SAUMUR
GRAPES: *Chenin Blanc,*
Chardonnay, Sauvignon
Blanc
TOURAINE
GRAPES: *Cabernet Franc,*
Gamay (reds); Chenin
Blanc, Sauvignon Blanc,
Chardonnay, Romorantin
(whites)

Saumur Two types of wine are important in Saumur – reds and sparklers. The Loire valley makes a speciality of the Cabernet Franc grape variety, one of the lesser players in red Bordeaux; the principal red appellations of Saumur and Touraine are permitted only that grape. In warm vintages, these wines have pleasant blackcurranty fruit, a lightish feel in the mouth (although by no means as light as, for example, Beaujolais) and gentle tannins. They can mature agreeably for several years. In less ripe years, though, they are pretty depressing, full of bitter green-pepper tannins and hard acids.

The best appellation for reds in Saumur is Saumur-Champigny. At their best, these are attractive, juicy-fruited wines, their upfront flavours of summer berries underpinned by considerable structure. In the good years, they are worth ageing.
PRODUCERS: Filliatreau, Dom. des Roches Neuves, Sauzay-Legrand.

The less distinguished area around Saumur-Champigny is designated straight AC Saumur Rouge. Its wines are drier and more astringent, with Filliatreau once again the best producer.

Sparkling Saumur is made by the same method as champagne, and is mainly made from Chenin Blanc. From good producers such as Gratien et Meyer (who also make a sparkling rosé from Cabernet Franc) or Bouvet-Ladubay, they have a tart but thirst-quenching crispness.

Some producers make a simple AC Saumur still white from Chenin Blanc that bears a not unexpected resemblance to Anjou Blanc Sec.
Touraine In the west of Touraine, the ACs of Chinon, Bourgueil and St-Nicolas-de-Bourgueil also make textbook Cabernet Franc reds, the last two in a distinctly lighter style. Chinon is the best of these three for structure and balance, but there are fine raspberry-fruited wines from the others too.
PRODUCERS: Couly-Dutheil, Dom. de la Tour, Raffault, Baudry (Chinon), Audebert, Dom. des Ouches (Bourgueil), Taluau (St-Nicolas-de-Bourgueil).

Chenin continues its sway into the area east of Tours, where its principal stamping-ground is Vouvray. Vouvray covers almost every stylistic manifestation that white wine can adopt – dry, medium-dry, semi-sweet, botrytized and sparkling. Confusingly, some producers are not always especially inclined to indicate the style on the label, so that what you thought was going to be a snappy, bone-dry white can have a perplexing degree of residual sugar in it. However, the picture is slowly changing, and Vouvray – despite being very vintage-sensitive – is capable of making some of the most appetizing Chenin wines of the Loire.

When the labelling does work, the designations are: sec, demi-sec, moelleux and 'Sélection' for the botrytis-affected *cuvées*. PRODUCERS: Fouquet (Dom. des Aubuisières), Brédif, Champalou, Ch. Moncontour, Prince Poniatowski. Huët makes by far the best Vouvray fizz, a wine as deeply rich and complex as good champagne.

Montlouis is an AC to the south of Vouvray on the other side of the river. It makes Chenin wines in the same repertoire of styles as Vouvray, but with somewhat less finesse.

Cheverny, in the northeastern corner of Touraine, was promoted from VDQS to AC in 1993. Its whites may use Chardonnay, Sauvignon or Chenin, but there is also a separate appellation – Cour Cheverny – for wines made from the residual plantings of a high-acid local grape called Romorantin. Cheverny also makes a crisp-edged red wine that may use Cabernet Franc, Gamay or Pinot Noir.

The regional appellation, Touraine AC, is for other reds and whites, usually labelled with the variety: Gamay or the Cabernets for reds, fruit-driven Sauvignon for whites. Look for the well-made wines of Dom. de l'Aumonier.

Upper Loire Here, at the eastern end of the Loire, in almost the dead centre of France, Sauvignon Blanc comes into play for the most fashionable ACs of the entire region. The two most lauded of the Sauvignon appellations are Sancerre and Pouilly-Fumé, which face each other on the left and right banks of the river respectively. They are both capable of producing some of the world's most intriguing Sauvignon – full of intense green flavours of apples and asparagus, nettles and parsley, as well as wisps of beguiling smoke – but they do fall short of greatness uncomfortably often for the prices they command. PRODUCERS: Gitton, Mellot, Roger, Vatan, Crochet, Bourgeois, Cotat (Sancerre); Didier Dagueneau, Châtelain, de Ladoucette, Ch. de Tracy (Pouilly-Fumé).

Travelling westwards from Sancerre, three less illustrious but noteworthy Sauvignon

appellations are to be found. Menetou-Salon, bordering on Sancerre, is the best and its prices are beginning to climb as it establishes a reputation. Pellé is the best producer. Across the river Cher are Quincy and Reuilly, making lighter, much less piquant Sauvignon wines.

Many producers in Sancerre, Menetou-Salon and Reuilly also make a red and/or rosé wine from Pinot Noir, perhaps with varying amounts of Gamay in the latter. These are nowhere near as powerful as the Pinots of Burgundy, but can be appealing in their grassy, cherry-fruited way.

Pouilly-sur-Loire is a little-seen dry white made from the humdrum Chasselas grape. South of the whole region, but north of the ancient town of Poitiers, is a VDQS area – Haut-Poitou – for good, simple whites and reds from Sauvignon, Chardonnay, Gamay, etc.

Any wine made outside the demarcated ACs, or using grape varieties not permitted within the specified AC (often fair-quality Sauvignon Blanc, Chardonnay, Chenin Blanc or Gamay) takes the rather florid regional designation of Vin de Pays du Jardin de la France.

VINTAGE GUIDE

The dry whites are not by and large for ageing. *2004* is good across the board, from Muscadet to the Upper Loire. The small harvest of *'03* produced exceptional wines, with fine Vouvray, and crisp, classic Sauvignon. *2002* was largely one to avoid. The best recent vintages for reds have been the gloriously ripe *2003* and *2000*, and the underrated *'02*. As with Sauternes, the Loire's best dessert wines last for aeons. The greatest recent vintages are *2003, 1990, '89* and *'88*, but *2000, 1997, '96* and *'95* are good too.

UPPER LOIRE
GRAPE: Sauvignon Blanc (whites)
SANCERRE, MENETOU-SALON AND REUILLY
GRAPES: Pinot Noir, Gamay (reds/rosés)

Sparkling rosé, made from Cabernet Franc (left), resting in pupîtres *at Gratien et Meyer, Saumur.*

CHAMPAGNE

The name alone conjures an image of celebration, of romance. The most northerly of France's fine wine regions, Champagne is the source of the world's finest sparkling wines.

THE NIGHT THEY invented champagne was about 350 years ago. It didn't take place overnight, and they didn't actually invent it as such, but it was around the middle of the 17th century that the fashion for wines that frothed took hold of smart café society – in London.

Although it was the winemakers of the Champagne region itself who perfected the various techniques indelibly associated with producing quality sparkling wines the world over, they would not have done so had the metropolitan English not developed a taste for deliberately spoiled wine. For there were no two ways about it: effervescence in the wine was considered an exasperating liability in the cold northerly climate of Champagne.

The problem often arose when the slow fermentation of the delicate and high-acid wines was interrupted by plummeting cellar temperatures as winter came on. When the time came to bottle the wines the following spring, there was very often a certain amount of residual sugar left over from the uncompleted fermentation. As the weather warmed up again, the yeasts that

had lain dormant in the wine over the winter now came back to life in the bottle and began feeding on the sugars once more. This time, however, the carbon dioxide gas that the fermentation process creates had nowhere to escape, so it dissolved into the wine until such time as the bottle was opened, whereupon hearts would sink at the discovery of another wretchedly fizzy disaster.

Much of the highly regarded still wine of the Champagne region was exported to Britain at this time. It was shipped in cask and would be bottled soon after its arrival by the London merchants. The British trade had, for some time, been used to adding brandy and a little sugar to the wines it imported because it was the only way to save them from turning rank during the long sea voyages they had to endure. (This practice is the origin of the great fortified wines, as we shall see in the chapter on Portugal.)

Champagne was the only wine – with the possible exception of burgundy – not to undergo this treatment as a matter of course, for the simple reason that, being the closest fine wine

The four vineyard areas of the Champagne region (below), with the warmer Aube valley tucked away to the south.

1. VALLÉE DE LA MARNE
2. MONTAGNE DE REIMS
3. CÔTE DES BLANCS
4. AUBE

Reims

Cumières

Bouzy

Epernay

Marne

Aube

Seine

Troyes

Les Riceys

region to the British Isles, the journey was nowhere near as arduous as that made, for example, by the wines of Portugal's Douro valley.

Since there was a marked British predilection, however, for sweetness and potency in wine, some merchants undoubtedly added a little sugar and a slug of spirit to the wines they brought in from Champagne as well. Given the fact that many of the wines were biologically unstable to begin with, this treatment, followed by early bottling, would have virtually assured anything from gentle pétillance to volcanic eruption when the bottle was broached.

Indeed, explosions in the cellar would have been quite commonplace and the injuries sustained thereby were viewed by the French as just desserts for the latest preposterous English fad. Not ones to be deterred by a bit of flying glass, the English responded by inventing stronger bottles.

Unbeknown to itself, the London *demi-monde*, having a rollicking good time drinking fashionable fizz in the cafés and playhouses, was assiduously developing the image that the champagne industry has traded on for most of the last three centuries. Fizzy wine is fun. All those little bubbles help it get right into the bloodstream without hanging about (which is why it "goes to the head" more quickly than whisky), and so champagne came to play a matchless role in partying and celebration.

Barrels holding unblended grape must (above). The markings show which area the grapes came from – VZY stands for Verzenay, on the Montagne de Reims.

Blanket of snow covers the walled Clos du Mesnil vineyard owned by Krug (left). Planted solely with Chardonnay grapes destined for Krug's prestige blanc de blancs.

Pinot Noir vines on the slopes of the Montagne de Reims (above). That puff of smoke in the distance is the prunings being burned.

Champagne going through the remuage *process (below) in traditional* pupîtres, *twisted and tipped by hand over many weeks.*

If you visit the headquarters of the largest and most famous champagne producer of all, Moët et Chandon, in Epernay, you will encounter a rather stern-looking statue in the forecourt. It stands in commemoration of Dom Pérignon, as does the wine at the top of Moët's range, which is named after him. Pérignon was a Benedictine monk who, in 1668, was appointed treasurer at the Abbey of Hautvillers near the town of Epernay, which is now the nerve-centre of the region as a whole.

Brother Pérignon's duties included overseeing the running of the cellars and the wine-making that was an important part of monastic life in the period. Among his formidable achievements were the perfecting of the technique of making a still *white* wine entirely from red grapes, refinement of the art of blending wines from different vineyards in the region to obtain the best possible product from available resources, and advances in clarification treatments to ensure a brighter wine than was the turbid norm at the time.

Dom Pérignon also devoted much effort to researching ways to avoid the dreaded refermentation that resulted in so many turbulent wines. His seminal place in the region's history is unquestionably merited, but not as the inventor of sparkling champagne.

As the process for making sparkling wines was rationalized, the inducement of the all-important second fermentation in the bottle was achieved by the addition of a little sugar solution to an already fully fermented wine. This then gave the surviving yeasts something more to chew over. The drawback to this was that the sediment of dead yeast cells then created remained trapped in the wine and gave it the cloudiness that Dom Pérignon had worked so sedulously to prevent. The house of Veuve Clicquot, founded in 1772, may take the credit for the solution to that particularly sticky problem.

Nicole-Barbe Clicquot-Ponsardin took over the running of the firm after her husband – the founder's son – left her widowed in her 20s. Her formidable promotional talents and encouragement of innovation in themselves would have made her one of the key figures in champagne history, but it was the development under her tutelage of the process of *remuage* that installed her unassailably in the region's hall of fame.

By this method, the bottles were placed in slots in wooden contraptions that look like large sandwich-boards. Over a number of weeks, cellar-workers would regularly give them a twist and a shake and in doing so gradually adjust their angles in the slots, until they were more or less upside down. As the bottles were slowly tipped, the sediment gradually sank towards the neck of the bottle until it all collected on the underside of the cap.

In time, the way to remove the accumulated deposit came to involve dipping the necks of the bottles in freezing brine so that the portion of wine containing the sediment is flash-frozen. When the metal cap is knocked away, the deposit flies out with it and the bottle is topped up and corked. All of this is automated now, of course, including the actual turning of the bottles, which is done by computer-programmed machines with the bottles packed in huge crates. Some houses make a virtue of the fact that they still painstakingly hand-turn all their wines. Whether this makes any noticeable difference in the finished wine is highly debatable, though great offence is occasioned if you dare to suggest otherwise.

The pre-eminence of champagne as the king of sparkling wines was well established by the end of the 18th century, but most of the world-famous houses we know today were founded in the first half of the 19th century. The region suffered horrendously during the Great War. The

rapid German advance through northern France in the early months of hostilities in autumn 1914 penetrated south of the river Marne. It was driven partially back by 1915 to a line north of the strategic city of Reims, where it was to remain virtually static until the Armistice.

With the coming of prosperity after World War Two, champagne began very gradually to trickle down the social scale and become less of a luxury. The industry lost its way somewhat in the 1980s when consumption in the UK reached unprecedented levels to coincide with relatively benign economic times. Some members of its controlling body felt that the wine was in danger of becoming too democratic and losing its aura of elite unaffordability. A more or less explicit attempt to ration consumption, using the sledgehammer of price inflation, was just beginning to work when the coming of severe recession did the job for them.

By the mid-1990s, champagne sales were once more on a gentle upward trajectory as prices moderated and a new quality charter came into effect to ensure that Champagne didn't just idly trade on its good name by selling wafer-thin, razor-sharp, watery wines as it had been tempted to do during the boom years. As a result, it is again possible to say that, when they play to the peak of their form, these are indeed the finest sparkling wines made anywhere.

THE WINES

Champagne production is dominated by members of the Club des Grandes Marques, the big houses such as Moët et Chandon, Bollinger, Mumm, Taittinger, Veuve Clicquot and Pol Roger. They have the highest profiles and their wines, in the main, sell for the highest prices. Additionally, there are a number of important co-operatives in the region who often make own-label champagnes for supermarket chains in the export markets. Increasingly, there are a number of go-it-alone growers who are making their own wines on an endearingly small scale.

The region divides into four broad areas, the Vallée de la Marne along the river at the heart of Champagne, the Montagne de Reims, a large hill overlooking the city where much of the Pinot Noir is grown, the Côte des Blancs where the concentrations of Chardonnay are found and – quite detached from the rest to the south – the Aube valley, with the most rustic wines. Throughout the region, the chalky soils are held to endow champagne with much of its finesse.

While most of the big houses own some vineyard land, they nearly all rely on buying in grapes from contract growers in the various vineyards. In the 1980s, the balance of power was radically shifted in the direction of the growers; previously bound by an annual price-fixing agreement, they are now free to negotiate for what they can get within much more discretionary guidelines. The initially dire impact on costs this entailed led to some swingeing price hikes, but things have lately moderated somewhat as the growers realize that champagne is their livelihood too.

Of the three grapes permitted in the wine, two are red, although most champagne is white. Pinot Noir brings weight and richness to a blend and helps it to age productively, while those who use a greater percentage of Chardonnay, such as Henriot, value it for the elegance and gracefully lighter feel it can impart.

Pinot Meunier is a less distinguished grape in itself, but does lend a distinct fruity immediacy to many blends. Some houses try to play down the influence of this grape; others, such as Krug, makers of expensive crème-de-la-crème champagne, openly celebrate the function it serves. (Its image isn't helped by the fact that it may not be planted on the best vineyard sites, designated *grand cru*.)

The aim for quality enshrined in the Chartre de Qualité that came into effect in the 1990s stipulates that only the first free-run juice of the harvested grapes, followed by the juice of one gentle pressing, may now be used in the wines of the charter's signatories. (Previously, the harsher, more astringent juice of a second pressing went in as well, and did a lot to coarsen the taste of many champagnes.)

Summer at Verzenay, on the Montagne de Reims (above). The sunny slopes of the Montagne are planted mainly with Pinot Noir.

CHAMPAGNE

GRAPES: *Pinot Noir, Pinot Meunier, Chardonnay*

Hand-harvesting ripe Pinot Noir grapes at Mailly on the Montagne (above).

Pruning vines in early March (above), and burning the cuttings on a portable fire.

Most champagne is labelled "Brut", which is the standard, bone-dry style. The dryness or sweetness of a champagne is determined at the last moment before the cork goes in, when a quantity of sugar in solution known as the *dosage* is added to create the final taste. Even the Brut contains some sugar, since unadorned champagne is naturally a very acidic wine. A very few wines receive no *dosage* at all, and may be labelled "Brut Zéro": the intrepid should look out for Laurent-Perrier's version for an acceptable taste of the style.

Alternatively, an above-average amount of sugar can be added to create a sweeter style – either medium-dry, labelled "demi-sec", or positively sweet, and labelled either "doux" or possibly "rich". Not many of these are especially attractive, although Louis Roederer makes a nicely balanced Rich.

Some still wine is made in the Champagne region, and goes under the appellation Coteaux Champenois. Red wines from the villages of Bouzy and Cumières may be good in a rasping, rustic sort of way. The rest are rather charmless. In the south of the region, in the Aube valley, is an appellation for still pink wines, Rosé des Riceys. Its tiny production constitutes one of the more arresting pink wines made anywhere in France, but the astronomical prices will act as a strong deterrent to the curious.

Non-vintage The benchmark style of champagne, and the brand that the reputations of the houses live or die by, is the non-vintage blend. Each year, a certain quantity of base wine is held back in reserve, and small amounts of this older, maturer wine, known as *vin de réserve*, is used to give a softer feel and more complex flavour to what would otherwise be very raw, acidic wine. When there has been a run of good vintages, as there was from 1988-90, the quality of the non-vintage (or NV) goes up significantly. Styles vary enormously from one producer to the next, but the ridiculous fluctuations in quality that were the norm in the 1980s seem to have been ironed out to a heartening extent now.
BEST HOUSES: Charles Heidsieck, Bollinger, Pol Roger, Lanson, Piper-Heidsieck, Veuve Clicquot, Billecart-Salmon, Ayala, Dumangin, Tarlant.

Vintage This is the produce of a single year's harvest, with the year stated on the label. The minimum ageing time it must spend on its sediment in the cellars is three years, although the better houses will give it longer. Like port, vintage champagne should theoretically only be

made in the best years, maybe three or at most four times a decade, but it seemingly takes a spectacularly rotten vintage to dissuade everybody from producing a vintage wine.

On average, vintage wines are released at around five years old, although they don't really come into their own until after eight to ten years. In 1995, for instance, it was quite clear that the exceptionally good '88s, which had been on the market for some considerable time, still needed at least another three years. Bear this in mind when you buy it; these wines are too expensive to waste by drinking them immature.
BEST VINTAGE PRODUCERS: Charles Heidsieck, H Blin, Bollinger, Lanson, Piper-Heidsieck, Louis Roederer, Veuve Clicquot, Billecart-Salmon, de Venoge, Henriot.

Rosé Pink champagne suffers somewhat from being seen as an unnecessarily frivolous wine, a little infra dig. Many could benefit, though, from a little frivolity, since in general they are nowhere near as attractive to taste as they look. Most of the wine is made by adding a little still red wine from the locale to the white champagne. A very small amount (Laurent-Perrier is the most famous example) is made by staining the white juice by allowing the red grapeskins to soak in it for a short while. At their best, rosé champagnes have an exhilarating strawberry or peachy fruit that makes them glorious for summer drinking.
BEST: Pol Roger, Jacquart, Veuve Clicquot, Ruinart, Gosset and – at the expensive end – Belle Epoque, Krug and Roederer Cristal.

Blanc de Blancs Champagne that utilizes only the Chardonnay grape. These are the lightest and most graceful wines of the lot. Many certainly do feel less mouth-filling than the blended champagnes, but vintage examples that are aged take on a gorgeous toasty richness that quite belies the lightness argument.
BEST: Billecart-Salmon, Nicolas Feuillatte, Drappier, Dom Ruinart, Salon, Taittinger Comtes de Champagne, Krug Clos de Mesnil.

Blanc de Noirs White champagne made from the black grapes, Pinot Noir and Pinot Meunier, usually with a noticeably darker tone to it, although it is never pink. Not an immediately attractive wine, certainly not beginner's champagne, too many of these wines taste muddy and leaden. When good, though, their richer style can be impressive.
BEST: Bollinger Vieilles Vignes, de Venoge, Billiot.

Prestige Cuvée Most of the big houses make a top-drawer special bottling. These are usually – though not always – a vintage wine, produced just to show how good they can really get. They are often aged for longer than ordinary vintage wine or come from particularly favoured parcels of vineyard land. The packaging may be quite diverting, as witness Perrier-Jouët's Belle Epoque in its flower-painted bottle, or the multi-faceted crystal effect of Nicolas Feuillatte's Palmes d'Or. Even more than straight vintage wines, these champagnes have to be aged properly. If it's cost you a day's wages, the incentive should be there.

BEST: Bollinger RD, Roederer Cristal, Pol Roger Cuvée Sir Winston Churchill, Krug Grande Cuvée, Perrier-Jouët Belle Epoque, Gosset Grande Réserve, Veuve Clicquot La Grande Dame, Mumm René Lalou, Pommery Cuvée Louise, Laurent-Perrier Grand Siècle, and Nicolas Feuillatte Cuvée Palmes d'Or.

VINTAGE GUIDE

2002 **** Not yet released at the time of writing, but should be great.

2000 ** Modest vintage from the better houses.

1999 ** Not a stunner, but some acceptable wines.

1998 *** Better than initially feared, with many wines now showing impressive maturity.

1997 *** These are well-balanced, attractive wines with real depth, and are drinking well now.

1996 **** Intensely lush, honeyed wines that reached maturity sooner than the '95s.

1995 **** A great vintage of harmonious, structured wines, drinking now.

1993 *** Underrated but decent vintage.

1990 **** Fine vintage that has matured into rich and full-flavoured champagnes.

1989 ***** Intensely lush, honeyed wines.

1988 **** Sturdy, long-lived, full-bodied vintage.

Earlier vintages worth trying if you see them, from houses that specialize in disgorging old stocks, are: *1985 **** 1982 ***** 1979 *****

Autumnal glow of the Champagne region (below) with the golden-coloured vineyards spreading across the hills.

ALSACE

A richly endowed wine region that deserves greater recognition, Alsace is a unique blend of the best of Germanic and French culture and grape varieties, and offers some of France's most idiosyncratic wine styles.

OF ALL OF FRANCE'S principal wine regions, Alsace is culturally the most distinct. Its political history has been a literal tug-of-war between the two great powers of continental Europe: since 1870, it has been run by France, Germany, France, Germany and France again. Now undeniably French in its cultural outlook, despite the Germanic names of its inhabitants, Alsace shelters between the Vosges mountains and the river Rhine and grows both French and German grape varieties.

The village of Hunawihr, Alsace (above), with its 15th-century church, and the grand cru *vineyard of Rosacker on the slope beyond.*

Alsace, bordered by the Vosges mountains and the river Rhine (right), has one overall AC, with specified grand cru *vineyards. The marked villages are where the cellars of most of the region's top producers are located.*

The wines it produces have no precise equivalents, however, in either the rest of France or Germany. They are among the most idiosyncratic styles made anywhere, and are greatly valued as such by those who know them. What Alsace is very bad at, unfortunately, is winning new converts. When people who have been introduced to wine via sugared-up German products like Liebfraumilch decide to branch out and try something more sophisticated, they tend to leave German wine behind. The wines of Alsace, bottled as they are in tall, Germanic green flutes by producers with Germanic names from vineyards with names like Pfingstberg, do not exactly make the novice customer think "France". When the grape variety is Riesling, the wine's fate is sealed. The assumption is that it will be sweet.

Ironically, Alsace should be just about the easiest French region to understand, because it is the only part of France where the wines have traditionally been named after their grape varieties, rather than villages (as in Burgundy) or the names of properties (as in Bordeaux). Furthermore, despite the demarcation of the *grands crus* in the 1980s, there is essentially one overriding regional appellation – AC Alsace – much as there is in Champagne or Cognac.

Although the location of these vineyards in a northeastern corner of France does mean that the growing season is relatively cool, it is also – because of the shelter of the mountains – particularly dry. Alsace has as little annual rainfall as parts of the broiling Midi down south (although vintages of the early 1990s were uncharacteristically damp). That means that, even when a harvest has been rather poor in much of the rest of France, Alsace tends not to take quite the caning that other regions suffer.

It is in these sometimes too arid conditions that clay-based soils, such as Alsace has in some of its lower-lying vineyards, are beneficial. Clay absorbs what moisture there is during wet spells and doesn't allow it to drain away as freely as other soil types – a nuisance if you have persistent rain, but a precious asset when summer drought is a real possibility.

Alsace's wines deserve a wider audience. Some producers border their neck labels in the blue, white and red of the *tricolor*, but short of actually changing the shape of the bottle – which there is no serious proposal to do – these wines will sadly continue to languish in mistaken identity. That could, in theory, be good news for those of us who have discovered the joys of Alsace wines and do want to drink them, but for the fact that the very lack of demand means that scarcely any mainstream wine merchants bother to list anything more than the lowest-common-denominator produce of the co-operatives.

THE WINES

Nearly all Alsace wine is dry to medium-dry varietal white, produced from one of the following varieties, and labelled as such. The first four listed here are considered the noblest of them all, and are the only ones permitted on the vineyard sites designated *grand cru*.

Gewürztraminer This is the variety most readily associated in people's minds with the region's wines. Intensely aromatic, with a range of musky, floral scents underpinned with ripe fruit and sweet spice, Gewürztraminer is usually a deeply coloured wine with low acidity and rumbustious levels of alcohol. Despite its headstrong personality, it is a sympathetic partner to many foods but, perhaps best of all, the richly flavoured pâtés and terrines for which Alsace cuisine is famous. The wines can benefit from some bottle-ageing, although in very ripe years, such as 2003, the acidity level in the finished wine may be so low to start with that prolonged ageing will only turn it mushy.
PRODUCERS: Zind-Humbrecht, Hugel, Trimbach, Kuentz-Bas, Willm.

Riesling The starkest, most unnervingly pure dry Rieslings in the world come from Alsace. They are almost painfully austere in youth, and a period of bottle-ageing is mandatory for most examples. The fruit flavours are acerbic lime-peel and grapefruit, held together by exemplary levels of steely acid and noticeably higher alcohol than even Germany's driest Riesling Trocken tends to attain. They make an appetizing accompaniment to simply prepared freshwater fish dishes. In their maturity, they can be overcome with a bewitching fume of freshly pumped petrol and damp earth, but never quite losing the outline of that nervy acidity. The buzzword for them is "racy".

PRODUCERS: Trimbach, Schlumberger, Josmeyer, Louis Sipp, Zind-Humbrecht, Dopff au Moulin, Léon Beyer.

Pinot Gris Once termed Tokay-Pinot Gris on the labels, after some misbegotten fable which had a soldier bringing back vines from the Tokaji region of Hungary (which doesn't have Pinot Gris), this is a much misunderstood variety. In some producers' wines, it can have all the spicy pungency of Gewürztraminer, with the fruit just a little sharper – orange perhaps rather than the mushy peach of Gewurz. Then again, it can have a fat, buttery texture to it and a layer of honey that can make it seem curiously like Chardonnay. Like Gewürztraminer, the acidity is generally fairly low, and that should be taken into account when deciding how long to age a Pinot Gris.
PRODUCERS: Zind-Humbrecht, Beyer, Schlumberger, Kreydenweiss, Albrecht.

Husseren-les-Châteaux, a typical Alsace village, surrounded by vineyards (above), with the three ruined towers on the hill behind.

The steeply sloping grand cru *Rangen vineyard at the village of Thann (right), Alsace's most southerly grand cru.*

Muscat Muscat is the name of one of the oldest known grape varieties, in fact a many-membered family as opposed to a single variety. Two of its scions are present in Alsace, one of them not surprisingly known as Muscat d'Alsace and the other Muscat Ottonel. No distinction is made between them on the labels. Muscat is one of the great sweet-wine grapes, the only one by consensus to actually smell and taste of grapes. Vinified dry, it can be bracingly tart and much thinner in texture than the three grapes listed above. There is very little of it planted compared to the others, but in a good year, from low-yielding vines, it can make a pleasantly sharp, refreshing white with something of the musky spice the region rejoices in.
PRODUCERS: Trimbach, Rolly-Gassmann, Weinbach, Schleret.

Pinot Blanc Not an especially aromatic grape, but definitely an underrated one. Pinot Blanc makes a creamy, slightly appley wine that provides an unstartling introduction to the region for those nervous of plunging headlong into the giddy waters of Gewurz. Sometimes it has a taste of bland tropical fruit like guava as well. Drunk young, these have far more character than many another unoaked dry white. Not for long ageing. (A minority of growers insists on calling the wines Klevner or Clevner.)
PRODUCERS: Rolly-Gassmann, Hugel, Mann, Zind-Humbrecht, Weinbach.

Sylvaner The speciality grape of Franken, in western Germany, makes a pungently vegetal, often distinctly cabbagey wine in Alsace. Not the most attractive flavour in the world, but the odd one can have a honeyed quality and unexpected richness that makes it worth trying.
PRODUCERS: Zind-Humbrecht, Becker, Weinbach, Domaine Ostertag, Seltz.

Auxerrois This is the grape variety that nobody really talks about, although there is certainly plenty of it about. An anomaly of the appellation regulations says that it can be considered as interchangeable with Pinot Blanc, so that a wine labelled simply Pinot Blanc may be blended with Auxerrois (or indeed in theory be nothing but Auxerrois). By itself, it gives very simple, though fairly full-textured wines with a vaguely soapy flavour. You won't see it mentioned on labels very often.
PRODUCERS: Albert Mann, Rolly-Gassmann.

Chasselas Very rarely seen on labels, this undistinguished grape makes extremely light, neutral-tasting wine. Schoffit works miracles with it to produce an impressively lush-textured wine from old vines.

Edelzwicker The name used for blends of any of the above grapes (with the exception of Pinot Blanc and Auxerrois). Since the varietals are generally so sharply delineated, there seems little point in drinking one of these if you can have a single-grape wine.

Pinot Noir The only red grape in Alsace makes some exceedingly light reds and tiny amounts of rosé. Not a lot of it shows much pedigree, it has to be said. Perhaps it's the climate, perhaps it's the soils, but the variety just doesn't have the same class here as it does in Burgundy. There may be some sharp cherry fruit in the better ones, but in the cooler years it has an unpalatably green tinge to it that can be quite off-putting. Marcel Deiss makes about the only reasonably consistent one.

Crémant d'Alsace Alsace makes some of the most impressive sparkling wine in France outside the Champagne region – generally of higher quality than either of the two corresponding Crémants of Burgundy or the Loire. The principal grape used is Pinot Blanc, but the small plantings of Chardonnay found in the region go into the sparklers too. The method is the same as that used for champagne, with a second fermentation taking place in the bottle. The result is often attractively nutty, full-flavoured wines of considerable depth.

PRODUCERS: Wolfberger, Dopff au Moulin, Dopff & Irion, Turckheim co-operative.

Vendange Tardive This is the less rich of the two sweeter styles of Alsace wine. The name means "late harvest" to denote grapes that have been left on the vine to overripen, and thereby achieve higher levels of natural sugar. The designation applies only to the first four noble grapes mentioned above. They can be addictively delicious, perfectly balanced between the tang of ripe fruits and the lightest trickling of spicy syrup. In the great vintages of 1989 and 1990, they were particularly rich, honeyed and decadently creamy. In lesser years, they can be pretty close to the dry wines, but with a just perceptible extra depth to the texture.

Sélection de Grains Nobles The "noble" in the name of this category refers to the noble rot, botrytis, that stalks the vineyards in some years and allows the growers to make Alsace's richest and most unctuous wines. They are powerfully alcoholic and glutinously sweet, and should theoretically age beautifully. The only slight vitiating factor is that, particularly with reference to Gewurz and Pinot Gris, the acidity – low enough in the dry wines – plummets even further when the rotted berries are left on the vine for so long. Once again, only the big four grapes may be used, with Muscat by far the most seldom encountered.

Grands Crus Since 1983, a *grand cru* system has been in use in Alsace, covering the most prestigious vineyard sites of the region. In the mid-1990s, this was still being painstakingly argued and negotiated over, but there will almost certainly be somewhere between 50 and 60 names on the list by the time it is finalized. Yields permitted under the *crus* at the outset were fixed too high, but have now been reduced to the 60 hectolitres per hectare worthier of a *grand cru* wine. Eventually, the wines from these named vineyards should begin to justify the extra premium that such a badge of quality commands, and even those *grand cru* growers who currently feel they have no need of the classification, such as Hugel, may be won over. Riesling, Gewurztraminer, Pinot Gris and Muscat are the privileged quartet of grapes allowed on these specified sites, and since the individual vineyards are quite distinct from each other in terms of soil, exposure and microclimate, the *grand cru* wines should give us a beguiling insight into the versatility that Alsace is undoubtedly capable of.

VINTAGE GUIDE

2004 *** Good picking conditions redeemed a poor summer, and the wines mostly have good acidity and ripeness.

2003 **** An absolute heatwave resulted in a small, superripe vintage. Fine Muscat, approachable young Riesling, but Gewurz and Pinot Gris may lack acid balance.

2002 **** Elegant, aromatic wines of obvious class, though sometimes lighter than the norm. The sweet wines are especially well-balanced.

2001 **** Late-summer warmth redeemed this vintage, and nearly all varieties (plus sweet wines) look great.

2000 *** Not as good as they seemed at first, these are now tiring.

1998 **** Very attractive, ripe vintage with some especially good Rieslings.

1990 ***** Great vintage of massively concentrated wines. Rieslings in particular are superb.

1989 **** Another dry, searing summer created the conditions for many splendidly intense wines. The late-harvest versions are sumptuous.

1985 ***** Excellent year that produced many monumental wines capable of long maturation. As good as the 1990s, and worth paying the price if you find any.

The village of Riquewihr, dominated by its church spire (above), seen from the Schoenenburg grand cru.

Half-timbered Alsace building (below), Hugel's cellars in Riquewihr.

BURGUNDY

Lovers of great Pinot Noir and classic Chardonnay speak the name with reverence.
Burgundy's vinous history dates back for centuries, tied up in the division of land
and the role of the négociant.

BURGUNDY IS THE region that arouses the most passionate controversies within French wine. In times gone by, connoisseurs of French wine divided amicably into devotees of Bordeaux and Burgundy, the one traditionally seen as a cerebral, contemplative wine, the other as the stuff of hedonistic sensuality. In latter times, however, while claret has largely maintained its equilibrium, burgundy has been plunged into conflict – over how it should be made, whether the small growers are better than the big-time merchants, and whether it is now being consistently outstripped by producers from outside Europe.

The autumnal colours of the
Charmes vineyard at Gevrey-
Chambertin on the Côte de
Nuits (above).

The great names of
Burgundy (right) are concen-
trated in a line north-south
between the towns of Dijon
and Lyon; Chablis lies alone
to the north.

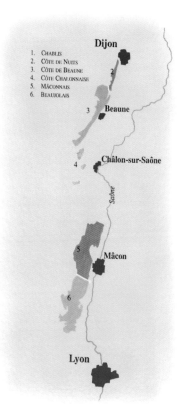

1. CHABLIS
2. CÔTE DE NUITS
3. CÔTE DE BEAUNE
4. CÔTE CHALONNAISE
5. MÂCONNAIS
6. BEAUJOLAIS

Dijon

Beaune

Châlon-sur-Saône

Mâcon

Lyon

What makes the debate all the more poignant is that the annual production of fine burgundy is microscopically small compared with the output of Bordeaux. Its premium wines – the equivalents of the classed growths of Bordeaux – come almost entirely from the narrow limestone ridge of the Côte d'Or, less than 48km (30 miles) from north to south and not more than 8km (5 miles) across at its widest point. (Most of the wines mentioned on the following pages are commercially unavailable, because the tiny production is snapped up immediately by contract customers, restaurants and hotels. Compare that with the oceans of unsold claret that built up in the Bordeaux region in the early 1990s.)

Furthermore, what land there is has been relentlessly subdivided over the generations. It is now quite common for a single proprietor to own no more vines than could be fitted into a decently sized back garden.

Before the French Revolution, large parcels of the land were owned by the nobility, as it had been when Burgundy was an autonomous ducal state in the 14th and 15th centuries, and the rest by the church. The Revolution saw that land sold to large numbers of the newly enfranchised bourgeoisie. The Napoleonic Code that was effected in the aftermath of the Revolution's demise decreed that, on the death of a landowner, property was to be divided equally among his offspring. Two hundred years later, where even a modest château in Bordeaux can put around 3000 cases of wine on to the market each year, a Burgundy grower may struggle to make two dozen.

It is hardly surprising, given this pattern, that the region came to be dominated by large merchant houses known as négociants. These would simply buy lots of wine, or even just harvested grapes, from the growers and blend what they bought to produce their own bottlings. The period since the Second World War, however, has seen the emergence of the *propriétaires-viticulteurs*, go-it-alone operators making infinitesimal quantities of wine from their own vineyard holdings and selling it independently. Some of these are unquestionably fine, indeed have a legitimate claim to be the region's best wines. Others vary from the mediocre to the extremely ropey, often because they can't or won't invest in the kind of up-to-the-minute hygiene technology that the quality-conscious négociants have at their disposal.

This chapter moves from north to south to take in Chablis, historically considered a viticultural part of Burgundy, the two sections of the Côte d'Or (the Côte de Nuits and the Côte de Beaune), the Côte Chalonnaise and Mâconnais.

CHABLIS

The Chablis vineyards to the northwest of the main Burgundy region are geographically closer to the southern end of Champagne than they are to the Côte d'Or. As such, they represent one of the most northerly outposts of still Chardonnay wine in the world. Not surprisingly, the style that has come to be associated with the area is one of light-textured wines with scything acidity and either a very restrained use of or – classically – complete absence of oak.

Chablis's claim to fame is a geological formation of limestone and clay that it shares with parts of southern England, and which is known as Kimmeridgian after the Dorset village of Kimmeridge. This is held to endow the wines with their celebrated minerality, an austere hardness that makes them worth ageing for a few years.

The class structure of the wines of Chablis is much the same as in the rest of Burgundy. The top vineyard sites are designated *grand cru*, the next best *premier cru* and then come the wines of the basic appellation. In Chablis, this is supplemented by a basement category of Petit Chablis. This covers wines from land just outside the main appellation, and wines from within it where the vines have not attained the minimum age for Chablis proper.

Grands crus There are seven of these, all located on the same south-facing slope just to the north of the town of Chablis itself. They are: Blanchots, Bougros, Les Clos, Grenouilles, Les Preuses, Valmur and Vaudésir. (If you come across Chablis from a vineyard called La Moutonne, consider it *grand cru*, even though it officially isn't. It has the misfortune to straddle Les Preuses and Vaudésir and therefore escapes the classification.) These are the richest and weightiest Chablis, and quality is by and large very reliable. They should be at least five years old before drinking, and many will have had

their naturally more opulent flavours enhanced by oak ageing. If you are trading up from basic Chablis, go all the way up to *grand cru*.

Premiers crus There are around 40 vineyards specified for *premier cru*, although many of them shelter under larger collective names. The more commonly encountered of these are: Fourchaume, Beauroy, Vaillons, Montée de Tonnerre, Montmains and Côte de Léchet. The numbers of the *premiers crus* have gone on increasing steadily as consortia of growers in vineyards that hitherto came under straight AC Chablis have persuaded the appellation authorities to upgrade them. In far too many cases, it has to be said, these promotions were either very borderline or else wholly unjustified. The result is that a lot of *premier cru* tastes no different to normal Chablis, and can't therefore justify the extra premium it charges: 40-50 per cent on top of the price of AC Chablis.

CHABLIS

GRAPE: *Chardonnay*

Four of Chablis's seven grand cru vineyards (below): looking from Grenouilles towards Vaudésir, Preuses and Bougros beyond.

Chablis The basic appellation is the most extensive area of the total vineyard. At its best, it is a faintly appley, sometimes attractively vegetal wine, with fresh lemony acidity and powerful but not overwhelming alcohol – the essence of unoaked Chardonnay. It is a style that is often imitated elsewhere by picking the grapes earlier to attain higher acid levels, but good Chablis shouldn't ever be bitter or green. Indeed, at its centre, there is a paradoxical softness. As it ages, it often assumes a richer, more honeyed quality, as if it had spent some time in barrels on its way from vine to bottle, though it may have done no such thing.

Petit Chablis Just as a lot of simple Chablis was elevated to *premier cru*, so a lot of Petit Chablis has miraculously become Chablis, with the result that there is very little land planted in the Petit Chablis designation. The wines generally lack concentration and breeding, with the (very) occasional shining exception.

CHABLIS PRODUCERS: René Dauvissat, François & Jean-Marie Raveneau, Denis Race, Daniel Defaix, Robert Vocoret, Louis Michel, Jean Durup, la Chablisienne co-operative. For the best of the oak-influenced Chablis, go to William Fèvre.

BEST RECENT VINTAGES: *2004, '03, '02, 2000, 1999.*

COTE DE NUITS

GRAPES: *Red – Pinot Noir; White – Chardonnay, small amount of Pinot Blanc*

COTE DE NUITS

The northern half of the Côte d'Or, starting just south of Dijon, is the Côte de Nuits. The area is particularly noted for its red wines, although a small amount of white is produced in some appellations. For many aspirant red winemakers around the world, the Côte de Nuits is *the* true heartland of Pinot Noir. The majestic intensity (and scarcity) of the wines makes the highest among them – the legendary *grands crus* – among the most sought-after and highly-valued red wines on the planet.

This guide to the appellations runs from north to south. Some of the villages have individually designated vineyard sites within their appellations, *premiers crus* and (at the top of the tree) *grands crus*. I have listed here the names of the *grands crus* (GC) followed by the number of *premiers crus* (pc), where they are appropriate.

Marsannay An AC since 1987, Marsannay has always been famed for its light, strawberryish rosé, but it can come in all three colours. The reds are getting better. Good value.

PRODUCERS: Roty, Jadot, Bruno Clair.

Fixin Meaty reds with considerable depth and structure, if not always great finesse. Some humdrum white. (5 pc.)

PRODUCERS: Bruno Clair, Moillard.

Gevrey-Chambertin The first of the great appellations (reds only). Powerful, strongly scented, beefy wines with richness and ageability at their best. GC: Mazis-Chambertin, Ruchottes-Chambertin, Chambertin Clos-de-Bèze, Chapelle-Chambertin, Griotte-Chambertin, Charmes-Chambertin, Le Chambertin, Latricières-Chambertin. (28 pc.)

PRODUCERS: Rossignol-Trapet, René Leclerc, Joseph Roty, Roumier, Dom. Dujac, Jadot, Faiveley.

Morey-St-Denis Somewhat lighter than Gevrey, but still having that beef-stock character over fruit like dark-skinned plums. Tiny amounts of white. GC: Clos de la Roche, Clos St-Denis, Clos des Lambrays, Clos de Tart, Bonnes Mares. (20 pc.)

PRODUCERS: Groffier, both Lignier brothers, Roumier, Dom. Rousseau, Serveau.

Chambolle-Musigny Generally over-light reds with sweet strawberry fruit, atypical for the Côte de Nuits. GC: Bonnes Mares (overlapping with the above), Le Musigny (which can also be white). (24 pc.)

PRODUCERS: Roumier, Serveau, Hudelot-Noëllat, Faiveley, Drouhin, Prieur.

Vougeot Small production of sound wines from the basic AC, totally overshadowed by the *grand cru*. Also some fair whites. GC: Clos de Vougeot. (4 pc.)

PRODUCERS: Leroy, Méo-Camuzet, Mugneret.

Vosne-Romanée Superbly aromatic, gamey Pinot, intensely ripe raspberry fruit and huge structure. Demands ageing. The *grands crus* – famously from the celebrated Domaine de la Romanée-Conti – are the best reds in Burgundy, made in tiny quantities at prices to induce a blackout. No whites. The neighbouring commune of Flagey-Echézeaux has two *grands crus* but its village wine is labelled Vosne-Romanée. GC: Grands Echézeaux, Echézeaux, Richebourg, Romanée-St-Vivant, Romanée-Conti, La Romanée, La Grande Rue, La Tâche. (13 pc.)

PRODUCERS: Dom. de la Romanée-Conti, Leroy, Méo-Camuzet, Jayer, Gros, Grivot, Daniel Rion, Clerget, Confuron.

Nuits-St-Georges Famous for decades in the UK. At best, classically meaty, cherry-fruited reds with great depth and complexity, but can be patchy. Some rather solid whites. (27 pc.)

PRODUCERS: Leroy, Gouges, Dom. de l'Arlot, Chevillon, Chopin-Groffier, Moillard, Jadot, Jaffelin, Rion, Grivot.

Hautes-Côtes-de-Nuits A group of little villages in the hills to the west of the Côte de Nuits is bunched together under this appellation, a reliable starting-point for those wanting a gentle run-up to the more extravagant stuff. The fruit on the reds is generally excellent and the wines hint at the sinewy structure of the top Côte de Nuits. The whites are soft and hazelnutty, if unspectacular.

PRODUCERS: Jayer-Gilles, Verdet, Cave des Hautes-Côtes.

Côtes de Nuits-Villages An appellation that gathers in a handful of villages from the extreme northern and southern ends of the Côte de Nuits area itself. Usually well-made, if lightish reds.

PRODUCERS: Philippe Rossignol, Chopin-Groffier, Daniel Rion.

COTE DE BEAUNE

This is the southern stretch of the Côte d'Or, an area particularly famed for its white wines, although there are many good reds too. Burgundy's highly reputed oak-aged Chardonnays come mainly from the southern end of the Côte de Beaune, while the best reds from further north are fully the equals of those from the Côte de Nuits. They tend to be slightly softer and more immediately approachable, however, emphasizing red fruit flavours first and the classic Burgundian meatiness second.

Once again, this is a north-to-south listing of the appellations, with the *grands crus* (GC) named and the number of *premiers crus* (pc) stated, where appropriate.

Pernand-Vergelesses Delicate whites and slimline reds can both be very attractive when a lighter style is required, but this is not generally the appellation to choose for the full-throttle Burgundy experience. Some of Burgundy's unsung alternative white wine, Aligoté (from the grape of that name), comes from around this village: expect lemon-sharp acids over a softer sour-cream base. GC: about a quarter of the *grand cru* Corton-Charlemagne lies within this appellation. (4 pc.)

PRODUCERS: Delarche, Pavelot, Rollin, Chandon de Briailles.

Ladoix Rarely seen appellation of the village of Ladoix-Serrigny, almost all lean, simple red. Now for the confusing part. GC: about one-eighth of Le Corton (nearly all red) and a tiny part of Corton-Charlemagne (white only) lie within Ladoix, although they are officially the *grands crus* of Aloxe-Corton (see below). Similarly, some of Ladoix's *premiers crus* are claimed by Aloxe-Corton, leaving it with 5 pc to call its own.

PRODUCERS: Ravaut, Chevalier, Capitain-Gagnerot.

Aloxe-Corton Good, muscular reds from the village appellation and a minuscule quantity of underwhelming white. GC: Le Corton (the only *grand cru* for red wines on the Côte de Beaune) may have any one of up to 21 vineyard names attached to it, eg. Corton-Bressandes, Corton-Perrières, Corton-Clos du Roi, etc. Corton-Charlemagne (the *grand cru* for whites only) is shared, as above, with Ladoix and Pernand-Vergelesses. (12 pc, some technically in the village of Ladoix.)

PRODUCERS: Chandon de Briailles, Bonneau du Martray, Remoissenet, Rapet, Louis Latour, Voarick, Tollot-Beaut.

The château of Gevrey-Chambertin (above), the first of the great red Burgundy appellations in the Côte de Nuits.

COTE DE BEAUNE
GRAPES: *Red – Pinot Noir; White – Chardonnay, some Pinot Blanc and Aligoté*

The famous Hôtel de Dieu (above), glimpsed through the entrance to the Hospices de Beaune in the village of Beaune.

Savigny-lès-Beaune On the western side of the Côte, this was once considered rather rustic and forgettable, but improvements in winemaking have begun to alter that perception. Still relatively sanely priced. Good red-fruit Pinot. A very little decent white. (11 pc, on either bank of the Rhoin, a trickle of a river that runs through Savigny.)
PRODUCERS: Chandon de Briailles, Bize, Tollot-Beaut, Drouhin.

Chorey-lès-Beaune Underrated, and therefore generally affordable, reds (and tiny amounts of white). The best have the ripe red fruit of good Beaune Pinot, with some depth and ageability to boot. Worth looking out for.
PRODUCERS: Tollot-Beaut, Senard, Arnoux.

Beaune The village after which this part of the Côte is named. Famous for soft, strawberry-scented reds of great elegance. Also some initially hard but eventually impressive Chardonnay. (28 pc.)
PRODUCERS: Morot, Germain, Prunier, Hospices de Beaune (holder of Burgundy's annual wine auction in aid of several charities), Jadot, Drouhin.

Pommard Classy, long-lived red wines with as much authoritative weight as some Côte de Nuits reds. In the wrong hands, can be rather clumsy. Price-quality ratio not currently very favourable. (27 pc.)
PRODUCERS: Dom. de la Pousse d'Or, Comte Armand, Boillot, de Montille, Lafarge.

Volnay Top-drawer Beaune Pinot, at best perfectly capturing the combination of creamy red fruit (raspberries, loganberries) with underlying savoury depth. Arguably the finest red of the Côte de Beaune. Expensive, but overall standard of achievement very good. (35 pc.) PRODUCERS: Dom. de la Pousse d'Or, Blain-Gagnard, Comte Lafon, de Montille, Lafarge, Ampeau, Hospices de Beaune.

Monthélie Suffers from its position between Volnay and Meursault, both of which are far more famous, this is nonetheless a good village for sturdy, if not noticeably elegant reds. (9 pc.)
PRODUCERS: Potinet-Ampeau, Doreau, Jadot.

St-Romain On the western flank of the Côte, St-Romain makes both white and red burgundy, its earthily dry Chardonnays distinctly better than its light and often inconsequential Pinot Noirs.
PRODUCERS: Thévenin, Gras, Germain.

Auxey-Duresses Quality for both reds and whites was on something of a roller-coaster in the 1980s, but things are looking up with some

gentle, strawberryish Pinot and pleasantly buttery Chardonnay. (6 pc.)
PRODUCERS: Leroy, Diconne, Ampeau, Duc de Magenta, Prunier.

Meursault First of the important white-wine villages, and the only one with no *grand cru*. The wines of Meursault are hugely fat and rich, heavily oaked golden creations, full of honey and butterscotch. Increasing overproduction, however, has meant that surprisingly cheap-looking Meursault is likely to be poor value. (13 pc, two of which – Blagny and Santenots – are also for red wine, in which case they don't mention the name Meursault. Santenots then counts as a *premier cru* of Volnay.)
PRODUCERS: Comte Lafon, Coche-Dury, Boisson-Vadot, Roulot, Michelot-Buisson, Jobard, René Manuel's Clos des Bouches Chères (marketed by Labouré-Roi).

Puligny-Montrachet The village wines are leaner than Meursault, though still creamy and hazelnutty, and rounded with plenty of new oak. From here on in, all the wines bask to some degree in the reflected glory of the greatest white burgundy of them all, the *grand cru* Le Montrachet, which makes hauntingly powerful, smoky, palate-blasting Chardonnay at second-mortgage prices. There is a little fairly dull red Puligny. GC: Le Montrachet, Bâtard-Montrachet (both shared with AC Chassagne-Montrachet – see below), Chevalier-Montrachet and Bienvenues-Bâtard-Montrachet. (14 pc.)
PRODUCERS: Sauzet, Dom. Leflaive, Carillon, Drouhin and, for *grands crus*, Dom. de la Romanée-Conti, Amiot-Bonfils, Bachelet-Ramonet, Niellon, Lequin-Roussot and Drouhin's Montrachet Laguiche.

St-Aubin Out west, this up-and-coming appellation is making some fine, smoky, pedigree Chardonnay and a larger quantity of light, strawberry Pinot at very attractive prices. Should be on every shopping-list. Most of the appellation is *premier cru*. (10 pc.)
PRODUCERS: Thomas, Bachelet, Clerget, Albert Morey, Prudhon, Lamy.

Chassagne-Montrachet Last of the great white-wine villages, perhaps the least spectacular for its basic village wines – though they still have the imprint of fine Burgundian Chardonnay – but producing some memorable *grands crus*. Reds are pretty much run-of-the-mill. GC: Le Montrachet, Bâtard-Montrachet (both shared with AC Puligny-Montrachet), Criots-Bâtard-Montrachet (all its own). (16 pc.)

PRODUCERS: Blain-Gagnard, Dom. Ramonet, Bachelet-Ramonet, Duc de Magenta, Ch. de la Maltroye, Jaffelin.

Santenay In the south of the Côte, Santenay produces mainly reds of no conspicuous finesse. Can be a satisfyingly hearty glass of basic Pinot, though, from the better growers. (8 pc.)
PRODUCERS: Dom. de la Pousse d'Or, Lequin-Roussot, Girardin, Drouhin.

Maranges An AC created in 1988 that unites three villages – Dezize, Sampigny and Cheilly – each suffixed by -lès-Maranges, although the wines may simply be labelled Maranges. Production is overwhelmingly red, and fairly rustic stuff it is too, though scarcely overpriced.
PRODUCERS: Drouhin.

Hautes-Côtes-de-Beaune As in the Côte de Nuits, there is a scattering of villages among the hills to the west of the Côte de Beaune that take this appellation. Quality is generally very good, notably for the soft, cherry-fruited reds.
PRODUCERS: Mazilly, Joliot, Caves des Hautes-Côtes.

Côte de Beaune-Villages Red-wine appellation that covers most of the Côte, and may be used by any of the individual villages (with the big four exceptions of Aloxe-Corton, Beaune, Pommard and Volnay) or for any wine blended from two or more villages, a practice not much in evidence on the Côte de Beaune now.
PRODUCERS: Lequin-Roussot, Jaffelin.

Côte de Beaune The simplest appellation in the area takes in vineyards on the hill overlooking the village of Beaune itself – but not from anywhere else on the Côte, perplexingly. The wines may be red or white and are mainly of undistinguished quality.

CÔTE CHALONNAISE

The large bulk-producing area in the south of Burgundy, the Mâconnais, is separated from the southern tip of the Côte d'Or by a strip of vineyard called the Côte Chalonnaise. It takes its name from the town of Chalon-sur-Saône on the banks of the river Saône to the east. As well as producing some basic Bourgogne Rouge and Blanc, there are five important village appellations here. Because their reputation is nothing like as exalted as the villages of the Côte d'Or, these generally represent good value, although they don't have quite the class of their northern neighbours. This list runs north to south.

Bourgogne Aligoté de Bouzeron Although white wines from the enigmatic Aligoté grape are made further north in Burgundy, the village of Bouzeron was granted its own appellation for such wines in 1979. The popular aperitif, Kir, is traditionally made from Aligoté with a slug of crème de cassis (blackcurrant liqueur) in it, but Bouzeron's Aligoté is considered a cut above that sort of treatment. Even so, it should be drunk fairly young to capture its challenging lemon-and-crème-fraîche character.
PRODUCERS: de Villaine, Chanzy, Bouchard père et fils.

Rully Increasingly fashionable lately, the whites and reds of this village have now eclipsed its erstwhile reputation as a source of cheap and cheerful fizz. Its whites are lighter and drier than from the Côte de Beaune, but well-made by and large, as are its simple, plummy reds. (19 pc.)
PRODUCERS: Jacqueson, Dom. de la Folie, Faiveley, Jaffelin.

Mercurey The lion's share of Chalonnaise production comes from this village, which is why you will sometimes see the whole region referred to as the "Région de Mercurey". Mostly well-balanced, concentrated reds, though whites

COTE CHALONNAISE
GRAPES: White – Chardonnay, Aligoté; Red – Pinot Noir

Dusk falls over the vineyards of the Hautes-Côtes-de-Nuits AC, in the hills of the Côte d'Or (below).

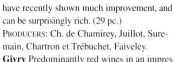

MACONNAIS/
OTHER WINES

GRAPES: Red – *Pinot Noir,*
Gamay, César, Tressot;
White – Chardonnay,
Aligoté, Pinot Blanc, Pinot
Gris, Sacy

Chardonnay grapes arriving
at the Caves de Buxy co-
operative (below) in the
Montagny AC, Côte
Chalonnaise.

have recently shown much improvement, and can be surprisingly rich. (29 pc.)

PRODUCERS: Ch. de Chamirey, Juillot, Suremain, Chartron et Trébuchet, Faiveley.

Givry Predominantly red wines in an impressively scented raspberry style, with good structure. Small amount of intriguingly spicy white. (5 pc.)

PRODUCERS: Delorme, Chofflet, Lespinasse, Mouton.

Montagny Quality in this appellation for white wines only is decidedly patchy. Some possess convincing intensity; many taste pretty similar to anonymous Mâcon Blanc-Villages. Ridiculously enough, the designation *premier cru* applies not to specific vineyards in Montagny but – uniquely in France – to any wine that attains a minimum alcohol level of 11.5 per cent.

PRODUCERS: Caves de Buxy co-operative, Vachet, Roy, Louis Latour.

MACONNAIS

The southernmost region of Burgundy is the Mâconnais, opposite the town of Mâcon, which is in many ways the commercial hub of the region. The majority of Burgundy's co-operatives are found in the Mâconnais and further south in Beaujolais. Predominantly everyday whites, with one or two stars, the production is very much geared to bulk markets and is easily outshone in many instances by low-priced Chardonnays from elsewhere in the world. The following wines are listed in descending order of quality rather than geographically.

Pouilly-Fuissé A whites-only appellation that carries the quality torch for the Mâconnais as a whole, and prices its wines in accordance with its ambition. At their classiest, they are richly oaked and fleshy, and do display some pedigree. Neighbouring appellations of Pouilly-Vinzelles and Pouilly-Loché are not quite in the same class.

PRODUCERS: Forest, Manciat-Poncet, Ch. de Fuissé, Guffens-Heynen.

St-Véran In the dead south of the region, overlapping into Beaujolais and wholly enclosing the appellation of Pouilly-Fuissé, St-Véran is a somewhat underrated source of dry, chalky Chardonnay wines with a certain amount of Burgundian flair.

PRODUCERS: Lassarat, Dom. des Deux Roches, Drouhin, Duboeuf.

Mâcon-Villages The umbrella appellation for the Mâconnais covers a total of 43 villages, all of which have the right to append their names to the word Mâcon on the label. Otherwise, the wine is simply labelled Mâcon-Villages, red or white. Some of the more famous villages are Lugny, Viré, Prissé, Montbellet, Clessé, Uchizy, La Roche-Vineuse and – tantalizingly – Chardonnay. Red wine labelled Mâcon, rather than Bourgogne, is almost always likely to be made from the Beaujolais grape Gamay.

PRODUCERS: Lassarat, Manciat-Poncet, Guffens-Heynen, Josserand.

Below Mâcon-Villages are the basic appellations of Mâcon Supérieur (reds and whites) and simple Mâcon (reds only).

OTHER WINES

The basic appellation for the whole region, top to bottom, is AC Bourgogne – Blanc or Rouge. Some of the more northerly village wines, notably those from the Auxerre region near Chablis, should eventually receive individual ACs. Some, such as Chitry, Irancy and Epineuil, already have the right to add their names to the basic Bourgogne designation. In the whites, Chardonnay may be joined by leavenings of Pinot Blanc and Pinot Gris, while reds – generally unblended Pinot Noir – may also contain Gamay and even a couple of historical oddities from near Chablis – César and Tressot.

A little-seen label, Bourgogne Grand Ordinaire, is rock-bottom stuff under which a cocktail of ignoble grapes may be used for both red and white. Bourgogne Passetoutgrains is the AC for a blend of just Pinot Noir and Gamay, in which the former should account for not less than a

third of the *assemblage*. Pink wines from anywhere in the region are labelled Bourgogne Rosé or Bourgogne Clairet.

The champagne-method sparkling wine is Crémant de Bourgogne. Made from any of the region's grapes, but principally Chardonnay and Pinot Noir, it is entitled to use the terms Blanc de Blancs and Blanc de Noirs for white wines made from all white grapes or all black grapes respectively. There is also some Crémant rosé.

VINTAGE GUIDE
Vintage conditions in Burgundy affect the red wines far more than the whites. An off-year for Chardonnay may result in dilute but perfectly drinkable wines, whereas unripe Pinot Noir may be feeble in colour, flimsy in texture and hopelessly lacking fruit.

REDS
2004 ** Early indications are not great. Many thin wines with brittle acidity.
2003 *** Hard to generalize. A very hot vintage produced some fruit-drenched stunners, but many are over-alcoholic, with tough tannins.
2002 *** A middling vintage of juicy reds with plenty of appealing fruit.
2001 ** Similar to 2000, very dependent on the individual producer. Côte de Nuits the safest bet.
2000 ** Distinctly underwhelming. Wet conditions resulted in a major letdown.
1999 **** This has turned into a very attractive vintage, with classic Burgundian depth and roundness. Still needs a good few years though.
1998 *** Patchy vintage, better in the Côte de Nuits than elsewhere. Drink now.
1997 **** Another lovely vintage that nearly rivals '88, '89 and '90.
1996 ***** The best since 1990. Expressive, aromatic wines that began developing early.
1995 **** Fine, ripe, well-structured wines.
1990 ***** Superb, immensely rich and concentrated wines for the cellar.
1989 **** Very charming, supple wines that began to blossom quite early on in their careers.
1988 **** Big, chunky, often quite tannic reds.
1985 ***** A classic Pinot vintage of beautifully soft, supple and ripe-fruited wines.
EARLIER HIGHLIGHTS: *1978* ***** *1971* ***** *1959* *****

WHITES
BEST RECENT VINTAGES: *2004, '03, '02, 1999.*

The rock of Vergisson (above) towers over the Pouilly-Fuissé vineyards, source of Mâconnais's finest white burgundies.

Barrels awaiting the new vintage (left) at Louis Latour's cellars in Aloxe-Corton, Côte de Beaune.

BEAUJOLAIS

Burgundy's southernmost wine region, the huge Beaujolais area, is devoted to the red grape Gamay and one of the winemaking world's most individual red wine styles. The winemakers here offer much more than just "Nouveau".

The hilly Beaujolais region (above), the most southerly of Burgundy's wine areas.

BEAUJOLAIS
GRAPES: *Red – Gamay; White – Chardonnay*

IT IS THE FATE OF Beaujolais never to be taken quite seriously. It is such a lightweight wine that few bother to age it, and certainly most retail outlets only ever sell the last couple of vintages. This means that the occasional pleasure that can be afforded by drinking a relatively mature Beaujolais with roast meats, or even a firm-textured fish like salmon, is denied to most. Then again, the fact that the regional industry happily sells about a third of its annual production hot off the presses as Beaujolais Nouveau doesn't exactly send out a message that this is a wine worth dwelling on.

All this is something of a shame, because when Beaujolais is on song – and it does fall woefully short of the mark too often – it is an incomparably charming wine. It can be as light-textured as the thinnest Italian reds such as Bardolino or red Lambrusco, and yet it still manages to have more substance than those because of its alcoholic weight and the easy, accessible ripeness of its juicy strawberry fruit. The drawback of very young Beaujolais is that it is extremely acidic, a trait the French themselves tend to be more relaxed about than most other wine consumers.

As we saw in the grape variety section on the Beaujolais grape, Gamay, there are moves in some quarters to give some of the *cru* wines more depth and power by varying the vinification method (traditionally *macération carbonique*, as explained under *Gamay*) to allow a little tannin into the wines. Those used to the chilled light reds of summer may find these wines something of a shock to the system. So, too, may those used to seeing Beaujolais as an oak-free zone when they first taste the barrel-matured wines of a producer such as Guy Depardon in Fleurie.

By and large, though, Beaujolais remains pre-eminently an unchallenging summer tipple, easily made and bottled early. In the light of that, it is hard to see why it should be priced quite as forbiddingly as it is, especially now that it has clear stylistic rivals from elsewhere in Europe.

The more basic the quality and the younger it is, the colder Beaujolais should be drunk. The best *cru* wines, however, when aged for six or seven years, can achieve a positively Burgundian gamey complexity. Négociants dominate the Beaujolais scene (most notably the excellent Georges Duboeuf) but there are many fine small growers to watch out for too.

The top wines, known as *cru* Beaujolais, come from ten villages thought to have the best vineyard sites. From north to south, they are:

St-Amour The one traditionally drunk on Valentine's Day, of course. Intensely fragrant, but with a hint of Burgundian structure to it as well, it is often one of the best-balanced of the *cru* Beaujolais.
PRODUCERS: Dom. des Ducs, Saillant, Ch. de St-Amour, Trichard.

Juliénas One of the less charming wines, often rather hard and insufficiently endowed with fruit, but made in a softer style by some.
PRODUCERS: Ch. de Juliénas, Pelletier, Perraud, Tête, certain of the Duboeuf cuvées.

Chénas At this point, the *cru* wines start becoming bolder and sturdier than the popular image of Beaujolais allows for. These are prime candidates for ageing, being clenched and dour in their first flush of youth but ageing to a meaty, sinewy richness.
PRODUCERS: Champagnon, Perrachon, Ch. de Chénas, Dom. des Brureaux, Lapierre.

Moulin-à-Vent The Beaujolais that seems to think it's a Rhône wine, Moulin-à-Vent is always the biggest and burliest of the *crus*. From a good producer, the wines can take ten years' ageing in their stride, but they can be just as enjoyable at three or four years, with ripe blackberry fruit and often a fair bit of tannin.
PRODUCERS: Janodet, Ch. des Jacques, Duboeuf's Dom. de la Tour du Bief, Siffert, Dom. Diochon, Dom. de la Rochelle.

Fleurie Still the best-loved of the *crus* – and therefore inevitably usually the most expensive these days. Classic Fleurie is summer-scented with strawberries and roses, light-textured and creamy and soft. A lot isn't. Depardon's atypical wines will shock the purists, but are masterpieces of violets-and-ginger-and-Turkish-Delight seductiveness, and need ageing for a decade.

PRODUCERS: Depardon, Duboeuf's Dom. des Quatre Vents and La Madone, Verpoix, Chignard, Berrod's Les Roches du Vivier.

Chiroubles Light and attractive wines, not much seen outside France, but worth trying if you come across one.

PRODUCERS: Passot, Méziat, Boulon, Ch. de Raousset, Cheysson, Dom. de la Rocassière.

Morgon Morgon's wines are famous for their capacity to age very quickly into a light, but interestingly meaty Burgundian maturity, an experience worth seeking out. To capitalize on this, some is released with the designation Morgon Agé – it is cellared for 18 months before it hits the market. Even in youth, there is a savouriness to them, and the fruit is often Cabernet-like blackcurrant rather than Gamay strawberry.

PRODUCERS: Janodet, Didier Desvignes, Duboeuf's Dom. Jean Descombes, Aucoeur, Ch. de Pizay.

Régnié The new *cru* on the block, since 1988 anyway. To put it charitably, Régnié was very lucky to be upgraded (there are other, more deserving villages such as Lancié).

PRODUCERS: Duboeuf, Rampon, Durand.

Brouilly Silky-soft, cherry-fruited charmers at their best, the wines of Brouilly are the most approachable of all *cru* Beaujolais. They don't generally need ageing, as their youthful fruit is too attractive to waste. Has by far the biggest production of the ten.

PRODUCERS: Large, Ch. de la Chaize, Jambon, Duboeuf's Ch. de Nevers and Dom. de Combillaty.

Côte de Brouilly Hillside vineyards in the middle of Brouilly, but possessing unique soil and exposure, and consequently making distinctive wine. Deeper cherry fruit and richer texture than Brouilly itself, and some have a touch of gingery spice to them. Underrated and not much exported, but this is definitely one to try.

PRODUCERS: Ch. de Thivin, Chanrion, Pavillon de Chavannes, Verger.

Wines from any of 39 villages in the northern part of the region may be sold as Beaujolais-Villages, with the village name mentioned if the wine comes solely from that vineyard. The rest is basic Beaujolais and represents a significant drop in quality. Buy a Villages wines if you are not in the market for a *cru*. There are small amounts of usually rather feeble Beaujolais rosé, and often pretty impressive, if austere, Beaujolais blanc made from Chardonnay.

As to Nouveau, it is the wine of the new vintage, released on to the market on the third Wednesday of November. In occasional years, it can be good, but it mostly stinks of fermentation and will make you queasy with acid-stomach syndrome. Yum.

BEST RECENT VINTAGES (but note that Beaujolais rarely has disasters): *2004, '03, '01, 1999.*

Gamay vines under an autumnal mist in the village of Juliénas (below), one of the more northerly of the Beaujolais cru villages.

RHONE

Overshadowed for centuries by Bordeaux and Burgundy, the Rhône Valley is nonetheless the source of formidable spicy, rich reds and intriguing whites from its two distinct areas – the Syrah-dominated north and the mixed culture of the south.

THE RHONE VALLEY consists of two quite distinct viticultural districts about 50km (30 miles) apart, and referred to simply as Northern and Southern Rhône. Back in the 14th century, when the papacy was temporarily moved for political reasons from Rome to Avignon, in the southern Rhône valley, the local wines found immense favour with the papal retinue. Such was the wines' popularity that they ended up drinking more of them than the beloved and much prized burgundy.

Despite such lofty endorsement, however, the region never quite attained the premier status of Bordeaux and Burgundy. The odd wine, principally Hermitage from the northern Rhône and, to a lesser extent, Châteauneuf-du-Pape from the south, were known among British connoisseurs, but that was about it.

In the last 20 years or so, all that has changed. The Rhône has been "discovered", and deservedly so, since its finest red wines are as long-lived and opulent as top-flight claret, while its small production of dry white wines includes some quixotic and arresting flavours that can offer welcome relief to those suffering from Chardonnay-fatigue.

NORTHERN RHONE

GRAPES: *Red – Syrah; White – Viognier, Marsanne, Roussanne*

The Rhône river lends its name to the long stretch of the Rhône valley wine region (below), divided into two distinct viticultural districts – northern and southern Rhône.

THE NORTHERN RHONE APPELLATIONS
(from north to south)

Côte-Rôtie What distinguishes the reds of the north from those of the south is that they are made purely from Syrah, whereas the southern wines are always a mix, with Syrah usually a fairly junior partner in the blend. Having said that, Côte-Rôtie is permitted to include up to 20 per cent of the white grape Viognier (see Condrieu, below). Not all producers use it, but those that do add a little – and it is hardly ever the full 20 per cent – produce perfumed wines of astonishing intensity.

The appellation's name, the "roasted slope", refers to its steep southeast-facing hillside on the left bank of the river, where the vines are sheltered from the worst the weather can do, and enjoy their own little sun-trap. In the hotter years, Côte-Rôtie is an uncommonly concentrated wine, crammed full of blackberry fruit and tannin, but with layers of spice and chocolate underneath, just waiting for a decade's maturation. It is arguably even more highly prized than Hermitage itself these days, with the inevitable consequence that prices for the wines of the best growers have shot through the roof. At the pinnacle of ambition are the wines of Marcel Guigal, who makes not only a straight AC Côte-Rôtie, but also three wines from single vineyards (La Landonne, La Mouline and La Turque) for which he charges the earth.
OTHER PRODUCERS: Jasmin, Jamet, Delas (especially the Seigneur de Maugiron), Rostaing, Gentaz-Dervieux, Champet.

Condrieu The sole grape of this white-wine appellation is Viognier, suddenly fashionable in the last few years as the wine world looks for a variety that can supply the broad textures of good Chardonnay with some distinctive aromatic personality. Condrieu is its true home, making wines that set the pace for all other growers of the variety. The wines initially seem rather heavy and creamy on the nose, but then a wonderfully musky scent of squashed ripe apricots comes through, followed by subtle spice notes that are often reminiscent of Indian cooking – cardamom pods, sticks of cinnamon,

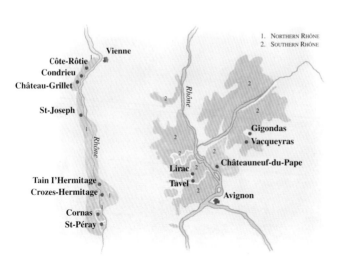

1. NORTHERN RHÔNE
2. SOUTHERN RHÔNE

Vienne
Côte-Rôtie
Condrieu
Château-Grillet
St-Joseph
Rhône
Gigondas
Vacqueyras
Lirac
Tavel
Châteauneuf-du-Pape
Tain l'Hermitage
Crozes-Hermitage
Avignon
Cornas
St-Péray

ginger root – but all bound by that thick, clotted-cream feel. Many producers achieve this, moreover, without resorting to oak. Opinion tends to divide on the best moment to drink these wines. I think they are at their best fairly young, up to two years old. Once again, they are expensive, but worth trying at least once.
PRODUCERS: La Côte-Chéry, Vernay, Guigal, Dumazet, Cuilleron, Ch. du Rozay, Perret.

Château-Grillet Single-vineyard enclave of four hectares within Condrieu, wholly owned by the Neyret-Gachet family, awarded an appellation all of its own. The wine is aged in cask, and is intended to be far longer-lived than Condrieu. Consensus is that its performance is patchy, often not as good as the top Condrieus.

St-Joseph Red and white wines. The reds may not be as distinguished as those of Côte-Rôtie or Hermitage, but do have a raspberry-fruited immediacy to them and some modest ageing potential. Some producers make a practically Beaujolais-like lighter red, but even the heavier ones are nothing like as dense as other northern Rhône reds. Whites are made from a pair of grapes often found together in these parts – Marsanne and Roussanne. There isn't much made in St-Joseph, but what there is is fairly chunky, walnut-dry in style.
PRODUCERS: Chave, Grippat, Trollat, Le Grand Pompée from Jaboulet (one the most important and reliable companies in the Rhône).

Crozes-Hermitage The largest output, mostly of red wines, of the north comes from this appellation. Usually considered to be at the foot of the ladder for quality, but in fact its wines are remarkably well-made, even at the basic co-operative level, and can therefore represent outstanding value. Peppery, plummy and firm-textured, they are capable of ageing for a few years. Up to 15 per cent white grapes (Marsanne and Roussanne) may be added to them, though rarely are. The white wines themselves are rather hefty and uninspiring.
PRODUCERS: Graillot, Jaboulet's Dom. du Thalabert, Ferraton, Chapoutier's Les Meysonniers, Combier, Pochon, Cave des Clairmonts.

Hermitage The great hill of Hermitage pops up in the middle of the Crozes appellation, and its steeply shelving vineyards form the famed AC of Hermitage itself. Often among the most majestically proportioned red wines made anywhere in France, they are huge, powerfully concentrated, full-on Syrah, with tannin and extract to spare and demanding the best part of

a decade to begin to unwind. When they do, one of the causes of these wines' success is revealed: their fruit remains as vibrantly fresh as the day they were bottled, so that even at 12 years old they can gush forth blackberries and raspberries in abundance, backed up by dark chocolate and the most savoury herbs – thyme and rosemary. Whites, a blend of Marsanne and Roussanne, are rich and heavy, with flavours of roasted nuts and a twist of liquorice.
PRODUCERS: Guigal, Jaboulet's Hermitage La Chapelle, Chave, Delas, Sorrel, Ferraton, Vidal-Fleury, Chapoutier's La Sizeranne.

Cornas Enigmatic appellation for densely textured, tannic Syrah reds that never quite seem to open out into the fruit-filled glories of Hermitage. Tasted blind, they can often resemble the burlier versions of blended Châteauneuf-du-Pape, with roasting-meat aromas filling out the expected black-pepper character.
PRODUCERS: Clape, Colombo's Dom. des Ruchets, Verset, Voge, Jaboulet.

St-Péray Mainly noted for rather tough, unfriendly sparkling wine, made from the white Hermitage grapes (plus another, fairly rare variety, Roussette) using the champagne method, but lacking elegance. Some strangely cheesy but often likeable still white is also made.
PRODUCERS: Clape, Grippat, Juge.

Vineyards of Côte-Rôtie, "the roasted slope" (above), on the sunny left bank of the Rhône, overlooking the village of Ampuis.

Picking Viognier grapes at the four-hectare AC Château-Grillet (above), a single vineyard within Condrieu.

Vineyards of Châteauneuf-du-Pape (above), the most famous red wine of the southern Rhône.

SOUTHERN RHONE

GRAPES: *Red – Grenache, Cinsaut, Mourvèdre, Syrah, Carignan, Gamay;*

White – Clairette, Picpoul, Bourboulenc, Grenache Blanc, Roussanne, Marsanne, Muscat, Viognier

THE SOUTHERN RHONE APPELLATIONS

Châteauneuf-du-Pape The most famous red wine of the southern Rhône, named after a palace built for one of the Avignon popes in the 14th century and flattened by Nazi bombers during the war, Châteauneuf is recognizable by the symbol of crossed keys embossed on its bottles. It embraces a wide stylistic range, from almost Beaujolais-light to fairly weighty, although these days it is never quite the blockbuster that old textbooks would lead you to believe. Principally Grenache, it can draw on 13 varieties, though most producers make do with three or four. It matures quite quickly too, and is perfectly drinkable at three years old, rarely possessing the fearsome tannins of young Hermitage. The white wines come from a cocktail of varieties led by such unlikely stars as Picpoul, Bourboulenc, Clairette and the white version of

Grenache. They tend to be fairly neutral in aroma, but appreciably fat, structured and alcoholic on the palate. Some exceptions, notably Ch. de Beaucastel, have real character and are worth keeping for three or four years. De Beaucastel also makes one of the very best reds.
OTHER PRODUCERS: Chante-Cigale, Dom. du Mont-Redon, Clos du Mont-Olivet, Ch. Rayas, Dom. du Vieux Télégraphe, Chapoutier's La Bernardine, Bonneau, Dom. de la Janasse.
Gigondas Seen as Châteauneuf's understudy, but a much fiercer, black-hearted wine, often rigidly tannic and head-clobberingly alcoholic. It needs plenty of time to soften up, but many of the wines are too austere to make the wait worthwhile.
PRODUCERS: Dom. du St-Gayan, Clos des Cazaux, Dom. Raspail, Jaboulet, Santa Duc.
Lirac On the opposite bank of the Rhône to Châteauneuf, this unfairly overlooked AC makes wines in all three colours – and all of them highly reliable. The reds have good fruit and considerable substance, the rosés are agreeably ripe and graceful and the whites are strong and flavourful. Good bargains.
PRODUCERS: Dom. les Garrigues, Dom. de la Tour, Maby, Ch. St-Roch.
Tavel An AC, unusually, for rosé wines only. They tend to look more beige than pink and have a lot of alcohol, but are not exactly overflowing with fruit. Most sit far too heavily on the palate to be considered refreshing summer quaffers. Try them with richly sauced shellfish and crustacean dishes.
PRODUCERS: Dom. de la Ginestière, Ch. d'Acquéria.
Vacqueyras Plucked from the mass of Côtes du Rhône-Villages in 1990 to become an appellation in its own right, Vacqueyras may be red, white or pink, although there is virtually no white to speak of. The reds are good spicy, gingery wines with a degree of rough-edged charm.
PRODUCERS: Dom. des Tours, Clos des Cazaux, Vidal-Fleury.
Côtes du Rhône-Villages A whole swathe of villages, from the Ardèche and the Drôme in the centre of the Rhône valley down through the southern section, are entitled to this appellation. Of those, 16 are allowed to append their names to the basic designation, among them Cairanne, Séguret, Sablet, Chusclun and Vinsobres. There are many conscientious winemakers, so quality across the board is quite dependable and the price is mostly right.

Côtes du Rhône This is the basic AC that covers all other villages, including those in the northern Rhône. Styles vary from light and fruity to tannin-driven reds, via some delightful rosé to a scant quantity of vaguely milky white. Quality, too, is all over the place, but at least the wines aren't costly. Reds to watch out for are Guigal's Côtes du Rhône, Dom. de Fonsalette and any wine labelled with the village name Brézème, from the area between the northern and southern zones, but which is made entirely from Syrah.

Other large areas around the southern Rhône make up a fair amount of the annual production, some of it at VDQS level (the next step down from AC), some of it not long promoted. Most of it is uncomplicated everyday stuff, but there are occasional stars. Côtes du Ventoux is a good area south of Vacqueyras (Jaboulet makes a fine red from there). Bordering it, the Côtes du Lubéron is less distinguished but quite acceptable. The Coteaux de Tricastin to the north makes reasonable wines, as does the VDQS Côtes du Vivarais. Costières de Nîmes is technically in the Languedoc, further south, but considers itself part of the Rhône, and its wines can be superb (look for those of the smartest producer, Paul Blanc).

In the central sector are two wine regions, the Coteaux de l'Ardèche and the Drôme, named after the one of the Rhône's tributaries. The former can be a source of good varietal wines (though not necessarily from the Rhône varieties – Mr Beaujolais, Georges Duboeuf, makes a good Gamay there).

The Drôme encompasses the small but good appellation of Châtillon-en-Diois, which makes Gamay reds and Chardonnay and Aligoté whites. There is also an interesting sparkling wine called Clairette de Die, made from the neutral Clairette grape, but often blended with grapey Muscat to make Clairette de Die Tradition – a dead ringer for sparkling Italian Asti to the uninitiated.

VINS DOUX NATURELS

These are sweet wine specialities of southern France. They are made naturally sweet by interrupting the fermentation of super-ripe grapes with the addition of spirit to produce a lightish fortified wine – basically the same method as is used for port.

Muscat de Beaumes-de-Venise The most celebrated of the fortified Muscats is a rich, golden dessert wine, tasting of ultra-sweet grapes and oranges, with a tongue-coating barley-sugar quality as well. They should be drunk young and fresh, and served very well chilled. PRODUCERS: Dom. de Durban, Dom. de Coyeux, Jaboulet, Vidal-Fleury, Delas.

Rasteau This comes as either red or white, from the respectively red or white versions of the Grenache grape. The red can be good in a rough, young port-like style; the local co-operative makes a passable example.

VINTAGE GUIDE

For northern Rhône reds, the best recent vintages are *2003, '01, 2000, 1999, '98, '97, '95, '91, '90, '89, '88* and *'85.*

In the south, the chance for blending means that more vintages are likely to produce something acceptable than if you have to pin all your hopes on the ripening of one grape variety. GOOD RECENT VINTAGES: *2003, '01, 2000, 1999, '98, '95, '94, '93* and *'90.*

Harvested Muscat grapes being taken to the local co-operative in Beaumes-de-Venise (below), to make the luscious, rich, golden sweet wine of the same name.

PROVENCE *and* CORSICA

Traditionally known for its pale rosés, the Mediterranean region of Provence now grows a wider and better choice of grape varieties that are bringing some fine reds and whites to market.

PROVENCE

GRAPES: *Red – Grenache, Mourvèdre, Cinsaut, Syrah, Carignan, Cabernet Sauvignon, Tibouren, Braquet; White – Clairette, Ugni Blanc, Grenache Blanc, Rolle, Sauvignon Blanc, Marsanne, Terret*

The broad sweep of the Provençal wine region, running from the cooler inland hills along the sun-soaked but Mistral-blown Mediterranean coast (below).

I**T IS HIGHLY PROBABLE** that the much-loved Mediterranean region of Provence, in southeast France, was the cradle of French viticulture. Its ancient seaport of Marseilles was founded around 600 BC by Greek settlers, who brought their own wines with them, probably sourced from their colonies in what was eventually to become Rome. Later, when France – as Gaul – had become a major component of the Roman Empire, cultivation of the vine spread slowly westwards and northwards.

Today, despite the fondness of European tourists, especially the British, for the region as a whole, Provençal wines remain largely unknown to the outside world, although a good quantity is exported. There is an unusually high production of rosé wine, and nearly all the wine is blended from a handful of grape varieties, some of them quite obscure, so that they don't have varietalism on their side. Provence has been the scene of much healthy experimentation and commitment to quality in recent years, however, and the region should soon see the greater prominence that it deserves.

Côtes de Provence By far the biggest appellation, covering the whole region, Côtes de Provence embraces a number of totally diverse areas in a broad sweep that runs from near

Aix-en-Provence down via the coast at St-Tropez and back up to a mountainous enclave north of Nice. The greater part of the production is pink wines – known locally as "little summer rosés" – targeted specifically at the tourist hordes. The wines are largely based on the Midi varieties Grenache and Cinsaut, but there is a good quality local grape, Tibouren, that is used on its own by some producers, and makes characterful rosés that are a cut above the basic slosh.

Reds have traditionally been based on that ubiquitous dullard, the Carignan grape. In an effort to raise the profile of Provence's reds, the regulations were amended in the 1980s to stipulate that a maximum of 40 per cent Carignan was allowed into any Côtes de Provence red. As the more forward-looking growers are ripping out their Carignan vines, and replacing them with Cabernet Sauvignon, Syrah and more of the much better Mourvèdre (one of the indigenous grapes), that 40 per cent will with any luck shrink still further. Only a small amount of white wine is made, but it can be unexpectedly good.

PRODUCERS: Dom. de Courtade, Ch. de Selle, Mas de Cadenet, Dom. Ott, Dom. Richeaume.

Coteaux d'Aix-en-Provence The area around the old university town of Aix-en-Provence produces wines in all three colours that are quite as varied as those from the main regional appellation, but at a higher overall standard of quality. It was demarcated in the mid-'80s, and its performance has since been on a steady upward trajectory. Again, Cabernet and Syrah are beginning to make their presences felt, and some of the reds from this westernmost part of Provence have a tantalizingly claret-like profile. Rosés account for about a third of the output, while whites are very few and far between.

PRODUCERS: Ch. Vignelaure and Ch. du Seuil are the two front-runners.

Les Baux de Provence This appellation was finally demarcated from the above in 1994. Situated at the western end of the Coteaux, it is a mountainous outpost of rare and highly individual red and rosé wines, some of them from relatively recently planted vineyards. Cabernet

1. COTEAUX D'AIX-EN-PROVENCE
2. LES BAUX DE PROVENCE
3. PALETTE
4. CASSIS
5. BANDOL
6. CÔTES DE PROVENCE
7. COTEAUX VAROIS

Nice

Aix-en-Provence

Marseilles

Cassis

Bandol

St-Tropez

and Syrah combine to do their stuff once more among the more traditional Provençal varieties, and there has been a widespread move towards organic viticultural methods (eliminating the use of pesticides and herbicides on the vines). PRODUCERS: Dom. de Trévallon and Mas de Gourgonnier lead the pack.

Bandol Potentially the weightiest and most age-worthy reds in Provence come from this coastal appellation that also makes some good savoury rosé and a little crisp, appley white (some containing a good dollop of Sauvignon Blanc). The reds have to be cask-aged for a minimum of 18 months, and they include a generous proportion of the distinguished Mourvèdre grape to achieve a dense-textured wine full of black plum fruit and herbs. They are slowly but surely acquiring a reputation outside the region – largely thanks to the first-named producer below – and represent a serious alternative to Bordeaux on grand gastronomic occasions.
PRODUCERS: Dom. Tempier, Ch. Pibarnon, Ch. Pradeaux, Dom. de l'Olivette.

Cassis Nothing to do with the blackcurrant liqueur of the same name, this tiny appellation a little further westwards along the coast from Bandol makes mainly white wines from a fascinating grab-bag of southern Rhône varieties – Marsanne among them – and Sauvignon Blanc. Mainly sold locally, they can be quite sturdy, but often possessed of an uncommonly beautiful aromatic allure. Reds and pinks use proportionately about as much Mourvèdre as those of Bandol.
PRODUCERS: Dom. Clos Ste-Magdelaine.

Bellet Perched high up in the hills to the north of Nice, near the border with Italy, Bellet's wines are only very infrequently seen outside Provence. Because of its altitude, this is a cooler area and the small production of reds, whites and rosés reflects that in slightly higher acid levels. The grape varieties are shared with parts of western Italy, so that the Rolle of Bellet's whites is Vermentino to the Italians, while the Braquet used in its pinks is called Brachetto over the border. Outposts of Grenache and Cinsaut make their appearance in the reds.
PRODUCERS: Ch. de Bellet, Ch. de Crémat.

Palette An historic enclave near Aix-en-Provence, about 80 per cent of which is owned by one property, Ch. Simone. In addition to the usual southern grape varieties, there are some microscopic plantings of all-but-forgotten local grapes on very aged vinestock, producing reds,

Carefully tended vines at Dom. Clos Ste-Magdelaine (left), in the hot coastal hills of Cassis.

whites and rosés. Reds and rosés can both make quite an impact in the best years.

Coteaux Varois Named after the *département* of the Var in which it is located, the Coteaux Varois – once simple AC Côtes de Provence – was made an AC in 1993. The usual mixture of southern grape varieties is employed to mostly good effect, although the whites can be a shade dull. The wines of Ch. St-Estève are worth looking out for.

CORSICA

The Mediterranean island of Corsica may be French-controlled, but its vine culture owes much to neighbouring Italy. Once the source of basic slosh for the European wine lake, it set about radically improving its ways in the 1980s, with cautiously encouraging results to date.

Corsica has a wide range of grapes, principally the reds of the southern Rhône and Languedoc, as well as more fashionable international varieties. In the white Vermentino (known as Rolle in Provence) and two characterful reds (Nielluccio and Sciacarello), it has a handful of good indigenous grapes.

Only a small percentage of the island's production goes under one of the eight ACs available. They are Patrimonio, Ajaccio, Vin de Corse (making emphatic use of the local grapes), and five subdivisions of Vin de Corse (Coteaux du Cap Corse, Calvi, Figari, Porto Vecchio and Sartène). Coteaux du Cap Corse includes a *vin doux naturel*, Muscat du Cap Corse.

A fair proportion of the rest is made by powerful co-operatives as Vin de Pays de l'Ile de Beauté. Over half, though, is still simple table wine and can only hold back Corsica's ambitions as a quality region.

Houses tumble down the hillside (above) in the Corsican town of Sartène that gives its name to the local AC, Vin de Corse Sartène.

LANGUEDOC-ROUSSILLON

Better grape varieties and modern technology are assisting producers across Languedoc-Roussillon in their efforts to move away from vin de table *to greater quality, with clean, stylish varietal wines.*

Tradition bush-trained vines near Caramany in Côtes du Roussillon-Villages (above). Behind are the Pyrenees.

France's largest wine region (below), taking in Langue-doc and the Côtes du Roussillon – once known as the Midi – that touches the Spanish border.

THE CENTRAL-SOUTHERN swathe of France that comprises the twin regions of Languedoc and the Côtes du Roussillon – often referred to by its old name, as the Midi – is where the most dynamic developments in the recent history of French wine have been taking place. This is the traditional grape-basket of France, source of the surplus production that came to constitute much of the European wine lake in the 1980s. Now it is the scene of frantic innovation, inspired in large measure by the arrival of wine technicians from other regions and countries.

A debate of gathering ferocity has been going on as to whether roving winemakers, with their technocratic ways, jetting in from Australia and elsewhere, and stopping just long enough to oversee the harvest, the grape-crushing and the juice becoming wine, are not guilty of standardizing the taste of these wines. Consumers will have to vote with their purses eventually, but it should at least be acknowledged that the new wines being produced today in the Languedoc are certainly cleaner and more palatable than the old-fashioned stuff, for which the word "rustic" was the politest description.

Even before the advent of the so-called flying winemakers, the Languedoc's potential was only just beginning to emerge. Some of its key appellations were upgraded from VDQS only as recently as the mid-'80s, while a lot of the running has been made by growers working outside those regulations. They have been planting varieties that were not the norm in the region – Cabernet Sauvignon, Chardonnay, Sauvignon Blanc, even the odd outbreak of Pinot Noir. In consequence, the Languedoc is – with the exception of Alsace and its handful of traditional white grapes – the best bet for the varietally-minded wine lover starting out in France.

Vin de Pays d'Oc/de l'Hérault The Languedoc is doing a good job of turning wine tradition on its head (after the fashion of many Italian quality producers) by bottling much of its best wine under the catch-all generic designation of *vin de pays*. Theoretically inferior to wines of AC and VDQS status, these would-be "country wines" are, in many cases, putting the produce of the appellations to shame in terms of quality. Prices are rising too, as growers realize that an oaked Cabernet Sauvignon (whether country wine or no) has more cachet than the fanciest Fitou.

Furthermore, the fact that the climate in these southern parts is so much more reliable than in most of the classic French regions means that a relatively high success rate has been achieved by the conscientious operators. Deep, blackcurranty Cabernets are often far better than cheap claret, Chardonnays range from the lightly oaked and lemony to strapping young things full of smoke and butterscotch, and Sauvignon Blancs can be improbably crisp and fresh for such a warm climate, and yet still full of tempting gooseberry fruit. Soft, juicy Merlots, peppery, plummy Syrahs and – excitingly – some ripely apricotty Viogniers (half as good as Condrieu for a quarter the price) fill out the picture.

The prize for the *grand cru* of the *vins de pays* must go to an estate in the Hérault in eastern Languedoc called Mas de Daumas Gassac, producer of a powerful and complicated white, as well as thick, strong, mountainous reds of uncompromising intensity.

OTHER PRODUCERS: Fortant de France (especially Viognier), Chais Baumière (fine Chardonnay and Merlot), Dom. Virginie, Dom. de Condamine-l'Evêque, Dom. de Limbardié, Peyrat.

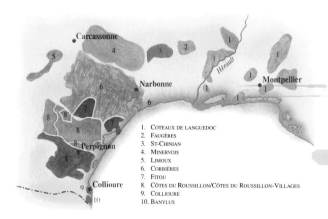

1. COTEAUX DE LANGUEDOC
2. FAUGÈRES
3. ST-CHINIAN
4. MINERVOIS
5. LIMOUX
6. CORBIÈRES
7. FITOU
8. CÔTES DU ROUSSILLON/CÔTES DU ROUSSILLON-VILLAGES
9. COLLIOURE
10. BANYULS

Coteaux du Languedoc A rather sprawling designation for some of the best village wines of the Hérault, flanked by the eastern edge of the Aude and the western fringe of the Gard *départements*. In time, more of the villages that are currently only entitled to credits on the bottle label – such as La Clape, Pic-St-Loup, Vérargues and Montpeyroux – may come to attain their own ACs, as others did before them. There is still a lot of fairly undistinguished stuff – textbook red and white blends of southern grape varieties, with a bit of pale pink rosé thrown in for good measure. The overall picture is improving all the time, though, and with Grenache, Syrah and Mourvèdre staking a claim to a larger share of the red blends, at the expense of the humdrum Carignan, things can only get better. Meanwhile, the appellation boasts a white wine of extraordinary versatility in Clairette du Languedoc. It ranges in style from light, neutral and dry to heavily sweet and oxidized. Take your pick.
PRODUCERS: Mas Jullien, Pech-Redon, Dom. de la Roque, Dom. de l'Hortus, the co-operatives in the villages of St-Saturnin and Cabrières.

Working our way around in a southwestern arc from just north of Cabrières, the other appellations for unfortified wines are as follows:
Faugères An AC since 1982, Faugères preserves its distinction from the umbrella Coteaux du Languedoc tag by making big, rich reds from Syrah, Grenache, Mourvèdre and a proportion of Carignan that had been edged down to a 40 per cent maximum by 1997. Small amount of fairly ordinary rosé. Excellent value.
PRODUCERS: Alquier, Vidal, Louison, Barral.
St-Chinian A little further west in the foothills of the Cévennes, St-Chinian shares the same history and grape varieties as Faugères, with light rosés and impressively long-lived reds.
PRODUCERS: La Dournie, Dom. Madalle, Ch. Viranel, the Berlou co-operative.
Minervois As for Faugères and St-Chinian, with the addition of a little white. Quality has steadily improved since it gained its AC in 1985. There are now some richly aromatic and age-worthy reds in particular beginning to shine.
PRODUCERS: Dom. Ste-Eulalie, La Combe Blanche, Villerambert-Julien, Ch. d'Oupia, Big Frank (a Polish-born ex-Bostonian!).
Cabardès/Côtes de la Malepère These two former VDQS regions to the north and west of the city of Carcassonne are situated on the very cusp of Languedoc and the southwest. They have

a variety of different soils and microclimates and, not surprisingly, they are allowed to utilize both the Midi grapes and those from Bordeaux for their red and rosé wines. Some diverting wines are coming out of both, although only in small quantities, fully justifying their promotions to AC status, Cabardès in 1999, Malepère in 2005.
PRODUCERS: Ch. de la Bastide, Dom. Jouclary (Cabardès); Caves du Razès, Ch. de Festes (Malepère).
Limoux Created in 1993, this appellation for white wines represents a determined attempt to give the oaked-Chardonnay brigade a run for their money, so much so that oak-barrel treatment is compulsory. There are also plantings of the Loire grape Chenin Blanc and the interesting, crisply appley local variety, Mauzac.
PRODUCERS: Best so far is Sieur d'Arques.

The old farmhouse at Mas de Daumas Gassac (above), star of the Vins de Pays de l'Hérault.

LANGUEDOC-
ROUSSILLON
(PLUS OTHER NATIVE VARIETIES)
GRAPES: Red – Carignan,
Grenache, Cinsaut, Mour-
vèdre, Syrah, Merlot,
Cabernet Sauvignon, Malbec;
White – Clairette, Rolle,
Terret, Bourboulenc,
Picpoul, Muscat, Maccabéo,
Marsanne, Viognier, Sauvi-
gnon Blanc, Chardonnay

Bush vines growing high in the hills of the Côtes du Roussillon (above), with the snow-capped Pyrenees and the Spanish border in the near distance.

Blanquette de Limoux/Crémant de Limoux The former is the traditional sparkling wine of the region, left to re-ferment in the bottle the spring after vinification, and claiming an older lineage than champagne. Blanquette is a synonym for the local Mauzac grape, although there has always been a little Chardonnay in the wine. Since 1990, any wine that contains up to 30 per cent of Chardonnay, Chenin, or both, goes under the Crémant appellation. Delmas and Collin make two of the more appetizing examples.

Corbières One of the larger and more famous Languedoc appellations covers a range of good, sturdy, often spicy reds as well as small amounts of white and pink wine from southern varieties. Here again, the general picture has been of demonstrable improvement on the past, with sloppy, ropey wines being shunted aside by some of the more fascinating – and fairly priced – examples of modern French winemaking. Some of the less convincing reds are made with partial recourse to the Beaujolais technique of carbonic maceration (see Gamay section).
PRODUCERS: Ch. les Ollieux, La Voulte-Gasparets, Ch. Cabriac, Dom. des Caraguilhes, Dom. du Révérend, Ch. de Lastours.

Fitou The oldest AC in the Languedoc makes red wines on the border of Languedoc and Roussillon, in two separate zones that are divided by part of Corbières. While the general pattern of improvement has certainly touched Fitou, a lot is still made in the rather indifferent, rough-old-red style beloved of students.
EXCEPTIONS: Dom. du Mont-Tauch, Colomer.

Roussillon/Côtes du Roussillon/Côtes du Roussillon-Villages The area south of Perpignan, bordering on Catalan country, is home to some rather more run-of-the-mill offerings. By far the best of these three designations is the last, which is for red wines only, and comprises the northern section of Roussillon, nearest to Fitou.
PRODUCERS: Vignerons Catalans, Ch. de Jau, Ch. Corneilla.

Collioure A beautiful coastal appellation of vertiginously steep vineyards, making some remarkable and thoroughly original reds in an ultra-ripe, expansive style, principally from Grenache and Mourvèdre. One to try.
PRODUCERS: Dom. du Mas Blanc, Dom. de la Rectorie, Les Clos de Paulilles.

OTHER WINES

There are a number of *vins doux naturels* produced in this region, both white and red. Winemaking techniques are the same as those for Muscat de Beaumes-de-Venise (see entry, Rhône) and the whites here all use either of two strains of Muscat. Frontignan, together with three other Muscats suffixed respectively by de Mireval, de Lunel and de St-Jean-de-Minervois, all use the Muscat à Petits Grains grape, and produce lightly fragrant, barley-sugar sweet wines of varying degrees of intensity. The chunkier, less attractive Muscat d'Alexandrie is permitted as well in Muscat de Rivesaltes, made north of Perpignan.
PRODUCERS: Dom. de la Peyrade (Frontignan); Dom. de Barroubie (Muscat de St-Jean-de-Minervois); Brial (Muscat de Rivesaltes).

Sweet red wines, usually made entirely from or heavily based on Grenache, are made in Rivesaltes, Maury to the west of Fitou, and Banyuls, down on the Roussillon coast and overlapping with Collioure. Of those, Banyuls is considered to be about the best, with sweet strawberry fruit and a heady perfume sometimes reminiscent of good ruby port, but much less aggressive on the palate.
PRODUCERS: Dom. de la Rectorie, Mas Blanc (Banyuls); Mas Amiel (Maury).

GASCONY *and* THE SOUTH-WEST

These small wine areas, scattered from Bordeaux down to the Spanish border, offer a diverse and exciting range of wines that have been little influenced by passing fashions. These winemakers are proud of their traditions.

WHEREAS MOST OF the appellations of the sprawling Languedoc region make use of the same basic collections of red and white grapes for their wines, a much more diverse picture prevails in the southwest. There is an umbrella organization for the wines of the southwest, but each appellation retains its own fiercely guarded identity, and many have one or two local grape varieties they are proud to call their own.

They also have a culinary tradition to be proud of. After Burgundy, this is probably the most celebrated gastronomic corner of France, home of magnificent pork and poultry, chunky Toulouse sausages, foie gras, prunes and armagnac.

The producers have been considerably less susceptible to the influence of foreign technologists, the flying winemakers, around these parts than further east, and are consequently more fearful that their often little-known wines will continue to be swept aside in the varietal mania that has overcome the world markets. However, there is at least a sporting chance that a wine-drinking generation will discover Petit Manseng and Négrette, and then the southwest will have its day.

Wending our way circuitously down from just south of Bordeaux to the far southwest corner, the main appellations are as follows:
Bergerac/Côtes de Bergerac The first few ACs in the immediate vicinity of Bordeaux were once considered part of its overall catchment area. They use the same grape varieties (chiefly Cabernet Sauvignon, Merlot and Cabernet Franc for reds and rosés, Sauvignon Blanc and Sémillon for whites). Bergerac and the theoretically slightly superior Côtes de Bergerac are to the east of the Côtes de Castillon sector of Bordeaux, on the river Dordogne. There are a few stars here, though a lot of the wine is pretty basic stuff from the local co-operative.
PRODUCERS: Ch. la Jaubertie, Ch. Belingard, Ch. Court-les-Mûts, Ch. Tour des Gendres.
Montravel/Côtes de Montravel/Haut-Montravel White-wine appellation at the western end of Bergerac, mainly planted with Sémillon. The three designations refer to dry, semi-sweet and very sweet wines respectively. The dry Montravel wines are best, and much improved of late.

Château de Crouseilles peering majestically over its vineyard in the Gascon red-wine enclave of Madiran (above).

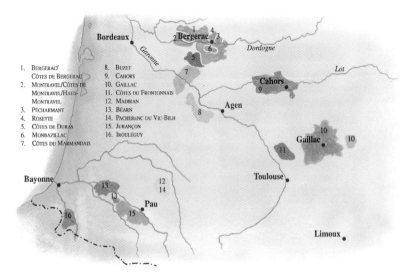

1. BERGERAC/CÔTES DE BERGERAC
2. MONTRAVEL/CÔTES DE MONTRAVEL/HAUT-MONTRAVEL
3. PÉCHARMANT
4. ROSETTE
5. CÔTES DE DURAS
6. MONBAZILLAC
7. CÔTES DU MARMANDAIS
8. BUZET
9. CAHORS
10. GAILLAC
11. CÔTES DU FRONTONNAIS
12. MADIRAN
13. BÉARN
14. PACHERENC DU VIC-BILH
15. JURANÇON
16. IROULÉGUY

The scattered appellations of Gascony and the southwest (left), from Bergerac, close to Bordeaux, down to Irouléguy on the border with Spain.

Pécharmant Red wines from near Bergerac itself, using Bordeaux grapes with a preponderance of Merlot. Overall quality is high, with Ch. Tiregand the main exporter of reliably classy claret lookalikes.

Rosette Sweet-whites appellation overlapping into Pécharmant using Sémillon, but now sadly dwindling towards extinction.

Côtes de Duras South of the Dordogne, the Duras makes some passable wines in the style of simple Bordeaux. The best shots are the Sauvignon whites, which can be agreeably crisp and clean. Here, the co-operative makes a good range called Le Seigneuret, and Dom. Petitot is also good.

Monbazillac One of the secrets that escaped from the region in the 1980s was the potentially glorious botrytized wine of Monbazillac. While Sauternes prices soared, this appellation further east along the Dordogne suddenly looked a ringer for great dessert wines at affordable prices. Sensational vintages in 1988, '89 and (especially) '90 brought its name to a much wider audience. Made from nobly-rotted Sémillon, with Sauvignon Blanc and flowery Muscadelle, the best can hold their heads up in the company of Sauternes without embarrassment.
PRODUCERS: Ch. les Hébras, Ch. Haut-Bernasse, Ch. la Borderie, Ch. La Brie.

Saussignac Tiny appellation for sweet Sémillon-based whites, just west of Monbazillac. Of no great pedigree, though Ch. Court-les-Mûts produces an eminently passable one.

Côtes du Marmandais Elevated from VDQS to AC in 1990, the Marmandais appellation straddles the river Garonne, south of Bordeaux. It makes principally reds (with a smidgeon of rosé and white) in a no-nonsense, easy-drinking style. The Bordeaux varieties are allowed to constitute up to 75 per cent of the red blends, with the remainder made up by Syrah, Gamay, the rough-natured southwestern grape Fer Servadou and Marmandais speciality, Abouriou. A couple of co-ops make nearly everything the appellation produces.

Buzet Although south of Marmandais, Buzet returns once again to the Bordeaux varieties for all colours of wine. Once again, the co-operative predominates, but its versatile range (Cuvée Napoléon and Baron d'Ardeuil are particularly good) is of high quality. The austerely concentrated reds are often as good as *cru bourgeois* claret.

Cahors Situated northeast of Agen, the appellation of Cahors spans the river Lot. Historically one of the more famous southwest names, it was known as the "black wine" because the grape juice was boiled to concentrate its colour. Now more sensitively vinified, it is made from a minimum 70 per cent of the Bordeaux variety, Malbec (here known as Auxerrois, but nothing to do with the white Alsace grape of that name), backed up by Merlot and a fierce local grape, Tannat, used only in judicious dashes. Light red fruits and modest tannins are the hallmarks of the wines, but the best producers achieve an intriguing floral note as well – something like violets.
BEST: Clos Triguedina, Ch. de Haute-Serre, Dom. Poujol, Dom. de Quattre, Ch. des Bouysses from the Côtes d'Olt co-operative.

Gaillac A large appellation northeast of Toulouse, Gaillac makes a wide range of styles, from bone-dry as well as slightly sweet whites, some sparkling wine using the same method as nearby Blanquette de Limoux (see entry, Languedoc-Roussillon) to firm, full reds. Its proximity to Limoux means that Mauzac is an important variety and the dry whites and sparklers have the same sort of tart, Granny Smith bite to them. It is supplemented by local grapes Len de l'El and Ondenc, as well as a soupçon of Sauvignon. The fizzes may be either just pétillant (and labelled Gaillac Perlé) or fully refermented and released with the yeast sediment still sloshing around in them. Reds include the local Duras and Fer Servadou,

together with some Syrah and Gamay, as well as the big three Bordeaux varieties.
PRODUCERS: Plageoles, Cros, Dom. de Labarthe, Ch. Larroze.

Côtes du Frontonnais Distinctive reds made from the local grape Négrette, which has a deliciously savoury pepperiness to it, fleshed out with the two Cabernets and Fer Servadou. Some of these can give any other full-bodied country reds a real run for their money for sheer concentration and personality. Also makes a small amount of rosé.
PRODUCERS: Ch. Montauriol (very high-flying young grower who puts leather labels on his top *cuvées*), Ch. Bellevue-la-Forêt, Ch. Flotis.

Tursan VDQS producing roughish, everyday reds, mainly from the muscular Tannat grape, and an oak-matured white made from the local Baroque. (Three-star Michelin chef Michel Guérard at Eugénie-les-Bains makes most of the white!)

Côtes de St-Mont VDQS for all shades of wine, dominated by the very good Caves de Plaimont co-operative. Reds use Fer Servadou and Tannat among others, while indigenous white grapes include such delights as Ruffiac and Petit Courbu. Some highly interesting flavours and some oak experimentation are to be found.

Madiran The unforgivingly brutal Tannat grape comes into its own in these fiery reds that almost invariably need a few years to settle, but never quite lose the power to intimidate. When fully ripe, however, they can have a spicy elegance. The two Cabernets are used to provide some fruit relief.
PRODUCERS: Dom. Laplace, Ch. Montus, Ch. Peyros, Ch. d'Aydie, Dom. Capmartin.

Béarn To the west of Madiran, and using the same grapes for reds and rosés. These are softer than Madiran but not particularly characterful. A co-operative at Bellocq makes most of the wine on the separately demarcated land, but over half of Béarn's grapes are vinified within the districts of Madiran and Jurançon.

Pacherenc du Vic-Bilh A separate appellation within Madiran for generally sweet white wines made from the local grapes Ruffiac, Petit Courbu and Gros Manseng, together with Sémillon and Sauvignon. Depending on the vintage conditions, Pacherenc may be made dry, but its sweet offerings made from grapes that are left to shrivel on the vine can occasionally be as distinguished as the sweeter wines of Jurançon.
PRODUCERS: Ch. Boucassé, Ch. d'Aydie.

Jurançon Much underrated appellation south of the town of Pau, making white wines principally from a blend of the twin varieties Gros Manseng and Petit Manseng (the latter the better for its piercing pineapple and apricot aromas), together with some Petit Courbu. The wines may be refreshingly dry and full of exotic fruit ripeness, or lusciously sweet from raisined grapes, as in Pacherenc. Excellent-value wines that are definitely worth seeking out.
PRODUCERS: Dom. de Cauhapé, Clos Uroulat, Clos Lamouroux, Clos de la Vierge.

Irouléguy Practically on the Spanish border in the Pays Basque, this far-flung appellation takes in a number of newly established vineyards carved out of the Pyrennean rock by growers motivated by great regional pride. Tannat raises its brutish head in the reds and rosés, but is tempered by some Cabernet, while the whites use the Jurançon varieties. As elsewhere, the regional co-operative makes a fair amount of the wine, but Dom. Brana is also good.

Vin de Pays des Côtes de Gascogne Surplus grapes not used in the production of armagnac, the brandy of the southwest, go into white wines under the Côtes de Gascogne designation. Much comes from the Ugni Blanc grape, which makes nice brandy but yawningly dull wine, although there is also some Sauvignon Blanc and both Mansengs to add aromatic appeal, and even a little Chardonnay. Dom. de Tariquet and Dom. de Plantérieu are good wines, as are some of the offerings of the Caves de Plaimont co-operative and the crisp, green-fruited whites of Dom. St-Lannes.

The stunning Château de Monbazillac (above). The finest sweet wines of Monbazillac can rival those of Sauternes.

Cabernet Sauvignon grapes arriving at the Buzet co-operative (above). The Bordeaux varieties are used to make concentrated claret-style reds.

JURA, SAVOIE *and* BUGEY

To the east of Burgundy lie the three little-known regions of Jura, Savoie and the Bugey. Tucked up against the French Alps, the areas are dominated by white wines, and the unique styles of vin jaune *and* vin de paille.

THESE THREE EASTERLY regions are among the most obscure and insular of all France's wine-growing areas. Not much of their wine is exported, and what is makes few compromises to modern tastes.

JURA

The remote high-altitude vineyards of the Jura, not far from the Swiss border, harbour some of France's most individual wines. They do crop up in minute quantities on the export markets, but tend to be highly priced, and the house style of the region is not an especially fashionable one. That said – *vive la différence*.

There are two regional specialities – *vin jaune* and *vin de paille*. Vin jaune, "yellow

The vineyards of Jura and Savoie (below) lie on the lower slopes of the French Alps, close to the Swiss border.

wine", is made in a similar way to sherry in that it matures in cask for six years under a *voile*, or film, of yeast culture. As the wine oxidates, it turns yellow. About one-third also evaporates. The resulting wine is heavy-textured, dry as chalk-dust and alcoholic – rather like fino sherry to the uninitiated. *Vin de paille*, "straw wine", is equally rare, made from raisined grapes. These are rich, alcoholic wines, and again capable of some bottle-age. Both wines are only made in good years, and in small quantities, and are therefore pricey. Much of the *vin de paille* is found in Arbois, while *vin jaune* reigns supreme in L'Etoile and Château-Chalon.

Arbois The greatest volume of Jura wine is produced under this appellation in the northern part of the region, centred on the town of the same name. They may be red, white or rosé, and there are three important local grapes: two red varieties – Trousseau, which gives a deeply rich if unsubtle wine, and thin-skinned Poulsard, quite the opposite and good for rosés – as well as a white, the gloriously musky Gewürztraminer relative, Savagnin.

The Pinot Noir and Chardonnay grapes of Burgundy are also grown, the latter more extensively in recent years. Some of the wine is made sparkling by the champagne method, and labelled Arbois Mousseux, while wines from the best village, Pupillin, are allowed to add its name as a suffix. The most visible producer from Arbois is Henri Maire.

Côtes du Jura The central and southern parts of the region take this appellation, but make the same broad range of styles from the same grapes as Arbois. Ch. d'Arlay is one of the bigger names and a good producer of *vin jaune*.

L'Etoile Tiny appellation largely represented by the local co-operative and specializing in hazelnutty sherry-like *vins jaunes* made from Savagnin. There is also some straight red and white and some sparkling wine.

Château-Chalon The only AC which is entirely for *vin jaune* from the Savagnin grape. Château-Chalon sits on a little hilltop and remains completely aloof from the modern wine world. Wine is only made in years when the producers

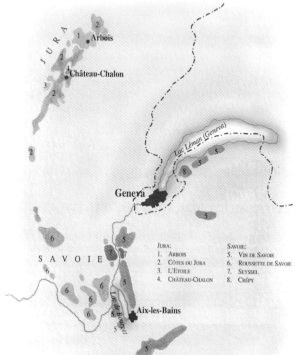

JURA:	SAVOIE:
1. ARBOIS	5. VIN DE SAVOIE
2. CÔTES DU JURA	6. ROUSSETTE DE SAVOIE
3. L'ETOILE	7. SEYSSEL
4. CHÂTEAU-CHALON	8. CRÉPY

The vineyards of Château-Chalon (left), the tiny AC in the heart of Jura that makes only vin jaune.

deem the harvest to be good enough to bother. Bourdy is one of the best growers.

SAVOIE

The region lies due south of Geneva. Home to some indigenous grape varieties, many of its wines have character but are not much exported.

Vin de Savoie The overall appellation for any wine produced within the *départements* of Savoie and Haute-Savoie. Most are whites and are made from the local Jacquère grape in a crunchy-fresh style, supported by Chardonnay, some of the Roussanne of the northern Rhône, and the neutral-tasting Chasselas much favoured in Switzerland. Reds use Pinot Noir and Gamay, as well as a local variety called Mondeuse, which makes something a little fleshier than the light-bodied norm. Certain privileged villages (17 of them) may add their names to the basic designation; they include Apremont, Abymes, Montmélian and Chautagne.

Roussette de Savoie The Savoyards consider the Roussette to be their best asset among white grapes. It has its own AC, though it covers the whole region, like Vin de Savoie. The wines have a diverting floral perfume and should be drunk young to catch their tingling acidity at its freshest. In four villages – Frangy, Marestel, Monthoux and Monterminod – the wines must be 100 per cent Roussette; elsewhere they can be up to 50 per cent Chardonnay.

Seyssel Small appellation taking in dry white wines from Roussette and the local Molette. There is also a sparkling version, Seyssel Mousseux, that is based on Molette, but has to contain at least 10 per cent of Roussette. Varichon & Clerc is the only exporter of note.

Crépy Chasselas makes the wines of this dry-whites appellation, and jolly dull they are too.

BUGEY

Just west of Savoie, in the Ain *département*, is the Bugey. Historically part of Burgundy, it now constitutes a mini-region of its own, its grape varieties marking its identity as a sort of cross between Savoie and the Jura. Finding any outside the region is something of a teaser, though it is reputed that some make it as far as Lyon.

Vin du Bugey One designation covers the whole region, although it only has VDQS status as opposed to full AC – a situation that may very well change before long. An entire range of styles is made, from aromatic, crisply textured dry whites, through delicate rosés, to lightish reds using Gamay, Pinot Noir and also some Mondeuse. There are additionally two styles of fizz – lightly prickly (*pétillant*) and fully sparkling (*mousseux*). Much praise has been heaped on the region's Chardonnay varietals. Cerdon is perhaps the best of the handful of individual village names that may appear on the labels.

JURA
GRAPES: White – Savagnin, Chardonnay;
Red – Trousseau, Poulsard, Pinot Noir

SAVOIE
GRAPES: White – Jacquère, Roussette, Molette, Roussanne, Chasselas, Chardonnay;
Red – Mondeuse, Gamay, Pinot Noir

The alpine town of Seyssel, in Savoie, on the river Rhône (left), that has given its name to the local white-wine AC.

VIN *de* PAYS

The vin de pays *designation was created to encourage production of higher quality, easy-drinking red, white, and rosé wines, "country wines" that display the character of their region.*

MANY FRENCH WINES – about one bottle in five – fall just below the two strictest categories for quality wine production, AC (*appellation contrôlée*) and VDQS (*vin délimité de qualité supérieure*). Vin de pays (literally "country wine") is a designation drawn up in the 1970s to denote wines that had some sort of regional identity, but for one reason or another, perhaps because the grower was using grapes not officially sanctioned in the locality, or perhaps because the vines were too young under the appellation regulations, didn't quite make it to AC or VDQS status.

The most basic quality category of all is straightforward table wine (*vin de table*). This is the generally insipid bulk production, mostly from the south, that did so much to swell the European wine lake in the last couple of decades. *Vin de pays*, intended in its way to be as representative of regional characteristics as the appellation wines, should therefore be several rungs up the quality ladder from *vin de table*, and most of it is.

There are three levels of *vin de pays*, depending on how specific the individual producer wants, or is able, to be. At the broadest,

most inclusive level, the designation may cover a whole region, such as the commercially pre-eminent Vin de Pays d'Oc, the regional VdP for Languedoc-Roussillon (see the relevant section). Some are given slightly cloying, flights-of-fancy names that the authorities hope will prove marketable. The VdP for Corsica is Vin de Pays de l'Ile de Beauté (Island of Beauty), while the one that covers the whole of the Loire valley goes by the name Vin de Pays du Jardin de la France (Garden of France).

Then there are VdPs that use the name of the *département*, such as Alpes-Maritime in Provence, Gers in Gascony, or l'Hérault in the Languedoc. To use these, the wines must have been sourced from vines grown entirely within that *département*. Within the confines of those, there are named patches of vineyard land, particular hillsides, and so forth, that take the specificity of the VdP designation almost to appellation levels.

There are more than 100 such VdPs, including the following. Coteaux de l'Ardèche in the centre of the Rhône valley refers to a particular stretch of slopes within the departmental Ardèche VdP, Côtes de Thongue falls within the

Vins de pays *that use the name of a* département, *such as Ardèche (right), must contain grapes sourced only from within that district.*

Vin de Pays de l'Hérault, while Vin de Pays des Marches de Bretagne is a Loire VdP whose borders overlap three *départements* – Loire-Atlantique, Maine-et-Loire and the Vendée.

To qualify as a *vin de pays*, the wines must be made from certain grape varieties, and are not to be blended with grapes from other areas. With the exception of wines from the Alsace region, *vins de pays* are likely to be the only French wines you will come across that are labelled with the name of a grape, many of them being single varietals. (To be sure, some producers making basic AC Bourgogne Blanc are beginning to state the magic word Chardonnay on their labels in acknowledgement of varietal recognition among consumers, but they are still very much a minority.)

The *vin de pays* producers are obviously concerned to combat whatever inferiority complex they feel their wines may have in an appellation-dominated market-place, and varietal identification is one of the easiest routes to a higher market share.

Within the Vin de Pays d'Oc designation, there are many fine varietal wines – not all, as we have seen, made exclusively by French producers – and some of the bigger operators, such as Fortant de France, have established enough of a quality reputation to charge more ambitiously for their wines. Thus is born the anomaly by which a lightly oaked Chardonnay, officially styled "country wine", may sell for more than a white AC Coteaux du Languedoc made just up

the road. Whatever we may think about the encroaching international Chardonnization of the world of white wine, there has undoubtedly been a certain payoff in terms of improving the general quality level of wines produced under some of the less distinguished ACs.

With lesser-known grape varieties, such as Marsanne or Viognier from the northern Rhône, the VdPs have introduced consumers to some important, slightly offbeat flavours that were previously only known to a handful of experts who could afford the white wines of Hermitage or Condrieu. Elsewhere, *vin de pays* has provided producers of cognac and armagnac with a handy outlet for surplus production of white grapes. (The respective VdPs are Vin de Pays Charentais and Vin de Pays des Côtes de Gascogne, with the latter representing distinctly better quality across the board.)

By the mid-1990s, production of *vin de pays* had risen to such a level that it had virtually matched the annual capacity of *vin de table*. That's fine as long as the wine is of distinctly more exalted quality, and the designation is not just being used as a way of getting higher prices for bottom-drawer plonk. About three-quarters of all *vin de pays* is red. At the bargain-basement end of the market, it is a long-established truism that it is considerably easier to produce a palatable red wine than it is to make a decent white within the same budget.

All in all, the *vin de pays* movement has been one of the more exciting developments within French wine in recent times, and one that offers a compelling opportunity for consumers to familiarize themselves with the tastes of some significant grape varieties.

These vineyards of Château Capion, in Hérault (above), grow Cabernet Sauvignon, Chardonnay and Merlot for Vin de Pays d'Oc.

Hand-picking of grapes near Reuilly in the upper Loire (above), destined for one of the region's comparatively rare red vins de pays.

Grapes growing in the spectacular Ardèche gorge for use in the region's highly regarded Vin de Pays des Coteaux de l'Ardèche (left).

EUROPE, AFRICA AND THE EAST

The 11th-century Castillo de Milmanda (above), owned by the famous winemaking family, Torres, in Catalonia.

Picking grapes for Vinho Verde (above), on Portugal's "Green Coast".

As the winemaking cultures of north America and the Southern Hemisphere have emerged over the last 20 years to compete with their European antecedents, the struggle for supremacy (and it has been seen as nothing less in some quarters) has been billed as France versus the "New World". The countries included in that now outdated category – an illogical assemblage of the United States and Canada, South America, South Africa, Australia and New Zealand – are usually portrayed as storming the holy citadel of traditional wine production, falsely seen as an exclusively French preserve.

The plethora of French-inspired varietal wines from countries outside Europe has led many consumers to neglect the wines of the rest of Europe. In this respect, each of the European wine countries is saddled with its own particular image problem. When drinkers whose only previous knowledge of German wine is Liebfraumilch, or for whom Italy always meant fizzy pink Lambrusco, graduate on to South African Chardonnay or California Merlot, they have little incentive to explore the *quality* wines of Germany, Italy and the rest.

As we have seen, the great majority of the internationally grown grape varieties are French in origin, and it is only recently that Italian and Spanish varietals have begun to be found outside their traditional homelands. If a wine like Chablis can suffer from the fact that consumers don't realize it is made from Chardonnay, what chance have wines from Ribera del Duero, Carmignano or Bairrada?

As the varietal trend shows no sign of abating (it is, if anything, strengthening), so Europe's traditional wines are finding it increasingly

difficult to gain market shares outside their immediate regions of production. Drunk solely by locals and holidaymakers, they may all come to occupy the same niche as many of the wines of Provence and eastern France (indeed, many have been quite happy to dwell in precisely such obscurity).

A handful of mainly southern European wines have actually established themselves as brand names. They include Spanish Rioja, Vinho Verde from Portugal, certainly Chianti, Valpolicella and Barolo from Italy. Beyond these, however, European wine represents an uncharted hinterland for most consumers.

It would be misleading to deny that a large part of the problem has been quality. Just as the poorer regions of southern France were the last to modernize themselves as the 20th century drew to a close, in terms of their vinification techniques and their understanding of what today's wine market expects of even a modestly priced bottle, so the countries of southern and central Europe also languished for too long. They relied on the bulk production of indifferent wine made by frankly unhygienic and insensitive methods and sold at very cheap prices. What these areas were producing primarily was not wine but alcohol, a bottom-line commodity intended to be as roughly consistent from one year to the next as was biochemically possible.

Consistency is, of course, a consideration. But, much more than this, wine is an expression of the environment and the conditions in which it is made, or it is nothing. That pride in the sense of place, a celebration of the flavours of native grapes, and what nature and the individual have combined to make of them in a particular vintage, should be reflected in every bottle of wine that a grower or merchant or co-operative sends out into the market. It isn't any longer just a question of keeping a few wine connoisseurs happy.

The fact is that, in commercial terms, there is no other way forward for the modern winemaker. Now that there is every chance that a Vin de Pays d'Oc may taste as excitingly fruit-filled and satisfying as something from South Australia or Chile, nobody wants ropey old reds and weary little whites from far-flung corners of southern Italy or the Iberian peninsula.

The signs are that the light of the quality revolution is at last penetrating some of Europe's dustiest cupboards. As the tendency gathers pace, and assuming that prices don't quickly shoot through the roof, many of the old wines of Europe will be ripe for rediscovery.

If a renaissance in Italian wines is at all likely, it might well turn out to have been nurtured in California. What became known as Mediterranean cuisine, founded on the olive oil, sundried tomatoes, balsamic vinegar and basil of Italian domestic cooking, originated on the west coast of America. As California growers sought to produce wines to match it, they began to try their hands at the Sangiovese, Nebbiolo, Barbera and Dolcetto grapes of Italy. The California speciality grape Zinfandel is actually a southern Italian variety (they call it Primitivo back home).

For red wines at least, there is certainly more untapped potential in Italy than in any other European wine country. Quality whites will probably continue to be dependent on the likes of premium Chardonnay, as the widespread reliance on neutral Pinot Grigio, and the monotonous Trebbiano traditional in white wines the length and breadth of Italy, do little or nothing to inspire.

Spain is still struggling to emerge from its old image as a producer of dirt-cheap oily reds, more often than not aged for years in musty old casks until whatever fruit they possessed at the outset was completely bleached out of them. There is still a tendency to assume that great age equates with quality in Spanish wine, but producers in some of the more dynamic regions – notably Ribera del Duero, Navarra and even dear old Rioja – are beginning to produce some vibrant young reds and whites with gratifying levels of fruit that should unerringly point the way ahead.

Portugal too has been looking to its laurels. Although its production is only a fraction of Spain's, it has a broader palette of indigenous grapes to draw on, many of them of genuine quality. The modern wine scene has perhaps been a little too dependent on big corporations with massive investment power, but there are some talented small producers emerging.

Germany remains a prisoner of the structure of its export industry, which is still massively geared to producing commercial slosh for the unsophisticated end of the market. As long as that is unchanged, the efforts of its most prodigiously talented growers (by no means working exclusively with Riesling, either) will continue to be sold short. In central Europe, Austria is streaking ahead of Germany in overall quality

terms. Where once its reputation rested solely on dessert wines from the northeast of the country, it is now rapidly gaining ground as a producer of premium varietal wines, many of them from indigenous grape varieties that offer some challenging flavours.

The countries of the former Soviet bloc have had mixed fortunes since the break-up of the old state monopolies. Hungary and the Czech Republic are coming along in leaps and bounds, with tasty, inexpensive varietal wines often made by foreigners, while Romania probably always did have good wines that have only just started finding their way to a wider audience. Bulgaria, sadly, faltered after the collapse of the Soviet bloc. During the communist era, its heavily subsidised varietals blazed some sort of trail for affordable quality, but with new investment flooding in from Australian, French, German and Russian sources, things are again on the up.

Meanwhile, countries such as Moldova and Greece, benefiting from an influx of expertise and technology, are poised for promotion to Europe's second division. A willingness to absorb lessons from outside, together with enough internal investment to back up the more forward-thinking practitioners, should see some exciting results emerge over time. And as the volume of annual production inexorably grows, and assuming the summers continue to be benevolent, not even the UK need be left out of the European wine movement.

Autumn arrives in the vineyards of Germany's Mosel region (above), above the town of Piesport.

The dramatic modernist bodega (below), built in 1918 for Spanish producer Raimat.

ITALY

The invading Greeks called it "Oenotria", the land of wine. Italy has remained steeped in viticulture, and today usually produces more wine than any other country in the world.

VITIS VINIFERA, the wine-grape species, has been growing on what is now the Italian mainland since centuries before the birth of Christ. For a long time it was believed by archaeologists that cultivation of the vine was introduced to these parts by the Greeks in the centuries before the rise of the Roman Empire. It is now thought that some tribal cultures, notably the Etruscans whose domain extended along the western coast of the peninsula, already possessed viticultural knowledge and that the Greeks did little more than introduce new vine varieties when they arrived.

However that may be, the name the Greeks gave to the new territories in what was to become Rome was Oenotria, meaning literally "land of wine". That alone suggests what a centrally

Italy's foremost agricultural industry is grape-growing. Vines are planted across the country, from the northern borders to its heel in the south (below).

important role wine has played in this part of the world since the very earliest civilizations. By the time the Roman Empire was at its height, the origins of wine connoisseurship were clearly apparent. Key texts of the period refer to particularly good vintages, while wines from specific regions, such as Lazio in the vicinity of Rome itself, Tuscany to the north and Campania, centred on Naples to the south, came to be especially highly valued.

The expansion of the Roman Empire into western Europe opened up busy trade routes, which not only kept the occupying armies supplied but also greatly expanded the practice of viticulture in such outposts as Spain and Gaul (in what is now France). Even Britain, with the relatively benevolent climate it enjoyed at the time, learned from the Romans how to tend vines and make wine. This was a habit Britain wasn't to lose until around the time of the disso-lution of the monasteries.

Nowadays, in terms of volume, Italy remains in most years the most significant wine-produc-ing country in the world, knocking France effortlessly into second place. Even more than in France, too, wine is an integral part of every-day life. The average Italian family consumes prodigious quantities of wine at both mid-day and evening meals, and it is a vital ingredient in traditional cookery.

Whereas there are whole swathes of France – notably northern parts such as Brittany and Nor-mandy – that are climatically unsuited to wine production, there is no part of Italy at all that is a no-go area for the vine. From the Alpine bor-der with Switzerland and the Tyrolean region abutting Austria, down to the tip of Italy's toe in Calabria – not to mention the islands of Sicily and Sardinia – Italian agriculture is about wine first and foremost.

What holds the country back is the lack of a coherent quality-control system that everybody can respect. The equivalent of the French *appel-lation contrôlée* is DOC, which stands for *denominazione de origine controllata*, and its upper subdivision DOCG (*denominazione de origine controllata e garantita*). These

1. PIEDMONT
2. VALLE D'AOSTA
3. LIGURIA
4. LOMBARDY
5. TRENTINO-ALTO ADIGE
6. VENETO
7. FRIULI
8. EMILIA-ROMAGNA
9. TUSCANY
10. THE MARCHES
11. UMBRIA
12. LAZIO
13. ABRUZZI
14. MOLISE
15. PUGLIA
16. CAMPANIA
17. BASILICATA
18. CALABRIA
19. SICILY
20. SARDINIA

designations were created in the 1960s, but were rather randomly applied to whichever wines were of particular commercial value at the time. Consequently, as an overall indication of quality, they were at best useless and at worst positively misleading.

Since 1992, there has been a painfully slow campaign to redesign the system, known as the Goria Law after the former Agriculture Minister who instigated it. This should in theory tighten up on quality within the DOC and DOCG regions, by making all wines subject to approval by a professional tasting panel.

The Goria Law also made provision for classifying the best regional wines with a designation broadly analogous to *vin de pays* – IGT (*indicazione geografica tipica*). Everything else is *vino da tavola* (table wine), although it should be noted that some of Italy's very finest wines have been made with flagrant disregard for the regulations for their areas. These wines are defiantly labelled as humble VdT, in much the same way that the monumental Mas de Daumas Gassac of southern France is proud to be labelled as a mere Vin de Pays de l'Hérault.

PIEDMONT

The northwestern region of Piedmont, in the foothills of the Alps, is one of Italy's very best wine-growing districts. Styles made range from the lightest of whites through sweet sparklers to thundering reds of great longevity; they are listed here alphabetically.

Arneis DOC since 1989 for white wines made from the grape of the same name. They are more sternly constituted than many Italian whites, with a fruit like tart pears, often mixed with a discernible hint of almond. Grown in the Langhe hills around Alba, and also in Roero to the northwest of the town.
PRODUCERS: Castello di Neive, Voerzio, Giacosa, Vietti.

Asti Formerly known as Asti Spumante, the famous sweet fizz produced around the town of Asti is one of Italy's classic styles. Low in alcohol (usually about 7 per cent) and full of the flavours of ripe green grapes and sugared almonds, it is one of the most approachable sparkling wines in the world. Quality is extremely reliable across the board, although it has suffered from a certain vulgarity of image, presumably on account of its sweetness.
PRODUCERS: Fontanafredda, Martini, Sandro, most supermarket own-labels.

Barbaresco This and Barolo (see below) are the two most important reds produced from the brilliant Nebbiolo grape. Centred on the village of the same name, the Barbaresco DOCG is often held to produce slightly more elegant Nebbiolos than its longer-established sibling Barolo, but the difference is pretty subtle. These are huge, tannic, exotically scented wines, monstrously tough in youth, but ageing well to a savoury, chocolatey maturity.
PRODUCERS: Gaja, Giacosa, Pio Cesare, Marchesi di Gresy, Scarpa.

Barbera d'Alba/d'Asti/del Monferrato The Barbera grape variety, suffixed by any of these regional names in Piedmont, produces a sharply acidic, but agreeably cherry-fruited, red that is usually fairly light in both body and alcohol. Best drunk young and fresh, its undeniable potential is what has made certain California growers try their luck with it.
PRODUCERS: Viticoltori dell'Acquese, Guasti, Conterno, Borgogno.

Barolo King of the Piedmontese reds, Barolo is one of Italy's most travelled DOCG wines. Its supporters are among the most dedicated of wine fans, as it is often very difficult to know when to drink Barolo to catch it at its best. In its youth, it is absolutely rigid with tannin, although its colour starts to fade surprisingly quickly. It then begins to acquire an extraordinary range of flavours that includes violets, black plums, bitter chocolate and wild herbs, but even at 20 years old (when it may have gone quite brown), it obstinately refuses to let go of that heavyweight tannin. In the main, its growers have declined to compromise with contemporary tastes, so that Barolo remains one of the world's most gloriously unreconstructed red wines. Best vineyard sites may be specified on the label.
PRODUCERS: Aldo Conterno, Giuseppe Mascarello, Prunotto, Ceretto, Voerzio, Altare, Cavallotto.

The Barbaresco DO (above) in Piedmont, "the foothills" of the Alps.

Scything poppies in springtime (above) in Barolo.

PIEDMONT:
ARNEIS
GRAPE: *Arneis*
ASTI
GRAPE: *Moscato*
BARBARESCO
GRAPE: *Nebbiolo*
BARBERA D'ALBA/
D'ASTI/DEL
MONFERRATO
GRAPE: *Barbera*
BAROLO
GRAPE: *Nebbiolo*

ABRACHETTO D'ACQUI
GRAPE: Brachetto
DOLCETTO
GRAPE: Dolcetto
FAVORITA
GRAPE: Favorita
FREISA D'ASTI/
DI CHIERI
GRAPE: Freisa
GATTINARA
GRAPES: Nebbiolo, Bonarda
GAVI/CORTESE DI GAVI
GRAPE: Cortese
MOSCATO D'ASTI
GRAPE: Moscato
SPANNA
GRAPE: Nebbiolo

LOMBARDY:
OLTREPO PAVESE
GRAPES: Red – Barbera,
Bonarda, Croatina, Uva
Rara, Pinot Nero; White –
Riesling Italico, Pinot Bianco,
Pinot Grigio
VALTELLINA
GRAPE: Nebbiolo
FRANCIACORTA
GRAPES: Red – Cabernet
Sauvignon, Merlot, Pinot
Nero; White – Chardonnay
LUGANA WHITE
GRAPE: Trebbiano di Lugana

*High on the alpine slopes of
Valle d'Aosta, vines are often
still trained up traditional
low pergolas (above).*

Brachetto d'Acqui Oddball pink wine from the aromatic Brachetto grape, usually slightly pétillant.
Carema Tiny DOC for lighter Nebbiolo reds, in the far north. Look for Ferrando's wines.
Dolcetto Seven DOCs in Piedmont make red wine from the Dolcetto grape. They are Dolcetto d'Alba (the best), Diano d'Alba, Dogliani, Dolcetto d'Acqui, Dolcetto d'Asti, Ovada and Langhe Monregalesi. The wine is a bright purple, light-bodied, exuberantly fresh product for drinking young, crammed with a sharp berry-fruit flavour like blueberries. Compared to Beaujolais, young Dolcetto is nearly always a more attractive and more gently priced alternative.
PRODUCERS: Mascarello, Clerico, Vajra, Ratti, Viticoltori dell'Acquese.
Erbaluce di Caluso Light, fairly soft dry whites as well as a famed but rare golden dessert wine (Caluso Passito), made from the not especially distinguished Erbaluce grape.
PRODUCERS: Boratto, Ferrando.
Favorita White variety making pleasantly lemony varietal wine on both banks of the river Tanaro. Best grower is Malvira.
Freisa d'Asti/di Chieri A pair of DOCs, the latter very near Turin, for an intensely scented, floral red of appealing lightness, from the grape of the same name.
Gattinara Most important of the lesser-known red DOCs based on Nebbiolo. Gattinara's wines are intense and potentially long-lived.
PRODUCERS: Brugo, Travaglini.
Gavi/Cortese di Gavi Ambitiously priced dry whites from the herbaceous Cortese grape. Gavi (in particular its most illustrious manifestation Gavi di Gavi) is held in preposterously high esteem locally, which helps to explain its outlandish price. When all's said and done, the wine is not noticeably special.
PRODUCERS: Deltetto, Chiarlo, Arione.
Grignolino Light, quaffable varietal red made near Asti, only mildly less fruity than Dolcetto.
Moscato d'Asti Made in the same region and from the same grape as Asti, but much less fizzy than its more famous cousin, Moscato d'Asti is noted for its appetizing citric freshness.
PRODUCERS: Chiarlo, Ascheri, Vietti, Gatti.
Ruchè Small DOC making full-bodied, herbal-scented reds in the Monferrato region. Not often seen.
Spanna Widely used synonym for the Nebbiolo grape, often seen on richly textured Piedmont reds from a number of localities. Travaglini makes a good example.

VALLE D'AOSTA
The far northwestern corner of Italy is occupied by a small river valley bordering on both France and Switzerland. Wines produced here are made from a number of native grapes, backed up by a smattering of Nebbiolo and Moscato and plantings of Burgundy and Alsace varieties. They are almost all consumed locally.

LIGURIA
An arc-shaped mountainous region that runs along the Mediterranean coast of northwest Italy, Liguria's main commercial centre is Genoa. In terms of exports, it is not a particularly significant winemaking district, and many of its traditional wines, such as the syrupy dessert wines made from raisined grapes, are dying out. Cinqueterre is a dry white based on the local Bosco grape, usually blended with Vermentino (known as Rolle in France, where it is a major player in the wines of Bellet in Provence). Rossese is an important native red variety, and has its own DOC, Dolceacqua, in the west of Liguria. Some Dolcetto is produced under the local name of Ormeasco.

LOMBARDY
The Lombardy region (or Lombardia) is centred on Milan, and runs from the alpine border with Switzerland down to the river Po, which forms its southern extremity. It is geographically the largest of Italy's wine regions, and has been in recent years one of the quality leaders.
Oltrepò Pavese In classic Italian fashion, this name covers almost any style of wine, from sparkling to sweet, only some of which qualifies for the DOC. The best is a good, sturdy red based on Barbera, while the dry whites from the Riesling Italico (nothing to do with the noble Riesling, confusingly) are largely forgettable. The champagne-method fizzes tend to use the various members of the Pinot family.
Valtellina The largest volume of Nebbiolo in Italy is produced in this DOC near the Swiss border. As well as basic Valtellina and the slightly better Valtellina Superiore, there are four recognized sub-regions that are responsible for the best wines – Inferno, Grumello, Sassella and Valgella. These are much lighter Nebbiolos than those produced in Piedmont, but the best do attain a purity of fruit and staying-power on the palate. Some powerful wine is made from shrivelled grapes fermented until fully dry, and bottled under the name Sforzato.

The castle of Soave (left), in the Veneto, that gives its name to one of Italy's most famous dry white wines.

Franciacorta Created a DOCG in 1995 for potentially excellent champagne-method sparklers that are worth investigating. The still wines are labelled DOC Terre di Franciacorta, and tend to use classic French varieties and techniques.
PRODUCERS: Ca' del Bosco, Bellavista, Cavalleri. Berlucchi is a benchmark fizz producer.
Lugana White DOC for dry wines based on a local variant of the dreaded Trebbiano grape – the Trebbiano di Lugana. The odd one has a little herbaceous snap to it. Zenato makes some half-decent examples. (Lugana overlaps into the Veneto region.)

TRENTINO-ALTO ADIGE
Hard by the Austrian border is Italy's northern-most wine region. The Alto Adige is known to the Austrians, as well as the many German-speaking Italians in these parts, as the Südtirol or South Tyrol. The lower half of the region takes its name from the city of Trento.

In the last couple of decades, producers here have made a name for the region by making some light but impressive wines from inter-national varieties, most notably the Cabernets Sauvignon and Franc, Merlot and Pinot Noir, as well as Chardonnay, Pinot Gris and Pinot Blanc. The Australian winemaker, Geoff Merrill, has

produced some outstanding wines here.

Some of the Chardonnay is barrel-aged and aims to carve itself a niche in the international market for oaky white wines, but prices for these wooded wines have tended to be too stiff for their own good. Local red varieties of particular note are the sour-cherry-flavoured Marzemino, the richly chocolatey Lagrein (which can make sinewy reds such as Lagrein Dunkel, as well as graceful rosés known as Lagrein Kretzer) and the blackcurranty Teroldego, which has its own DOC in Teroldego Rotaliano.
PRODUCERS: Haas, Lageder, Tiefenbrunner, Walch.

VENETO
The Veneto is the major wine-producing region of northeast Italy, extending from east of Lake Garda across to Venice and up to the Austrian border. There are some important DOCs and commonly recognized names like Soave and Valpolicella, but overall quality is dragged down by excessive production and some ill-conceived matching of grape varieties to vineyard sites. However, the potential for improvement is clearly there, and some enterprising growers are showing signs of healthy impatience with the general level of mediocrity.

Drying grapes for Amarone and Recioto (above) at the Masi winery, in Veneto's Valpolicella DOC.

Cases of Soave leaving the packing shed (right).

VALPOLICELLA CLASSICO

VENETO:
BARDOLINO
GRAPES: *Red – Corvina, Molinara, Rondinella*
BIANCO DI CUSTOZA
GRAPES: *White – Trebbiano Toscano, Garganega, Tocai Friulano*
BREGANZE
GRAPES: *Red – Cabernet Sauvignon, Cabernet Franc, Merlot; White – Tocai Friulano, Pinot Bianco, Sauvignon Blanc, Chardonnay*
PIAVE
GRAPES: *Red – Merlot, Cabernet Sauvignon; White – Tocai Friulano, Verduzzo*
SOAVE
GRAPES: *White – Garganega, Trebbiano di Soave, Chardonnay, Pinot Bianco*
VALPOLICELLA
GRAPES: *Red – Corvina, Molinara, Rondinella*

Bardolino Featherlight reds from a trio of local grapes for drinking young and fresh but not for lingering over. Wines labelled Superiore should have a bit more oomph. The rosé version is called Chiaretto, but is rarely very nice.
PRODUCERS: Masi, Boscaini, Le Vigne di San Pietro.

Bianco di Custoza Mostly neutral dry whites from a cocktail of grape varieties, none of which seem able to contribute much character. Occasionally, a vague hint of tutti-frutti enlivens some wines, but not often.
PRODUCERS: Zenato, Le Vigne di San Pietro, Portalupi, Tedeschi.

Breganze One of those DOCs making waves by trying out international varietal wines, though there is plenty of humdrum stuff from local grapes too. The red wines made from the Bordeaux blend can be extraordinarily good in a genuinely claretty way. Maculan stands head and shoulders above other producers in the area.

Gambellara Dry whites that bear a marked resemblance to Soave, owing to their being made from the same grapes. Most are very bland indeed.

Piave The area immediately behind Venice produces large quantities of indifferent varietal wine, the lion's share of it thin, grassy Merlot.

Prosecco di Conegliano/di Valdobbiadene Made near Piave, Prosecco can be a still dry white, but its more celebrated manifestation is as a simple sparkler, using the Charmat method in which the second fermentation is induced in a large tank before bottling. A lot of it is just off-dry and can be agreeably refreshing. In the bars of Venice, they mix it with peach juice to make the famous Bellini cocktail.
PRODUCERS: Collavini, Carpene Malvolti.

Soave One of Italy's most famous dry white wines, often synonymous with the bone-dry, totally neutral, flavour-free image of Italian whites that many wine-drinkers have. Increasing amounts of Chardonnay in the blend have added a little interest, even if we may be allowed some scepticism as to how traditional it is. If you're lucky, you may find a hint of almond paste on the nose that contributes some interest. Some producers are experimenting with ageing in oak – a difficult balancing-act to bring off. Recioto di Soave is a sweet but austere version made from raisined grapes.
PRODUCERS: Pieropan, Anselmi, Costalunga, Pasqua, Zenato, Tedeschi, Santi.

Valpolicella Red wine DOC that covers a multitude of styles, from very dilute pinkish wines of no discernible character to some deliciously concentrated, gamey, chocolatey reds of considerable ageing potential. As well as the basic style (and the slightly more alcoholic Superiore version), there are some high-octane traditional Valpolicellas produced from grapes that have been dried on straw mats.

Recioto is a silky-sweet version that can resemble port, while Amarone is fermented out to full dryness, is hugely alcoholic (often 15-16 per cent without fortification) and almost painfully bitter – its name coming from the Italian word for bitter, *amaro*. Ripasso is a sort of compromise, an ordinary Valpolicella that has been allowed to run over the skins of grapes used to make Amarone or Recioto.
PRODUCERS: Allegrini, Quintarelli, Tedeschi, Masi, Le Ragose, Dal Forno.

FRIULI
The easternmost wine region of Italy borders Austria to the north and Slovenia to the east, and forms part of the Adriatic coastline that extends down to Trieste. It is sometimes known as Friuli-Venezia Giulia. This is another region that has achieved some notable successes with international varieties, and the main production within DOC regions such as Collio or the Colli Orientali is of varietally named wines.

Best reds so far have been Cabernet Sauvignon and Merlot, particularly from the commercially important DOC of Grave del Friuli, Cabernet Franc from Collio, and local grapes Refosco, which makes a sharp-textured but appetizing red, and spicy Schiopettino. Successful dry whites have been Pinot Grigio, the tantalizingly flowery Tocai Friulano, crisp

Sauvignon and even some subtly perfumed Gewürztraminer. The improving DOC of Isonzo has scored with most of these varieties too. There is also a very rare, austerely almondy, golden dessert wine that is made by the raising method from a variety called Picolit: snap it up if you see it, but don't expect it to be cheap. BEST REGIONAL PRODUCERS: Collavini, Jermann, Puiatti, Schiopetto, La Fattoria, Borgo.

EMILIA-ROMAGNA

A sprawling region south of the river Po, comprising Emilia in the west and Romagna on the Adriatic coast, and with the ancient city of Bologna at its heart, Emilia-Romagna is one of the bulk-producing wine regions of Italy. Very little of the wine is of DOC standard, and much of it is drunk in a slightly fizzy state, whatever the provenance. The epitome of this tendency is Lambrusco, which comes in all colours but is usually sparkling, high in acidity and often of little discernible quality.

A hillside district bordering on Lombardy, in the northwest of the region, the Colli Piacentini, is one of the better zones for quality wine. Gutturnio (made from Barbera and Croatina grapes) is a good, hearty red, and there are some refreshing white varietals, including Sauvignon Blanc. Down in the southern part of Romagna, Albana di Romagna is noteworthy only for being the first white wine to receive the exalted DOCG classification, a questionable choice for an unexceptional wine made from the workaday Albana grape. Some steadily improving red wine is made from Sangiovese, the great red grape of Tuscany. Labelled Sangiovese di Romagna, it is best drunk young while there is still a bracing acid edge to it.

TUSCANY

Along with Piedmont, Tuscany is the most significant part of Italy in quality wine terms, and occupies a special place at the cultural heart of the country. In addition to the beautiful old cities of Florence and Siena, the rolling landscape of olive trees and vines is one of the best-loved on the European tourist circuit.

For many newcomers to wine in the 1960s, Chianti – as often as not coming in straw-covered bottles like something from the tourist shops – came to be synonymous with Italian red wine. More than any other region, however, it was here that the Vino da Tavola revolution really took off, with the launch of a generation of

wines made without reference to the DOC stipulations. These proved once and for all that Italian growers are capable of producing genuinely world-class wines.

Bolgheri The Tuscan wine scene was transformed in the 1970s with the release of the first vintages of Sassicaia, the brainchild of the Incisa della Rochetta family. Blended from the two Cabernets, it was an explicit attempt to produce a premium wine in the image of a classed-growth Bordeaux. For all that there are no Italian varieties in it, it does still taste quintessentially Tuscan, the rich cassis-and-plum fruit always having a savoury edge like bitter herbs that proudly announces its provenance. It was a mere *vino da tavola* until 1994, when the Bolgheri DOC was drawn up to include it. Fiendishly expensive, but truly memorable wine.

Brunello di Montalcino Created single-handedly by the Biondi-Santi family in the late 19th century, Brunello is made from a particularly fine clone of the Chianti grape Sangiovese. It is only since the last war that any name other than Biondi-Santi has been involved in the production of this wine. Brunello is one of Tuscany's greatest red wines – deeper and richer than Chianti, full of sour black cherries and pungent herbs, and capable of long evolution. It has to be aged for three years in cask under the regulations, which many feel is too long, and prices are stratospherically high, but the quality is there. A separate DOC, Rosso di Montalcino, has been created for wines released at one year old; these represent much better value. PRODUCERS: Biondi-Santi, Val di Suga, Talenti, Il Poggione, Argiano, Castelgiocondo.

Merlot vineyard in the Bolgheri DOC (above), destined for the "super-Tuscan"Tenuta Ornellaia.

TUSCANY:
BOLGHERI
GRAPES: Red – Cabernet Sauvignon, Cabernet Franc
BRUNELLO DI MONTALCINO
GRAPE: Red – Sangiovese

CARMIGNANO
GRAPES: *Red – Sangiovese,*
Cabernet Sauvignon
CHIANTI
GRAPES: *Red – Sangiovese,*
Cabernet Sauvignon,
Canaiolo; White –
Trebbiano, Malvasia
VERNACCIA DI SAN
GIMIGNANO
GRAPES: *White – Vernaccia,*
Chardonnay
VINO NOBILE
DI MONTEPULCIANO
GRAPES: *Red – Sangiovese,*
Canaiolo; White –
Trebbiano, Malvasia
VIN SANTO
GRAPES: *White – Trebbiano,*
Malvasia, Pinot Grigio,
Pinot Bianco, Sauvignon
Blanc, Chardonnay

Grapes hanging from the
rafters (above) to dry out for
the sweet Tuscan wine,
Vin Santo.

Carmignano Cabernet was allowed into Carmignano before it gained admittance to any other Tuscan red, including Chianti. The proportion isn't great, but the Sangiovese is generally ripe enough not to need the extra dimension of intensity conferred by Cabernet. Impressive quality was rewarded in 1988 by elevation from DOC to DOCG. Capezzana is the major name on the export markets, and is highly reliable.

Chianti Inevitably for such a high-volume wine region, Chianti spans the quality range from heavenly wines of tremendous, often oak-powered concentration to vapid, thin apologies for red wine that have only helped over the years to undermine its reputation. Part of the problem is that the boundaries of the region are much too inclusive. It comprises seven sub-zones: Chianti Classico (the heart of the region between Florence and Siena), Chianti Rufina in the northeast, Chianti Montalbano, and four hillside areas named after the cities they adjoin – Colli Fiorentini (Florence), Colli Senesi (Siena), Colli Aretini (Arezzo) and Colli Pisane (Pisa).

Of these, only the first two are genuinely dependable for quality, and will always carry their regional names. Wines given longer in cask from any of the sub-zones are labelled Riserva, not necessarily an infallible indicator of a fine wine, since much Chianti is too frail to withstand long periods in wood. The traditional Sangiovese and Canaiolo blend has been joined by Cabernet, but the allowance of the white grapes Trebbiano and Malvasia has only hindered the production of quality wine, and many of the better producers don't bother with them.

Typically, Chianti is an orangey-red wine with an aroma of dried berry fruits, perhaps even a little plum tomato, and savoury herbs, feeling quite sharp on the palate from high acidity and a slight peppery edge. Modern production methods are now seeing wines with much richer colour, obvious Cabernet presence and longer finishes than has been the norm.
PRODUCERS: Castello di Volpaia, Castello di Fonterutoli, Villa di Vetrice, Isole e Olena, Castello di San Polo in Rosso, Badia a Coltibuono, Berardenga, Fontodi, Selvapiana.

Galestro When the conscientious producers stopped diluting their Chianti with Trebbiano, something had to be done with this redundant, widely planted grape. Galestro, a water-white, low-alcohol, flavourless dry white, was the answer. Malvasia can add some interest.

Vernaccia di San Gimignano The local Vernaccia grape forms the base for this highly prized but low-volume white wine made within sight of the famous towers of the town of San Gimignano. It was actually the first wine to gain the new DOC classification in 1966, and was elevated to DOCG in 1993. Chardonnay may constitute no more than 10 per cent of the blend. At its best, it has an intriguingly waxy texture and attractive almond-paste character, but – as with many Italian whites – the generality is bland, anonymous quaffing stuff.
PRODUCERS: Terruzzi e Puthod, Falchini, San Quirico.

Vino Nobile di Montepulciano There is an Italian grape variety called Montepulciano, but it isn't part of this DOCG wine, which is made in the hills southeast of Florence from the classic Chianti grape mix (minus Cabernet). Although the wines can be powerfully intense, with strong purple fruit and a dash of liquorice, they tend to stop just short of the pedigree of top Chianti or Brunello. Two years' cask ageing is required; again, the better producers ignore the white grapes. As with Brunello, younger wine may be released as Rosso di Montepulciano, under its own DOC.
PRODUCERS: Avignonesi, Trerose, Boscarelli, Fattoria del Cerro.

Vin Santo Undoubtedly the best manifestation of the undistinguished white grapes of Tuscany is as Vin Santo, an often lusciously sweet *passito* wine. It is made from grapes that have been raisined by being hung up in the warmest part of the winery to lose their moisture. A small amount is fermented out to a nutty dryness like the driest sherry. There are two DOCs for Vin Santo – Val d'Arbia, and Colli dell'– Etruria Centrale. It is the latter that permits the use of the non-Italian varieties. Long cask ageing of the wines is the norm, and many are made in a deliberately oxidized style.
PRODUCERS: Isole e Olena, Avignonesi, Selvapiana.

THE MARCHES

An eastern region on the Adriatic coast, with the city of Ancona its main commercial centre. Its best wines are a pair of red DOCs, Rosso Conero and Rosso Piceno, made from blends of the eastern Italian variety Montepulciano with Tuscany's Sangiovese. (In the case of Rosso Conero, the local grape predominates, while Rosso Piceno must be not less than 60 per cent Sangiovese.) Both are full-bodied, spicy reds with notable ageing potential. Verdicchio is the regional white grape, most often seen in Verdicchio dei Castelli di Jesi, one of those infuriatingly neutral-tasting whites that Italy seems to specialize in (although a producer like Garofoli can coax some peanutty aromatic quality out of it). Verdicchio di Matelica is a superior version but not much of it is made. The house of Umani Ronchi makes good wines across the board.

UMBRIA

Wedged between Tuscany and the Marches, the small landlocked region of Umbria is centred on the city of Perugia. Its most famous wine is Orvieto, which lays claim to a distinctive local grape variety in Grechetto. Unfortunately it is swamped with admixtures of Trebbiano and Malvasia. It comes in three basic styles, a simple dry wine (*secco*) which often has the tartness of Conference pears, a medium-sweet, in-between version (*abboccato*) and a fully sweet, often rotted dessert wine (*amabile*). Overall quality is uninspiring; Barberani, Palazzone and Bigi make the best ones.

Torgiano is the best red wine, now classified a DOCG. It is made from Sangiovese in an almost improbably concentrated style (one producer, Lungarotti, has blazed this particular trail). Montefalco is a DOC for Sangiovese reds made near Assisi and blended with a little of the local variety Sagrantino. Vinified alone in this region, this latter grape also has its own DOCG, Sagrantino di Montefalco.

LAZIO

Lazio is the region surrounding Rome, chiefly responsible for large quantities of indifferent white wine, the most famous of which, Frascati, is – with Soave – virtually synonymous with Italian white on the export markets. The Trebbiano and Malvasia grapes hold sway here, so most Frascati is fairly dull stuff. Colli di Catone in the frosted bottle is about the best, having a bewitching tang of *crème fraîche*, but Fontana Candida is also good; both must be drunk as young as you can find them. The most overbearingly named white wine in Italy – Est! Est!! Est!!! di Montefiascone – is also Trebbiano-based, and rarely tastes as if it justifies one exclamation mark, let alone six. Some Cabernet Sauvignon and Merlot is grown in this region, but otherwise there are no particularly remarkable reds.

ABRUZZI

The reputation of this mountainous region on the Adriatic coast, south of the Marches, rests on a pair of DOC wines, one red and one white. The red, Montepulciano d'Abruzzo, is by far the more famous of the two. Made from the grape of the same name, it is always a softly plummy, low-tannin, easy-going wine with a strange but unmistakable waft of sea air about it. Despite its strong reliability, it has never become expensive on the export markets, and is often a surefire bet for a modestly priced Italian red with more depth than most of its equals. Umani Ronchi and Mezzanotte make fine ones.

The white wine, Trebbiano d'Abruzzo, is hampered by its name alone. It actually contains, in a typically Italian paradox, no Trebbiano at all, but is made from a southern variety with the rather splendid name of Bombino. A producer called Valentini has single-handedly made a name for this DOC with a hazelnutty dry wine of quite uncommon intensity.

Bottles of Montepulciano d' Abruzzo being packed at the Illuminati winery in eastern-central Italy (below). The wine is regularly one of the country's most reliable and reasonably priced reds.

Vines compete for space with houses on the coastal cliffs at Amalfi (above), in Campania.

MOLISE

Small and quantitatively unimportant region south of the Abruzzi, specializing in *vini da tavola* from international varieties such as Chardonnay and Riesling. Biferno is a regional DOC for wines in all three colours, the reds and rosés based on the Montepulciano grape, the whites on Bombino, Trebbiano and Malvasia.

PUGLIA

Puglia is the heel of Italy, incorporating the Adriatic port of Bari, and responsible for one of the largest annual productions of any of the country's wine regions. Only a small proportion of this is of DOC standard, however. The extreme southeastern province of Salento is where the finest reds come from. Here the spicily exciting Negroamaro grape is the claim to fame. Its best DOC is Salice Salentino, a richly plummy, often interestingly honeyed red wine of enormous appeal (Candida's Riserva is an especially good example). It also crops up in the wines of Copertino, Squinzano and Brindisi among others, sometimes given extra bite with another local grape, Malvasia Nera.

Primitivo di Manduria makes colossally alcoholic reds from the Primitivo grape, which has been identified as the Zinfandel of California. Castel del Monte is another red DOC with its own local grape, the intriguing Uva di Troia. Otherwise, the grapes of Abruzzi are relatively important for reds and whites, and there is the usual smattering of international varieties.

CAMPANIA

The Neapolitan southwest of Italy has the most venerable winemaking tradition of any part of Italy, but the lowest percentage of wine qualifying as DOC. That seems a shame because the DOC areas have undoubted potential. Taurasi is a fierce and exciting, if tannic, red made from a fine local variety called Aglianico. Falerno del Massico is a new DOC seeking to re-create the lost glory of Falernian, the much-revered wine of classical antiquity that is mentioned repeatedly in the literature of the period; it is a blend of Aglianico and the local Piedirosso with Primitivo and Barbera.

The main white DOCs are Greco di Tufo, a mildly lemony wine of some charm, and Fiano d'Avellino, which can have a haunting taste of ripe pears. Both are named after their grape varieties. Lacryma Christi del Vesuvio is one of the region's more famous wines, appearing in both red and white versions, both fairly unpalatable. Mastroberardino makes wines in most of the DOCs of Campania, and is certainly the best producer.

BASILICATA

This very poor southern region makes only minuscule quantities of wine, and indeed there is only one DOC, although it is a good one. Aglianico del Vulture is made from the red grape of that name also seen in Campania. Here it is grown in vineyards around the extinct Vulture volcano, and produces an astonishingly lush-textured wine with a strange coffee-like aroma, worth seeking out.

CALABRIA

Cirò is the only DOC wine you might see outside the region that forms the toe of Italy's boot. Based on the local Gaglioppo grape, it comes in red and rosé styles and may, as with many other Italian reds, be blended with some white grapes, inevitably including Trebbiano. On the south coast, a rather sophisticated DOC dessert wine is produced from semi-dried Greco grapes – Greco di Bianco – although, again, you'll be lucky to see it outside Calabria.

SICILY

The island of Sicily is one of the most copiously productive regions of Italy. Much of its produce is of no more than table wine standard, but there are isolated pockets of improving quality that suggest that, some time in the future, Sicilian wines could be among Italy's finest.

Its most celebrated product is the fortified wine Marsala, produced in the west of the island. Although it is of declining commercial importance now, in common with southern Europe's other classic fortified wines, it remains one of the great original wine styles, quite unlike any other. Various methods of fortification are used, including a rather clumsy one that uses cooked concentrated grape juice known as *mosto cotto*. The best grades of Marsala, however, are Superiore and Vergine, which are not permitted to use this method.

Styles range from the austerely dry (*secco*) to the liquorously sweet (*dolce*) but common to all of them is a smoky, almost acrid burnt-toffee tang that is Marsala's unique selling point. These days, most of it probably goes into zabaglione or tiramisù, but the best Marsalas, such as those from de Bortoli, deserve to be appreciated on their own as stimulating alternatives to the more familiar after-dinner tipples.

Two of the white grapes used in Marsala make good dry table wines elsewhere on the island. They are Inzolia and Catarratto, both capable of producing lightly aromatic wines of some character. Nero d'Avola is about the best of the native red grapes, and blended reds with a healthy percentage of that grape are often among Sicily's best.

Regaleali is one of the leading Sicilian producers of quality wines. Its reds can be monumentally complex and ageworthy, as can Corvo Rosso, a long-lived, excitingly spicy red made by the house of Duca di Salaparuta. Settesoli, the main co-operative on the island, produces some well-made simple reds.

The tiny island of Pantelleria, halfway between Sicily and Tunisia, has revived one of the legendary dessert wines of history in Moscato di Pantelleria, made from dried Moscato grapes given delicious richness with extended oak-ageing.

SARDINIA

Sardinia's wine production continues to be hampered by its very insular approach to marketing, and the ridiculously high yields permitted under the DOC regulations for what could otherwise be quite interesting, characterful wines. Cannonau is one of the most important red varieties (claimed by some to be related to Grenache) and can make an inky, full-bodied red if yields are restricted. Monica produces a much lighter, almost Beaujolais-like red for early drinking.

Nuragus is one of the more significant white grapes, but its wines tend to the classic Italian neutrality, partly because of the massive yields obtained. Vernaccia di Oristano can be a diverting curiosity for those on holiday – a bone-dry, nutty, often oxidized white that may remind you of a basic fino sherry.

OTHER CLASSIC WINES OF ITALY

As the redesigning of Italy's wine classification system continues apace, one of its central concerns has been to draw into its embrace all of those quality wines that were being defiantly produced outside the regulations as *vini da tavola*, many of them selling for prices comparable to the most illustrious wines of France. The ground-breaking Sassicaia, as explained above, is now DOC Bolgheri, as is Ornellaia. The other wines listed here have all been designated IGT under the new rules. A lot depends on whether

the individual producers care to play a part in the official system. Many don't as yet.

Balifico (Castello Volpaia): Sangiovese-Cabernet Sauvignon blend aged in French oak.

Cepparello (Isole e Olena): Attractively ripe varietal Sangiovese fleshed out with new oak.

Flaccianello della Pieve (Fontodi): 100 per cent Sangiovese similar in style to Cepparello, but with a slightly more obvious Tuscan bitterness to it.

Grifi (Avignonesi): Sangiovese-Cabernet Franc from the celebrated producer of Vino Nobile di Montepulciano.

Ornellaia (Lodovico Antinori): Massively concentrated blend of Bordeaux grape varieties, built for a long life.

Sammarco (Castello dei Rampolla): Three-quarters Cabernet, one-quarter Sangiovese.

Solaia (Piero Antinori): Cabernet-Sangiovese of great distinction, not as sweet and lush as some, but full of classical intensity.

Tignanello (Antinori): A Sangiovese-Cabernet blend from one of the finest houses in Tuscany, Tignanello is a hugely exciting, long-lived red that combines gorgeously ripe purple fruits with chocolatey richness.

RECENT VINTAGES FOR REDS

Piedmont: *2004* ***** *2003* ****** *2002* **
2001 ****** *2000* ***** *1999* ***** *1998* ****
1997 ****** *1996* ***** *1990* ******

Tuscany: *2004* ***** *2003* ****** *2002* *
2001 ****** *2000* ***** *1999* ***** *1998* *****
1997 ****** *1995* **** *1990* ******

Ancient farmhouse in the hills of Basilicata (above), surrounded by ploughed land ready for planting with new vines.

Sicilian vineyard (below) planted on black volcanic soils in the shadow of Mount Etna.

SPAIN

A proud winemaking tradition, and the producers' commitment to quality, are placing Spain at the forefront of Europe's great wine nations. Freshness and fruit are now the bywords for the best wines, rather than old-fashioned wood flavour.

The castle of Peñafiel (above) perches above the vineyards of the dynamic Ribera del Duero region.

Renowned for its sherries and oaked wines, the arrival on the map of new wine regions is bringing impressive still and sparkling Spanish wines to the market (right).

1. RIOJA
2. NAVARRA
3. RIAS BAIXAS
4. RIBEIRO
5. VALDEORRAS
6. EL BIERZO
7. TORO
8. RUEDA
9. CIGALES
10. RIBERA DEL DUERO
11. CHACOLI DE GUETARIA
12. CALATAYUD
13. CAMPO DE BORJA
14. SOMONTANO
15. TERRA ALTA
16. COSTERS DEL SEGRE
17. PRIORATO
18. TARRAGONA
19. CARIÑENA
20. CONCA DE BARBERÁ
21. PENEDÉS
22. ALELLA
23. AMPURDÁN-COSTA BRAVA
24. MÉNTRIDA
25. LA MANCHA
26. VALDEPEÑAS
27. UTIEL REQUENA
28. VALENCIA
29. ALMANSA
30. JUMILLA
31. YECLA
32. ALICANTE
33. MONTILLA-MORILES
34. MÁLAGA
35. CONDADO DE HUELVA
36. JEREZ

A S IN MUCH OF THE rest of southern Europe, vine-growing is a matter of considerable antiquity in Spain. The vine is known to have been cultivated on the Iberian peninsula since about the fourth millennium BC. By the time Spanish territory came to be fought over by the Romans and Carthaginians in the third and second centuries BC, a winemaking culture had long been established. Modern Spain has more land devoted to vine cultivation than any other country in the world, although its average annual production of wine is normally behind those of both Italy and France.

The viticultural industry has slowly but surely come to terms over the last 30 years with what the contemporary market expects of wine. Time-honoured practices such as the extended cask-ageing of both red and white wines, typified by the overwhelming oak flavour of classic Rioja, has gradually given way in many regions

to a more sensitive approach that seeks to emphasize fruit flavours and youthful vibrancy over the desiccating impact of years in wood.

In addition to that, Spain's quality wine system, similar to that coming into operation in Italy, has been taken rather more seriously by the mass of producers than has been the case in Italy. The old DO designation (*denominación de origen*, the equal of *appellation contrôlée* in France) now has an upper level, DOCa (*denominación de origen calificada*) for the very best wines. Rioja was the first region declared a DOCa in 1991. Below those, an equivalent of *vin de pays* has been created – *vino de la tierra* – for wines that come from any of a series of large but geographically specific zones. After that comes a broader regional designation, *vino comarcal*, and then basic *vino de mesa*, or table wine.

As well as its rapidly improving reds and whites, Spain also boasts one of the world's

greatest fortified wines, namely sherry, together with the lesser-known Montilla and Málaga. Throw in some fine indigenous grape varieties, led by the ubiquitous but excellent Tempranillo, and it all adds up to a dynamic wine scene crammed with potential.

RIOJA

Spain's most visible export wines for years have come from the Rioja region surrounding the river Ebro in the northeast of the country. The red wine in particular, with its typically oily texture, strawberry-flavoured fruit and thick, creamy texture derived from ageing in oak, became a much-loved style in the 1970s, and remains the pre-eminent Spanish red for many wine-drinkers. When the new super-category of DOCa wines was created, Rioja was its first recipient, reflecting its pre-eminence in Spanish wine history.

The region is subdivided into three districts, the Rioja Alta west of Logroño (generally held to produce the wines of highest pedigree), the Rioja Baja southeast of the same town, and the Rioja Alavesa, which forms part of the province of Alava, in the Basque country. All three regions make reds, whites and rosés, the last known as *rosados* in Spanish.

The hierarchy of classification for the wines depends on the length of maturation in barrel and bottle they receive before being released on to the market. At the bottom of the pile, young new wine may be released as *joven* (meaning "young"). Not much is exported in that state, but it can have a delicious sweet-cherry appeal, and responds well to chilling.

Crianza wines must be aged for one year in barrel and a further year in bottle before release. Many commentators feel that this is probably the optimum period for those looking for an oaky red that still retains some decent fruit flavour. Reserva spends a year in barrel, but a further two in the bottle, while Gran Reserva is aged for at least two years in wood before being held in the bottle for a further three.

Traditionally, the type of wood favoured for the production of both red and white Rioja was American oak, which gives a much more pronounced sweet vanilla flavour to the wine than the softer French oak. More producers are now turning to French coopers, however, in order to achieve a subtler wood influence in their wines, and the innovation seems to be paying off in terms of yielding more balanced wines.

Tempranillo is the principal grape of the reds, contributing flavours of summery red fruits to young wines, but often turning fascinatingly gamey (almost like Pinot Noir) as it ages. It is supported mainly by Garnacha (Grenache), which usually lends a spicy edge to the softer Tempranillo fruit.

There are two distinct schools of thought in white Rioja. The traditional preference is for heavily oaked and deliberately oxidized wines of golden-yellow hue. They often smell tantalizingly like dry sherry, yet possess a bitter tang like dried citrus peel. Sipped in small quantities, they can be impressive wines to mull over, but "refreshing" is not one of the descriptions that springs to mind for them.

The newer style is all about squeaky-clean fermentation in stainless steel, at low temperatures, to maximize fruit flavours and freshness. Often made entirely without the use of oak, these light, lemony creations may not be as imposing as their barrel-fermented cousins, but they do chime more harmoniously with modern tastes in white wine. Rioja's white grapes are the relatively neutral Viura (often seen alone in the more modern-style whites) and the muskier, more headily perfumed Malvasia.

The rosados tend to be a little on the hefty side, rather in the manner of the rosés of the southern Rhône and the Midi over the border, but the odd one can be agreeably ripe and peachy.
PRODUCERS: Marqués de Murrieta (in the traditional oaky style), López de Heredia, Marqués de Cáceres, Campo Viejo, Bodegas Palacio, Montecillo, Amézola, La Rioja Alta SA.

Oak barrels piled up outside the winery at Rioja producer Bodegas López de Heredia (above).

RIOJA
GRAPES: Red – Tempranillo, Garnacha, Mazuelo, Graciano; White – Viura, Malvasia

Splashes of red mark the autumnal vineyards of Valdeorras (above), where increasingly characterful wines are being created.

NAVARRA

GRAPES: Red – Garnacha, Tempranillo, Cabernet Sauvignon, Merlot; White – Viura, Chardonnay

RIAS BAIXAS

GRAPES: Albariño, Treixadura, Loureiro, Caiña Blanca

RIBEIRO

GRAPES: White – Treixadura, Torrontés, etc; Red – Garnacha, etc.

VALDEORRAS

GRAPES: White – Palomino, Godello, etc; Red – Garnacha, Mencía, etc.

EL BIERZO

GRAPES: Red – Mencía

TORO

GRAPES: Red – Tinto de Toro

NAVARRA

Just to the northeast of Rioja, but also on the river Ebro, is the increasingly trendy DO region of Navarra. While Navarra grows essentially the same grapes as neighbouring Rioja, its wines are quite different. There has also been increasing interest shown in incorporating some of the classic French varieties into the more ambitious oak-aged wines, so that it is not uncommon to see a white wine labelled Viura-Chardonnay. Unlike the traditional oaky wines of white Rioja, these wines are much fresher, with a gently buttery quality somewhat reminiscent of the lighter wines of Burgundy.

Navarra makes a much higher proportion of rosado than Rioja, and most of it benefits from attractively juicy strawberry fruit flavours and exemplary freshness. Red wines range from the relatively light in style, rather like Côtes du Rhône, to the seriously weighty and alcoholic. PRODUCERS: Bodegas Ochoa, Chivite, Nekeus, Agramont from Bodegas Príncipe de Viana, and many of the co-operative wines produced under the auspices of the experimental research station EVENA.

RIAS BAIXAS

Rias Baixas has lately been one of the more talked-about wine regions of northern Spain. Situated in Galicia, in the northwest of the country, its reputation has been founded on some unexpectedly fragrant, positively floral dry white wines, mainly based on a fine local grape variety called Albariño. The DO is subdi-

vided into three distinct areas: Val de Salnes on the western coast, and O Rosal and Condado de Tea on the Portuguese border. As in much of the rest of Spain, the typical yields are low, and although other varieties are permitted in the wines under the Rias Baixas DO, they do not generally account for much of the blend. These are quite expensive but highly attractive modern white wines.
PRODUCERS: Lagar de Cervera from Lagar de Forlelos, Bodegas Morgadío, Codax.

RIBEIRO

The region's name means "riverside", and the vineyards occupy the land around the river Miño, which extends from northern Portugal. There is some fairly inconsequential red made here, but – as in Rias Baixas – the main business is white wine, and here quality is much improved of late. Some recently established plantings of Torrontés should add character to the whites in future. This is a florally aromatic grape with strong notes of orange blossom in it. Added to the Treixadura, the result is pleasantly fresh, fruity whites.

VALDEORRAS

Small wine-producing area in the east of Galicia that, in common with other regions, is progressing slowly but surely from making dull, bland plonk to wines of burgeoning character. Palomino, the sherry grape, has long been the scourge of northwestern whites, but is now being replaced by more appropriate varieties such as the local Godello, which gives good dry whites with a certain amount of aromatic personality. The ubiquitous Garnacha is responsible for many of the reds, but some attractively grassy, fresh-tasting reds are being made from the native Mencía grape in a style not dissimilar to the lighter reds of the Loire valley.

EL BIERZO

Just to the northeast of Valdeorras, El Bierzo is also beginning to explore its potential. The main focus of interest so far is good, ripe Loire-like reds made from the local Mencía grape. Watch this space.

TORO

The wines of Toro are produced in some of the most inhospitable conditions of any of Spain's vineyard regions, in a country that isn't short on climatic challenges for the vine. Planted at high altitude along the river Duero, the grape responsible for the thunderously powerful Toro reds, Tinto de Toro, is a local mutation of Spain's main red variety, Tempranillo. Alcohol levels are typically around 13.5 per cent, and can go even higher, but the wines mostly wear it well, the thick, liquoricey flavours of the grape more than adequately supporting the almost spirity strength. One producer has dominated the region above all others – Bodegas Fariña. Fortunately, its wines – best exemplified by the darkly brooding, sweetly oaky Gran Colegiata – do not let the side down. Insignificant quantities of rosado and white are also produced.

RUEDA

A DO region since 1980, Rueda's regulations stipulate that it can produce white wines only. The old traditional style of wine was an oxidized fortified wine made from the Palomino grape that bore a passing resemblance to cheap, dry sherry. Nowadays, the region is carving out a reputation for producing some of Spain's freshest and most agreeable light dry whites. The native variety here is Verdejo, which gives generously full-textured wines. It is sometimes given a little citrus tang with a dash of the Rioja grape Viura, or increasingly brought into even sharper focus with a dose of nettly Sauvignon. Basic Rueda must be at least 25 per cent Verdejo, while wines labelled Rueda Superior have to contain a minimum of 60 per cent of the grape.
PRODUCERS: Marqués de Riscal, Marqués de Griñon.

CIGALES

North of the river Duero, Cigales is not much known to the outside world. It principally makes dry rosados and a little red from the two main red grapes of Rioja.

RIBERA DEL DUERO

For many, this dynamic, forward-looking region is now ahead of the Spanish pack. Across the board, its wines are increasingly more dependable than those of Rioja, and its producers appear to have absorbed more readily the lessons to be learned from current world tastes in red wine. Its principal variety is yet another local variation of Tempranillo, Tinto Fino, often making up 100 per cent of the wine. Controlled plantings of some of the Bordeaux varieties are permitted only in specific sections of the DO area, which was created in 1982. A proportion

of juice from the local white grape, Albillo, may be used to soften the intensity of the red wine, but the DO does not extend as yet to the production of white wines.

The best wines of Ribera del Duero have concentrated blackberry or plum fruit and usually a fair amount of oak influence. This is either the blowsy vanilla of American oak or the more muted, subtler tones of French oak. The system of ageing in cask and bottle is analogous to that of Rioja (from youngest to oldest: Joven, Crianza, Reserva and Gran Reserva).

In the west of the region is a property called Vega Sicilia that makes an enormously expensive, totally individual range of red wines, using Tinto Fino with the French varieties and a modicum of Albillo. Valbuena is a five-year-old oak-aged red with an astonishing and unforgettable mixture of perfumes – orange essence, loganberries and milk chocolate. Unico is its top wine, only made in the most promising vintages. The wine is released at about ten years old, after undergoing an elaborate ageing procedure in various types of wood (including large old casks that allow a fair amount of oxygen to seep into the wine) and in bottle. Vega Sicilia has been making wines in this way since modern Ribera del Duero was just a twinkle in an entrepreneur's eye, and has been fairly compared to the top classed growths of Bordeaux, in majesty if not in flavour.
OTHER PRODUCERS: Pesquera, Callejo, Arroyo, Torremilanos, Pago de Carraovejas.

RUEDA
GRAPES: *White – Verdejo,*
Viura, Sauvignon Blanc,
Palomino
CIGALES
GRAPES: *Red – Tinto del País*
(Tempranillo), Garnacha
RIBERA DEL DUERO
GRAPES: *Red – Tinto Fino*
(Tempranillo), Garnacha,
Cabernet Sauvignon, Merlot,
Malbec; White – Albillo

The church of Santa Maria
la Mayor in Toro (left). On
Spain's high central plain,
the wine region of Toro
makes big, powerful reds.

The 17th-century castle of Raimat, in Catalonia (right), where the Raventos family has extensive high-altitude vineyards.

CHACOLI DE GUETARIA
GRAPES: White – Hondarrabi Zuri; Red – Hondarrabi Beltz

CALATAYUD
GRAPES: Red – Garnacha, Tempranillo, Mazuelo, Graciano; White – Viura, Malvasia

CAMPO DE BORJA
GRAPES: Red – Garnacha, Cariñena, Tempranillo; White – Viura

CARINENA
GRAPES: Red – Garnacha, Tempranillo, Cariñena; White – Viura, Garnacha Blanca, Parellada

SOMONTANO
GRAPES: Red – Moristel, Garnacha, Tempranillo, Cabernet Sauvignon, Merlot; White – Viura, Alcañón, Chardonnay, Chenin Blanc, Gewürztraminer

TERRA ALTA
GRAPES: White – Garnacha Blanca, Macabeo; Red – Garnacha

COSTERS DEL SEGRE
GRAPES: Red – Tempranillo, Garnacha, Cabernet Sauvignon, Merlot, Pinot Noir; White – Chardonnay, Parellada, Macabeo

CHACOLI DE GUETARIA
A tiny DO region (Spain's smallest) in the Basque country to the west of San Sebastian. Its mainly white wine is light and snappy and made in such minute quanitites that it is not viable as an export product. The equally light red is even rarer.

CALATAYUD
In the Aragon region on the river Jalon, Calatayud is dominated largely by co-operatives but not as yet geared for export. The varieties are essentially the same as Rioja and the wines come in all three colours, the unsubtle, alcoholic reds being the surest indicator of local taste.

CAMPO DE BORJA
Stunningly alcoholic reds are the speciality of Campo de Borja, near the town of Borja in the province of Aragon. Made mainly from Garnacha, they must attain at least 13 per cent alcohol to qualify for the DO. Again, co-operatives rule the roost, and again, most of the wine is drunk in the vicinity.

CARINENA
Much the most promising so far of the DO regions of Aragon, Cariñena – southwest of Zaragoza – is actually named after the grape variety that originated and once flourished there. (In its other guises, it is the Carignan of southern France, and is known as Mazuelo in Rioja.) Garnacha is star of the show currently for the big, opulent reds in which the region specializes, and, as in other parts of Aragon, they can attain spine-tingling levels of alcohol. Some Tempranillo is being blended in to soften the impact. Whites are largely fresh and clean, and some use a little of the Chardonnay-like Parellada grape more typically associated with the white wines of Penedés further east. A small quantity of champagne-method sparkling wine (known as cava in Spain) is made in Cariñena, although it too is more at home in Penedés. Monte Ducay from the Bodegas San Valero co-operative is a characteristic Cariñena red offered on the export markets.

SOMONTANO
A healthily outward-looking DO region in the Pyrennean foothills to the east of Navarra, Somontano makes reds, whites and rosados from a tempting mixture of local grapes (including the indigenous red Moristel and white Alcañón) and a catholic range of French varieties, including some convincingly perfumed Gewürztraminer. The Covisa winery in particular is finding its experimentation paying dividends. Espiral is another good name. As in Cariñena, a small amount of cava is produced.

TERRA ALTA
As its name suggests, Terra Alta is a high-altitude vineyard region in the west of Catalonia currently making the familiarly northern Spanish shift from heavy fortified wines to light, dry whites in the modern idiom. Reds are galumphing Garnachas in the jammy old style.

COSTERS DEL SEGRE
Split rather messily into four separated sub-regions, Costers del Segre has made waves outside Spain, despite its starting life as inauspicious desert land. These waves have been created almost exclusively through the efforts of the Raimat winery in Lerida, which makes a range of excellent varietals from softly velvety Tempranillo to densely meaty Merlot, as well as some Chardonnay fizz of impressive richness.

Some bottlings have successfully blended French and Spanish varieties in what has come to be characteristically Catalan fashion, notably Gran Calesa (Tempranillo-Cabernet) and Abadía (Cabernet-Tempranillo-Garnacha). Other producers are starting to enter the lists, and seem to be putting Costers del Segre on a vigorous upward trajectory.

PRIORATO

Practically a legend in its own right, Priorato makes one of the most uncompromising styles of red wine anywhere in Europe. Yields from the older vines in the region are minuscule and the rules specify a minimum alcoholic strength of 13.75 per cent for the wine to be true DO Priorato. The result is not hard to imagine – fiercely concentrated and heady wine, with a pugnacious peppery edge to it, capable of ageing for many years in the bottle. A Penedés producer, René Barbier, has planted some French varieties in the most promising vineyard sites, and may help to bring Priorato kicking and screaming into the modern wine world. The old-style stuff is still worth a flutter, though.
PRODUCERS: Scala Dei, Masia Barril, de Müller.

TARRAGONA

Tarragona once enjoyed a reputation for sweet, red, port-style fortified wines, but now contents itself largely with producing unambitious blending material for bulk producers elsewhere. Its limited local wine production, in all three colours but most of it white, is quite undistinguished.

CONCA DE BARBERA

Considered virtually a western extension of Penedés, Conca de Barberá produces some pleasantly fresh dry whites from the Catalan varieties (see Penedés below), as well as some hearty reds, but is mainly a source of sparkling cava. The region is a recently established DO that has benefited from substantial investment by the hugely important Penedés wine company of Miguel Torres.

PENEDES

Penedés, the largest of the DO regions of Catalonia, has two main claims to fame. It is the centre of the Spanish sparkling wine, or cava, industry, and it is the base of one of the most successful wine dynasties of Europe – the house of Torres.

Cava is a peculiarity in terms of its regulations, in that it can technically be made else-where in Spain – the DO is not specific to Penedés. In practice, most of it is made in this northeastern region near Barcelona. The method used is the same as that in champagne, but the grapes are nearly all native varieties: Parellada, Macabeo and the rather assertively flavoured Xarel-lo. In addition to those, Chardonnay is being grown to a much greater extent than hith-erto for cava production, and some cava (often labelled with the borrowed champagne term "blanc de blancs") is entirely Chardonnay.

Cava has to be aged on its yeast sediment for a minimum of nine months (two years in the case of vintage cava). It once typically had a strange rubbery aroma, but most export stuff is much fresher and more graceful now, in a nutty, lemony style. Significant amounts of cava rosado (deeply coloured with Monastrell and/or Garnacha grapes) are now being seen too. The best of these have convincing raspberry-ripe fruit.
PRODUCERS: Codorníu, Rovellats, Segura Viudas, Mont Marçal, Condé de Caralt, Juvé y Camps.

The pioneering work of Miguel Torres, who died in the early 1990s, established Penedés as the most outward-looking wine region in the country. He planted international grape varieties alongside the indigenous ones, in many cases blending them together for certain wines, and created a formidable reputation for his company, and for Penedés.

Among the more successful Torres whites are the basic Viña Sol (made from Parellada, out of which Torres manages to tease more flavour than seemingly anyone else), Gran Viña Sol (a lightly oaked blend of Parellada and Chardonnay), Gran Viña Sol Green Label (Parellada with Sauvignon in a mouth-wateringly crisp, often slightly pétillant style), Viña Esmeralda (a honey-and-lemon, off-dry blend of Muscat and Gewürztraminer) and Milmanda (a highly opulent, uncannily Burgundian oaked Chardonnay).

The notable reds include Gran Sangre de Toro (earthy Garnacha and Cariñena), Atrium (a soft varietal Merlot), Mas Borrás (a classically cherry-scented, gamey Pinot Noir) and Mas la Plana, sometimes known as Black Label (a premium bottling of intensely dark, austerely tannic, unblended Cabernet Sauvignon).

Jean León is the other grower of note to have followed the international varietal trail here. His Chardonnay and Cabernet Sauvignon varietals are made in the thoroughly modern style, with lashings of ripe, vibrant fruit and unabashed levels of oaky richness.

PRIORATO
GRAPES: *Garnacha,*
Cariñena
TARRAGONA
GRAPES: *Red – Garnacha,*
Cariñena; White – Macabeo,
Xarel-lo, Parellada,
Garnacha Blanca
PENEDES
Numerous Spanish and
French red and white
varieties

Old Garnacha and Cariñena vines yield powerful, heady reds that have drawn atten-tion to the small Priorato region in Catalonia (above).

ALELLA
GRAPES: White – Pansa
Blanca, Chardonnay, Chenin
Blanc
**AMPURDAN-COSTA
BRAVA**
GRAPES: Red – Garnacha,
Cariñena; White – Xarel-lo,
Macabeo
MENTRIDA
GRAPES: Red – Garnacha
LA MANCHA
GRAPES: White – Airén,
Chardonnay; Red – Cencibel
(Tempranillo), Cabernet
Sauvignon
VALDEPENAS
GRAPES: White – Airén; Red
– Cencibel (Tempranillo)
UTIEL-REQUENA
GRAPES: Red – Bobal,
Tempranillo
VALENCIA
GRAPES: White – Merseguera,
Muscat of Alexandria; Red –
Monastrell, Garnacha

ALELLA

Alella is a tiny DO north of Barcelona, in which the Marqués de Alella co-operative is the pre-eminent producer. The output is light dry whites, in which the rather vegetal flavours of Xarel-lo (here known as Pansa Blanca) are frequently softened with a modicum of Chardonnay, and sparkling cava labelled Parxet, which may also contain a freshening soupçon of Chenin. A good varietal Chardonnay is also made.

AMPURDAN-COSTA BRAVA

This is a small DO situated on the opposite side of the border to the French Côtes du Roussillon. Nearly all the wine made here is drunk in situ – mostly simple rosados for the tourist market. There are also some rustic reds and, this being Catalonia, some cava made from the traditional Spanish varieties. A recent innovation was rush-released Vin Novell, an Iberian answer to Beaujolais Nouveau, although what the beach-bums on the Costa Brava make of it is anybody's guess.

MENTRIDA

A DO region immediately to the south and west of Madrid in central Spain, Méntrida's principal business is rough-and-ready Garnacha reds of no obvious pedigree. The excellent winery of Marqués de Griñon is also situated near here. As it is not within the DO boundaries, the wines – including an oaky Chardonnay and a pitch-black, awesomely concentrated Cabernet Sauvignon – are labelled as table wines of Toledo.

LA MANCHA

The largest DO region in Spain is also the largest individual appellation in Europe. La Mancha occupies the broiling, arid dustlands of the centre of Spain from Madrid down to Valde-peñas, about 200km (125 miles) from top to bottom. The pre-eminent grape variety grown here, the white Airén, is actually the most extensively planted wine grape in the world. Given that it is grown virtually nowhere outside Spain, that gives some idea of the sprawling vastness of La Mancha's vineyards.

Once seen as a workhorse area, dedicated as much to producing alcohol for industry as everyday table wines, La Mancha is now set on an upward course to quality. The Airén grape, previously dismissed as boringly neutral, turns out to make quite refreshing, simple, lemony whites in the right hands, and since the pre-

dominant red grape is Tempranillo (here adopting another of its many pseudonyms, Cencibel), the prospects for classy reds too are good. They are generally somewhat lighter than those of Rioja, but have the pronounced strawberry fruit of the grape, together with appealingly smooth contours. The cosmopolitan duo of Cabernet and Chardonnay are beginning to make their presence felt in the vineyards of La Mancha too, reflecting the scale of ambition among many of the small proprietors.

In short, the region is set fair to prove that, even in the world of wine, big can be beautiful. It is expected, however, that sooner or later the region will have been broken up into a handful of more manageable chunks.

VALDEPENAS

Valdepeñas is the southernmost outpost of the huge central region of La Mancha. Its wines are thought sufficiently distinctive to merit a separate DO, and the growers have been quicker off the draw in penetrating the export markets than their neighbours to the north. Red wines from Tempranillo are the main business. Often given long cask-ageing, and labelled as Reserva or Gran Reserva, they can suffer from an excess of petrolly oak flavours on a basically rather light fruit base, but the better producers have managed to achieve good balance. (Señorio de los Llanos and Viña Albali are labels to look for.) Some straightforward, thin dry white is also made from the much-favoured Airén, but a fair amount of it, depressingly enough, goes into the red wines below Reserva level, reducing them to distinctly insipid specimens.

UTIEL-REQUENA

In the province of Levante, to the west of Valencia, Utiel-Requena's speciality is the Bobal grape – a good red variety that yields fairly meaty wine with a distinctive raisiny flavour. The reds can be a little clumsy, but the rosados are improving, and can be agreeably thirst-quenching on the right occasion.

VALENCIA

The eastern port of Valencia lends its name to a DO region inland from the city. White wines run the gamut from dullish dry wines, made from the less-than-inspiring local Merseguera grape, to the well-known sweet wine Moscatel de Valencia. The Moscatel doesn't undergo normal fermentation but is made by adding grape spirit to freshly pressed Muscat juice (a product known as *mistela* in Spanish). Red wines can be surprisingly thin and acidic when made from the Garnacha variant grown in these parts (rosados are better), but the Monastrell grape – Spain's second most widely planted red variety after Garnacha – produces a firmer, beefier style of red. Gandía is one of Valencia's better producers, making finely crafted reds as well as a very drinkable Moscatel de Valencia.

ALMANSA

A relatively unimportant Levantine DO that has concentrated much of its effort hitherto on making blending wine for other regions. When it does bottle its own red wines, they tend to the heavyweight end of the spectrum. Varietal Tempranillos are the best bets. Bodegas Piqueras is one producer intent on raising the reputation of the DO with some conscientiously made reds.

JUMILLA

Much the same applies in Jumilla as for neighbouring Almansa. A lot of blending wine is produced, alongside some strong-limbed Monastrell reds and Merseguera whites that lack excitement. Improvements seem to be afoot, though, particularly among the red wines. A huge co-operative, San Isidro – the second biggest in Spain – bestrides Jumilla like a colossus.

YECLA

Another DO making large quantities of blending wine, with a vast co-operative at the centre of operations. Big, beefy reds are the name of the game once more, supplemented by weedy Merseguera whites. Bodegas Castaño is one of the more reputable producers.

ALICANTE

The typical Levantine pattern of giant co-operatives producing mainly blending wine is repeated again in the Alicante DO that extends inland from the coastal city of the same name. A sweet fortified wine, Fondillon, using the same ageing method as in sherry, brightens the picture a little, and Tempranillo is beginning to make an appearance and lend some sophistication to the generally rustic reds.

BINISSALEM

The holidaymakers of the Balearic islands are kept well-supplied with wine by the Binissalem DO, the first to be created outside the Spanish mainland, on the island of Majorca. Two indigenous grape varieties, plus the white grapes of Catalonia, make some pretty rasping reds, simple, gluggable rosados and undistinguished whites. Nothing to get excited about in other words, but if the sun's shining and the price is right, who cares?

ALMANSA
GRAPES: Red – Monastrell, Garnacha, Tempranillo
JUMILLA
GRAPES: Red – Monastrell; White – Merseguera
YECLA
GRAPES: Red – Monastrell, Garnacha; White – Merseguera
ALICANTE
GRAPES: Red – Monastrell, Garnacha, Bobal, Tempranillo; White – Merseguera
BINISSALEM
GRAPES: Red – Manto Negro; White – Moll, Xarel-lo, Parellada

La Mancha, in the hot, arid centre of Spain (below left). This vast vineyard area is Europe's largest single appellation.

SHERRY

GRAPES: Palomino, Pedro Ximénez, Moscatel

The finest vineyards of the sherry region, as here at Osborne's Viña el Caballo west of Jerez (below), are planted on chalk-white albariza *soil.*

SHERRY AND OTHER FORTIFIED WINES

The province of Andalucía, in the south of Spain, is home to a range of traditional fortified wines, the most celebrated of which is sherry. At one time, fortified wines were produced all over Spain, but as the fashion in this century has gradually shifted towards lighter table wines, so the other regions have abandoned their frequently poor efforts, and Jerez and its satellites have cornered the market.

It is, to be sure, a dwindling market. Tastes have changed, and the image of sherry has suffered from its exasperating association with inferior products, such as the commercial pale and dark cream sherries that maturing tastebuds quickly grow out of. The profligate use of the word "sherry" to describe sub-standard sweet brown slosh from other countries has not helped. The latter problem was belatedly addressed by the European Union when, at the beginning of 1996, a ruling came into effect that rightfully reserved the word "sherry" for the produce of the Jerez region alone.

Sherry The wine takes its name from the city of Jerez de la Frontera in Andalucía, but the region also encompasses the major towns of Puerto de Santa María and Sanlúcar de Barrameda. These are the three principal locations for the maturation of the region's wines. Their quality rests fundamentally on the geology of the Jerez DO. The soil at the heart of the region is a mixture of limestone, sand and clay that looks deceptively like chalk, so blindingly white does it glare at you in the brilliance of a summer day. The local name for it is *albariza*, and most of the best

vineyard holdings are planted on this type of soil. Because of its proximity to the ocean, moreover, Jerez does not suffer quite the summer heat-stress that, say, La Mancha does. Although the summer months are relentlessly dry, cooling Atlantic breezes waft across the vines and the falling night-time temperatures mitigate the roaring heat of day.

Palomino is the main grape variety in sherry production. Nearly all of the wines, from the palest and driest up to the most liquorously treacly, are based on that grape. The variable element lies in how the producers decide which lots of the base wine will end up as which style.

After the light Palomino base wine has completed its fermentation, it is fortified with grape spirit up to anything from 15 to 20 per cent alcohol. Generally, the lighter fortification will be used for wines that are destined to be sold as fino, the palest, most elegant version of dry sherry. This is because fino sherries are matured in casks underneath a film of naturally forming yeast called *flor*, derived from wild yeasts that are present in the atmosphere of the cellars. The *flor* protects the developing wine from the influence of too much oxygen, and also imparts a characteristic nutty taste (like plain peanuts) to classic fino. Fortification above 15 per cent will inhibit the growth of *flor*, which is why fino sherries are lower in alcohol than darker and sweeter styles.

Sometimes the *flor* doesn't quite form a solid enough layer to produce fino. It breaks up and sinks to the bottom of the cask, and the more direct exposure to oxygen causes the wine's colour to darken. This becomes the style known as amontillado. (The best amontillados are still bone-dry, the popular conception of it as a medium-sweet style being derived from commercial brands that have been sugared up.)

The heaviest, darkest version of sherry is oloroso, which is fortified to the highest alcoholic degree of all, and is aged with maximum oxygen contact so that the colour is a deep burnished brown. Most olorosos are given a sweetening dose of juice pressed from raisined grapes, Pedro Ximénez (or PX) giving the best quality although Palomino may be treated in this way too. As with amontillado, however, there is a certain amount of totally dry oloroso made (labelled *oloroso seco*). Austere and intense, with a flavour of strangely bitter walnuts, it is one of the greatest taste experiences wine can offer.

Other sherry styles commonly encountered are *palo cortado* (which is a kind of naturally evolved median stage between amontillado and oloroso and is generally given some sweetening), Cream (sweetened, blended brown sherries, eternally symbolized by Harvey's Bristol Cream) and Pale Cream (a sweetened fino epitomized by Croft Original). Manzanilla is the official name of fino sherries matured in the town of Sanlúcar de Barrameda. They are popularly supposed to have a distinct salty whiff of the local sea air in them; on a good day, with a spanking-fresh bottle, it's possible to believe there is an element of truth to that.

Some houses make a speciality of bottling their raisined PX wine unblended. The result is an oleaginous, nearly-black essence of mind-blowing sweetness, so glutinously thick that it can scarcely be swirled in the glass. Everybody should try at least a mouthful, but it is admittedly hard to know what to do with a whole bottle of it. (The fashionable thing of late has been to pour it over vanilla ice-cream, which is indeed embarrassingly delicious.)

The traditional method of sherry maturation, now extensively abandoned by many houses, was in the so-called *solera* system. This consisted of massed ranks of barrels containing wines that went back a century or more. With each bottling, a third of the wine would be drawn off the oldest barrels, which would then be topped up with wine from the next oldest. This would in turn be replenished from the next oldest, and so on up to the youngest at the top of the pile, which would be topped up with newly made wine.

Given the painstaking labour involved in operating and maintaining such a system, it isn't entirely surprising that modern economics have decreed the abandonment of it in many cases. Wine that has been aged in a *solera*, however, will be labelled with the date of the oldest wine in it; there will of course be some 1895 wine in a bottle so labelled, but only a microscopic quantity sadly.

A note about serving the different types of sherry. Fino and manzanilla sherries *must* be served well-chilled, or they will taste hopelessly stale, but no other sherries should be. Equally as important with the paler sherries is to drink them as soon as possible after opening. Just treat them exactly as you would leftover white wine – they aren't that much more alcoholic, after all.

BEST SHERRIES: FINO: Tio Pepe, Don Zoilo, Hidalgo, Lustau, Williams and Humbert, Valdespino Inocente.

MANZANILLA: Barbadillo Príncipe, Hidalgo La Gitana and La Guita, Don Zoilo, Valdespino, Lustau Manzanilla Pasada (an older, darker version than the norm).

AMONTILLADO: Gonzalez Byass Amontillado del Duque, Valdespino Tio Diego and Coliseo, Hidalgo Napoleon, Lustau Almacenista.

OLOROSO: Gonzalez Byass Matúsalem and Apostoles, Valdespino Don Gonzalo, Williams and Humbert Dos Cortados, Lustau Muy Viejo Almacenista.

Montilla-Moriles A region to the northeast of Jerez that makes entirely analogous styles of fortified wine to sherry. However, it is generally somewhat behind the best sherries in terms of quality because of its inland location and less promising soils, and also the fact that the main sherry grape Palomino has not been able to make itself at home here. The wines can be good and are always cheaper than the corresponding sherry.

Málaga Made in the hinterland behind the Mediterranean port of the same name, the fate of Málaga stands as a salutary warning to what can happen to an original and inimitable style of wine when nobody wants to drink it any more. In the 19th century, it was highly revered, particularly in Britain where it was known as Mountain, owing to the steep hillside locations of its vineyards. By the 1990s, however, hardly anybody had heard of it and the last major producers in the region were close to shutting up shop. Málaga makes much more from tourism these days. This is a great pity, as the wine has a style all of its own, more often than not mahogany-coloured and full of a gentle raisins-in-caramel sweetness that is somehow never cloying.

Condado de Huelva A historically significant region for fortified wines situated to the west of Jerez towards the border with southern Portugal, Condado de Huelva is now sunk in obscurity as far as the outside world is concerned. It still makes some fortified wine, only very vaguely comparable to sherry; there is a kind of fino that develops under *flor* called Condado Palido, and a darker oloroso-type wine, Condado Viejo, that is aged in a *solera* system. Hardly any of it is exported, though. The emphasis is slowly shifting to the production of an unfortified table wine, Viño Joven. First impressions suggest it won't exactly set the world on fire.

MONTILLA-MORILES
GRAPES: *White – Pedro Ximénez, Muscat of Alexandria*

MALAGA
GRAPES: *White – Pedro Ximénez, Airén, Muscat of Alexandria, Palomino*

Fino sherry is matured in oak butts (above) under a film of flor, a natural yeast that imparts a characteristic nutty taste to classic fino.

PORTUGAL

Shaking off its old-fashioned attitudes, Portugal has rediscovered its greatest treasure – a range of exciting grape varieties – to prove that it can produce more than the world's top fortified wines.

P ORTUGAL'S ROLE IN the history of European wine is of an importance quite belied by the relative unfamiliarity of most of its table wines to today's consumers. Its reputation was founded primarily on the success of its fortified wines, port and madeira, in the lucrative markets of England and what was to become the United States. The 14th-century alliance between England and Portugal became significant when hostilities broke out between the English and French. Preferential tariffs for Portugal's wines were formalized in the

Methuen Treaty of 1703, and drinking port rather than French wines became a matter of patriotic observance in English society.

In the centuries since then, Portugal's influence has declined as French wines once again became pre-eminent. Its economy was not easily able to support the kind of technological investment needed by every wine-producing country in order to make the wines the modern trade demands. For many years Portugal remained quite insular in its approach to wine, largely satisfying itself with the income generated by sales of port and, in Mateus Rosé, its own version of the semi-sweet sparkling wines usually guaranteed to be popular.

It is only in the last 20 years or so, since Portugal joined the European Union and the funds started to flow, that its other traditional table wines have begun to be appreciated across Europe. There is still a long way to go, and it is fair to say that the Portuguese have not been the most dynamically outward-looking among European winemakers. But they have a great asset in the broad range of high-quality indigenous grape varieties, many of which are capable of turning out some truly original wines at sharply competitive prices.

The classification of Portuguese wines follows the four-tier system that EU regulators have devised on the basis of the French model. At the top, the equivalent of *appellation contrôlée* is DOC (*denominação de origem controlada*). Then comes IPR (*indicação de proveniencia regulamentada*), a sort of Portuguese VDQS, *vinhos regionais* for regional wines like the *vins de pays*, and finally simple table wines, *vinhos de mesa*.

VINHO VERDE

This is Portugal's largest DOC region by far, up in the northwest corner of the country around Oporto. The sheer volumes produced and exported have made Vinho Verde one of Portugal's better-known wines internationally. At least, it is the *white* version that is popular; many consumers are unaware that just over half of all Vinho Verde is red, probably because the

At their best, traditional aged Portuguese reds (above) are liquoricey and spicy in character.

1. VINHO VERDE
2. PORTO/DOURO
3. DÃO
4. BAIRRADA
5. OESTE
6. RIBATEJO
7. BUCELAS
8. COLARES
9. PALMELA
10. ARRÁBIDA
11. ALENTEJO
12. ALGARVE
13. SETÚBAL MOSCATEL
14. CARCAVELOS
15. MADEIRA

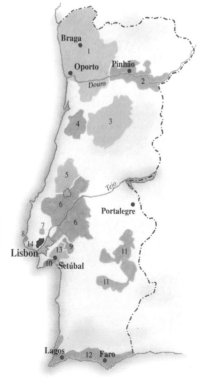

Portugal offers a striking range of wine styles (right), the two most renowned – port and Vinho Verde – coming from the north.

VINHO VERDE

GRAPES: *White – Loureiro, Trajadura, Arinto, Avesso, Alvarinho; Red – Vinhão, Azal, Espadeiro, etc.*

Portuguese keep nearly all of it to themselves. The name means "green wine", but that doesn't refer to the greenish tinge in many of the whites, but to the fact that the wine, both red and white, is released young for quick consumption. Its youth means that there is usually a slight pétillance, even a positive sparkle, in many bottles (indeed some are deliberately carbonated before bottling), as well as generous dollops of raw, palate-scouring acidity.

Most wines are blends of various local grapes, and each sub-region has its own particular specialities, Loureiro and Trajadura for example being especially favoured in the central part of the DOC. The whites have a simple, bracing, lemony charm that can be appealing enough at the height of summer. Sensitive souls may gag on the reds, however, which are astringently dry as well as slightly fizzy, not a combination familiar from any other European wine (which is why they hardly ever leave the region).
BEST WINES: Quinta da Tamariz, Terras de Corga, Gazela, Quinta de Aveleda Grinalda.

DOURO

Named after the river Douro, which has its origin in Spain (where they call it the Duero), the Douro valley's most celebrated product is port (see below), but the DOC for the region also encompasses some rapidly improving table wines. Growers here are not exactly short of choice when it comes to finding the right grape to grow on each particular patch – they have nearly 100 at their disposal, including all of the varieties used in port. A number of the port shippers have now diversified into the production of red and white unfortified wines.

Just as Spain has its premium red wine in Vega Sicilia, Portugal has one too, in Barca Velha, launched in the 1950s by the port house of Ferreira. It is a complex, subtly spicy wine made only in the best vintages and given long cask-ageing – a profound and inspired creation. Ferreira now belongs to the large wine combine Sogrape, which has itself pioneered many of the better Douro wines, and has achieved notable successes with international varieties such as Cabernet Sauvignon. The non-traditional grapes are not allowed DOC status, the wines taking the regional designation Terras Durienses. Quinta do Cotto is one of Sogrape's best labels for good, meaty reds, while its white Douro Reserva made from Portuguese grapes is an aromatic triumph. Raposeira is another company achieving results.

DÃO

Dão, a large mountainous DOC just north of the centre of Portugal, makes one of the country's higher-profile red wines, as well as a small quantity of fairly undistinguished white. During the 1950s and '60s, it came to be dominated by co-operatives, whose regressive winemaking techniques were responsible for a corresponding drop in the quality of what had been a highly regarded wine. Extended ageing in casks of often dubious cleanliness robs a lot of the reds of their fruit, and they are often disappointingly dried-out before they even get to the bottle, let alone the market. When good, though, they can possess that spicy, liquoricey appeal that characterizes the finest Portuguese reds. The whites were traditionally also overaged and reached the consumer in an oxidized state, tasting flat and dull.

More conscientious small growers are slowly but surely elbowing the co-operatives and their outdated methods aside, and some fresher, more modern wines are emerging. Sogrape has a finger in the Dão pie as well, and makes good wines in both colours, its Grão Vasco white a real trail-blazer. Caves Aliança and the Terras Altas label of another large concern, José Maria da Fonseca, are also noteworthy.

The port house of Ferreira has gained a reputation for a fine red wine, from grapes grown on the steep hillsides (above) of the Douro valley.

DOURO
GRAPES: Red – *Touriga Nacional, Tinta Roriz, Tinta Cão; White – Gouveio, Malvasia, Viosinho*
DÃO
GRAPES: Red – *Touriga Nacional, Bastardo, Tinta Pinheira, Tinta Roriz, Alfrocheiro Preto, etc; White – Encruzado, Bical*

A timeless scene outside the 19th-century bodega (above) at Bairrada's most innovative producer, Luis Pato.

BAIRRADA
GRAPES: *Red – Baga;*
White – Maria Gomes, Bical
OESTE
GRAPES: *Red – Arruda*
RIBATEJO
GRAPES: *White – Fernão*
Pires, Arinto;
Red – Periquita

BAIRRADA

To the west of Dão, the Bairrada DOC shares some of the same problems as its neighbour in that its production is dominated by poorly equipped co-operatives using rather backward vinification methods. The picture will slowly brighten, however, as more of the small growers decide to cut out the co-ops and bottle their own wine. Three-quarters of Bairrada is red, and the major red-wine grape, Baga, is one of Portugal's more assertive red varieties. Sloppily vinified, it can be depressingly tannic and rough, but the smarter operators are managing to coax some ripe, plummy fruit out of it and show its potential. White Bairrada, given a gentle touch of oak by one or two producers, can be splendidly smoky and appley, but the majority is still fairly bland.

This is also the region in which Sogrape makes its famed Mateus Rosé. Sweetish pink fizz may not be the mood of the moment just now, and the wine has recently been relaunched in a drier version, its clean peachy fruit refreshing enough on a hot day.

PRODUCERS: Luis Pato (one of the region's great innovators), São João, Caves Aliança, Sogrape, Vilharino do Bairro.

OESTE

Quantitatively but not yet qualitatively important, Oeste is the collective name for a group of six IPR regions on the western coast of Portugal,

north of Lisbon. They are, from north to south, Encostas d'Aire, Alcobaca, Obidos, Alenquer, Torres Vedras and Arruda. European Union funds are showering on the region like winter rainfall, so things may improve, but so far, apart from the odd, rustically meaty Arruda red, not much of any note has braved the export markets. The presence of a little Chardonnay and Cabernet in the vineyards indicates one of the likely avenues of progress.

RIBATEJO

Inland from the Oeste, also north of Lisbon, Ribatejo is similar to Oeste in two respects. It is a huge volume producer, and it is subdivided into six IPR regions. Working downwards, these are Tomar, Santarém, Chamusca, Almeirim, Cartaxo and Coruche. The potential for better quality in the Ribatejo is quite distinct, however. Many of its wines have been sent to other regions to form the base for the long-aged reserve reds of Portugal known as *garrafeiras*. The main red grape, Periquita (locally called Castelão Frances) is a good one, giving deeply coloured, spicy wine, while the whites are based on Fernão Pires (the Maria Gomes of Bairrada). They can be enticingly fresh, and even lightly oaked from those with the resources.

PRODUCERS: Margaride, Bright Brothers (where the winemaker is Australian Peter Bright). The Almeirim co-op's Leziria label is pretty reliable too.

BUCELAS

A tiny DOC to the south of Oeste's Arruda, Bucelas came perilously close to extinction in the 1980s. Caves Velhas was its last producer in fact, although there are now one or two new estates determined to restore it to the lofty reputation it historically enjoyed. It is a white-wine region only, its light, crisply acidic wines based on Arinto, which crops up in white port, and Esgana, which – as Sercial – is one of the four noble grapes of Madeira.

COLARES

Another of the DOC minnows of Portugal, Colares perches high on the wind-battered clifftops above the Atlantic Ocean, northwest of the capital. Its claim to fame, the noble Ramisco grape, makes some fine, concentrated, age-worthy reds, both on the coast as well as further inland. Whites are less interesting. Overall production is sadly declining, largely because most of the vineyards are too inaccessible to maintain.

PALMELA

Palmela, in the northern part of the Setúbal peninsula, was made an IPR in 1990 and has gradually made a name for itself as one of the quality regions of Portugal. The fine red Periquita grape makes some intriguingly spicy and peppery wines with good plum and raisin fruit, as well as a small amount of fresh rosé. Some of the country's best large wine companies are based here – J. P. Vinhos (which makes a highly

acclaimed dry Muscat as well as some good savoury reds) and José Maria da Fonseca the two most notable. Sparkling wines are also becoming a speciality. This is a region to watch.

ARRABIDA

In the south of the Setúbal peninsula, the hilly Arrábida region is – like Palmela – producing some highly progressive wines from Portuguese grapes, as well as a handful of international varieties, which seem to have bedded in very well. The same big companies, Fonseca and J. P. Vinhos, are leading the way here too, and the region became an IPR at the same time as Palmela. Cova da Ursa, an intensely smoky barrel-aged Chardonnay from Peter Bright, is typical of the philosophy. Arrábida and Palmela form part of the Vinho Regional area known as Terras do Sado.

ALENTEJO

In the southeast of the country, not far from the Spanish border, the Alentejo region has become one of the hottest names on the Portuguese wine scene. Indeed, Alentejo was really where Portugal's latter-day wine revolution began. Much experimentation has taken place, and the evident quality of the predominantly red wines speaks for itself. The VR is divided into eight sub-regions, five of DOC status (Portalegre, Borba, Redondo, Reguengos and Vidigueira) and three IPR (Evora, Granja-Amereleja and Moura).

In addition to the co-ops, José Maria da Fonseca is once again playing a leading role, and the Esporão estate at Reguengos is also producing some impressively world-class wines. Tinto da Anfora, a Periquita-based red for the João Pires brand blended from various Alentejo sub-regions, took the British market by storm a few years ago. Cartuxa's wines, and those of João Portugal Ramos, are also top-drawer. Roupeiro is the favoured local white grape, showing particular promise in the scented dry whites of Esporão.

ALGARVE

The southern coastal strip of Portugal may be much-loved as a holiday destination, but it tends not to produce much in the way of quality wine. It consists of four DOCs – from west to east Lagos, Portimão, Lagoa and Tavira – mostly making burly reds of no particular charm. A long-forgotten pale, dry fortified wine is still made by the local co-operative.

BUCELAS
GRAPES: White – Arinto,
Esgana Cão
COLARES
GRAPES: Red – Ramisco;
White – Malvasia
PALMELA
GRAPES: Red – Periquita
ARRABIDA
GRAPES: Red – Periquita,
Espadeiro, Cabernet
Sauvignon, Merlot;
White – Moscatel de Setúbal
(Muscat of Alexandria),
Arinto, Esgana Cão,
Chardonnay
ALENTEJO
GRAPES: Red – Aragonez,
Trincadeira, Moreto,
Periquita;
White – Roupeiro

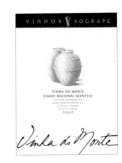

Ripe bunches of Periquita grapes (left) destined for Tinto da Anfora, a blended red from the Alentejo region.

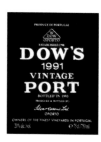

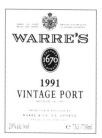

Taylor's Quinta da Vargellas, source of one of the most successful single-estate ports (above).

PORT

The origins of port, as of all fortified wines, lie in the need to stabilize and protect light table wines from spoilage during long sea voyages. When the English merchants found themselves having to pay punitive tariffs to import French wines, as a result of the 17th-century wars with France, they turned to Portugal as their next best source. The thin white wines of northern Portugal (the modern Vinho Verde DOC) were not much to anyone's taste but, venturing into the Douro valley, the importers chanced upon the fiery red brews of what was to become port country.

Imported in barrel, the wines had inevitably spoiled by the time they reached England, and so the shippers learned to add a little brandy to them in order to preserve them. At this point, therefore, port would have been a potent but dry wine. It wasn't until some while later that the English systematically began adding the brandy *before* the red wine had finished fermenting. That stopped the yeasts dead in their tracks before all of the grape sugars had been consumed, and so port became naturally sweet as well as strong. A legendary fortified wine was born.

Today, the fortifying agent is a more neutral, colourless grape spirit rather than actual brandy, but the production process is otherwise not much changed since the 1600s. In the mid-18th century, in a drive to protect port from poor imitations from other regions, the Douro valley was demarcated as the only area that could produce genuine port. It was thus the first denominated appellation, predating the French system by about 180 years.

Of all the European fortified wines, port is the most confusing to the unsuspecting. The following is a summary of the range of port styles now made.

Ruby The most basic style of all, blended from the produce of several harvests and aged for no more than a couple of years. Many shippers produce a house brand that may or may not call itself Ruby – the term is somewhat debased now – but if it has no other description, that is what it will essentially be.

Vintage Character If ever a wine term were ripe for abolition, it is Vintage Character port. These are basic rubies, aged for longer (about five years on average), that theoretically have something of the depth of flavour of true vintage port. In practice, they simply never do, and if you are going to trade up from basic ruby, it is far more advisable to move on to the next category, Late Bottled Vintage.

Late Bottled Vintage (LBV) Unlike Vintage Character, these really are the produce of a single vintage which will be specified on the label. They are basically the years that are not quite deemed good enough to make true vintage port, but the quality is nonetheless generally good. They are aged for between four and six years, and the best ones will have been bottled without being filtered, so that the wine throws a sediment and requires decanting. Some companies filter their LBVs in order to avoid the need for that, largely because many consumers wrongly assume that decanting is more technical than it is (see the introduction for advice on the process). Buy an unfiltered LBV in preference to a filtered one; the flavours are far more resonant and complex.

Vintage port At the top of the pyramid, vintage port is the product of a single year, stated on the label as with ordinary table wine, that is bottled after two or three years' cask ageing. Each shipper must decide within two years of the harvest whether the wine of a particular year is going to be fine enough to be released, unblended, as a vintage port. This is known as "declaring" the vintage. Good years such as 1985 may result in a universal declaration among the major shippers. Vintage port requires ageing in the bottle by the customer, and will always throw a sediment. Some, such as the relatively light 1980s, will only need a few years; other vintages, like the legendary 1977, may take a quarter of a century and more before they are ready for drinking (many were still nowhere near ready as the century turned).

Single Quinta Vintage wines made from the grapes of single estates or *quintas*. Since these grapes normally play a part in a shipper's best vintage port, the single-estate wines tend to be produced in the marginally less good years but quality is still good (and above LBV in most cases). Names to look for are Quinta do Bomfim from the house of Dow, Quinta da Vargellas from Taylor and Quinta da Cavadinha from Warre.

Crusted port So-called because it forms a crust of sediment in the bottle, crusted or crusting port is a kind of cross between vintage port and LBV. It is not the produce of a single year, but is treated like a vintage port and bottled unfiltered. The style is a creation of the British-owned port houses, and is intended as an economically kinder alternative to true vintage port.

Tawny port Traditionally a basic blended port that is aged for several years longer than ruby, so that its colour drops out and the flavour goes almost drily nutty with oxidation. Some tawny is now made by simply adding a little white port to a base of paler red wines to lighten the colour.

Aged Tawny These are invariably true tawny ports, aged for many years in cask. The difference from basic tawny is that the label will state the average age of the wines that have gone into the blend, calculated in multiples of ten. A ten-year-old tawny, such as the perennially superb example from Dow, may very well be the optimum age. Twenty-, 30- and 40-year-old wines will increase correspondingly in price, but may yield diminishing returns as to drinking pleasure.

Colheitas A *colheita* port is essentially a vintage tawny. The wines from a single year receive a minimum of seven years in cask, so that their colour fades. Many are only released at grand old ages, and the prices – compared to early-bottled vintage port – can look immensely attractive.

White port Among the cocktail of 80-plus grape varieties that are permitted in port are a handful of white ones. Some houses produce a port solely from white grapes (largely Arinto, Gouveio, Malvasia and Viosinho) that is fortified by the same method as the red. They may be dry or sweet and are not particularly great wines. The dry port has nothing like the pedigree of good fino sherry for instance, but can be refreshing served well-chilled in small quantities.

BEST NAMES IN PORT: Dow, Taylor, Graham, Cálem, Fonseca, Warre, Ferreira, Niepoort, Burmester. Quinta do Noval makes a famously brilliant vintage wine called Nacional from ancient vines, selling at a once-in-a-lifetime price.
PORT VINTAGES: *2003* ***** *'01* *** *2000* **** *1997* *** *'94* **** *'91* **** *'85* **** *'83* **** *'77* ***** *'75* **** *'70* ****

Back-breaking manual harvesting in the terraced vineyards of Quinta do Bomfim in the Douro (above).

A traditional barco rabelo sails through Oporto (below), on the Portuguese coast. These boats were used to carry the pipes of port down the Douro to the port houses.

MADEIRA

The history of madeira is perhaps the single most remarkable example of human dedication to the cause of fine wine. The island of Madeira is a volcanic tropical outcrop in the Atlantic Ocean, nearer to the coast of north Africa than to the Portugal of which it forms an auto- nomously governed province. Its soil contains a great quantity of ash from a conflagration that raged across the island many centuries ago, and its mountainous terrain means that its vineyards are among the most inaccessible in the world.

Like port, Madeira's wines were once light table wines that came to be fortified so that they might better survive long sea transportation. In the case of madeira, though, the shippers stum- bled on an extraordinary discovery. Carried aboard the great trading vessels of the Dutch East India Company, the wine's voyage east was a more arduous matter than simply ferrying port from northern Portugal to the south of Eng- land. It was noticed that, when the wine arrived in India, it was unspoiled; in fact it was posi- tively improved. So, just for good measure, the shippers left some to complete a round trip back to Europe, and that turned out even better.

No other wine has ever, before or since, proved so improbably masochistic. It sailed the heaving oceans in raging heat for weeks at a time, the barrels clattering around in the hold, and nothing could destroy it. For many decades, every bottle of madeira sold had been on this round-the-world cruise, until a way was found to simulate those conditions in its place of origin.

In the 19th century, a maturation system known as the *estufa*, or stove, was introduced. The *lagares* – the storage houses in which the wine is aged – were equipped with central-heat- ing systems, hot-water pipes that ran around the walls (or occasionally through the vats of wine themselves) in order to cook it as it had been in its maritime days. Some wines, reputedly the best, were cooked by simple exposure to the tropical summer sun.

Simple blended madeira is often based on a grape variety called Tinta Negra Mole that used to find its way into any of the four varietal styles of madeira. Those must now, as a result of intervention by the European Union, be made up of no less than 85 per cent of the named varietal, and so Tinta Negra Mole is, at least in theory, in decline.

All of Madeira's agriculture, including its vineyards, is planted in terraces on sheer hillside land such as this (right). The fearsome gradients mean that any form of mechanized harvest- ing is out of the question.

The varietal wines are, from lightest and driest to richest and sweetest, Sercial, Verdelho, Bual and Malmsey, the last name being an Anglicized corruption of Malvasia. Even at its very sweetest, madeira always has a streak of balancing acid running through it to complement the amazing flavours of treacle (molasses), toffee, Christmas cake, dates and walnuts. There is also often a telltale whiff of mature cheese about it, rather like old dry Cheshire, and just to complete its range of peculiar attributes, it generally has a distinct green hue at the rim.

Labels may state the age of the blend (ten-year-old is significantly more rewarding than five), or may use such vague-sounding but in practice fairly precise terminologies as Finest (about three years old), Reserve (five), Special Reserve (ten) or Extra Reserve (15).

A small quantity of vintage-dated madeira is made, which sells for a fraction of the price of vintage port. As the history of this fabulously unique wine suggests, it is virtually indestructible.

BEST NAMES IN MADEIRA: Blandy, Henriques & Henriques, Barbeito, Cossart Gordon, Rutherford & Miles, Leacock.

SETUBAL

Three variants of the Muscat grape, the main one being Muscat of Alexandria, make a port-method sweet fortified wine on the Setúbal Peninsula. After the fortification, the skins of the grapes are left to infuse in the new wine for several months so that a particularly pronounced aroma and flavour of fresh Moscatel grapes is imparted to it. It is usually aged in cask for five years or so before bottling, though some premium wines are given up to 25 years' maturation, resulting in a nuttily oxidized, deep brown wine. Most examples taste fairly heavy on the palate, and don't quite attain the graceful balance of the best southern French fortified Muscats. José Maria da Fonseca is the main producer of note.

CARCAVELOS

Decreasingly important coastal DOC just west of Lisbon that once tried to rival port as a producer of quality fortified wine. The wines are made in much the same way, from both red and white grapes, and generally resemble basic tawny. Quinta dos Pesos is a recently established estate determined to keep the flame alive.

Traditional thatched A-frame houses, like this one at Palheiros (below), are a characteristic feature of Madeira's vineyards.

GERMANY

Germany's wines have struggled to earn respect abroad, yet the country's ultra-efficient producers can offer the very best of fine, light wines in a whole range of styles.

IT MAY SEEM SOMETHING of an anomaly to today's wine-drinkers to reflect that Germany once occupied a place in the connoisseur's hall of fame scarcely lower than that of France. In the Middle Ages, Rhenish – named after the river Rhine – was highly prized in the countries of northern Europe. Nor was it necessarily a white wine. Shakespearean references to it make it quite clear the wine was principally thought of as red; much of it would have been made from Pinot Noir. At this time, of course, Germany included all of the Alsace region, and many merchants held that the wines from that side of the Rhine were the finest of all.

A combination of factors, not least the ravages of the Thirty Years War in the early part of the 17th century, caused a general decline in German viticulture. That was thrown somewhat into reverse in the 1700s, but by the turn of the 20th century the country's vineyards were in wholesale retreat. Other forms of agriculture were more profitable, and the brewing industry generated considerably greater income than winemaking. The reparations demanded from Germany after the Great War in the Treaty of Versailles played their devastating part in the wine industry as much as any other sector. It was only by selling cheap blended wines, sourced from many regions and sweetened up to appeal to the broadest possible customer base (Liebfraumilch being the most famous, or perhaps notorious, example), that German wine survived at all as an export proposition.

Its principal problem ever since has been how to shake off the Liebfraumilch legacy. Seasoned wine-lovers may sniff at the very name, but the obstinate fact remains that sweetened German wine is still by far the largest sector of the British wine market. If consumers who develop a taste for those wines would just look towards Germany's premier varietal wines – best exemplified by Riesling – they would discover an unsuspected world of much subtler, and ultimately more rewarding, sweet wines.

Similarly, if those who have left German wines behind altogether because of the Liebfraumilch association, but who have learned to admire the Rieslings of Alsace or Australia, would give Germany another chance, they would find some of the most uncommonly beautiful, and stylistically unequalled, light white wines in the world in the best Riesling vintages of the Mosel or the Pfalz.

The German wine classification system underwent a number of mutations in the 20th century, the most recent set of amendments being introduced in 1993. It was in 1971, however, that the foundations for a system comparable to that now used throughout the European Union were laid.

At the lowest level are the basic table wines, labelled *Deutscher Tafelwein*. This is only applied to a tiny fraction of Germany's annual production and may be blended from anywhere in the country. A step up is the *vin de pays*

Germany's famous wine regions hug the river Rhine and its tributaries, along the southwestern borders (below). Saale/Unstrut and Sachsen are two additions since the fall of the Berlin wall.

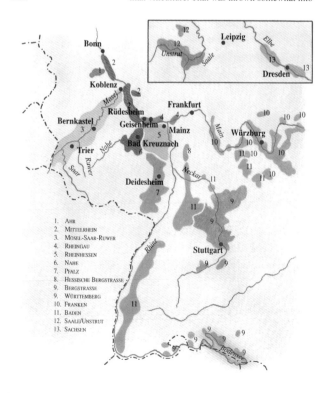

1. AHR
2. MITTELRHEIN
3. MOSEL-SAAR-RUWER
4. RHEINGAU
5. RHEINHESSEN
6. NAHE
7. PFALZ
8. HESSISCHE BERGSTRASSE
9. BERGSTRASSE
9. WÜRTTEMBERG
10. FRANKEN
11. BADEN
12. SAALE/UNSTRUT
13. SACHSEN

category, *Landwein*. This may come from any one of 20 large demarcated regions, and is used with greater frequency these days. Above that is QbA (*Qualitätswein bestimmter Anbaugebiete* or "quality wine from a specified region"). This is the volume category, in which the juice of underripe grapes may be sweetened to increase the final alcohol level, and the wine itself may be sweetened with unfermented grape juice before bottling to produce an easy-going commercial style.

At the top is QmP (*Qualitätswein mit Prädikat* or "quality wine with pedigree"). These wines are subdivided according to how much natural sugar the harvested grapes possess. In order of ascending sweetness, they are: Kabinett, Spätlese, Auslese, Beerenauslese and Trockenbeerenauslese. The separate category Eiswein ("ice wine" made from frozen ultra-ripe berries picked in the dead of winter) also counts as a *Prädikat* wine; it usually falls somewhere between the last two categories in terms of sweetness.

The fashion of late has been to ferment out some of the sugar in QmP wines, either all the way to dry (Trocken) or semi-dry (for which style the newly minted term Feinherb replaces the old Halbtrocken).

It remains true that its Rieslings are still Germany's best shot, but there are other varieties to contend with, many of them grown in several different regions. In an effort to find grapes that will ripen more dependably than Riesling in the cold, northern climate of Germany, viticultural researchers have worked at crossing varieties – and even crossing the crosses. The results have been decidedly mixed, and many of these new creations remain unheard of outside the country. We shall look first at these other grapes, and then at the wine regions.

Silvaner Particularly valued in the Franken region around Würzburg, Silvaner is one of the best of the uncrossed grapes after Riesling. Ripening much earlier than Riesling, it gives wines with a whiff of cabbage leaves when young, but that can age to a silky, honey-laden maturity.

Müller-Thurgau A Riesling-Silvaner mix, this was the first of the crossings, developed in the 1880s by a Swiss scientist working in Germany. So grateful were the growers for its early-ripening properties that they fell upon it with unconfined zeal – so much so that it became the most widely planted grape in Germany, a

position it still occupies. Indeed it could have been the Holy Grail were it not for the fact that the wines it produces almost invariably taste watery and flat.

Kerner One of the more successful new varieties, Kerner is a crossing of Riesling with a red grape called Trollinger. Although it was only conceived in the late 1960s, it is now planted on more German vineyard land than Riesling itself. One of the higher-quality crosses, it makes a crisply lime-zesty wine, without quite having the elegance of properly ripened Riesling.

Scheurebe Here is another Riesling-Silvaner cross, but a much more refined one than Müller-Thurgau. When properly ripe, Scheurebe has a distinct flavour of grapefruit, with the corollary that, if the summer hasn't been kind, Scheurebe wines are agonizingly tart. In the right conditions, it gives excellent noble-rotted dessert wines.

Rieslaner Probably the best Riesling-Silvaner crossing of them all, the clumsily named Rieslaner can be stunning, full of almost tropical fruit from the best growers. Rieslaner occupies only a tiny percentage of vineyard; it is a shame there isn't more planted.

Among more internationally known white varieties, Germany also grows Weissburgunder (aka Pinot Blanc), Grauburgunder or Ruländer (Pinot Gris), Gewürztraminer and even a little Chardonnay (see grape variety section).

The sundial (above) that gives the terraced Wehlener Sonnenuhr vineyard, one of the Mosel's premier sites, its name.

A misty winter morning dawns over the vineyard of Schwarzerde, near Kirchheim, Pfalz (above). German wines have to survive some of the severest cold-weather conditions anywhere in the world.

The village of Zeltingen (above), caught between the Mosel river and the steeply rising vineyards.

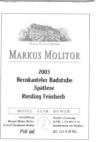

Dornfelder A fine red variety produced from two other crossed red grapes, Dornfelder is making inroads into various German regions, particularly along the Rhine. Its wines can be light and cherryish, a little like young Beaujolais occasionally but without the high alcohol. Some producers are attempting to coax a fuller, richer style from it suitable for oak-ageing.

Portugieser Not a Portuguese grape despite the name, it gives rather coarse reds with high acidity and is generally in decline.

Limberger Known as Blaufränkisch in neighbouring Austria, this is a good, characterful red grape that produces light, but appetizingly spicy, even violetty wines, with plenty of fresh acidity.

There are also significant quantities of Pinot Noir planted in Germany, where they call it Spätburgunder or Blauburgunder. A bit thin in the northerly Ahr region, it is beginning to produce impressively fuller-bodied wines along the Rhine and in the southerly Baden region.

THE REGIONS

Ahr This small northerly wine region, lying just south of the city of Bonn, specializes in red wines, mostly from Spätburgunder (Pinot Noir). They are inevitably light, in both texture and colour, as a result of being asked to ripen in such a marginal climate, but there are a few good examples – notably from late-picked grapes that

retain a gentle natural sweetness. The region's production is overwhelmingly dominated by co-operatives. There are also some good Ahr Rieslings, but the grape is losing ground as a percentage of total plantings.

Mittelrhein A small production area that extends from Bonn to south of Koblenz, the Mittelrhein is three-quarters Riesling – a high proportion for any German region. Vineyards are planted on both banks of the Rhine, often on steep hillsides. Müller-Thurgau makes up most of the non-Riesling wine. Quality is good, but most of the wine is drunk in situ by the locals, or by tourists, as this is one of the most unspoiled parts of Germany. Toni Jost is a fine Mittelrhein winemaker, who is exporting some of his sharply defined, exciting Rieslings.

Mosel-Saar-Ruwer The Mosel valley runs southwest of Koblenz, down past the city of Trier, and stops short at the intersection where Germany borders Luxembourg and France. The region's full name includes two small tributaries of the river Mosel, the Saar and the Ruwer. It includes some of the most historically celebrated vineyards in German wine history, many of them located in the Bernkastel district in the centre of the valley. These are some of the world's more dramatically sited vineyards, clinging vertiginously to sheer hillsides on either bank of the river, completely inaccessible to any form of machine-harvesting. Here the Riesling achieves some of its great glories, wines that are almost miraculously subtle expressions of the variety, extremely low in alcohol and yet possessed of a fragile purity all their own.

The best vineyard sites (preceded by their village names) have been Erdener Treppchen, Wehlener Sonnenuhr, Graacher Himmelreich, Bernkasteler Doktor, Brauneberger Juffer and Piesporter Goldtröpfchen. Some of these, notably Piesport, have suffered by association with bland, mass-market products that are blended from the general district (or *Bereich* in German). Always choose a single-estate wine in preference to anything else.

Around the Saar, Wiltinger Scharzhofberg, Ockfener Bockstein and Ayler Kupp are the leading vineyards, while Maximin Grünhaus and Eitelsbacher Karthäuserhofberg are the jewels in Ruwer's crown.
PRODUCERS: Haag, Dr Loosen, von Schubert, J J Prüm, Dr Thanisch, Schloss Saarstein.
Rheingau The Rheingau mostly occupies the right bank of the Rhine to the east of the Mittelrhein region. In some ways, it represents the nerve-centre of German winemaking. Rheingau boasts some of the most highly regarded wine estates in the country, growing a great preponderance of Riesling. At Geisenheim, the viticultural research institute has been responsible for so much of the work in creating new vine varieties.

A range of disparate vineyard conditions makes up the Rheingau. Around Rüdesheim, steeply-shelving slaty soils produce some ethereally light Rieslings, while more robust wines, known and much favoured in history as "hock", come from the more gently contoured land around Hochheim.

At the heart of Rheingau production is a group of about four dozen winemakers, calling itself the Charta Association. To qualify for the Charta seal of approval, wines must pass a rigorous tasting examination; only Rieslings are allowed to enter. It is a quality initiative that other German regions would do well to imitate.

The two most famous wine properties are the ancient castles of Schloss Vollrads and Schloss Johannisberg. In a region dominated by small producers rather than co-operatives, the names of outstanding individual growers are a better guide to quality than the vineyard sites themselves. They include Weil, Ress, Breuer and Künstler.

Rheinhessen South of the Rheingau, the Rheinhessen is where a lot of the mass-market wines of Germany originate. Half of all Liebfraumilch is made here, and there are other regional names that will be familiar to British and American consumers, such as Niersteiner Gutes Domtal. Much of Germany's acreage of crossed grape varieties is planted in the Rheinhessen too, with Müller-Thurgau leading the way. Production is much larger than the neighbouring Rheingau, and this is not by and large a quality region. There are, however, some exceptions, increasingly in the production of surprisingly sturdy reds from Spätburgunder (Pinot Noir) and Dornfelder. Silvaner also makes good wine, although somewhat less of it than hitherto.
PRODUCERS: Villa Sachsen, Guntrum, Heyl zu Herrnsheim.
Nahe The Nahe region, named after its river, lies to the west of the Rheinhessen. It is a fine, and considerably under-recognized, player on the German wine scene, its best estates as good as those in the Rheingau or Mosel. Some astonishingly concentrated Rieslings are made within the vicinity of the town of Bad Kreuznach, with Silvaner and Müller-Thurgau making up most of the rest of the plantings. A concerted campaign to raise the profiles of the best growers is under way, which will inevitably lead to a rise in prices, but for the time being, the Nahe represents one of the best-value regions in Germany.
PRODUCERS: Dönnhoff, Diel, Crusius, Plettenberg.

A tiny patch of red earth at the foot of the towering Rotenfels cliff (above) at Bad Münster, in the Nahe, yields intensely flavoured wines.

Assmannshausen, at the western end of the Rheingau (below). This wine region, like Burgundy, can trace an unbroken history back to the early days of the Benedictine and Cistercian monks.

*Decorative architecture
typical of Germany's wine
villages (above).*

*Looking down over the town
of Würzburg on the river
Main in Franken (right),
from the Marienberg
vineyard.*

Pfalz Formerly known as the Rheinpfalz, and before that the Palatinate, the Pfalz is a fast-improving and dynamic region to the south of Rheinhessen. The range of grapes grown is very broad. Not only Riesling, but Grauburgunder, Gewürztraminer, Scheurebe, Spätburgunder and Dornfelder are all producing good things. Among the more famous wine villages are Deidesheim, Ruppertsberg and Wachenheim, but good wine is proliferating all over the Pfalz now. Some of the new-style Pinot Noir reds could give some négociant burgundy a run for its money these days; not only do they have richness and body, but they can often match Burgundian Pinot for alcohol too. Decent sparkling wine, known in Germany as Sekt, is also becoming something of a speciality.

The very best Pfalz estate is Müller-Catoir, whose range of varietals is frankly world-class. Not only does it make breathtaking Rieslings and Rieslaners, as well as some convincingly spicy Gewürz, but the estate has even been known to cajole some display of personality from that old dullard Müller-Thurgau.
OTHER PRODUCERS: Bürklin-Wolf, Bassermann-Jordan, Lingenfelder, von Buhl, Köhler-Ruprecht.

Hessische Bergstrasse This small region, to the east of Rheinhessen, does not export much of its wine, but quality is impressively high. About half the vineyard is Riesling, and the better growers manage to achieve levels of concentra-tion similar to those around Hochheim. This has been one of the sectors of Germany that has most wholeheartedly embraced the latter-day trend for fermenting wines of QmP standard to a dry (Trocken) or semi-dry (Feinherb) final style. The vineyards owned by the state of Hesse are producing some of the best wine.

Württemberg A large region centred on Stuttgart, Württemberg is not greatly renowned beyond its own boundaries. Riesling, Kerner and Müller-Thurgau are the principal white varieties, Trollinger the main red. The region specializes in red wines (some made from Pinot Noir) that are so light in both colour and body that they don't seem appreciably far from the style of other producers' rosés.

Franken Otherwise known as Franconia, the region through which the river Main runs was traditionally famous as the mainstay of the Silvaner grape, although this grape now accounts for only about a fifth of the area under vine. The local taste is for austerely dry wines, the best of which come in a flat, round bottle called a *Bocksbeutel*. Nowadays, Müller-Thurgau has made inroads into the vineyards, but there are some delicately floral wines from a crossing called Bacchus. The wines are exported to some degree, but the prices tend to be off-putting.
PRODUCERS: Wirsching, Ruck, the church-owned Juliusspital.

Baden The principal region of southwest Germany, just over the border from Alsace, Baden

has been on most people's lists as one of the more exciting European wine areas of recent years. It encompasses a long stretch between Franken and the border with Switzerland, with some vineyards situated in the vicinity of Lake Constance (or the Bodensee in German). Although there is a fairly high percentage of Müller-Thurgau in the vineyards, there is also some fine, boldly delineated Riesling, musky dry Weissburgunder, spicy Gewürztraminer and – perhaps most promising of all in these warmer southern climes – some intensely ripe, deep-flavoured Spätburgunder.

PRODUCERS: Johner, Huber, the Königschaff-hausen co-operative.

Saale-Unstrut One of two small wine regions that fell within the boundaries of the old GDR, or East Germany, Saale-Unstrut is named after two rivers at whose confluence it lies. Müller-Thurgau, Weissburgunder, Silvaner and others are used to make dry, relatively full-bodied wines, but the region wasn't much blessed with investment by the old state authority and it can still only be considered emergent as yet.

Sachsen The most northerly, the most easterly, and also the smallest wine region in Germany, Sachsen (known in English as Saxony) is cen-tred on the old city of Dresden, its vineyards planted along the banks of the river Elbe. Like Saale-Unstrut, it makes dry white wines from good varieties, but the prospects for quality wine are noticeably higher. Müller-Thurgau

rules the roost, but Riesling, Weissburgunder, Gewürztraminer and Ruländer all play their parts. The wine is mostly made by a single large co-operative of numerous small growers.

SPARKLING WINES

German sparkling wine covers a multitude of sins. It comes in four basic categories, the best of which is *Sekt bestimmter Anbaugebiete* or Sekt bA. The grapes are sourced from one par-ticular district, indicated on the label (eg. Pfalz Sekt); some of the wine is even made by the champagne method. The sparkling Rieslings from producers like Dr Richter are wonderfully fresh, like sparkling alcoholic limeade.

Deutscher Sekt is a step down, and may be blended from anywhere in the country. Lila, from the large wine company Deinhard, is a good, tasty Riesling. Basic *Sekt*, the great majority of German fizz, does not have the adjective "Deutscher" for the simple reason that it will contain wines shipped in from other countries, mainly Italy and France's unwanted slosh. Lowest of the low is the unbelievably atrocious *Schaumwein*, a term that covers virtually anything else that fizzes.

RECENT GERMAN VINTAGES: *2004 **** '03 ***** '02 **** '01 **** 2000 ** 1999 *** '98 *** '96 **** '95 **** '92 *** '90 ******

Netting keeps birds off the sweet shrivelled Riesling grapes left on the vine after harvest to botrytize (above), in the Ungeheuer vineyard at Forst, in the Pfalz.

UNITED KINGDOM

In the relatively short period of the last 30 years, the UK's wine industry has developed dramatically. It may not ever become prolific but when the weather is kind, the quality is there.

A mechanical harvester at work at Denbies, in Surrey (above), the UK's largest producer at 250ha.

Most of the UK's vineyards (below) are clustered in the southeast, and are tiny, averaging less than one hectare.

IT WOULD BE EASY TO believe that wine-making in the British Isles was an innovation of the 20th century, a belated attempt to get in on the act in the face of stiff climatic odds. In fact, England once boasted a small but thriving viticultural sector, thanks – almost certainly – to the Roman invasion in the 1st century AD. Some have suggested that winemaking may even have predated the Romans, but as yet there is no firm evidence to support the contention.

What is certain is that, by the time the Venerable Bede came to write his *Ecclesiastical History* in the 8th century, he was able to note that there were vineyards in various parts of England. The advent of Christianity provided an impetus for the production of wine for use in church ceremony, and many of the monasteries established their own vineyards. Not all of the wine was for religious use, though. Much was drunk, and warmly praised, in secular life.

A number of factors contributed to the whole-sale decline of English viticulture. The first was the marriage of Henry II to Eleanor of Aquitaine, which brought tracts of southwest France under English jurisdiction, thus providing a ready pipeline of reliable and cheap bulk wine. That was followed, in the 14th century, by a dramatic cooling in the British climate. Until this time, the average summer temperatures had been conducive to vine cultivation, but the cooler, damper weather that was to stay at least until the era of global warming made ripening grapes a much trickier proposition. The final nail in the coffin was the dissolution of the monasteries under Henry VIII, and the consequent abandonment of the vineyards.

Nothing much then happened between the 16th and 20th centuries, except that the United Kingdom, as it came to be, became the epicentre of the international wine trade. A culture of connoisseurship developed that could afford to be expansively broad-minded precisely because all the wine being drunk was imported. It is only in the years since the Second World War that English viticulture has been speculatively revived.

Volumes produced are still microscopic compared to the European countries we have so far looked at, although some sort of milestone was reached in 1992 when that year's output exceeded 25,000 hectolitres. That is the magic figure above which the European Union rules state that an appellation system has to be brought into being. So far the only two designations have been England and Wales, which are used for the Quality Wine category. Anything else is UK Table Wine, or if it contains any non-*vinifera* grapes, Regional Counties wine.

Britain's cool northerly climate is such that the range of grape varieties that can be successfully grown, in even relatively hot summers, is pretty narrow. Conditions being roughly comparable to those of Germany, England and Wales have, not surprisingly, had to rely on Germanic grapes, including some of the crossed varieties

of rather dubious repute. The great tragedy, in a sense, of UK winemaking is that Riesling – hero of the German vineyards – just won't ripen.

Notwithstanding that, some pretty torrid summers in the mid-1990s and, most recently, 2003, gave a tantalizing glimpse of what English winemakers could achieve given half a chance. In years such as these, the autumnal weather has provided the right circumstances for the development of botrytis, and some outstanding dessert wines have been made.

Best prospects of all, however, lie in traditional-method sparkling wine, which is now beginning to receive due acclaim. The soils in swathes of southern England are part of the same geological chalk deposits as are found in Champagne. A cool climate is auspicious for yielding just the kind of low-alcohol, high-acid base wine that good fizzes need. The omens could scarcely be better.

The single most important determining factor in the style of an English or Welsh wine is the grape or grapes that go into it. Regional characteristics are not sufficiently sharply delineated as yet, but the varieties do play an important part. Some of the most commonly planted are listed below.

Müller-Thurgau The most widely planted grape in Germany turns out also to rule the roost in England. Not unexpectedly, its wines are no more thrilling than they are in the Rheinhessen. Some producers add a little sweetening to it before bottling to create a more commercially appealing style. Those wines can be palatable enough.

PRODUCERS: Breaky Bottom, Staple St James, Wootton, Bruisyard St Peter.

Seyval Blanc Seyval is something of an albatross to the English wine industry in the sense that it is a hybrid variety. This means that it has some non-*Vitis vinifera* parentage, thus outlawing it within EU rules from any wine classified under the approved appellation system. As a varietal, it gives generally dull, thin, neutral-tasting wine, and is best blended with grapes that have a little more to say for themselves. Breaky Bottom in East Sussex makes about the best unblended Seyval.

Reichensteiner A three-way cross, Reichensteiner very often turns out rather lifeless wine, but can occasionally make a more scented (and often slightly sweetened) varietal. Some wineries, such as Northbrook Springs, have achieved partial success with it by giving it a period in oak.

Other better-quality, but not widely planted white grapes include Ortega, Schönburger, Bacchus (all three of which can provide attractively perfumed wines), grapefruity Scheurebe, a little Gewürztraminer, and increasing quantities of good old Chardonnay. Reds include the Pinot-like Triomphe d'Alsace, as well as increasing plantings of Pinot Noir itself, and Rondo, which has produced some surprisingly robust reds.

Among England's better wineries are: Breaky Bottom, Camel Valley, New Wave Wines, Three Choirs and Valley Vineyards. Nyetimber and Ridgeview make sparkling wines every bit as good as decent champagne.

Only a tiny amount of wine is made in the south of Wales, and most is consumed locally, but Monnow Valley has made some good, crisply refreshing whites.

Breaky Bottom, in Sussex (above). Frost and birds are two menaces facing growers.

CENTRAL EUROPE

Led by Austria, the wine regions of Central Europe – stretching from Switzerland to Slovakia – are becoming increasingly important in the international arena. Internationally familiar grape varieties will help them to compete.

This highly ornamental gateway (above) leads to the wine cellars of Gustav Feiler at Rust, in the Burgenland region of eastern Austria.

THE CENTRAL EUROPEAN countries, some of them former constituents of the old Soviet bloc, were of only marginal importance to the international wine scene at one time, but with new trade agreements in the air and an influx of expertise in the shape of the so-called flying winemakers, things are changing fast. As elsewhere, the lesson has been absorbed that only the relentless quest for quality can equip unfamiliar wines with a fighting chance of survival in the jungle of today's market.

AUSTRIA

Undoubtedly the most exciting developments in central European wine are taking place in Austria. Its recent wine history is a tale of remarkable resurgence after an adulteration scandal in the mid-1980s that made its wines commercial poison for a decade. It takes time to recover from that sort of setback, but the country's many conscientious wine-growers are now being rewarded for their efforts as Austrian wine keeps winning international awards.

The vineyard regions are all concentrated in the eastern half of the country, along its borders with the Czech Republic, Slovakia, Hungary and Slovenia. Germanic as well as French grape varieties are grown, but being that much more southerly than most of Germany's wine regions, Austria's climate allows for a wider spectrum of wine styles than is the case in Germany.

The local grape made good in Austria is a white variety called Grüner Veltliner; it occupies more vineyard land than any other. The wine it yields is quite unique, mediumweight on the palate, but with an extraordinary dry spice like white peppercorns that may almost remind you of an Alsace wine.

Otherwise among whites, there's Müller-Thurgau (slowly being abandoned), Riesling, Gewürztraminer, Pinot Gris and a sprinkling of Chardonnay and Sauvignon Blanc. Welschriesling, which is nothing to do with the real Riesling, has achieved some improbably tasty results in parts of Austria. It crops up in Italy and Hungary too where its wines are mostly deadly dull. Then there are Rotgipfler and Zierfandler, the Rosencrantz and Guildenstern of the grape world: together, they go into a peculiarly heavy wine called Gumpoldskirchner, made just south of Vienna.

Red varieties are led by the indigenous Zweigelt, which gives an often purple-hued wine with a Dolcetto-like taste of blueberries. The German varieties Portugieser and Blaufränkisch also appear, as well as some impressive Cabernet Sauvignon and Pinot Noir, the latter known as Blauer Burgunder. St Laurent is a central European grape gaining a reputation for itself. Once used to produce lightweight quaffing material, it is now making some slightly spicy, raspberryish wine not a million miles from the style of classic meaty burgundy.

Austria's vineyards lie in the eastern half of the country (right), producing mainly full-bodied dry white wines, now being joined by some rapidly improving reds. Around the Neusiedlersee lake in Burgenland, the regular occurrence of noble rot provides some of Europe's best-value dessert wines.

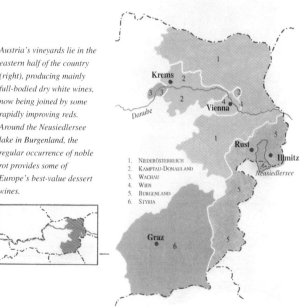

Krems

Danube

Vienna

Rust

Illmitz

Neusiedlersee

1. NIEDERÖSTERREICH
2. KAMPTAU-DONAULAND
3. WACHAU
4. WIEN
5. BURGENLAND
6. STYRIA

Graz

The crown jewels of Austrian wine, though, are its botrytized dessert wines. These are mostly produced around the Neusiedlersee, a large, shallow lake on the border with Hungary. Conditions for the development of noble rot are so obliging most years that they enable Austria to sell its sweet wines for much less than the top German examples. The categories for dessert wines are essentially the same as Germany's, including Eiswein, though with one extra classification – Ausbruch – inserted between Beerenauslese and Trockenbeerenauslese. A speciality is *Strohwein* (meaning "straw wine") made from naturally overripe grapes that are dried on straw mats, as in the production of Spanish *mistela* or the French *vin de paille*.

Prädikatswein is the designation for the top-quality wines, although – unlike Germany – it excludes wines classified as Kabinett, the sweetness category below Spätlese. A small amount of regional wine, made from specified grape varieties, is labelled as *Landwein*, and the basic stuff is *Tafelwein*, which means in practice the majority produced in any given year.

The northernmost wine zone is Niederösterreich or Lower Austria, north of the Danube. Its wines are predominantly dry or medium-dry whites from Grüner Veltliner, Riesling and Welschriesling. Kamptau-Donauland on the western fringe, north of Krems, makes some of the most richly intense Grüners of any Austrian region. Just to the south, in Wachau, some fine, sharply defined Rieslings (some botrytized) are rivalling those of the Rhine valley.

The capital city, Vienna (Wien to the Austrians), is a little wine region in itself, not a claim that any other European capital can make. Grüner, Riesling and Pinot Blanc are the best wines, and are almost exclusively snapped up by the Wieners, not surprisingly. Traditional taverns, known as *Heurigen*, in which much of wine is drunk are cheery hostelries in the city's outskirts where growers' families sell the wines of the new vintage, many of them unclarified and still cloudy from the tank.

Burgenland, on the Hungarian border, is the region that includes the Neusiedlersee. A versatile range of dry table wines is made here as well as fabulously opulent dessert wines from grapes such as Welschriesling, Gewürztraminer, the local Bouvier and so on. Whites take in some firmly textured Pinot Blanc and Welschriesling, as well as creamy oaked Chardonnay and gooseberryish Sauvignon, while Zweigelt and

Blaufränkisch reds are often packed with savoury spice and are increasingly being barrel-matured. One or two growers have attained astonishing levels of concentration in Cabernet Sauvignon wines.

The southernmost viticultural sector is Steiermark or Styria. It is predominantly white-wine country and, while geographically extensive, only accounts for a modest fraction of Austria's total output. The style, whether for Sauvignon, Chardonnay (often known by one of its rarer pseudonyms, Morillon), Gewürztraminer or dry Muscat from Gelber Muskateller (Muscat Blanc à Petits Grains), is extremely dry, often tart, with sharply emphasized acidity. In the west, around Graz, a red grape called Blauer Wildbacher makes Schilcher – a highly regarded rosé. NOTABLE PRODUCERS: Opitz, Kracher, Moser, Stiegelmar, the Winzerhaus range from co-operatives in Lower Austria.

The imposing white church gives its name to the village of Weissenkirchen (above) in the Wachau region of Austria, source of some of the country's finest Riesling wines.

*Trimly tended vineyards
cluster around the village
church at Conthey (above),
in the Valais, western
Switzerland.*

*Through the heart of Europe
stretches a band of cool
vineyards (right). Once
under the rule of empires
and some now emerging
from Communist control,
they produce mainly white
wines.*

SWITZERLAND

The wine-growing areas of Switzerland are concentrated near the country's borders – with
France in the west, Germany in the north and
Italy in the south. Its wines are not exported in
any great quantity, and tend to be horrifyingly
expensive even in situ. Unless a path to better
value can be found, they are only ever likely to
have curiosity status in external markets.

Around the continuation of the river Rhône in
the west, the Valais and Vaud regions specialize
in French varieties, although the favoured white
grape, Fendant (Chasselas to the French), is not
much prized in its mother country, yielding a
thin, unassuming, sometimes minerally but not
conspicuously fruity white. Sylvaner does well
here, and there are isolated outposts of
Chardonnay and Pinot Gris.

Pinot Noir makes some reasonably tasty light
reds, sometimes in a blend with a smaller proportion of Gamay and labelled Dôle in the
Valais, Savagnin in the Vaud. With avoidance of
maceration, a white version of the Valais blend,
Dôle Blanche, is made. East of France's Jura is
Neuchâtel, where the local claim to fame is a
delicate Pinot Noir rosé, Oeil-de-Perdrix
("partridge-eye").

Ticino in the south is the Italian-speaking
section of Switzerland, interesting because its
production is overwhelmingly dominated by
Merlot reds. Some are light and grassy, others
have a bit of sinew to them, helped along by
judicious application of oak.

LUXEMBOURG

Müller-Thurgau (known here as Rivaner) and a
pallid-tasting variety called Elbling are backed
up by most of the Alsace varieties in Luxembourg's vineyards. Nearly all the wine is white,
with a little Pinot Noir for frail rosés, and is
labelled by variety. There is just one appellation,
Moselle Luxembourgeoise. Perhaps the most
interesting wine is Crémant de Luxembourg, a
denomination that came into effect in 1991 for
the country's champagne-method fizz, both
white and rosé. Quality is good, but you'll probably have to go to the Grand Duchy to taste it.

CZECH REPUBLIC/SLOVAKIA

Both halves of the former Czechoslovakia are
emerging, blinking, into the modern wine world
after decades of insularity under the state-controlled Soviet-bloc system. The Czech Republic
is the lesser of the two players as yet. Its vineyards are largely concentrated in the
southeastern region of Moravia, on the Austrian
and Slovakian borders, although an insignificant
quantity of wine is made north of Prague.

International varietals to look for are Cabernet Sauvignon and Pinot Noir for reds, and
Sauvignon Blanc, Pinot Blanc, Riesling and
Traminer (Gewürz) for whites. Sporadic plantings of the Austrian Grüner Veltliner, together
with Müller-Thurgau, are responsible for quite a
lot of Czech white. St Laurent makes appetizingly rustic red, and the violetty Blaufränkisch
crops up as Frankovka.

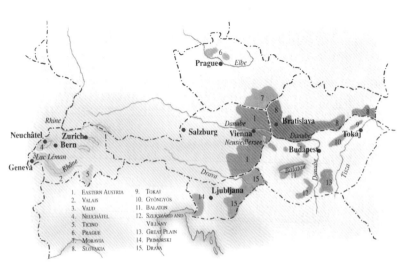

1. EASTERN AUSTRIA
2. VALAIS
3. VAUD
4. NEUCHÂTEL
5. TICINO
6. PRAGUE
7. MORAVIA
8. SLOVAKIA
9. TOKAJ
10. GYÖNGYÖS
11. BALATON
12. SZEKSZÁRD AND VILLÁNY
13. GREAT PLAIN
14. PRIMORSKI
15. DRAVA

Slovakia's vineyard regions extend in a virtually unbroken line along the country's southern borders, all the way from Austria to Russia. Varieties grown are mostly as in the Czech Republic. A local curiosity is the Irsay Oliver grape, which makes fragrantly graceful white wines, with more than a whiff of scented soap about them, especially in the Nitra region – strange but attractive. Pinot Gris does well too. As with its western neighbour, the principal impetus for Slovakia's improvement will be the visits of international wine consultants.

HUNGARY

Hungary was once famous only for Tokaji (previously spelt Tokay), occasionally great, often stalely oxidized, brown dessert wines that bore an uncanny resemblance to sherry. Produced in the northwest of the country, they are made in a range of styles, from basically dry to lusciously sweet. Tokaji is matured in large casks under a film of naturally formed yeast comparable to the *flor* of the Jerez region, hence the wines' similarity to sherry.

The sweeter styles, labelled Aszú, involve the addition to the base wine of rotted grapes pounded into a paste. They are measured out in custom-made hods called *puttonyos*; the label states the number added (from 3 *puttonyos* up to a sticky-sweet 7). Tokaji Essencia, sweetest of all, appears only in occasional vintages, and is made from free-run juice cask-aged for at least five years. Inward investment in the Tokaji region in the last few years, including French and German interests, has gone a long way to restoring the wines to their former exalted reputation.

As well as Tokaji, Hungary's table wines are gaining ground, again because of the initial input at key wineries by foreign producers. Hugh Ryman, born in Britain, trained in Australia, introduced a range of good dry white varietals, including Chardonnay and Sauvignon from Gyöngyös in northeast Hungary. The Balatonboglar winery, near Lake Balaton in the west, has turned out some well-made oaked Chardonnay, as well as a range of easy-drinking, top-value sparklers under the Chapel Hill label.

Most of the major varieties of Burgundy, Bordeaux and Alsace are now planted in Hungary, and are yielding encouraging results. Native white grapes include the Furmint and Hárslevelü used in Tokaji, but also in some straight dry whites, and the crisp but unremarkable Ezerjó. The principal red is Kadarka,

which makes beefy reds in the southern regions to the west of the Danube such as Szekszárd and Villány. (It is also the backbone of Bull's Blood, once thought the height of racy sophistication in Britain.) Blaufränkisch is successful as well; it is known in Hungarian as Kékfrankos.

SLOVENIA

The northwestern province of the old Yugoslavia became an independent country in 1991, neatly escaping the ravages of the war further south. It was from here that one of the biggest-selling wine brands of the 1970s came – the palatable but undistinguished Lutomer Laski Rizling, made from the Welschriesling grape common throughout central Europe. These days, Slovenian wine production is trying hard to enter the international quality league with a range of classic varietals. Expertise and influence are being absorbed from neighbouring Italy and Austria, in the Primorska and Drava regions respectively. Sipon (Hungary's Furmint), Sauvignon Blanc, Cabernet Sauvignon and Merlot are all doing well, while the best of the Muscat family – Muscat Blanc à Petits Grains – can make refreshing, simple sweet wines.

Vineyards at Nova Gora in Slovenia (above), one of central Europe's emergent wine nations.

Checking on the development of sweet Tokaji in the mould-coated cellars of the Tokaji Wine Trust, Hungary (above).

EASTERN EUROPE

Through the great empires of the Greeks, Byzantines and Ottomans who crossed Eastern Europe, the vine has flourished and faded. Centuries on, winemaking is again enjoying a new momentum.

AS WE MOVE TOWARDS the eastern fringes of Europe, we are nearing the birthplace of wine itself, the first homeland of the winemaking grape *Vitis vinifera*. If history ever paid lip-service to the notion of precedence, then Greece would have been the pre-eminent wine country in Europe ever since classical antiquity.

But it didn't happen that way. The Greeks took their expertise into Rome and parts of southern Europe, and the Roman Empire carried it on northwards and westwards. In time, the native varieties of what was to be France became the most highly prized of all wine grapes; the vineyards in which they grew were painstakingly selected for the most sympathetic matches of soil and climate, and French wine ascended to greatness.

In the Middle Ages, Greece became part of the Byzantine Empire. At this stage, it still had a thriving viticultural tradition, particularly on certain of its islands in the Aegean. One single piece of administrative short-sightedness in the

The swathe of Eastern Europe, crossing Bulgaria, Romania and Moldova, Turkey and Greece (below), offers a vast range of styles and native grape varieties.

11th century, however, was to undermine it for centuries to come. The Emperor Alexius decided to grant Venice, long since detached from Byzantium, favourable trading status in certain key cities of the Empire. From 1082, the Venetians were exempted from paying duties on commodities they exported to the east. As Greek wine, along with everything else, was thus deprived of the ability to compete, the entire economic edifice of the Empire came clattering about its ears.

When an enterprise becomes obsolete because others are able to practise it more cheaply, the inevitable decline is accompanied by a critical loss of skills and knowledge, even where they have been possessed for many generations. So it was with Greek wine. As the collapsing Byzantine Empire was overrun by the Ottoman Turks, its fate was sealed. The nation that had, in large measure, taught Europe how to make wine saw its viticulture regress to a helpless infancy that was to endure until the period after the Second World War.

In the eastern countries formerly in the Soviet sphere of influence, a quality wine industry was not seemingly viewed as anything approaching an economic necessity when the agricultural sector as a whole was so perennially fragile. The one exception was to be Bulgaria, where an experiment in flooding western markets with heavily subsidized state-produced wines was to be one of the more conspicuous economic successes of the Soviet era.

Today, eastern Europe is struggling somewhat to keep pace as wines from the Southern Hemisphere have caught the imaginations of British consumers in particular. Bulgaria and Romania are dedicated to the cause, however (the former still trading to some extent on its success in the 1970s and '80s), while Greece – with a little help from western friends – is learning all over again how to make good wine.

GREECE

When Greece joined the European Union in the 1980s, it had put in place an appellation system so devotedly modelled on the French that the

1.	MACEDONIA	13.	TROODOS
2.	THRACE	14.	ISTANBUL
3.	EPIRUS	15.	IZMIR
4.	THESSALY	16.	ANKARA
5.	PELOPONNESE	17.	KHAN KRUM
6.	CEPHALONIA	18.	SUHINDOL
7.	PAROS	19.	HASKOVO
8.	SANTORINI	20.	DAMIANITZA
9.	SAMOS	21.	MURFATLAR
10.	LEMNOS	22.	COTNARI
11.	RHODES	23.	TEREMIA
12.	CRETE		

French terms *appellation contrôlée* and *vin de pays* are often seen on labels. As in other countries, the better wines that have been treated to prolonged ageing in cask are named Reserve wines, again in French – Réserve or Grande Réserve. Table wines, including branded wines of dubious repute, make up the rest. There are now approaching 30 appellations throughout the country, from Macedonia in the north down to the island of Crete.

Macedonia and Thrace The northern regions are especially noted for red wines. Xynomavro is the main indigenous red grape, making intense, oak-aged, raisiny reds in Náoussa and Goumenissa. One of the first reds to be taken seriously in the early stages of the renaissance of Greek wine was Château Carras, from the slopes of Mount Meliton on the Thracian peninsula. Here, the great Bordeaux wine professor Emile Peynaud played a part in creating an authoritative Greek version of classic claret, based on good Cabernet Sauvignon. The result has been a new appellation, Côtes de Meliton, and subsequent feverish experimentation with blending French and local grape varieties. Prospects look extremely healthy.

Epirus and Thessaly Vineyards are rather thinly spread over the central regions of Greece. In the west, not far from the Albanian border, a local variety called Debina makes a slightly pétillant white wine at Zitsa. On the Aegean coast, the Xynomavro grape crops up again, this time in a blended, cask-aged red, Rapsani, made in the shadow of Mount Olympus. Further south, Ankhíalos is a crisp dry white made from native grapes Rhoditis and Savatiano, a combination also much favoured in retsina (see below).

Peloponnese The southern peninsula is home to more of Greece's appellations than any other zone. The extensive vineyards of Patras in the north produce wines that span the stylistic spectrum, from Patras itself, a light dry Rhoditis white, through fortified Muscat of Patras (made in the same way as Beaumes-de-Venise), to the fairly widely known Mavrodaphne, Greece's answer to port. Mavrodaphne is the name of the grape that plays the greatest part in the blend, and the vinification is the same as that for port. Extended cask-ageing is the norm, although the wine tends to retain its deep red colour. The best, such as those from the Kourtakis company, are a match for a good LBV.

At Nemea in the northeast, another good red grape – Agiorgitiko – comes into its own, mak-

ing full-bodied, concentrated, oaky reds at high altitudes. Some of the less good wine from this region is made slightly sweet.

On the central plateau of Mantinia, some of Greece's more arrestingly original wine is made from Moscophilero, one of the rare varieties of grapes that may accurately be classed as pink, rather than red or white. Most of the wine is a highly scented, viscous white full of musky orange aromas like a heavier version of dry Alsace Muscat. The pigmentation in the skin, however, means that a period of maceration can yield a full-fruited rosé.

Hot and dry, Cephalonia, in the Ionian Sea (left), makes both fortified and varietal white wines.

Picking Cabernet Sauvignon on the slopes of Mount Meliton, in Thrace (below), for the Château Carras red. Styled on claret, this wine marked the birth of Greece's modern wine industry.

Pruning vines (above). Old-fashioned methods still rule in many of Cyprus's remote hilltop vineyards.

Almond trees in blossom among the vines in the foothills of the Troodos mountains (below), home of Cyprus's legendary fortified sweet wine, Commandaria.

Greek islands In the Ionian Sea off the west coast of Greece, the island of Cephalonia makes its own versions of the fortified wines of Patras, as well as a strong-limbed, heavy-going varietal white from the northern Italian Ribolla, here called Robola.

The Cycladean islands of Paros and Santorini each have their respective appellations, the former for a red wine curiously blended from the red Mandelaria grape with some white Malvasia, the latter for a dry, refreshingly acid white made from the local Assyrtiko.

Greece's most celebrated fortified Muscats, from the top-flight Muscat Blanc à Petits Grains, come from two islands in the Aegean. Muscat of Samos, from the island just off the Turkish coast, is the better-known, and comes in a variety of styles from gently sweet to an almost unbearably concentrated nectar, made from fully raisined grapes. The version most often seen abroad is somewhere in the middle, a *vin doux naturel* like Beaumes-de-Venise. Further north, the island of Lemnos makes a similar style of sweet wine, as well as a small quantity of dry wine for local consumption and a resinated Muscat made like retsina.

Rhodes has a trio of appellations, representing different wine styles. The dry white is made from a grape called Athiri, the red is from the

Mandelaria seen on Paros, and there is also the inevitable dessert Muscat.

Crete, which has been making wine since early antiquity, has a good showing of native grape varieties. Peza, in the centre of the island, is the principal appellation, making both red and white wines from grapes such as red Liatiko and white Vilana.

Retsina The wine that was entirely synonymous with Greece in the early days of mass tourism was, for many, the very definition of the phrase "acquired taste". The style is based on techniques that date back to classical times, when the stone jars known as *amphorae* were lined with pine resin in order to preserve their contents. Today, however, retsina is a simple dry white wine that has had lumps of resin, specifically from the Aleppo pine, infused in it during its fermentation. It is made all over Greece, but principally in the area immediately around Athens to supply the tourist industry.

Retsina's improbable popularity among the first influx of tourists was perhaps based as much on its challengingly foreign nature as any genuine appreciation. It became well enough known to sell in the UK, however. Served extremely cold, in sherry-like quantities, it can be an interesting alternative, but a little does go a very long way.

CYPRUS

Winemaking on the island of Cyprus leaves much to be desired. Production is virtually cornered by four large industrial concerns whose installations are located near to the port of Limassol for easy export. That, of course, means that the vineyards themselves, mainly up in the hills, are far enough away to require temperature-controlled transportation, but this is a luxury not deemed entirely necessary in the cash-strapped Cypriot wine industry. There are very tentative signs of improvement, but Cyprus has no ready market for its wines since the end of its trade agreements with the old Soviet bloc.

Two indigenous grape varieties dominate the vineyards. Both could make reasonably good wine given half the chance. The red is Mavro, at its best when the wine is still fairly young and fresh; the white is Xynisteri, a bit of a rough diamond but certainly capable of giving wines with at least some aromatic personality. Southern French grape varieties, as well as the inevitable Chardonnay, are being tried, with reputedly encouraging results.

Melnik, in the torrid south-western region of Harsovo, Bulgaria (left). The native Melnik grape makes characterful, dark reds for ageing.

The only commercially visible Cypriot wines on the export markets were traditionally its sherry equivalents. Even they have had to contend with the banning in the EU from 1996 of the term "sherry" for anything other than the produce of Jerez. The sweet brown liquor was never going to win any prizes for subtlety, but there is some fino-style wine matured under *flor* and aged in a *solera* system, exactly like the best examples of the real thing. For those visiting the island these are worth seeking out.

As in other Mediterranean regions, Cyprus has a legendary, now little-known dessert wine. Commandaria, a fortified sweet wine made from sun-dried Mavro and Xynisteri grapes, is made in the foothills of the Troodos mountains. It is aged for a minimum of two years – often much longer – in casks, arranged in some cases into a *solera* system. After years of decline and abuse, the name was at last finally protected in an edict of 1993 that defined its geographical origin and method of production within strict guidelines. As other European fortified wines flounder, Commandaria could just be poised to make a well-deserved comeback.

TURKEY

Turkey's viticultural history goes back at least to Biblical times, when – as the story has it – Noah established the first vineyard on Mount Ararat after the Flood. Excavations in this area have lent strong support to the theory that some

of the very earliest systematic wine-growing did indeed arise here. Today, it is mostly very basic state-controlled slosh for the tourists that accounts for Turkey's efforts. There are plantings of some of the southern French grapes, and even Riesling and Pinot Noir, in the west of the country, while Anatolia produces wines from mainly indigenous varieties that can withstand the climatic extremes.

The privately owned Doluca company makes some half-decent reds and whites, but for the time being there is nothing like the level of expertise, or indeed will, to get Turkey off the ground as a significant producer. It will have to wait until the travelling circus of international winemaking consultants discovers its potential, at which point grape names like Papazkarasi and Oküzgözü may be on all our lips.

BULGARIA

Bulgaria's phenomenal export success in the 1970s and '80s was built on a winemaking tradition among the most venerable in the world. The Ottoman interdiction on alcohol consumption during the period that Bulgaria came under its sway contributed to a certain decline, but it was undoubtedly the investment in state-owned vineyards that communist Bulgaria initiated in the years after the Second World War that set the ball rolling once again.

A combination of uprooting and neglect, coupled with the economic upheaval following the

A truckload of freshly picked Chardonnay at Blatetz (above), in the sub-Balkan region of Bulgaria.

At Cernavoda, east of Constanta in Romania, the vineyards lie alongside the canal (above right).

reforms of the *Perestroika* era in the former Comecon countries, has led to troubled times for Bulgaria's wine industry. As the vineyards have been sold back into private hands, many smallholders cannot readily afford to ship their grapes to the central vinification plants established under the old state system. The result has been a considerable setback in terms of the quality of exported wine.

The equivalent of *appellation contrôlée* in Bulgaria is *Controliran*, denoting specific vineyard sites that may only grow approved grape varieties. There were getting on for 30 such designated areas by the 1990s. The varieties with which Bulgaria shot to prominence were classic French reds led by Cabernet Sauvignon and Merlot, together with a small amount of Pinot Noir (blended bizarrely with Merlot at the central Sliven winery). Whites included Chardonnay that could occasionally be good, in a fairly cheesy sort of way (from wineries like Khan Krum in the northeast), Sauvignon Blanc that tended to lack aromatic definition and rather flabby Riesling.

These are supplemented by some good native red grapes such as Mavrud and Melnik, which both give appetizingly meaty wines, and Gamza, which turns out to be the same as Hungary's grape Kadarka. Native white grapes are less inspiring, and include a variety called Dimiat of no noticeable character, which has

been crossed with Riesling to produce Misket, but still contrives to be resolutely tasteless. Welschriesling is there too.

The country divides into four basic regions, the eastern (including the Khan Krum and Schoumen wineries), northern (Suhindol, Svischtov, Russe), southern (Haskovo, Stambolovo, Assenovgrad) and southwestern (Damianitza, Harsovo). There are considerable climatic variations between them, the northern having the most temperate climate while the southwestern, bordering Greece, is pretty torrid. Some of the central wineries have, over the years, established reputations with particular varieties, such as the often distinctly claretty Cabernets of Russe and Svischtov, the voluptuously plummy Merlots of Stambolovo and the fiery Mavruds of Assenovgrad.

ROMANIA

Romania's vineyard regions are comprehensively scattered across the country, from Teremia in the west to Murfatlar on the Black Sea coast. The vast majority of the wine produced – even after the breaking of the economic deadlock with the fall of the Ceausescus – is still consumed within its borders, however.

There is now a drive to transform this picture by the accepted strategy of seeking western investment, which has begun to flow, and planting international varieties. In time, runs the

current consensus, Romania could become the most reliable producer of quality wine of all the old Comecon countries. Its climate is far more dependable than that of Bulgaria, for example, and it does have some excellent indigenous styles of wine.

Cabernet Sauvignon has established an extensive base all over the country, far more so than in Bulgaria, and there is some already famed Pinot Noir, together with Merlot, Welschriesling, Burgundy's Aligoté, Sauvignon Blanc and Pinot Gris. Two versions of a white grape called Feteascǎ represent the most widely planted varieties of all, and are used in some of the sweet wines in which Romania has a long and distinguished tradition. Tǎmaîioasǎ and Grasǎ are the two native ingredients of Cotnari, Romania's greatest and most assertively flavoured botrytized dessert wine, which is made in the northeast of the country, near the border with Moldova.

North of the capital Bucharest, the Dealul Mare region has made waves with its often sensational Pinot Noirs. At their most carefully vinified, they can be uncannily close to the style of good rustic burgundy. Cabernet and Merlot, meanwhile, have made some hearty reds in Babadag and Istria nearer the Black Sea. Lower down on the coast, Murfatlar also has a dessert wine tradition, but its wines are almost invariably less opulent than those of Cotnari, being much less prone to noble rot.

MOLDOVA

Moldova was an integral part of Romania until the USSR took a large bite of its eastern sector during the war. It is now an independent state, but one that retains strong cultural ties with Romania and speaks its language. Moldova's vineyards are hugely extensive and, like its western neighbour, it looks set fair to ascend the quality scale in time. A very catholic range of grape varieties is grown, including most of the major French names, some Russian varieties such as the white Rkatsiteli and the red Saperavi, plus a few of its own. Cabernet, Chardonnay and Sauvignon have inevitably been the first successful Moldovan wines seen in the west.

As well as promising table wines, Moldova also makes sparkling wine, together with some high-potential fortifieds similar both to sweet sherry styles and to the Liqueur Muscats of Australia. A small splash was made in the UK in the early 1990s with the importation of some deeply traditional, extensively aged red from the 1960s – Negru de Purkar and Roshu de Purkar. The wines were pretty oxidized and heavily browned, but some thought they detected in them something of the faded splendour of long-matured claret.

OTHER EASTERN EUROPEAN COUNTRIES

Wine is still of great commercial importance in the sections of the former Soviet Union that now comprise the Confederation of Independent States. As well as Moldova (see above), Russia, Belarus, the Ukraine and Georgia are the major producing areas. Rkatsiteli and Saperavi are the two principal indigenous varieties (white and red respectively), but there are also widespread plantings of Cabernet Sauvignon, Riesling and the Aligoté of Burgundy. Crimean reds were once celebrated far beyond the boundaries of the Ukraine, and may come to be once again if the investment currently flowing in begins to pay dividends.

Visitors to the old USSR may remember the great quantities of Soviet sparkling wine, fancifully referred to as *champanski*, that were available. Despite the name, the fizz was made by a technique known as the Russian Continuous Method. The yeast-boosted base wine was passed through a series of connected tanks over several weeks, depositing dead yeast cells as it went, until it emerged clarified and sparkling at the end. It is still produced in gargantuan quantities, the quality generally quite acceptable.

Hay-making in the Tîrnave region, in central Transylvania, Romania (left). The high, cool vineyards produce mainly white wines.

Gigantic fermentation tanks at the bulk-producing Sliven winery, Bulgaria (above), typify the large-scale postwar investment the country conferred on its wine industry.

MIDDLE EAST, NORTH AFRICA *and the* FAR EAST

Israel and Lebanon are extending their reputation with classic grape varieties, while the wines of North Africa and the Far East remain little-known beyond their borders.

Historic barrels outside the Carmel winery (right), a huge co-operative that produces most of Israel's wine.

BEYOND THE CONFINES of Europe is a handful of countries that have been making wine for centuries, small amounts of which may find their way into the export trade. In Israel and Lebanon, western know-how has contributed enormously to the creation of quality wines, while the north African countries, by and large, await the arrival of the flying winemakers.

ISRAEL

The modern Israeli wine industry was effectively founded by Baron Edmond de Rothschild, owner of Château Lafite in Bordeaux, in the late 19th century. He conferred on the returning Jewish settlers a huge endowment for agricultural purposes, including the establishment of vineyards for the production of kosher wine. For most of the 20th century, that was the industry's main concern: it was exported to Jewish communities worldwide. Since the beginning of the 1980s, however, Israel has moved to capitalize on its favourable grape-growing climate to produce an expanding range of wines for general consumers.

Carmel is the label most often seen on export markets. The fairly basic wines come from the first co-operative winery founded with the Rothschild money in the 1880s. Perhaps the most exciting development to date was the establishment of the Golan Heights winery in northern Israel. It makes a number of good international varietals – Cabernet Sauvignon, Chardonnay, Sauvignon Blanc and Riesling among them – under the brand names Golan, Gamla and (best of all) Yarden.

LEBANON

The story of Lebanese wine in recent times has basically been the story of the Château Musar winery in the Bekaa valley. Owner and winemaker Serge Hochar trained in Bordeaux and makes what is undoubtedly the region's most celebrated red wine, exporting virtually every bottle produced. A blend of Cabernet Sauvignon and Cinsaut, it is matured in both barrel and bottle for several years before release, and is a ferociously dark, intensely spicy and cedary wine with plenty of alcohol and a haunting, savoury character that lingers on the palate.

It is all the more remarkable for being made in the gruesome circumstances of invasion and civil war that, until recently, dogged the region. Hochar's winery has been shelled and, in one year, used as a bomb shelter by local villagers, but his tenacity is legendary and it is only in very occasional vintages that he has been prevented from making a wine altogether. He also makes small quantities of oaky white wine from a mixture of Chardonnay, Sauvignon and a local grape called Meroué. Ksara is another Bekaa winery exporting to western Europe.

Lebanon's Bekaa Valley and Israel's Golan Heights (below), in the Middle East, offer especially favourable climes for grape-growing.

Beirut

Tel Aviv
Jerusalem

1. BEKAA VALLEY
2. GOLAN HEIGHTS
3. GALILEE
4. SHOMRAN
5. SAMSON
6. JUDEAN HILLS
7. NEGEV

Ploughing a young vineyard at Enfidaville, Tunisia (left). Most of the country's vines are southern French varieties.

NORTH AFRICA

Algeria's vineyards are principally concentrated on the Mediterranean coast in the northwest of the country. It was once a hugely important bulk producer, sending much of its wine north to the former colonial power, France, where a lot of it undoubtedly ended up in bottles that bore impeccably French labels. Algerian viticulture is now declining, largely as a result of the onward march of Islamic fundamentalism. This may well reduce its industry to an export-only business, in which case it will collapse the more rapidly since external markets will be very hard to find.

Not since the launch in the 1970s of the colourfully named brand Red Infuriator has anyone paid much attention to Algerian wine. Its winemaking goes back to antiquity, although it has suffered in the modern era from under-investment. One of its better inland regions, the Coteaux de Mascara, makes cheerfully abrasive reds from a fistful of southern French grape varieties.

Morocco's wine industry benefits from intensive tourism, producing a fairly broad range of French varietals, including Cabernet Sauvignon, Syrah, Chenin Blanc and Chardonnay, for the holiday crowds. To show it means business in the quality stakes, it has devoted the most assiduous effort of all the north African countries to honing its nascent appellation system (AOG, or *appellation d'origine garantie*) to approximate to European standards. Low-priced raisiny reds, typified by the palatable Domaine de Cigogne seen recently in British retailers, are the norm, and there is a little Cinsaut rosé as well. The honeyed fortified Muscat de Berkane could well turn out to be an eye-catcher in the future.

Tunisia also has tourists' thirsts to slake, and does so with pretty rough-and-ready red and rosé wines, again made largely from southern

French grape varieties. Whites include a rather leaden dry Muscat (made from the less good Muscat of Alexandria). For the time being, it probably needs to be sipped ice-cold in order to taste good, but if vinification practices improve, it may win converts abroad.

INDIA, CHINA AND JAPAN

India's repute as a wine producer rests solely on the sparkling wine of Maharashtra, Omar Khayyam, launched with expertise from the champagne house Piper Heidsieck. It can be appetizingly full, dry and nutty but has been too variable for commercial comfort.

China is awash with native grape varieties and has plenty of good vineyard land, but so far not much in the way of solid viticultural knowledge. The state wineries produce sweetened-up plonk for a country that naturally prefers grain wine like *shaoshing*, made from rice. However, French and Australian money is coming in, and enterprises like the Huadong winery at Qingdao are testing the international waters with varietal Chardonnay, Riesling and the like.

Japan makes grape wine on three of its four islands (with northern Hokkaido having the largest plantings), although local predilections have only recently made it a viable industry. Japanese investors have in recent years discovered a taste for the finest wines of France, in the sense that some are actually drinking them now rather than merely buying and selling them. Giant industrial concerns such as Suntory have been responsible for much of the investment to date. The country's own vineyards are, for the time being, hampered by the fact that they are largely planted with north American hybrid grape varieties, which can give some very peculiar flavours, but tastebuds weaned on *sake* may not mind that.

Vineyard worker thinning out grape bunches in early summer (above) in Suntory-owned vineyards, Japan.

REST OF THE WORLD

Vine leaves reddening with the onset of autumn in the Napa Valley, California (above).

The dramatic landscape of Marlborough, New Zealand (below).

No single factor has done more to change the world of wine in the modern era than the advent of wines and winemakers from North America and the Southern Hemisphere. These are the countries that comprise a great unwieldy region still known as the "New World" in many European minds.

For a time, the presence of wines from California and Australia in the major wine markets of Europe was blithely ignored by winemakers in the old countries, especially the French. What have we to fear, they asked themselves, from the products of wine cultures invented no more than 150 years ago in some cases, when we've been at it for centuries? The answer, as always, lay in the bottle.

In the end it wasn't sheer novelty value that induced wine consumers, the British in particular, to turn to the wines from these new countries so enthusiastically. That would have worn off in time in any case. It was the fact that the wine tasted so exuberant.

Australia led the way with its Chardonnay and Cabernet. Whether it was the staggeringly rich, sunny, butterscotch flavours of the one or the velvet-soft, creamy blackcurrant essence of the other, no European wine had ever tasted like this. And not only were the wines largely free of the tart, unripe acidity or the hard, mouth-furring tannins of the European run-of-the-mill

offerings, their fruit flavours were so appealingly easy to understand.

To capitalize on that instantly recognizable taste profile, the new wines were varietally labelled. Consumers came to see that Chardonnay meant lemon and butter and maybe vanilla, Cabernet was blackcurrants and plums and perhaps some melted chocolate, Pinot was raspberries and cherries, Sauvignon was gooseberries, and so on. By emphasizing those fruit characteristics, the so-called New World wines did a valuable job in educating people in one of the essential factors that influence the way wines taste – the grape types they are made from.

Although the term "New World" may understandably have offended the sensibilities of American winemakers who didn't see the logic in bracketing them with Australians and vice versa, the concept did in one sense do everybody a favour. Consumers came to believe there was such a thing as a New World style, one that was in direct contrast to anything they might find in Europe. This led them to try the wines of far more countries than they would otherwise have done had the style been fixed as, say, Australasian. The common identifying factor was that varietal labelling.

In this way, the non-European winemaking countries kicked down the door and started to rewrite the rules. It wasn't simply that many of these wines came from places that had good, reliable climates in which the annual vintage was usually nothing like the lottery that the French have to contend with. There were new approaches in the vineyards and wineries that were playing an integral part in shaping the flavours of the wines: cold fermentations, artificial yeast cultures, stainless-steel tanks instead of huge age-old casks, cold maceration of red grapeskins in the juice before fermentation to extract maximum concentration, sterile bottling conditions.

Some of these techniques were in use among quality-conscious European winemakers, to be sure, but the generality still worked exactly as their forebears had done, by picking the grapes at a predetermined time, pressing as much juice as possible out of them and closing the lid on the cask to let nature get on with it.

Nowadays, the once entrenched opposition between old and new ways is becoming a meeting of minds. Château Lafite's Gilbert Rokvam winters in Chile, South Australia's Geoff Merrill does Teroldego in Trentino, his compatriot Peter Bright works wonders in Portugal, while

Moët et Chandon – one of the biggest wine names of all – now makes bubbles not just in Champagne, but in California, Australia and Spain. The world of wine is becoming a global vineyard.

There are some who regret this and seek to blame the New Worlders for what they see as the creeping internationalization of wine. If it hadn't been for them, hallowed traditions would have remained undisturbed.

What the complaint about standardization is in danger of ignoring, though, is that the greatest individual wines of old Europe were the very ones that most people never knew because they couldn't afford them. What they were left with was the mediocrity and the outright dross. If California Chardonnay and Australian Cabernet helped to elbow aside the likes of the ropiest St-Véran and the bitterest Bordeaux Supérieur, then they did us all a good turn. But more than any of us, they did the Burgundians and the

Bordelais a favour because they put a bomb under the complacency that was steadily crushing the life out of those regions.

That said, it would be remiss not to deplore the growing homogenization of international wine that the non-European countries are largely responsible for. When a glass of pale, lightly oaked, reasonably ripe Chardonnay tastes as though it could have been made absolutely anywhere, then something has been lost, and a major point about wine's individuality is being missed.

What should give us hope is that winemakers in the United States and Australia particularly are trying their hands at grapes that have previously only enjoyed minority acclaim in their birthplaces. Napa Valley Barbera, Oregon Pinot Gris, Barossa Grenache and Victorian Marsanne represent the strongest evidence to date that the new countries are intent on breaking the mould again. Watch this space.

California poppies, the state flower (above), provide a splash of colour beneath the wire-trained vines of Kenwood Vineyards, Sonoma County.

South Australia's Clare Valley (left), splashed with spring flowers and newly planted vineyards.

UNITED STATES

Enthusiasm and the willingness to experiment has brought great success to the winemaking states of North America. Led by California and the Pacific Northwest, America's vineyards have made a great impact on wine-drinkers around the world.

The US's top winemaking regions are centred on the west coast, in California, Washington and Oregon, but other areas are gaining reputations for fine wines.

ALTHOUGH THE contemporary wine industry in the USA dates back only to the first half of the 19th century, Nature always intended the States to be a wine producer. Exactly whose ship made the earliest landfall at precisely which spot may never be known, but the Norse settlers who discovered the North American continent a millennium ago christened the place Vinland, after the wild vines that luxuriantly carpeted the lands on the eastern seaboard.

The first permanent European settlements were not established until the late 1500s, and it was to be fully two centuries later before anything like an embryo wine industry could be identified. By this time the settlers included Germans, Spaniards, Italians and Greeks. What dogged the early attempts was the realization that the vines that grew wild in America were not *Vitis vinifera*, the European wine grape species, but a collection of weird and mostly unwonderful native species, such as *Vitis labrusca*, *Vitis riparia* and *Vitis rupestris*. Wines made from these are nothing like *vinifera* wines; they often have a strangely animal smell to them, for which the common coinage for many years was "foxy".

Once the problem was identified, colonists from the wine countries decided that all they needed to do was to ship over some of their good old *vinifera* vinestock from home, and start again. They reckoned without a whole host of pests and diseases that were at that happy time unknown in European viticulture. Various forms of mildew and rot, as well as the devasting phylloxera vine louse, which feeds on sap in the vine's roots with fatal consequences, visited the first *vinifera* vines in America like the ten plagues of Egypt. And as if all that weren't enough, many decades of trial and heartbreaking error went into finding the right climatic zones in which the European varieties could survive.

Initially, the answer seemed to lie in cultivating hybrid mixtures of *vinifera* and one of the American species, the hybrids first occurring by chance cross-fertilization, and then as a result of deliberate botanical engineering. Such magical names of 19th-century American viticulture as the Catawba, Isabella and Concord grape varieties, hybrids all, might have remained the whole story of wine in the USA, were it not for the annexation of the Spanish colonies in the south and west. The Spanish had been practising relatively trouble-free *vinifera* cultivation in what is now New Mexico, and to a lesser extent California, for generations.

One of the key pioneers of the period was a central European entrepreneur, Agoston Haraszthy, who arrived in California just in time to grab a piece of the Gold Rush action. Although not quite the undisputed godfather of California wine that some of the histories have portrayed him as, Haraszthy did undeniably exert a seminal influence in the expansion of winemaking in the state. Apart from anything else, he was responsible for shipping cuttings of many European grape varieties into the region, then struggling to make the best of less than brilliant performers such as Mission, an indigenous South American grape brought northwards by the Spanish to provide the California monasteries with communion wine. (It is still widely grown in Chile, where they call it País.)

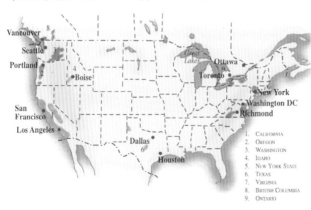

Vancouver 8
Seattle 3
Portland
Boise 4
San Francisco
Los Angeles
Dallas 6
Houston
Great Lakes
Ottawa 9
Toronto
New York
Washington DC
Richmond

1. CALIFORNIA
2. OREGON
3. WASHINGTON
4. IDAHO
5. NEW YORK STATE
6. TEXAS
7. VIRGINIA
8. BRITISH COLUMBIA
9. ONTARIO

The flat valley floor of Salinas in California's Monterey County (left). Monterey is cool, yet one of the state's most prolific grape-growing areas.

In the 20th century, the emerging American wine industry was dealt a near-fatal blow by the advent of Prohibition in 1920. Although vineyards were kept going for the production of grape concentrate, used to make non-alcoholic juice, the expertise the winemakers had acquired withered on the vine. The banning of alcohol lasted just long enough – 13 years – for the bare bones of the US wine industry to have crumbled to virtually nothing. As a result, it was to take another four decades before first California, and then the United States as a whole, assumed its rightful place as a major player on the world wine scene.

Even now, American winemakers are not without their problems. Falling sales in recent years have meant that their quality wines have become increasingly expensive, both at home and abroad. California is still recovering from a further outbreak of phylloxera – the old enemy – in the 1990s. It is a very difficult pest to detect in advance, both because it is microscopically small and because it mainly lives underground, sucking on the vines' roots, and so the first you tend to know about it is when your vines start looking brown and shrivelled. Once things have gone that far, there is no alternative but to pull them up and replant at great expense.

Perhaps most perniciously of all, there is a new mood of Prohibitionism in the United States. It is more virulent and hysterical than anything seen in Europe, where even France has succumbed to controls on alcohol advertising. The hidden agenda of the anti-alcohol campaigners, who have already won the battle to label wine-bottles with health warnings, is to stop others from exercising freedom of choice.

Hope, however, springs eternal in the winemaker's heart, as any European grower studying the summer weather forecasts can attest. The economy will turn around as the wineries' prices moderate to keep pace with the foreign competition. Phylloxera is being vanquished once more as the new vines are grafted on to hardier, more resistant rootstocks. And when American TV showed a documentary programme about the findings of Dr. Serge Renaud, the Lyon cardiologist who has established that wine plays a definite part in reducing the risk of coronary heart disease, consumers all over the country turned back, albeit briefly, to drinking red wine in healthy quantities.

A further sign of the increasing maturity of the industry came in 1983, when the United States began to implement a sort of appellation system consisting of geographically defined American Viticultural Areas (AVAs). Although that wording does not as yet appear on the labels, the system decrees that wines using the individual AVA names must be made from no less than 85 per cent of grapes grown in that area.

There are many who say that the USA is probably foremost among the non-European winemaking countries now: for the diversity its regions are capable of, its willingness to absorb the lessons of that old French concept *terroir* in choosing the best grape varieties for each specific site, instead of just planting cash-crop Cabernet and Chardonnay everywhere, and in terms of the sheer dynamism its winemakers are driven by. There appear to be no vinous challenges these days the Americans are unwilling to take on, and if that isn't the authentic pioneering spirit, I don't know what is.

Modern technology in the vineyard and winery includes sterile winemaking equipment such as this crusher-destemmer (above).

California's own red grape variety, Zinfandel, arriving at the winery (above).

California's wine country (below) stretches the length of the state. Vineyards are planted on cool, hillside sites, in hot, inland valleys and close to the ocean.

CALIFORNIA

To say that the state of California is at the epicentre of the United States wine industry would be something of an understatement. Nine out of every ten bottles of American wine come from there. From Mendocino County north of San Francisco to the San Diego and Imperial Valley areas on the Mexican border, it's wine country practically all the way. Cross the Golden Gate Bridge heading north out of San Fran, and you soon enter the Napa Valley, California's Bordeaux, where it's difficult to find anybody growing anything other than vines. From world-class champagne-method sparklers to idiosyncratic fortified Muscats and even brandy – if it's possible to make it, California does.

For a long time, all the European markets ever saw was pretty basic stuff, known as "jug wine" in its homeland for the inelegant flagons it used to be packaged in. Paul Masson was one of the more visible brands in the UK, as often as not sold in de-alcoholized versions that didn't win many friends. E & J Gallo of Modesto was another large brand. Founded by two brothers in

the wake of Prohibition's repeal, it had become the largest wine producer in America by the middle of the century, and is now the biggest on the planet. Gallo now has some ambitious wines, but the backbone of its commercial success was unashamed jug wine.

The revolution began in the 1970s, in 1976 to be precise, when, at a comparative tasting in Paris, two California wines – a Chardonnay and a Cabernet – beat all comers in a scrupulously blind taste-off. They were Chateau Montelena Chardonnay 1973 and Stag's Leap Cabernet Sauvignon 1973, their names forever deserving to be invoked because they sparked the tidal wave that swept California wine into Europe. What was so indigestible to the French was that, quite apart from the fact that many *cru classé* clarets and *grand cru* white burgundies were relegated to runner-up status, it was the French themselves that did it. There were no American judges. There could be no greater plaudit.

Since then, California has gone from strength to strength. It is beyond any doubt one of the most innovative wine-growing regions on earth and is now set fair to startle us all – not just the French – with what it can do.

As in most of the wine regions outside Europe, California is making the running with international, largely French, grape varieties. The rollcall includes Chardonnay and Cabernet Sauvignon, of course, the hugely fashionable Merlot (which has established a varietal reputation for itself as a sort of Cabernet without tears), some of the finest Pinot Noir anywhere (including Burgundy), cool, crisp Riesling, some often ill-defined Sauvignon Blanc and small amounts of jet-black Syrah.

Its one peculiar claim to fame is a red variety called Zinfandel. In recent years, the cautious theory that the grape was the same as a southern Italian variety seen in and around Puglia, where they rather unfeelingly call it Primitivo, seems to have firmed up into confident fact. It could very well have been brought over by Italian settlers as early as the 18th century, and was certainly in currency at the onset of modern California viticulture in the mid-1800s.

Styles of Zinfandel wine vary. There is a lot of deeply coloured purple-red wine of high alcohol and tremendous fruit concentration, displaying ripe berry flavours like blueberries, together with something strangely herbal (sometimes even compared to fresh tea leaves). Some is much lighter, made in a quasi-

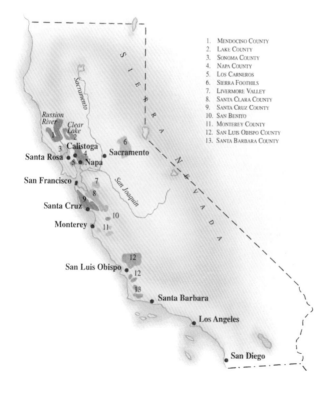

1. MENDOCINO COUNTY
2. LAKE COUNTY
3. SONOMA COUNTY
4. NAPA COUNTY
5. LOS CARNEROS
6. SIERRA FOOTHILS
7. LIVERMORE VALLEY
8. SANTA CLARA COUNTY
9. SANTA CRUZ COUNTY
10. SAN BENITO
11. MONTEREY COUNTY
12. SAN LUIS OBISPO COUNTY
13. SANTA BARBARA COUNTY

Beaujolais idiom, and not generally as impressive. Then there is a usually slightly sweet pink style called "blush", which can be as refreshing as raspberry-ripple ice-cream, and just as sickly taken in quantity.

Enterprising growers are trying their hands at almost anything that takes their fancy, from native Italian and Spanish varieties to Rhône-style Viognier and the aromatic grapes of Alsace.

Mendocino and Lake Counties These two counties, through which runs the Russian River, lie at the northern end of California wine country. Mendocino, on the Pacific coast, encompasses a very broad range of micro-climates as it extends inland, meaning that the styles of wine produced take in everything from delicately spiced Gewürztraminer and lightly leafy Sauvignon to big, meaty Cabernets and Zinfandels. As far as defined AVAs (American Viticultural Areas) go, there is one large catchall designation for the whole of Mendocino, within which are three valley areas – the coastal

Anderson and inland McDowell and Potter.

In Lake County to the east, Clear Lake is the main AVA, with the smaller Guenoc Valley, consisting of only one winery of the same name, founded around the time of the Great War. Lake County, being that much smaller than Mendocino, is climatically less diverse, but has built a reputation for pleasantly green-fruited Sauvignons and soft, approachable Cabernets.

MENDOCINO PRODUCERS: Fetzer (the biggest Mendocino winery, making a fistful of fine varietals, including nutmeggy organic Bonterra Chardonnay, juicy Barrel Select Cabernet, damson-rich Pinot Noir and gorgeously brambly Zinfandel), Jepson Vineyards, Parducci, Handley Cellars and Roederer (the last two producing fine champagne-method Chardonnay-Pinot fizz).

LAKE PRODUCERS: Kendall-Jackson (whose fine, savoury Chardonnay comes from vineyards much further south in Santa Barbara), Konocti (good smoky Sauvignon), Guenoc (for Chardonnays and red and white Bordeaux blends called Meritage in California).

The herb garden at Fetzer winery (below), in Mendocino County, planted with hundreds of varieties of herbs.

(Above) State-of-the-art sparkling winemaking at Domaine Chandon, in Napa Valley, owned by champagne house Moët & Chandon (right). The fertile valley floor of Napa Valley is considered by many to be the state's premier site for Cabernet and Chardonnay.

Sonoma Sonoma is a coastal county north of San Francisco Bay, encompassing a valley of the same name that forms its main sub-region. For a long time, the Sonoma region existed in the shadow of its eastern neighbour, Napa County, but its growers and wineries have worked assiduously to define its undeniable potential for quality, now reflected in ten demarcated AVAs.

The Alexander Valley AVA has seen the most intensive programme of plantings in Sonoma in the last quarter-century. Grape varieties that grow nowhere near each other in France flourish here in happy proliferation. The Simi winery makes one of northern California's more diverting Chardonnays here, while Jordan Vineyards has hit the headlines with an elegant champagne-method sparkler called "J".

The Sonoma Valley AVA itself includes some of California's oldest wineries, such as Buena Vista (established in the 19th century by the pioneering Mr Haraszthy) and Sebastiani. Running north to south, the valley is blessed with subtle gradations of microclimate as it moves away from the cooling influence of the Bay. This means that a highly disparate range of grapes can be grown. At the southern end, it takes in a section of the celebrated Carneros region, which it shares with Napa County (see below).

One of the coolest Sonoma areas is the Russian River Valley, which forms its own AVA within Sonoma County. The impact of the morning fogs that roll in off the Bay is most keenly felt here, with the result that Pinot Noir is notably successful (especially from practitioners like Williams-Selyem, Dehlinger, Iron Horse and Rod Strong). Chardonnay can be superbly balanced from the likes of De Loach, and there is fine sparkling wine too.

Dry Creek Valley AVA, formed around a little tributary of the Russian River, is making a name for itself with some sharply delineated Sauvignon from Preston and Dry Creek Vineyards, as well as one of the more memorable Zinfandels from Quivira. The other AVAs are Chalk Hill, Knights Valley, Sonoma-Green Valley, Sonoma Coast, Sonoma Mountain and Northern Sonoma (the last an important redoubt of E&J Gallo).

OTHER GOOD SONOMA WINERIES: Laurel Glen, Chateau St Jean, Arrowood, Ravenswood, Carmenet, Kenwood.

Napa If California is the premier state for American wine, the Napa Valley is its regional frontrunner. So much land has been planted with vines that the area is almost at capacity, forming a virtual grape monoculture. The Napa is the Côte d'Or of California, if such comparisons can mean anything. Like Burgundy's best

patch, it is barely more than 20 miles from end to end, but embraces a dizzying degree of climatic variation. As with Sonoma, the southern end near the Bay is relatively cool and foggy, while the northern end at Calistoga is fiercely hot.

The overall Napa AVA was, by the mid-1990s, being organized into a string of smaller appellations, based on the main towns along the valley highway. From north to south, they will be Calistoga, St Helena, Rutherford, Oakville, Yountville and Napa. Some of the very best Chardonnays, Cabernets and Merlots are made along this trail, varying in style as much because of their geographical location and altitude as because of the philosophies of individuals. A rollcall of the great and the very great would have to take in Robert Mondavi, Heitz Cellars, Niebaum-Coppola (owned by Francis Ford Coppola of cinematic fame), Beaulieu Vineyards, Beringer, Swanson and many others.

Other Napa AVAs are the qualitatively important Stags Leap District, just to the north of the town of Napa (including fine Cabernets and Merlots from Stag's Leap Winery itself, Clos du Val and Shafer), Howell Mountain in the east of the valley (where La Jota makes some sensationally concentrated Cabernet), Mount Veeder, between Napa and Sonoma (with the Hess Collection producing its most distinguished

Chardonnays and Cabernets), and the emerging Wild Horse Valley, east of Napa itself.

OTHER GOOD NAPA WINERIES: Newton, Silverado, Caymus, Joseph Phelps, ZD, Vichon, Grgich Hills, Silver Oak, Trefethen, Cuvaison, Duckhorn, Franciscan. Domaine Mumm's Cuvée Napa and Schramsberg are the two leading producers of champagne-method sparkling wine.

Carneros The Carneros district overlaps the southern ends of both the Napa and Sonoma regions and forms a distinctive AVA of its own. Being immediately to the north of San Francisco Bay, its climate is continually influenced by the dawn fogs that roll in from the Pacific, often not clearing until around mid-morning. They mitigate the ferocious heat of summer to such a degree that Carneros qualifies as one of the coolest areas on average in all of California.

It shot to prominence in the 1980s for a handful of exquisitely crafted Pinot Noirs and Chardonnays from wineries such as Acacia, Saintsbury and Carneros Creek. The quality of the Pinots in particular – angular in youth, but packed with deep red fruit and roasted meat intensity – served notice that the citadel of Burgundian Pinot was about to be stormed.

Carneros has developed a reputation as a good producer of sparkling wines as well, with the champagne house Taittinger (Domaine Carneros) and cava producer Codorníu (Codorniu Napa) representing the European vote of confidence.

Sierra Foothills The foothills of the Sierra Nevada mountain range that forms the border with the state of Nevada encompass some of the oldest vineyard land in California, dating from the Gold Rush that began in 1849. Within the overall Foothills AVA are a number of subdivisions. El Dorado County forms one, while Amador County to the south takes in Shenandoah Valley and Fiddletown. The usual diversity of grapes is grown, but the acreage of Zinfandel vines is among California's more venerable. The North Yuba AVA consists only of the Renaissance winery, famed for delicate Rieslings and Sauvignons and a totally contrasting Cabernet – a pitch-black study in rip-roaring tannins.

Livermore Valley East of the Bay in Alameda County, the Livermore Valley AVA was historically famed for its Bordeaux-style white blends, but has since followed the path of California diversity. One of the Livermore's oldest wineries is the 100-year-old Wente Brothers, acclaimed now for its best cuvées of Chardonnay as well as some tasty sparkling wines.

Clos Pegase, in Napa Valley (above). This striking modern building contains not only the winery but an art gallery too.

New vines waiting to bud against a stark California landscape at Au Bon Clinat, Santa Barbara (above).

Vineyards of Wente Brothers in Livermore Valley (above), east of San Francisco Bay in Alameda County.

Santa Clara Valley South of Alameda, the Santa Clara Valley is now rather more about micro-electronics than wine, although it was one of the first AVAs. Ridge Vineyards is the big name around here: winemaker Paul Draper makes succulent Montebello Cabernets and a show-stopping Lytton Springs Zinfandel, from Sonoma grapes. The Mount Eden winery is, among others, keeping the flag flying with top-notch bottlings of Cabernet and Chardonnay.

Santa Cruz A coastal AVA south of the city of San Francisco, the Santa Cruz mountain vineyards have been a notably dynamic contributor to the California scene. This was one of the first regions to try producing great Pinot Noir, the proximity to the ocean making its climate cool enough not to overstress that notoriously fragile variety. Now all sorts of grapes have moved in, many of them under the creative aegis of Randall Grahm at the Bonny Doon winery. His entertainingly off-the-wall labels and wine names announce some genuinely original wines. Plantings of Marsanne, Roussanne, Syrah, Grenache and Mourvèdre, just as everyone else was going hell-for-leather with Cabernet, earned him the nickname of the Rhône Ranger, and helped to blaze a particularly fruitful trail. If it's Cabernet you're after, though, Klein Vineyards and Ahlgren make some of the most opulent.

San Benito San Benito is a smallish inland wine region west of Fresno, whose brightest star is Calera Vineyards. Calera's Josh Jensen is the sole proprietor in the tiny San Benito AVA of Mount Harlan, where he produces hauntingly scented Mills Vineyard Pinot Noir, a lovely, buttercream Chardonnay and the most extraor-

dinary Viognier made anywhere in the world outside Condrieu. It sells for about the same sort of giddy price as Condrieu, but the aromatic intensity of the wine is powerfully persuasive.

Monterey County Monterey, on the so-called Central Coast, is marked by both coolness and aridity, so that grape-growing has always been something of a challenge. Notwithstanding that, the county is one of the more densely planted California regions. Cool-climate grapes such as Pinot Noir, Riesling and even Chenin Blanc are now doing well there. Within its all-encompassing AVA, there are three flagship zones with their own designations that represent Monterey's premier division: Chalone, Arroyo Seco and Carmel Valley. The first of those is home to Chalone Vineyards, maker of benchmark Chardonnay, surprisingly full Pinot Blanc and richly gamey Pinot Noir.

San Luis Obispo The next AVA along the coast south of Monterey is San Luis Obispo. The county covers the climatic extremes, with the most highly regarded wines tending to come from the cooler coastal areas such as Edna Valley, which enjoys its own AVA. The Edna Valley winery makes pace-setting Chardonnay here. North of Edna is the large, elevated plain of Paso Robles, where the fiercer conditions are better for Cabernet and Zinfandel. South of the Edna Valley, in the Arroyo Grande AVA, the champagne house Deutz has established one of its overseas outposts, Maison Deutz (the other is in New Zealand).

Santa Barbara The southernmost of the Central Coast wine counties is fog-shrouded Santa Barbara, not far north of Los Angeles. Its best vineyards congregate in the two valleys that constitute the AVA land: Santa Maria and Santa Ynez. Both enjoy the cooling influence of the ocean and make good showings of Pinot Noir and Chardonnay, much as Carneros does, as well as some crisply textured Sauvignon and Riesling. Au Bon Climat and Sanford wineries have set a tough standard with their effortlessly concentrated, raspberry-fruited Pinots, while Zaca Mesa has done improbably good things with Syrah and Byron Vineyards scores highly for Sauvignon and Chardonnay.

In the south of the state, three regions of no enormous viticultural significance are located: Riverside County (which includes the Temecula AVA), San Diego County (including the tiny San Pasqual Valley AVA) and the inland Imperial Valley.

PACIFIC NORTHWEST

Three states in the far northwest of the USA have emerged in recent years from the long shadow cast by California's status as the Number One wine region in America. Of the three, it is the challenging climatic circumstances of Oregon that have caused the most excitement so far, but Washington State and – to a much lesser extent – Idaho are now making strong showings as well. From here will come the next wave of American wines to break upon European shores in significant volumes.

Oregon Although *Vitis vinifera* vines were first planted in Oregon over a century ago, it is only comparatively recently that the state's potential as a quality wine producer has been taken seriously. Even then, it was in the face of considerable scepticism from their southern neighbours in California that a handful of indomitable visionaries put their state on the world wine map. The picture began to change when a vintage of David Lett's Eyrie Vineyards Pinot Noir wiped the floor with a few red burgundies in an international blind tasting.

Pinot Noir, the Holy Grail of aspirant winemakers everywhere at the time, became the Oregon buzz wine *par excellence*, so much so that there are probably too many growers producing mediocre Pinot reds when they could be giving a better account of themselves with something easier. Alsace varieties have done remarkably well, providing some dry, spicy, fragrant wines from Riesling, Gewürztraminer and – most successfully of all – Pinot Gris.

One long valley area dominates Oregon production – the Willamette Valley. It occupies a northwestern corner of the state, near the Pacific coast, and enjoys the kinds of cool growing conditions that are to be found in parts of northern France. All of the finest Oregon producers are located here. Adelsheim, Ponzi and Eyrie make full-blown, creamy Pinot Gris (Eyrie is also tops for Chardonnay with its subtle, baked apple-flavoured Reserve bottling).

As to the celebrated Pinot Noirs, Elk Cove, Bethel Heights, Ponzi, Argyle and Sokol Blosser all make state-of-the-art, sweetly cherryish but ageworthy wines. Burgundy négociant Robert Drouhin bought a piece of Oregon real estate after absorbing the Eyrie Vineyards lesson in the '70s. His daughter Véronique has been making Pinot at the Oregon Domaine Drouhin since 1991, and has propelled it into a sharp upward swing.

Washington State In volume terms, Washington's production of *Vitis vinifera* wine is second only to that of California, and some say it is also first runner-up for quality. The two halves of the state are, climatically, chalk and cheese. While the seaward side has temperate, dampish conditions, the eastern half has sweltering summers and unforgivingly cold winters.

Notwithstanding that, nearly all the vineyard land is in the east, where the overall Columbia Valley AVA accounts for most of the wine produced. An important sub-region of Columbia – the Yakima Valley AVA – is home to some of the state's oldest vineyards.

Cabernet, and particularly Merlot, have proved themselves adept at coping with the climatic torments of eastern Washington, and generally yield round, emphatically fruity wines that are drinkable quite early on. Riesling, perhaps surprisingly, does well, and can produce outstandingly graceful dry and medium-dry styles – it seems a shame that the variety isn't especially popular among American consumers.

The inevitable Chardonnay, however, sells like hot cakes, and good, gently buttery stuff it is too. Semillon, not previously much lauded in the USA, looks like becoming something of a fad in Washington; the style is somewhat similar to the minerally dry, unoaked examples of Australia's Hunter Valley.

Oregon's cool Willamette Valley (above) dominates the state's wine industry, with the top producers clustered at the northern end of the valley.

While Oregon's vineyards lie close to the ocean, Washington's major wine regions are in the east, where the temperatures are more extreme, as in neighbouring Idaho (below).

1. WILLAMETTE VALLEY
2. COLUMBIA VALLEY
3. YAKIMA VALLEY

Half of all Washington production is accounted for by one giant combine, Stimson Lane, which puts out wines under a number of labels such as Columbia Crest, Chateau Ste Michelle, Snoqualmie and so forth. Quality is good, if rarely idiosyncratic. Best of the smaller wineries include Hogue Cellars (which makes a beautifully subtle, lightly oaked Chardonnay), Staton Hills and Kiona (look for its delightfully well-made late-harvest sweet wines from the Alsace varieties Muscat, Gewürztraminer and Riesling).

Idaho Washington's eastern neighbour shares much the same climate as the Columbia Valley, except that Idaho's vineyards are planted at very high altitudes, making winter conditions here extremely severe. High-acid white varieties do better than Chardonnay, so Riesling and Chenin Blanc can be impressive. Against all the omens, Cabernet is beginning to yield some reassuringly ripe reds now. A single high-volume producer, Ste Chapelle, rules the Idaho roost, and its wines are generally good. However, most of the state's production doesn't travel much further than Washington State.

Riesling vines of Idaho's main producer, Ste Chapelle (above).

Vineyards spreading towards the water's edge in New York State's Finger Lakes AVA (right).

OTHER STATES

New York State Unlike the west coast states, in New York State the wine industry still relies to a significant extent on the native American vine species that grow wild in such profusion on the eastern side of America.

New York viticulture only really got underway in the early years of the 19th century, not much before California's, although the eastern state had of course been settled for much longer. The principal growing region is the Finger Lakes AVA, a group of long, thin bodies of water in the centre of the state, south of Rochester. Long Island also has fairly extensive vineyards, and a pair of AVAs in The Hamptons and North Fork.

Seyval Blanc is important in New York State, as is the red variety Concord. Best of the international grapes have been Chardonnay (particularly good from the Finger Lakes winery Wagner and Long Island's Bridgehampton), Cabernet and Merlot (Hargrave, one of the Long Island pioneers of *vinifera* grapes, makes pedigree Cabernet) and some classically steely Riesling.

Texas The Lone Star state develops apace, and now has six AVAs. Its wine industry is essentially a recent creation dating from the 1970s, when the Llano Estacado winery set the ball rolling, making fine Cabernet, Chardonnay and Sauvignon near Lubbock. Now there are also Pheasant Ridge, Fall Creek and the ambitious Ste Genevieve – a joint venture with a négociant company in Bordeaux. Fall Creek makes a particularly good fist of varietal Carnelian, a crossing of Cabernet, Grenache and Carignan that has yielded disappointing results elsewhere.

Virginia Despite the fact that it has an uncompromisingly hot climate, some are tipping Virginia as a forthcoming story in American wine. Unusually, given the pretty torrid conditions, it has proved itself most adept so far at white wines. The Chardonnays are luscious enough to give the best of California a run for their money, while Semillon and Riesling also look promising. Reds are faltering for the time being.

Other states that may soon be capable of causing a stir in wine circles are **Missouri**, **Maryland** and **Pennsylvania**.

A coming region is the state of Virginia (above), where new plantings of classic white varieties are proving successful.

CANADA

Canada first attracted attention for its award-winning Icewines. Now, with plantings of popular international varieties, the country's producers are surging forward with an impressive range of styles.

Harvesting frozen Vidal grapes (above) in winter for Canada's speciality, Icewine.

Canada's two important wine-growing regions are divided by the vast country itself, with Ontario on the east coast, bordering New York State, and British Columbia on the west.

WHILE OTHER EMERGENT wine countries have targeted European markets with huge sales drives and promotional campaigning, Canada has quietly been developing its own industry at a rate that suits itself. The first wines to be released in the UK were made from hybrid grape varieties similar to those found in the eastern United States. They found the going pretty rough, as those who bothered to try them at all found the weirdly pungent flavours of wines like Maréchal Foch red quite baffling, even repellent. The impression was given that Canada couldn't really be a serious wine-producing country.

Happily, Canadian wine is poised in the new century to begin definitively reversing that notion. The way forward, as it will turn out to be in New York State, is with *Vitis vinifera* varieties. That hasn't necessarily been an easy solution in the harsh northern climate of Canada. Its summers are perfectly benign, but the several degrees of frost that can be relied on year in, year out in the winter months can be highly dangerous for the dormant vines. Nonetheless, patient perseverance has identified the most suitable sites for a clutch of international varieties, and early results – many of these vines only came into full production in the last decade – are encouraging indeed.

At least one of the hybrids may still have a role to play in one important respect. The white Vidal grape has yielded some of the most lusciously concentrated examples of Icewine, which is rapidly turning out to be Canada's major speciality. After all, if you have sub-zero winters as a matter of course, you may as well put them to good effect. Canada's Icewine is made in exactly the same manner as Germany's, from grapes that are left to overripen on the vine and then freeze as night-time temperatures start to plummet with the onset of winter. When the frozen berries are harvested, they are quickly pressed so that the ice-pellets of water remain behind in the presses, and the sweet, concentrated juice runs free.

So favourable are the conditions for making Icewine that Canada has become the foremost world practitioner of the frozen arts. Most of it is made from either the hybrid Vidal or from Riesling. It easily attains the kind of sugar

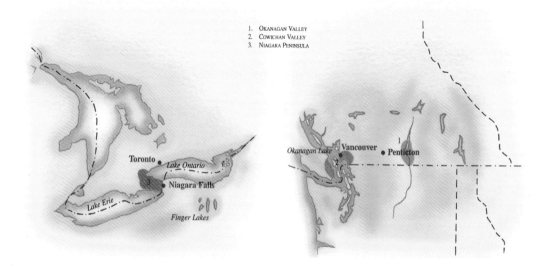

1. OKANAGAN VALLEY
2. COWICHAN VALLEY
3. NIAGARA PENINSULA

Toronto
Lake Ontario
Niagara Falls
Lake Erie
Finger Lakes

Okanagan Lake Vancouver • Penticton

concentration (or "must weight", to give it its technical term) found in all but the very sweetest German and Austrian versions. Good acidity balances the apricot-syrup sweetness of the wines, so that, although irresistibly easy to drink on release, they are also capable of ageing in the bottle.

Dry table wines from hybrid grapes are not a noticeably attractive proposition. As well as Vidal, there is some of the Seyval Blanc grown in New York State and England, while the red grape Maréchal Foch is supported by the even less lovely Baco Noir. These varieties are the legacy of Canada's early wine pioneers in the 19th century. It is only since the 1970s that grapes more familiar (and more acceptable) to international tastes have been planted on anything like a significant scale.

Chardonnay and Riesling are the best whites so far, though some of the Alsace varieties are showing promise. Pinot Noir and a certain amount of light-textured Cabernet Sauvignon show progress among the reds. Cabernet Franc, with its naturally more delicate profile, may yet prove a better bet than its Cabernet cousin, making cranberryish Loire-style reds.

To demonstrate the seriousness of their endeavours, Canadian winemakers instituted a rudimentary appellation system in 1988, the Vintners Quality Alliance. To make the VQA grade, wines have to be sourced entirely from grapes grown in the defined regions and to have achieved minimum levels of ripeness. As plantings increase, so should the number of wines made under the auspices of the VQA system.

Canada's vineyards are located in four of its provinces. Of these, the first two listed below are by far the most important for quantity.

Ontario The province that borders New York State has similarly cool, marginal growing conditions. A degree of natural protection is afforded by a high ridge overlooking the main vineyard area that mitigates the worst effects of the climate. Riesling is a star performer here, from crisp dry styles to the celebrated Icewines, and Chardonnay too achieves good things in the style of steely Chablis and softer, gently oaked examples. Pinot Noir grown in these cool climes may very well turn out to be among North America's finest.

It was in Ontario's Niagara peninsula that the modern Canadian wine industry got going, with the innovative Inniskillin winery's first plantings in the 1970s. Its standard bottlings of

Chardonnay and Riesling are well-made wines, and – for those with a sense of gustatory adventure – Inniskillin does still make a Maréchal Foch varietal. Henry of Pelham is another of the more dynamic producers.

British Columbia Whereas most of Canada's vineyards lie in the Atlantic east of the country, the western province of British Columbia, way out on its own Pacific limb, is also participating in the quality wine movement. The Okanagan Valley in the southwest of the province is where the vineyards are found. Good varietals have been produced from Alsace grapes such as Pinot Blanc and Gewürztraminer, as well as Riesling of course, although some of the delicate Chardonnay has tended to be rather smothered with oak. Mission Hill is a name to look out for.

Quebec and Nova Scotia The other two eastern provinces to make wine have only a sparse scattering of vineyards. So far they are largely dedicated to the production of wines from hybrid grape varieties, although there are tentative plantings of Chardonnay.

The beautiful Okanagan Valley in British Columbia (above) is carving a name for itself for Alsace grape varieties.

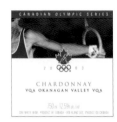

SOUTH *and* CENTRAL AMERICA

Led by the great successes of Chile and Argentina, South America has become an important player in the Southern Hemisphere. Mexico, from where vines initially headed south with the Spanish, is also enjoying a revival.

ALTHOUGH WILD VINES flourished in Central America just as they did in the north, there is no indication, archaeological or otherwise, that winemaking was practised on the continent in pre-Columbian times. It took the arrival of the Spanish and then the Portuguese to develop systematic viticulture in Central and South America. The progress of vine cultivation occurred in a rapid southward march from Mexico, down through Peru to Chile and Argentina. Today, organized wine industries are to be found in around ten Latin American countries, from the major production of Argentina, whose export efforts are gathering momentum, to the very minor cultivation of mostly native species in Venezuela.

Climatically, Chile and Argentina offer the best wine-producing conditions in South America (below). There are also pockets of vineyards in Brazil and Uruguay.

1. BAJA CALIFORNIA
2. SONORA
3. HERMOSILLO
4. QUERETARO
5. ACONCAGUA
6. CENTRAL VALLEY
7. MENDOZA
8. RIO GRANDE DO SUL
9. CARPINTERIA
10. CERRO CHAPEU

For the purposes of the export markets, however, the flagship of South American wine so far has been Chile. Although its annual production is smaller than that of either Argentina or Brazil, Chile's wine industry moved up a gear in the 1980s. It won renown with its Cabernets and Chardonnays of course, and to a lesser extent with some Sauvignons and Merlots. Chile was proud not only to be producing wines that could hold their heads up in the best international company, but also to be attracting some big European names into the country. However, not the least powerful card in its hand was that Chile was virtually the only wine producer in the world never to have been invaded by phylloxera.

The worldwide epidemic of phylloxera began in the 1860s when it was carried to Europe on cuttings of North American vines. Within a very few years, it had swamped the continent, devastating vineyards, and forcing many growers beyond the limits of commercial survival. The antidote was eventually found in grafting new plantings of European varieties on to roots from American vine species, which had become immune to the louse. What was also observed, however, was that the one type of soil where it doesn't survive is sand. Those vineyards planted in coastal areas, where sandy soils predominate, tended to find the attack passed them by.

Chile's main protection lay in the circumstances of its geography. Since the country is, in essence, one long, narrow strip of Pacific coast, nearly all of its soil is sand-based. Furthermore, the natural bulwark of its border with Argentina, the Andes mountains, prevented what limited outbreaks of phylloxera arose in Argentina from spreading westwards. Chilean vines have, as a consequence, never had to be grafted, so that the wine being made today should still resemble – at least in theory – the wine of a century ago. (The fact is, of course, that modern viticultural and vinification practices mean that it would be very odd if it didn't taste considerably better.)

It only took a decade or so before Argentinian wine started making the same sorts of headlines

New vineyard plantings of Cabernet in Chile (left). Vines do not need grafting on to phylloxera-resistant roots as the pest cannot thrive in the sand-based soils.

as Chile had done in the 1980s. Unlike Chile, the country has not significantly benefited from foreign investment, and the leaders of its wine industry were wary of straying into the new-kid-on-the-block trap that saw Chile fawned over and then dropped as the global wine circus moved on in search of the next novelty.

What has undoubtedly helped Argentina is that it isn't entirely hidebound as to the varietals it produces. Malbec, one of the minor varieties in red Bordeaux, is accorded a status that it doesn't quite enjoy anywhere else outside Cahors (see southwest France). The perfumed white variety Torrontés, a relative of the one grown in Galicia in northwest Spain, is very widely planted and can make intensely fragrant wines with cleanly defined acidity.

The Andean mountains provide the vineyards of Mendoza in western Argentina, as well as the wine regions of central Chile, with one important viticultural advantage. In the searing, arid climates of South America, vines may very often be deprived of water at the point in the growing season when they most need it. There is sufficient rainfall in most of Europe for irrigation to be forbidden under EU wine regulations (although there are ways around the ban for the truly determined), but the hotter, drier countries couldn't manage without it.

The Spanish colonists and Jesuit missionaries bequeathed to the winemakers of Argentina and Chile a complex but highly efficient system of channelled irrigation, using the water that ran down from the mountains when

the snowcaps melted. To this day, it flows through the vineyards in carefully laid trenches, providing measured relief to the vines' roots.

The large Brazilian wine industry is, despite its scale, not geared for export at all, other than to one or two of its neighbours. That is mainly because it relies to such a far-reaching degree on hybrid grapes, principally Isabella, once common in California. With the steady increase in plantings of *Vitis vinifera* that recent years have seen, this could eventually change dramatically. Certainly, the volumes are there, although finding the right sites – even within the colossal Brazilian interior – is not the most straightforward of operations, owing to the enervating heat and humidity most of the country endures. Nearly all of the vineyards have been established in the relatively mild southern regions.

Mexico, the only other wine producer of significant scale on the continent, is where the whole American wine story started. Planted by Spanish *conquistadores* in the 1500s, the country's vineyards had gone into a seemingly terminal decline by the beginning of this century. Fiery spirits like mescal and tequila were for a long time the staple alcohol of the Mexicans, but in the last 30 years or so they have rediscovered an enthusiasm for wine, perhaps as a result of migrant workers who went to labour in the California vineyards coming back with a taste for it.

The revival is a happy event, as Mexico has provided ample proof within just one generation that it can make some superlative wine, especially from the southern French red varieties.

All over central Chile, new vineyard holdings are being established, making the country currently the most dynamic in South America (above).

Ploughing the old-fashioned way (above) in Argentina.

(Right) Three-quarters of Argentina's wines, and the finest, come from the western province of Mendoza, in the foothills of the Andes. Of the other four regions, Salta is producing the most notable wines.

1. MENDOZA
2. SAN JUAN
3. LA RIOJA
4. SALTA
5. RIO NEGRO

ARGENTINA

The vast majority of Argentina's vineyard land is in the western province of Mendoza, in the foothills of the Andes. The earliest vines were established here by Jesuit monks in the mid-16th century. It is a very dry region, and depends greatly on irrigation from melting mountain snow to prevent the vines from becoming terminally parched.

In the past, wine quality suffered from the fact that the slow, manual harvest was followed by an often arduous, hot journey to the nearest central winemaking plant, by which time the grapes were in less than prime condition. As elsewhere, the chief priority in bringing the country's viticulture into the modern era has been investment in new technology that can speedily and hygienically process the grapes at wineries constructed much nearer to the growing areas.

For many years, the mainstays of the Argentinian wine industry were a clutch of pink grape varieties that represent the hoi-polloi of South American winemaking: two variants of a grape called Criolla – Grande and Chica (the latter, known as País in Chile, was the important early Californian variety Mission) – and another called Cereza, whose name means "cherry".

These grapes can be vinified to produce a heavy, flat-tasting white wine with a distinct pinkish tinge or they can be blended with something a little darker to make a still fairly bloodless red. They are the typical locally consumed wines that potential importers from abroad prefer to draw a veil over, and the grapes that make them will inevitably continue to yield ground in the vineyards to the international stars.

White grapes are dominated by an undistinguished variety called Pedro Giménez (not to be confused with the Pedro Ximénez of Jerez) and the humdrum Muscat of Alexandria, which makes rather leaden sweet wines. The promising, aromatically citric Torrontés, as well as Chardonnay and Semillon, produce the higher-quality whites.

Malbec leads the field among reds, and is responsible for many of Argentina's most sophisticated, ageworthy red wines. Italian red grapes from Piedmont and Tuscany do well in this climate, as does Spain's Tempranillo. Cabernet and some outstandingly successful Syrah add to a rollcall that would make up most people's lists of pedigree red varieties.

Mendoza This is where about three-quarters of all Argentinian wine is made, and where all of the companies that have so far come to notice in the export markets are based. The much-favoured Malbec heads the list of grapes planted, and is supported by Barbera, Sangiovese, Tempranillo and Cabernet. By and large, Mendoza Malbecs are rich, opulently damsony reds, with pronounced but controlled tannins and fairly overt oak influence. The Cabernets can be denser and darker still, often reminiscent of good *cru bourgeois* Médoc. White wine exports are, not unexpectedly, dominated by Chardonnay – fine, lightly buttery Chardonnay with beautifully weighted oak, in the case of Trapiche's top bottling – and there is even a little Sauvignon.

The Trapiche label is owned by a giant combine called Peñaflor, but its various cuvées offer both quality and value. Other good producers include Cavas de Weinert, Norton, Esmeralda, Santa Julia, Lopez and Cateña.

San Juan The area north of Mendoza is important in terms of volume but not of the quality to balance it. With a much less forgiving climate to contend with than the Mendozans, San Juan's wineries have contented themselves with supplying the domestic market only.

La Rioja The scattered vineyards of La Rioja lie to the northeast of San Juan. Although this is where Argentinian wine probably started, there isn't much to stimulate the imagination now. There is not much call for flabby Muscats.

Salta The northwestern province of Salta is currently producing the best Argentinian wine after Mendoza. Here, some convincingly ripe Cabernet is produced, and the speciality Torrontés comes into its own. Etchart makes a fine example at Cafayate in the Calchaquies Valley, all orange-blossom and cinnamon on a crisp, appley base.

Rio Negro This southern region, as yet largely untapped, looks to have the best potential of all. Its cooler climate and more propitious soil types should make it a happy hunting-ground for new investors when the bandwagon starts to roll. White varietals such as Torrontés, Sauvignon, Chenin and the obligatory Chardonnay could well be among Argentina's finest, while sparkling wine production has been given a substantial fillip by the arrival of a posse of Champagne VIPs with money to spend.

Irrigation channels in a Mendoza vineyard (below). The water is sourced from the melting snowcaps of the Andes mountains.

Huge old oak fermentation vats at a vinery in Rio Grande do Sul, Brazil (above).

BRAZIL

Brazil's viticultural history fits the general pattern of most of the Americas. Colonists (Portuguese in this case) and missionaries planted the vine, slow vineyard expansion led to hybrid grapes churning out basic plonk by the 19th century, foreign investment arriving in the 20th century transformed the scene with sprinklings of Chardonnay and Cabernet and a splodge of Welschriesling.

In Brazil's case, the progress has been more lumbering than most, despite the fact that it is now one of the top three South American producers. Most of the country is simply too tropical for *vinifera* vines to cope with. Raging humidity and extremely high rainfall are not what even Chardonnay is used to, but in Rio Grande do Sul in the deep south of the country, conditions are more temperate. In the regions of Serra Gaucha and Frontera, the latter near the intersection of the borders of Brazil, Uruguay and Argentina, the best results so far are being achieved.

The greater part of the Brazilian vinescape is still planted with native species and hybrids, pre-eminent among them being Isabella (she once hung around California's vineyards, before

the smarter *vinifera* set moved in). As well as Chardonnay, most of the Bordeaux grapes, red and white, are planted, as well as a little optimistic Pinot Blanc and Gewürztraminer. Sparkling wine is made, mainly to cater for local tastes, although Moët has enough faith in it to have a commercial interest here, just as it does in Argentina.

Consumers availing themselves of one of the rare opportunites to taste Brazilian wine in the export markets may be surprised to find it all rather light and delicate – not at all what the climate would lead you to expect. That is because most of the winemakers are currently overcompensating by picking their grapes while they still have plenty of acidity in them. The theory is that they thereby retain fruity freshness; the unkind way of looking at it is the wines simply taste unripe. In the case of the reds, the lightness is of almost Bardolino proportions.

The Palomas company is about the most intensive exporter as far as Europe is concerned.

CHILE

The meteoric rise of Chilean wine in both European and North American markets in the late 1980s was one of the more sensational (and also more salutary) tales from the world of wine in latter times. Just as the consumer craze for Southern-Hemisphere wines was taking off, first and foremost within the UK, the prices of wines from Australia particularly were suddenly given a stiff hike. California wine has never been especially cheap in the first place, but bargain Chardonnays full of oak and sunshine from the valleys of South Australia were very much the name of the game. As prices elsewhere rose, Chile was poised to step into the breach.

With the exception of Shiraz, the Chilean industry had most of the big-name varietals that Australia produced, the fruit flavour was strong and convincing, and the national economy – working hard to emerge from its embargoed isolation under Pinochet – needed hard currency. Furthermore, not to be outdone by the Americans, Chile had its own French-bashing story to trail before the international wine press.

One of its premium Cabernet Sauvignons, from the Los Vascos winery in Rapel, went to Bordeaux, muscled in among the top châteaux and set their annual winefair alight. Breathless notices in the French press called it "Chile's *premier cru*". And so Chile found itself hailed as the hot new property.

Certain members of the international wine aristocracy had, to be sure, been convinced of the potential of Chile's vineyards as far back as the 1970s, when the Torres family of Catalonia bought some land. Château Lafite now has a stake in Los Vascos, flying winemaker Hugh Ryman has helped out with the Discover company's Montes wines, while Napa Valley winery Franciscan is a force in Casablanca. In some ways, however, the stampede to Chile was a case of too much, too soon.

It wasn't that Chilean wine turned out to be disappointing, exactly. It was more the case that it proved initially more limited in stylistic range than Australia, to which it was unfairly being compared. What is fascinating now is to see the meeting of North and South that, between them, Chile's top Cabernets and Chardonnays represent. Many are made in a distinctly French style, the red wines with austere, backward tannins in their youth, the whites showing tantalizingly subtle oak seasoning and taut acidity. Others have nailed their colours to the Southern-Hemisphere mast, with voluptuous, essence-of-blackcurrant Cabernets and galumphing, wood-driven Chardonnays with plenty of attitude.

As to other varietals, Chile is now emerging as a producer of world-class Merlot (with the best wines showing enveloping aromas of black fruits and well-hung game à la Pomerol) and some vastly improved Sauvignon. The Merlots, much better-balanced in many cases than the Cabernets, are probably the country's strongest suit for red wines, for the time being, with even Reserve wines very competitively priced for their outstanding quality. One can only wish they wouldn't release them so young (frequently less than 12 months old). Sauvignons are often distinctly Loire-like, all gooseberries and asparagus, although where grown in the hotter regions, they can lack fruit and focus.

Chile has oodles of Semillon, but that has traditionally gone into roughly made plonk for domestic consumption. Small quantities of Riesling make fresh, simple, dry wine not too far from the New Zealand style, while Viognier is muscling in on the fashion for big, aromatic whites, with a little delicate Gewürztraminer tagging along behind. Among reds, recent success stories have been fiery, full-throttle Pinot Noir, good enough to compete with California's efforts eventually, and richly concentrated Syrah. These latter could be very exciting in time. Sparkling *champaña* probably won't be.

The most widely planted grape of all, however, is País, the feeble pink variety that is equally widespread as Criolla Chica in the vineyards of Andean neighbour Argentina. It produces precisely the same sort of thin, tasteless semi-red here as it does in Argentina, but is deeply traditional, and will thus take a generation or two to die out.

Most of Chile's vineyards lie in the climatically benign central section of the country, immediately south of the capital, Santiago. The smouldering heat of summer is mitigated to a significant degree by the proximity of the vineyards to the cooling influences of the Pacific Ocean, and irrigation is virtually as widely practised here as it is in Argentina. And no description of Chilean viticulture would be complete without mention of the celebrated fact that these mountain-protected, sandy vineyards are a no-go zone for the dreaded phylloxera.

Cabernet grapes arriving at the Santa Rita bodega (left), in Chile's Maipo Valley.

PRODUCE OF CHILE

1993
VILLA MONTES
Sauvignon Blanc

A long narrow strip of land caught between the Pacific and the Andes, Chile (below) is blessed with sandy soils. The vineyards lie mainly in the centre of the country, where the climate is benign.

Valparaiso

Santiago

1. ACONCAGUA
2. CASABLANCA
3. MAIPO
4. RAPEL
5. MAULE
6. BIO-BIO

Curicó

Stainless-steel tanks at Montes winery, in Maule's Curicó area (above), symbolic of the investment in and influence of modern technology in Chile.

one of Chile's most far-sighted winemakers, Ignacio Recabarren. Casablanca's Sauvignons and Chardonnays are masterpieces of tropical fruit intensity, and there is also a Gewürztraminer that veers from forgettably dilute in one vintage to gorgeously aromatic and *alsacien* in the next. The Cabernets are cool-climate giants, stuffed with brooding tannins and chewy damson fruit.

Central Valley South of Aconcagua, the vineyards of the Central Valley and its various sub-regions are concentrated midway between the Andes and the Pacific. At the northern end is Maipo, just south of the capital. Cabernet is king once again, but there are some improving Sauvignons too, and the Chablis grower William Fèvre has also set up shop.

Recabarren of Casablanca makes more everyday wines here, under the Santa Carolina label. Viña Carmen is a promising enterprise of the long-established Santa Rita winery. Santa Rita itself produces an ultra-reliable range of basic varietals and Reservas, including top Cabernets. Canepa has made a splash with a ground-breaking Zinfandel, while the house of Cousiño Macul is a bastion of tradition with its Antiguas Reservas Cabernets that can age for 20 years to a gamey, claret-like venerability.

Next south is Rapel, comprising the two valley districts of Cachapoal and Colchagua. The latter has been more important for export wines so far, with brilliant Merlots, the distinctive Cabernets of Los Vascos and innovative Pinot Noirs from Cono Sur. In Cachapoal, California's Clos du Val has invested in a winery called Viña Porta, which is making some world-class Cabernet and Chardonnay.

The Maule area is cooler again than Rapel, and includes the important wine centres of Curicó and Lontué, both of which are good for white wines, crunchy Sauvignons as well as lightly creamy Chardonnays. In Maule itself to the south, Merlot has long shown real class as a varietal, particularly from the Terra Noble winery in Talca. Terra Noble's winemaker is from the Loire and, not surprisingly, makes a good Sauvignon Blanc too.

Aconcagua/Casablanca The northernmost region for export wines is the Aconcagua, north of Santiago. It is named after both a river and the highest peak in the Andes. Cabernet Sauvignon is the grape best suited to the arid, broiling conditions here, where it achieves massive, pitch-black concentration in the premium wines of Errazuriz.

Southwest of the Aconcagua, nearer to the coast and the city of Valparaiso, the Casablanca district has been the main talking-point of Chilean wine in recent years. Here, the climate is much cooler, so much so that frosts in the spring are not at all uncommon, and the summer swelter is constantly mitigated by ocean breezes. Concha y Toro, which has a good range of Cabernets and Chardonnays (the Don Melchor Cabernet is the top cuvée), is located here, as is the Casablanca winery itself, brainchild of

Bio-Bio The largest wine region, Bio-Bio, south of the Central Valley, is also the least interesting to date. It is considerably cooler and damper than Maule to the north, and is mostly carpeted with País. Undoubtedly, though, there is potential for the classic grapes, as soon as the big companies venture this far south.

MEXICO

When the *conquistadores* arrived from Spain in the wake of Columbus's voyages of discovery, Mexico was where they started their long triumphal sweep through Central and South America. Wherever anyone settled, vineyards were planted, so that something like the life back home could be replicated in the brave new Spanish world. The wine may not have tasted much like the produce of the motherland, but at least it was wine.

Wine production has always taken a back seat to distillation in Mexico, and the cactus spirits tequila and the originally hallucinogenic, now sanitized mescal were supplemented by brandy. Mexico actually produces one of the world's largest export brandies, Presidente, and much of its vineyards' yield is destined for the stills. However, faint flickerings of domestic interest, followed by the usual sporadic foreign investment, have created the bare bones of a modern wine industry.

Since the Spanish also once occupied what is now California from their Central American base, it comes as no surprise to find most of the vineyard land concentrated in the north of the country near the United States border. The Mexican state of Baja California is its premium growing area; along with the other main northern region, Sonora, this is where most of the wines with any chance of competing internationally will come from.

Southern French red varieties make up much of the vineyards, together with outposts of California grapes both old and new, including the historically significant Mission (Chile's País), a variety called Petite Sirah (nothing to do with Syrah, but actually another dark-skinned French grape Durif) and a spot of Zinfandel. Petite Sirah

has shown particular promise in producing a thick, savoury red at the L. A. Cetto winery, which also makes excellent Cabernet. Plantings of white grapes have not so far been of the more distinguished varieties. Sparklers may one day get a foot in the door, if the presence of the Spanish cava company Freixenet is anything to go by.

URUGUAY

If Brazil doesn't emerge to join Chile and Argentina as the next big South American wine country, then Uruguay could well be in the frame. The usual drawback of widespread hybrid vines is present, but a very broadminded range of international *vinifera* varieties now supplements them. Just as Argentina has its Malbec, so Uruguay has made something of a speciality of one of the other lesser-known southern French grapes in Tannat, the often brutal red menace of Madiran. Uruguayan Tannat, however, seems better suited to its surroundings, and the Castel Pujol bottling, which spends several productive months in oak barrels, is a beauty – full of ripe purple fruits and dark chocolate richness.

Vineyards are planted in most parts of Uruguay, with those at Carpinteria in the centre of the country and Cerro Chapeu near the Brazilian border showing the most exciting promise. The industry has a long way to go before it can think seriously of exporting in any quantity, and a lot more investment is needed, but given the current outside interest in South America, that should certainly come.

Other South American wine producers, of no real significance outside their own national boundaries, are Peru (which was once the dominant source of wine on the continent), Bolivia, Ecuador and Venezuela.

An old timber-roofed wine bodega at Ensenada, Baja California, Mexico (above).

Traditional low-trained vines in Uruguay (left). Viticulture is practised all over the country.

SOUTH AFRICA

After a century of political strife, the South African wine industry is developing fast. The potential for quality wines is vast, and exciting times lie ahead for the country's winemakers.

VITICULTURE WAS among the very first enterprises of the Dutch settlers who arrived on the Cape of Good Hope in the mid-17th century. We don't know what grapes they brought with them, though it seems likely the cuttings would have come from Bordeaux. Early results were not immediately seized on with glee when they found their way back to the settlers' homeland, but a start had been made. What first put Cape winemaking on the map was the creation of one of those legendary dessert wines with which vinous history is littered.

Constantia was the name of an estate near Cape Town planted by colonial governor van der Stel barely 40 years after the new territory had been claimed by the Dutch. It made sweet wines in both colours from grapes that were left to overripen and then dry out on the vine. There is some uncertainty as to whether they were fortified, although analysis of the contents of antique bottles opened a few years ago suggests not. Perhaps some of the wine exported by sea was fortified to preserve it, as indeed was the developing practice at the time.

However that may be, the wines took Europe by storm. In the 18th and 19th centuries, they enjoyed a reputation so exalted that higher prices were paid for them than for any of the classic dessert or fortified wines of Europe. In

1861, Great Britain was the colonial power in the Cape. The Whig government of William Gladstone abolished the tariff relief that imported goods from outposts of the Empire had, until then, qualified for. This forced South African wines to compete on the same terms as those from suppliers much nearer their target market. It then only took the advent of the vine pest phylloxera, swinging through the Cape 25 years later on its triumphal world tour, to smash what was left of Constantia's edifice.

As South African wine found itself unable to compete in world markets, a colossal wine lake began to accumulate. Corporate action to deal with the resulting chaos and wastage was taken in 1918 with the establishment of the Ko-operatiewe Wijnbowers Vereniging, or KWV (Co-operative Winegrowers Association). This huge organization exercized swingeing powers over the industry. It declared what could be planted where, how much of it could be produced and what the growers could sell it for. The initiative worked, but at the cost of steamroller-ing diversity. For many years, the only wines likely to be seen in export markets were bottled under the auspices of the KWV.

Excess production was sent for distillation into brandy, or was fortified to produce a range of wines – some with a resemblance to port, others more like madeira – that became something of a Cape speciality. The table wines were generally based on grapes that didn't enjoy

The Cape of Good Hope has always been the focus of wine-growing in South Africa (below). Even so, inland from the cooling Atlantic and Indian oceans, the climate here can still be hot and humid.

1. OLIFANTS RIVER
2. SWARTLAND
3. PAARL
4. DURBANVILLE
5. CONSTATIA
6. STELLENBOSCH
7. ELGIN
8. WALKER BAY
9. WORCESTER/TULBAGH
10. ROBERTSON
11. KLEIN KAROO

huge cachet in knowledgeable circles. Acidic Chenin Blanc (known in South Africa as Steen) and thin red Cinsaut were not really anybody's flavour of the month. The chance to branch out was now stymied by two factors. One was the stranglehold that the KWV still had over all Cape production, and the other was the worldwide trade boycott of the apartheid era.

Boycotts are never wholly effective. The longer they persist, the more holes are punched in them by those determined to make money where others refuse to tread. But the boycott of South African goods was unusually tenacious. While European governments declined to take part, individual consumers shunned Cape produce almost as an article of faith. The effect, on the wine industry in particular, was crippling. It was unable to attract any significant outside expertise and, although it was powerful enough to export its wines at prices that should have enabled them to compete with the very humblest of European rustic slosh, they basically failed to sell.

With the political settlement of the early 1990s came the long-awaited denuding of the powers of the KWV. Small private growers began to plant the varieties they chose, inward

investment started to flow and South Africa is consequently poised to move in among the giants of the Southern Hemisphere and ruffle a few feathers. The current picture is one of happy confusion, with growers going off at their own tangents all over the place, but some of the wines reaching Europe – Chardonnays, Gewürztraminers, Merlots and even Pinot Noirs – are evoking gasps of astonishment that so much has been achieved in such a short time.

The appellation system that South Africa inaugurated in 1973 remains a very imprecise one. It is broadly geographically based, and involves certification of wines by panels of tasters, but doesn't make any imposition as to yields. Vintage-dated wine is generously allowed to contain up to 25 per cent of wine made in the years immediately before and after that stated on the label.

Regional definitions are often so loosely drawn as to be meaningless. If a wine entered for classification is passed, it receives a special seal that proclaims it to be a Wine of Origin (WO). As the industry gets into its stride, this system will presumably be tightened up, and something more closely analogous to the *appellation contrôlée* system will be formulated.

Harvesting Sauvignon grapes at Klein Constantia (above), in the Cape.

The manor house at Klein Constantia (below), the smallest of the three producers that make up the small, yet famous, Constantia wine region.

Looking out across the stunning Paarl region from Fairview Estate (above). Paarl produces the full range of South African wine styles.

It is quite plain that the century-long nightmare that South African winemaking suffered has been put firmly behind it. Producers may be forgiven for regretting the fact that their chance to shine has come at a time when there are more competitors in the field of wine than at any other period in viticultural history. That a resurgence of Cape wine is in the offing is not in any doubt.

In a country whose climate is so propitious for the production of concentrated, rich red wines, it may come as some surprise to learn that no less than 82 per cent of the vineyard land is planted with white varieties. The South African preference, however, beyond the speciality fortified market, was for light white wines to quench the thirst, rather than complex reds for ageing in the bottle. It is expected the balance of red to white varieties will gradually change as the Cape begins to win plaudits for its Bordeaux-style blends and Shiraz.

Chief among the whites is Steen (what most of the rest of the world knows as Chenin Blanc). It is encouraged to perform with as much versatility as it does in France's Touraine. Its repertoire ranges from almost excruciatingly sharp, young dry wines, through the ever-

popular off-dry style (like demi-sec Vouvray) at which the grape excels, all the way up to honeyed, liquorous dessert wines made from grapes picked after the main harvest. Colombard, a French import from the Cognac region, was traditionally important in South Africa's brandy industry too, and is often used to make light dry whites. As a varietal, however, it has little character other than a waxy coarseness not designed to endear it to the Chardonnay set.

Chardonnay itself is spreading like wildfire, as is Sauvignon Blanc which, in some of the cooler areas, is turning out some superbly complex, smoky Loire-style whites. Crouchen is a French variety the French have long since forgotten but that South Africa found a place for in its history; they confusingly call it Cape Riesling. The real Riesling is here as well, generally known as Weisser (White) Riesling. Ugni Blanc (Italy's Trebbiano) is just the sort of neutral grape beloved of brandy producers, but only contributes to diluting any character in a blended white wine. Both of the two main Muscats are used for producing sweet and fortified wines. Most promisingly, some growers are achieving highly impressive results with Gewürztraminer, especially in the Paarl region.

devices, it doesn't amount to much, but it was one of the minor components of Constantia, and is still grown on part of the old estate in readiness to play a role in the wine's resurgence.

Most of South Africa's wine regions are located in the southwest of the country, where the vineyards benefit to greater and lesser degrees from the cooling maritime influence of both the Atlantic and Indian Oceans. Most of the interior is too hot for successful viticulture, although there are some recently established vineyards around the Orange River in the centre of the country. Although winters are usually damp and windy, the growing season is characterized by prolonged hot and arid weather conditions. Irrigation is routinely practised by most Cape vineyards, although not quite to the extent that South American growers have to resort to.

Vergelegen's highly functional cuvier (below), in Stellenbosch, where viticulture dates right back to the Dutch colonists' arrival in the 17th century.

As to red grapes, the most widely planted variety traditionally was Cinsaut, one of the important red grapes of southern France. The pedigree gang are all here, too: Cabernets Sauvignon and Franc, Merlot, Syrah (given its Australian name, Shiraz, on the Cape), Pinot Noir and even a little Gamay. There is even a smattering of Zinfandel.

South Africa's equivalent of Zinfandel, a grape they can call their own, is Pinotage. It is a crossing of the ubiquitous Cinsaut with Pinot Noir. If that sounds a rather clumsily arranged marriage, many would agree. Like Zinfandel, there are three Pinotage styles: simple rosé, light, Beaujolais-like red and a deeper, often barrel-aged version. At its most basic, it has a hard-to-pin-down fruit flavour veering towards little pippy berries like cranberries or redcurrants. Made in the more lavish idiom, it can be almost Rhône-like, with lush raspberry fruit and sinewy density of texture, reflecting at least one half of its parentage.

The Cape pantheon of red grapes includes a French variety long since abandoned in its homeland. Pontac, named after one of the more illustrious families in Bordeaux history, is actually rather a rustic grape. Left to its own

La Concorde (below), head-quarters of the KWV (Co-operative Winegrowers Association) in Paarl.

The following guide to the regions moves anti-clockwise around the Cape.

Olifants River Primarily a source of bulk wine for distillation, the mountainous Olifants River area is home to several of the major Cape co-operative producers. The biggest of these, Vredendal, is actually one of the better practitioners, with some appetizing Chardonnays and Sauvignons. Its Goiya Kgeisje is an early-bottled fruity-fresh Sauvignon-based white, its flavours presenting considerably less of a challenge to European tongues than its name. Sweet Muscat wines are locally popular. Red wine production is only a marginal activity.

Swartland The blackish scrubland of this large, mostly very hot region gives the area its name (meaning "black land"). Notwithstanding the heat, Sauvignon Blanc is curiously one of its best varietals, as in the smoky and nettly Reuilly or Quincy lookalike from the Swartland co-operative for example. Pinotage does well, achieving some of its more concentrated results here. A measure of how promising this sort of climatic context is for thick-skinned red varieties that can take more ripening than most is the

success of Tinta Barroca. One of the mainstay grapes of port production, it makes an intriguing, plums-and-pepper varietal at the Allesverloren estate.

Paarl With Stellenbosch, this is one of the Cape regions that has made the headlines in the export trade in recent years. It is where the once all-powerful KWV is based, and still represents the epicentre of the whole South African wine enterprise. One of the hotter regions as a result of lying completely inland, Paarl nonetheless produces the full range of South African wine styles, from crisp, light dry whites and sparklers to full, long-lived reds and excellent fortified wines, as well as some of the country's premium brandies.

All of the major varietals are made in Paarl. The Nederburg estate is one of the largest private producers, making some succulent Chardonnay and some not-so-succulent Pinotage. Fairview Estate is representative of the modern South African outlook, making an impressively diverse range of top varietals. These include cherry-fruited Gamay rather like a young Brouilly, minerally Semillon, steely Chenin Blanc and a particularly well-crafted Gewürztraminer that, sometimes seasoned with a dash of Riesling, comes close to the fullness and weight of Alsace versions.

Villiera also does good Gewürz, as well as sensationally intense Sauvignon (sometimes with as much exuberant fruit as New Zealand growers typically obtain), while Backsberg makes creditable Chardonnay and Shiraz. The Glen Carlou estate is notable for one of the Cape's best Pinot Noirs to date, with a headily perfumed Turkish Delight quality, as well as persuasively Burgundian Chardonnay.

In the southeast of the region is a valley enclave called Franschhoek (meaning "French corner", after its original settlers). It could be that some of Paarl's best wines will come from here in future, or perhaps that it will simply come to be seen as a region in its own right. High flyers so far have been Dieu Donné, whose superb Chardonnay is in the buttered-green-bean Côte de Beaune mode, La Motte with its brambly Shiraz, and the big-scale Boschendal operation, renowned for plump Merlot, richly oaky contemporary Chardonnay and crisp, well-made sparkling wine. Clos Cabrière is a specialist in champagne-method fizz.

The KWV still makes its sherry-style fortifieds in Paarl, maturing the dry ones under a *flor*-style yeast layer and putting them through a *solera*

Meerlust Estate in Stellenbosch (left), with the Helderberg mountain beyond.

Modern equipment and new oak barrels (above) at Klein Constantia.

system. Its portfolio doesn't stop at wine, however, but goes on to encompass several spirits, as well as the once-popular Van der Hum, a kind of South African Grand Marnier whose name translates as something like Whatsisname.

Durbanville Like many another small vineyard region that lies in the shadow of a major city, Durbanville's existence is being threatened by the urban expansion of Cape Town. It won't consequently play a significant role in South Africa's wine renaissance.

Constantia The old, sprawling estate where South Africa's greatest wines were made was eventually broken up and divided among three proprietors, the largest of them – Groot Constantia – state-owned. The result is that Constantia is effectively now a little wine region, rather than a single property. Of the two privately owned portions, one is in German hands, while the smallest of them all, Klein Constantia, has so far proved itself the most visionary. As well as producing splendid modern varietals in the shape of Sauvignon and Chardonnay (together with a less than compelling Cabernet), it has been the first to make a serious attempt to revive the fortified Constantia of blessed memory. The early efforts – rechristened Vin de Constance – are hugely encouraging.

Stellenbosch Viticulture in the coastal Stellenbosch region, south of Paarl, dates back to the first generation of Dutch colonists. Today, it is home to more of South Africa's first-division

wine estates than any other district. Benefiting from their proximity to the ocean, the vineyards of Stellenbosch regularly produce the best-balanced red wines of the Cape. At the heart of the region is the town of Stellenbosch itself, headquarters of the Republic's principal viticultural research institute.

Blended red wines, often using all three of the main Bordeaux varieties, are usually a better bet than varietal Cabernet, which characteristically lacks the class of other examples from the Southern Hemisphere. Warwick Farm's Trilogy bottling is a good blend, as are the sumptuous Rubicon from Meerlust, and the Paul Sauer cuvée from Kanonkop. The latter estate also makes one of the more charming Pinotages. Neetlingshof is an enterprising producer, making a couple of aromatic Alsace varietals as well as expressive late-picked sweet wines.

Sauvignon Blanc from the Uitkyk estate is impressive, while Thelema has won plaudits for its rounded, golden Chardonnay and a voluptuously silky Merlot of great power and presence. Avontuur's Reserve is one of the more convincing varietal Cabernets. Mulderbosch's Sauvignons are everything good Sauvignon should be – either oak-fermented or *au naturel* – and Stellenzicht makes an enterprising, though fairly tart, light Zinfandel, plus some lusciously intense dessert wines, including a botrytized Sauvignon-Semillon labelled Noble Late Harvest.

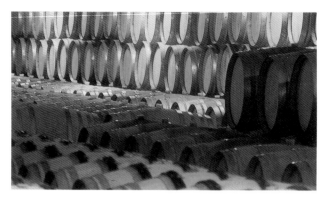

Barrel cellar of Graham Beck Winery in the Robertson region (above), renowned for its Madeba Sauvignons.

Elgin One of South Africa's newer wine regions, following the recent trend to plant vineyards at higher altitude in order to benefit from cooler growing conditions. Elgin may turn out to be a good source of varietals from northern French grapes such as Sauvignon, Chenin and especially Pinot Noir.

Walker Bay Further east along the coast, near the town of Hermanus, Walker Bay is already ahead of Elgin in the race to produce cool-climate varietals, and with greater subtlety than has been the norm hitherto. Chardonnay and Pinot Noir are both looking good, and one of the larger Burgundy négociant houses has entered into a joint venture, Bouchard-Finlayson, to bring a little piece of the Côte d'Or to the Cape. Their wines, as well as those of Hamilton Russell, show what can be done. Not all of the vintages to date have been spot-on, but the potential is indisputable. Bouchard-Finlayson also makes a clean, snappy Sauvignon. The Wildekrans estate weighs in with some highly typical Pinotage.

Worcester The Worcester and Tulbagh regions lie well inland, northeast of Paarl, and are largely occupied by volume-producing co-operatives making old-fashioned fortifieds. The Muscat and Muscatel varieties (the latter may be red or white) are responsible for producing sweet wines in a number of styles. Jerepigo is made either from red or white Muscatel, the production method similar to that used in Moscatel de Valencia and certain Portuguese equivalents. Intensely sweet, fresh grape juice is fortified with the addition of grape spirit before it has had a chance to ferment, resulting in a not unexpectedly grapy sweet wine at around 17 per cent alcohol. The whites are lightly refreshing, the reds more seriously blood-warming.

The Tulbagh sub-region, to the northwest of Worcester, has produced one of the most admirable sparkling wines yet with the Krone Borealis Brut from the Twee Jongegezellen winery, despite the fact that this is not theoretically the right sort of climate for fizz.

Robertson Robertson is another of South Africa's up-and-coming wine regions. Located well back in the hinterland, it is hot and steamy, its vineyards heavily dependent on irrigation. Nonetheless, it has emerged as a premier-league producer of white wines rather than red. Pre-eminent among these are Chardonnays, with plenty of fleshy, chunky Colombards and more of that super-ripe, eminently fortifiable Muscat and Muscatel.

De Wetshof has worn the yellow jersey so far in the Tour de Chardonnay, its Danie de Wet cuvées aged on their lees to produce an indulgently rich, buttercream style with powerful appeal. Van Loveren's are almost as good. Sauvignons from this region are now exhibiting plenty of lush tropical fruit, and the Madeba bottling from Graham Beck is replete with pretty convincing gooseberry character. Beck also makes fine Chardonnay called Lone Hill and one of the region's more conspicuously successful sparklers, Madeba Brut. Among reds to look out for are the full-blooded Shirazes of Graham Beck and the Zandvliet estate.

Klein Karoo Sprawling landlocked region where fortified Muscatels are best suited to the indomitable heat, though a few producers are chancing their arm with dry varietal table wines.

Mossel Bay Like Walker Bay and Elgin, this easterly coastal area is a newly established wine region designed to benefit from the ameliorating sea breezes, in this case blowing in from the Indian Ocean. Cool-climate varieties are what the growers are putting their faith in, with Pinot Noir at the pinnacle of ambition as usual, supplemented by Riesling and Sauvignon Blanc. Given time to find a foothold, the wines should be excellent.

Orange River To the west of the landlocked state of Lesotho, the Orange River region is South Africa's climatically fiercest wine area, its riverside vineyards further from maritime influence than any on the Cape itself. Volume production is the chief activity; since the vines have to be so intensively irrigated, the amount of fruit they bear is correspondingly far too high for quality. Nobody is going to make great varietals around here.

SPARKLING WINES

South Africa is continually growing in confidence as a producer of sparkling wines, and has come a long way in the few short years since all it could really offer was KWV Mousseux. So important has the current generation of Cape fizzes become that a new country-wide term, Méthode Cap Classique (MCC), has been instituted to describe any sparkler produced using the traditional bottle-fermentation method of Champagne. A measure of the maturity of the nascent industry is that nobody tries to label their wines as "Champagne" for the domestic market, where the EU writ doesn't apply. (If only all non-European fizz producers could claim as much.)

Some of these sparkling wines are made from the classic Chardonnay-Pinot Noir blend, others may have a dash of something non-*champenois* like Chenin in them, but the overall quality is becoming frankly breathtaking. Indeed, we may not be too far away from being able to claim that they are the best such wines made anywhere outside Champagne itself. Given that the traditional method is literally only a product of the 1980s in South Africa, this achievement is highly commendable. There are now around 40 wineries making MCC sparklers, and the atmosphere of healthy competition is acting as a powerful impetus for excellence.

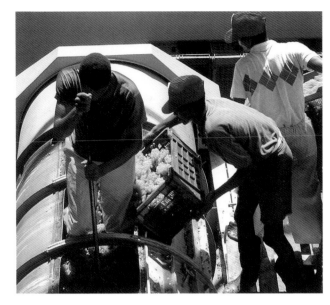

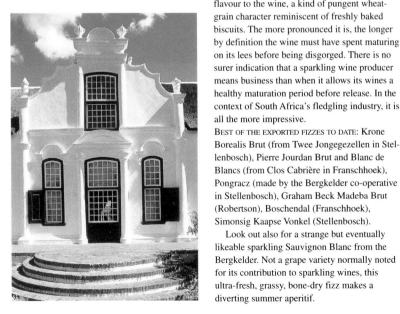

What has been notably striking about many of the early releases is the degree of yeast autolysis they display. Autolysis is the name for the biochemical interchange that takes place within the wine as it undergoes its second fermentation in the bottle. As the active yeasts die off, the dead cells impart a distinctive aroma and flavour to the wine, a kind of pungent wheat-grain character reminiscent of freshly baked biscuits. The more pronounced it is, the longer by definition the wine must have spent maturing on its lees before being disgorged. There is no surer indication that a sparkling wine producer means business than when it allows its wines a healthy maturation period before release. In the context of South Africa's fledgling industry, it is all the more impressive.

BEST OF THE EXPORTED FIZZES TO DATE: Krone Borealis Brut (from Twee Jongegezellen in Stellenbosch), Pierre Jourdan Brut and Blanc de Blancs (from Clos Cabrière in Franschhoek), Pongracz (made by the Bergkelder co-operative in Stellenbosch), Graham Beck Madeba Brut (Robertson), Boschendal (Franschhoek), Simonsig Kaapse Vonkel (Stellenbosch).

Look out also for a strange but eventually likeable sparkling Sauvignon Blanc from the Bergkelder. Not a grape variety normally noted for its contribution to sparkling wines, this ultra-fresh, grassy, bone-dry fizz makes a diverting summer aperitif.

Pressing Chardonnay grapes (above) destined for the Cap Classique sparkler, Madeba Brut, at Graham Beck Winery in Robertson.

This gleaming white, intricately gabled façade (left) belongs to the manor house of the Boschendal estate in Franschhoek, Paarl.

AUSTRALIA

Leaders in the triumphal march of the varietal movement, Australia's winemakers have taken Chardonnay and Cabernet Sauvignon, added Shiraz to the list, and recreated them in styles all of their own.

ONE NAME MORE than any other is responsible for keeping Europe's winemakers awake at night. The shudders of apprehension that the mere mention of Australia evokes are not hard to understand. It isn't just the speed with which its wines went from a mere trickle in Northern-Hemisphere markets at the beginning of the 1980s to an unstoppable surge by the end of the decade. It isn't just the indignity of having squadrons of Australian consultants arriving in the Midi, in Trentino, in the Alentejo, to point out how things could be done better. It is, at bottom, the fact that of all the newer non-European winemaking countries, Australia is the least in thrall to European ways of doing things.

Australia's wine industry is effectively scarcely any older than that of the USA and quite considerably younger than South Africa's. (In fact, some of the earliest vine cuttings to be brought into the country came from the Cape, including the all-important Shiraz.) Unlike North America, Australia had no wild vines, and

nor has its industry ever had to go through the painful process of freeing itself from hybrid varieties like California's Isabella and the others.

By the early years of the 20th century, Australian wine was finding its way to Britain through the channels of the Commonwealth in significant quantities. There was a certain amount of unsubtle table wine, but the bulk of what was coming in was fortified – passable approximations of port that were long forgotten by the time the contemporary wine boom began. One of the first red wine brands to brave the British wine trade in the postwar era was marketed as Kanga Rouge, exhibiting about the same level of self-esteem as Algeria's Red Infuriator.

What changed everything was the advent of Chardonnay and Cabernet Sauvignon. While California wines from those two grapes were winning prizes in French tastings, Australia's growers were just about planting their first experimental cuttings. But if Chardonnay and Cabernet have become the Esperanto of the

Australia's vineyards run in a swathe across the southeast of the continent, as well as popping up in enclaves in Western Australia and on the island of Tasmania.

modern wine-drinker, they have done so more as a result of their Australian manifestations than any of their rivals. Winemakers in the Barossa and Hunter Valleys, in the Adelaide Hills and Victoria, taught the non-specialist wine consumer varietal recognition by making the wines so easy to love. They took the red-hot, mouth-drying tannins out of Cabernet, and the steely acidity out of a lot of traditional Chardonnay, and marinated them both in the sweet vanillin of brand new oak, and the rest is history.

Fuelling this development was the importance within Australia itself of wine shows. All of the wine-producing states regularly hold their own regional competitions, in which wines are tasted blind and awarded medals, rather in the manner of the UK's International Wine Challenge organized by *Wine International* magazine.

The awards have a high profile within the domestic trade, with gold-medal bottles flying off retailers' shelves as fast as they can sell them. Consequently, many winemakers have come to fashion their wines in a style that will help them to command attention in a long line-up of other similar wines. These have become known, not always flatteringly in some circles, as "show wines" – big, brash, love-me-or-leave-me types designed to make an immediate impact but not always easy to drink in any quantity.

To some extent, there is justice in this case. Australia makes the richest, oakiest, yellowest, most upfront Chardonnays in the world, wines that have no trouble in attaining 14 per cent alcohol. But it would be entirely misleading to suggest that all Australian Chardonnay tastes like that. Revolutions need to be ushered in by some headline-grabbing act that stirs the hearts of potential followers, and the zeal with which those first wines were seized on by British (and even American) consumers told its own story.

The Chardonnays were followed by Cabernets and Shirazes and blends thereof. Those who are phobic about red wine because they associate it with harsh tannins and vinegary sourness were encouraged by these wines to abandon their prejudices. Then there were sparkling wines that tasted of ripe summer fruits, mango-scented whites and strawberry-perfumed rosés, selling in Britain for as little as a third the price of non-vintage champagne at a time when the champagne producers were having one of their collective dizzy spells.

Behind them came a phalanx of fortifieds, liqueur Muscats unlike any other *vins de liqueur* on earth, headily redolent of smoky tangerine and creamy milk chocolate. It all added up to a non-stop scattergun strategy, and it worked like a dream.

Opening the vintage (above) at the annual Barossa Festival, in South Australia.

Morning sunlight over the northern slopes of the Great Dividing Range (below), in Victoria.

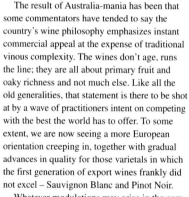

Margaret River (above) is one of Australia's cooler wine-growing regions.

the equator, have a correspondingly fiercer climate to contend with, in which the spring can bring virtual drought while the harvest season suffers torrential rains.

The vineyards are strung throughout a swathe of southeast Australia, from north of Adelaide in the state of South Australia, through Victoria and up to the Hunter Valley north of Sydney. There is a small outpost on a high plateau called the Granite Belt just into Queensland, as well as small but important plantings in the state of Western Australia. The island of Tasmania, in the Tasman Sea between Australia and New Zealand, has isolated vineyards, mainly on its northern edge.

There is a regulatory system in Australia's wine industry. It covers the expected three principal features of labelling: region of origin (a minimum of 85 per cent of wine so labelled must come from the specified area), grape variety (85 per cent again) and vintage (95 per cent). To an even greater extent than in California, however, Australian wine is often made from grapes that are grown in areas quite distant from the winery itself, with the produce of different areas being blended in the same cuvée. A rough-and-ready appellation system allows wines to be considered of GI (Geographic Indication) status if the 85% rule for grape sourcing is observed, but the process of mapping out the GI regions has been bedevilled by non-stop wrangling.

Australia's premium white grape varieties are led by Chardonnay, planted more or less wherever vines are grown. At best, it produces the broad-beamed, sunny, golden wines the world has to come to adore, with subtle variations of style according to sites chosen and the vinification regimes of individual winemakers. Some is kept back for blending as a crowd-pulling component with other grapes such as Semillon and Colombard.

After Chardonnay comes Riesling, originally referred to on labels as Rhine Riesling. In many ways the backbone of fine white wine, it is still top dog in South Australia, but has been overtaken nationally in the last few years by the vogue for Chardie. Riesling gives a fatter, riper wine here than in Europe, but one that is quite as capable of developing interestingly in the bottle. Semillon shares that characteristic, but is very much an Australian original in its dry, unoaked and unblended guise. Always popular in Australia itself, it has had to be patient in awaiting international recognition.

The result of Australia-mania has been that some commentators have tended to say the country's wine philosophy emphasizes instant commercial appeal at the expense of traditional vinous complexity. The wines don't age, runs the line; they are all about primary fruit and oaky richness and not much else. Like all the old generalities, that statement is there to be shot at by a wave of practitioners intent on competing with the best the world has to offer. To some extent, we are now seeing a more European orientation creeping in, together with gradual advances in quality for those varietals in which the first generation of export wines frankly did not excel – Sauvignon Blanc and Pinot Noir.

Whatever modulations may arise in the coming years, Australia has established itself a solid bridgehead into the global wine village, and it did so more quickly and decisively than was achieved by any other emergent nation in wine history. In recent years, indeed, supply has even fallen short of global demand.

Most of Australia's regions experience reliably hot, dry growing conditions year on year. Within the overall pattern, however, there are cooler pockets where more temperate summers have a consequent effect on wine styles. They include the Margaret River area of Western Australia, inland regions such the Clare and Eden valleys in South Australia and much of Tasmania. By contrast, the vineyards of New South Wales and Queensland, being that much nearer

Sauvignon Blanc is occasionally blended with Semillon, as in Bordeaux, but more is often seen on its own. It is a grape that many winemakers are only just learning how to handle, early examples often suffering from a lack of clarity or inappropriate and excessive oaking.

Other classic white grapes planted in small quantities include Gewürztraminer, the Rhône grape Marsanne, and Chenin Blanc.

In addition to those, there are widespread plantings in the irrigated Murray River region of South Australia of an indifferent white variety called Sultana. As its name implies, much of it ends up being processed as dried grapes, but a lot is still used for wine, often the bulk output of bag-in-box wines that account for an important proportion of the domestic market. Muscat of Alexandria, which goes under the local name of Muscat Gordo Blanco, also plays a role in volume production, and is not an ingredient of the premium liqueur Muscats. Colombard is grown too, but on nothing like the scale that it appears in South Africa.

Chief among reds is Shiraz (the Syrah of the northern Rhône), another grape that Australia fashioned in its own image. The reds of the northern Rhône are varietal Syrahs too of course, but the Southern-Hemisphere style is hugely rich, creamy and blackberryish, with little or none of the black pepper or sharp tannins of young Hermitage. It is best exemplified by the wines of Barossa. At its least sensitively vinified, Shiraz can turn out roaringly alcoholic wines with a blurred, cooked flavour like jam, the sweetness of which is then made the more cloying with extended oak-ageing. Thankfully, these wines are by no means the norm for exports.

Shiraz is frequently blended with Cabernet Sauvignon, generally forming the greater element in the mix. The effect can be to stiffen the sinew of the otherwise soft-centred ripe Shiraz, or to mitigate some of young Cabernet's severity where Shiraz is the minor partner. Cabernet is also valued as a varietal in its own right, though, and can offer incontrovertible evidence to those inclined to be sceptical about the winetaster's vocabulary that Cabernet Sauvignon really can taste intensely of blackcurrants.

Increasingly, if Cabernet is blended, it is with its traditional claret bedfellows, Merlot and Cabernet Franc. They are both currently grabbing themselves ever-increasing shares of vineyard land across Australia. One consequence may well be more varietal Merlot, not

hitherto – and unusually in the Southern Hemisphere – one of Australia's specialities.

Grenache looked until recently as if it might be doomed to die out as a humdrum variety used to bulk everyday reds. Just lately, however, it is beginning to hog a share of the limelight as certain winemakers discover it will make a hugely concentrated Shiraz-style red of undeniable pedigree. Pinot Noir is coming on apace as well. Much of it goes into premium bottle-fermented sparkling wines conceived in the champagne image, but there are doughty souls, as there are wherever quality red wine is made, determined to make world-class red varietal Pinot. The first signs of success are with us already, as suitable sites are identified for the famously unforgiving grape.

Minority red grapes take in the Mourvèdre of the southern Rhône and Languedoc – here usually known as Mataro – and Tarrango, a crossing of white Sultana with the port grape Touriga Nacional. It is vinified by some (notably Brown Brothers) in the style of a muscular Dolcetto.

The grounds of St Hallett's in Barossa Valley (below), where 100-year-old Shiraz vines still yield fabulous wines.

Red gum trees in Western Australia (above) flower at grape-harvest time, distracting birds from eating the grapes.

Western Australia's vineyards lie at the southwestern tip of the state (right), with the top producers clustered in the Margaret River region close to the Indian Ocean.

WESTERN AUSTRALIA

Swan Valley One of the very hottest wine regions in a hot country, the Swan Valley was once the main growing area of Western Australia. It is now of declining importance as a result of the identification of cooler sites further south. Notwithstanding that, the Houghton winery still makes a range of decent generic wines here, together with improbable varietals bottled under the Moondah Brook label, such as Chenin Blanc and Verdelho (the latter one of the white grapes of Madeira). Evans & Tate makes a Semillon that bears a positively uncanny resemblance to smoky Sauvignon.

1. SWAN VALLEY
2. MARGARET RIVER
3. LOWER GREAT SOUTHERN
4. SOUTHWEST COASTAL PLAIN

Margaret River One of the great talking-points of Australian wine lately, the milder climate of the Margaret River district has led to the production of some intriguing wines in a considerably less upfront style than is traditionally associated with Australia. Cooling breezes off the Indian Ocean exert a moderating influence here, in a country that doesn't generally receive the same maritime amelioration that, say, South Africa or the western US states do. Consequently, the Margaret River's Chardonnays have an almost Burgundian profile and may require much less acid adjustment than those from South Australia, while the Cabernets are leaner and more closed in their youth. Sauvignons are briskly fresh and herbaceous, while the Semillons are crisp but healthily rounded.

Cullens is one of Margaret River's best estates, making nutty, savoury Chardonnay in a restrained style. Moss Wood makes a slightly richer version that, in some vintages, has the unmistakable waft of shredded cabbage familiar to lovers of Puligny-Montrachet. Cullens also makes a benchmark toasty Semillon without oak (as well as one with) and impressive Pinot Noir. Cape Mentelle, the winery that founded the show-stopping Cloudy Bay in New Zealand, has its Australian base in this district, where it produces an apple-and-melon blend of Semillon and Sauvignon and even has some plantings of Zinfandel.

Leeuwin Estate is one of the most ambitious wineries in all of Australia. Its expensive but indisputably brilliant Chardonnay is an object-lesson to others. A varietally intense Cabernet and deep, resonant Pinot show its versatile abilities to the full. The long-established Vasse Felix winery's Shiraz is plump and rich, without slumping into jamminess.

Lower Great Southern Western Australia's largest wine area is situated a little to the east of the Margaret River. In the sub-regions of Mount Barker and the Frankland River, it is beginning to demonstrate its promise quite emphatically. An entire range of grapes succeeds here, including the finicky Pinot and Sauvignon. The potential for Rieslings in particular looks extremely exciting.

Mount Barker winery, Plantagenet, does all sorts of things well, including a meaty Cabernet to age, tropically juicy Riesling and lemon-butter Chardonnay. Goundrey, also at Mount Barker, has raised some eyebrows with its good-value bottlings of creamy Chardonnay and cassis-scented Cabernet. Another sharply focused, lime-zesty Riesling is made by the Howard Park winery.

SOUTH AUSTRALIA

The most copious wine-producing state of Australia is home to many internationally famous wineries. Its vineyard regions are fairly widely scattered throughout the southeast of the state, with the result that pronounced differences between them can actually be tasted in the glass. In the southern district of Coonawarra, South Australia boasts one of the most distinctive growing regions anywhere in the Southern Hemisphere. Almost every major variety performs well, and botrytized dessert wines – from Semillon and Riesling – have lately become a notable South Australia speciality.

Clare Valley One of the cooler growing regions, Clare actually consists of four interconnected valleys, the Clare, Skillogallee, Watervale and Polish River. The premium varietal here has to be Riesling, which achieves diamond-bright, intensely defined lime-juice and petrol characteristics from the best growers. Semillon is good too, in the austere, minerally, unwooded style, while Chardonnays can be a little on the shy and retiring side, unusually for Australia. Reds are lean as well, often with pronounced tannins and acidity, but for that reason do perform well if bottle-aged.

Tim Knappstein's Riesling is indicative of the Clare style – smoky, full-bodied and zesty, and ageing to a delicious pungency. His Caber-

net is good too. Skillogallee and Pike are textbook Riesling specialists (the latter also makes a first-division Chardonnay.) Another Tim, Tim Adams, makes spectacularly concentrated Semillon and deep, long-lived Shiraz. Jim Barry attracts followers for his crisp Rieslings and Sauvignons, as well as a hauntingly aromatic Shiraz labelled Armagh. The Leasingham label, owned by the Hardy conglomerate, is a good source of simple Clare varietals, including a ripely blackcurrant Shiraz.

Riverland The backwash area of South Australian wine, making bulk produce for the bargain end of the market, is located on heavily irrigated vineyard land along the Murray River. This is where plantings of the more mundane varieties such as Sultana and Muscat of Alexandria (Gordo Blanco) are concentrated.

The Berri-Renmano combine, owned by the godfather of Australian wine, BRL Hardy, pumps out tasty enough varietals. These are led by a powerfully vanillary, but often rather oxidized Chardonnay and light, approachable Cabernet. Angoves makes a lot of generic wine for supermarket own-labels and is probably more reliable. The greater part of Riverland production, though, goes into wine-boxes. By no means of unacceptable quality, these are best glugged back round the barbie rather than lingered over before dinner.

Spring-time scene (above) in the Polish Hill area of South Australia's Clare Valley, home to fine whites.

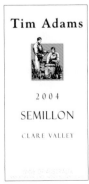

*Penfolds' space-age
Nuriootpa Winery (right)
in the Barossa Valley,
South Australia.*

*The most prolific wine-
producer in Australia, South
Australia's vineyards extend
across the state (below),
offering distinctively
different styles of wine.*

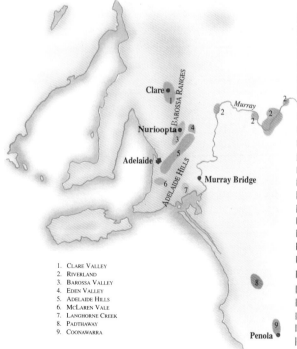

1. CLARE VALLEY
2. RIVERLAND
3. BAROSSA VALLEY
4. EDEN VALLEY
5. ADELAIDE HILLS
6. McLAREN VALE
7. LANGHORNE CREEK
8. PADTHAWAY
9. COONAWARRA

Barossa Valley Probably the first regional name in Australian wine that overseas customers came to recognize, the hot Barossa Valley, northeast of Adelaide, is in many ways the epi-centre of the whole industry. It was settled and planted by Germans and Poles in the 19th century, and today is where much of the harvest from neighbouring regions finds its way to be crushed. A high proportion of Barossa's wineries, therefore, are not necessarily making exclusively Barossa wine.

The bottom of the valley has the hottest microclimate, and is the source of some of Australia's most intensely coloured and alco-holic reds. Shiraz from this region attains incomparable levels of concentration, the epitome of which is Penfolds Grange, the Barossa's legendary *grand cru*. Growers in search of cooler conditions for the Rieslings and Chardonnays for which the area is equally famed have latterly begun planting higher up on the valley hillsides.

Penfolds remains the pre-eminent Barossa name for a comprehensive range of varietals and blends to suit all pockets, as they say. From its simple, zesty Riesling and oak-driven full-on Chardonnay, to its versatile and splendidly crafted reds, quality exudes from every bottle.

Among the red highlights are the top-value Bin 28 Kalimna Shiraz, always a supple, brambly masterpiece, Bin 389 Cabernet-Shiraz and the sensationally concentrated, ink-black Bin 707 Cabernet Sauvignon. Grange (known at home as Grange Hermitage) is nearly all Shiraz, a colossal and yet immaculately graceful wine, full of the aromas of preserved purple fruits, soft leather and wild herbs, and capable of age-ing in the bottle for decades. It isn't cheap, but it's still a fraction of the price of the Château Pétrus to which it is often compared. Penfolds' bottlings of Coonawarra wines (see below), especially the Cabernet, are more purely indica-tive of the region than virtually any others.

Other large-scale operators include Orlando-Wyndham, maker of the best-selling Jacob's Creek range, and Seppelt, whose extraordinarily diverse portfolio takes in premium sparkling wines such as the bone-dry Salinger and trail-blazing sparkling Shiraz (like alcoholic fizzy Ribena), together with authoritative fortifieds, among which the sherry styles are tops (see below).

A list of excellent smaller wineries would have to include Grant Burge (appetizingly nutty Zerk Vineyard Semillon and a soft, plummy Hillcott Merlot), St Hallett (famously intense Old Block Shiraz from century-old vines), Peter

Lehmann (minty, almost claret-like Stonewell Shiraz), Basedow (musclebound, unapologeti-cally oaky Chardonnay), Rockford (idiosyncratic, smooth-contoured Basket Press Shiraz) and Wolf Blass (a comprehensive range including some musky, aromatic Cabernets).

Eden Valley A group of high valleys in the Barossa Ranges, Eden is properly speaking a continuation of the Barossa region itself. It is considerably cooler than the Barossa Valley floor, and those gentler conditions show up in the wines, especially in the significant quantities of Riesling the area produces.

One of the biggest names in Eden is Yalum-ba, which owns the Hill-Smith, Heggies and Pewsey Vale labels, as well as bottling under its own name. The Hill-Smith Sauvignon is an especially poignant wine, an eloquent riposte to those who claim that Australians don't under-stand the grape. Pewsey Vale and Heggies Rieslings both represent benchmark lemon-and-lime versions of that variety. Yalumba's own Family Reserve Shiraz is a triumph, a superbly complex red with a beguiling waft of coffee. The company's sparklers, such as its supremely quaffable Angas Brut wines and the more seri-ous Yalumba D and Pinot-Chardonnay, and fortifieds like the chocolatey, caramelly Clock-tower, are also to be reckoned with.

Hot, dry Barossa Valley (above) is South Australia's premier wine region.

Henschke is another name to drop. It owns some of the oldest vineyard land for miles around, its shatteringly profound Hill of Grace Shiraz made from 100-year-old vines. Its Mount Edelstone is another top-drawer Shiraz, while Cyril Henschke is fine, concentrated Cabernet that demands ageing. The whites are good too, particularly the pungent, petrolly Riesling, another one to age.

Adelaide Hills The hill ranges east of the city are fairly sparsely planted, but represent another favourable microclimate for growers looking for relief from South Australia's heat. Petaluma is the most widely-known name around here, although its most celebrated bottlings come from Coonawarra fruit (see below). Bridgewater Mill is its alternative label, and includes a good, citrus-fresh Chardonnay. Pirramimma's Cabernet has an attractive eucalyptus note.

McLaren Vale South of Adelaide, this flat, expansive district is carving out a regional identity for itself with wines that are increasingly being made in a much subtler style than was once the case. It is part of a wider, though not precisely enough defined area known as the Southern Vales.

The Chapel Hill winery is making the running with some exquisitely honed reds from Cabernet and Shiraz. Chateau Reynella makes powerhouse Basket Press Shiraz here too under the auspices of the Hardy conglomerate, in whose crown this is the jewel. Among Cabernets, Wirra-Wirra's Angelus bottling exhibits all the cassis intensity looked for in South Australia, while Ryecroft's Chardonnay is a curvaceous charmer. Wandering winemaker Geoff Merrill is here too, making a range of good-value varietals under the Mount Hurtle label, including a raspberryish rosé from Grenache and some melony Sauvignon-Semillon.

Langhorne Creek The Langhorne Creek district is east of McLaren Vale, but shares much the same characteristics. Too much of its production finds its way into blended Southern Vales wines at present, but as the inherent quality of the region comes to be appreciated, that will hopefully change.

Padthaway Padthaway is a sort of northern outpost of the more famous Coonawarra region. Lying in the southeast corner of the state of South Australia, it is nearly as cool as its neighbour and has a little of the sought-after *terra rossa* soil of Coonawarra. Whereas the latter has developed a reputation for red wines, Padthaway has become something of a white-wine enclave – specifically Chardonnay, Riesling and Sauvignon. Most of the vineyard land is owned by companies based in other areas, but who make special cuvées that carry the regional name on the bottle label.

A camel sanctuary amid the vines (below) in the flat expanse of South Australia's McLaren Vale.

Orlando, Seppelt and Penfolds all have interests in Padthaway. Penfolds Chardonnay from the region is one of the most richly buttery; the company also now owns the long-established Victoria winery Lindemans, whose Padthaway Chardonnay is almost as powerful.

Coonawarra Just south of Padthaway is the region that got everybody so excited about Australia in the first place. Declared a GI in 2001, Coonawarra's unique blend of cool climate and *terra rossa* soil – the paprika-coloured red loam that lends the vineyards such a striking appearance – is without doubt responsible for the obvious class of its wines.

Coonawarra's finest bottles provide the answer to that interminable rhetorical question that still fuels debates between the so-called Old and New Worlds: does vineyard siting or *terroir* make a difference outside Europe? Not all of Coonawarra's vines are planted on the red soil, and those that aren't do seem to lack that extra dimension of perfume and complexity boasted by those that are.

It is the reds, Shiraz and (most notably) Cabernet Sauvignon that best demonstrate the regional identity, although there are good Chardonnays and even some Riesling as well. The Cabernets are made in a positively French idiom, in that their youthful tannins can be decidedly severe and the aromatic components stubbornly refuse to show themselves. When they do open out, however, there is nothing remotely French about them. They have a pronounced savoury quality, often resembling

mocha coffee beans, sometimes a deliberate slight volatility like Worcestershire sauce, but underlying them is that dry, subtly spiced dark fruit, with the odd date or prune thrown in with the basic blackcurrant.

There are a few more wineries actually based here than in Padthaway, but the headline-hitting wines have tended to be made by outsiders owning priceless Coonawarra land. Penfolds makes some of its most extravagantly beautiful Cabernet from grapes grown here; its range is as good a place to start as any. (Lindemans' bottling, now under the Southcorp umbrella with Penfolds, is also very fine, though.) Petaluma has long had a reputation for a hugely intense Cabernet-Merlot blend, simply called Petaluma Coonawarra. The premier-league Rosemount company from New South Wales has a well-made Coonawarra Cabernet too.

Among wineries located in the region, Hollick makes a glorious, challenging Ravenswood Cabernet, as well as a more immediately accessible Cabernet-Merlot blend and fresh, limey Riesling. Katnook Estate makes tobaccoey Cabernet and a big, fleshy Chardonnay, while Penley is a relative newcomer making dense-textured Cabernet and a brambly, gamey Shiraz. Wynns is a well-known name, now also under Southcorp's wing, and is an ultra-reliable producer of ripe-fruited unoaked Shiraz, smoky Chardonnay, a sweetly limey Riesling and a pitch-black, massively structured, top-of-the-range Cabernet called John Riddoch (it needs about ten years to come round).

The name that everyone recognizes as uniquely Australian (above), Coonawarra is the most southerly of South Australia's wine regions.

VICTORIA

Victoria's vineyards are no longer as extensive as they were a century ago (they suffered badly in the worldwide phylloxera plague that South Australia managed to escape), but the cooler southern reaches of the state are now producing fine varietals and sparklers to compete with the best. In the northeast, Australia's celebrated fortifieds reach their apogee.

Drumborg Very cool western region, dominated by Seppelt, which uses grapes from here to make one of its extensive range of sparkling wines, Drumborg Brut.

Great Western The area known as Great Western is further inland than Drumborg, and consequently somewhat warmer. It too has a sparkling wine tradition, immortalized in the name of Great Western Brut, yet another fizz from Seppelt. Increasingly, though, it is becoming clear that the potential for Australia's best two red grapes, Cabernet and Shiraz, is most exciting of all. Chardonnays tend to be fashioned in the rounded and richly oaked style.

Mount Langi Ghiran is one of the high flyers of this region, with a Shiraz in an intriguingly restrained style and Cabernet with plenty of extract. Its Riesling has long been one of the best, and is structured for ageing. Cathcart Ridge makes a particularly lush, chocolatey Shiraz, while the Best's winery has a portfolio of cheap and cheerful varietals with good, lemon-meringue Chardonnay but thinnish reds.

High-altitude cool vineyards of Victoria's Great Dividing Range (above), source of delicate Riesling and subtle Chardonnay.

From the cooler coastal areas, to the hot inland regions, the smaller state of Victoria (right) produces a wide range of wine styles, including the famous liqueur Muscats made in the northeast.

1. DRUMBORG
2. GREAT WESTERN
3. GEELONG
4. YARRA VALLEY
5. MORNINGTON PENINSULA
6. GOULBURN VALLEY
7. GLENROWAN-MILAWA
8. RUTHERGLEN
9. MURRAY RIVER
10. LAUNCESTON
11. BICHENO
12. HOBART

Geelong First of a ring of small regions surrounding Melbourne (Geelong is just west of the city) that are home to some of the more far-sighted and ambitious of Australia's current generation of winemakers. The winemaker at the Bannockburn estate doubles as a Burgundy vigneron during Australia's winter months, so it comes as no surprise to find him a dab hand at Chardonnay and Pinot Noir. Nor does his Cabernet lack for anything in varietal richness. There are eloquent Cabernets and Chardonnays too from the Idyll winery.

Yarra Valley The temperate Yarra is Victoria's answer to South Australia's Coonawarra, a prime site for highly individual winemaking and superlative cool-climate varietals. This is one of the most promising areas in Australia for Pinot Noir, with Green Point, Coldstream Hills and Tarrawarra leading the pack. Mount Mary's is coming up fast on the inside. There was a tendency in the past to overoak the wines, which is now thankfully being resisted. Green Point (the export name for Moët's Domaine Chandon) also makes a very fine, lightly buttery, nutmeggy Chardonnay – not a million miles from the Sonoma County, California, style – as well as its much-praised fizz. The Cabernets and Shirazes of Yarra Yering winemaker Bailey Carrodus are idiosyncratic creations fully worth the high asking price. St Huberts makes a deep, satisfying Cabernet to last.

Mornington Peninsula There are not far off 100 wineries crowded on to this little peninsula southeast of Melbourne. Like the Yarra, it is a region of stylistic pioneers who are making waves. Dromana is a winery with a versatile portfolio, including a soft, strawberryish Pinot Noir and plushly textured Cabernet-Merlot. Its soundly made cheaper range is bottled under the Schinus Molle label. Stonier's Merricks has textbook Chardonnay and Cabernet in the full-blown opulent style.

Goulburn Valley North of the Yarra, Goulburn is an expansive valley region that contains some of the oldest wineries and vineyards in Australia, whose vines miraculously escaped the worst of the phylloxera wave. Château Tahbilk has some 100-year-old vines, its Private Bin bottlings of Shiraz and Cabernet bursting with venerable class. This is one of the properties that pioneered varietal Marsanne in Australia. The Mitchelton winery produces both oaked and unoaked versions of Marsanne. It certainly has a style all of its own, but its clinging, top-heavy, buttery banana quality is too much for some. Delatite offers a more broad-minded range from its high-altitude vineyards. Snappy Riesling, delicately scented Gewürztraminer and rose-petally Pinot Noir supplement the excellent Shiraz and Cabernet.

Glenrowan-Milawa As you head into the northeastern sector of Victoria, you are heading towards fortified country (see below). At Milawa, though, table wines are made in quantity, the most important producer being Brown Brothers, one of the vanguard companies that blazed the trail for Australian wines in the UK. Its range is wide and fairly stolid, but some wines stand out: buttery King Valley Chardonnay, the juicy-fruited Dolcetto lookalike Tarrango, deliciously peachy late-picked Muscat, and hazelnutty Semillon.

Rutherglen Pre-eminent for liqueur Muscats and Tokays (see under Fortified Wines).

New vineyards planted by Brown Brothers (below), one of hotter, inland Glenrowan-Milawa's top producers of table wines.

Vineyards of the Lower Hunter (above) suffer more from tropical rain storms than those in its more northerly partner, the Upper Hunter.

1. MURRUMBIDGEE IRRIGATION AREA
2. COWRA
3. MUDGEE
4. HUNTER VALLEY

The hot Hunter Valley, north of Sydney (right), is New South Wales' finest wine region.

NEW SOUTH WALES

Although it contains the Hunter Valley region of worldwide repute, New South Wales only accounts for a relatively tiny fraction of Australia's annual wine production. Its climate is as hot and hard for growers to contend with as parts of South Australia.

Murrumbidgee Irrigation Area (MIA)
The world's least attractively named wine region is responsible largely for volume output destined for boxes and own-brand bottlings. Botrytized Semillon is an unlikely exception to the humdrum rule, and is especially distinguished from de Bortoli.

Cowra Small region supplying much of the Hunter Valley's raw material. Hunter winery Rothbury makes an impressive regional Cowra Chardonnay, though.

Mudgee The Mudgee district is sufficiently proud of its regional pedigree to have invented its own appellation. A pity then that much of the produce of this hot, dry district goes to beef up Hunter's wines when their harvests are hit by rain. Firm Cabernet and stout Shiraz are the baseline (Botolobar's Shiraz is a stunner), but gathering potential is being observed in Chardonnays too.

Hunter Valley Divided into the Upper and Lower Hunter, this hot, extensive valley is the premium wine region of New South Wales. The Upper section is quite a way to the north of the Lower, and manages to escape the tropical rains that can disrupt the Lower Hunter vintage. Dry Semillon, practically an indigenous Hunter style of great lineage, is the proudest boast. It's usually fairly low in alcohol, austerely hard and minerally and famously takes on a burnt-toast quality as it matures in the bottle. This has fooled many a blind taster into thinking it has been aged in charred oak, when it may very well be entirely innocent of the stuff. Red wines can be a bit muddy – a lot of that sweet plum-jam style of Shiraz comes from the Hunter – but they are improving.

Good Semillon producers include Rothbury, Rosemount, McWilliams Elizabeth, Tyrrell's Vat 1 and Brokenwood. Rothbury also make a slim but beguiling Shiraz, Rosemount a show-stopping, vegetally Burgundian Roxburgh Chardonnay, Tyrrell's an exciting, offbeat range sold under Vat numbers (such as the famed Vat 6 Pinot and the butterscotchy Vat 47 Chardonnay) and Brokenwood a reverberating Shiraz sombrely called Graveyard Vineyards.

QUEENSLAND

Right on the border with New South Wales is a an area unromantically known as the Granite Belt. Only its altitude makes it a propitious place to grow grapes, and the wines don't tend to travel much further than Sydney.

TASMANIA

Led by the visionary and multi-talented Andrew Pirie at Pipers Brook vineyard, a small band of Tasmania producers intends to show the world that the island can make sharply defined varietals, especially Pinot Noir and Chardonnay, in a distinctively European (i.e. French) idiom. The two centres of production are Launceston in the northeast and Hobart in the south; they are delineated by an appellation system that Tasmania has drawn up for itself and its modest output.

Pipers Brook winery, in the northern region of the same name, makes exemplary Pinot Noir, hard in youth and needing time, a subtly steely Chardonnay and some crisp, zesty Riesling. Moorilla Estate produces good, beefy Pinot, and is trying its hand at Gewürztraminer. Heemskerk was traditionally known for big but fairly brittle-centred Cabernet, and is now set on making fizz after some initial input from champagne house Louis Roederer.

FORTIFIED WINES

There are two basic styles of Australian fortified wine. One derives from the days when the hot Southern-Hemisphere countries all had a shot at imitating the traditional methods and flavours of port and sherry. Indeed, those terms were until recently in widespread use in Australia itself, though they are now on the wane. Among the port-styles are some extremely sweet strawberry-jam-like wines made from fortified Shiraz; McWilliams, Seppelt and Montara offer typical examples, of which some are vintage-dated. Extended wood-ageing washes out the colour of some, which are then referred to – as in the Douro – as tawny. The sherry styles are not as widely seen on the export markets, but can be even better. Seppelt makes a comprehensive range of tangy, salty fino (labelled DP117), hazelnutty amontillado (DP116) and toffeeish oloroso (DP38).

The other styles are unique to Australia. Liqueur Muscat and Liqueur Tokay are breath-takingly rich fortified wines made from, respectively, the Muscat Blanc à Petits Grains (here known as Brown Muscat for the dun-skinned variant locally grown) and Muscadelle, the minority grape of Sauternes. The production area is mainly in northeast Victoria around the town of Rutherglen, although some Muscats are also made in Glenrowan, a little to the south.

Their production seems to combine a little of every traditional method for making liquorous dessert wines. Firstly, the grapes are left to overripen and partially shrivel on the vine. They are then pressed and the viscous juice partially fermented but fortified with grape spirit long before the piercing sweetness has even begun to soften. After that, they are aged and blended from a barrel system something like the *soleras* of Jerez.

The Muscats, especially, are shockingly intense. Pure orange marmalade on the nose, they dissolve in the mouth into a glutinous amalgam of milk chocolate, sticky dates and candied orange rind, with a finish that persists on the back of the palate for minutes on end. There are many fine producers, the more notable of whom are Stanton & Killeen, Chambers, Morris, Yalumba and Campbells of Rutherglen.

Heemskerk Vineyards in the Pipers Brook region of Tasmania (above), makers of notably well-built Cabernet and elegant sparkling wines.

NEW ZEALAND

In just 20 years, New Zealand's winemakers have taken the world by storm to become the fastest growing wine country in the world. Undaunted by geographical isolation, they have established a strong regional identity.

THIS IS WHERE the global wine tour makes its final stop, at the world's most southerly vineyards on the North and South Islands of New Zealand. Any further, and we would be trying to make Icewine in Antarctica.

Australia may be a relative junior in the international wine industry, but New Zealand really is the new kid on the block among the major producing countries. Its potential for fine winemaking only began to be taken seriously in the 1970s but, undoubtedly helped to a great degree by the successful rise of its ambitious northern neighbour, it now has one of the most rapidly growing viticultural sectors anywhere. Although winemaking will never be as

The world's most southerly vineyards operate in a damp, cool climate. Except for South Island's Central Otago, New Zealand's wine regions (below) lie on or close to the coast.

important to it as sheep- or dairy-farming have famously been, there is nonetheless an infectious and widespread atmosphere of experimentation, such as overtook California in the 1960s and Australia in the 1970s.

It has to be said that the domestic market in New Zealand has not, until very recently, been a conspicuously favourable one in which to sell wine. At about the same time as it was introduced in the United States, New Zealanders briefly experimented with Prohibition. National licensing laws have, for most of the century, been the most restrictive in the English-speaking world. High-street wine shops are a post-war phenomenon, while supermarkets have only been allowed to sell the country's home wine produce since the beginning of the 1990s.

Viticulture was tentatively practised in the 19th century. Its earliest pioneers were British settlers, led by the enterprising James Busby. He created a thriving little vineyard in the north of the country that lived off sales to the local garrison. Phylloxera, the vine louse that built an empire of destruction in the world's vineyards in the closing decades of the 19th century, was careful not to pass New Zealand by. The wholesale replanting that followed was of hybrid grape varieties of mixed *vinifera* and American vine parentage, so that, until well after the Second World War, the dowdy Isabella held sway over both islands.

What eventually catapulted New Zealand into the limelight was, of course, Sauvignon Blanc. There is an oft-expressed feeling among wine commentators that Sauvignon is not quite a major-league grape variety, owing to its brash and relatively unmalleable character. If any region is likely to persuade consumers to come down on the other side of the argument, it will be the Marlborough district of New Zealand's South Island. There is more uplifting, happy fruit flavour in New Zealand Sauvignon than in any other dry white wine on earth.

Sauvignon was followed by fruit-fuelled Chardonnay and Riesling. Reds lagged behind for a while, the varieties not carefully enough matched to the planting areas; much of the

1. AUCKLAND
2. GISBORNE
3. HAWKES BAY
4. WAIRARAPA
5. NELSON
6. MARLBOROUGH
7. CANTERBURY
8. CENTRAL OTAGO

Auckland

Gisborne

MT RUAPEHU *Hawkes Bay*
Napier

Wellington
TASMAN
MTS
Blenheim

Christchurch

Queenstown

Dunedin

Cabernet Sauvignon was excessively light and herbaceous, its inescapable whiff of green pepper skin complaining bitterly in the glass of climatic indignities in the vineyard. Producers have addressed that problem now with better site selection, and some wineries are achieving even faster improvements with Pinot Noir, always a likelier bet than Cabernet in a cool climate. The latest development is the appearance of that other cool-climate classic, fine *méthode traditionelle* sparkling wine, promptly followed by a Champagne delegation looking to invest.

At the moment, the New Zealand wine industry is still very much in a state of germination. It has proved that it can make a range of commercially successful varietal wines, whites especially, and some of those Pinots are now beginning to achieve internationally acknowledged greatness. There is certainly a small clutch of wineries ahead of the field, whose wines (Cloudy Bay is the most prominent example) are sufficiently sought-after that export allocations have to be severely restricted and the proprietors have only to name their price.

The country's wine infrastructure, however, is still in its infancy in the sense that much of the annual harvest still has to travel unconscionable distances to reach the winery at which it will be pressed. The journey may very well include a rough crossing of the Cook Strait, the body of water that separates the two islands. While that is being addressed, party-pooping phylloxera is on the march again, gnawing its way through precious Marlborough vinestocks.

Preferential duty rates for home produce do not prevent the Australians from selling a healthy quantity of wine in New Zealand, and then there is the problem of how to get the world to beat a path to your door when you are so off the beaten track. For the time being, the industry's ruling body, the Wine Institute of New Zealand, has sensibly decided to target the greater part of its export effort at the UK, but that does mean that the influential American wine constituency remains largely sceptical or completely ignorant of what the country is capable of.

Eventually, all of these problems will be resolved. Investment in new installations is increasing faster than ever before, so that a greater percentage of each vintage will be processed close to the vineyard where it was grown. The replanting that the latest bout of phylloxera will entail should be on resistant American rootstocks. Home consumption will

The love-affair with Marlborough Sauvignon Blanc began with the wines of Montana. Machine-harvesters at work (above) picking Sauvignon grapes at Montana's Brancott Estate, Marlborough, North Island.

Stunning landscape of inland South Island (left), on the shore of Lake Wanaka in Central Otago.

increase as the industry's overall capacity grows. As to the preference for the UK market, it is currently paying dividends, so why upset the applecart?

The next step is an appellation system to cover New Zealand's widely dispersed vineyard regions. A start was made in the mid-1990s with the identification of regional names, although at the outset, any wine that was composed of grapes from more than one region, rather than being denied a regional designation, was simply allowed an amalgamated one. That of course

Ngatarawa Winery and vineyards (above) in the well-established Hawkes Bay region of North Island.

defeats the object of having an appellation name in the first place (imagine the French allowing two growers in the Loire to pool their Sauvignon and officially call the resulting wine Menetou-Sancerre) and should be tightened as soon as practically possible.

When all is said and drunk, though, New Zealand has no greater asset than the fact that its wines have recognizable national identity. And it is that irresistible factor on which the repute of any wine-producing region, old or new, is inevitably founded.

Not only does New Zealand have a cool climate, it also has a damp one. Annual rainfall is plentifully distributed throughout the year, with the result that vines often yielded too vigorously, giving low-quality fruit, or that the grapes were diluted by water penetration during the all-important ripening phase. New techniques in vineyard management introduced during the 1980s have widely rectified those particular problems. This allows many growers to harvest earlier, leading to riper, fuller and more concentrated flavours in the glass.

The growing regions are scattered throughout an extensive stretch of the North and South Islands, for all that the total acreage is still very limited compared to that of Australia, which annually produces about ten times more wine than New Zealand. With the exception of southerly Otago, they are all situated on or near the coast, mostly on the Pacific side. The whole show began in the far north of the North Island, in area now logically enough known as Northland, just about the warmest section of the country. Although most of the recent activity has been in vineyards much further south, there

are moves afoot to re-investigate Northland as a possible site for warm-climate varietals.

Müller-Thurgau once occupied pole position in the vineyards, but has now been put in its place rather decisively by Chardonnay and Sauvignon spreading like wildfire. The former achieves more overt fruit quality in New Zealand than it does seemingly anywhere else. Aromas of peach, banana and pear are quite common, and not especially disguisable by oak treatments. Some wineries are attempting to capture a more Burgundian ethos, with buttery richness as opposed to fruit-salad freshness, but they are not yet the norm. Müller can, surprisingly, yield a soft, gently fruity wine from the best exponents but its poor reputation elsewhere means that it is likely to continue declining here.

Sauvignon Blanc is the great white hope of New Zealand wine – better here than in the Loire, many think, for sheer fruit-powered dynamism. There are quite dramatic stylistic differences between wineries, some emphasizing the green, herbaceous flavours of gooseberries, asparagus and freshly-washed watercress, others plunging headlong into tropicality with mango, passion fruit, pineapple and musky Charentais melon. I have tasted Marlborough Sauvignons that smelt of red peppers, grated carrot, the purest blackcurrant juice, even glacé (candied) cherries. It is one exciting wine when it wants to be.

Riesling achieves classical steeliness, without quite the petrolly pungency of Australian versions. Then there's a dash of Chenin Blanc, which should enjoy the climate, some delicate but recognizable Gewürztraminer and limited plantings of so far rather unremarkable Semillon, better blended than made as a varietal.

Cabernet Sauvignon, once the most widely planted red, now plays second fiddle to Pinot Noir. Those vegetal flavours that have dogged its image are still too easy to find, but some offerings are showing much deeper, plummier concentration than before, so there is hope. Pinot itself is now flexing its muscles on the world stage, producing wines as complex, thrilling and distinguished as any from Carneros or Oregon. As well as being built on good, solid, raspberry fruit foundations, they also display a distinctly Burgundian reluctance to charm in their first flush. Merlot is striking out on its own in some parts, while playing its historically sanctioned role of chaperoning Cabernet in others.

NORTH ISLAND

Auckland The area in the immediate vicinity of Auckland was at one time in decline as a wine region, as attention was resolutely turned to more fashionable districts further south. In the last few years, it has started gaining in status as the most auspicious region for well-built reds. It is warm, but prone to harvest rains, which means that fruit from other regions often has to be bought in to beef up the blends, but in the kinder years Auckland reds are looking good. The region includes a subzone called Matakana, north of the city, as well as Waiheke Island, situated in the harbour.

Persuasive Bordeaux-blend reds come from Te Motu, Goldwater and Stonyridge. Kumeu River makes a profoundly Burgundian and quite atypical Chardonnay as well as a striking red with more Merlot than Cabernet.

Gisborne On the east coast of the North Island, Gisborne has begun to find its feet as a quality region after years of languishing as a bag-in-box bulk area. Copious plantings of Müller-Thurgau still testify to that, but Gisborne has become so good at premium white varietals, and won so many awards, that it now styles itself – without a blush for modesty – Chardonnay Capital of New Zealand. As well as Chardonnay, Gewürztraminer has performed creditably, and the smart money is now on champagne-method sparkling wines. The town of Gisborne stands on Poverty Bay, sometimes used as an alternative name for the region.

New Zealand's two biggest wine companies, Marlborough-based Montana and Corbans from near Auckland, both have footholds in Gisborne. Millton Vineyards is a partially organic producer, making some of its wines according to the biodynamic principles followed by Nicolas Joly in Savennières (see Loire section). Its Chardonnay is a thunderously rich, lemon-curd wine. Auckland family producer Nobilo makes a more restrained and smokily oaked Poverty Bay Chardonnay.

Hawkes Bay Further down the coast, in the environs of the town of Napier, Hawkes Bay is one of New Zealand's longer-established vineyard regions. Like Gisborne, it has a high reputation for Chardonnay, as well as some subtler, gentler Sauvignon than is commonly met with on the South Island. There is plenty of Müller still, as there is in Gisborne, but red Bordeaux blends are improving significantly in what is one of the country's sunnier vineyards.

Hawkes Bay winery Te Mata makes what is probably the most authoritative range of wines in the region, taking in soft, gooseberryish Sauvignon (Castle Hill), discreetly buttery Chardonnay (Elston) and full-frontal, muscular Cabernet-Merlot (Coleraine). To indicate the measure of the ambition, Te Mata has also planted some Syrah. The Villa Maria conglomerate, which owns both the Vidal and Esk Valley labels, makes some tasty Sauvignon and modest, approachable red blends. Ngatarawa (the "g" is silent) makes ripely expressive Cabernet-Merlot and, in some years, a good stab at dessert Riesling from noble-rotted grapes. Auckland's Babich winery makes a regional Hawkes Bay Chardonnay (Irongate) in the oaky buttercream mould.

The damp climate encourages vines to grow too vigorously. Pruning and leaf-trimming help control their growth here at Esk Valley vineyards in Hawkes Bay (above).

Vines were only planted in Marlborough (below) as recently as the 1970s, by big producer Montana. The region is now synonymous with fruit-rich Sauvignon.

Wairarapa At the very southern tip of the North Island, near the New Zealand capital of Wellington, Wairarapa is home to some of the country's best small wine-growers. Reds are the declared speciality, whether from Cabernet or Pinot Noir, and the challenge has been taken sufficiently seriously that the export wines, at least, have been hugely impressive. A sub-region within Wairarapa, Martinborough, has emerged as particularly promising for Pinot Noir, and is being mentioned in the same breath as California's Carneros by some.

Martinborough Vineyards, having taken its name from the region, does the area proud by producing its most celebrated Pinot Noir, a clean, raspberry-fruited, deeply complex wine with Burgundian levels of acidity and – perhaps – longevity. Its Chardonnay and Riesling are also finely crafted. Ata Rangi's Pinot is another resonant performance, subtly spiced and meaty; this is another winery with a bit of Syrah, which it uses to plump its fine Cabernet-Merlot blend. A slightly lighter, more cherryish Pinot is made by Palliser Estate, whose bold Sauvignons and Chardonnays have plenty of guts.

SOUTH ISLAND

Nelson A hilly region on the fringes of the Tasman mountains, Nelson is Chardonnay country *par excellence*. Only a handful of wineries have made their homes here, in a damp but otherwise promising cool-climate district, but the quality of the white varietals is very persuasive. Neudorf makes a finely honed Chardonnay and some pretty good, positively flavoured Pinot, while Seifried (aka Redwood Valley) has crisp Riesling in both dry and lightly sweet versions and a heartwarming, bright golden Chardonnay with overtones of banana.

Marlborough Over the last decade and a half, Marlborough (centred on the town of Blenheim at the northern end of the South Island) has emerged as the greatest of all New Zealand regions. Little matter that it doesn't have a particularly elevated reputation for red wines, it is the origin of many of the country's most sharply definitive white wines, with Sauvignon Blanc at the head of the pack. The region is cool but relatively dry, and its misty autumns mean that botrytized wines from Riesling are a possibility in most vintages. Chardonnay plays an important role too.

Montana, the New Zealand wine colossus, basically invented Marlborough as a wine region in the 1970s when it planted the first vines here, and its top-value benchmark Sauvignon has become a contemporary classic wine. For all that it may wax and wane from year to year, it is never less than riotously fruity. Montana's Chardonnay is a peachy little number, there's good botrytized Riesling and some quietly impressive single-estate Pinot Noir.

Cloudy Bay was the second winery to startle the world with its Sauvignon from Marlborough. Those in the know fight over the limited quantities. It is expensive, but profoundly eloquent wine, thrown into relief by a little Semillon. Its Chardonnay is deep and complex, and the Cabernet-Merlot a damson-rich powerhouse of long, refined flavour.

Hunters Estate is another great name for opulent Sauvignon and Chardonnay, Jackson Estate makes soft, biscuity Chardonnay and an emphatic, explosive Sauvignon, Vavasour (and its alternative label Dashwood) has high-octane Sauvignon and Chardonnay, Delegats' Oyster Bay range from Marlborough includes a smoky, peachy Sauvignon, Matua Valley's Shingle Peak label offers gooseberry-crammed Sauvignon, Wairau River has a taut, orchard-fruited

New Zealand's cool climate is showing itself adept as a source of méthode traditionnelle *sparklers, especially in the Marlborough area (left).*

Sauvignon and melt-in-the-mouth Chardonnay... but you get the picture.

Marlborough is also where most of New Zealand's champagne-method sparklers are being made, often with expertise and investment from champagne houses such as Veuve Clicquot and Deutz. Pinot Noir and Chardonnay are the grapes used, and the examples so far released show just how distinguished sparkling wines can be when made in a cool climate.

Pelorus is the Cloudy Bay fizz, undoubtedly the best to date, for its limpid, toasty richness derived from maturation on the yeast lees. Deutz Marlborough Cuvée, released by Montana, is extremely crisp and dry, a touch more knowing than its everyday Lindauer fizz (though the Lindauer rosé is expressive enough). Cellier Le Brun, a sparkling specialist, could yet outstrip them all.

Canterbury Centred on the city of Christchurch, Canterbury's vineyards are cooler still than those of Marlborough, with the Waipara zone north of the city producing the most elegant wines to date. Chardonnay and Pinot Noir are the varietals of choice, but there is good Riesling too. Waipara Springs offers an ample-fleshed Chardonnay, as does Giesen, which also makes noble-rotted Riesling when the weather performs. Pinot Noir looks ostentatiously good from the recently established Mark Rattray winery. Innovative St Helena has planted Pinot Gris and Pinot Blanc.

Central Otago East of the town of Queensland, on South Island, Central Otago is New Zealand's smallest, and most southerly, wine region. It is also the only inland region, with a handful of producers. The vineyards are only at a tentative stage of development as yet. The two foremost grape varieties so far are the intriguing duo of Pinot Noir and Gewürztraminer.

BEER

INGREDIENTS

Beer, like many things we take for granted, is little understood. It is a much more complex drink than many realize. Beer is the juice of the good earth. Its colours, from deep copper and ruby black to pale-yellow, reflect the passing of the seasons – from bare soil through to the golden harvests of barley and wheat.

THE FOAMING HEAD on a glass hides many mysteries, not least of which are beer's basic ingredients. Malt and hops feature regularly on beer labels and in promotional photographs, but how many drinkers would recognize the aromatic hop cone, one of the most unusual species in the plant kingdom? Apart from a few Belgian gourmets, nobody eats them today. Besides, how many know what malt really is? It may begin life as a waving field of cereal, but the grain has to undergo a complex series of changes – germination, roasting, and mashing – between its initial harvest and reaching the drinker's glass. There are many different types of malt. Each varies in colour, flavour and sugar content, depending upon the precise methods used to produce it. Each beer has its own "signature" combination of different malt types.

Yeast is the crucial, "magical" ingredient and its role in the transformation of the sugar in a brew to intoxicating alcohol remained a mystery for centuries. Again, there are many varieties to choose from, each with its own characteristics – its speed of action, flavour and the amount of alcohol and carbon-dioxide that it produces.

Hops are a relatively recent addition to the list of essential ingredients. The natural oils that are contained within the hop cones impart the bitterness that many drinkers demand, and help to preserve the brew. There is a mind-boggling range to choose from.

In addition to the basic ingredients, brewers sometimes add more unexpected ingredients to the recipe, such as cherries or ginger, to impart an individual flavour to their particular beer. The result of the vast number of permutations of ingredients available to the beer brewer is a mouth-watering world of choice in the global bar for the lucky beer drinker.

Above: A photograph dated 1910 shows hops being delivered to an oast-house in Kent, England.

Above left: Drip mats and labels commonly use the ingredients of beer as a motif.

Left: A stained-glass window at the Sapporo brewery in Hokkaido, Japan. It shows water, hops and barley, some of the ingredients used to make beer.

Opposite: A golden field of barley ripening in the summer. Barley is the traditional cereal used in beer making.

WATER

Ask any group of drinkers what beer contains, and they may mention malt and hops. They rarely remember the greatest ingredient of all – water. Yet without a good supply, brewing good beer is impossible.

BEER IS MADE UP mainly of water, and its quality and mineral content directly affect the character of the brew. Brewers have even given water their own name – liquor.

Water contains six main component salts: bicarbonate, sodium, chloride, calcium, magnesium and sulphate. The proportions of these in the liquor used will greatly affect the flavour and sometimes the colour of the finished product. High levels of bicarbonate, for example, can produce a highly acidic mash, which will give a poor rate of sugar extraction from the malt. Too much sulphate will produce a sharp, bitterness in the brew and magnesium is an essential nutrient for the yeast.

Many brewers like to boast about the refreshing source of the water they use to brew their beers. Hürlimann of Switzerland, for example, sells the liquor used at its Zurich brewery as a bottled mineral water under the tradename "Aqui".

In the United States, Coors of Colorado built its sales and reputation by proclaiming that its water poured from the snow-capped Rocky Mountains. To reinforce the point, a waterfall plunges from its cans and bottle labels. And in parched Australia, Tasmanian Breweries make a similar appeal with their Cascade Lager.

Some breweries have unusual water sources. Rodenbach in Belgium, famous for its sour red ales, uses underground springs to feed an ornamental lake which then supplies the West Flanders brewery, and on the parched, rocky island of Malta in the Mediterranean, where every drop of water is precious, one brewery has a rooftop reservoir in order to catch and store each brief shower of rain.

JEALOUSLY COVETED LIQUOR

A good water source was a particularly key requirement for the earliest breweries. Many of the great brewing towns sprang up around a good liquor supply. The town of Plzen in the Czech Republic, for example, had very soft water, perfect for brewing the

Above: The label for Cascade Lager from Tasmania uses an image of a local waterfall to emphasize the pure source of the water contained in the brew.

Below: The unique taste of Guinness was often mistakenly attributed to the River Liffey, in the heart of Dublin. In fact Guinness is brewed with water from the Grand Canal.

Pilsner-style lagers, and the water in Burton-on-Trent in England had exactly the right mineral content for brewing the pale ales which made the town so famous.

In England, London brewers were so jealous of the water in the small Staffordshire town of Burton that they built their own breweries there, and a Lancashire brewer miles away transported Burton water to his brewery by rail.

This fine liquid was drawn from wells sunk deep into the layer of gypsum beneath the town. Purified by slow, natural filtration, it contains high levels of trace elements of gypsum (calcium sulphate) which make for clear, bright bitters, because the calcium increases malt extraction during the mashing process.Today, breweries all over the world that want to produce pale ales usually "Burtonize" their water first by artificially adding gypsum salts.

Burton's leading independent brewer Marston's, founded in 1834, still draws more than four and a half million litres (a million gallons) each week from 14 wells, the shaft of the deepest descending nearly 300 m (1,000 ft). The family firm analyses its water daily in their laboratories, and its composition has not varied in any significant way since the company records began.

KEEP OFF OUR LIQUOR!

Good water can take on mythical properties. Many Irish beer drinkers, for example, swear that the Guinness brewed in Dublin is far superior to that produced at its sister stout plant in London. They attribute the difference to the River Liffey which runs through the Irish capital. In fact, since 1868 the Guinness Brewery at St James's Gate in Dublin has taken its water from the Grand Canal which flows from St James's Well in County Kildare.

The supply of liquor to the world-famous brewery was threatened with being cut off by the Dublin Corporation in 1775. When Arthur Guinness saw that he was in danger of losing his liquor supply and potentially his livelihood, he seized a pickaxe from a workman and dared the Corporation to continue over his dead body – they backed away.

Good water is so essential for brewers that it has to be protected at all costs. So in 1994, when a concrete company planned to fill in a nearby quarry with rubbish, the Burton brewers, who feared that the scheme, would pollute their pure supply, banded together to oppose it.

MORE RELIABLE SUPPLIES

Many breweries today have abandoned traditional wells and springs because of the threat of contamination, particularly by farmers' fertilizers. Instead, they use treated town water from the mains supply and can add the minerals that they require. It is not as romantic as a well, but it is more reliable. Breweries need vast amounts of water on tap. For every litre of beer produced, at least five more are required for cleaning and cooling.

Above: A water treatment plant may not be romantic, but it is a reliable source of good water.

Below and left: Fresh, fast flowing water straight from the Rocky Mountains of Colorado is illustrated on the Coors label.

MALT

Malt is the body and soul of a brew. It is this partially germinated, roasted grain that provides not only the alcohol, but also much of the flavour and nearly all of the colour in a glass of beer.

Above: Barley is the grain most commonly used for malting.

Right: Oakhill's Mendip Gold label reminds us of the grain at the heart of the brew.

Below: Part-germinated grains are baked in a kiln for two days to produce the malt.

MALT IS MUCH MORE than the harvested grain. Raw ears of barley, for example, will barely ferment, and are of little use to the brewer. First they need to pass through the hands of the maltster, and in ten days a grain of barley can be turned into a grain of malt, ready to make beer. It is possible to malt other cereals besides barley: wheat, oats and rye may also be used. In fact some beer styles, such as German wheat beers, demand a wheat malt. Oats were widely used for brewing during the Second World War when barley was scarce. Barley, however, provides the best extraction rate of sugars and is therefore by far the most favoured by brewers the world over.

Barley itself comes in many forms, not all of them suitable for malting. Maltster Robert Free observed in 1888, "The art of making good malt from bad barley has not yet been found."

To produce good malt the barley must have plump, sound grains and must germinate at an even rate. It should also be low in nitrogen, as nitrogen can affect fermentation.

THE MALTSTER'S MAGIC

When batches of barley first arrive with the maltster from the field, they are screened and sieved to remove straw and dirt. Next, the barley is dried in order to reduce the moisture that it has retained, so that the harvested grain can be stored for use throughout the year. If the grain is too damp, it may go mouldy or start to germinate prematurely. Maltsters prefer to keep the barley dormant for at least a month, because this improves later germination.

Soaking the grain

In traditional floor malting, the grain is soaked in large water cisterns containing up to six tons (6.1 tonnes) of barley and 1,500 gallons (6,800 litres) of water. This steeping process takes two to three days. The barley is not kept under water the whole time. It is soaked for half a day, then the tank is drained so that the grain can breathe for between six to 12 hours before it is immersed in water again.

Germination

Next, the damp grain is emptied on to huge germinating floors, and evenly spread to a depth of 6–9 in (15–20 cm). Here it stays

for five days to allow the seeds to begin to sprout and grow. This is the all-important process of germination, which turns inaccessible starches in the seeds into sugar.

The germinating grain is turned and raked regularly to ensure adequate aeration and an even growth, and to prevent the seed roots from becoming tangled together. If the workers at the maltings didn't turn the grain three times a day, you could roll it up like a coconut mat. In former times, this back-breaking work would have been done with a shovel, but today, electrically powered tools or turning machines are usually used.

Baking the green malt

After five days, when the sprouting shoots reach three-quarters the length of the grain, germination is brought to a sharp halt. The maltster does not wish to lose the newly created sugars, which the brewer will later turn to alcohol. This "green malt" is then sent to the kiln where it is baked for two days at high temperatures; the exact temperature determines the type of malt that results. Some Bavarian maltings still use wood-fired kilns, giving the malt a smoky flavour.

Nothing is wasted and the malt is screened after baking to remove the rootlets – known as "malt culms", which are sold as animal feed.

Final transformation

Once the roots are removed, the malt looks little different from the original grain.
However, one bite will reveal the miraculous

transformation in its flavour. The baked grains are no longer hard but good to eat, with a crunchy, nutty texture.

This delicious final product is used not only to brew beer, but also to make malted drinks, biscuits and breakfast cereals, and as an essential ingredient in malt whisky.

THE MODERN INDUSTRY EMERGES

Traditional floor malting was the system used in most countries until well into the 20th century. The buildings can be seen in many grain-growing areas, usually alongside watercourses or railway lines. Some maltings are substantial – long and heavily built with thick walls and narrow windows, and layer upon layer of germinating floors. Some breweries once had their own maltings, larger than the brewhouse itself, but nearly all have now been converted to other uses such as a bottling hall or warehouse. Others have been demolished, turned into industrial units or converted into shopping malls.

In general, traditional floor malting, which was highly labour-intensive and seasonal, has been abandoned. As mechanization spread

Left: Wheat, oats and rye can all be used to produce brewing malt, as well as barley. Oat Malt Stout is a traditional brew from Alloa, Scotland.

Below: A combine harvester cutting a field of barley. Malting barley is subject to rigorous quality controls to ensure that it is low in nitrogen.

Above: The Estonian Saku brewery celebrates the grain harvest on this bottle label.

Right: The Efes brewery of Turkey gets its barley from the plains of Central Anatolia and processes over 100,000 tons a year at its malting plants. Their malt is exported to breweries in South America and Africa.

Below: There are several types of malt, differing in flavour and appearance according to the precise way that the barley has been kilned.

throughout industry in the 19th century, some maltsters began to look for new methods.

A Belgian maltster named Galland developed drum malting in the 1870s. This system transferred the grain from steeping tanks into huge, airtight metal cylinders that slowly revolved to turn the grain.

About the same time, a Frenchman called Saladin introduced the efficient drying method – the "Saladin Box" system that forced air through the perforated floor of a box containing grain to the depth of 2 to 3 ft (60 cm – 1 m). This technique was later further developed in Germany into the Wanderhaufen or "moving piece" process, in which the grain slowly flows through the box.

The new systems saved space and labour, and could operate throughout the year. However, they caught on quite slowly, partly due to mechanical problems, and also because of the expense of buying new equipment. Many brewers believed that floor malting was best and indeed some still insist on traditionally made malt.

The global market

It wasn't until after the Second World War that mechanical malting methods were widely adopted, bringing in their wake even larger-scale malting plants and concentration in the industry. By the 1970s in Britain, for example, two huge companies – Associated British Maltsters (ABM) and Pauls &

Sandars – had come to dominate the malting trade, accounting for more than half of all sales. Some companies operated maltings in several countries and exported far and wide.

In fact only a third of beer-making countries produce significant amounts of malt, and only eight countries supply three-quarters of the world's needs (see table). Malting depends on a reliable supply of barley. There is a huge international market – a grain-growing country such as Australia supplies its neighbours, including the Philippines. Some major brewing nations, such as Japan, have no large malting industry and the brewers there import the bulk of their requirements.

The brewers' search for a particular quality of barley resulted in an international grain market. In the 19th century, Denmark and France were regarded as excellent grain-growing countries, and barley from there was highly coveted. An area of central Europe covering Moravia, Silesia and Bohemia also developed an excellent reputation. Grain from here was known as Saale barley, and sold well, mainly through the Hamburg market. By the 1930s, brewers were competing with each other all around the globe to purchase sun-ripened crops from California, Chile and Australia.

Barley varieties

Surprisingly, much of this worldwide market was in barley that came from a few original varieties. In the 1820s, the Reverend J.B. Chevallier spotted a barley growing in an English labourer's cottage garden in Debenham, Suffolk. He was struck with the barley's extraordinary quality, and saved the

Pale malt

Crystal malt

seed. From that the Chevallier barley strain was developed. Archer was another popular English variety.

The barley plant produces kernels of grain which grow in either two or six rows. Chevallier and Archer are both two-rowed barleys. In the United States, six-rowed barley is preferred.

After the Second World War, Archer and its hybrids Spratt-Archer and Plumage-Archer gave way to Proctor, which was better suited to mechanized farming. Modern varieties include Triumph, Kym, Klages, Halcyon and Pipkin.

Some more traditional brewers have remained true to lower-yielding (for the farmer) but more characterful and reliable grains (for the brewer), for example Maris Otter and Golden Promise.

GLOBAL MALT PRODUCTION

US	2.85
Germany	2.16
Britain	1.67
France	1.18
China	1.08
Canada	0.76
Belgium	0.76
Australia	0.64
Others	4.62
Total	15.72

(All figures in millions of tons. 1 ton = 1.016 tonnes)

TYPES OF MALT

Malt comes in a variety of styles, depending on how it is kilned. The higher the temperature, the darker the colour and more profound the flavour. The brewer skilfully blends different malts to produce different beers.

Pale malt

This is the standard malt in most beers. The barley is baked in the kiln over 48 hours with a slowly rising temperature. Pale malt is ideal for both light-coloured ales and golden Pilsners. Some specific Pilsner types are known as lager malts. Other varieties tend to be used in small amounts in conjunction with pale malt.

Amber and brown malts

This barley is heated to higher temperatures than pale malt to give more coppery colours to the brew. Amber and brown malts are rarely used today. In Continental Europe, Vienna malt provides a reddish tinge to the beer.

Crystal malt

An exceptionally rapidly rising temperature in the kiln dries out the barley husk, leaving behind a hard, sugary, crystalline core. Crystal malt adds a fuller, sweeter flavour to beer. Dark varieties are called caramel malts; lighter ones, carapils malts.

Chocolate malt

The barley is steadily heated to about 200°C (400°F). This deep chocolate malt generates a complex mix of roasted flavours as well as a dark colour.

Above: Autumn Frenzy's label evokes the harvest season.

Black malt

Black malt is chocolate malt that has been taken almost to the burning point. Because of its powerful bitter taste, it is used sparingly, even in stouts and porters.

Chocolate malt

HOPS

The cones of the hop plant were originally added to beer as a preservative. They prevent the brew from going sour, but also bring a characteristic bitter flavour and aroma to the drink.

IF MALT PROVIDES BEER with its body and colour, hops add immeasurably to its flavour by countering the cereal's sweetness with a sharp, bitter tang. The hop also gives beer its heady aroma. It is the seasoning and spice in the barley meal.

Medieval holy communities in central Europe are credited as having been the first to brew with hops. But while the monastic brewers may have welcomed the hop plant, which preserved the life of their beer, various vested interests strongly resisted its development. The powerful Archbishop of Cologne, for example, enjoyed a monopoly on the herbs used for flavouring beer and so tried to suppress the use of hops. Only in 1500 did he agree to take a rent in lieu of his rights.

In the Netherlands in the 14th century, many drinkers were developing a taste for hopped Hamburg beer from over the border in Germany, in preference to their locally brewed gruit ales. The Dutch nobility, who had vested interests in the sale of herbs, tried to exclude foreign beers or impose high import duties. But the barrel barrier failed and soon many Dutch brewers were brewing hopped beer to compete with Hamburg. In response, the Emperor Charles IV granted the nobles a tax on hops.

The hop spread from the Low Countries into England. Hopped beer was imported into Winchelsea in Sussex by 1400, and before long brewers from Flanders followed, setting up their own beer breweries, much to the disgust of the English ale makers.

Above: The type of hop used affects the flavour of the resulting beer. The Hogs Back Brewery is proud of the Goldings variety that it uses in its Traditional English Ale.

Below: Hops may be added either slightly crushed (as shown), or as condensed pellets.

Above: In the days before mechanical harvesting stilts were necessary in order to reach the cones of the tall, spindly hop vine.

Their concern was understandable, for hopped beer kept much better than the sweeter ale, especially in summer. For a while they had the backing of the authorities – Henry VIII banned the royal brewer from using hops in 1530. Nevertheless, by 1600, the use of the hop was widespread. True unhopped ale was in decline. James Howell, a Royalist imprisoned during the Civil War, wrote in 1634, "In this island, the old drink was ale, noble ale, but since beer hath hopped in amongst us, ale is thought to be much adulterated."

CULTIVATING THE HOP

The hop plant (*Humulus lupulus*) is a tall, climbing vine that is a member of the hemp family. It is distantly related to both cannabis and the nettle.

A single plant carries either male or female flowers. Only the female flowers form the vital cones required by the brewer.

The female cone is made up of a number of petal-like structures called bracts. As the cones ripen, the bases of these bracts bear glands

Left: Tallying up the day's work – from a 1910 postcard. The hop harvest in Kent, England was the traditional holiday for gypsies and workers from the East End of London.

that are filled with a yellow resinous substance known as lupulin. It is this complex oil, found nowhere else in the plant kingdom, that contains the alpha acids which give the hop its characteristic bitterness.

The hop plant needs deep soil to grow, as its roots can go down for over 6 ft (2 m). It can thrive in any temperate climate, as long as there is sufficient heavy rainfall during the growing period, and plenty of sun to help the flowers ripen.

Growing at breakneck speed

Each year the plant is cut back to the rootstock, then in the spring shoots covered with hooked hairs called bines surge upwards. The hop farmer provides a support network of poles and wires for the hairy shoots to wind around and form the characteristic tall, leggy plants. Shoots can grow as much as 1 ft (35 cm) in a single day, and eventually reach 15–18 ft (5–6 m) in height.

The flowers appear in summer and are followed by the cones which are harvested in early autumn. Traditionally this was done on stilts, but today mechanization has made the task much easier.

AN ANCIENT PROFESSION

At one time, hordes of hop-pickers came from the cities to carry out the work by hand, living in tents or wooden huts on the land. For many poor families from the industrial towns, this was their annual holiday – a breath of fresh

country air away from the grime and smoke. Nowadays, the labourers have been replaced by machines.

Once harvested, the hops are dried gently in kilns, then pressed into tall sacks or pockets (bales), as long as 6 ft (2 m), ready for the brewery, or for further processing. These pockets usually carry the emblem of the growing area.

HOP BY-PRODUCTS

Many traditional brewers still prefer to use whole hop cones in their recipe, but processed derivatives are commonly used today. About two-thirds of the world's hop crop is treated in some way before it is used by a brewer.

Below: Modern harvesting methods and short-growing varieties have revolutionized the previously labour-intensive business of hop picking.

Above: The hop, Humulus lupulus, *is the raw ingredient which provides beer's bitter flavour.*

Below: The distinctive witch's-hat-shaped cowls, wind vanes and hot air outlets of traditional oast-houses became a characteristic feature of the landscape in hop-growing regions.

The simplest by-product is made by grinding the cones into powder, which is then pressed into pellets that are easy to transport and work well with modern equipment. However, pellets do not provide the filter bed of hops required by some older breweries.

Hop extract is another alternative. This treacle-like substance is sold in a can. It is very stable and highly efficient, but can give the beer a more cloying flavour than whole or pelleted hops.

TYPES OF HOP

Traditional aroma hop varieties give beer a subtle, fine flavour and an enticing nose. In recent decades, the emphasis has been on extracting more bitterness by developing "high-alpha" varieties.

Because many hop farms have been badly hit by fungal infections, notably Verticillium Wilt, creating disease-resistant varieties is now a research priority in many countries.

Bramling Cross
A 1920s cross between an English Golding and a Canadian wild hop. It was unpopular in the past because of its "blackcurrant" nose, but its character is more appreciated today.

Cascade
A fruity American aromatic hop first introduced in 1972.

Above: Brewers throughout the world feature hops on the labels of their beer.

Crystal
A mildly aromatic American hop.

Fuggles
Propagated by Richard Fuggle in Kent in 1875. It is also grown in Oregon, US, and Slovenia. In Slovenia it has adapted to local conditions and is known as "Styrian Goldings".

Goldings
Originated in East Kent in the 18th century. It has a flowery bouquet and is used for dry-hopping traditional English ales in the cask.

Left: At the Hop Exchange in London, England hops of many different varieties were traded from all over the world.

High-alpha hop varieties

Admiral (England)
Brewers' Gold (England, Belgium and Germany)
Centennial (US)
Challenger (England, Belgium and France)
Chinook (US)
Cluster (US)
Eroica (US)
Galena (US)
Magnum (Germany)
Northdown (England)
Northern Brewer (Germany, England)
Nugget (US, Germany)
Orion (Germany)
Phoenix (England)
Pride of Ringwood (Australia)
Super Styrians (Slovenia)
Target (England, Germany and Belgium)
Yeoman (England)

Hallertauer Mittelfrüh
A traditional aroma hop from the Hallertau district in Bavaria, the world's largest hop-growing area (responsible for a fifth of global production). This hop has been almost wiped out by disease.

Hersbrucker
A traditional variety from the Hersbruck hills, this has now replaced Hallertauer as the most popular German aroma hop in the brewing industry. It is grown throughout the Hallertau region in Bavaria.

Huller
Huller is a new German aromatic variety, which was developed at the Hull Research Institute in Hallertau.

Mount Hood
Based on the German Hallertauer, this American aroma hop was introduced in 1989.

Perle
Perle is a newer German aroma hop. It is also grown in America.

Progress
This Wilt-resistant hop was introduced in the 1950s in England as an alternative to Fuggle.

Quingdao da Hua
Derived from Styrian Goldings, this is the predominant Chinese hop.

Saaz
The classic aroma hop from Zatec in the Czech Republic provides just the right flowery bouquet for Bohemian Pilsners.

Select
The Hull Research Centre in Hallertau developed this new German aromatic variety.

Spalter
A traditional German variety mainly grown in the Spalt region near Nuremberg.

Styrian Goldings
Slovenia's main aromatic hop.

Tettnanger
This is a delicately aromatic German hop, mainly grown in the Tettnang region by Lake Constance on the Swiss border.

Tradition
Despite its name, Tradition is a new German hop variety.

WGV
Whitbread Goldings Variety was widely planted in the 1950s in England, as it can survive Wilt attacks.

Willamette
An American variety related to the English Fuggle, introduced in 1976.

YEAST

Without yeast, malt, hops and water will never make beer. It is the catalyst that transforms the hopped cereal solution into a potent drink, hiding its magic beneath a living cloak of froth and foam.

YEASTS ARE LIVING ORGANISMS, members of the fungus family. Their scientific name is *Saccharomyces Cerevisiae*. Each yeast plant consists of a tiny, single cell, invisible to the naked eye. It is only when many millions are massed together that they become visible – as when they multiply to make beer.

The spherical yeast cells reproduce by budding. A bud forms on the parent, then, when it has grown to the same size, it separates to form another cell. Multiplying in this way, under good conditions (such as in a nutritious sugar solution) the cells can reproduce every two hours.

THE BREWER'S FRIEND

During the fermentation process, the yeast cells clump together (flocculate). In top-fermenting beers such as stout, the yeast cells rise to the surface of the liquid in the fermenting vessel. By contrast, in bottom-fermenting beers such as lagers, they sink.

The yeast gets the energy for its growth during brewing by consuming the sugar solution in the mash provided by the malt. Alcohol and carbon dioxide are the waste products of its reproduction cycle. In fact, the yeast growth and the fermentation of the brew slow down, and

Below: Louis Pasteur, from the portrait by Albert Edelfelt, 1885. Pasteur, who gave his name to pasteurization, was the French scientist who discovered that yeast was a living organism.

Above: Gazing down a powerful microscope the tiny, single, living cells of the yeast fungus become clearly visible.

eventually stop, once the solution contains too much alcohol.

Many brewers use the same yeast, jealously guarded, for years. Each different strain has its own characteristics. Some work especially quickly, while others ferment to a greater degree. Each gives its own unique flavour, and particular types produce specific types of beer.

Some brewers even leave the yeast in the beer to give extra flavour; the cloudy Hefe wheat beers of Germany are classic examples of this technique.

At the end of each brew the brewer skims off some of the yeast, ready for use in the next batch. But the vast bulk is pressed, dried, and sold as nutritious yeast extract.

UNRULY ORGANISM

When yeast is working it can quickly run riot. This unpredictable organism often surprises even modern laboratories, and causes deep despair for brewers as they search for consistency.

Yeast may be a plant, but it can be a beast to control, and anyone who has seen a vigorously fermenting vat of beer, popping and heaving, will understand this fear. Yeast has a life of its own. Some brewers talk about yeast as though it were a difficult friend, and most agree that it can be awkward. Yeast can be greedy and troublesome and liable to let the brewer know if it is not being treated correctly.

SECRET LIFE

Scientists have spent many years peering through microscopes in order to uncover the workings of this secret beer agent. A Dutch-man named Leeuwenhoek first described the appearance of yeast in 1685; however, it was not until Frenchman Louis Pasteur's work in the 19th century that its true role in fermentation was understood.

LOUIS PASTEUR

French scientist Louis Pasteur is the father of modern brewing. His work on yeast allowed brewers to understand for the first time exactly what happened during fermentation. Previously, it had been almost as big a mystery at the start of the 19th century as it had been in medieval times or even in ancient Egypt. Beer frequently went off and became undrinkable, and the brewers had no idea why. Most companies expected losses of 20% or more through waste, and regularly had to destroy whole batches of sour beer.

Beer of national revenge

Pasteur was already a world-famous scientist when he started to study beer in 1871. His work was motivated by national pride in the aftermath of France's humiliating defeat by German forces in the Franco-Prussian war. He started his researches "with the determination of perfecting them and thereby benefiting a branch of industry wherein we are undoubtedly surpassed by Germany," he wrote in the preface to his ground-breaking work *Etudes sur la Bière*, published in 1876. He called his resulting brew, which he went on to patent, "Bière de la Revanche Nationale" (Beer of National Revenge).

By examining yeast through a microscope, Pasteur demonstrated that yeast was a living organism, and he was able to identify and isolate the contaminants that had been causing brewers so many problems.

His work prompted J.C. Jacobsen to build a magnificent laboratory at the Carlsberg Brewery in Copenhagen in the late 1870s, where another great scientist, Emil Hansen, was able to break yeasts down to single strains.

Left: Top-fermenting yeast boils and heaves itself to the top of the fermenting vessel.

Above: Dormant dried yeast.

Above: Ten minutes later, after water and sugar are added, the yeast is frothing and bubbling.

Hansen also showed that by isolating and using the right strain of yeast, brewers could produce dependable beers. The art of brewing was never the same again.

The main bottom-fermenting yeast, *Saccharomyces Carlsbergensis*, is named after the Danish brewery in honour of the innovative work that Hansen carried out there.

MULTIPLE STRAINS

Although pure, single yeast strains are more predictable to brew with, many brewers still prefer to use multiple yeast strains. Each reacts with the others to produce the final beer. Bass of England, for example, uses two strains, while Palm of Belgium juggles with four.

Belgian brewers of lambic beers still use wild yeasts. They rely on the natural spores of yeast carried in the air spontaneously to ferment their beer – as their ancestors did centuries before.

Handle with care

Yeast must always be handled with care. It is all too easy to break the delicate balance of multiple strains through chance infection by other microbes – or even by the introduction of new equipment. Cleanliness is vital. Even the introduction of new equipment or a change in the shape of the fermentation vessel can alter the characteristics of the yeast, and therefore the taste of the beer.

Left: The Carlsberg brewery, where Emil Hansen carried out his ground-breaking research on brewing yeasts.

OTHER INGREDIENTS

Although the basic four ingredients – water, malt, hops and yeast – are all that you need to brew beer, many brewers add other substances to their recipe, perhaps to produce a distinctive flavour and aroma, or simply to save money.

A BREWER IS NOT RESTRICTED to the four main ingredients. There are as many recipes and potential ingredients as there are brews. As well as the great variety to be found within malt, hops and different water compositions, there are also many extra ingredients that can be added to the brew to produce a highly individual recipe. As a result, flavours can vary enormously even within one beer type. As well as flavour variations, however, there are other reasons for including additional ingredients in the brew – to reduce costs or to improve the colour, for example.

ADJUNCTS

Some brewers add other substances to the mash besides malt. These "adjuncts" are added to the grist, when the malt is cracked in the mill. Adjuncts can be used to provide a cheaper substitute for part of the malt, or when malt is in short supply. Sometimes, however, the extra ingredients can simply be added to enhance the flavour of the beer. Light beers in particular tend to use additional unconventional grains in their mash. Brewers who spurn the temptation of using adjuncts boast that they produce "all-malt" beers.

Below and right: Kriek is a traditional Belgian recipe that includes cherries in the brew to produce a tart, fruit-flavoured, red beer.

Sugar

The most common adjunct is sugar, in blocks or as syrup. It ferments easily and quickly to give more alcohol, but leaves little in the way of body. Heated sugars or caramels are sometimes used instead of coloured malts to darken beers. Belgian brewers often use a less-refined candy sugar. This adjunct is particularly favoured in Africa, where barley is scarce. For example, sucrose is one of the main ingredients in Castle Lager from South African Breweries.

Flaked maize

Maize (corn), usually processed into flakes, is widely used. In some American breweries it accounts for as much as half the mash, giving a very dry, light-coloured beer.

Rice

Rice, like maize, can be a partial alternative to malt. The world's best-selling beer, Budweiser, from Anheuser-Busch of the US, uses rice to give a clean, crisp finish.

Torrefied wheat

This heated cereal, or popcorn, is added to help head retention.

Malt extracts

Malt syrups are sometimes used to make a larger brew than the capacity of the mash tun allows. They are also popular in home-brew kits, since using extract allows the home brewer to miss out the process of mashing altogether.

Roasted barley

Unmalted roasted barley is sometimes used to blacken brews. It gives a harsh, dry flavour. The classic Irish stout Guinness uses a small amount of roasted barley in the mash to give the beer its distinctive bitter flavour.

FLAVOUR ENHANCERS

Adding extra flavourings in beer is an old tradition. In the days before the hop, brewers made their own flavouring called gruit. The recipe for each brewer's mix was a secret but it would often contain herbs, spices or fruit, such as juniper or bog-myrtle. In some countries the tradition of adding extra ingredients for flavour died out, but some brewers clung on to their tradition and the Belgian brewers, for example, never gave up their age-old fruit beers. With the revival of small-scale breweries, unusual flavourings are also making a comeback.

Spices

Ginger beer is a familiar non-alcoholic relic from prohibition. However, ginger is also used to flavour alcoholic beer.

Herbs

Adding herbs such as coriander to flavour the brew is an ancient tradition that has been revived by Hoegaarden.

Fruit

Orange and lemon peel, apples, raspberries, cherries and bananas have all been added to beer with various degrees of success. Some of the newer fruit-flavoured brews were conceived by modern marketing departments and often use fruit juice or extract simply as a flavouring. However, some traditional recipes use the fruit to spark a natural secondary fermentation as well as to add flavour. Two ancient Belgian recipes, Kriek and Frambozen, use cherries and raspberries.

Below: Hoegaarden is spiced with coriander seeds and curaçao orange peel.

Honey

Honey is one of the oldest flavour enhancers known to man, and it has been used in cooking and in drink making for centuries.

Chilli

Beers with whole chillies in the bottle are a relatively new innovation, presumably a follow-on from the craze for Mexican lagers in the 1980s. It is an unusual taste sensation.

ADULTERANTS

Unscrupulous brewers seeking to maximize their profits by using inferior ingredients in the brew have long been a problem that the authorities have tried to legislate against for centuries. One common illegal additive in the 19th century was salt, which was used to "bob" the beer – to make two or three casks from one good one. It is shown here in the *Illustrated London News* in 1850, being added to the brew in blocks. Other common substances used to make the beer go further were treacle and water.

STYLES OF BEER

The title "beer" runs the gamut from dark, hearty ales to tangy, spritzy gueuzes.
The myriad different tastes, colours, flavours and aromas can, to some extent, be
squeezed into groupings with similar characteristics and methods of production.

Above: The names of abbey beers may be misleading since most are now brewed under licence by commercial breweries.

Below: Ale is a convenient, catch-all term that is generally used to mean beer made using top-fermenting yeast.

NEWSPAPERS AND MAGAZINES have had tasteful columns about the mysteries of wine for many years, but it is only recently that writers have begun to discuss beer in the same way. Beer is much more complex than wine. Wine is based on a single ingredient – grapes. Beer is a fine balance between two – malt and hops. The variety of hops is as great as the variety of grapes and there are many different styles of malt and different cereals. In addition, there is an exotic store of extra spices for the more adventurous brewer. Today, interest in local styles and different qualities has never been greater. Drinkers increasingly appreciate that there is a rich variety of beer tastes to explore around the world.

ABBEY BEERS

Strong fruity ales, abbey beers are brewed in Belgium by commercial companies, sometimes under licence from religious communities. They copy the style of the surviving beers produced in monasteries, or name their brews after a church or saint. Examples include Leffe from Interbrew, Grimbergen from the Union Brewery and Maredsous from Moortgat. (See Trappist.)

ALE

Nowadays this is a vague term meaning any top-fermented beer. It is one of the two main branches of the beer family, the other being lager. Of the two, ale is the older, dating back thousands of years. England is the country where ales are now most commonly brewed.

ALT

Alt is the German word meaning "traditional" or "old", and in the context of Altbier it indicates a bitter-tasting brew produced by the ancient style of brewing using top-fermentation. Alt is a copper-coloured aromatic ale, made in the city of Düsseldorf and a few other cities in northern Germany. It is a firm-bodied but quite bitter beer that contains just over 4.5% alcohol. Major, well-known brands include Diebels, Schlosser and Uerige.

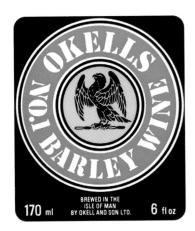

BARLEY WINE

Barley wine is the English name for a powerful, almost syrupy, strong ale, that is usually sold in small nip-size bottles. These well-matured brews can be golden or dark in colour. The darker versions of barley wine were once called Stingo.

BERLINER WEISSE

A light, sharply acidic German wheat beer made predominantly in Berlin, this refreshing brew is relatively low in alcohol and is often laced with a dash of green woodruff or raspberry juice to add colour to its cloudy white (weisse) appearance.

BIÈRE DE GARDE

A top-fermenting "beer for keeping" from north-west France, this was originally made in farmhouses, but is now produced by commercial breweries. This style produces medium to strong, spicy ales; some are bottle-conditioned, and many are sealed with champagne-style wired corks.

BITTER

The distinctive style of draught ale in England and Wales is generally served in pubs. It is usually

dry and hoppy with an alcohol content of 3–5%. Traditionally reddish amber in colour, paler varieties are now proving popular in England. Stronger versions used to be called Best or Special.

BLACK BEER

In Germany, Schwarzbier is a strong-tasting, bitter-chocolate lager. It is not a stout but a very dark lager and is a speciality of eastern Germany, particularly around Bernau. The town of Kostritz in the former East Germany is noted for its black lager, and Kulmbach and Erlangen are also known for their deep brown beers. This style is also made in Japan.

In England, especially Yorkshire, black beers are strong, pitch-black, treacly malt extracts, usually bottled for mixing with lemonade to make distinctive shandies.

BOCK

A strong malty, warming German beer of about 6.5% alcohol, bock was originally brewed for the colder months. Traditionally dark in colour, today it is more likely to be golden-bronze. This powerful smooth brew originated in Einbeck in Lower Saxony, but is now more associated with Bavaria. Bock is also produced in Austria, the Netherlands and other countries surrounding Germany. The word bock means "billy goat", and a goat's head often features on the label. The brew is sometimes linked with seasonal festivals, such as Maibock which celebrates the arrival of spring. Extra-potent versions are called doppelbocks (and are chiefly associated with Bavaria), with more than 7% alcohol, such as Paulaner Salvator. Eisbocks, in which frozen water is removed from the beer, are even more powerful. This brew (10%) is the speciality of Reichelbrau of Kulmbach.

BROWN ALE

A sweetish, bottled mild ale, dark in colour and low in alcohol, from England, brown ale was once a popular workers' drink, although sales have declined heavily in recent years. The north-east of the country produces stronger,

Above: Bitter is not bitter in taste as its name might suggest. It usually has a floral, fruity flavour.

Above: Bocks were originally drunk by fasting monks because they were considered nutritious.

Above: Brown ale was one of the traditional drinks of the working classes in England. Nowadays sales have declined.

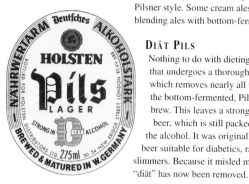

drier versions like the well-known Newcastle Brown Ale.

Belgium boasts its own sweet-and-sour brown ales from East Flanders. The main producer is Liefmans of Oudenaarde. The sour taste comes from a slow simmering rather than a boil, and from the addition of a lactic yeast. Other producers include Cnudde, also of Oudenaarde, the nearby Roman Brewery and Vanden Stock.

CHILLI BEER

Produced by only a handful of American breweries this is an odd, slow-burning speciality. The Pike Place Brewery of Seattle produces an occasional Cerveza Rosanna Red Chilli Ale, while the hotter Crazy Ed's Cave Creek Chilli Beer of Phoenix, Arizona, has a whole chilli pod in each bottle. It reputedly goes well with Mexican food.

CREAM ALE

A sweetish, smooth, golden ale from the United States, cream ale was originally introduced by ale brewers trying to copy the Pilsner style. Some cream ales are made by blending ales with bottom-fermenting beers.

DIÄT PILS

Nothing to do with dieting, diät pils is lager that undergoes a thorough fermentation, which removes nearly all the sugars from the bottom-fermented, Pilsner-derived brew. This leaves a strong, dry-tasting beer, which is still packed with calories in the alcohol. It was originally brewed as a beer suitable for diabetics, rather than slimmers. Because it misled many, the word "diät" has now been removed.

DOPPELBOCK

An extra-strong bock beer; doppelbock is not double in strength, but usually around 7.5% alcohol. It is rich and warming. The names of the leading Bavarian brands usually end in "ator", Salvator from Paulaner of Munich, for example.

DORTMUNDER

Dortmunder is a strong, full-bodied export style of lager from Dortmund in Germany, the biggest brewing city in Europe. It was originally brewed for export and was once sold under this name across the globe, but is now declining in popularity. Malty, dry and full-bodied, these brews usually have an alcohol strength of around 5.5%, being firmer and less aromatic than a Pilsner. The leading examples include DAB, Kronen and DUB.

DRY BEER

First produced in Japan by the Asahi Brewery in 1987, this is a super diät pils with a parching effect, which was widely adopted in North America. The beer taste is so clean it has been swept away almost entirely through further fermentation.

Dry beer, in which more of the sugars are turned to alcohol leaving little taste, was developed in Japan and launched in America in 1988. After an initial surge in sales when Anheuser-Busch introduced Bud Dry, the market has faded almost completely away.

DUNKEL

German lagers were traditionally dark, and these soft, malty brown beers are associated with Munich, often being known as Münchner. Like the paler hell, they contain around 4.5% alcohol. Most of the major Munich breweries produce a dunkel.

Duppel/Double

This is a term used to describe dark, medium-strength Trappist and abbey beers in Belgium.

Eisbock

An extra-potent bock, eisbock is produced by freezing the brew and removing some of the frozen water to leave behind more concentrated alcohol. The most notable producer is Kulmbacher Reichelbrau in Northern Bavaria. Eisbock is the original ice beer.

Export

This term was originally used to denote a better-quality beer, worth selling abroad. The Dortmunder style is also known as Dortmunder Export, since it became popular around the world. In Scotland, the term export is widely adopted for premium ales.

Faro

Once the most common manifestation of Belgian lambic beer, faro is a weak lambic sweetened with sugar. Now this style has largely disappeared.

Framboise/Frambozen

These are Flemish and French names for a Belgium fruit beer made by adding raspberries to a lambic. Framboise has a sparkling, pink champagne character and the raspberries impart a light, fruity flavour. Because the whole fruit is too soft, producers usually add raspberry syrup. In recent years a whole variety of other fruit juices have been tried, from peaches to bananas, with varying degrees of success.

Ginger Beer

Despite its name, this is a refreshing, low or no-alcohol soft drink flavoured with root ginger. However, long before the hop appeared, ginger was used in beer and some pioneering micro-brewers are trying it again: Salopian in England adds ginger to its dark wheat beer, Gingersnap.

Green Beer

Any young beer which has not had time to mature is known as a green beer. The term is also used to denote a beer made with organic malt and hops. Organic green beer is known as biologique in France (where Castelain makes an organic beer called Jade) and biologisch in Germany. In Scotland, the Caledonian Brewery of Edinburgh has pioneered organic ale with Golden Promise.

Gueuze

This is a ripe blend of old and new Belgian lambics. By blending young and old lambics, a secondary fermentation is triggered. The resulting distinctive, sparkling beer, often sold in corked bottles like champagne to withstand the pressure, packs a fruity, sour, dry taste. Blending is such an art that some producers do not brew, but buy in their wort. Often this beer is matured for many more months in the bottle. In some cases the secondary fermentation is triggered by the addition of various fruits. Traditionally gueuze should not be filtered, pasteurized or sweetened, though some more commercial brands do all three.

Heavy

Scottish brewers use this term to describe a standard strength ale, between a Light and an Export. A "wee heavy" is a bottled strong ale, the wee referring to the small nip-size of the bottle.

Hefe

The German word for yeast is used to describe a beer that is unfiltered, with a sediment in the bottle. Draught beers "mit Hefe" are usually cloudy.

Hell

This word means pale or light in German and indicates a mild, malty golden lager, often from Munich. Notable examples include Hacker-Pschorr and Augustiner.

Honey Beer

The Celts and other ancient peoples used to make mead from

Above: Several breweries have sprung up producing "green" beer using only organic ingredients.

Below: The word "Hefe" on a label indicates that the beer still contains yeast.

*Right: The attractively named
Waggle Dance honey beer
brewed by Ward's of Sheffield is
a revival of an old traditional
drink of the Celtic people.*

Far right: A selection of IPAs.

*Below: US brewers have
followed the Canadian
innovation of ice beers.*

fermented honey. They also produced a beer,
bragot, to which honey was often added as a
soft sweetener. A hazy honey brew called
Golden Mead Ale was produced in England by
Hope & Anchor Breweries of Sheffield, and
was widely exported until the early 1960s.
Today, a few breweries have revived the style,
notably Ward's of Sheffield with Waggle
Dance and Enville Ales of Staffordshire. Some
new American brewers also use honey, as do
the innovative Belgian De Dolle Brouwers in
their Boskeun beer.

ICE BEER

A chilling innovation of the early 1990s; the
brew is frozen during maturation to produce a
purified beer, with the ice crystals removed to
increase the strength.

Many ice beers were originally developed
in Canada by Labatt and contain around
5.5% alcohol. Canadian brewers Labatt
and Molson introduced the new beer style
in 1993 in which the beer is frozen after
fermentation, giving a cleaner, almost
smoothed away flavour. Sometimes the
ice crystals are removed, concentrating
the beer. Most major US brewers have
launched their own brands such as Bud
Ice and Miller's Icehouse, but ice beer
still accounts for less than 4% of the
beer market.

In 1996, Tennent's of Scotland
produced a Super Ice with a strength
of 8.6%.

IMPERIAL STOUT

See Stout.

IPA

The words behind the initials betray IPAs
imperial origins – India Pale Ale. This strong,
heavily hopped beer was brewed in Britain,
notably in Burton-on-Trent by companies like
Allsopp and Bass. The recipe was designed to
withstand the long
sea voyages to
distant parts of the
British Empire like
India. According to
legend, a cargo of
300 casks of
Bass's East
India Pale Ale
was wrecked
off the port of
Liverpool in
1827. Some of
the rescued beer
was sold locally
and won instant
fame among
English
drinkers.

Specialist American brewers like Bert Grant's
Yakima Brewing Company now probably
produce the most authentic versions.

IRISH ALE

A soft, slightly sweet reddish ale from the
"Emerald Isle". Top and bottom-fermenting
versions are brewed commercially. This ale
followed many of the Irish in migrating to
other lands. George Killian Letts, a member of
the Letts family who brewed Ruby Ale in
County Wexford until 1956, licensed the
French brewery Pelforth to produce George
Killian's Bière Rousse and the American
brewers Coors to produce Killian's Irish Red.
Smithwick's of Kilkenny (owned by Guinness)
is the best-known ale in Ireland today.

KÖLSCH

The refreshing golden beer of Cologne may
look like a Pilsner (though it may sometimes
be cloudy), but its light, subtle fruity taste
reveals it to be a top-fermenting ale. Its
fleeting aromatic nature masks an alcohol
content of 4–5%.

Kölsch is produced only by some 20
breweries in and around the busy cathedral city
of Cologne and it is usually served in small
glasses. The leading producers include
Kuppers and Fruh.

KRIEK

In this Belgian lambic beer, secondary fermentation is stimulated by adding cherries to give a dry, fruity flavour and deep colour. This is not a novelty drink, but draws on a long tradition of using local fruit to flavour an already complex brew, balancing the lambic sourness and providing an almond character from the cherry stones. The kriek is a small dark cherry grown near Brussels.

KRISTALL

This term, taken from the German word for a crystal-clear beer, usually indicates a filtered wheat beer or Weizenbier.

LAGER

Lager is one of the two main branches of the beer family. The word lager is derived from the German word "to store". In Britain it refers to any golden, bottom-fermented beer, but elsewhere it has little meaning, apart from a general word for beer.

LAMBIC

The wild beers of Belgium have their roots deep in history. One of the most primitive beers brewed on earth, these spontaneously fermenting beers are unique to Belgium, or to be more exact, to an area to the west of Brussels in the Senne Valley.

Lambic brewers use at least 30% unmalted wheat in order to produce a milky wort from the mash. Old hops are used, as they are only required for their preservative value, not for their flavour or aroma.

Unlike most other beer styles, in which a carefully cultivated yeast is used to ferment the wort, the wheat brew used to produce lambic beer is left exposed to the air to allow spontaneous fermentation to happen from wild

yeasts in the atmosphere. As in previous centuries, this beer is only brewed in the cooler months of the year, as the wild yeasts would be too unpredictable in summer. The fermenting wort is then run into large wooden casks and left to age in dark, dusty galleries from three months to many years.

The result is a unique, tart, sour beer, probably similar to the ales made in ancient times. The taste is almost like a flat, acidic cider, which attacks the tongue and sucks in the cheeks. It has an alcohol content of around 5%. This can be drunk young on its own, often on draught in cafés in the Brussels area, but it is usually blended with older lambics to produce gueuze. Sometimes fruit is added to create framboise (raspberry) or kriek (cherry) beers. The lambic range of beers is mainly produced by small, speciality brewers, like Boon, Cantillon, De Troch, Girardin and Timmermans. But there are a few more commercial brands, notably Belle-Vue (part of Interbrew) and St Louis.

LIGHT ALE

In England, this term indicates a bottled low-gravity bitter. In Scotland, it means the weakest brew, a beer light in strength although it may well be dark in colour.

Far left: Apart from in Britain, the term lager is used generally for beer.

Below: The term lambic indicates a Belgian wheat beer that is spontaneously fermented by wild, airborne yeast.

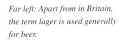

Above: In Miller Lite more of the sugar is turned to alcohol in the brewing process to produce a lower-calorie beer.

LITE
In North America, this term is used to describe a thin, low-calorie beer, the best-known being Miller Lite. In some countries, Australia for instance, lite can mean low in alcohol.

LOW ALCOHOL
Since the late 1980s, many breweries throughout the world have added low- or no-alcohol brews to their beer range, usually in response to increasingly strict drink-driving laws. Low alcohol (or LA) can contain as much as 2.5% alcohol. Alcohol-free brews should contain no more than 0.05%. Some of these near beers are produced using yeasts which create little alcohol, or the fermentation is cut short.

In others the alcohol is removed from a normal beer by distillation or reverse osmosis. It has proved difficult to provide an acceptable beer taste. Some of the more successful brews, Clausthaler from Frankfurt in Germany and Birell from Hürlimann of Zurich in Switzerland, now sell or licence their low- or no-alcohol beers across many countries.

Below: Relatively low alcohol, mild is usually a dark brown ale which was originally brewed for English workers.

MALT LIQUOR
In the United States, this term indicates a strong lager, often made with a high amount of sugar to produce a thin but potent brew. These beers are designed to deliver a strong alcoholic punch (around 6–8%) but little else. They are light beers with a kick, often cheaply made with a high proportion of sugar and using enzymes to create more alcohol. Sales of malt liquor account for about 4% of the total American beer market.

MÄRZEN
A full-bodied copper-coloured lager, this beer style originated in Vienna, but developed in Munich as a stronger Märzen (March) brew (6% alcohol), which was laid down in March, to allow it to mature over the summer for drinking at the Oktoberfest after the harvest. It has largely been replaced in Germany by more golden "Festbiere". Smooth and malty, most are now stronger versions of the golden hell, containing more than 5.5% alcohol. Notable examples include Spaten Ur-Märzen and Hofbrauhaus Oktoberfest.

MILD
Mild was the dominant ale in England and Wales until the 1960s, and later in some regions. It is a relatively low-gravity malty beer, usually lightly hopped, and can be dark or pale in colour. Mild was traditionally the workers' drink and would be sold on draught in the pub or club. Today, the style has vanished from many areas; it survives mainly in the industrial West Midlands and the north-west of England.

MILK STOUT
See Stout.

MÜNCHNER
The German name for a beer from Munich traditionally refers to the city's brown, malty lager style.

OATMEAL STOUT
See Stout.

OLD ALE
This strong, well-matured, rich, dark ale is usually sold as a seasonal beer in England as a winter warmer. Sometimes such ales are used as stock beers for blending with fresher brews.

OUD BRUIN
Old Browns in the Netherlands are weak, sweetish lagers.

OYSTER STOUT
See Stout.

PALE ALE
An English bottled beer, pale ale is stronger than light ale and is usually based on the brewery's best bitter. See IPA.

PILSNER

Strictly speaking, Pilsner is a golden, hoppy, aromatic lager from the Bohemian Czech town of Plzen (Pilsen in German), where this classic style was first produced in 1842. The original Pilsner Urquell (original source) is still brewed there. Czech Pilsner has a complex character with a flowery hop aroma and a dry finish.

This golden classic has spawned a thousand imitators, some excellent, others pale, lacklustre imitations of the original. Variations on the style now dominate the world beer market.

Pilsner is now the predominant lager beer of Germany. German Pilsners are dry and hoppy with a light, golden colour. They contain around 5% alcohol and often lack the smooth maltiness of the original Czech version.

Leading German brands include Warsteiner, Bitburger and Herforder.

Left: The original Pilsner comes from Plzen in the Czech Republic, but it has spawned many imitators.

PORTER

The origins of porter are shrouded in myths and legends. It was said to have been invented in London in 1722 by Ralph Harwood when he grew tired of making Three Threads, a popular drink of the day, by mixing strong, brown and old ales. He decided to brew one beer – or entire butt – combining the characteristics of all three.

In fact, porter was the product of the world's first major breweries, which were rising in London at this time. By brewing on a large scale with huge vessels, they were able to concoct a beer that was much more stable with far better keeping qualities than previous ales – porter.

The first porter was a traditional London brown mild ale which was much more heavily hopped than usual in order to improve its keeping qualities. The beer was then matured for months in vast vats, to increase its alcoholic strength. Older brews were then blended with fresher ones to produce an "entire" beer.

Only major brewers, such as Barclay, Truman and Whitbread, could afford to build the expensive plants that were necessary to produce beer on this scale and to tie up so much capital in maturing beer. In return for their investment, they captured the English capital's beer market, as porter was much more reliable than previous ales. The economies of scale in its production also made it cheaper.

Porter proved so successful that it was widely distributed and exported.

Enterprising brewers elsewhere, like Guinness in Dublin, followed this example and began to brew their own porter. Sales gradually declined in the 19th century as it was replaced in popularity by paler ales and only the stronger or "stouter" porters survived. The name is still used around the world today to indicate a brown beer.

In the Baltic countries, strong porters are still made, based on the original export brews. Some new micro-brewers have also tried to revive the dark, dry style in England and North America.

Porter, however, was never a craft beer. It flowed from the Industrial Revolution. It was the first mass-produced beer.

RAUCHBIER

The intense smoky flavour of these German smoked beers from the region of Franconia comes from malt that has been dried over moist beechwood fires. There are nine breweries in the town of Bamburg that produce this dark, bottom-fermented speciality. Leading examples include Schlenkerla and Spezial.

Below: Dark porters have diminished in popularity relative to when they were first introduced.

Above: The Campaign for Real Ale celebrated its tenth anniversary with a traditional brewed beer.

Above: The De Dolle brewery in Silly, Belgium, produces a strong, dark, Scotch-style ale.

REAL ALE

The British drinkers' consumer organization, CAMRA, the Campaign for Real Ale, devised this name for traditional cask-conditioned beer which continues to mature in the pub cellar. Real ale is not filtered or pasteurized.

RED BEER

The reddish sour beers of West Flanders in Belgium are sometimes dubbed the Burgundies of Belgium. The colour comes from using Vienna malt. The prime producer is Rodenbach of Roeselare, who matures its beers in a remarkable forest of huge oak vats.

Younger brews are blended with old to create the distinctive Rodenbach brand. Some of the more mature beer is bottled on its own as the classic Grand Cru. Other brands include Petrus from Bavik and Duchesse de Bourgogne from Verhaeghe of Vichte.

ROGGEN

Only a few breweries make this German or Austrian rye beer. Some English and American breweries have started to use rye to add flavour to barley malt, and one American brewer produces its own Roggen Rye.

ROOT BEER

An American temperance soft drink, not a beer, it was originally flavoured with sassafras root bark. Root beer is boiled but not fermented.

RUSSIAN STOUT

See Stout.

SAISON/SEZUEN

This Belgian speciality beer is now hard to find. A refreshing, slightly sour summer style, saison (which means "season" in French) is mainly made in rural breweries in the French-speaking Wallonia region, some of which have closed in recent years.

The orange, highly hopped, top-fermenting ales are brewed in winter and then laid down to condition in sturdy wine bottles for drinking in the hot summer months. They are sold in corked bottles after ageing. Some also contain added spices like ginger.

Small producers include Silly, Dupont and Vapeur. The larger Du Bocq brewery makes Saison Régal, while in Flanders Martens of Bocholt produces Sezuens.

SCHWARZBIER

See Black Beer.

SCOTCH ALE

Scotland's ales, brewed many miles from the nearest hop field, tend to be more malty in character than English beers. Bitters are called Light, Heavy, Special or Export in Scotland, depending on their strength, or are sometimes rated 60/-, 70/- or 80/- shillings according to an old pricing system.

Bottled Scotch Ale in Belgium is the name given to a powerful, rich ale, which is often brewed in Belgium itself.

STEAM BEER

An American cross between a bottom-fermented beer and an ale, steam beer was originally made in the Gold Rush days in California. It was brewed with lager yeasts at warm ale temperatures, using wide, shallow pans. Casks of this lively brew were said to hiss like steam when tapped. Now it is brewed only by the Anchor Steam Brewery of San Francisco.

STEINBIER

German "stone beer" is brewed using a primitive method of heating, in which red-hot rocks are lowered into the brew to bring it to the boil. The sizzling stones become covered in burnt sugars and are then added back to the beer at the maturation stage to spark a second fermentation. This smoky, full-bodied brew is made only by Rauchenfels at Altenmünster near Augsburg.

STOUT

One of the classic styles of ale, originally a stout porter, stout has survived and prospered thanks to its sharp contrast in taste and colour to the popular Pilsner – and also to the determined marketing and enterprise of one brewer, Guinness of Ireland.

This dry black brew is made with a proportion of dark roasted barley in the mash and is heavily hopped to give its distinctive taste. Draught stout tends to be much creamier and smoother than the more distinctive bottled beer, because it uses nitrogen gas in its dispenser. Guinness also produce a much heavier Foreign Extra Stout for export. Some other countries also produce dry stout, notably Australia, with fine examples from Cooper's of Adelaide and Tooth's of Sydney.

Besides dry or bitter stout, there are a number of variations of this dark style:

Milk or Sweet Stout

This is a much weaker and smoother bottled English stout, originally called Milk Stout because of the use of lactose (milk sugar). The name was banned in Britain in 1946 because of the implication that milk is added to the brew, though it is still used in some countries such as South Africa and Malta. The leading brand, Whitbread's Mackeson, still maintains a creamy connection through the sketch of a milk churn on the label. The Boston Beer Company in America produces a Samuel Adams Cream Stout. In addition, there are stronger tropical sweet stouts, notably Dragon brewed in Jamaica and Lion which comes from Sri Lanka.

Oatmeal Stout

Many sweet stouts were sold as nourishing, restorative drinks for invalids. Some were further strengthened by the addition of oats. Once a popular bottled brew, most oatmeal stouts have vanished, but a few have been revived, including Sam Smith's Oatmeal Stout from Yorkshire in England and Maclay's Oat Malt Stout from Scotland. The latter claims to be the only beer in the world to be brewed using malted oats, rather than oatmeal added to the mash.

Above: The characteristic dark, heavy, opaque hue of stout is unmistakable in the glass.

Below: Stout is a derivative of porter. There are many varieties within the general category.

Oyster Stout

Stout has always been seen as an ideal accompaniment to a dish of oysters. Some brewers went further and added oysters to their beer. Famous examples from the past include Castletown on the Isle of Man and Young's of Portsmouth in England, who boasted that their oyster stout contained the "equivalent to one oyster in every bottle". The seaport brewers used concentrated oyster extract from New Zealand. Some American and English brewers have occasionally revived the style, but the main bottled oyster stout today from Marston's of Burton-on-Trent contains no oysters.

Russian or Imperial Stout

Originally brewed in London in the 18th century as an extra-strong, export porter for the Baltic, this rich, intense brew with a fruit-cake character was reputed to be a favourite of the Russian Empress Catherine the Great, hence the Russian Imperial title. Many Baltic breweries took up the style, including Koff in Finland, Pripps of Sweden (whose porter was sold under the Carnegie brand name) and Tartu in Estonia.

In England, Courage still produces an occasional Imperial Russian Stout, which is matured for more than a year in the brewery. The nip-size bottles are year-dated, like vintage wines.

TARWEBIER

This is the Flemish word for the Belgian style of wheat beer. See Witbier.

TRAPPIST

Trappist is a strict designation referring only to beers from the five Trappist monastery breweries of Belgium and one in the Netherlands. These silent orders produce a range of strong, rich, top-fermenting ales. The Chimay, Orval, Rochefort, Westmalle and Westvleteren breweries are in Belgium, while Koningshoeven (La Trappe) is Dutch. All the complex, spicy brews are bottle-conditioned. Some number their beers in strength, terming them dubbel or tripel.

Commercial breweries producing ales in the same style, or under licence from the religious communities, have to call their brews abbey beers.

TRIPLE/TRIPEL

These are Flemish or Dutch terms, usually indicating the strongest brew in a range of beers, especially in Trappist or abbey beers. They are hoppy, golden brews, stronger than the darker doubles or dubbels.

Below: The term Trappist is an "appellation". By law only beers produced by the Trappist monasteries can carry this mark.

URQUELL

Urquell is the German word meaning "original source". The term should be used to show that the beer is the first or original in its style, such as Pilsner Urquell from the Czech Republic. Often only Ur is used, as in Einbecker Mai-Ur-Bock.

VIENNA

The term Vienna indicates the amber-red lagers developed by the Austrian brewing pioneer Anton Dreher, but these beers now have little association with the city. The style is best found today in the Märzen beers of Germany.

WEISSE OR WEIZEN

This wheat beer style has grown from almost nothing to a quarter of Bavaria's beer market in 20 years since the early 1970s. The white or wheat beers of Bavaria are made with 50–60% malted wheat. These ghostly pale, often cloudy brews have become a popular summer refresher in Germany. They have the quenching qualities of a lager but, as they are top-fermented, all the flavour of an ale.

This is particularly true in the more popular unfiltered cloudy version containing yeast in suspension, Hefeweizen. Filtered wheat beers are Kristall. Stronger brews are called

Weizenbock; dark ones Dunkelweizen. Notable Bavarian wheat beer brewers include Schneider and Erdinger. There is also a stronger Weizenbock at around 6.5% alcohol compared to Weissbier's usual 5%. In north-eastern Germany, a weaker, sourer style made with about half the wheat is Berliner Weisse. Fruit syrups are often added to Berliner Weisse by drinkers to provide a sweet and sour summer refresher. The leading brewers are Kindl and Schultheiss.

WITBIER

The white wheat beers of Belgium are also known as "Bières Blanches" in French. These are brewed using around 50% wheat, but then a variety of spices are added, notably orange peel and coriander. This style is also known as tarwebier.

The witbier or bière blanche style has risen like a pale ghost from the dead to haunt every corner of the market, and the best-known example is the pioneering Hoegaarden. When Pieter Celis revived the art of brewing this spiced wheat beer in the small town of Hoegaarden in 1966, he could not have imagined how it would grow. Now many breweries in Belgium and other countries have copied the style.

Hoegaarden is brewed from roughly equal parts of raw wheat and malted barley. The cloudy top-fermented brew differs from German wheat beers through the use of coriander and curaçao (orange peel) to give a spicy, fruity flavour and enticing aroma. Other leading brands include Brugs Tarwebier (Blanche de Bruges) from the Gouden Boom brewery, Dentergems Witbier from Riva, and Du Bocq's Blanche de Namur.

Left: Triple beers are a sub-category of the abbey style.

Above: Hoegaarden is one of the best-known examples of Witbier or bière blanche.

IRELAND

When people think of Irish beer, they picture a dark glass of stout. Ireland is the only country in the world where this creamy brew is the most popular drink, consumed in great quantities in the famous Irish pubs.

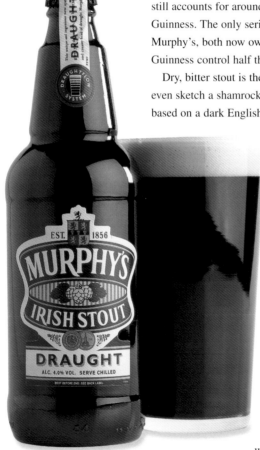

THE IRISH HAVE PROBABLY BEEN BREWING since the Bronze Age. Although spirits have always been popular, beer is very much a traditional tipple and brewing is a major industry, with the majority of the malting barley crop going directly into whisky and beer production. One particular type of beer – stout – still accounts for around half of all beer sold in Ireland, the vast bulk of it Guinness. The only serious competition comes from Cork where Beamish and Murphy's, both now owned by foreign companies, brew rivals. But even in Cork, Guinness control half the market.

Dry, bitter stout is the quintessential Irish drink and some obliging barmen will even sketch a shamrock leaf in the foam, to prove it. But Irish stout is actually based on a dark English beer, porter, imported into Ireland in the 18th century. Irish brewers copied the increasingly popular style, then in the early 19th century Guinness introduced its own, bigger-bodied, drier version – Extra Stout Porter – which eventually became known simply as stout.

In Ireland drinking is a highly sociable tradition. The nation is full of bars and pubs, famous the world over for their good music and convivial atmosphere. It is here that beer is generally consumed, rather than at home, and as a result most beer (more than 80%) is still served on draught. Up until the 1950s, stout was served through a two-cask system. One wooden cask contained fresh, still-fermenting stout, while another contained more mature stout. The glass was filled with the fresh brew, and then, when the foam had settled, was topped up with the older, flatter stout. This system was replaced in the 1960s by pressurized containers which used nitrogen to give a smoother, creamier texture.

The beer was served from one keg and was filtered and pasteurized. At the same time weaker porter was phased out and the strength of stout was lowered from around 5% alcohol by volume to 4%. Today, there is an increasing tendency to chill it, thereby reducing its flavour and aroma.

Above: Drinking in Ireland generally means a pint of stout in the pub. But brewers have tried to bottle the experience to be enjoyed at home.

THE BEERS

Beamish Red Ale
This recent addition to the Beamish range is a smooth, traditional Irish-style red ale (4.5%). It has a rich, red colour, created by the black and crystal malts that are used in the brew. It has a full, sweet flavour.

Beamish Stout
The chocolatey Beamish Stout (4.2%) is the only stout brewed nowhere but Ireland. In fact it is not even brewed outside the town of Cork. Its distinctive flavour is partly due to the use of malted wheat, as well as barley, in the mash. Beamish is exported to Britain, Europe and North America.

Black Biddy Stout
A rare, cask-conditioned stout (4.4%) brewed at the Biddy Early pub, County Clare.

Caffrey's Irish Ale
This strong, creamy, traditional, Irish ale (4.8%) is brewed at the Ulster brewery in County Antrim. It is named after Thomas R. Caffrey, who founded the brewery in 1891. Caffrey's pours like an old-fashioned stout and takes about three minutes to settle from a creamy liquid to a rich auburn colour, topped with a creamy head. The beer is served chilled like a lager, but has the flavour of an ale. It was launched in the UK on St Patrick's Day 1994.

Great Northern Porter
This rare cask Irish porter (4%) is a black, traditional seasonal brew with a rich, sweetish, burnt flavour, from the Hilden brewery.

Guinness Draught
Draught Guinness (4.1%) is a smooth and creamy stout (partly due to the nitrogen-dispensing system) with a refreshing, roasted flavour and a rich black hue. It is filtered and pasteurized. In 1989, canned "draught" Guinness was launched, after five years' research, so that dedicated Guinness drinkers could enjoy the smooth brew in the comfort of their homes.

Guinness Extra Stout
This quality bottled stout (4.3%) uses unmalted, roasted barley and is heavily hopped to give a ruby-black colour and a complex, bitter flavour. It is still unpasteurized in Ireland. One of the world's classic beers.

Guinness Foreign Extra Stout
A strong export stout with a richly astringent taste (7.5%), it is a partly blended brew, using specially matured stout.

Guinness Special Export
This delicious, strong, mellow export stout (8%) is produced exclusively for the Belgian market.

Harp Export
This is a stronger (4.5%) version of Harp Lager and is produced at Guinness's Great Northern Brewery in Dundalk.

Harp Lager
This pioneering golden lager (3.6%) was developed by Guinness in 1959, to mark the bicentenary of the firm. Harp was launched in 1960 and was named after the company's famous Irish harp logo. It is brewed at the Great Northern Brewery in Dundalk.

The *Craic*
Irish pubs are famous the world over for their great beer and convivial atmosphere. The pub, as much as the church, is the traditional meeting place for the local community and is a place for good talk, good music and good drink. "The *Craic*" as it is known is one of the country's best known exports as "Irish pubs" spring up as far afield as Milan and Sydney.

Hilden Ale

This cask bitter (4%), produced by the Hilden brewery, is a hoppy, light-amber brew, which is mainly exported to Britain.

Hilden Special Reserve

A dark, amber mild (4.6%), brewed using dark malts, by the Hilden brewery.

Hoffmans Lager

This lager (3.3%) is produced in Waterford for south-east Ireland.

Irish Festival Ale

This amber-coloured, fruity bitter (5%) was originally brewed for important calendar events and beer festivals, but it is now a regular offering from the Hilden brewery.

Kaliber

This is a non-alcoholic lager brewed by Guinness.

Kilkenny Irish Beer

This red ale (4.3%) is a creamy, premium ale, initially produced for export in 1987 by Smithwick's. It was launched in Ireland in 1995. A stronger version (5%) is exported to the United States.

Macardles Ale

This Irish ale (4%) is produced at the small traditional Macardle Moore brewery in Dundalk.

Murphy's Irish Stout

This is a relatively light, smooth stout (4%). It should be served cooled to lager temperature, with a head about 1½ cm (½ in) deep.

Murphy's Red Beer

This pressurized red ale (5%) was launched by Murphy's in 1995. Its distinctive red hue is entirely natural.

Oyster Stout

This classic Irish beer (4.8%) includes real oysters in the boil. It is produced by the Porter House brewpub in Dublin. In its first year this stout won two awards.

Phoenix

This traditional Irish ale (4%) is produced at Macardle Moore of Dundalk.

Plain Porter

This classic light stout (4.3%) has a dry, roast flavour and an uncompromising black colour. Yet another quality brew from the Porter House brewing company, Parliament Street, Dublin.

Porter House Red

A traditional Irish red ale (4.4%) with a hoppy, caramel flavour. Produced by the Porter House brewery.

Smithwick's Barley Wine

Despite its name, this barley wine (5.5%) is actually brewed at Macardle's brewery in Dundalk.

Smithwick's Export

This auburn Irish ale (5%) is brewed in Ireland for the Canadian market.

Whitewater Mountain Ale

This cask-conditioned Irish ale (4.2%) is produced by the Whitewater brewery, a new brewery founded in 1996 in Kilkeen, County Down.

Wrasslers XXXX Stout

This stout (5%) is made to a recipe using four different types of malt, originally brewed by Deasy's of West Cork in the 1900s. The Hilden brewing company bills it as "a stout like your grandfather used to drink".

THE BREWERS

Beamish and Crawford

The Cork-based brewers first produced porter in 1792 and early in the 19th century they were the largest brewers in the land, bigger than Guinness. However, by the mid-20th century the brewery was run down and since 1962 it has been owned by a succession of foreign breweries. A modern brewhouse now stands alongside the half-timbered city centre offices. As well as Beamish Stout, it also produces a Beamish Red Ale.

Guinness

This international giant is, perhaps, one of the most renowned brewers in the world. The name has become almost synonymous with Irish stout (see next page).

Hilden brewery

This small brewery located alongside a Georgian country house in Lisburn, County Antrim, was set up in 1981. It is the oldest surviving independent brewery in Northern Ireland.

Letts

The Ghost Brewer of Ireland, Letts, ceased brewing at Enniscorthy in County Wexford in 1956, but an enterprising member of the family – George Killian Letts – licensed two major foreign brewers to produce their Ruby Ale. Pelforth of France produce George Killian's Bière Rousse, while Coors of the United States brew a lighter Killian's Irish Red. English brewers Greene King have since also rolled out Wexford Irish Cream Ale brewed to a Letts recipe.

Murphy's

Murphy's was established in 1856 by the Murphy brothers, on the Lady's Well site in Cork. Following a disastrous trading agreement with English brewers Watney's in the 1960s to sell keg Red Barrel in Ireland, the Lady's Well brewery had to be rescued by the Irish Government and a consortium of publicans before being bought by Dutch giants Heineken in 1983. Today Murphy's Stout (4%) is exported to more than 50 countries.

Above: A village pub advertises its wares – beer, food and music – in Killarney, County Kerry.

Porter House

A brewpub brewing classic Irish beers. Porter House opened in 1996 in the heart of Dublin in Parliament Street. Its brews include Porter House Plain Porter (4.3%), Porter House Red (4.4%), 4X Stout (5%) and an Oyster Stout (4.8%).

Smithwick's

Ireland's oldest brewery, built around the impressive ruins of Kilkenny's St Francis Abbey, dates from 1710. It is now owned by Guinness. The soft, red Smithwick's (3.5%) is Ireland's best-selling draught ale. It also produces Kilkenny Irish Beer (4.3%), mainly for export.

THE GUINNESS STORY

Arthur Guinness began brewing in Dublin in 1759.

For many, Guinness is the first, last and only word on Irish beer. Initially Arthur Guinness produced ale, but seeing the success of imported porter from England, he completely switched to brewing the dark drop by 1799. He reversed the beer trade, sending exports to England. By 1815, Guinness was so well known that wounded officers at the Battle of Waterloo were calling for the beer by name.

In the 1820s, the second Arthur Guinness (1768–1855) perfected an extra stout porter which eventually became known simply as stout. He made Guinness the largest brewer in Ireland. His son Benjamin (1798–1868) turned St James's Gate into the largest brewery in the world. Its stout sold around the globe.

A franchise was granted to McMullen of New York in 1858; Speakman Brothers of Melbourne started distribution in Australia in 1869. The familiar buff label with its harp trademark first appeared in 1862, and in 1878 a completely new brewhouse was built under Edward Guinness (1847–1927).

By 1910, the ever-expanding plant was producing two million hogsheads (54-gallon/245-litre casks) of stout a year. A quarter of a million wooden barrels were stacked in mountains on the 64-acre (26-hectare) site.

In 1936 a second brewery was opened at Park Royal in London to meet demand in England. Since 1962, Guinness has built breweries around the world: in Nigeria, Malaysia, Cameroon, Ghana and Jamaica. In addition, the stout is brewed under licence from North America to Australia.

In the 1950s, Guinness re-entered the ale trade through Irish Ale Breweries, with a beer called Phoenix from Waterford. The firm celebrated its bicentenary in 1959 by planning its own Harp lager. The black stuff, however, remains at the heart of the business.

Guinness stout varies in strength and character, depending on the market that it is being sold in. Stronger stouts are brewed for export, partly blended using specially matured stout. St James's Gate also exports concentrated versions of mature stout to blend into Guinness brewed abroad to provide the characteristic flavour and

Above: By the 19th century the St James's Gate brewery had become a city within a city, complete with its own power station and internal railway system, and employing an army of men.

colour. Sweeter and stronger Guinness is especially popular in Africa and the Caribbean.

Besides its Dublin brewery, Guinness in Ireland also owns ale and lager breweries at Kilkenny, Dundalk and Waterford.

Since it merged with United Distillers in 1986 and Grand Metropolitan in 1997 it has become one of the world's top drinks companies.

Below: Altogether, Guinness is brewed in 50 countries and is on sale in a further 100.

NUTRITIOUS AND DELICIOUS

Dublin's famous stout brewer Guinness was one of the first brewers to achieve international recognition. It had little choice, since it had already saturated its home market. By 1959, when the Irish brewer celebrated its bicentenary, 60% of production at its huge Dublin plant was for export.

Despite its huge success Guinness never ceased its search for new sales, and as a result its distinctive advertising campaigns have become well known the world over.

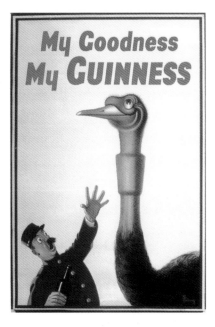

Above: The Guinness toucan.   *Above: A drink to come home to.*   *Above: A cartoon by H. Bateman and J. Gilroy.*

Above: Guinness has used several effective slogans but this one probably made the most lasting impact.

WALES

As you step from the train in the Welsh capital of Cardiff, you cannot miss the heady aroma of malt and hops drifting across the platform from Hancock's brewery behind the station and Brains old brewery in the city centre.

THE WELSH have a long brewing tradition. However, a chilling draught of takeovers and closures swept through the industry in the 1960s. Today, two English companies, Bass and Whitbread, dominate South Wales, alongside the family brewery, Brains of Cardiff. Further west, in Llanelli, another two breweries – Felinfoel and Crown Buckley – still operate, though in 1997 Brains took over Crown Buckley.

The Welsh beer trade was built in the 19th century on the raging thirst of miners and steelworkers who worked in the heavy industries of the valleys. At the same time, however, there was a strong temperance movement led by the powerful Methodist chapels of the area. Demon drink was top of the sin list during the religious revivals of the 19th century. At a temperance meeting in Tredegar in 1859, 7,000 signed the teetotal pledge. That summer the receipts of the local Rhymney brewery plunged by £500 a month.

The twin influences of heavy industry and temperance ensured that the typical Welsh ale was a low-gravity brew, relative to English beers. It was brewed for drinking in quantity. The two leading brands today, Allbright from Welsh Brewers (Bass) and Welsh Bitter from Whitbread, reflect this weak tradition: both are light-processed beers.

However, some tastier traditional brews still survive, notably Brains Dark and Worthington Dark.

When Welsh brewing recovered somewhat in the early 1980s, 20 new breweries frothed up to meet the demand for traditional cask ale. Most, however, found it difficult to establish a reliable trade and went rapidly to the brewhouse wall. The only survivors from this period are the Bullmastiff brewery in Cardiff and Plassey near Wrexham.

In the mid-1990s, a second wave of new ventures appeared, led by Dyffryn Clwyd of Denbigh, Cambrian of Dolgellau and Tomos Watkin of Llandeilo.

Above right: Roberts of Aberystwyth is one of the many breweries which have vanished.

Above: The Brains brewery of Cardiff has long kept the flag of cask-conditioned ales flying. It has only recently released its premium brew S-A in bottles.

THE BEERS

Allbright
This is the most popular beer in Wales. It is a standard, pale-amber keg bitter (3.2%), produced by Bass-owned Welsh Brewers in Cardiff.

Archdruid
This flavoursome ale (3.9%) is one of a range of beers from the small Dyffryn Clwyd brewery, located in the old, stone butter market in the centre of Denbigh.

Brains Bitter
This hoppy, golden-amber cask bitter (3.7%), is Brains' best-selling brew.

Brains Dark
This lightly hopped, dark mild (3.5%) is traditionally served with a creamy head. Brains Dark is a smooth brew that is less sweet than most beers of the dark mild type, a stronger (4%) processed version is sold as Dark Smooth.

Brenin
Crown Buckley's low-gravity keg bitter (3.4%) takes its name from the Welsh word for "king".

Brindle
A strong, tasty ale (5%), produced by the small Bullmastiff brewery.

Buckley's Best Bitter
This well-balanced bitter (3.7%) has a pleasing, hoppy character. It has been famous for generations in west Wales and is still Crown Buckley's best-selling brew. Buckley's Best Bitter is available in cask, keg and cans.

Bullmastiff Best Bitter
A malty, fruity beer (4%) brewed by Bullmastiff of Cardiff.

Cambrian Original
Hoppy, session bitter from the Cambrian brewery of Dolgellau. They also brew a malty Best Bitter (4.2%) and full-bodied Premium (4.8%).

CPA
Crown Pale Ale is the light-amber, refreshing bitter (3.4%) that was once known as "the champagne of the valleys", when it slaked the thirsts of the miners. It is brewed by Crown Buckley.

Cwrw Castell
The name of this beer (4.2%) means "Castle Bitter" in Welsh. It is produced by Dyffryn Clwyd.

Cwrw Tudno
This is Plassey's malty premium bitter (5%). "Tudno" is the patron saint of the seaside resort of Llandudno.

Dr Johnson's Draught
This traditional draught beer (3.6%) is one of the range from Dyffryn Clwyd.

Double Dragon
Felinfoel's famous full-bodied premium bitter (4.2%) won the Challenge cup for cask beer at the Brewers' Exhibition in London in 1976. A stronger version of the dark-amber, moderately malty, delicately hopped brew is bottled for export, mainly to the US.

Dragon's Breath
This is Plassey's fiery, spicy-flavoured, dark-amber winter warmer (6%).

Ebony Dark
This distinctive, rare cask ale (3.8%) comes from Bullmastiff in Cardiff.

Felinfoel Bitter
An amber, lightly hopped session bitter (3.2%) brewed using pale pipkin malt in the mash by the Felinfoel brewery.

Felinfoel Dark
This deep, dark beer (3.2%) is brewed using extra caramel to produce a slightly sweeter brew than the standard.

Gold Brew
This amber-coloured, tasty, cask ale (3.8%) is produced by the Bullmastiff brewery in Cardiff.

Hancock's HB
Hancock's HB is a malty, cask bitter (3.6%) from the Bass-owned Hancock's brewery in Cardiff.

Jolly Jack Tar Porter
This is Dyffryn Clwyd's dark, dry traditional porter (4.5%).

Main Street Bitter
This is the Pembroke brewery's fine, cask-conditioned bitter (4.1%).

Off the Rails
This strong beer (5.1%) is produced at the Pembroke brewery, for the free trade. It is available at the Station Inn at Pembroke Docks.

Old Nobbie Stout
A dark beer from the Pembroke brewery (4.8%). It is available for the free trade and at the Station Inn.

Pedwar Bawd
This strong ale (4.8%) comes from Dyffryn Clwyd of Denbigh. The name means "four thumbs". In 1994, it won the CAMRA accolade of "Welsh Beer of the Year".

Plassey Bitter
A straw-coloured beer (4%) with a fruity flavour from Plassey brewery.

Reverend James
Buckley's full-bodied,
warming, spicy, fruity
premium ale (4.5%) is
named in honour of the
Reverend James Buckley.
A Methodist minister,
Buckley combined saving
souls with satisfying thirsts
when he inherited the
brewery in Llanelli from his
father-in-law in the 1820s.

BRAGOT

Centuries ago, Welsh ale was a highly prized commodity throughout Britain. For example, when King Ine of Wessex in southern England drew up a law concerned with payments in kind received in return for land, some time between 690 and 693 AD, he decreed that for every ten hides of land, the food rent paid should include 12 ambers (an ancient liquid measurement) of Welsh ale.

Records of the Saxon period divide ale into three types – clear, mild and Welsh. Welsh ale, which was known as Bragawd or Bragot, was more highly valued than either clear or mild ale. It was recognized as a separate style, and did not necessarily have to be brewed in Wales. The savoury brew, which was flavoured with expensive spices and honey, was driven west by the invading Saxons, but then welcomed back into England by the new masters who greatly appreciated its heady flavour. In ancient Britain, Welsh ale was second only to mead, that other honey brew.

S-A
Brains' best-known beer is a dark-amber, malty, fruity premium bitter (4.2%) that is affectionately known as "Skull Attack" by Welsh drinkers. However, its name actually comes from the initials of the brewery's founder, Samuel Arthur Brain. S-A is exported to the United States under the name Traditional Welsh Ale.

SBB
Special Best Bitter (3.7%) is brewed by Crown Buckley in Llanelli. This rounded, mature, cask-conditioned bitter is particularly popular with beer drinkers in the Cynon valley.

Son of a Bitch
This full-bodied and dangerously drinkable ale is the strongest, regularly brewed, cask beer in Wales (6%). It comes from Bullmastiff of Cardiff.

Watkin BB
A malty bitter (4%) from Tomos Watkin of Llandeilo.

Watkin OSB
A slightly stronger old style bitter (4.5%) from Watkin.

Welsh Bitter
Whitbread's well-known weak keg bitter (3.2%) from its vast plant at Magor.

Worthington Dark
Welsh Brewers' dark-ruby, creamy mild (3%), named after the famous Burton brewers. It is popular in the Swansea area.

Worthington Draught
A smooth, creamy bitter (3.6%) from Welsh Brewers with subtle bitterness and pear-and-peach aroma.

THE BREWERS

Brains

This traditional family brewery has been operating in Cardiff since 1882. The brewery is famous for its slogan "It's Brains you want". It produces three cask ales for its 189 pubs.

Above: The Williams brothers toast the success of their fledgling Cambrian brewery.

Bullmastiff

Bob Jenkins founded this colourful brewery in 1987, and named it in honour of his pet dogs. Now located in Cardiff, this small brewery produces distinctive but hard-to-find cask beers, including Gold Brew and Ebony Dark, Best Bitter, Brindle and the infamous Son of a Bitch.

Cambrian

Brothers Kevin and Keith Williams set up the only brewery in north-west Wales in 1996, to serve the mountainous Snowdonia National Park. Based in Dolgellau, the small brewery produces Cambrian Original, Best Bitter, Premium and Mountain Ale, as well as various seasonal brews.

Crown Buckley

Buckley's brewery in Llanelli claims to be the oldest in Wales, dating back to 1767. Crown brewery, which was previously D.T. Jenkins of Pontyclun, has been rolling out barrels as Crown since 1919. D.T. Jenkins became Crown when the local clubs banded together to buy their own brewery in an attempt to overcome shortages of beer caused by rationing. In 1989 Crown and Buckley merged, and the brewing was then concentrated at the former Buckley site in Llanelli. The old Crown site is used for bottling and kegging. In 1997 the company was taken over by Brains of Cardiff and is now known as Brain Crown Buckley.

Above: Vans load up with barrels of Brains for the pubs (c. 1930).

Dyffryn Clwyd

A small brewery located in the old, stone butter market in the centre of Denbigh.

Felinfoel

This village brewery, situated just outside Llanelli, is one of only two surviving breweries in west Wales. In 1935, it became the first brewery to can beer in Europe, in an effort to help the local tinplate industry during the Depression. Felinfoel is best known for its robust and patriotically named Double Dragon ale (a red dragon is the symbol of Wales). It also brews a fine bitter and a tasty dark (both 3.2%) for its 85 pubs.

Hancock's

William Hancock took over North and Low's Bute Dock brewery in Cardiff in 1883. From there the company expanded by taking over several other breweries around South Wales, until eventually it could easily claim to be the largest brewer in Wales. When this regional force was taken over by the English giant Bass in 1968, Welsh Brewers was born through a merger of Hancock's with Webb's of Aberbeg and Fernvale of the Rhondda. Today only Hancock's Brewery in Cardiff remains.

Pembroke

David Lightley set up this small brewery in 1994, in converted stables behind his 18th-century guest house. Pembroke mainly supplies his pub, the Station Inn, on the railway platform at Pembroke Docks. Beers produced include a rare cask-conditioned lager (4.1%).

Plassey

This small brewery was set up in a caravan site at Eyton in 1985. Plassey produces a hoppy Plassey bitter (4%), a dry stout (4.6%) and two stronger ales for the three bars on the caravan site, as well as for the local free trade.

Watkin

Tomos Watkin and Sons is named after a former Llandovery brewery. It was established in 1995 in Llandeilo in south-west Wales by Simon Buckley, a member of the famous Buckley brewing family. The plant produces two cask beers: Watkin's Brewery Bitter and Watkin's Old Style Bitter. Watkin has ambitious plans to expand to larger premises and to build up a pub estate.

Welsh Brewers

Bass's South Wales subsidiary is based in Cardiff.

Whitbread

This famous company is England's third largest brewing group. It has a weighty presence in Wales through its huge plant at Magor. As well as the best-selling Welsh Bitter, it also brews many foreign beers at the plant for the Welsh market.

Below: Tin plating was a traditional industry of West Wales. Its decline prompted Felinfoel to adopt beer in cans more readily than most in a bid to boost the tin industry and the pockets of its local drinkers.

HOME-BREW PUBS

Wales has four pubs that brew their own beers:

• The Joiners Arms, Bishopston. The Swansea Brewing Co. was set up behind this pub in 1996. The main beer is Bishopswood Bitter.

• The Nag's Head, Abercych, near Newcastle Emlyn, is a restored old smithy producing Old Emrys (4.1%).

• The Red Lion, Llanidloes, Powys, brews Blind Cobbler's Thumb (4.2%), Witches' Brew (7.5%) and, at Christmas, the powerful barley wine Blind Cobbler's Last (10.5%).

• The Tynllidiart Arms, Capel Bangor, near Aberystwyth, is a cottage brewpub that produces Rheidol Reserve (4.5%).

WREXHAM LAGER

Wrexham was once the centre of beer making in Wales, as its springs provided ideal water for brewing. The town boasted 19 breweries, and its beers were famous across Britain. The last of the Wrexham ale breweries, Border, closed in 1984 – but one unique concern remains.

German and Czech immigrants established the Wrexham Lager Beer Company in 1882. When it first began brewing, it claimed to be the first lager brewery in Britain. Much of its early production was shipped abroad, particularly by the army.

Burton brewer Ind Coope took over Wrexham in 1949, and it switched to producing foreign lagers under licence. It was the first brewery in Britain to brew American Budweiser. It still brews a light Wrexham lager for the local trade and occasional export.

Below and above: The Wrexham brewery struggled to convert Britain's ale drinkers with its lager beer.

225

ENGLAND

In the first half of the 20th century, the main beer in England was mild, the worker's drink. Since the Second World War mild has been replaced by another top-fermenting ale, the stronger, more heavily hopped bitter.

DESPITE THE FACT that the golden tide of lager has washed over the shores of England, in the shape of imitations of the Pilsner style from overseas, ales are still very popular and account for around half the market. No country in the world drinks more. Ale, which varies in colour from pale gold through to dark ruby, is a social drink, usually of modest strength, from 3.5 to 4.5% alcohol by volume. It is brewed for drinking in quantity (usually in pints or halves) in company.

To find the native beers of England, walk into an English pub (public house) where the bulk of beer is still enjoyed on draught, served over the bar usually from a tall handpump, rather than being bought in a bottle or a can in a shop or supermarket and drunk at home. Traditional English beer is cask-conditioned – it is a living beer which continues to ferment and mature in the cask in the pub cellar after leaving the brewery. This allows the beer's flavour to develop fully.

English beer has a reputation for being "warm", but though it should not be heavily chilled, like lagers, it should always be served cellar cool.

In the 1960s the major breweries in England tried to replace cask beer with easier-to-handle keg beer, which was filtered and pasteurized at the brewery (to make it easier to store), then served chilled and carbonated at the bar. But the beer drinkers of England rose in revolt. Many objected to losing their traditional local tastes. They wanted cask beer's fuller flavour. A campaign was launched in the early 1970s called CAMRA – the Campaign for Real Ale. It sparked a major revival of cask beer. As a result around 55 traditional local and regional breweries have survived, and some of the national companies have relaunched their own cask beers. CAMRA began a brewing revolution, and following that hundreds of new breweries have been set up since the 1970s, some reviving old styles of ale such as porter.

Above: English beer is brewed to be drunk in quantity. Stronger ales such as Fuller's 1845 are for special occasions.

THE BEERS

Abbot Ale

This robust, bright-amber, fruity premium bitter (5%) from Greene King is named after the last abbot of Bury St Edmunds in East Anglia – the brewer's home town.

Adnams Bitter

Adnams bitter is a dark-gold classic of its type (3.7%), with a hoppy, orangey flavour. Adnams also brews a smooth, malty, dark mild (3.2%), Regatta Ale (4.3%), a light summer ale, and its Extra, a pleasant best bitter with a dry, hoppy flavour, was voted Champion Beer of Britain in 1993.

AK

This long-established and popular ale (3.7%), produced by McMullens of Hertford, is a refreshingly light bitter.

Amazon Bitter

Additive-free beer (4%) from the Masons Arms brewpub, Cartmel Fell, Cumbria.

Ansells Mild

A liquorice-tasting, dark mild (3.4%) brewed by Ind Coope at Burton-on-Trent.

A Pint-a Bitter

A tasty, cask-conditioned bitter (3.5%) from the Hogs Back brewery in Surrey. Also known as APB.

Archers Best

A malty, fruity bitter from Archers of Swindon.

Arthur Pendragon

A full-bodied, fruity, premium ale (4.8%) from the Hampshire brewery in Andover, Hampshire.

Arundel Best Bitter

This gold-coloured, additive-free bitter (4%) is produced by Arundel of Sussex.

Badger

The popular name for a range of beers by the historic Hall and Woodhouse brewery in Blandford Forum, Dorset.

Ballard's Best

Copper-coloured malty ale from the Sussex country brewery, Ballard's of Nyewood.

Banks's Ale

A reddish-amber mild (3.5%), made with Maris Otter malt, Fuggles and Golding hops and caramel.

Banks's Bitter

A bittersweet, crisp bitter (3.8%) from Banks's brewery in Wolverhampton.

Banner Bitter

A flavoursome, light-brown bitter (4%) from the Butterknowle brewery in Bishop Auckland.

Barn Owl Bitter

A darkish-brown, fruity, rich bitter (4.5%) from the Cotleigh brewery, Somerset.

Batham's Best

Sweetish, golden bitter (4.3%) from the famous Black Country brewery, Batham's, of Brierley Hill.

Battleaxe

A smooth, slightly sweet cask beer (4.2%) from the Rudgate brewery, near York.

Beacon Bitter

A refreshing bitter (3.8%) brewed by Everard in Narborough, near Leicester.

Beast

A potent winter brew (6.6%) from the Exmoor brewery in Wiveliscombe, Somerset.

Beaumanor Bitter

This light-brown, strong-tasting bitter (3.7%) is brewed by the Hoskins brewery in Leicester.

Beechwood

A full-bodied draught beer (4.3%) with a nutty character from the Chiltern brewery.

Benchmark

A pleasantly bitter, malty ale (3.5%) produced by Bunces brewery, Wiltshire.

Bishops Ale

A potent, full-flavoured, warming barley wine (8%) from Ridleys brewery near Chelmsford.

Bishops Finger

A ruby-red ale (5.4%) with a fruity flavour and a malty aftertaste from the Shepherd Neame brewery in Kent.

Black Diamond
A dark-ruby-coloured, rich, malty bitter (4.8%) from the Butterknowle brewery in Bishop Auckland.

Black Jack Porter
A rich, black, winter beer (4.6%) with a fruity, sweetish flavour, from Archers in Swindon, Wiltshire.

Black Magic
Bitter stout (4.5%) from Oakhill brewery of Somerset.

Black Rock
A strong ale (5.5%) from the Brewery-on-Sea, Lancing, Sussex.

Black Sheep Best
A hoppy bitter (3.8%) fermented in traditional Yorkshire stone squares at the Black Sheep brewery, Masham, North Yorkshire.

Blunderbus
An intense porter (5.5%) from the Coach House brewery in Warrington.

Boddingtons
A straw-coloured brew (3.8%) from this famous Manchester brewery. It was once worshipped for its parch-dry bitterness, but it now has a smoother flavour.

Bodgers
A bottle-conditioned barley wine (8%) from the Chiltern brewery, near Aylesbury.

Bombardier
A mild, smoky, malty cask beer (4.3%) from the Charles Wells brewery in Bedford.

Boro Best
A full-bodied cask beer (4%) from the North Yorkshire brewery in Middlesborough.

Bosun Bitter
This smooth, amber, cask beer (4.6%) has a strong malt flavour. Brewed by the Poole brewery, Dorset.

Bosun's Bitter
A refreshing, amber cask bitter (3.1%) with a bitter, hops taste from the St Austell brewery, Cornwall.

Brakspear Bitter
A well-hopped, aromatic light bitter (3.4%) produced by this Oxfordshire brewery.

Brakspear Special
A golden-brown, malty, dry bitter (4.3%).

Brand Oak Bitter
This well-balanced cask beer (4%) has a dry finish and a citrus, sweet flavour. It is brewed by the Wickwar brewery in Gloucestershire.

Branoc
An amber bitter (3.8%) brewed by Branscombe Vale in Devon using the local spring water.

Brew XI
A sweetish, malty cask bitter (3.8%) from the Mitchells & Butlers brewery in Birmingham.

Brew 97
A full-bodied, malty cask beer (5%) with a good hops taste, from the Moles brewery, Wiltshire.

Bishop's Tipple, The
A strong, rich, deep-amber barley wine (6.5%) with a sweet and smokey, complex flavour brewed within view of the city's towering cathedral spire by Gibbs Mew of Salisbury.

Black Adder
This dark stout (5.3%) with a roast-malt character, from the Mauldon brewery, was voted Champion Beer of Britain in 1991.

Black Cat Mild
A dark, full-tasting cask bitter (3.2%) from the Moorhouse brewery, Lancashire.

Black Sheep Special
A full, amber ale (4.4%) brewed in traditional stone squares. It is sold bottled as Black Sheep Ale.

Brewer's Droop

A strong ale (5%) available on draught and in bottles from the Marston Moor brewery, North Yorkshire.

Brewer's Pride

An amber, light, refreshing, fruity cask bitter (4.2%) from the Marston Moor brewery, North Yorkshire.

Bridge Bitter

A fruity, hoppy bitter (4.2%), brewed by Burton Bridge in Burton-on-Trent.

Bristol Stout

A tasty, seasonal stout (4.7%) from the Smiles brewery, Bristol. It has a red-brown hue and a pleasant roast malt taste.

Broadside Ale

Adnams' strong garnet-coloured, bitter, hoppy ale (4.7%) was brewed to mark the 300th anniversary of the battle of Sole Bay in 1672. The ale in its bottle version (6.3%) packs more cannon fire than the draught beer.

Buccaneer

A light, pale gold bitter with a sweet malty taste (5.2%) brewed by Burtonwood.

Bullion

Fruity dark ale (4.7%) from the Old Mill brewery, Snaith, Yorkshire.

Bulldog Pale Ale

A strong, yellow-coloured, hoppy, bottled pale ale (6.3%), produced by Courage in Bristol.

Bunce's Best Bitter

This aromatic, fresh and fruity bitter (4.1%) is brewed in a watermill in Netheravon, Wiltshire.

Burton Porter

This tawny-brown, dry porter (4.5%) has a light, malty taste. It is also available as a bottle-conditioned beer. Brewed by the Burton Bridge brewery in Burton-on-Trent.

Burtonwood Bitter

A smooth, smoky-tasting bitter (3.7%), brewed near Warrington at the Burtonwood brewery.

Butcombe Bitter

A dry, hoppy bitter (4%) brewed near Bristol in the Mendip Hills.

Buzz

A cask beer primed with honey (4.5%) produced by the Brewery-on-Sea, Lancing, Sussex.

Cains Bitter

A dry, spicy, amber bitter (4%) from this popular Merseyside brewery in Liverpool.

Cambridge Bitter

A traditionally brewed, amber, hoppy bitter (3.8%) from the Elgood brewery in the Fens at Wisbech.

Camerons Bitter

An orange-coloured, light, malty bitter (3.6%) from the Hartlepool brewer, which is very popular with the local workers.

Carling Black Label

This smooth, sweet lager (4.1%) is Britain's best-selling beer. It was introduced to England from Canada in 1953 and was adopted by Bass as its leading lager brand.

Castle Eden Ale

An amber-coloured, sweet, malty ale (3.8%) from the Durham-based brewery owned by Whitbread.

Castle Special Pale Ale

One of a range of bottled beers (5%) from the McMullen brewery in Hertford.

Challenger

A premium bitter (4.1%), which despite carrying the name of a hop, has a fruity, malty flavour. It is brewed by the Ash Vine brewery, Trudoxhill, Somerset.

Chiltern Ale

A tangy, light draught beer (3.7%) from the Chiltern brewery of Terrick.

Chiswick Bitter

A refreshing bitter (3.5%) with a subtle, floral, smoky flavour, from Fullers of London, this is much acclaimed.

Coachman's Best

A medium-coloured full-bodied bitter (3.7%) with a hoppy, fruity flavour, from the Coach House brewery in Warrington.

Cocker Hoop

A golden, refreshing bitter (4.8%) with a hoppy, fruity flavour, from the independent Jennings brewery in the Lake District.

College Ale

A strong seasonal, winter cask ale (7.4%) from the Morrells brewery, Oxford.

Conciliation

This dark, tawny-brown bitter (4.3%) has a good, hoppy taste. It is the flagship brew of the Butterknowle brewery in Bishop Auckland, County Durham.

Coopers WPA

A popular, refreshing, yellow-gold cask beer (3.5%) with a hoppy, citrus tang, which comes from the Wickwar brewery in Gloucestershire.

Country Best Bitter
A full and fruity, clean-tasting bitter (4.3%) from the McMullen brewery in Hertford.

Country Stile
A mid-brown draught beer (4.1%), produced by Daleside brewery in Harrogate, Yorkshire.

Courage Best
A traditional golden-brown, malty, dry cask bitter (4%) brewed in Bristol by Courage.

Craftsman
A hoppy, gold, premium ale (4.2%) from Thwaites brewery in Blackburn, Lancashire.

Cromwell Bitter
A gold, fruity cask bitter (3.6%) from the Marston Moor brewery, North Yorkshire.

Cumberland Ale
A gold-coloured bitter (4%) with a delicate flavour, from the Jennings brewery in Cockermouth in the Lake District.

Daredevil Winter Warmer
A smooth, fruity brew (7.1%) with a strong, mature flavour, produced by Everards in Narborough, near Leicester.

Deacon
A pale-gold, orangey, dry bitter (5%) from the Gibbs Mews brewery in Salisbury, Wiltshire.

Deep Shaft Stout
This black stout (6.2%) produced by the Freeminer brewery, Gloucestershire, has a roast-malt flavour.

Devon Gold
A straw-coloured, fruity, summer brew (4.1%) from Blackawton in South Devon.

Director's
A traditional dark, rich, cask bitter (4.8%) brewed in Bristol by Courage.

Dolphin Best
This dry, amber, cask bitter (3.8%) is brewed by the Poole brewery, Dorset.

Dorset Best
Also known as Badger Best Bitter (4.1%). This Hall and Woodhouse cask ale has a bitter hop and fruit flavour.

Double Chance
A malty bitter (3.8%) from the Malton brewery of North Yorkshire.

Double Diamond
Ind Coope's famous dark-amber bottled pale ale from Burton-on-Trent, which after a period of promotion as a weak keg beer, has seen its reputation restored as a bottled ale (4%), particularly in the stronger export version (5.2%). Also occasionally available as a cask beer.

Double Maxim
A classic, strong, amber-coloured brown ale (4.7%) with a smooth, fruity taste from the giant Vaux brewery.

Double Stout
An old-fashioned stout (4.8%), revived in 1996 after 79 years by the Hook Norton brewery in Banbury.

Dragonslayer
A yellowish real ale (4.5%) with a dry malt and hops flavour, from B&T, Bedfordshire.

Draught Bass
A superb bitter (4.4%) with a malty flavour and light hop bitterness. This is the biggest-selling premium ale in the country.

Draught Burton Ale
A full-bodied ale (4.8%) from the Carlsberg-Tetley brewery in Burton-on-Trent.

Drawwell Bitter
A cask beer (3.9%) from the Hanby brewery in Shropshire.

Eagle IPA
A sweet, malty, amber-coloured cask beer (3.6%) from the Charles Wells brewery in Bedford.

Eden Bitter
A smooth, sweet bitter (3.6%) from the Castle Eden brewery in County Durham.

Edmund II Ironside
A tasty, cask-conditioned bitter (4.2%) from the Hampshire brewery in Andover.

Elizabethan
A golden, barley wine (8.1%) originally brewed to mark the Queen's coronation in 1953 by Harveys brewery.

Enville Ale
One of a range of honey beers produced by the Enville Farm brewery in Staffordshire. The pale-gold ale (4.5%) is primed with honey after a rapid initial fermentation and then lagered. The brewery uses its own honey and barley.

Enville White
A golden wheat beer (4%) with a clean, sweet flavour from Enville Farm brewery.

ESB
The revered Extra Special Bitter (5.5%) from Fuller's of London is much stronger than most bitters. It has great character with a complex malt, fruit and hops flavour and has won the Champion Beer of Britain title an unprecedented three times.

ESX Best
A fruity cask bitter (4.3%) produced by Ridleys brewery, near Chelmsford, Essex.

Everard Mild
A dark mild (3.3%) which forms an unusually large head when it is poured. It is brewed in Narborough, near Leicester by Everard.

Exmoor Ale
This pale-brown, malty bitter (3.8%), from the Exmoor brewery in Wiveliscombe, Somerset, won the best bitter award at the Great British Beer Festival in 1980.

Exmoor Gold
An amber bitter (4.5%) from the Exmoor brewery.

Fargo
A rich, amber-coloured cask ale (5%) with a soft hop and roast-malt taste, from the Wells brewery in Bedford.

Farmer's Glory
A dark, fruity premium bitter (4.5%) from Wadworth's of Devizes, Wiltshire.

Fed Special
This bright, pale-amber, filtered bitter (4%) is brewed for the working men's clubs by the Federation Brewery in the north-east of England.

Festive
A fruity premium ale (5%) from the King & Barnes brewery, Horsham, Sussex.

Flowers IPA
A coppery-coloured, creamy pale ale (3.6%) produced by Whitbread in Cheltenham.

Flowers Original
A tasty bitter (4.5%) with a good malt and hop balance, produced by Whitbread in Cheltenham, Gloucestershire.

Flying Herbert
This red, refreshing, malty cask bitter is from the North Yorkshire brewery.

Formidable Ale
Strong golden-coloured ale (5%) with a full taste from Cains brewery, Liverpool.

Fortyniner
A well-balanced, fruity bitter (4.8%) from the Ringwood brewery, Hampshire.

Founders
A pale-brown bitter (4.5%) with a slight citrus and sweet-malt taste, from the Ushers brewery in Wiltshire.

Franklin's Bitter
A distinctive floral, aromatic, hoppy bitter (3.8%) brewed in Harrogate, Yorkshire.

Freedom Pilsener
This fresh, slightly fruity Pilsner (5.4%) is brewed by the Freedom brewery in Fulham, London.

Freeminer Bitter
A pale, hoppy bitter (4%) from the Forest of Dean, Gloucestershire.

Fuggles Imperial
A pale, strong, premium bitter (5.5%) from Whitbread's Castle Eden brewery, County Durham.

Gargoyle
A tasty cask bitter (5%) from the Lichfield brewery in the Midlands.

GB Mild
A smooth, malty, fruity brew (3.5%) brewed by the Lees family brewery in north Manchester.

Georges Bitter Ale
A light, refreshing bitter (3.3%) from the Courage brewery which was formerly Georges, in Bristol.

Gingersnap
A dark, orangey-coloured wheat beer (4.7%), brewed with fresh root ginger from Shrewsbury.

Ginger Tom
A ginger-flavoured ale (5.2%) from the Hoskins & Oldfield brewery, Leicester.

Gladstone
A refreshing, smooth bitter (4.3%) from the McMullen brewery, Hertford.

Golden Best
A fine mild (3.5%) from the Timothy Taylor brewery, Keighley, Yorkshire.

Golden Bitter
A fruity bitter (4.7%) from Archers in Swindon.

Golden Brew
A golden, aromatic, bitter (3.8%) from the Smiles brewery, Bristol.

Gold Label
England's best-known bottled barley wine. This spicy, warming brew (10.9%) is produced by Whitbread.

Gothic Ale
A dark ale (5.2%) from the Enville Farm brewery, Staffordshire.

Governor
An amber bitter (4.4%) from the Hull brewery.

Graduate
A roasted-malt-flavoured premium bitter (5.2%) from the Morrells brewery, Oxford.

Granary Bitter
An amber-coloured brew with a bitter, fruity character (3.8%), from the Reepham brewery near Norwich.

GSB
A dry, fruity bitter (5.2%) from the Elgood brewery near Wisbech.

Gunpowder
A liquorice-black mild (3.8%) from the Coach House brewery, Warrington.

Hammerhead
A robust, strong, rich, malty ale (5.6%) brewed by Clark's of Wakefield, West Yorkshire.

Harrier S.P.A
A light-brown bitter (3.6%) with a light, hoppy taste, from the Cotleigh brewery, Somerset.

Harvest Ale
A staggeringly strong bottled ale (11.5%) that is produced each year from the new season's malt and hops by the Lees brewery in Manchester. This vintage brew can be laid down to mature in the cellar for several years.

Harveys Christmas Ale
A strong warming ale produced annually by the Harveys brewery, Lewes, Sussex.

Harveys Firecracker
This brew was bottled in honour of the emergency services who fought a disastrous fire at the Harveys brewery in 1996. It is a strong, dark pale ale with a smoky flavour (5.8%).

Harveys Sussex Best Bitter
A golden, hoppy bitter (4%) from Harveys of Lewes.

Harveys Sussex Pale Ale
A light, hoppy ale (3.5%) from the Harveys brewery.

Harveys Tom Paine
A strong pale ale (5.5%), from Harveys brewery.

Hatters
A fine, light mild (3.3%) from the Robinson's brewery, Stockport.

Headstrong
A fruity bitter (5.2%) from the Blackawton brewery in Devon.

Heritage
A full-bodied beer (5.2%) with a roast-malt, fruity flavour from the Smiles brewery, Bristol.

Hersbrucker Weizenbier
A light wheat beer (3.6%) from the Springhead brewery, Nottinghamshire.

Hick's Special Draught
Also known as HSD, this full-bodied, fruity cask bitter (5%) is produced by the St Austell brewery, Cornwall.

High Force
A complex, smooth beer (6.2%) with a sweet, malt flavour, from the Butterknowle brewery in Bishop Auckland.

Highgate Dark Mild
A dark-brown, smooth mild (3.2%) produced in this Victorian tower brewery in Walsall, West Midlands. It is fermented using a vigorous four-strain yeast to give a complex flavour.

Highgate Old Ale
A dark, red-brown, fruity ale (5.6%) with a complex flavour, brewed in winter by this Walsall brewery.

High Level
This sweet and fruity, bright, filtered brown ale (4.7%) is brewed for the working men's clubs by the Federation Brewery in the north-east of England. It is named after the bridge in Newcastle which crosses the River Tyne.

Hobgoblin
A robust, red ale (5.5%) sold in the cask and bottle in Britain and also in Europe and North America. It is produced by the Wychwood brewery, Oxfordshire.

Holden's Black Country Special Bitter
A sweetish, full-bodied bitter (5.1%) from Holden's brewery in Woodsetton in the West Midlands.

Holt's Bitter
This uncompromising dry bitter (4%) is sold at a relatively low price and still supplied in huge hogsheads (54-gallon casks) by Holt's brewery of Manchester.

Hook Norton Best Bitter

A dry, hoppy, cask-conditioned beer (3.4%) from this old Oxfordshire village brewery.

Hop and Glory

Complex bottle-conditioned beer (5%) from Ash Vine brewery, Somerset.

HSB

Famous, full-bodied bitter (4.8%) from Gale's of Horndean, Hampshire.

Imperial Russian Stout

A classic beer from Scottish Courage, the dark-brown, smooth brew (10%) has a rich malty flavour.

Indiana's Bones

A rich, dark, cask ale (5.6%) which is sold both as a cask beer and a bottled brew, from the Summerskills brewery, South Devon.

Innkeeper's Special

This smooth, malty brew (4.5%) has a rich, ruby-port hue and a crisp, hop taste. It is produced by the Coach House brewery in Warrington.

Inspired

A dark, malty cask bitter (4%) from the small Lichfield brewery.

Ironbridge Stout

A dark, rich stout (5%) from the Salopian brewery, Shrewsbury.

Jennings Bitter

A light, dry malty bitter (3.5%) from Jennings brewery in Cumbria.

John Smith's Bitter

A dark-amber, sweet, malty cask bitter (3.8%) with a creamy texture, from Yorkshire. One of the most popular beers in England.

Kimberley Classic

A light-coloured premium bitter (4.8%) with a dry, hoppy taste, from Hardys & Hansons brewery, Nottinghamshire.

King Alfred's

A hoppy cask beer (3.8%) from the Hampshire brewery.

Kingsdown Ale

This powerful, fruity, draught beer (5%) is produced by the Arkell's Kingsdown brewery, Swindon.

Lancaster Bomber

A straw-coloured cask ale (4.4%) from the Mitchell brewery in Lancaster.

Landlord

A classic, amber-coloured, premium bitter (4.3%) with a buttery flavour, from Timothy Taylor's brewery in Keighley, Yorkshire. It won the Champion Beer of Britain award in 1994.

Larkins Best Bitter

A full-bodied, fruity bitter (4.4%) from this Kent brewery.

London Pride

Fuller's fine, deep-red best bitter (4.1%) has a rich, dry, malty, hoppy taste.

Lynesack Porter

This is very dark, even for a porter (5%) with a sweet, malty finish. It is produced by the Butterknowle brewery in Bishop Auckland.

Mackeson's Stout

England's best-known bottled sweet stout (3%) from Whitbread is a blackish colour with a sugary, fruity taste. It was originally brewed by the firm of Mackeson in Hythe, Kent, in 1907. At that time it was claimed to be a tonic for invalids because it contained milk sugar or lactose. The sugar does not ferment, so the beer is low in alcohol.

Mackeson's was called milk stout until the British Government banned the term in 1946. However, Whitbread continues the connection through a milk churn on the label. It is still the leading brand in a declining sweet stout market and was once exported to 60 countries, and brewed under licence in Belgium, Jamaica, New Zealand and Singapore.

Above: A 1940s advertisement for Mackeson's before the British Government banned the term "milk stout" as misleading.

Magnet
A nutty-tasting premium bitter from the John Smith's brewery, Tadcaster, North Yorkshire.

Malt and Hops
A lively, seasonal ale (4.5%) made by Wadworth's, in Devizes, Wiltshire. It is one of a range of seasonal brews made using the new season's unkilned fresh hops.

M&B Mild
A reddish, full-bodied cask mild (3.2%) from Mitchells & Butlers brewery in, Birmingham.

Mann's Original
England's best-known bottled, sweet brown ale (2.8%) has a sticky, sugary texture and a fruity taste, and is now brewed by Ushers in Wiltshire.

Mansfield Bitter
This refreshing, sweetish bitter (3.9%) is brewed using traditional Yorkshire squares by the Mansfield brewery, Nottinghamshire.

Marston's Bitter
A light-brown, hoppy cask bitter (3.8%) from Marston's brewery, Burton-on-Trent.

Mauldon Special
A very hoppy cask beer (4.2%) from the Mauldon brewery in Suffolk.

COMMEMORATIVE BEERS

Brewers often make one-off brews to commemorate special occasions. Harveys of Lewes in Sussex, for example, bottled a special strong pale ale, called Firecracker, in honour of the emergency services who fought to save it from disaster when a fire broke out in the brewery in 1996. Many brewers bottled ales to keep for the Queen's Coronation in 1953 and later royal marriages.

Millennium Gold
This fruity, amber, cask beer (4.2%) is produced by Crouch Vale brewery, Essex.

Ministerley Ale
A complex, pale, cask bitter (4.5%) from the Salopian brewery, Shrewsbury.

Mitchell's Bitter
An amber-coloured, mild-tasting, hoppy bitter (3.8%) from Mitchell's of Lancaster.

Moles Best
A fruity cask bitter (4%), the leading beer from the Moles brewery, Wiltshire.

Monkey Wrench
A smooth, dark, sweetish, potent beer (5.3%) which is produced by Daleside brewery in the spa town of Harrogate, Yorkshire.

Moonraker
A rich, strong, orangey ale (7.5%) from the J.W. Lees brewery, Manchester.

Morocco Ale
This dark, rich, spicy bottled ale (5.5%) is said to be based on a 300-year-old recipe. It is produced by the Daleside brewery, Harrogate, Yorkshire.

Morrells Bitter
A golden-brown cask bitter (3.7%) from the Morrells brewery in the university town of Oxford.

Mutiny
A reddish, full-bodied cask ale (4.5%) from the Rebellion brewery, Buckinghamshire.

Natterjack
An aromatic, golden ale (4.8%), named after the natterjack toad, produced by the Frog Island brewery, Northampton.

Newcastle Amber
This less-well-known cousin of Newcastle Brown was introduced in 1951 as a lighter version. It has a malty, sugary taste.

Newcastle Brown
This pioneering northern brown ale (4.7%) has a nutty, caramel taste. It was first produced by Newcastle Breweries in 1927. Newcastle Brown is strong, dry and light in colour. Drinkers usually expect a small glass so they can keep topping up. This best-selling bottled beer is exported to more than 40 countries. It is now brewed by Scottish Courage on Tyneside.

Nightmare Porter
A smooth, dry porter (5%) with a roast-malt and liquorice taste from the Hambleton brewery near Thirsk, North Yorkshire.

Noel Ale
A Christmas ale (5.5%) from the Arkell's Kingsdown Brewery, Swindon.

Norfolk Nog
The 1992 Champion Beer of Britain. This tasty old ale (4.6%) is produced by Woodforde's of Norfolk.

Norman's Conquest
A dark, strong ale (7%) from the Cottage brewery in West Lydford, Somerset. It won the Champion Beer of Britain title at the Great British Beer Festival in 1993.

North Brink Porter
A special, reddish-black winter beer (5%) from the Elgood brewery in Wisbech.

Nut Brown
A nut-brown ale with a nutty, sweet flavour (4.5%) from the Whitby brewery, North Yorkshire.

OBJ
An intense, fruity, winter ale (5%) produced by the Brakspear brewery.

Old Baily
A copper-coloured, fruity, malty bitter (4.8%) from the Mansfield brewery in Nottinghamshire.

Old Bircham
An amber, sweet, malty winter beer (4.6%) from the Reepham brewery, near Norwich.

Old Bob
A dark-amber strong bottled pale ale (5.1%) from Ridleys brewery.

Old Brewery Bitter
A malty, nutty cask bitter (4%) from Samuel Smith's who also brew a distinctive orangey-coloured bottled pale ale (5%).

Old Buzzard
This winter beer (4.8%) is almost black. It has a smooth, rich flavour and is produced by the Cotleigh brewery, Somerset.

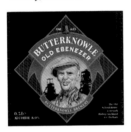

Old Ebenezer
A dark, tawny-coloured, rich ale (8%) from Butterknowle brewery in Bishop Auckland, County Durham.

Old Expensive
A strong, fruity winter barley wine (6.7%) brewed by Burton Bridge in Burton-on-Trent.

Old Growler
A complex porter (5.5%) with a sweet fruit and malt taste and chocolatey character, which comes from the Nethergate brewery, Suffolk.

Old Hooky
A strong, reddish-brown beer (4.6%) with a honey, orange and malt flavour. This cask brew is produced by the Hook Norton brewery in Oxfordshire.

Old Knucker
An additive-free rich, dark old ale (5.5%) from the Arundel brewery, Sussex.

Old Masters
A dry, tawny bitter (4.6%), brewed by Morland's of Abingdon.

Old Mill Mild
A dark-red, malty mild (3.5%) from the Old Mill brewery, Snaith, Yorkshire.

Old Nick
A devil of a bottled barley wine (6.9%) with a dark-reddish-brown hue and a pungent, but mellow, fruity flavour from Young's.

Old Original
A premium bitter (5.2%) with a strong, rich, malty character from Everard.

Old Peculier
Theakston's famous, rich, dark old ale (5.7%) with a roast-malt flavour, comes from Masham, North Yorkshire. The odd name refers to the Peculier of Masham, the town's ancient ecclesiastical court.

Old Smokey
A warming, malty dark ale (5%) with a slightly bitter, liquorice taste, brewed by Bunces brewery, Wiltshire.

Old Speckled Hen
A deep-gold, premium pale ale (5.2%) with a good malt, hop balance from Morland's of Abingdon, Oxfordshire. It is named not after a farmyard fowl, but an old MG car made in the town which was speckled black and gold.

Old Spot Prize Ale
A reddish, fruity cask ale (5%) from the Uley brewery in Gloucestershire. The spent grains from brewing go to a local pig herd, and the ales have retained the porky connection. Others include Hogshead, Pig's Ear and Severn Boar.

Old Stockport Bitter
A malty, fruity cask bitter (3.5%) from Robinson's brewery, Stockport.

Old Thumper
A pale-coloured, strong ale
(5.8%) with a rounded grain
and hops flavour, from
Ringwood, Hampshire.

Old Tom
Robinson's rich, fruity,
barley wine (8.5%) from
Stockport, Cheshire, was
originally named after the
brewery cat. It was first
brewed in 1899.

Olde Merryford Ale
A light-brown, full-bodied,
sweet bitter (4.8%), with a
good malt and hop balance,
from the Wickwar brewery in
Gloucestershire.

Olde Stoker
A dark-brown, smooth
winter bitter (5.4%) from the
Branscombe Vale brewery,
Devon.

Original Porter
A ruby-brown porter with a
roast-malt and liquorice
flavour from the liquorice
used in the recipe (5.2%).
Produced by the Shepherd
Neame brewery, Kent.

Owd Rodger
A rich, strong, creamy winter
ale (7.6%) from Marston's
brewery, Burton-on-Trent.

Oyster Stout
A creamy, bottle-conditioned
stout which, despite its name,
doesn't contain oysters, by
Marston's, Burton-on-Trent.

Pedigree
A classic, coppery-
coloured pale ale (4.5%)
with a dry hop and malt taste
and woody, spicy
overtones, from
Marston's of
Burton-on-Trent. It
is brewed using the
traditional Burton
Union system.

**Pendle Witches
Brew**
A tasty, full-bodied
ale (5.1%) which
comes from the
Moorhouse brewery
in Burnley, Lancashire.

Penn's Bitter
A reddish, sweet bitter
(4.6%) from the Hoskins
brewery in Leicester.

Peter's Porter
A seasonal porter (4.8%)
brewed in autumn and winter
by the Arkell's Kingsdown
brewery, Swindon.

Phoenix Best Bitter
A light-tawny, hoppy cask
bitter (3.9%) from the
Phoenix brewery, near
Manchester.

Prize Old Ale
This remarkable bottle-
conditioned ale (9%) from
Gales of Horndean,
Hampshire, is
intensely warming
with a hop and fruit-
cake flavour. It is
matured for six to
twelve months
before being put
into corked bottles,
where it
continues to
mature for
several years.

Progress
A malty ale
(4%) from the
Pilgrim
brewery,
Reigate, Surrey.

Rain Dance
A golden,
fruity wheat

beer (4.4%) from the
Brewery-on-Sea, Lancing,
Sussex.

Ram Rod
A full-bodied ale (5%) with
a bitter hops and malt
flavour, produced by Young's
brewery in Wandsworth,
London.

Ramsbottom Strong
A tawny-brown, rich and
complex bitter (4.5%),
brewed using local spring
water by the Dent brewery in
the Yorkshire Dales.

Rapier Pale Ale
An amber, malty, fruity cask
ale (4.2%) from the
Reepham brewery, near
Norwich.

Rebellion IPA
This refreshing, sweet, malty
pale ale (3.7%) comes from
the Rebellion brewery in
Marlow, Buckinghamshire.

Ridley Champion Mild
A dark cask mild (3.5%)
with a fruity, malt flavour
and a dry, hops finish,
brewed by Ridleys, near
Chelmsford, Essex.

Riggwelter
A complex, dark ale (5.9%)
with a roasted flavour. It is
fermented in traditional
Yorkshire stone squares by
the Black Sheep brewery,
North Yorkshire.

Roaring Meg
A malty, light-brown cask bitter (5.5%) from the Springhead brewery, Nottinghamshire.

Robinson's Best Bitter
A hoppy, amber, malty, fairly bitter beer (4.2%) from this Stockport brewery.

Rooster's Special
A challenging, amber-coloured, malty, hoppy ale (3.9%) from this Harrogate brewery, Yorkshire.

Royal Oak
A red-brown, fruity, sweet ale (5.0%) produced by Thomas Hardy of Dorset.

Ruddles Best Bitter
A characterful cask bitter (3.7%) from this famous Rutland brewery in Langham.

Ruddles County
A full-bodied, malty, strong cask bitter (4.9%) from Ruddles.

Rumpus
A ruby-coloured nutty ale (4.5%) with a fruit and malt flavour, from the Ridleys brewery, near Chelmsford.

Ryburn Best Bitter
A fine, hoppy cask bitter (3.8%) from the Ryburn brewery, Sowerby Bridge, West Yorkshire.

Rydale
A brown, malty cask bitter (4.2%) from the Ryburn brewery.

Salem Porter
A deep, dark porter with a nutty, dry taste (4.7%) from the Bateman family brewery in Wainfleet, Lincolnshire.

Salisbury Best
A sweetish bitter (3.8%) from the Gibbs Mews brewery in the cathedral town of Salisbury, Wiltshire.

Salopian Bitter
A fruity, hoppy cask bitter (3.5%) from the Salopian brewery, Shrewsbury.

Samuel Smith's Imperial Stout
A rich, heavy, bottled stout (7%) from this famous North Yorkshire brewery in Tadcaster, which is best served and enjoyed as a liqueur.

Samuel Smith's Oatmeal Stout
A distinctive stout (5%) with a thick, dark texture and chocolatey, fruity flavour.

SAS
Strong Anglian Special is a dry, well-balanced cask bitter (5%) produced by the Crouch Vale brewery, Essex.

SBA
A malty bitter from the Donnington brewery, Stow-on-the-Wold.

Shakemantle Ginger
A cloudy, ginger wheat beer (5%) produced by the Freeminer brewery, Gloucestershire.

Shefford Bitter
A good, well-balanced, real ale (3.8%) from B&T, Bedfordshire.

Shropshire Lad
A flavoursome bitter (4.5%) produced by the Wood Brewery, next to the Plough Inn, Wistanstow.

Shropshire Stout
A deep-red, rich, dry cask beer (4.4%) from the Hanby brewery, Shropshire.

Single Malt
A powerful, seasonal ale (7.2%), which uses whisky malt in the brewing process, from Mitchell's brewery in Lancaster.

Slaughter Porter
A dark, roasted, malty porter (5%) produced by the Freeminer brewery, Gloucestershire.

Smiles Best Bitter
A rich, brown-coloured, clean-tasting, sweetish bitter (4.1%) with a dry, bitter finish from this Bristol brewery.

Smuggler
A bitter-sweet, hoppy, fruity beer (4.1%) from the Rebellion brewery, Buckinghamshire.

Sneck Lifter
A rich, dark malty premium bitter (5.1%) from the Jennings brewery in the Lake District. Also available in a bottle.

SOS
Shefford Old Strong is a malty, fruity real ale (5%) from B&T, Bedfordshire.

Spinnaker Bitter
This smooth, hoppy ale (3.5%) is one of the Brewery-on-Sea's range of cask beers. Brewed at Lancing, Sussex.

Spitfire
An amber-coloured, mild, smoky malt ale (4.7%) from the Shepherd Neame brewery, Kent.

Stabber's
A brown, strong bitter (5.2%) with a rich, malty flavour from the Ryburn brewery, West Yorkshire.

Stag
A light-brown, malty, sweet bitter (5.2%) from the Exmoor brewery in Wiveliscombe, Somerset.

Steeplejack
A light-brown cask bitter
(4.5%) with a fresh, hoppy
taste, from the Lichfield
brewery in the Midlands.

Stig Swig
A golden, seasonal ale (5%)
brewed by Bunces brewery,
Wiltshire, using the herb
Sweet Gale (bog-myrtle), an
old Viking ingredient.

Stones Bitter
This famous straw-coloured
bitter (3.9%) with a sweet,
malt and hops flavour was
introduced by the Cannon
Sheffield brewery in the
1940s.

Strongarm
Camerons premium ruby
bitter (4%) with a smooth,
creamy head from Hartlepool
was originally brewed for the
steelworkers of Teesside.

Stronghart
A rich, dark, strong beer
(7%) produced by the
McMullen brewery in
Hertford.

Strong Suffolk
An intriguing, unique,
complex bottled ale (6%)
which comes from Greene
King of East Anglia. It is
produced by blending an old
ale that has been matured in
oak vats for at least two
years with a fresh brew of
dark beer.

Summer Lightning
A striking, strong pale bitter
(5%) which comes from the
Hop Back brewery, near
Salisbury, Wiltshire.

Summerskills Best Bitter
A good, brown-coloured,
malt and hops bitter (4.3%)
from this South Devon
brewery.

Sussex Bitter
A light-coloured, tasty bitter
(3.5%) from the King &
Barnes brewery in Horsham,
Sussex.

Sussex Mild
A dark-brown, malty mild
(3%) from Harveys brewery,
Lewes, Sussex.

Taddy Porter
A distinctive dark-brown,
rich, dry, bottled porter (5%)
from Samuel Smith's,
Yorkshire.

Tally Ho
A rich, warming barley wine
(7%) brewed by Adnams at
Christmas. Palmer's of
Dorset also brew a dark nutty
ale (4.7%) which is sold
under the same name.

Tanglefoot
A toe-tingling strong, sweet,
amber bitter (5.1%) brewed
at the Badger brewery,
Blandford St Mary, Dorset,
by Hall & Woodhouse.

Tetley Bitter
This pale-amber, hoppy,
fruity bitter (3.7%) is
traditionally served through a
tight tap to give a creamy
head. Brewed by Tetley in
Leeds, Yorkshire.

Tetley Mild
This amber, hoppy mild
(3.3%) with a malt finish, is
produced by Tetley, Leeds.

Theakston Best Bitter
A bright-gold, soft bitter
(3.8%) with a nutty flavour,
which originally came from
the North Yorkshire
Theakston brewery in
Masham. It is now also
brewed by Scottish Courage
in Newcastle.

Thomas Hardy's Ale
This bottle-conditioned ale
(12%) was introduced by
Eldridge Pope of Dorset in
1968 to celebrate that
summer's Thomas Hardy
festival in Dorchester,
marking the 40th anniversary
of the novelist's death. It was
brewed the previous autumn
"about as strong as it is

possible to brew" by head
brewer Denis Holliday to
match Hardy's description of
Dorchester strong ale in his
novel *The Trumpet Major*:
"It was of the most beautiful
colour that the eye of an
artist in beer could desire;
full in body yet brisk as a
volcano; piquant, yet without
a twang; luminous as an
autumn sunset; free from
streakiness of taste; but,
finally, rather heady." After
maturing in casks for six
months, the highly hopped
ale was filled into bottles,
corked, sealed with wax and
displayed with velvet
ribbons. The brewery said it
would continue to mature
for up to 25 years. It was
only expected to be a one-off
special brew, but such was
interest and demand that it
was repeated, and now
drinkers compare different
vintages. Each bottle is year-
dated and gradually changes
from a rich, fruity brew
when young to a deeper,
mellower flavour, like a
spicy Madeira wine.

Three Sieges
A winter ale (6%) flavoured with liquorice, from the Tomlinson brewery in the Yorkshire town of Pontefract.

Thwaites Best Mild
This smooth, dark mild (3.3%) is the best-known brew from Thwaites brewery in Blackburn, Lancashire, which still uses shire horses for local deliveries.

Tiger Best Bitter
A good malt-and-hops-flavoured bitter (4.2%) brewed by the Everard brewery in Narborough, near Leicester.

Tinners Ale
A good, light, hoppy cask ale (3.7%) from the St Austell brewery, Cornwall.

Toby
A light mild (3.2%) brewed by the giant Bass group.

Tolly's Strong Ale
This reddish-coloured, mild, creamy bottle-conditioned ale (4.6%) has a slightly sweet taste. Brewed by the Tolly Cobbold brewery, Suffolk.

Tom Hoskins Porter
A traditional porter (4.8%), brewed using honey and oats by the Hoskins and Oldfield Leicester brewery.

Top Dog Stout
A dark, strongly roasted winter brew (5%) from the Burton Bridge brewery, Burton-on-Trent.

Top Hat
A malty, nutty bitter (4.8%) brewed by Burtonwood near Warrington.

Topsy-Turvy
A dangerously drinkable strong ale (6%) from the small Berrow brewery at Burnham-on-Sea, Somerset.

T'owd Tup
A dark-coloured, strong old ale (6%) from the Dent brewery in the Yorkshire Dales.

Traditional Ale
This light-brown ale (3.4%) is one of a range of cask beers from the Larkins brewery in Kent.

Traditional Bitter
A smooth, hoppy, copper-coloured bitter (3.8%) with a strong malt character and a dry after-taste, produced by Clark brewery in Wakefield, West Yorkshire.

Traditional English Ale
A light-brown, malty, fruity ale (4.2%) from the Hogs Back brewery in Tongham, Surrey. It is commonly known as TEA.

Trelawny's Pride
A light, mild-flavoured cask bitter (4.4%) from the St Austell brewery, Cornwall.

Umbel Ale
A coriander-spiced brew (3.8%) from the Nethergate brewery in Clare, Suffolk. There is also a stronger version, Umbel Magna (5.5%).

Ushers Best Bitter
A golden-brown, hoppy bitter (3.8%) from this Wiltshire brewery.

Valiant
A golden, slightly fruity bitter (4.2%) with a bitter hops flavour, from the Bateman brewery in Lincolnshire.

Varsity
A cask beer with a good balance of sweet and bitter tastes, from the Morrells brewery, Oxford.

Vice Beer
A wheat beer (3.8%) brewed by Bunces brewery, Wiltshire.

Victory Ale
A full, fruity pale ale (6%) first brewed in 1987 to celebrate the Bateman brewery's narrow escape from closure after a family split.

Viking
A hoppy, malty, cask beer (3.8%) with a fruity finish, from the Rudgate brewery, near York.

Village Bitter
A light, hoppy bitter (3.5%) brewed by Archers of Swindon.

Waggle Dance
A golden honey beer (5%) brewed by Ward's of Sheffield for Vaux.

Wallop
A fresh, fruity, light bitter (3.5%) with a hoppy finish, from the Whitby brewery, North Yorkshire.

Ward's Mild
A malty cask ale (3.4%) brewed by Ward's, a traditional Sheffield brewery.

Wassail
A full-bodied draught and bottled beer (6%) from Ballard's, Sussex.

Wherry Best Bitter
The 1996 Champion Beer of Britain. This amber-coloured, hoppy cask bitter (3.8%) is produced by Woodforde's of Norfolk.

Whistle Belly Vengeance
A malty reddish ale (4.7%) from Summerskills of South Devon.

White Dolphin
A fruity wheat beer (4%) from the Hoskins & Oldfield brewery in Leicester.

Willie Warmer
A fruity cask beer (6.4%) produced by Crouch Vale brewery, Essex.

Wilmot's Premium
A strong ale (4.8%) brewed by the Butcombe brewery near Bristol.

Wiltshire Traditional Bitter
This dry, malty, hoppy bitter (3.6%) is produced by the Gibbs Mews brewery in Salisbury, Wiltshire.

Winter Royal
Wethered's famous rich, fruity brew (5%) now brewed by Whitbread at Castle Eden, County Durham.

Winter Warmer
A red-brown seasonal ale (5%) with a rich fruit and malt flavour and a sweetish aftertaste, produced by Young's in London.

Wobbly Bob
A robust cask beer (6%) from the Phoenix brewery, Heywood, near Manchester.

Worthington White Shield
This bottle-conditioned, pale ale (5.6%) has a delicate, yeasty, hoppy, malt flavour. It is now brewed at Mitchells and Butlers in Birmingham. For years White Shield was the only widely available bottled pale ale which retained a sediment of yeast. This meant it was a living beer – a brewery in a bottle. It developed a complex character and required careful handling. Bar staff had to pour the ale steadily into the glass without disturbing the sediment – but some drinkers preferred their glass cloudy and added the yeast anyway. It was not just a beer but a ritual.

Wye Valley Bitter
A bitter, hoppy cask bitter (3.5%) from the Wye Valley brewery in Hereford.

XL Old Ale
A bottled Christmas beer (6.9%) from Holden's brewery in Woodsetton, West Midlands.

XXX
A rare, dark, sweet, mild (3.6%) with a fruity finish, from the Donnington brewery near Stow-on-the-Wold, Gloucestershire.

XXXB Ale
A complex-tasting premium bitter (4.8%) from the Bateman brewery in Lincolnshire.

XXXX Mild
A dark, malty beer (3.6%) from the St Austell brewery, Cornwall.

THE BURTON UNION SYSTEM

In the Burton Union brewing system the beer is fermented in several linked oak casks – in union – with the fermenting beer rising through a swan-neck pipe connecting each cask to a top trough which runs the length of the whole system.

From the trough, the beer then runs back down into the casks, leaving any excess yeast behind in the trough. This constant circulation while the beer is fermenting ensures a vigorous fermentation and fully aerates the beer, giving the yeast enough oxygen to work properly.

The Burton-on-Trent giants Bass dropped the Burton Union system in 1982, claiming that it had become too expensive to maintain. In contrast, however, the traditional Marston's brewery has heavily invested in new unions and still uses the Burton Union system to brew its Owd Rodger and some of its Pedigree. The system is also used to provide the yeast for some of Marston's more conventionally fermented beers.

Yates Bitter
A fruity, straw-coloured bitter (3.7%) from this Cumbrian brewery.

Young's Ordinary
A classic bitter (3.7%) from this traditional London brewery.

2XS
An aptly named strong real ale (6%) from B&T, Bedfordshire.

3B
A draught beer (4%) from Arkell's Kingsdown brewery, Swindon.

4X
A winter warmer (6.8%) from Hydes in Manchester.

6X
Wadworth's premium fruity bitter (4.3%) from Devizes in Wiltshire, which has become well known way beyond the south-west of England. It is also sold in bottles in a stronger export version which clocks in at (5%).

1066
A strong pale ale (6%) which is available in bottle from the Hampshire brewery in Andover, Hampshire.

THE BREWERS

Adnams

This seaside family firm from Southwold, dating from 1872, sprang to fame outside Suffolk in the real ale revival of the 1970s. Adnams is now one of the top quality brewers of Britain. Most production is devoted to its traditional draught beers.

Ansells

This Birmingham brewery, known for its Aston ales, closed in 1981. However its liquorice-tasting dark mild lives on, brewed by Carlsberg-Tetley at Burton-on-Trent.

Archers

Enterprising brewery set up in the old Great Western Railway workshops in Swindon, Wiltshire, in 1979.

Arkell

In 1843 after John Arkell returned from Canada, where his family had founded the village of Arkell near Toronto, he established the Arkell company. Its Kingsdown brewery in Stratton St Margaret, Swindon, is a classic Victorian brewhouse still with its steam engine.

Badger

Hall & Woodhouse's historic Dorset brewery in Blandford Forum, established in 1777, now goes by the popular name of "Badger", after its traditional "Badger" beers.

Ballards

This Sussex country brewery, founded in 1980, is famous for producing an annual bottled beer with a staggering strength to match the date. In 1997 the brewery at Nyewood

produced Old Pecker (9.7%). Each new year's beer, with its cartoon label, is launched at a charity walk on the first Sunday of December.

Bass

England's best-known brewery was founded by William Bass in 1777 in Burton-on-Trent. The firm's flagship ale in England, Draught Bass, lost a little of its reputation when the Burton Union system of brewing was abandoned in 1982. Bass's Burton home also houses England's leading brewing museum, which includes a pilot brewing plant used to produce special ales.

Bass is Britain's largest brewing group and if the proposed merger with Carlsberg-Tetley in 1997 is allowed by the Office of Fair Trading, Bass would control 40% of Britain's beer business. Besides Burton, it also owns notable breweries in Birmingham (Mitchells & Butlers), and Sheffield (Stones). Outside England it controls Tennents in Scotland, Hancock's in Wales and the Ulster Brewery in Ireland. In addition to exporting to 70 countries, in the 1990s Bass took over brewing groups in the Czech Republic, notably Staropramen in Prague and launched a joint venture with Ginsberg Brewery in China.

Bateman

This Lincolnshire brewery was founded in Wainfleet in 1874 and narrowly survived a family split in the mid-1980s thanks to the determination of Chairman George Bateman to keep brewing his "Good Honest Ales".

Batham

A traditional Black Country family brewery which was founded at Brierley Hill, near Dudley, in 1877.

Black Sheep

When Paul Theakston of North Yorkshire's famous brewing family lost control of Theakston's Masham brewery, he was determined to start brewing again. The Black Sheep brewery, founded in an old maltings at Wellgarth, Masham, in 1992, is the result. Built on a much larger scale than most new breweries, it installed equipment taken from the former Hartley's brewery in Cumbria. Black Sheep brewery ferments its beer in traditional Yorkshire stone squares and boasts its own visitor centre, making Masham a place of pilgrimage for serious beer drinkers.

Boddingtons

This Manchester brewery, founded in 1778, was once worshipped for the parch-dry bitterness of its straw-coloured bitter. It was taken over by Whitbread in 1989.

Brakspear

A traditional brewery dating back to the 17th century in Henley-on-Thames, Oxfordshire. Its pubs pack the streets of the small town that is famous for its rowing regatta. It is one of the least spoilt breweries in Britain.

Burtonwood

A north-west regional brewery dating from 1867. It built a new brewhouse in Burtonwood, near Warrington, in 1990.

Butcombe

One of the most successful new breweries, set up in the Mendips near Bristol in 1978.

Above: A beautifully decorated English pub with the handpumps for serving traditional draught beer visible on the curving bar.

Cains

This Liverpool brewery has enjoyed a history as elaborate as its towering Victorian brewhouse. After many years as Merseyside's most popular brewery, Higson's, the site is now owned by a Danish brewing group, who restored it to its original title of Robert Cain.

Camerons

The north-east's major brewer of real ales was bought by the Wolverhampton & Dudley Breweries in 1992 as part of their expansion programme. The Hartlepool brewery is best known for its ruby-red ale Strongarm, which once sustained the many steelworkers in the area.

Below: Draught Strongarm from Camerons brewery.

Castle Eden

Whitbread's specialist ale brewery in County Durham produces a wide range of limited-edition brews, often using imaginative flavourings and spices. Formerly Nimmo's Brewery, this County Durham plant also brews beers from breweries closed by Whitbread like Wethered's, Fremlin's and Higson's.

Courage

Originally Courage was a London brewer, founded in 1787. It developed into a national combine before being taken over by a series of multinational companies starting with Imperial Tobacco in 1972 and ending up with the Australian brewers, Foster's. Control of Courage was brought back to Britain in 1995 when Scottish and Newcastle Breweries bought the company from Foster's to form Britain's second largest brewing group, which is now known as Scottish Courage. Courage's traditional cask bitters are today brewed in Bristol.

Donnington

Described as the most picturesque brewery in Britain, time seems to have stood still since the Cotswold stone buildings were first built as a medieval cloth mill near Stow-on-the-Wold, Gloucestershire. Trout rise in the mill pond and ducks nest in the reeds. The brewery was added in 1865 by Richard Arkell. The plant is powered by a waterwheel.

Elgood

This classic Georgian riverside brewery in the Fens at Wisbech has been run by the Elgood family since 1878. It uses open trays for cooling the beers, and also has its own small pilot plant for brewing special beers.

Everard

A family brewery established in 1849 which originally brewed in both Leicester and Burton-on-Trent. Everard opened a new plant in Narborough in 1991 and since then has concentrated its brewing there.

Exmoor

A venture set up in the old Hancock's brewery in Wiveliscombe, Somerset, in 1980, which won the best bitter award at the Great British Beer Festival in its first year.

Federation

The only surviving clubs brewery in England was set up in 1919 in Newcastle by working men's clubs because of a postwar beer shortage. The co-operative opened a brewery at Dunston on the south side of the Tyne in 1980. It brews mainly bright, filtered beers for the clubs.

Flowers

The former Stratford-upon-Avon brewer was taken over and closed by Whitbread. The name is now used for the group's Cheltenham brewery.

Fuller's

This famous family brewer has been in Chiswick, London, since 1845. Fuller's had to boost its brewing capacity in the 1990s to keep up with demand for its traditional ales. The three main brews – Chiswick Bitter, London Pride and ESB – have won more awards at the Great British Beer Festival than the beers of any other brewer.

Gales

Hampshire family brewery at Horndean with an impressive tower brewery built in 1869.

Greene King

The East Anglian regional giant based at Bury St Edmunds, Suffolk, was founded in 1799. In 1995 it added a range of seasonal cask ales to its well-known IPA and Abbot Ale.

Hardys & Hansons

Two Nottinghamshire breweries started in the 19th century in Kimberley, that merged in 1930. The firm is still family controlled.

Harveys

Founded in 1790, this quality family brewer still brews at its attractive riverside site in Lewes, Sussex, despite a damaging fire in 1996.

Highgate

A West Midlands Victorian tower brewery in Walsall, famous for its Dark Mild. Since being bought out by the management from Bass in 1995, Highgate has added a Saddlers Best Bitter to its range of beers.

Holden

Black Country family brewery in Woodsetton in the West Midlands which goes back four generations.

Holt

This Manchester family brewery since 1849 is famous for the uncompromisingly dry bitterness of its bitter. Holt is also known for its low prices. One of the few breweries to still use hogsheads (huge 54-gallon casks) in its pubs.

Hook Norton

This dramatic Victorian tower brewery in a small Oxfordshire village near Banbury still retains much of its original equipment.

Hydes

A traditional family brewer in Manchester since 1863, turning out ales under the Anvil trademark. Unusually, Hydes still brews two milds, light and dark.

Ind Coope

This historic brewing group was originally based in Romford, Essex. It became part of Allied Breweries in 1961, and merged with Carlsberg in 1993 becoming

Above: A 1952 advertisement for Ind Coope's Arctic Ale, a famous rich, strong ale which is no longer brewed.

Carlsberg-Tetley. The proposed merger with near-neighbours Bass is currently awaiting approval from the Office of Fair Trading. It brews a range of specialist beers under the Allsopp name.

Jennings

The only surviving long-standing brewer in Cumbria, dating back to 1828.

J.W. Lees

A well-established north Manchester family brewery since 1828, still committed to delivering its beers in oak casks.

King & Barnes

A Sussex family firm in Horsham, dating back to 1800, which has extensively modernized its brewery.

McMullen

A Hertford family brewer since 1827, located in a fine Victorian brewhouse.

Mann's

This famous east London brewer's Albion brewery was taken over by Watneys in 1958 and closed in 1979. But the name lives on in England's best-known bottled, sweet brown ale, Mann's Original, which is now brewed by Usher's in Wiltshire.

Mansfield

A regional brewery in Nottinghamshire, founded in 1855, which has expanded considerably since opening its new brewhouse in 1984. It still uses traditional Yorkshire squares to ferment its ales.

Marston Thompson & Evershed

This is the last brewery in Britain that still uses the Burton Union system and the last major independent company brewing in Burton-on-Trent. Besides its famous Pedigree, it now brews a range of special cask beers under the Head Brewer's Choice label.

Mauldon

This Suffolk brewing family from Sudbury started brewing in 1795. The brewery closed in 1960 but restarted brewing in 1982.

Melbourn

This brewery in Stamford, Lincolnshire closed in 1974 and became a museum under Samuel Smith. Since 1993 Melbourn have brewed fruit ales in the old brewery, using wild yeasts from Belgium.

Mitchell's

Traditional family brewer in Lancaster since 1880.

Mitchells & Butlers

Often just known as M&B, Mitchells and Butlers are the dominant Birmingham brewers and merged with Bass in 1961. Their Cape Hill brewery in Smethwick, near Birmingham has been heavily modernized.

Morland

The second-oldest English brewery founded in 1711. The Abingdon firm sprang to fame outside Oxfordshire in the 1990s with the success of its strong pale ale, Old Speckled Hen.

Morrells

The only brewery left in the university town of Oxford which has been run by the Morrell family since 1782.

Oakhill

A historic stout brewery founded in 1767 at Oakhill, near Bath, which was badly damaged by fire in 1924, and then closed. In 1984 the brewery was restarted and moved to the Old Maltings, a larger site in 1993.

Palmer

England's only thatched brewery which was founded at Bridport, Dorset in 1794.

Ridleys

This family brewery was established in 1842 by Thomas Ridley at Hartford End, near Chelmsford, Essex.

Ringwood

Set up by Peter Austin in 1978 in the Hampshire town. In 1995 Ringwood moved beyond the micro-brewery stage with the opening of a 125-barrel modern brewhouse.

Robinson's

A major regional family firm from Stockport, near Manchester, founded in 1838.

Ruddles

One of the most famous names in English brewing, Ruddles lost its independence in 1986 when Watneys bought up the Rutland brewery in Langham. Since 1992, it has been owned by the Dutch brewers, Grolsch.

St Austell

Cornwall's only remaining long-established independent family brewery, founded in 1851. The solid Victorian brewery dominates the town.

Shepherd Neame

England's oldest brewery dates back to 1698. It is fittingly to be found in the

Above: A game of cards is a traditional accompaniment to a pint.

hop garden of Kent, at Faversham. Shepherd Neame still uses steam engines and two teak mash tuns from 1910. It produces a range of cask and bottled beers.

Smith, John

A magnificent Victorian building in Tadcaster, North Yorkshire, built in 1884, houses the John Smith's brewery. The company is now owned by Scottish Courage. Today the towering stone buildings house a modern brewhouse.

Smith, Samuel

Samuel Smith was the first of the two Smith brewers of Tadcaster and the firm is still brewing in the Old Brewery which dates back to 1758. The family firm has remained fiercely independent. The beer is still fermented in Yorkshire stone squares and racked into wooden casks.

Stones

The Stones brewery has quenched the fire of the steel city of Sheffield in Yorkshire since 1865. It was taken over by Bass in 1968.

Taylor

One of the top quality brewers of England. Timothy Taylor began brewing in Brontë country at Keighley, Yorkshire, in 1858.

Tetley

England's leading brewer of bitter was founded in Leeds, Yorkshire, in 1822. A modern brewhouse was built in the 1980s and more Yorkshire squares for fermenting the beer were added in 1996. It became known as Carlsberg-Tetley in 1993 following the merger with Carlsberg.

Theakston

This North Yorkshire brewer has been at Masham since 1827. Theakston is famous for rich, dark Old Peculier. The family lost control in the late 1970s, and after a succession of takeovers the country brewery is now owned by Scottish Courage. Most Theakston beers are brewed at its Tyne brewery in Newcastle, as well as at the original Masham brewery.

Thomas Hardy

Formerly Eldridge Pope of Dorchester, this grand brewery, founded in 1837, was renamed after their most famous customer, the novelist Thomas Hardy.

Thwaites

A major Lancashire regional brewer founded in Blackburn in 1807 that still uses shire horses for local deliveries.

Tolly Cobbold

A Suffolk brewer since 1746 in a fine Victorian brewhouse in Ipswich which was closed in 1989 – but was then saved by a management buyout. The popular name comes from the merging of Cobbold with another well-known Ipswich brewery, Tollemache, in 1957. The grand Cobbold brewery in Ipswich was built on Cliff Quay on the banks of the River Orwell in 1894–6. It is a classic example of a tower brewery, and still retains many fine old brewing vessels. Following the management buyout in 1990, the brewery has become one of the main tourist attractions in the town, with guided tours. The offices alongside have been turned into the Brewery Tap pub.

Ushers

This Wiltshire brewery was founded in Trowbridge in 1824. After being taken over by Watneys of London in 1960 it lost its local identity. A management buyout in 1991 restored its independence.

Vaux

The giant northern brewery which is based in the town of Sunderland on the River Wear. Vaux also owns Ward's of Sheffield.

Wadworth

A traditional family brewery whose towering brewhouse has dominated the Wiltshire market town of Devizes since 1885. The brewery includes a rare open copper.

Ward's

A traditional Sheffield brewery which was founded in 1840, 15 years before the better-known Stones brewery in the steel city.

Watneys

This once-famous London brewery ruined its reputation by leading the movement to processed keg beers. It is now part of Scottish Courage. Its Mortlake brewery is used by Anheuser-Busch to brew Budweiser. Most remaining Watneys beers are brewed abroad for foreign markets.

Wells

Enterprising Bedford family brewers since 1876 who rebuilt their brewery in 1976. Wells brews various foreign lagers under licence, including Kirin from Japan and Red Stripe from Jamaica.

Whitbread

This famous London brewer since 1742 closed his brewery in the capital city in 1976. Originally Whitbread was known for its porter. It is England's third largest brewing group, brewing foreign lagers under licence, notably a weak version of Heineken and Stella Artois. It also produces a wide range of cask beers under local names such as Wethered, Fremlins and Higsons, now produced at Flowers brewery in Cheltenham, Gloucestershire, and at Castle Eden, County Durham. Whitbread also owns Boddingtons in Manchester.

Wolverhampton & Dudley

Wolverhampton is the home of this brewery, famed for its reddish-amber Banks's mild, a favourite in the industrial West Midlands. It trades as Banks's and Hanson's in the Black Country. It is the largest regional brewing group in Britain, with around 1,100 pubs and in 1992 bought Camerons brewery in the north-east.

Wood

A small brewery behind the Plough Inn in Wistanstow, Shropshire.

Woodforde's

Quality Norfolk brewery since 1980 which has the rare distinction of having twice won the Champion Beer of Britain title.

Worthington

This famous Burton brewing name merged with Bass in 1927. The brewery has since been demolished, but the name lives on in a national bitter brand and more notably in the bottle-conditioned pale ale Worthington White Shield, now brewed at Mitchells & Butlers brewery in Birmingham.

Young's

A firmly traditional London family brewery situated at the Ram brewery in Wandsworth since 1831. Young's is noted for cask beers. Deliveries are still made by horse-drawn drays, a wonderful sight in south London, although these are now under threat from the increased traffic in the area. The Victorian brewery also houses geese, peacocks and a ram (the company mascot). In recent years Young's has added seasonal ales including a summer wheat beer. Its bottled ales are also sold abroad.

Below: Cheers!

SCOTLAND

Once Scotland was famous for its beer, and during the 19th century the capital Edinburgh ranked alongside Burton-on-Trent in England, Munich in Germany and Plzen in the Czech Republic as a notable brewing centre.

AT THE START OF THE 20TH CENTURY Edinburgh boasted 28 breweries, most packed into an area with an excellent water supply known as the "Charmed Circle". Alloa, just across the River Forth, was also a famous beer town.

In 1960, Edinburgh still had 18 breweries and Scottish brewers were vigorous exporters, but as the overseas trade dried up many companies fell into financial difficulties and were taken over and closed down like Robert Younger. Two giants – Scottish & Newcastle and Tennent's – came to dominate the market. This hastened the disappearance of traditional cask beer. Eventually only two breweries were left in Edinburgh. Overall, just three independent breweries survived in the whole of Scotland. A once-thriving industry had almost vanished. Since 1980 there has been a small revival, with the appearance of a number of new breweries bringing back welcome variety to the bar. Scottish beers are darker, more full-bodied, and sweeter than English ales. Perhaps because hops are not grown in the country, there is less emphasis on bitterness. Perhaps the malty warmth helps to keep out the northern cold. Local specialities include strong barley wines known as "wee heavys", as well as "oatmeal stout", made using a local cereal. The English terms of mild and bitter are not generally used north of the border. Instead, beers are traditionally rated in strength according to the invoice price charged per barrel in the 19th century. Under the "shilling system" the weakest beer is 60/-, an average-strength beer 70/-, and a premium brew 80/-. Strong ales are 90/-. These designations usually refer to cask beers. Keg beers are more popularly known as light (this refers to the light alcoholic content, not the colour, which may well be dark); special or heavy indicate mid-strength brews; and export is the name given to premium ales. Scotland also has its own individual dispensing system, which uses tall air-pressure fonts, rather than handpumps, to serve traditional ales.

Above: Traditional ales are still brewed in Scotland, despite its radically reduced brewing industry and the increasing popularity of lager.

THE BEERS

Ale of Atholl

A rich, malty beer (4.5%) from the Moulin brewery, near Pitlochry.

Arrol's 80/-

A fruity, cask-conditioned Scottish heavy (4.4%) with a hoppy aftertaste, brewed by the Alloa brewery.

Auld Alliance

Tart, hoppy refreshing bitter (4%) from the Fife brewery, Kirkaldy.

Bear Ale

This cask ale (5%) is fermented in oak vessels at the historic Traquair House manor brewery.

Black Douglas

This distinctive, dark, winter ale (5.2%) comes from the Broughton brewery.

Borve Extra Strong

A powerful, extra-strong ale (10%), which is matured in oak whisky casks at the Borve home-brew pub.

Broadsword

This golden cask ale (3.8%) with a fruity, malty flavour and bitter finish is brewed at Alloa by Maclay.

Buchan Bronco

This cask beer (4.6%) is produced by the Aberdeenshire brewery in Keith, fermented using Yorkshire squares. The brewery also produces the lighter Buchan Gold (4%).

Calder's

This is the brand name for keg beers made by the Alloa brewery, including Cream Ale (4.5%) and 80/-.

Caledonian

A range of beers from the Caledonian brewery. The weakest is a flavoursome, dark, malty 60/- beer (3.2%) with a refreshing hint of roast barley. Caledonian 70/- (3.5%) is a more tawny coloured, creamy brew and Caledonian 80/- (4.1%) has a complex malt and hops flavour.

Cuillin

Red Cuillin (4.2%) and Black Cuillin (4.5%) are two cask beers produced by the Isle of Skye brewery at Uig on Skye.

Dark Island

A rich, wine-coloured, refreshing beer (4.6%) with a fruity aroma, from the Orkney brewery.

Deuchars IPA

This very pale "pale ale" (4.4%) is late-hopped to produce a refreshing brew. Brewed by Caledonian.

Douglas

See Gordon's.

Dragonhead Stout

This smooth, classic stout (4%) is produced by the Orkney brewery.

Edinburgh Strong Ale

A strong, premium ale (6.4%) with a complexity of malt and hop flavours, but without the usual sweetness of strong beers. It is brewed by Caledonian.

Fraoch

Bruce Williams has been brewing Fraoch (the Gaelic word for heather) at Maclay's Alloa brewery every flowering season since 1993. Instead of adding hops – which are not grown in Scotland – to the boiling wort, he follows the example of the ancient Picts and uses native heather tips and myrtle leaves. The hot liquid is also infused in a vat of fresh heather flowers before fermentation. The spicy, floral brew that results comes in two strengths – Heather Ale (4.1%) and Pictish Ale (5.4%).

Gillespie's

First introduced in 1993, Gillespie's keg and canned creamy, sweet-malt stout (4%) is named after a closed Dumbarton brewery. It is produced by Scottish Courage in Edinburgh.

Golden Pale

A pale-amber-coloured, aromatically hoppy, organic beer (4%), from the Caledonian brewery.

Golden Promise

The first organic beer from Caledonian, Golden Promise is slightly stronger (5%) than Golden Pale. A quality brew, it is named after Scotland's traditional variety of barley.

Gordon's

This warming range of bottled, strong ales is brewed in Edinburgh by Scottish Courage, mainly for the Belgian market. It includes Gordon's Scotch Ale (8.6%), Christmas Ale (8.8%) and Gold Blond (10%). It is sold in France under the Douglas name.

Greenmantle

This distinctive, smoky, fruity ale (3.9%) is available in bottles and cask. It is produced by the Broughton brewery.

Grozet

First produced in 1996 by Bruce Williams at the Maclay brewery in Alloa, this hazy beer (5%) is a wheat ale to which whole gooseberries are added after fermentation.

Highland Hammer

This powerful, full-flavoured strong ale (7.3%) is a seasonal speciality of the Tomintoul brewery.

Jacobite Ale

This strong brew (8%) is fermented in oak and flavoured with coriander. It comes from the Traquair House brewery.

Kane's Amber Ale

This amber cask beer (4%) with a good malt and fruit flavour is produced in the brewing town of Alloa by the Maclay brewery.

Laird's Ale

The weakest cask ale (3.8%) from Tomintoul is a traditional, dark-mahogany 70/- ale, with a malty flavour and fine hop balance.

McEwan's Export

A sweet and malty Scottish ale (4.5%) produced by McEwan's in Edinburgh.

MacAndrew's

A strong, amber-coloured ale (6.5%) brewed for sale in the US by Caledonian.

Maclay

Maclay brewery's cask beers include a full-flavoured, malty, fruity 70/- ale (3.6%) with a sweet, fresh flavour. The flagship 80/- Export (4%) is a creamy, malty beer with a dry finish. There is also an oat malt stout (4.5%).

Malcolm's

A range of beers, named after King Malcolm III who slew Macbeth, including Malcolm's Ceilidh (3.7%), Folly (4%), and Premier (4.3%), from the Backdykes farm brewery in Fife.

Merlin's

This distinctive, hoppy, golden ale (4.2%) is one of a range of beers produced at the Broughton brewery.

Merman

A mellow, reddish-bronze, malty, fruity, bottled pale ale (4.8%) from Caledonian, based on an 1890 recipe.

Montrose

A tasty, tawny cask beer (4.2%) from the Harviestoun brewery.

Murray's Heavy

An amber-coloured, traditional Scottish heavy beer (4.3%), produced by Caledonian.

Old Jock

A distinctive dark-ruby, sweetish, fruity, bottled strong ale (6.7%). It is produced by the Broughton brewery in the borders.

Old Manor

This old ale (8%) is brewed each winter by the Harviestoun brewery. Molasses gives the beer a good ruby colour and a rich fruitiness. This is one of a range of seasonal brews.

Ptarmigan

An outstanding pale-golden, fruity, premium beer (4.5%) from the Harviestoun brewery. It has a light, refreshing flavour and is brewed using Saaz hops.

Raven Ale

An amber-red, nutty, dry ale (3.8%) from the Orkney brewery.

Red MacGregor

A full-bodied, smooth, red-brown beer(4.1%)from the Orkney brewery,

St Andrew's

A rich, brown, malty cask beer (4.9%) with a fruity butterscotch flavour, brewed by Belhaven.

Sandy Hunter's

A bitter-sweet, roasted-malt, hoppy cask beer (3.6%) from the Belhaven brewery. It was named after a former head brewer.

Schiehallion Lager

A cask-conditioned, Bohemian-style lager (4.8%), brewed using German Hersbrucker hops, from the Harviestoun brewery. It won a Gold Medal at the Great British Beer Festival in 1996. Schiehallion, a local mountain, was once climbed as part of an experiment by Astronomer Royal Neville Maskelyn.

THE OUTWARD-LOOKING SCOTS

Scottish brewers have always been enthusiastic exporters of their wares, partly because of the relatively small size of the home market. The strong, rich, dark brews have been widely drunk throughout Britain for centuries, and in the heyday of the British Empire they also reached the former colonies scattered across the world, from the US to Australia and India. The ales were dispatched overseas in great quantities to quench the thirsts of Scots who had emigrated. The "export" brews became well known and well regarded. They were so popular in parts of Europe that Belgian brewers began to produce their own "Scotch" ales – a style that persists today.

Left: At the beginning of the 20th century, many brewers produced beers for the export market but declining sales spelled the end for most of them.

Skull Splitter
An powerful, strong, dark-amber barley wine (8.5%), from the Orkney brewery.

Stag
A dark, malty ale (4.1%) from the Tomintoul brewery in the Highlands which is sold in cask and bottle.

Stillman's 80/-
This mid-gold, mild beer (4.2%) with a complex flavour is produced by the Tomintoul brewery. Its name reflects the local whisky distilling industry in the Spey valley.

Sweetheart Stout
This very weak (2%), sweet and fruity brew is produced by Tennent's, but bears little resemblance to a real stout.

Tennent's Lager
This fizzy, golden keg lager (4%) is the mainstay of the Tennent's brewery's lager range, which includes a grainy, pale-gold Pilsner (3.4%), a stronger Extra (4.8%), Gold (5%) and a weighty, amber-coloured, sweetish, strong Super (9%). Tennent's are Scotland's dominant lager brewers.

The Ghillie
This distinctive bottled ale (4.5%) is produced by the Broughton brewery.

Traquair House Ale
A dark, strong classic oak-fermented ale (7.2%) from the Traquair House brewery. It has a fruity, malt flavour and a slight dryness. This distinctive ale is exported to the US.

Triple Diamond
This is the special, extra-strong, export ale brand (8.5%) produced by the Alloa brewery.

Wallace IPA
A hoppy, fruity pale ale (4.5%) with a bitter finish, produced by Maclay.

Waverley 70/-
A chestnut-coloured, hoppy, cask beer (3.7%), from the Harviestoun brewery.

Wild Cat
A deep-amber ale (5.1%) with a complex flavour from the Tomintoul brewery.

Young Pretender
A golden, dry ale (4%) from the Isle of Skye brewery named after Bonnie Prince Charlie. It was first produced in 1995 to mark the 250th anniversary of the Jacobite rebellion.

Younger's Tartan
A dark-amber Scottish keg ale (3.7%) with a sweet and fruity flavour from William Younger of Edinburgh.

THE BREWERS

Alloa

Founded in 1810, the Alloa brewery became known in the 1930s for its lager, Graham's, then Skol (3.6%) after becoming part of Allied Breweries. It also produces keg ales under the Calder's name and special export brands such as Triple Diamond. Since 1982 it has brewed cask beer, notably Arrols 80/-.

Belhaven

Scotland's oldest brewery, Belhaven dates back to at least 1719. Built on former monastery land on the coast at Dunbar, its ales were sold way beyond Scotland and found their way to the Imperial Court of Austria, where the Emperor declared them "The Burgundy of Scotland". This claim is still carried by its robust 80/- ale (4.2%). Other malty cask beers include 60/- (2.9%), 70/- (3.5%), St Andrew's and Sandy Hunter's besides a rich, warming 90/- (8%).

Above: The Caledonian brewery in Edinburgh was restored after a fire in 1994. It produces a wide range of cask and bottled beers. Caledonian 80/- was the Champion Beer of Scotland in 1996.

Borve

Originally set up on the Isle of Lewis in 1983, this home-brew pub is now on the mainland at Ruthven.

Broughton

David Younger, a descendant of the George Younger brewing family of Alloa, set up the brewery in 1980 in the Borders region at Broughton.

ALLOA

The town of Alloa at the head of the Firth of Forth has long been a brewing centre, using water from the Ochil hills, local barley and coal from nearby mines. Early in the 20th century it boasted nine breweries, the most famous being George Younger's which closed in 1963. By 1996 only two were left, Alloa (now part of Bass) and the independent Maclays.

In 1995 it relaunched its distinctive cask and bottled ales as "Beers with Character".

Caledonian

Caledonian is the sole survivor from an era when Edinburgh boasted 30 independent breweries. The Victorian brewhouse still uses direct-fired open coppers, one dating back to 1869 when the firm was founded as Lorimer and Clark. Its wide range of quality cask and bottled beers includes 60/- (3.2%), 70/- (3.5%), 80/- (4.1%), Deuchars IPA, Murray's Heavy, Double

Amber, Merman, Edinburgh Strong Ale (6.4%) and two organic beers. The Caledonian 80/- was the first champion Beer of Scotland in 1996.

Harviestoun

A village brewery in an old stone dairy at Dollar, near Stirling, since 1985, Harviestoun produces a prize-winning range of cask beers including Waverley 70/-, Original 80/- (4.1%), Montrose, Ptarmigan and Old Manor.

McEwan's

A famous firm since 1856 which merged with Younger's in 1931 and is now part of Scottish Courage. McEwan's still brews at its Fountain brewery in Edinburgh which has recently been completely rebuilt. Though McEwan's is best known for its keg and canned beers (McEwan's Export is the best-selling canned beer in Britain), it also produces some cask-conditioned beers in the old classic Scottish shilling ratings – 70/- and 80/-.

Scotland boasts a handful of home-brew houses, most established in the mid-1990s:
- Aldchlappie Hotel, Kirkmichael, Perthshire.
- Harbour Bar, Kirkcaldy, Fife.
- Lugton Inn, Lugton, Ayrshire.
- Mansfield Arms, Sauchie, Alloa.
- Moulin Hotel, Moulin, Pitlochry.
- Rose Street, Edinburgh.

Above: Stirring the brew in modern shiny coppers.

Maclay's

The last independent family-owned brewery left in Alloa was founded in 1830. The traditional tower brewhouse was built in 1869. Maclay's still uses bore-hole water drawn from 300ft (100m) below ground for its brewing. Cask beers include 70/- (3.6%), the flagship 80/- Export (4%), Maclay's Oat Malt Stout (4.5%), Wallace IPA and also a strong, golden Scotch Ale (5%).

Orkney

Britain's most northerly brewery is located on the Orkney's main island off the north coast of Scotland. It was set up at Quoyloo in 1988 by Roger White. Its cask and bottled beers are Raven Ale, Dragonhead Stout, Red MacGregor, Dark Island and the powerful Skull Splitter.

Scottish Courage

This is Britain's second-largest brewing group. It is based in Edinburgh and was formed in 1995 when Scottish & Newcastle Breweries bought the Courage brewing group of England. It has only one brewery in Scotland, located in Edinburgh. Its beers are still marketed under the McEwan's and William Younger names.

Tennent's

Founded in Glasgow around 1776, the Wellpark Brewery became famous as Scotland's first lager brewers in 1885. Today, the brewery produces a range of lagers for the British and overseas markets. It also brews keg ales and bottled stout.

Tomintoul

This brewery in the heart of the Highlands malt whisky country, just a couple of miles from the Glenlivet distillery, claims to be the highest brewery in Britain. It was set up in 1993 in an old watermill by Andrew Neame, a member of the brewing family in Kent, England. Its cask beers include Laird's Ale (3.8%), Stag (4.1%), Stillman's 80/- (4.2%), Wild Cat (5.1%) and Highland Hammer (7.3%).

Traquair House

A rare survivor from an age when all great manor houses had their own breweries. Traquair House at Innerleithen, near Peebles, dates from the 12th century and is said to be the oldest

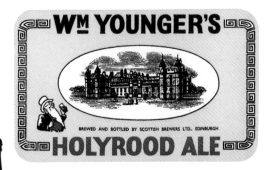

inhabited building in Scotland. Its beer was first recorded in an account of a visit to the house by Mary Queen of Scots in 1566. The present brewery, dating back to the 1730s, was revived in 1965 by the Laird, Peter Maxwell Stuart. A second brewhouse has since been added to keep up with demand. All the beer is fermented in oak vessels.

Younger's

William Younger founded his brewery in 1749. It is now part of Scottish Courage. The Holyrood brewery closed in 1986, and production moved to McEwan's Fountain brewery. Younger's is best known for its Tartan ale. Its cask ales, Younger's Scotch and Younger's IPA, are the same as McEwan's. Younger's No. 3 is McEwan's 80/- with added caramel.

DENMARK

Perhaps because it is further south and much more firmly attached to mainland Europe than its northern neighbours in Scandinavia, Denmark has always enjoyed a relatively relaxed attitude to beer and to its brewing industry.

WHEN DRINKERS THINK of Denmark, one name stands a thick foaming head above all others – the famous Carlsberg. Besides having a worldwide reputation, the Carlsberg group controls the domestic market. It absorbed its main rival Tuborg in 1970, and it also holds stakes in the other leading brewing groups. This domination by one brewery has restricted choice. Drinkers in Copenhagen have to look hard in their bars to find anything apart from Carlsberg and Tuborg. The variety of beer styles is also on a tight rein with Pilsners reigning supreme.

Denmark has played a major role in spreading the popularity of bottom-fermenting lagers and a malty, mild style of Pilsner is by far the most widely available beer today. Before this most brewers once produced top-fermenting wheat beers. Carlsberg, more than any other brewery, has popularized the golden lager style, devised in central Europe, around the world. In 1993 its worldwide sales were more than five times larger than its home sales. So profound has this company's contribution been to the development of lager, that the classic bottom-fermenting yeast used by brewers, *Saccharomyces Carlsbergensis*, has been named after the Copenhagen brewery.

As well as golden lagers, however, there are some seasonal brews and darker beers to be found in Denmark. You may even come across the occasional porter – a reminder of the days when English ale was sold in the Baltic. There is also a tradition of brewing an extremely weak, dark, top-fermented table beer called hvidtol, which is so low in alcohol that it escapes the tax levied on other beers. Despite the lack of variety and relatively high taxes on alcohol, the Danes certainly enjoy their beer – drinking more per head of population than any other nation, apart from the Czech Republic and Germany.

Above: There are occasional unusual brews to be found in Denmark, such as this red beer from Ceres. However it is Carlsberg's world-famous golden lager, that is associated with Danish beer, and lagers that dominate brewing and drinking.

THE BEERS

Albani Porter
A strong, smooth all-malt porter (7.8%) from the Albani brewery in Odense.

Bering
Bering is an unusual cross between a strong spicy stout and a lager blended with lemon and rum (6.3%), brewed by Ceres.

Bjørne Bryg
A bright-gold, strong lager (8.3%) with a bitter hops after-taste from Harboe. The name means "Bear Beer".

Buur
A deep-gold, strong, sweet, hoppy, Dortmunder-style beer (7.6%) from Thor, part of the Ceres brewing group.

Carlsberg Let
A light, golden, weak table-beer (2.7%) with a malty and bitter hoppy taste, from Carlsberg.

Carlsberg Master Brew
A highly alcoholic, strong, beer (10.5%) created for the firm's 150th anniversary.

Carlsberg Pilsner
Also known as Carlsberg Lager Beer (or sometimes as Hof after the royal court), this lager (4.6%) with the green label has a clean, soft flavour.

Ceres Royal Export
This strong golden lager (5.8%) produced by Ceres, has a ripe, malty flavour with a hoppy finish.

Dansk Dortmunder
A strong, malty, golden lager (7.7%) brewed by Ceres that is widely exported under the name Ceres Strong Ale.

Dansk LA
This low-alcohol beer is probably the best-known beer made by Wiibroe, a Carlsberg subsidiary at Elsinore, founded in 1840, which mainly produces lower-priced products.

Elephant
A rich golden lager (7.5%) in the German bock style, from Carlsberg. It is named after the brewery's elephant gates.

Faxe Premium
A malty lager with a soft, malt finish (5%) from the Faxe brewery.

Gamle Special Dark
This dark lager (4.2%) from Carlsberg recalls the brewery's original malty, Munich-style lager.

Gammel Porter or Imperial Stout
This strong, Baltic-style stout from Carlsberg (7.5%) is bottom-fermenting, and has a rich, roasted flavour. "Gammel" means old.

Giraf
A pale, strong lager (6.8%) with a long-neck label, produced by Albani of Odense. It was first brewed to help sponsor the purchase of giraffes for the local zoo.

Grøn
Tuborg's main brand is known as Grøn after the green colour of the label, with a premium Guld (gold) and a dark lager Rod (red).

Hof
See Carlsberg Pilsner.

The dominant bottle

One peculiarity of the beer market in Denmark is that the vast bulk is sold in returnable bottles and relatively little is available on draught. The litter-conscious Danes are vehemently opposed to the can, and they have banned its use for the sale of drinks on environmental grounds. This has brought the country into conflict with the European Union's free-market directives.

Kongens Bryg
This low-alcohol golden lager (1.7%) is produced by Tuborg.

Red Erik
This lager from Ceres is named in honour of the Viking who discovered Greenland and began brewing there.

Silver Pilsner
This tasty Pilsner is the selling beer from the Harboe brewery.

Sort Guld
Sort Guld or "Black Gold" is a malty, dark beer (5.8%) produced by Carlsberg.

THE BREWERS

Albani

One of the larger independent breweries in Denmark was founded in Odense in 1859. It is best known for its tall-necked pale, strong lager Giraf, and it also brews a porter, Albani Porter (7.8%), an Easter brew, Albani Påske Bryg, Albani Christmas Jule, as well as a range of Pilsners.

Apollo

A home-brew pub in Copenhagen near the famous Tivoli Gardens. This establishment first appeared in 1990 at the Hereford Beefstouw restaurant in co-operation with the Wiibroe brewery of Elsinore. It produces a range of unfiltered lagers.

Carlsberg

See panel opposite.

Ceres

After a merger with the Thor and Faxe breweries, Ceres of Aarhus in Jutland is now part of the second-largest brewing group in Denmark. The brewery was founded in 1856, and is named after the goddess of grain. Besides a range of Pilsners, it brews a strong, dark Ceres Stowt (stout, 7.7%) and a range of stronger golden lagers that are widely exported.

Faxe

This brewery at Fakse gained cult status in the 1970s with its Faxe Fad beer. "Fad" means draught, and the bottled brew was unpasteurized. The brewery has linked up with Ceres to form Brewery Group Denmark, the second largest combine in the country.

Harboe

The independent family-owned brewery was founded in Skaelskor on Zealand in 1883. It initially brewed the non-alcoholic hvidtol before starting to brew lager in 1890. Its modern brewery, built in 1960, is best known abroad for its powerful Bjørne Bryg ("Bear Beer") but its best-selling brew is its Silver Pilsner. It also brews a premium Harboe Guld (5.9%) and a range of seasonal beers. Harboe is the sole Danish producer of malt extract and still produces low-alcohol malt brews.

Danish dynasty

Some have said that the Carlsberg story is like a dynastic blockbuster. Danish television agreed and in 1996 made its most expensive production, a 12-part series based on the remarkable life of J. C. Jacobsen. It is simply called *The Brewer*.

Tuborg

Although Tuborg is less well known on the international market than its sister brewery Carlsberg, this Copenhagen brewery outsells Carlsberg in the home market and in the other Nordic countries. Tuborg was founded in Tuborg, to the north of Copenhagen, in 1873 by a group of bankers.

At first it sold the same dark Munich-style lagers that had been introduced by Carlsberg, but in 1880 the Tuborg brewer Hans Bekkevold launched Denmark's first Pilsner. The Tuborg brewery was also one of the first in Denmark to bottle its beers and the green-labelled Pilsner proved a major success with consumers – so much of a success in fact that in 1903, a new seven-storey brewhouse was built to keep up with demand. A clock looked down on the new shiny coppers, with the financiers' favourite words below the dial, warning slack workers, "Time is Money".

One of the odder features of the Tuborg brewery in Copenhagen which, like Carlsberg, has a large visitor centre, is a massive 26-metre (85-foot)-high beer bottle. This city landmark was originally built for the Great Nordic Industrial Fair in Tivoli Park in 1888, and was fitted with Denmark's first ever hydraulic lift. At its centenary in 1988, the towering bottle was shipped back to the town centre to stand alongside the city hall.

Throughout the 20th century Tuborg and Carlsberg co-operated closely, and finally in 1970 the two major brewers merged, and the combined company now accounts for about 80% of domestic beer sales. Each still retains its own independent management and takes control of its own marketing. Tuborg has also maintained production at its own brewery in Copenhagen. The company has made its mark on the international scene, being sold and brewed in more than 130 countries.

The Tuborg range of beers is similar to Carlsberg's, although its Pilsners tend to be a little lighter and hoppier. The main Tuborg brand is known as Grøn after the green colour of the label. There is also a premium Guld and a dark lager, Rod. Like Carlsberg, Tuborg also produces some seasonal brews and a dark, rich, creamy porter.

THE CARLSBERG STORY

Since 1901, four stone elephants have stood guard at the gates of the Carlsberg brewery in Copenhagen. They symbolize the enduring power of one of the most famous names in brewing and signify that this is no ordinary company. The story of Carlsberg is an epic tale.

The Carlsberg brewery was founded in 1847 by Jacob Christian Jacobsen on a hill at Valby just outside Copenhagen. He named it after his five-year-old son Carl and the Danish word for a hill – "berg". At the time, many small Danish breweries (including one run by his father) were producing top-fermented wheat beers, but Jacobsen was determined to brew on a grand scale – and to brew the new bottom-fermented lagers, which were then being pioneered in Bavaria.

Jacobsen travelled to Munich to study under the famous Gabriel Sedlmayr of the Spaten brewery and, according to legend, returned from one trip in 1845 with 2 litres (3½ pints) of the vital bottom-fermenting yeast, which he kept cool throughout the long stagecoach journey by frequently dousing it with cold water and covering the

containers with his stovepipe hat. After successful experiments to produce the dark, Munich-style lager, using the cellars under the city ramparts while his new brewery was being built, he began to brew the first batch at his plant at Valby on November 10 1847.

Jacobsen became one of the leaders of the new science of brewing and built a famous set of laboratories. It was here in 1883 that Emil Hansen isolated the first single-cell yeast culture *Saccharomyces Carlsbergensis*. This major development allowed brewers to control the quality of their beers by eliminating bad yeast strains. Jacobsen also established the Carlsberg Foundation in 1876, to promote scientific research. After his death in 1887, this foundation became the owner of the brewery. Jacobsen's son Carl, often in dispute with his father, set up his own brewery on an adjoining site to brew Pilsners. His interest lay in

the arts, and in 1901 he designed a new brewhouse on an elaborate scale, complete with Florentine flourishes and elephant gates. The Carlsberg Foundation took over this cathedral of beer in 1902. Today the company is uniquely run as a charity for the benefit of the sciences and, following Carl's intervention, for the arts. Its huge trust fund donates vast amounts of money. Carl Jacobsen helped develop Copenhagen as a city of soaring spires. In 1913, he donated the Little Mermaid statue, which has become the symbol of the city. Carlsberg first became known outside Denmark when its beer was shipped to Scotland in 1868. The other Scandinavian countries

and the West Indies soon followed. Carlsberg is a particularly big brand in the Far East. The first brewery outside Denmark was built in Malawi in Africa in 1968. In 1970, Carlsberg merged with Tuborg to form United Breweries, which in 1987 became Carlsberg.

Today, Carlsberg has about 100 subsidiary and associated companies, mostly abroad. More than 80% of its sales are outside Denmark. Its beer is sold in 150 countries and brewed in 40. In Denmark, where it serves four out of every five glasses of beer, it also owns Wiibroe of Elsinore, and in 1979 opened a new brewery at Fredericia to serve western Denmark.

Above: The imposing Carlsberg brewery in Copenhagen

NORWAY

The frozen lands of northern Europe might conjure up images of hard-drinking, ale-quaffing Vikings, but the truth is that few regions have done more to try to curb alcoholic drinks.

FEW COUNTRIES SQUEEZE THEIR DRINK into a tighter strait-jacket. Norway levies the highest and most punitive rate of duty on beer in the world. One result of this is that home-brewing is a potent tradition in Norway, with some rural recipes still incorporating home-grown juniper berries. The styles and strengths of commercial beers are strictly regulated by the State. The positive side of this strict regulation has meant the introduction of a beer purity law along German lines, which gives the all-malt Norwegian beers a smooth, clean taste.

Since 1995 there have been seven tax bands in operation, known by letters of the alphabet. The biggest leap is between the third level (for beers with an alcohol content of 2.75–3.75%) to the fourth level, (3.75–4.75%). Despite this price hike, the fourth level, (band D), is by far the most popular, accounting for more than three-quarters of all sales. Virtually all of this is Pilsner-style beer. A dark variety of Pilsner is also brewed, called baierol or bayer. The three stronger bands, up to a maximum 7%, include export-style lagers or gullol (gold beer) and some darker, seasonal brews, such as bokkol or juleol, at Christmas. Lower-alcohol beers are called brigg or lettol. All are bottom-fermented. There are few nationally sold brands. Instead, regional beers tend to dominate in their local areas. Dahls Pils rules Trondelag for instance; Tou Pils is pre-eminent in Stavanger; and Arendal Pils reigns supreme in the Sorlandet region. In the mid-1980s there were around 15 independent breweries. Since then the largest company, Ringnes, has been taking over its rivals and now controls all the dominant brands mentioned. This concentration in the industry has inevitably led to the closure of some plants.

Above: Norway taxes its beer heavily, and the variety of brews available is limited. The most popular beers tend to be light lagers, and the main brewery is Ringnes, founded in 1877.

THE BEERS

Aass Bock
A creamy, copper-coloured, malty bock beer (6.1%), from the Aass brewery.

Aass Classic Special Brygg
An aromatic, dark-gold lager (4.5%) with a crisp, clean hop taste from the Aass brewery in Drammen.

Akershus Irish Stout
This uncompromisingly black stout (4.6%) from Akershus has a smooth, rich chocolatey flavour.

Akershus Pale Ale
A copper-coloured, hoppy pale ale (4.6%) from the Akershus brewery.

Akershus Weissbier
This filtered, German-style wheat beer (4.6%) is brewed using wheat and barley by the Akershus brewery.

Arctic Pils
This golden, hoppy Pilsner (4.5%) is brewed by Mack.

Christmas Juleol
A seasonal celebration brew from Aass, Drammen. It has a deep-caramel colour and a toasted-malt flavour.

Frydenlund Pilsener
A well-hopped, traditional Pilsner now brewed by Ringnes following the closure of the Frydenlund brewery in Oslo in 1995.

Hansa Bayer
A tasty, dark, Bavarian-style brew (4.5%) from Hansa.

Hansa Eksportol
A tawny-gold lager (4.5%) with a salty, malt flavour. It is brewed for export.

Hansa Premium
A light-tasting wheat beer (4.5%), brewed by Hansa in Bergen, which is very popular in western Norway.

Lauritz
This Dortmunder-style beer is named after the founder of the Aass brewery Lauritz Aass.

Ludwig Pils
A golden, hoppy Pilsner from the Hansa brewery.

Lysholmer
Ringnes-owned Dahl's brewery in Trondheim produces this range of nationally popular brews which includes the golden special and an ice beer.

Mack Bayer
A Bavarian-style, dark chocolatey brew from the Mack brewery.

Mack Polar Bear
A hazy, amber lager with a malty taste, from Mack.

Pilsener Mack-Ol
This malty, golden Pilsner from the Mack brewery in the far north of the country is reputedly the best brew with which to wash down a local delicacy – seagulls' eggs.

Ringnes Pils
A golden Pilsner-style lager with a fresh, mild hop and malt flavour. This is the flagship brand for Ringnes.

THE BREWERS

Aass
Norway's oldest brewery was founded in Drammen in 1834. A medium-size independent company, it generates tremendous loyalty among local drinkers with its own beer club boasting more than 8,000 members. It also offers one of the widest range of beers, with more than ten different brews.

Akershus
This firm was founded in the Oslo suburb of Enebakk in 1992. It brews a variety of top-fermenting styles.

Hansa
The large Bergen brewery was founded in 1891 and is best-known for its Ludwig Pils, but it brews a large range of beers. It also runs a traditional farmhouse brewery for tourists and makes a juniper beer. The firm regained its independence in 1996, following the merger of Ringnes and Pripps.

Mack
The world's most northerly brewery at Tromsø, inside the Arctic Circle, was founded in 1877. As well as its flagship Pils, Mack also brews hoppier Mack Norges and Arctic Pils, besides other beers which have a more Bavarian accent.

Mikro
Norway's first home-brew pub, the aptly named Mikro Bryggeri, in Oslo, has brewed top-fermented English-style draught bitters and stout since 1990.

Ringnes
Norway's major brewery, founded in Oslo in 1877, also owns many other brands and breweries. Its main national beers are Ringnes Pils and Lysholmer Ice from Dahl's brewery in Trondheim. In 1995 it merged with Pripps of Sweden to form Pripps Ringnes.

SWEDEN

Brewers in Sweden have long struggled to keep their heads above water due to the strict laws that govern alcohol consumption. However, in recent years the rules have been relaxed and there has been a revival of small-scale brewing.

L IKE ITS NEIGHBOURS, Sweden has had to contend with a powerful temperance movement. Both politicians and church leaders regularly hold up alcohol as the source of the nation's moral ills. The production and sale of beer is tightly controlled, including strict demarcation according to strength. Beers are sold in three different strengths (Class I to 1.8%; Class II to 3.5%; Class III to 5.6%) – often with the same label. Only Class I and Class II beers can be sold in bars or food stores. Laws were introduced that severely restricted the sale of stronger, Class III beers. Under the legislation, stronger beers could only be bought in restaurants or from State shops (which are closed in the evenings and at weekends) and large taxes were levied on their consumption.

In 1960 there were 85 breweries in the country, but this strait-jacket on sales proved to be the final straw for many struggling companies, who went out of business in the years that followed. Many of the other brewers switched to producing medium-strength beers. At one stage, the State owned some breweries, including the leading brewer Pripps.

However, since Sweden's entry into the European Union in 1995, some of the State monopolies and restrictions have had to be relaxed, to conform with rules on free trade within the union. A ban on beer stronger than 5.6% was dropped, and the country is now adopting a uniform rate of duty on alcohol instead of the three-class system, which heavily favoured the brewing and sale of weaker brews.

Above: Swedish brewers have long struggled against a strong temperance movement. Spendrup's is one of the few hardy survivors.

A licence has been granted for a brewpub in Stockholm, and a growing number of new, small, local breweries has begun to spring up, mainly devoted to brewing the stronger Class III beers.

THE BEERS

Dart
This English-style copper-coloured, hoppy bitter is brewed by Pripps.

Falcon Export
This gold Pilsner has a bitter, hop taste and a light-malt finish. It is produced by Falcon, Falkenberg.

Gorilla
This new extra-strong beer (7.6%) is one of the potent brews that have arrived on the Swedish market since the relaxing of the beer laws. It is produced by the speciality Abro brewery, Vimmerby.

Pripps Bla
The best-selling Swedish beer in all three strength classes.
It is a honey-gold sweetish Pilsner. There is also a new Extra Strong Pripps Bla (7.2%) in the strongest beer class.

Royal Pilsner
This is the brand name for a range of hoppy, all-malt Pilsners from Pripps, whose label was designed by Prince Sigvard Bernadotte of Sweden.

Spendrup's Old Gold
This deep-gold, hoppy, all-malt Pilsner-style lager (5%) comes in a distinctive, ridged brown bottle. It is produced by the Spendrup's brewery in Grangesberg.

Spendrup's Premium
This flavoursome, full-bodied, all-malt premium Pilsner comes from the Spendrup's brewery in Grangesberg.

Tom Kelley
This is a potent and flavoursome brew (7.5%). Tom Kelley was introduced by Pripps when the regulations on strong beers were relaxed.

CARNEGIE PORTER – A SCOTTISH BREW IN SWEDEN

Many Swedish beers carry English names, but one of Pripps' more distinctive brews poured out of Scotland. A Scot called David Carnegie emigrated to Gothenburg in the early 19th century, setting up his own brewery there in 1836 to produce the popular porters of the day. The company was eventually absorbed by Pripps, but they never stopped brewing the top-fermented dark drop. Today, Carnegie Porter is brewed in Stockholm in two strengths – a richly roasted 5.6%, and a thin shadow of the full-bodied version at 3.6%. It has also introduced a vintage, year-dated stark (strong) porter, which is matured for a full six months. In 1992, the heavy, aromatic brew returned home to Britain to win a gold medal at the International Brewing Exhibition in Burton-on-Trent.

THE BREWERS

Abro
A family brewery at Vimmerby since 1856, Abro is known for its speciality products, notably a powerful Gorilla (7.6%) in the new extra-strong sector. Other brews include Abro Guld and a darker Abro Bayerskt.

Falcon
This large Falkenberg firm has been brewing since 1896. Besides a range of Pilsners, it also offers a malty Falcon Guldol, and a dark, Munich-style Falcon Bayerskt.

Gamla Stans
Sweden's first brewpub opened in Stockholm in 1995 brewing a fresh, unfiltered lager, Faerskoel (5%).

Gotlands
A small brewery in Visby on the island of Gotland which was revived by Spendrups in 1995. Besides a dry Munkeol lager, it also brews two Scottish-style beers, a creamy Oat Malt Stout (4.5%) and Scotch Ale (4.2%) plus the unfiltered, fruity Klosteroel (6%).

Pripps
The dominant force in Swedish brewing has absorbed many smaller breweries. It was founded in Gothenburg in 1828 and merged with Stockholm Breweries in 1963. At the time of the merger the combined company boasted 30 breweries. Its main plant is now at Bromma near Stockholm and the leading brand is the sweetish Pilsner Pripps Bla ("blue").

In 1995, Pripps merged with Norway's major brewer Ringnes. Pripps also has a stake in Hartwall of Finland, and the two companies have expanded heavily eastwards into the new Baltic states.

Spendrup's
In the difficult and restricted trading conditions that have prevailed in Sweden for many years, it seemed that this local brewery in Grangesberg, like a large number of others, was in danger of closing. The brewery, which was then trading as Grangesbergs, revived its fortune when it restored the old family name of Spendrup's and launched a range of all-malt Pilsners in distinctive bottles.

FINLAND

Finland has, more than any other Scandinavian country, managed to retain its ancient brewing traditions, and despite a vigorous anti-alcohol movement in the country, the modern industry is also thriving.

S UCH IS THE POPULARITY of the traditional Finnish beer *sahti* that it has moved out of remote rural farms into more commercial production. Many Finns like to drink sahti after a traditional sauna, and some households even make it in the sauna. The country also has a long history of more conventional brewing, but the development of the industry was heavily disrupted by anti-alcohol legislation. Like the United States, Finland endured a long period of Prohibition from 1919 until 1932. However, unlike its Scandinavian neighbours, the dry grip of the temperance movement shows little sign of relaxing in Finland and taxes on beer have remained high (as much as 40% on the strongest brews, with an additional value-added tax of around 16%).

Beer is divided into classes according to strength for regulation of sales and for tax purposes. Only the weakest, Class I (beers below 2.8% alcohol by volume), are allowed to be sold through ordinary shops, and may be advertised freely. The popular Class III (3.7–4.7%) is more restricted, through higher taxation and State-regulated distribution. Almost all Class III beer is of the Pilsner style.

As strength climbs, so the State's grip tightens, and sales of stronger beers (to 5.7%) are closely controlled by the State-owned retail monopoly, Alko. These export lagers can only be legally sold through Alko's shops and licensed restaurants. There are also a few speciality brews containing up to 7.8% alcohol. Despite these severe restrictions, the Finnish brewing industry has managed to remain quite vigorous, with two main groups, Hartwall and Sinebrychoff, dominating the tightly controlled market, and a growing number of small "restaurant-brewers" are now springing up all the time.

Above: Hartwall, Finland's biggest brewer, produces a golden lager Lapin Kulta, which, in its strongest form (5.3%), may only be sold in restricted outlets.

THE BEERS

Cheers

A copper-coloured, bottom-fermented ale, produced by one of the Finnish giants, Sinebrychoff.

Jouloulot Christmas Beer

A reddish-coloured, rich-flavoured, seasonal winter brew (5%), produced by Sinebrychoff.

Karhu 3

A dark, brownish lager (4.6%), with a strong, full flavour. This is one of a range from the Sinebrychoff's second brewery at Pori.

Karjala

This tawny-coloured, richly flavoured, spicy, hoppy Pilsner is brewed by Hartwall and is their best-selling brew after Lapin Kulta. The company have recently added Hartwall 1836 Classic, a full malt ale to their range, first produced in 1996.

Koff

Koff is the abbreviated name which is given to the beers from the Sinebrychoff brewery, these include a popular, light-brownish, pleasant-tasting Pilsner (4.5%), a powerful pale Extra Strong (7.5%) and an export lager (5.2%).

Koff
Porter

The Sinebrychoff brewery still brews one of its oldest beers (7.2%), a dense dark ale which was only revived after the Second World War, using a top-fermenting yeast cultured from a bottle of Guinness. Centrifuged but not filtered, it has a rich, roasted flavour. Four different malts are used in the mash, and the beer is conditioned for six weeks before it is pasteurized. It was once exported to the US under the name Imperial Stout.

Lammin Sahti

The best-known commercial sahti producer sells the Finnish speciality in a container resembling a wine box. The reddish, hazy drink (8%) has a spicy, tart taste.

Lapin Kulta

Hartwall's leading Pilsner from its most northern brewery trades on its fresh image using the icy waters of Lapland. Its strongest form (5.3%) is smooth and malty.

Leningrad Cowboy

This unusually named, golden export lager (5.2%) is brewed by Sinebrychoff and reflects the brewery's Russian connections.

Pilsner Nikolai

A sweetish, premium Pilsner (4.5%) brewed by the Sinebrychoff brewery. It is named in honour of the brewery's founder.

Postin Oma

Michael Jackson (*The Beer Hunter*) described this dark brew from the small Ravintola Wanha Posti brewery very favourably when he visited in 1995, saying, "It has a very attractive copper-brown colour and a good, dense head. The flavour has some nuttiness and some dark chocolate with a good development of malt flavours. It is very easily drinkable and soothing." The brewery was so pleased that it has immortalized Mr Jackson's complimentary write-up of their brew on the back of its beer mats!

Sahti

This is the traditional beer style of Finland. It is strong (usually around 8%), unfiltered, hazy, reddish-amber in colour and quite flat, with a spicy, bittersweet flavour. Rye, rather than barley, is used as the main component in the mash. This, combined with the main seasoning of juniper (rather than hops), gives the finished product a refreshingly tart tang. Juniper twigs are also traditionally used to strain the brew, and saunas are sometimes used to kiln the grains. Sahti production was originally a domestic enterprise, and the fact that baking yeast is often used in the recipe reflects its homely origins.

Sandels

Olvi's lightly hopped, light brown, traditional Finnish lager which has a smooth, malty taste. It is named after Colonel Sandels, a famous soldier in the Russian-Finnish War.

Vaakuna

This dark, golden, malty, toffeeish, Bavarian Märzen-style lager (4.5%) is produced by the Olvi brewery.

Sowing the seed

Finland's cold climate is well suited to cereal production, and it is one of the major barley growers of the world. Its malted grain is exported widely and may even end up in brews as far afield as Japan.

Above and below: The colours of Lapin Kulta's label are inspired by Finland's midnight sun.

THE BREWERS

Hartwall

The Hartwall company controls more than half of the beer market in Finland, with breweries in Helsinki, Lahti and Tornio. The brewery in Tornio was founded in this trapping and gold-rush town in 1873 and the Lapin Kulta name, meaning "Lapp Gold", was taken from an old mine. This brewery is one of the few breweries in the world to take its water from rivers.

Hartwall was a soft drinks manufacturer until 1966 when it bought its first brewery. Its main Pilsner brand is Lapin Kulta. but it also produces Karjala and Hartwall 1836 Classic. In 1991, Hartwall set up a joint venture with Pripps of Sweden, Baltic Beverage Holdings (BBH), to expand into the Baltic states, buying into breweries in Estonia, Latvia, Lithuania and Russia.

Kappeli Brasserie

The Kappeli Brasserie in Helsinki produces unfiltered lagers and seasonal specials.

Olvi

The third-largest brewing group in Finland is based in Iisalmi. Besides a range of Pilsners it produces a malty export lager, Vaakuna and the light brown Sandels.

Sinebrychoff

Finland's oldest brewery was established by a Russian merchant, Nikolai Sinebrychoff, in 1819 in Helsinki. Originally the brewery made porter, mead and top-fermenting beers, then it introduced lager to its range in 1853. It still trades on the

A northern industry

There are thousands of local sahti producers, churning out about four million litres (900,000 gallons) each year. The majority is made in the region the Finns call "the north" – the area stretching 150 km (100 miles) or so to the north-east and north-west of Tampere. The best-known commercial producers are Joutsa, Sysmä and Honkajoki.

Russian connection. The beers are mainly sold under the abbreviated Koff name, but there is also a premium Pilsner Nikolai and oddities such as an export lager called Leningrad Cowboy.

ICELAND

The small, northerly island of Iceland has a tradition of producing very weak beers as a result of prohibitive legislation that placed an effective brake on normal beer production for 74 years.

IN 1989, ICELAND finally came in from the cold when it ended a 74-year ban on beer imposed in 1915. Previously, companies such as the family-run Egill brewery of Reykjavík, produced only soft drinks and low-alcohol beers, but since the relaxation of the ban they have added a number of stronger brews for the country's tiny population of 250,000, half of whom live in the capital, Reykjavík. Since the repeal of the ban on beer, Reykjavík is fast gaining the reputation of being a fun-loving town, and an increasing number of well-heeled younger Europeans now visit to experience the hedonistic nightlife, particularly during the summer months. At the same time alcoholism is a growing social problem, which perhaps can be partly attributed to the long, dark winters during which there can be as little as four hours' daylight.

Above: Viking is a new beer that has appeared in Iceland since the repeal of the beer ban.

THE BEERS

Dökkur
This stronger (in Icelandic terms) beer (3.8%) was introduced by Egill after the ban on producing alcoholic drinks was lifted in 1989. The name means dark.

A Viking toast

Iceland is the home of the oldest "parliament" in the world – the Thingvellir. The ancient sagas handed down from Viking times tell of the annual meeting there to make laws, resolve disputes and strike deals. It was a great occasion accompanied by feasting and of course copious beer drinking.

Egils Malt
This old-fashioned style of low-alcohol beer (1%) is still brewed by Egill of Reykjavík.

Egils Pilsner
The weak, pale-gold Pilsner (2.25%) is produced by Egill brewery of Reykjavík. The refreshing beer is brewed with pure Icelandic water and is the most popular light beer in Iceland.

Gull
This golden, Pilsner export lager (5%) was introduced by Egill brewery following the repeal of the ban on strong beers. It is now the most popular beer in the country.

Viking Bjór
This pale-gold, clear Pilsner-style lager (5%) is produced by Viking.

THE BREWERS

Egill
Run by the Tomasson family since 1913, Egill concentrated on the production of low-alcohol beers such as Egils Malt until 1989. It still markets these, but since the repeal of the beer ban it has added the stronger Dökkur and Gull to its range, besides brewing Tuborg under licence.

Viking
Originally a soft drinks producer called Sanitas. Viking built a new brewery at Akureyri in 1988 to meet the demand for stronger beer when the ban was lifted in 1989.

BELGIUM

Belgium is the land of beer. No country offers such a rich variety of styles – from wild, spontaneously fermenting brews and fruit beers to spiced beers and blessed Trappist ales still produced in monasteries.

O N ONE LEVEL the Belgian beer market has become concentrated over the last century. The number of breweries has declined from around 3,000 in 1900 to little more than 100 today. Pilsner-style beers, such as Stella Artois and Jupiler, from the major brewers Interbrew and Alken-Maes, dominate domestic consumption, and while they are fine brews, they do not match the top-quality lagers available in the Czech Republic and Germany.

However the joy of Belgian beer lies not in its pils but in the fascinating range of other beers which can be found in its bars. What France is to wine, Belgium is to beer. It may be a small country, but it is vast in what it has to offer those thirsting after new tastes. For the adventurous, Belgium is heaven on earth, a beer drinker's paradise.

There are monasteries still producing strong, richly favoured, Trappist ales such as Chimay and Orval, which are now copied by some commercial breweries and sold as abbey beers. Near Brussels a region creates wild lambic beers which are allowed to ferment spontaneously. Some breweries add fruit to these ancient wheat brews to produce beers such as the deliciously dark kriek made using cherries, while others add spices or sour their beers in special ways.

It is in this colourful and complex speciality section that Belgium has earned its reputation. The speciality beers can be divided into seven main groups – lambic (sometimes spelled lambik), white beer, brown beer, red beer, ales, Trappist and saison. Within these categories the range of flavours, styles and strengths is bewildering and some brews are unique and defy categorization. Many cafés and bars offer a staggeringly long beer menu for the customer to choose from, and each beer is often served in its own special glass.

Above: Belgium's speciality beers have earned acclaim throughout the world. Cherry-flavoured kriek beers, with their luscious dark, red colour, are usually made using whole fruit.

THE BEERS

Abbaye d'Aulne

This is the name used by the de Smedt family brewery in Opwijk for some of its commercially produced abbey-style beers.

Abbaye de Bonne Espérance

This bottle-conditioned, cloudy golden tripel (7.5%) is better known as Floreffe tripel from the Lefebvre brewery in Quenast.

Adler

The third largest lager producer in Belgium, Haacht brews this strong, golden, premium lager (6.5%).

Affligem

The abbey beers from the De Smedt brewery of Opwijk are brewed according to original recipes from the ancient Benedictine Affligem Abbey in the region of Aalst. It produces a brown, dry Affligem Dubbel, a golden blonde (both 7%) and a fruity, amber tripel (8.5%).

Agnus Dei

A complex, strong, pale tripel (8%). This abbey-style beer is sold under the Corsendonk name. The brew, which dates from 1982, is brewed at the Du Bocq brewery. It is the brainchild of Jozef Keersmaekers.

Augustijn

The strong abbey-style beers from the Van Steenberge brewery of Ertvelde include Augustijn (8%) and a Grand Cru (9%).

Avec les Bons Voeux de la Brasseries

A strong, gold, spicy (9.5%) New Year beer with a long title. This brew comes from Dupont in Hainaut. An organic (biologique) version is also available.

Bel Pils

Considered one of Belgium's better Pilsners, Bel Pils (5.3%) is pale gold with a hoppy flavour. It is produced by the independent family brewery Moortgat, which also makes Duvel and Maredsous abbey beers.

Belle-Vue

Gueuze, kriek and frambozen (5.2%) from this large-scale brewer of lambic beers are pleasant but a little undemanding.

Blanche de Namur

This pale wheat beer (4.3%) with a spicy, fruity flavour is brewed in Namur province by the family brewery Du Bocq.

Blanche des Honnelles

A cloudy wheat beer (6%) that incorporates malted oats in the mash and is spiced with juniper, coriander and orange peel. Produced by Abbaye des Rocs.

Block Special 6

Brewed in Peizegem, Block produces this unique sour beer, Block Special 6 (6%), which is a blend of lambic and young and old pale ales. It also brews the range of Satan ales.

Bokkereyer

A strong (5.8%) Vienna-style lager from a Limburg family brewery, St Jozef, on the Dutch border at Opitter.

Bourgogne des Flandres

Lambic brewer Timmermans of Itterbeek produces this lambic-based, plummy, sour, red ale (6.5%).

Brigand

A robust, bronze-coloured ale (9%) with a sweetish taste. It is served in corked bottles by the Van Honsebrouck brewery of Ingelmunster, West Flanders. Brigand has gained a cult following.

Brugs Tarwebier

Also known as Blanche de Bruges, this cloudy wheat beer (5%) is the best-known brew from Gouden Boom in Bruges. Tarwe means wheat.

Brugse Straffe Hendrik

See Straffe Hendrik.

Brugse Tripel

This strong, golden beer (9.5%) comes from the small Gouden Boom brewery in Bruges (the brewery also boasts its own beer museum).

Right: Transferring casks of craft-brewed Belgian ale from the lorry to the bar earlier this century.

Bush

The strongest beer in Belgium, Bush (12%) is an amber-coloured, English-style barley wine from the Dubuisson brewery in Pipaix, Hainaut. Originally brewed in 1933, this dry, warming brew with a mellow, oaky taste, became the family firm's only regular beer. It is sold as Scaldis in the US in order to avoid confusion with brewing giant Anheuser-Busch. Dubuisson also brews a dark amber Bush Noël (12%) at Christmas. In 1994, the brewery marked its 225th anniversary with the launch of a weaker hoppy Bush Beer (7%).

Celis White

This wheat beer (5%) is now brewed by De Smedt under licence from the original producer of Belgian wheat beer, Pieter Celis, who now brews in America.

Chapeau

This range of weak, lambic fruit beers, including banana, strawberry and pineapple, is produced by De Troch.

Charles Quint

This strong, sweetish brown ale (7%) is produced by Haacht.

Chimay Blanche

See Chimay Cinq Cents.

Chimay Bleu

See Chimay Grande Réserve.

Chimay Cinq Cents

A golden, amber Trappist tripel with a malty flavour (8%). It is the hoppiest, driest offering from the Abbaye de Notre-Dame de Scourmont, near Chimay. In the smaller bottle size it is known as Chimay Blanche, and is so called after the white colour of the bottle cap.

Chimay Grande Réserve

This rich, fruity Trappist ale (9%) is the strongest and most complex ale from the Abbaye de Notre-Dame de Scourmont. The bottle has a blue cap and label. It was originally introduced as a Christmas beer, but has been brewed regularly since 1958. It is vintage-dated and benefits from being laid down for a few years. In the smaller size it is known as Chimay Bleu.

Chimay Première

A rich, red-brown Trappist ale (7%) with a spicy, fruity flavour from the Abbaye de Notre-Dame de Scourmont. The bottle has a red label and top. In the 33cl bottle is called Chimay Rouge.

Chimay Rouge

See Chimay Première.

Cochonne

An annual ale (9%) from the small Vapeur brewery in Pipaix in Hainaut.

A SINGULAR ALE

The Antwerp brewery De Koninck was founded in 1833. It uses a traditional Flemish brick-clad kettle with a hop sieve that is removed by a pulley system. The recipe is all malt (using no adjuncts) and incorporates Saaz hops. The best way to enjoy a glass of De Koninck is on draught in the Pilgrim café opposite the brewery, where locals often add an extra shot of yeast to their glass.

Corsendonk

These two abbey beers in their stylish brown bottles date from as recently as 1982. They are named after the former Corsendonk Augustinian priory near Turnhout, which was established in the 15th century and recently restored. The brews are the brainchild of a member of the well-known brewing family, Jozef Keersmaekers. The dark, chocolatey dubbel, Pater Noster, is brewed by the Van Steenberge brewery. The stronger, pale tripel, Agnus Dei (8%), is brewed at the Du Bocq brewery.

Cristal Alken

This unpasteurized beer is generally regarded as the hoppiest of the main Belgian Pilsners (4.8%). Brewed by the Alken-Maes group, it is the best-selling beer in its home province of Limbourg.

Cuvée d'Aristée

Unusual honeyed ale (9.5%) from the tiny Praille brewery in Peissant near Mons.

Cuvée de l'Hermitage

Cuvée, like the terms luxe and spéciale, has largely become a meaningless title, but this rich, russet ale (8%) from the Union brewery in Jumet deserves the accolade.

De Koninck

This all-malt, top-fermenting ale (5%) has been described as a cross between an English bitter and a German alt. It is matured in the cask, then pasteurized in the bottle. There is also a stronger version available, called Cuvée de Koninck (8%).

Delirium Tremens

This aptly named, notoriously strong, golden, spiced ale (9%) from the Huyghe brewery near Ghent is served in a glass painted with pink elephants.

Dentergems Wit

The Riva brewery of Dentergem launched this, one of the first rival white beers to Hoegaarden, in 1980. The pale, cloudy brew (5%) is more in the German wheat-beer style, with a delicate, wheaty, lemony taste.

Doppelbock Bugel

This is one of the strongest (8%) bottom-fermented beers in Belgium. A heavy Christmas brew, it is produced by Domus, the first home-brew house in Belgium, set up in Leuven in 1985 by a former Cristal Alken brewer. Other beers include a tasty, fresh lager and a cloudy wheat beer, Leuvens Witbier (5%).

Double Enghien Brune

This interesting, creamy, walnutty, strong, dark ale (8%) and the amber blonde come from the Silly brewery in the town of Silly.

Duivelsbier

An unusual beer (6%), produced by the Vander Linden brewery by blending a conventional pale ale and a lambic.

Duvel

This is a beer with a devil of a reputation, one of the best-known and most celebrated drinks in Belgium. A golden ale with a frothy white top, it appears attractive but unremarkable in its balloon goblets apart from its surging lines of bubbles. However, just one sniff of its heady hop aroma and one taste of its complex fruity flavour, together with its sustaining strength

(8.5%), make the beer drinker appreciate that this is a glass apart.

Duvel is brewed by the Moortgat brewery in Breendonk. After the First World War, the brewery attempted to brew a Scotch ale. The Moortgat brewers examined bottles of McEwan's ale from Edinburgh and made a dark ale using the McEwan's yeast. "It's a devil of a brew," claimed one taster, and the name Duvel was born in 1923. In 1968 Moortgat perfected a golden version.

Today, the devil appears in two guises: the delicious bottle-conditioned brew has a red-lettered label; a blander, filtered version has green letters. Other Belgian brewers have tried to copy the beer, but none can match the original.

Ename

A range of abbey beers brewed by the Roman brewery in East Flanders which includes a dark Dubbel (6.5%) and a golden Tripel (8%).

Felix

The Clarysse brewery of Oudenaarde produces this range of sweetish East Flanders brown ales. Beers include Felix Oud Bruin (5.5%), Special Oudenaards (4.8%), plus two kriekbiers (6% and 5%).

Floreffe

This range of quality bottle-conditioned abbey beers from the Lefebvre family brewery at Quenast, south-west of Brussels, is named after the Norbertine abbey at Floreffe.

The best, a mahogany-coloured spicy ale, is simply called La Meilleure (8%). A golden tripel (7.5%) is also sold as Abbaye de Bonne Espérance. Additional beers include a tasty dubbel and a blonde (both 7%).

Gildenbier

This strong, sweetish brown ale (6.6%) is produced by Haacht.

Goudenband

See Liefmans Goudenband.

Gouden Carolus

A distinctive, smooth, dark ale (7%) from the family-run Anker brewery of Mechelen, its name derives from a gold coin of the Holy Roman Emperor Charles V who grew up in the city. There is also a lighter, less spicy Mechelsen Brune (5.5%) and a yellow, pale ale, Toison d'Or Tripel (7%).

Grimbergen

This range of abbey beers from the large Alken-Maes group is brewed at its Union brewery in Jumet. They include a warming Optimo Bruno (10%), a sweet, winey, golden tripel (9%) and blonde (7%) and a dark,

fruity dubbel (6.5%). The beers are named after the abbey of Grimbergen in the northern suburbs of Brussels.

Hapkin

The Louwaege brewery of West Flanders produces this strong, bottle-conditioned golden ale (8.5%), which seeks to rival Duvel.

Het Kapittel

The Van Eecke brewery of Watou produces this range of quality abbey beers. Brews include a strong abt (10%) and darkly delicious prior (9%), plus a dubbel (7%) and pater (6.5%).

Hoegaarden

The renewed interest in cloudy wheat beers began with this beer, first brewed by Pieter Celis at his De

Kluis Brewery in Hoegaarden in 1966. It revived the art of brewing "white" beers spiced with coriander and curaçao. Hoegaarden's chunky glasses have become a familiar part of Belgian bars. Besides the refreshing cloudy, lemon-coloured Hoegaarden (5%), the brewery also produces a stronger, golden Grand Cru and a spicier orangey-coloured Julius (both 8.7%), plus a rich, fruity brown ale, Verboden Vrucht (8.8%). All are bottle-conditioned.

Horse-Ale
This is an English-style pale ale (4.8%), with an aromatic hop character brewed by Interbrew.

Ichtegems Oud Bruin
A refreshing, Flemish red ale, with a sweetish, malt taste from the Strubbe brewery of Ichtegem.

Jacobins
This range of sweetish lambic beers – Jacobins amber, sweet-and-sour gueuze, the red, cherry-flavoured kriek and raspberry frambozen (all 5.5%) – comes from the Bockor brewery of Bellegem.

Jupiler
Belgium's best-selling beer, the popular malty Pilsner (5.2%) comes from Jupille

near Liège. Founded in 1853, the brewery is now part of Interbrew.

Kasteel
A very strong, amber-coloured, bottled, rich dark ale (11.5%). It is laid down to mature by the Van Honsebrouck brewery in the cellars at Ingelmunster Castle, an 18th-century moated mansion owned by the brewing family. The taste is rich, almost like a port.

La Chouffe
This golden ale (8%) from the Achouffe brewery is spiced with coriander.

La Divine
This interesting, strong, dark, amber-coloured ale (9.5%) with a full, spicy flavour, is brewed by the Silly brewery.

La Gauloise
The distinctive strong ales from the Du Bocq brewery of Namur include an ambrée (6.5%), blonde (7%) and dark, red-coloured brune (9%). The larger-size bottles are corked.

La Meilleure
This mahogany-coloured, bottle-conditioned spicy ale (8%) is, as the name implies, the best brew from the Floreffe range of abbey ales.

Leffe
Interbrew produces this range of abbey beers, named after the Leffe abbey at Dinant, near Namur. Besides an amber-coloured blonde and a dark-brown, malty, fruity brune (both 6.5%), there's a golden tripel (8.4%) and two brown ales, Vieille Cuvée (7.8%) and Radieuse (8.2%).

Liefmans Frambozenbier
This pale-pink, sour, raspberry fruit beer (5.7%) can be served as an aperitif in place of champagne.

Liefmans Goudenband
An acidic, chocolate-brown-coloured, sweet-and-sour Belgian brown ale (8%) that is brewed by Liefmans using four different hop varieties and a 100-year-old yeast strain. Part of the brew is matured for six to eight months, then it is mixed with a younger version to make the distinctively flavoured finished product.

Liefmans Kriekbier
This traditional tart, cherry fruit beer (6.5%), produced by the Liefmans brewery in Oudenaarde, is a deep, cloudy red-brown colour. It is suitable for keeping for up to four years and will age and mature with time.

Limburgse Witte

This tasty wheat beer (5%) is produced by the family-owned Martens brewery.

Lucifer

This is one of the rival brews to Duvel. It is a strong, golden ale (8%) brewed by the Riva brewery in Flanders.

McChouffe

A complex, copper-coloured, creamy, malty Ardenne strong ale (8.5%) with a vague Scottish ancestry, from the Achouffe brewery.

McGregor

A dark, whisky-malt brew (6.5%) from the Huyghe family brewery in Melle.

Maes Pils

This popular, mass-market, deep golden Pilsner with a big hoppy flavour (5.1%) comes from the Maes brewery near Antwerp.

Marckloff

A hazy Walloon pale ale (6.5%) which comes from the homebrew café La Ferme au Chêne in Durbuy.

Maredsous

The range of abbey ales from the Moortgat brewery in Breendonk includes a strong, black quadrupel (10%), a dark tripel (8%), a mild-tasting blonde dubbel (6%) and a dark dubbel (6%) and a golden ale with an orange colour. These beers are identified by degree numbers, 10, 8 and 6. They are named after a Benedictine abbey at Denée, south of Namur.

Moinette

These strong ales from the Dupont brewery in Hainaut include a spicy, complex blonde and brune (both 8.5%) and an organic biologique (7.5%).

Mort Subite

These sweet, commercial lambics from the De Keersmaeker brewery include the gentle, amber Mort Subite gueuze, a sweet, cherry-flavoured kriek (both 4.5%), sweet framboise and pêche (both 4%) and a cassis (4%) made with blackcurrant juice. The name means "sudden death" after a card game.

Oerbier

This popular, dark, hazy amber, Scottish - style ale (7.5%) was the first brew produced by De Dolle Brouwers.

Op-Ale

This pale, sweetish, malty ale (4.8%) is produced by the De Smedt family brewery in Opwijk.

Optimo Bruno

This warming Grimbergen abbey beer (10%) comes from the Alken-Maes group's Union brewery.

Orval

This Belgian classic Trappist ale (6.2%) is the only brew made by the Abbaye d'Orval. It is orange, with a heady, hoppy aroma and an intense, dry flavour. Its complex character is in part due to three separate fermentations and dry-hopping.

Oud Beersel

These traditional unfiltered lambics, from the tiny Van-dervelden brewery at Beersel, near Brussels, include Oud Beersel Lambik (5.7%), gueuze (6%) and kriek (7%).

Oud Kriekenbier

This is the only non-lambic cherry beer (6.5%) to be made completely with whole cherries rather than using juice. It is produced by the small Crombe brewery.

Oudenaards Wit Tarwebier

This white wheat beer (4.8%) is produced by Clarysse at Oudenaarde in East Flanders.

Palm

Palm Spéciale (5.2%) is the biggest-selling ale in Belgium. It is brewed by the independent Palm brewery of Steenhuffel. It is an amber, fruity, refreshing beer. A darker version called Dobbel Palm (5.5%), is produced at Christmas. The village brewery, which dates back to 1747, also brews a more powerful, copper-coloured, bottle-conditioned ale, Aerts 1900 (7%), and a wheat beer, Steendonk (4.5%).

Pater Noster

A dark brown, smoky, malt-tasting dubbel (7%) from the Van Steenberge brewery sold under the Corsendonk name.

Pauwels Kwak

This warming, garnet-coloured ale (8%), named after an innkeeper, is served in a distinctive round-bottomed Kwak glass which has to be supported on a wooden stand.

Petrus

The top-fermented beers from the Bavik brewery include a dark imitation of Rodenbach which is matured in oak casks (5.5%). Bavik also brews a golden spéciale (5.5%) and tripel (7.5%).

Poperings Hommelbier

A creamy, hoppy, amber ale (7.5%), this seasonal drink is brewed by the Van Eecke brewery of Watou to celebrate the hop harvest in nearby Poperinge.

Primus Pils

A highly regarded, dry, yellow, hoppy Pilsner (5%), produced by Haacht.

Rodenbach

This distinctive ale (5%) is made by blending a vintage brew, which has been matured in oak casks for over a year, with fresh, young beer, which has only been matured for five to six weeks. A quarter of the old ale is mixed with three-quarters of the new. The resulting beer is so tart that it is sweetened with sugar to produce a refreshing sweet and sour taste. Some of the vintage brew is bottled

unsweetened and undiluted to create the much-bolder Grand Cru (6.5%). There is also a sweeter version, blended with cherry essence, called Alexander (6.5%).

Rose de Gambrinus

The most celebrated lambic frambozen (5%), which comes from the Cantillon brewery in Brussels. It contains a small proportion of cherries and a dash of vanilla, as well as raspberries. It is blood-orange-coloured, wih a tart, fruity flavour.

St Benoît

The fine abbey beers from the Du Bocq brewery of Namur include a yellow, wheaty St Benoît Blonde and amber-brown brune (both 6.5%) with a fresh, dry, woody flavour, besides a hoppy golden tripel (8%), which is also sold as Triple Moine.

St Idesbald

These unusual, sour abbey beers come from the Damy brewery in east Flanders and include a licht and dubbel (both 6%), as well as a dark tripel (8%).

St Louis

The Van Honsebrouck brewery produces this range of sweet commercial lambics, including a gueuze, kriek, framboise and cassis (all 5%). There is also a more characterful, unfiltered Gueuze Fond Tradition (5%).

St Sebastiaan

These abbey beers from the Sterkens brewery of Meer, close to the Dutch border, are sold in distinctive pottery bottles. The beers include a Grand Cru (7.6%) and a dark (6.9%) which is also sold as Poorter.

St Sixtus

See St Bernardus.

Saison de Pipaix

The small Vapeur brewery produces this refreshing spicy saison (6.5%).

Saison Régal

A spicy, hoppy saison-style, amber-coloured beer (6%) from Du Bocq in the province of Namur.

Saison de Silly

A fruity saison beer (5%) produced by the Silly brewery in Hainaut.

THE LAMBIC HELPER

Thousands of tiny yeast organisms are carried on cool evening air currents through the open windows of lambic breweries. Inside the dark, dusty interiors (for lambic brewers know better than to remove the cobwebs and moulds from the brewery walls) the yeasts settle on cobwebs and into damp nooks and crannies. Some find their way into the open vats of cooling beer, where they begin to feast on the sugars and ferment the brew. These untamed, wild helpers produce an ale that is tart and refreshing. Trusting to the action of wild yeasts borne invisibly in the air is the oldest fermentation method in the world, and their effect was once regarded by brewers as nothing short of magical. The lambic brewers of Belgium, though they now understand the source of their help, have maintained this ancient tradition.

Satan

Strong red, gold and brown ales (all 8%) from the Block brewery of Peizegem.

Sezuens

A hoppy, sunny, gold-amber, saison ale (6%) which comes from the Martens brewery of Bocholt. It follows the saison style of thirst-quenching beers, which are brewed during the winter for drinking in summer. Martens also brews a stronger, amber-red Sezuens Quattro (8%) and the less-powerful Sezuens Europe (6.5%).

Silly Brug-Ale
This fruity beer (5%) comes from the Silly brewery in the town of the same name.

Sloeber
The Roman brewery produces this rich, malty, strong, golden ale (7.5%) in the Duvel style. The name means "joker".

Steenbrugge Dubbel
This abbey ale (6.5%) comes from the small Gouden Boom brewery in Bruges.

Steenbrugge Tripel
This creamy, golden abbey beer (9%) from Gouden Boom is less heavy than the brewery's Brugse tripel.

Stella Artois
Belgium's best-known, golden lager is the flagship Pilsner (5.2%) of the brewing giant Interbrew.

Stille Nacht
Dolle Brouwers produces this strong, orangey, seasonal, bottle-conditioned ale (9%) in winter. The name comes from the German title for the popular carol, "Silent Night".

Straffe Hendrik
This heavily hopped pale ale (6.5%) is the only beer produced by Straffe Hendrick, Bruges.

Titje
A distinctive, cloudy, gold wheat beer (5%) with a fruity, spicy flavour from the Silly brewery.

Tongerlo
Abbey beers from Haacht brewery include a double blonde (6%), brune (6.5%) and amber tripel (8%).

Unic Bier
A characterful, weak table beer (3.2%) from Gigi, a fine example of this style.

Verboden Vrucht
The name of Hoegaarden's distinctive, strong, orangey-coloured dark ale (9%) means "forbidden fruit", and it is also sold as Fruit Défendu in France. When customs officials in the United States saw the sexy label of Adam and Eve, based on a Rubens painting, they tried to ban bottles of the revealing brew.

Vieille Provision
An excellent, hoppy, saison-style ale (6.5%) which comes from the farmyard Dupont brewery. It is also known as Saison Dupont and Vieille Réserve. This classic country beer has a complex, refreshing taste and a solid creamy head.

Vieux Temps
Interbrew's malty, pale ale (5%) from Leuven, is popular in the south of the country. Its name means "old times".

Vigneronne
A tart lambic (5%) made from green grapes and blended lambic beers, from the Cantillon brewery.

Westmalle
Both the dark dubbel (6.5%) and the golden tripel (9%) from this monastic brewery have a secondary fermentation. They are then primed with sugar and given a dose of yeast before being bottled. The dubbel is complex and surprisingly dry. The tripel has many imitators. It is extremely pale with a delicious citric and honeyed flavour.

Westvleteren
A range of much-sought-after beers produced by the small Westvleteren monastery, including a dark, fruity special (6.2%) and a similar and stronger extra (8%) leading up to a stern but rotund abt, which at 11.5% is one of the strongest beers in the country. All are on the sweetish side for Trappist ales. The bottles are identified by the colour of their crown corks – red for special, blue for extra and yellow for abt.

Witkap
This range of quality abbey ales, named after the monk's cowl, come from the Slaghmuylder brewery in Ninove, which was founded in 1860. The Witkap beers include the hoppy pale Stimulo (6%), a rich Dubbel Pater (7%) and a golden, bitter, fruity tripel (7.5%).

Yperman
A robust pale ale (6%), from the Leroy family brewery near Ypres.

THE BREWERS

Abbaye d'Orval

Abbaye d'Orval is the most attractive of the Trappist monasteries, set in woodland above a lake in the rolling hills of the Ardennes. Though an abbey has stood on this site near Florenville since 1070, it was repeatedly sacked and the present stone buildings were only planned in 1926. Five years later, construction was still not finished, so, to provide funds to complete the grand scheme, the community decided to add a brewery, the outside of which is designed like a chapel. It opened in 1931, and drinkers have been giving thanks for this brew ever since.

Orval means "Vale of Gold", and the true treasure of the Orval monastery is its one precious beer. Unlike the other Trappist breweries, Orval does not brew a range of beers, but produces one delicious, intensely dry ale. The monks at the monastery also produce a crusty bread and a fine cheese which go well when eaten as accompaniments to a bottle of Orval.

Abbaye des Rocs

This commercial brewery in Montignies-sur-Roc has been producing strong Walloon ales since 1984. It is best known for its dark, spicy Abbaye des Rocs and golden La Montagnarde (both 9%).

Achouffe

This farm brewery in the Ardennes uses its own spring water for brewing. Its bearded gnome symbol has been a familiar sight in this holiday area since 1982.

Alken-Maes

The Belgian arm of the French brewing giant Kronenbourg controls a fifth of the Belgian beer market through its Cristal Alken and Maes Pilsners, as well as other brands such as Grimbergen abbey ales and Mort Subite lambics.

Artois

Best known for its international Pilsner brand, Stella Artois (5.2%), Artois was founded in Leuven in 1366. Now it is part of Interbrew, the second-largest brewing group in Europe. A massive new brewery opened in Leuven in 1995, alongside the huge original plant.

Bavik

A regional brewery in Bavikove in West Flanders, Bavik was founded in 1894. It produces a range of Pilsners and a witbier, plus top-fermented ales under the Petrus name.

Belle-Vue

The largest brewer of lambics, Belle-Vue has two breweries on the edge of Brussels – a traditional plant at Molenbeek and another operation at Zuun. The Molenbeek brewery has more than 10,000 wooden casks filled with maturing lambic. The quality of these brews is largely unknown because they are diluted with immature young lambics which have been brewed in steel cylinders at Zuun. Since 1990, the Molenbeek plant has also produced an excellent, unfiltered Séléction Lambic (5.2%). Belle-Vue exports its beers to France under the Bécasse brand name.

Binchoise

This small Hainaut brewery was founded in 1989 in an old maltings. It produces a range of strong, spiced ales, notably the citric blonde, which is also sold as Fakir (6.5%) and a honey beer, Bière des Ours (9%).

Block

Brewers at Peizegem in Brabant since 1887 who are best known for their wide range of Satan ales.

Bockor

This regional brewery in Bellegem, West Flanders, founded in 1892, is best known for its Pilsner and Jacobins range of lambic beers. It also brews a brown beer, Bellegems Bruin (5.5%), in which corn is added to the mash and mixed with a lambic brew.

Boon

The pioneering brewer, Frank Boon, helped to revive interest in the ancient lambic style when he started to brew and blend in Lembeek in 1975. His beers include a sweetish Boon gueuze, kriek and frambozen, plus a sourer range which is sold under the Mariage Parfait label. He also brews a weak table beer (2%) called Lembeek and a heavy mix of lambic, pale ale and sugar called Pertotale Faro (6%).

Bosteels

The Bosteels family brewery has been operating in Buggenhout, East Flanders, since 1791. It is famous for its garnet-coloured Pauwels Kwak beer (8%) drunk from its distinctive round-bottomed glass. Bosteels also brews Prosit Pils (4.8%).

Brunehaut

A former African brewer, Guy Valschaerts, established this brewery in 1992 at Rongy in the Hainaut region of Belgium. Brunehaut's beers include an organic wheat Blanche de Charleroi (5%), a juniper brew Abbaye de St Amand (7%) and a golden Bière du Mont St Aubert (8%), besides its original blonde and ambrée ales.

Cantillon

This working brewery museum produces true lambics in the back streets of Brussels. Run by the Van Roy family since 1900, it is famous for its brewing open days. Its uncompromisingly sour beers include a Cantillon lambic, kriek, super gueuze and a gueuze matured in port casks, called Brabantiae (all 5%).

CHIMAY

Chimay is the largest and most internationally famous of the Belgian Trappist breweries. It has been brewing beer on a commercial scale at the Abbaye de Scourmont near Chimay since 1862. The brewery is located behind the walls of the abbey and uses its wells, but the work, as at other Trappist breweries, is carried out largely by secular staff under the monks' supervision. Bottling is handled at a modern plant in nearby Baileux. Chimay brews three distinctive ales, each known by the red, white or blue cap on the bottle. Chimay Rouge, or red (7%), was the original beer produced at the monastery, and was the only product for almost a century.

The quality of the beers owes much to a Belgian scientist, Professor Jean De Clerck of Leuven University, who helped the monastic brewery get back on its feet, after the disruptions of the Second World War, by developing its distinctive yeast strain. When he died in 1978, he was buried at the abbey.

The monastery also produces a range of foods, including some excellent cheeses, which go well with Chimay beer. One, called Chimay à la Bière, has a rind steeped in hops.

Caracole

A small brewery in Falmignoul, near Namur, Caracole produces a wide range of Walloon strong ales under the sign of the snail, including Caracole ambrée and brune (both 6.5%), an annual Cuvée de l'An Neuf for the New Year, and a good wheat beer called Troublette (5%).

Clarysse

Clarysse has been brewing in East Flanders at Oudenaarde since 1946. It produces mainly brown ales under the Felix name, and is a local rival to the neighbouring Liefmans Brewery. It also brews a wheat Oudenaards Wit Tarwebier (4.8%).

Crombe

A small village brewery in Zottegem near Ghent which dates back to 1798. Crombe is best known for its Oud Kriekenbier (6.5%), the only non-lambic cherry beer to be made completely with whole cherries rather than juice.

De Dolle

See panel opposite – *The Mad Brewers*

De Keersmaeker

This lambic brewery in Kobbegem mainly brews commercial lambics under the Mort Subite brand, but also produces a more traditional gueuze (5%) which is marketed under its own name.

De Koninck

The De Koninck brewery was founded in 1833 in Antwerp. It stuck to producing ale when most of its rivals switched to brewing Pilsners, and it has thrived.

De Smedt

A wide range of abbey beers, notably the Affligem range but also Abbaye d'Aulne, are produced by this enterprising family brewery which has been based in Opwijk since 1790. Other beers include a pale Op Ale and the wheat beer Celis White.

De Troch

One of the oldest lambic brewers, De Troch dates back to 1820 in Wambeek. It produces a rare orangey-coloured, sour gueuze and a sweet, fruity kriek (5.5%), but concentrates on a range of weak lambic fruit beers under the Chapeau brand.

Du Bocq

This family brewery, located at Purnode in Namur province since 1858, brews an excellent, if confusing, range of ales, often under a variety of labels. Best known for its La Gauloise beers, it also produces abbey ales under the St Benoît name, a wheat beer Blanche de Namur (4.3%) and a spicy, hoppy Saison Régal (6%).

Dupont

This family farmhouse brewery at Tourpes in Hainaut has been operating since 1850. It produces an excellent saison Vieille Provision (6.5%) and a range of Walloon strong ales under the Moinette label. It also brews organic (biologique) versions of these beers, as well as a strong New Year beer.

Eupener

An old brewery in the border market town of Eupen which has its roots firmly in Germany. This small German-speaking area east of Liège was taken over by Belgium after the First World War. Besides a pleasant pils (4.7%), Eupener brews a sweetish, tawny bock called Klosterbier (5.5%) and two dark, low-alcohol, table beers in the German Malzbier style.

Facon

A family brewery at Bellegem in West Flanders since 1874, which until recent years concentrated on Pilsners and weak table beers. Today it also brews specialist ales, including a dark Scotch Ale (6.1%) and an Extra Stout (5.4%).

Friart

An attractive, old, red-brick Hainaut brewery in Le Roeulx, which was closed in 1977 but reopened in 1988, Friart mainly brews abbey beers under the St Feuillien name. These include a heavy, roasted Cuvée de Noël brewed for Christmas. Some beers are sold in huge six-litre Methuselah bottles.

THE MAD BREWERS

When three brothers rescued an old brewery from closure in 1980 in Esen, near Diksmuide in West Flanders, their bank manager thought they were insane, but the success of their dark Scottish-style ale, Oerbier (7.5%), proved otherwise. De Dolle Brouwers now produce a range of strong and seasonal bottle-conditioned ales including the strong Christmas brew, Stille Nacht (9%), Ara Bier, Boskeun and Oeral.

Gigi

This old Gérouville brewery in Luxembourg province produces the best weak table beers in Belgium, notably the lightly hoppy Double Blonde (1.2%) and the characterful Unic Bier (3.2%). It also sells pale and brown ales (5%) under the La Gaumaise label.

Girardin

This small traditional farm brewery at St Ulriks Kapelle produces fruity lambics from its own wheat, notably Girardin lambic, gueuze and kriek (all 5%). It also produces an aromatic Framboos using raspberries in the brew.

Haacht

The largest independent brewery in Belgium has been operating in Boortmeerbeek in Brabant since 1890. It mainly produces a range of lagers, notably Primus Pils (5%) and a premium Adler (6.5%). It brews a wheat beer Haacht (4.7%), two strong, sweetish brown ales – Charles Quint (6.7%) and Gildenbier (6.6%) – plus a range of abbey beers under the Tongerlo name.

Interbrew

The Belgian brewing giant was formed in 1988 by the merger of Artois and Jupiler. It has bought up several smaller Belgian brewers and produces a large range of brews on home soil. Following the takeover of Canadian brewers Labatt in 1995 and expansion into Eastern Europe after the fall of the Iron Curtain, it is now one of the largest brewing groups in the world, with interests around the globe.

KWAK

The story of Kwak is a marketing lesson in how to make your beer stand out at the bar. In a land where every brew seems to have its own distinctive glass, the Bosteels brewery of Buggenhout went one better and

designed a glass which could not stand up on its own. Every time a customer asks for a Kwak, it is served in a tall glass with a round bulbous bottom held erect by a wooden stand. Everyone in the bar knows at a glance when you order a Kwak. Pauwels Kwak (8%) is a warming, garnet-coloured ale named after a famous innkeeper who used to serve beer in stirrup cups to horsemen, for drinking in the saddle.

Lefebvre

Brabant brewery in Quenast since 1876 which produces a wide range of ales, notably the Floreffe abbey beers.

Liefmans

Liefmans is the classic producer of East Flanders brown ales. Its stronger beers are sold in corked bottles, tissue-wrapped for laying down in the cellar to improve with age. All the beers are matured for three months in the bottle before leaving the brewery.

Lindemans

A farmhouse lambic brewer in Vlezenbeek since 1816, Lindemans now sells its beers as far from home as the US. The demands of the world market have led to a range of sweetish lambics including Lindemans faro, gueuze, kriek and framboise. It has recently launched a more distinctive range called Cuvée René, named after the owner.

Martens

This is one of the largest independent breweries in Belgium, but it is still family-owned. Martens has brewed at Bocholt in Limburg since 1758 and is best known for its Sezuens beer, though it also brews a wheat beer, Limburgse Witte (5%), a range of Pilsners and a tafelstout.

Moortgat

A family-owned brewery in Breendonk, north of Brussels, famous for its delicious flagship ale, Duvel.

Riva

Ambitious Flanders brewing group based in Dentergem which includes Liefmans. Best known for its Lucifer ale (8%) and Dentergems witbier.

Rochefort

The least known and most secretive of the Trappist breweries is situated deep in the Ardennes, at the Abbaye de St Rémy near the town of Rochefort.

The first brewery at the abbey, which used its own hops and barley grown in the grounds, dated from 1595, but the present one was built in 1960. More of the monks are involved in day-to-day brewing than at other blessed breweries, and three typically rich, dark Trappist beers are produced. These are all in the same basic style, but increasing in strength from the 6 (7.5%) through the 8 (9.2%) to the ultimate 10 (11.3%), and are known by their degree numbers.

Until quite recently, labels were not used; instead, the three beers were identified by the colour of their bottle caps – red for the 6, green for the 8 and blue for the 10. The chestnut-coloured and powerfully fruity 8, a complex, richly textured and richly rewarding beer is the most popular by far. The lighter, drier 6 is sold only locally, while the near-black 10 is overpowering in its heavy intensity.

Roman

A large, family brewery near Oudenaarde, Roman dates back to 1545. It brews a range of East Flanders brown ales including Oudenaards (5%), the soft, bitter special (5.5%) and bottle-conditioned Dobbelen Bruinen (8%). It also brews a Christmas ale and various Pilsners mainly under the Romy brand, a wheat beer, Mater, and abbey beers under the Ename name.

St Bernardus

This West Flanders brewery, founded in 1946 at Watou specializes in producing abbey beers, both under its own name and that of St Sixtus, after the nearby brewing monastery at Westvleteren. The beer is matured for three months and then bottled without filtering. At one time the monastery used to licence the brewery to produce imitations of its own beers. St Bernardus brews a dark pater (6%), prior (8%), a golden tripel (7.5%) and a strong abt (10%).

St Jozef

Limburg family brewery in Opitter which produces a strong reddish lager Bokkereyer (5.8%).

Silly

Brewery in the Hainaut town since 1950 which brews a vast range of beers including Saison de Silly (5%).

Slaghmuylder

Ninove brewery best known for its quality abbey beers sold under the Witkap label.

Straffe Hendrik

This small brewery in the centre of the city of Bruges brews one ale, Brugse Straffe Hendrik (6%), the classic, hoppy Belgian pale ale.

Timmermans

Lambic brewers in Itterbeek since 1888, their range of lambics includes a fine kriek and Gueuze Caveau (both 5%), plus lighter, aromatic framboise, pêche and cassis (all 4%). They also brew a refreshing lambic wheat beer (3.5%) and a red Bourgogne des Flandres (6.5%).

Vander Linden

A small lambic brewer in Halle since 1893, Vander Linden brews a stronger than average range of lambics, which include a frambozenbier (7%), and the Vieux Foudre gueuze and kriek (both 6%). It also produces Dobbel Faro (6%) and an unusual Duivelsbier.

Westmalle

This Belgian monastic brewery, more than any other, has influenced and defined the abbey style. The monastery near the village of Westmalle, close to the Dutch border near Antwerp, was founded in 1794 by monks from the La Trappe monastery in France. It has been brewing since 1836, but only on a commercial scale since the 1920s. It is now the second largest of the five Belgian Trappist breweries. The brothers brew the defining dark dubbel and tripel. There is also a single, but this everyday drinking beer (4%), also known as Extra, is kept mainly for the monks themselves. The monks also produce a range of cheeses for sale.

Westvleteren

The St Sixtus abbey at Westvleteren, near Ypres in West Flanders, has been brewing since 1839. It is the smallest of the Trappist breweries. Its old brewery is small and its brews are much sought after, partly because they are difficult to obtain. The local beer drinkers queue at a hatch when they hear that a batch of bottles is ready for sale.

In order to meet growing public demand after the Second World War, the Westvleteren abbey for a time licensed the commercial St Bernardus brewery in nearby Watou to brew imitations of its St Sixtus beers. This licensing arrangement has now ceased, but St Bernardus still brews Sixtus beers for the nearby St Sixtus abbey.

RODENBACH

Rodenbach is one of the most remarkable breweries of Belgium. When you walk down the lines of upright old oak tuns, it is like stepping back into another age. The great porter breweries of England once looked like this, but only in Rodenbach have the imposing vessels survived to this impressive extent. There are 300 altogether, filling several halls. Some hold as much as 60,000 litres (13,198 gallons) and are over 100 years old.

The brewery, in Roeselare in West Flanders, was founded in 1820 and came to specialize in the region's sour red beers. A reasonably conventional ale is brewed, using Vienna crystal malt to impart a red colour. Rodenbach's distinct character arises from the way it is then matured. After a second fermentation, the beer is left in huge oak tuns for at least 18 months. During this time, it ages and sours. The inside of the tun is bare and uncoated, so the beer is also flavoured through direct contact with the wood.

Rodenbach only produces three beers – Rodenbach, Grand Cru and Alexander – sometimes called the Burgundies of Flanders. Other more conventional breweries have attempted to imitate these classic ales, but rarely use the same demanding craft.

THE NETHERLANDS

Wedged between the quality brewing found in Germany and the rich variety of Belgium, Dutch beer has always been a little flat in comparison. The country is best known for its international brands.

THE NETHERLANDS has suffered more than most countries from the concentration of its brewing industry into just a few hands. In the late 19th century over 1000 breweries existed, mainly concentrated in the south of the country due to the influence of the anti-alcohol Protestant church in the north. Now only about 30 breweries remain. The standard product of the early breweries was a traditional sweet, weak, brown table lager called oud bruin and brown dark boks (a Dutch style in its own right), but these styles were mostly usurped in the 20th century by a ubiquitous, rather bland, golden lager beer.

The international giant Heineken now dominates the beer market, closely followed by the Belgian giant Interbrew which in 1995 took over Oranjeboom. The Netherlands is also the home of one of the largest privately owned breweries in the world, Bavaria, which produces own-brand lagers for supermarkets around Europe. However, as the Dutch interest in speciality beers grows, small brewers producing more interesting varieties appear all the time, influenced by both the Belgian and German traditions.

Ales are the main area of interest in the Dutch micro-brewery movement, with many new alts, Kölsch-style ales and the occasional wheat beer. Some major producers have also added meiboks and dark boks to their product lines. Abbey-style beers are brewed by some secular breweries, either under licence or independently. The Netherlands is also the home of the Koningshoeven "Schaapskooi" brewery – the sixth Trappist brewer (the other five are in Belgium) producing top-fermented ales.

Above: Dutch lager brands such as Amstel have become familiar in many countries. Their fame is mainly a product of the companies' effective marketing.

THE BEERS

Alfa

A range of all-malt beers from the brewery of the same name, including a full-flavoured Edel (Noble) Pils, which is lagered for two months (5%), and two of the better Dutch boks – Lente Bok, brewed in the spring, and the darker Alfa Bokbier, (both 6.5%), brewed in the autumn. Alfa also produces an unfiltered midzomerbier (3.9%) in June.

Amber

This amber-coloured, top-fermented, alt-style ale (5%) from Grolsch has a good bitter, hoppy flavour.

Amersfoorts Wit

This spicy wheat beer (5%) is brewed by Drie Ringen in Amersfoort.

Ammeroois

A strong, bottle-conditioned ale (7%) from the Kuipertje brewery in Heukelum.

Amstel

Heineken's second-string brand name covers a range of beers, including a light lager, a hoppy Amstel 1870 (5%), the stronger Amstel Gold (7%), a robust dark, malty Amstel bokbier (7%) and the pale Amstel Lentebok (7%).

Arcener

See Arcen.

Bavaria 8.6

The numbers in the name refer to the strength of the beer (8.6%). It is brewed by the independent Bavaria brewery.

Bethanien

The Kölsch-style Bethanien (4.5%) is brewed by the Maximiliaan brewpub.

Brand Dubbelbok

A ruby-red, bottom-fermented, bok-style beer from the Brand brewery. A gold, top-fermented meibok (7%) is also brewed.

Briljant

A malty, mellow dort (6.5%) produced by the Kroon brewery of Oirschot.

Budel Alt

A deep-amber, smooth, strong, German-style ale (5.5%) with a nutty, malt flavour from the Budel brewery.

Buorren

This copper-coloured, sourish ale (6%) is produced by Us Heit.

Capucijn

This opaque-amber, fruity, smoky, abbey-style beer (6.5%) is brewed by Budel. The name – meaning a monk's cowl – is a reference to the religious connection of the abbey beer style.

Casper's Max

A tasty, copper-coloured, malty, sweet tripel (7.5%) produced by the Maximiliaan brewpub in Amsterdam.

Château Neubourg

This "luxury" brew (5%) is the top Pilsner from the Gulpener brewery near Maastricht.

Christoffel Blond

This quality all-malt, bottom-fermented beer (5%) is dry and heavily hopped. It is unfiltered and unpasteurized, and is available in bottle-conditioned form, including 2-litre (3.5-pint), swing-stoppered jugs. The brewery also produces a good Munich-style lager.

Columbus

A strong, blond ale (9%) brewed by the home-brew house t'IJ in Amsterdam.

Dominator

A rich, fruity dort (6%) from the Dommelsch brewery. It is also sold under the brand name Hertog Jan Speciaal.

Drie Hoefijzers

See Oranjeboom Pilsner.

Drie Ringen Hoppenbier

A powerfully hoppy, rich fruit and malt-flavoured beer (5%) from the "Three Rings" brewery.

Egelantier

A copper-coloured, full-bodied, Munich-style lager (5%) which is produced by the Kroon brewery of Oirschot.

Enkel

See La Trappe.

Frysk Bier

This bitter, pale ale (6%) is brewed by Us Heit.

Gladiator

This strong, golden brew (10%) from the Gulpener brewery was launched in 1996.

Gouverneur

A bronze, sweetish Vienna-style lager from the Lindeboom brewery of Neer.

Grand Prestige

This powerful, dark, barley wine (10%) is produced by the Arcen brewery.

Grolsch Bokbier

This sweet, dark bok (6.5%) is a less well-known, but fine brew from Grolsch. There is also a dry, golden meibok.

Grolsch Pilsner

A fresh, hoppy Pilsner (5%), which is brewed using only malt, hops, yeast and water, and left unpasteurized in the bottle. (The canned premium lager is pasteurized.)

Gulpener Dort

A mellow, malty strong lager brewed using maize and caramel (6.5%) in the mash, which comes from the Gulpener brewery.

Heineken Oud Bruin

This smooth, lightly hopped weak table beer (2.5%) for easy drinking was first brewed over 50 years ago. There is also a stronger Heineken Special Dark (4.9%) for export.

Heineken Pilsner

A universally popular but rather bland Pilsner (5%). This is the Dutch giant's flagship brand.

Imperator

A quality all-malt, amber bokbier (6.5%), brewed using pale, chocolate and Munich malts by the Brand brewery of Wijlre.

Jubileeuw

An all-malt Pilsner (5%) from the Leeuw brewery.

Koningshoeven

See La Trappe.

Korenwolf

An aromatic, spicy, white beer (5%) from the Gulpener brewery. Korenwolf is made not only from wheat and barley but also oats and rye. It is named after the grain-loving hamster.

Kylian

Heineken's newly introduced top-fermented red ale (6.5%) with a smooth, gentle hops flavour, is based on the George Killian's Bière Rousse based on the old Irish recipe that is produced by its French subsidiary company, Pelforth.

La Trappe

A range of four Trappist top-fermenting, bottle-conditioned ales from the Koningshoeven Trappist monastery. The beers rise in strength starting from the pale-amber, fresh, fruity enkel (5.5%). Enkel is one of the few "single" strength Trappist ales brewed for the monks' everyday consumption that is available commercially. The dark, deep-red, dry dubbel (6.5%) is the next strongest brew, followed by a paler, bronze-coloured, spicier tripel (8%). The rich, reddish-coloured, vintage, heavyweight brew quadrupel (10%) makes an ideal nightcap for the dedicated beer drinker.

Lente Bok

One of the better Dutch boks, Lente Bok (6.5%) is brewed by Alfa.

Lingen's Blond

A weak table beer (2%) produced by Heineken.

Maltezer

A strong, malty dort lager (6.5%) from Ridder of Maastricht.

Maximator

A strong, spicy wheat beer (6.5%) produced by Maximiliaan, an Amsterdam brewpub opened in 1992, with the plant actually in the bar.

Maximiliaan Tarwebier

A sweetish tarwebier (5%) is brewed at the Maximiliaan brewpub. "Tarwebier" means "wheat beer".

Mestreechs Aajt

A refreshing sweet-and-sour, low-gravity summer brew (3.5%) from the Gulpener brewery. Mestreechs Aajt is a blend of oud bruin and a wild, spontaneously fermented beer, which has been aged in wooden tuns for a year.

Mug Bitter

This English-style Mug Bitter (5%) is brewed by the t'IJ micro-brewer.

Natte

This dark, abbey-style double ale (6%) is another beer brewed by the t'IJ micro-brewery.

Oranjeboom Pilsner
This mild, golden Pilsner (5%) is the main brew from the Drie Hoefijzers brewery in Breda.

Parel
A flavoursome, pale-gold, creamy, Kölsch-style beer (6%) from the Budel brewery of North Brabant.

Quintus
Rare old brown ale (6.5%) from the tiny Onder de Linden brewery in Wageningen.

Robertus
This reddish, malty bottom-fermenting beer (6%) from Christoffel is sold in bottle-conditioned form, unfiltered and unpasteurized.

Schele Os
This outstanding Belgian-style pale ale (7.5%) is an aromatic, orange ale made from barley, wheat and rye, by Maasland in Oss.

Sjoes
Some Dutch drinkers like to mix their dry Pilsner with a sweet oud bruin. Gulpener produced Sjoes (4.5%) with the two beers ready-mixed in one bottle.

Struis
This spicy, fruity dark brew (10%) is another strong ale from the t'IJ brewpub. The name means "ostrich" which is the brewpub's symbol.

Super Dortmunder
As strong as the name implies, this is the strongest Dutch dort available. At 7%, it is a ripe, fruity, export-style lager, brewed by the small Alfa brewery.

Superleeuw
This strong, rich, malty dort (6.5%) is brewed by the independent Leeuw brewery.

Sylvester
A strong, fruity, copper-coloured, top-fermented, winter ale (7.5%), from the Brand brewery of Wijlre.

Tarwebok
One of Heineken's new, more adventurous range of beers. This rich, dark wheat bok (6.5%) was introduced in 1992.

Urtyp Pilsner
This all-malt Urtyp Pilsner, also known as UP (5%), is brewed by Brand.

Valkenburgs Wit
A fruity, unfiltered wheat beer (4.8%), introduced in 1991, it comes from the Leeuw brewery of Valkenburg.

Van Vollenhoven Stout
Described as a stout, this full-bodied bottom-fermenting beer with added caramel and sugar is really a creamy, dark lager (6.5%). It is brewed by Heineken, and named after a brewery the giant company took over and closed down.

Venloosch Alt
A malty alt (4.5%) from the Leeuw brewery near Maastricht.

Volkoren Kerst
A Belgian-style, malty-brown winter ale (7%) from the Maasland brewery in Oss.

Wieckse Witte
Wieckse Witte is a softly spicy, lemony-tasting cloudy wheat beer (5%) from the Heineken subsidiary brewery, Ridder of Maastricht.

Witte Raaf
A tart, fruity wheat beer (5%) from the Raaf farmhouse brewery in Gelderland. The name Raaf means "raven".

Zatte
This abbey-style tripel (8%) with a spicy, hoppy taste is brewed by the home-brew house t'IJ.

Trading tradition

It should come as no surprise that the world's biggest beer exporter, Heineken, is a Dutch company. The Netherlands has a long history of vibrant overseas trade. It is one of the great maritime nations of the world, and its merchants have been shipping goods across the high seas for centuries.

THE BREWERS

Alfa
This independent family brewery at Schinnen has a reputation for quality all-malt beers, brewed using its own spring water.

Amstel
This Amsterdam brewery was bought by Heineken in 1968. Its name lives on as a Heineken brand.

Arcen
A pioneer of speciality beers in Limburg since 1981, Arcen's early emphasis on ales has recently switched to more mainstream lagers. Its beers appear under both the Arcener and Hertog Jan labels, including an abbey-style dark dubbel (7%) and an amber tripel (8.5%).

Bavaria
The large, independent Bavaria brewery has been brewing at Lieshout since 1719. It has flourished by brewing own-label Pilsners for supermarkets.

Brand

The Brand brewery at Wijlre, with its individual range of beers, claims to be the oldest in the country, dating back to the 14th century.

Budel

The small independent brewery at Budel near the Belgian border has been operating since 1870. It brews a Budel Pilsner and an unusual range of strong ales.

Christoffel

The small brewery was established by Leo Brand of the Dutch brewing family in Roermond in 1986 to brew quality all-malt beers. It is named after the town's patron saint. Its Pilsners are regarded as some of the best in the world.

De Kroon

The small independent brewery at Oirschot dates back to 1627. "The Crown" produces a range of full-flavoured lagers: light and dark bokbiers (all 6.5%), a brown Egelantier and a dort called Briljant.

Dommelsch

The brewery at Dommelen produces mainly Pilsners. Its Pilsner (5%) is also sold as Hertog Jan Pilsner. Dommelsch also brews a darker bokbier (6.5%).

Drie Ringen

"Three Rings" beers have been brewed in Amersfoort since 1989. It is now one of the larger of the new ventures. Its brews include a wheat beer, a pale ale, a meibok and an amber tripel.

Grolsch

Probably as well-known for its bottle as its beer, this large independent brewery in Groenlo was founded in the 17th century by Peter Cuyper. It stuck by its distinctive, swing-stoppered bottles, which date from 1897, when other breweries were phasing them out, claiming that they had become too expensive. However, the old-fashioned container became the company's most well-known characteristic. Grolsch's bottled Pilsner is sold unpasteurized, even in the export version. The company has been expanding into other countries since the early 1990s.

Gulpener

Brewing in the southernmost tip of the Netherlands, near Maastricht, since 1825, Gulpener is probably one of the most innovative of the country's more established companies. It produces a range of Pilsners, an oud bruin, and a dort. Gulpener has also developed two Dutch versions of Belgian-style beers.

Koningshoeven

The Gospel and the glass have never been more intimately connected than in the birth of the only Trappist brewery outside Belgium, established in 1884 in Koningshoeven, near Tilburg. The beer came first – the Schaapskooi (Sheep's pen) brewery was originally set up by the monks in order to fund the building of the monastery. Fortunately for the holy community, the blessed beer proved popular. The monastery's initial brews were lagers, thanks to a Bavarian brewmaster. The monastery introduced top-fermenting, bottle-conditioned ales in the 1950s. Today, there are four beers produced under the La Trappe brand, and also sold under the Koningshoeven label.

Leeuw

The independent Lion brewery was established in Valkenburg near Maastricht in 1886 on the site of a former gunpowder factory with a giant waterwheel. Today it brews a range of lagers including an all-malt Pilsner Jubileeuw brewed in honour of the centenary celebration in 1986, as well as an alt, an oud bruin, a winter wit, a meibok and a bokbier (6.5%).

Lindeboom

The small independent Linden Tree brewery was founded in 1870 in Neer, north of Roermond.

Today the brewery produces a variety of lagers including a Vienna-style Gouverneur, a quite bitter, dark, dry Lindeboom bokbier and a sweetish meibok (both 6.5%), as well as a dryish Pilsner (5%) and an oud bruin.

Maasland

This brewery was set up in 1989 in Oss and has been described as the Netherlands' best brewer of spiced ales. Besides the Belgian-style beers, there are two tasty boks.

Oranjeboom

The Orange Tree brewery, founded in Rotterdam in 1671, was once one of the largest breweries in the Netherlands. However, it was closed in 1990 and production moved to the Drie Hoefijzers (Three Horseshoes) brewery in Breda.

Oudaen

A grand brewpub in Utrecht, Oudaen is known for its wheat beers, including a strong tarwebok (6.8%).

Raaf

The Raven farmhouse brewery in Gelderland was revived in 1983, brewing a wide range of beers, including a tasty tripel (8.5%).

Ridder

The Knight brewery was founded in 1857 on the banks of the River Meuse in Maastricht. It brews a cloudy wheat beer, Wieckse Witte, a malty dort, Maltezer, a dark Ridder bokbier (7%) and a Ridder Pilsner (5%).

t'IJ

Probably the most striking home-brew house in the world. t'IJ, situated on Amsterdam's waterfront, is topped by a windmill. Established in 1984, the beers include two abbey-style beers and two strong ales – the blond Columbus and dark Struis. The last name means "ostrich", which is the brewpub's symbol. t'IJ also brews an English-style Mug Bitter.

Us Heit

Founded in a cowshed in Friesland in 1985, the Our Father brewery produces a good range of sourish ales. It also brews a bokbier (6%) and two Pilsners (both 5%).

THE HEINEKEN STORY

Heineken's giant strides through the world of brewing began on December 16, 1863, when 22-year-old Gerard Adriaan Heineken bought the Haystack brewery (founded in 1572) in Amsterdam. His intention, he told his mother, was to tackle the staggering problem of alcoholism by offering the public a light beer as an alternative to the widely consumed strong spirits like gin. He found a ready market. Haystack was the largest brewery in the city, but he soon outgrew it and five years later a larger brewery was opened in Amsterdam. By 1874 the ambitious brewer

was already exporting, and in 1886 Heineken employed Dr Elion, a pupil of Louis Pasteur, to help develop a consistent Pilsner.

Heineken began to export its beers as far as Indonesia after the First World War. In 1933 the brewery made the first legal beer shipment to the United States after Prohibition ended, and today Heineken is the leading imported brand in the United States.

Heineken has acquired stakes in local breweries around the world and built foreign plants, so that Heineken now has over 100 breweries throughout the world.

Only the American giant Anheuser-Busch brews

more beer, but while Anheuser is primarily a US brewer, Heineken is an international force. The vast bulk of its business is outside the Netherlands. It sold 6.7 million hectolitres (147 million gallons) in 1996 in its native land, compared to 1,553 million worldwide. Heineken beer is sold in 170 countries; its second brand Amstel is available in 85.

Heineken in the Netherlands operates two vast plants at 's Hertogenbosch and Zoeterwoude, as well as

owning Brand and Ridder. Its old city brewery in Amsterdam is now a visitor centre.

Heineken concentrates on producing beers which appeal to the widest possible taste. However, since the early 1990s it has started to produce all-malt beers, rejecting the cheaper adjuncts like corn used by many major brewers. It has also extended the variety of its beers.

LUXEMBOURG

The Grand Duchy of Luxembourg, despite its position in the heart of Europe's brewing lands, is not famed for its beers. However, this tiny country has a proud brewing history and rolls out a surprisingly large quantity of beer each year.

ALTHOUGH IT IS BORDERED by Germany and Belgium Luxembourg's brews are more similar to those of its other neighbour, France. Luxembourg beers have neither the exciting variety of Belgium nor the purity of Germany, (brewers often use adjuncts in the mash). Nevertheless, Luxembourg has a long brewing tradition that can be traced back to the abbey at Altmünster in 1083. The abbey is the site of Les Brasseries Réunies de Luxembourg Mousel et Clausen, one of Luxembourg's leading brewers.

BASCHARAGE (Gr. D. Luxembourg)

This small country has two other large brewing companies, Bofferding, which merged with Funck Bricher in 1975 to form Brasserie Nationale, the largest group, and Diekirch, which has brewed in the city of the same name since 1871. These breweries mainly brew a mild Pilsner and an export lager, and offer interesting specialities, such as strong seasonal Christmas beers or German-style dunkels.

A major family in the history of brewing in Luxembourg was the Funcks, in particular Henri Funck, whose name is commemorated on the lager Pils produced today by the Mousel group. The Brasserie Henri Funck, which he founded, was in the forefront of brewing technology for years and was among the first brewers to use refrigeration equipment and steel tanks. It became part of the Brasseries Réunies group in 1982.

Above: At the beginning of the 19th century Luxembourg had about 60 breweries. Diekirch is one of the handful of brewers that have managed to survive into the 20th century.

Two of the most interesting small breweries in Luxembourg are the Brasserie Battin, founded by Charles Battin in 1937, which produces four beers sold under the Battin label, and the Wiltz brewery, which has been owned by the Simon family since 1891. This was totally destroyed in the Ardennes offensive at the end of the Second World War and was rebuilt in 1954.

The domestic market in Luxembourg is small, and the main groups survive by concentrating on the export markets, particularly Belgium and France. Almost a third of all the beer produced is exported.

THE BEERS

Altmünster
A firm-bodied, Dortmunder-style beer (5.5%) from Brasseries Réunies.

Bofferding Christmas Béier
This brown, seasonal ale (5.5%) is produced annually by Bofferding.

Bofferding Lager Pils
This refreshing, Pilsner-style lager (4.8%) is brewed using pale malt and corn (maize) and is lagered for a month.

Diekirch Exclusive
A strong, Pilsner-style lager (5.2%) produced by one of the largest brewers in Luxembourg.

Fréijoers
A refreshing, unfiltered beer (4.8%) produced by Bofferding.

Hausbeier
A tasty, all-malt beer (5.5%) brewed by Bofferding.

Henri Funck Lager Beer
This Pilsner (4.8%) is brewed by Mousel to a similar recipe to Mousel Premium. Both use 10% rice in the mash, producing a light, refreshing, bright gold beer.

Luxembourg
Two beers are produced under this brand name, Luxembourg Lager (3%) and the stronger Luxembourg Export (4%). Both are brewed by Mousel.

Mansfeld
A malty Pilsner (4.8%) from Mousel.

Régal
The export-style beer (5.5%) from the Wiltz brewery.

Simon Noël
A rich, dark, Christmas beer (7.5%) from the small brewery in Wiltz, run by the Simon family. They also produce Simon Pils (5.8%) and Simon Régal (5.5%).

THE BREWERS

Battin
This is the smallest of the Grand Duchy's breweries which, along with the similar-sized Wiltz brewery, produces arguably the best beers. Founded in 1937 in Esch-sur-Alzette, it brews an Edelpils, Gambrinus, a fuller-bodied urtyp and darker Battin Dunkel.

Bofferding
The brewery in Bascharge dates back to 1842, and it merged with Funck-Bricher in 1975 to form the country's largest brewing group, Brasserie Nationale. Its main beer is a Bofferding Lager Pils (4.8%), but it also brews an all-malt Hausbeier, a brown Bofferding Christmas Béier (both 5.5%) and the unfiltered, refreshing Fréijoers.

Below: Bofferding, part of Brasserie Nationale, dates back to 1842.

Diekirch
One of Luxembourg's biggest three breweries, this company has brewed in Diekirch since 1871. Besides Diekirch Light (2.9%) and the pale Diekirch Premium Pilsner (4.8%), it brews a mellow, lager, Diekirch Exclusive (5.1%), the amber Diekirch Grande Réserve (6.9%) and a brune (5.2%).

Mousel
Les Brasseries Réunies de Luxembourg Mousel et Clausen brew two similar Pilsners, Mousel Premium and Henri Funck (both 4.8%), and a malty Mansfeld.

Wiltz
This small brewery, founded in 1824, was bought by the Simon family in 1891, who have run it since then. The buildings were totally destroyed during the Second World War.

GERMANY

Drinkers across the world tend to regard Germany as the land of lager, the country where bottom-fermenting beers reign supreme. There is, however, much more to German beer than overflowing steins at the Munich Beer Festival.

Above: *Much of the revival in the popularity of wheat beers has been due to the perceived health-giving properties of the cloudy, yeasty brew.*

No COUNTRY TAKES more pride in the quality of its beer, and although the rules of the beer purity law the Rheinheitsgebot, mean that German brewers cannot indulge in the wilder flights of fancy of the Belgian brewers, there is still plenty of variety to be found, and excellent quality.

Top-fermenting ales are still brewed, notably the alts of Düsseldorf and kölsches of Cologne. There has also been a revival in demand for wheat beers. Within the lager market, beers vary – from sharp, hoppy Pilsners in the north to the softer, maltier brews of Bavaria. The glasses shimmer with all the colours of the ripening barley field, from pale golden helles through copper-coloured marzens and darker dunkels and bocks to black beers. There are even a few exotic types, such as the smoked beers of Bamberg. All of these brews comply with the rules that prohibit the use of cheap adjuncts and inferior materials.

No people are more loyal to their local beers. The beer marketplace is fragmented, regionally oriented and highly conservative. Unlike most other countries, there are few national beer brands. People stick to their home-town brews. This has meant that many more breweries have survived in Germany than in other European countries, with around 1,200 still steaming away. Cologne, a city of only one million people, has 23 breweries, and there are some 700 in the Bavarian countryside, where the clock appears to have stopped in another era altogether and almost every village has its own brewhouse. Some local breweries have closed, but since the late 1970s a new wave has sprung up, with over 150 brewpubs opening in the last 20 years, catering for a wide range of tastes. About 30% of all the breweries in the world are in Germany.

THE BEERS

Abtstrunk
The word "Abt" (abbot) reveals the monastic links of the makers of this thick, potent, liqueur-like beer, (11.5%) which is brewed in a former abbey guesthouse at Irsee near Munich.

Achd Bambarcha Schwarzla
The name of this dark, mellow beer (5.3%) means "true Bamberg black". It is produced by the Klosterbräu in Bamberg, the oldest brewer of rauchbier, dating back to 1533. Its small plant was once run by monks.

Aecht Schlenkerla Rauchbier
This is a classic smoked beer (4.8%) from the Bamberg region. It has a light, fresh, smoked flavour and a dry malt aftertaste. It is produced by the Heller Brauerei in Bamberg for the Schlenkerla tavern.

Alt Franken
See Urfrankisch Dunkel.

Altstadthof Hausbier
A fruity, unfiltered but quite flat, dark lager (4.8%) produced by the small Altstadthof brewery in Nuremberg.

Alt Wetzlar
This is not an Altbier in style, but a dark lager, brewed by Euler in Wetzlar, north of Frankfurt.

Apostulator
A dark, ruby-coloured Doppelbock (7.5%) with a fruity, malt taste. This brew is produced by the Eichbaum brewery of Mannheim.

Arcobräu Coronator Doppelbock
An auburn-coloured Doppelbock (7.5%) with a strong malty flavour, from Graf Arco of Bavaria.

Arcobräu Dunkel Weisse
A cloudy, amber-brown wheat beer (5.2%) with a clean, citrus flavour, from this family owned company.

Arcobräu Urweisse
A refreshing, apple-tasting, unfiltered, cloudy, gold Bavarian wheat beer (4.8%) from Graf Arco.

Astra
A range of gold, hoppy Pilsners from the Bavaria St Pauli brewery of Hamburg. The Astra label also has a gold Bock with a light malt flavour.

Aventinus
This classic, extra-strong wheat beer (8%) or Weizen Doppelbock comes from the specialist wheat beer brewers Schneider of Bavaria. Conditioned in the bottle, Aventinus has a deep reddish-brown colour, a creamy head and a warming, rich, fruity taste.

Ayinger Altbayerische Dunkel
A deep-red lager with a malty flavour and pleasant aftertaste, produced by the quality Ayinger brewery.

Ayinger Bräu-Weisse
A pale wheat beer (5.1%) with a tart, fruity taste, produced by Ayinger.

Ayinger Maibock
A pale-gold, traditional maibock with a complex hop flavour, from the Privatbrauerei Franz Inselkammer in Aying.

Beck's
One of Germany's best-known beers on the international market, this crisp, dry Pilsner (5%) has been brewed in the northern port of Bremen since 1874. It is Germany's leading export beer, with more than six million hectolitres sold every year in more than 100 countries. It accounts for more than 85% of German beer exports to the United States. Beck's also brews a deep-amber, dark beer and a dry, malty Oktoberfest brew.

Bernauer Schwarzbier
This is a very dark, creamy, chocolate-tasting, smooth

Schwarzbier from the Berliner Bürgerbräu. It is named after the town of Bernau, once known for the black beer style.

Bitburger
Bitburger (4.8%) is a dry, aromatic and hoppy Pilsner from Bitburg in the Rhienland. It is allowed to mature for a three months, making it a classic of its style, and the second-best-selling Pilsner in Germany.

Brauhernen Pilsner
A pale-gold, dry, bitter Pilsner with a hoppy aftertaste (4.9%), produced by Einbecker.

Braumeister
This bright-gold Bavarian Pilsner is produced by the leading Munich brewer Hacker-Pschorr. It has a pleasant, toasted-malt and hop flavour.

Bremer Weisse
This refreshing summer beer with only 2.7% alcohol is a Bremen variation of a Berliner Weisse. The producer, Haake-Beck still delivers its beers locally by horse-drawn drays.

Brinkhoff's No. 1
A smooth, bright-gold, premium Pilsner from DUB of Dortmund, this beer is named after an early brewer.

EINBECKER BEER – A MEDIEVAL TRADITION

The reputation of Einbecker beer is said to have been built on a remarkable communal operation. The Lower Saxony town of Einbeck was once the major brewing centre for the medieval Hanseatic League of north German trading towns. It developed a style of strong beers – bocks – brewed to survive long journeys.

In the Middle Ages, every citizen in the town brewed, using a communal copper which was wheeled around 700 homes. The door arches of the old buildings had to be high to accommodate the vessel. The citizens then sold their beer to the town council, which traded it through the Hanseatic League. The strong beer gained a widespread following – even Martin Luther praised it. Its reputation caused the Bavarian dukes to entice an Einbeck brewmaster to Munich, so spreading the brewing of bock – or beck – beer to southern Germany, where it is mainly brewed today.

Broyhan Alt
A strong, malty Altbeer (5.2%) in the Düsseldorf style. This beer is produced by the Lindener Gilde brewery of Hannover and it is named after a famous Hannover brewer.

Busch Golden Pilsner
A golden Pilsner-style beer produced by the local Busch brewery in Limburg near Koblenz. Despite its name the brewery has no connection with America's brewing giant Anheuser-Busch.

Carolus
This very deep, ruby-brown-coloured strong Doppelbock (7.5%) has an unusual, complex, fruity taste. It is brewed by Binding of Frankfurt.

CD
A popular, brilliant-gold, sweetish Pilsner, named after Carl Dinkelacker, who founded the brewery in Stuttgart in 1888.

Celebrator
This export name is mainly used in the US for the classic, dark-red, velvety Doppelbock, Fortunator (7.2%), from the Ayinger brewery.

Clausthaler
This pioneering non-alcohol lager (0.5%) took Binding of Frankfurt years to develop before it was launched in 1979. It virtually created a whole new beer sector on its own.

Cluss Bock
This malty, dark-copper-coloured Bock is brewed by the Cluss brewery.

DAB Original
This is the premium version of Meister Pils from DAB in Dortmund. It is a golden, grassy, hoppy beer (5%).

Dampfbier
Dampfbier is an unusual top-fermented reddish ale (4.9%) from the Maisel brewery of Bayreuth in Bavaria, which is not unlike a fruity English bitter. The word "Dampf" means steam.

Delicator
This dark, fruity Doppelbock (7.5%) is brewed by the famous Hofbräuhaus of Munich.

Diebels Alt
A brown, biscuity Altbier (4.8%) from the Privatbrauerei Diebel in Issum Weidernhein.

Dom Kölsch
A leading kölsch beer in Cologne named after the cathedral.

Dom Pilsner
This dry Pilsner is brewed by the Euler brewery of Wetzlar.

DUB Export
Dortmunder Union Brewery brews this smooth, malty Export (5%). DUB also produces Pilsners, most notably its hoppy Siegel Pilsner and the premium Brinkhoff's No. 1.

Duckstein
An unusual, fruity, amber ale, matured over beechwood chips. It is produced by the Feldschlösschen Brewery of Brunswick.

Echt Kölsch
This delicate beer, regarded as the true Kölschbier, was originally produced at a home-brew pub, P. J. Früh's Cölner Hofbräu, near Cologne Cathedral. Demand became so great, however, that Echt Kölsch is no longer brewed behind the tavern, but at a brewery outside the city centre.

Einbecker Maibock
A deep, golden-amber-coloured, malty, seasonally brewed spring Bock (6.5%) produced by the Einbecker brewery.

Einbecker Urbock
This bright-gold, smooth, strong, hoppy Bock beer (6.5%) is produced by the Einbecker brewery.

EKU Pils

A soft creamy Bavarian Pilsner (5%) brewed by the Erste Kulmbacher Union of Kulmbach, a brewery best known for its heavy, extra-strong lager, Kulminator 28.

Erdinger Weissbier

This range of top-fermented wheat beers from the Erdinger brewery is brewed strictly according to the Bavarian purity law. It includes a cloudy Hefe (5.3%), a sparkling Kristallklar (5.3%) and a reddish-brown, strong, spicy, dark Dunkel (5.6%).

Euler Landpils

This Pilsner comes from the independent Euler brewery in Wetzlar.

Feldschlösschen

Feldschlösschen Pilsner is a leading Pilsner brand for Holsten. The large north German Feldschlösschen brewery in Brunswick is part of the Holsten group. Feldschlösschen also produces the distinctive Duckstein amber ale and Brunswick alt.

Fest-Märzen

This marzen-style beer (5.8%) is produced by Ayinger of Bavaria.

Feuerfest

This dark, fruity, warming "fire festival" Doppelbock (10%) is produced in limited-edition, wax-sealed bottles by Schäffbräu of Treuchtlingen, near Nuremberg in Bavaria.

First

A popular, pale-gold Pilsner (4.8%) with a grainy flavour, produced by Ritter of Dortmund.

Fortunator

This rich, dark-red, velvety Doppelbock (7.2%) is brewed by Ayinger.

Franz Joseph Jubelbier

This strong, dark lager (5.5%) is named after the monarch. It is brewed by the south Bavarian Altenmünster brewery near Augsburg.

Franziskaner

A range of wheat beers from the famous Spaten brewery of Bavaria. The wheat brews, which now account for more than half of Spaten's production, include the cloudy but refreshing hefe-weissbier, a filtered, grassy Kristallklar and a Dunkel (all 5%).

Freiberger Pils

This hoppy Pilsner is the best-known beer from the sizeable Freiberger Brauhaus in the old colliery town of Freiberg.

Fürstenberg Pilsner

The widely available, bright-gold, hoppy, dry premium Fürstenberg Pilsner (5%) is the best-known beer of the Fürstenberg brewery, which also produces a range of other brews including three wheat beers.

Gatz Alt

The brown, fruity Gatz Alt (4.8%) is produced by Gatzweiler, the family brewers of Alt, in Düsseldorf. There is also a non-alcohol version. The original Düsseldorf brewery was in the brewpub Zum Schlüssel and still brews.

Gilde Pils

This pale-gold Pilsner with a dry finish (5%) comes from Hannover's Lindener Gilde brewery. As its name implies, the brewery was once run by a city guild.

Hacker-Pschorr Edelhell

This is one of the stronger speciality beers (5.5%) from the Hacker-Pschorr brewery in Munich, which dates back to 1417. Its more popular lagers are fruity Hell (5%) and Dunkel (5.2%).

Hacker-Pschorr Oktoberfest Märzen

This Märzen beer (5.8%) is brewed in Munich for the famous Oktoberfest, by Hacker-Pschorr.

HB Hofbräuhaus München

The premium lager (4.9%) brewed at the former Bavarian Royal Court brewery in Munich.

Holsten Pils

The widely available premium Pilsner (5%) from the Holsten brewery is one of that firm's famous dry, hoppy range from Hamburg.

Hopf Dunkler-Bock

This unusually rich and tangy Dunkler-Bock wheat beer (6.3%) comes from the small Hopf family brewery in the Bavarian Alps at Miesbach that specializes in wheat beers.

Hopf Weisse Export

The fruity, but not hoppy, Weisse Export (5.3%) is a wheat beer from Hopf.

Hubertus

Hubertus is a robust, copper-coloured Bock (6.8%) from Hacker-Pschorr of Munich. The brewery's doppelbock is called Animator (7.5%).

Jahrhundert

A golden, export-style beer (5.5%) from Ayinger of Bavaria. It was originally produced to celebrate its centenary in 1978.

KALTENBERG CASTLE

Once upon a time, almost all aristocratic families brewed their own beer, and this tradition continues in the fairy-tale Kaltenberg Castle in the village of Geltendorf, 50km from Munich. The spires of Kaltenberg tower over the cellars where the beer is lagered. However, most Kaltenberg beers, including its Pilsner and Prinzregent wheat beers, are now produced at a modern brewery in Fürstenfeldbruck.

flavour. The Bamberg brewery also produces more conventional lagers, Extra-Dry (4.9%) and Pilsner (4.8%), as well as a delicious apricot-coloured Weissbier (5.3%).

Kaiser Pilsner
The black-labelled bottles of this premium Pilsner (4.8%) from Henninger of Frankfurt have become familiar around the world.

Kaltenberg
See König Ludwig.

Kapuziner
A range of wheat beers from the Mönchshof brewery of Kulmbach in Bavaria which has monastic origins. The name means "monk's hood" and the beers include two heady, unfiltered brews, Kapuziner Dunkel and Hefetrub (both 5.2%).

Kindl Berliner Weisse
The pale, sour, refreshing wheat beer (2.5%), once called "the champagne of the north" is a speciality of Berlin. It is often laced with fruit juices. The large Kindl brewery was founded in Berlin in 1872 and brews several conventional beers, including Kindl Schwarzbier. The main rival brewer of Berliner Weisse is Schultheiss.

Jever
This is probably the most bitter beer produced in Germany. Jever Pilsner underlines the general German rule that beers become drier as you travel north. The town of Jever is in Friesland. The brewery of the same name, dating back to 1848, is famed for its Pilsner (4.9%), which has a heady, hoppy aroma and an intense bitterness. Owned by Bavaria St Pauli of Hamburg since 1923, a modern brewery was built in 1992 in this old North Sea resort. Its other brews include Jever Light (2.7%) and the alcohol-free Jever Fun.

Kaiserdom
The most widely available Rauchbier (4.8%) (smoked beer) from Bamberg has been brewed by the Bavarian town's Bürgerbräu brewery since 1716. Although it is not the most intensely smoky beer of its type, it will still surprise the unsuspecting drinker with its fume-filled

Kloster-Urtrunk
The tasty, unfiltered marzen Kloster-Urtrunk (5.6%) is brewed by Irseer Klosterbräu near Munich.

Kloster Urweisse
Kloster Urweisse (5.2%) is a tasty wheat beer from Irseer Klosterbräu near Munich. The name means "original white".

König Ludwig
König Ludwig Dunkel (5.1%) is named after "mad" King Ludwig II of Bavaria. The Dunkel is one of the beers still brewed by Prince Luitpold, heir to the throne of Bavaria, at his Kaltenburg Castle brewery in Geltendorf.

König-Pilsener
A pleasant, dry Pilsner (4.9%), with a faintly appley flavour, from the König brewery, Duisberg.

Korbinian
This dark-amber Doppelbock (7.4%) with a rich, malt flavour, is produced by the Weihenstephan brewery, a former monastery brewery at Freising.

Köstritzer Schwarzbier
Köstritzer Schwarzbier (4.6%) is a smoothly chocolatey, bitter, bottom-fermented beer with a 450-year-old reputation as a sustaining drink for invalids. Goethe drank the revered drop while recovering from illness. It comes from the Köstritz black beer brewery in the former East German spa town of Bad Köstritz in Thuringia.

Kräusen
Kräusen is an unusual, unfiltered, cloudy version of the standard Pilsner, brewed by Haake-Beck of Bremen. It was introduced to the north German market in 1985.

Kronen Classic
This is the golden premium Pilsner (5.3%) with a slightly sour, hoppy taste, from the popular independent, family-owned Kronen brewery in Dortmund. It also brews a robust, malty export.

Kulminator 28

One of the strongest beers in the world, the threateningly named Kulminator 28 has an alcohol content of more than 12% – the highest gravity of any bottom-fermenting beer. The brew is matured for nine months, including a short period of freezing, to produce this intensely malty, heavyweight, amber beer.

There is a less threatening and darker conventional Kulminator Doppelbock (7.6%) without the number. Both of the beers are brewed by EKU in the Bavarian town of Kulmbach, and are widely exported.

Küppers Kölsch

This deep-gold sweetish kölsch comes from the largest brewer of kölsch in Cologne.

Kutscher Alt

A malty, copper-coloured Alt (5%) that is smooth and gently warming. This beer is brewed by Binding of Frankfurt. It is top-fermented, then cold-conditioned in the classic Altbier style.

Lammsbräu Pils

Lammsbräu's pale, amber, delicately fresh and citric organic Pilsner (5%) was introduced in the late 1980s. It is brewed by the small Lammsbräu brewery at Neumarkt, near Nuremberg, using barley and hops grown without artificial fertilizers or pesticides. Some claimed that it was purer than the requirements of the Rheinheitsgebot – much to the annoyance of larger brewers, although this did not prevent others trying their own "bio beers".

Leichter Typ

This light, low-calorie beer from Eichbaum has a strength of just 2%.

Löwenbräu Hefe Weissbier

An unpasteurized, unfiltered, slightly cloudy, wheat beer (5.0%) which comes from the best-known of the Munich breweries. The Hefe Weissbier is produced using Löwenbräu ale yeast, malted wheat, spring barley and Hallertau hops. A filtered version of the Hefe style, which is clear, is also available, called Klares Weissbier. This version has a distinctive flavour rather like a wheaty lager.

Löwenbräu Oktoberfest

A subtle, light, bottom-fermented Reinheitsgebot beer (6.1%) that is specially brewed each year for the Munich Oktoberfest.

Löwenbräu Premium Pils

This light, refreshing, golden lager is made in Munich under the Bavarian purity law, with Hallertau hops, spring barley and yeast.

Maisel Pilsner

This pale-gold, aromatic Pilsner with a good malt and hops taste (4.8%) is brewed by the Maisel brewery, the largest brewery in the famous Bavarian opera town of Bayreuth, which also produces a good range of fruity wheat beers.

Meister Pils

This gold Pilsner with a fresh, zesty taste, comes from DAB of Dortmund. The name, which means champion, is also used by the Schwaben brewery of Stuttgart for its Pilsner.

Mönchshof Kloster Schwarzbier

This deep-copper-coloured Schwarzbier with a smooth, malt flavour comes from the old Mönchshof brewery in Kulmbach, Bavaria. The brewery has monastic origins and is known for its strong, dark lagers.

Oberdorfer

This is a range of wheat beers from the Franz-Joseph Sailer brewery in Marktoberdorf in Bavaria, one of which is sold mixed half and half with lemonade.

Optimator

An orangey-coloured, strong Doppelbock (6.8%) with a smooth, roasted, malt flavour, brewed by Spaten of Munich.

Pikantus

This strong, russet-coloured Weizenbock (7.3%) is brewed by wheat-beer specialists Erdinger of Bavaria.

Pilsissimus

This hoppy Pilsner (5.2%) is very highly thought of by the patrons of the Forschungs brewpub.

Pinkus Hefe Weizen

This cloudy, gold, unfiltered wheat beer (5%) with a citrus and wheat flavour is an organic beer which is produced by the Pinkus Müller home-brew house in Münster.

Prinzregent

This range of wheat beers, named after Prince Luitpold, includes an unfiltered hell, and a brown, spicy, malt-flavoured Dunkel Weissbier (both of them 5%). They are brewed by Kaltenberg in Bavaria.

Radeberger Pilsner

This bright-gold, hoppy Pilsner is the flagship brew of the Radeberger brewery near Dresden in the former East Germany. It was once supplied to the King of Saxony.

Ratsherrn

A brand name that is applied to a hoppy, dry Pilsner and malty Bock from the Elbschloss brewery of Hamburg on the River Elbe. Both beers are unpasteurized.

Ratskeller Edel-Pils

This bright-gold, hoppy, premium Pilsner is brewed by the Lindener Gilde brewery of Hannover.

Rauchenfelser Steinbier

This unique speciality is brewed using an ancient process. When all brewing vessels were made of wood, it was risky to use direct flames to heat them, so instead rocks were fired to high temperatures and then placed in the wort to bring it to the boil. In 1983, Gerd Borges revived this process at Neustadt near Coburg. The white-hot stones not only make the brew bubble, but also cause sugars to caramelize on their surface. The top-fermented beer is then matured for two to three months with the sugar-coated rocks. The result is a tawny-coloured Steinbier (4.8%) that is both smooth and smoky. There is also a Steinweizen made using the same process. In 1993, as part of the Franz Joseph Sailer group, the brewing was moved to Altenmünster in southern Bavaria.

Reichelbräu Eisbock

This is a Bockbier (10%) that is strengthened by freezing for two weeks and removing the ice. The dark, warming brew is then matured in oak casks for two months. It is brewed by Reichelbrau in Kulmbach, Bavaria.

Romer Pilsner

A popular, yellow-gold, dry Pilsner (5%) with a classical image, brewed by the giant Binding brewery of Frankfurt. It is a quality brew with a dry, hop finish.

St Georgen Keller Bier

This is the speciality of the St Georgen brewery, an unfiltered lager (4.9%) bursting with hops, which is even exported in bottle to the United States. The small Bavarian village brewery in Buttenheim brews some of the hoppiest beers in the region, including a very dry marzen (5.6%).

St Jakobus

This quality pale Bock (7.5%) is produced by the Forschungs brewpub in the Perlach suburb of Munich. The brewpub is only open in summer.

Salvator

The pioneer of the Doppelbock style from the Paulaner brewery of Munich. This rich, ruby brew (7.5%) is overpowering with its fruit-cake aroma and deep, warming flavour.

Sanwald

The wheat beers from the Dinkelacker brewery of Stuttgart include a bright-gold, light, dry hefe weiss and a sparkling, tawny-amber Weizen Krone.

Schierlinger Roggen

This rare, red-amber rye (Roggen) beer (4.7%) is brewed by the local brewery in Schierling, Bavaria. Launched in 1988, it is similar to a dark wheat beer, but with a more tangy, grainy taste. The mash contains 60% rye. The brewery was once part of a convent.

Schlenkerla

The classic and most uncompromising Rauchbier (4.8%), this smoked speciality of Bamberg in Bavaria is brewed from malt kilned over beechwood fires. The result is a pitch-black brew with a pungent flavour of burnt malt. This dry, smoky beer used to be brewed on the premises at the Schlenkerla tavern in Bamberg, but is now produced at the nearby Heller brewery dating back to 1678.

Schneider Weisse

A refreshing, yeasty wheat beer (5.4%) brewed by the Schneider brewery. This is the classic example of the Weisse style. Besides the Original Hefeweizenbier the brewery also produces a filtered Kristall, a weaker Weizen-hell (4.9%), and a light (2.9%).

OKTOBERFEST

Mention Germany and beer, and many people envisage Munich's famous Oktoberfest, when in just 16 days, around six million litres (1,319,814 gallons) of beer will be drunk in huge canvas beer halls by thousands of visitors. It is the world's biggest beer festival – though it is not in October, but in the last two weeks of September. This mad annual party began when the Bavarian Prince Ludwig married Princess Theresa in 1810, and the city threw a huge celebration. It was such a success that it has been repeated ever since. Only the six major breweries in Munich are allowed to supply beer – to the annoyance of many other Bavarian brewers. In 1882 Spaten created the amber-coloured, Oktoberfest beer which caused such a sensation that it has been served ever since!

Above: A happy participant of the Munich Oktoberfest at the end of the 19th century, complete with his stein of beer and tobacco pipe.

Left: The Hacker-Pschorr beer tent at the Oktoberfest. Only the six main breweries of Munich are allowed to supply beer at the festival.

Below: One of six million litres of beer being drunk at the Oktoberfest. In fact, the festival takes place at the end of September.

SPATEN AND THE LAGER REVOLUTION

Spaten is a Munich brewery whose name means "spade". It was at the heart of the bottom-fermenting lager revolution, which swept the world in the 19th century. Brewer Gabriel Sedlmayr pioneered the production of dark and amber lagers in the 1830s and later developed the use of refrigeration and steam power. Spaten is still justly proud of its lagers today, notably its malty Münchner Hell (4.8%) and dunkel (5%) and its classic, full-bodied Ur-Märzen (5.6%). It also brews a dry Pilsner (5%), a golden maibock (6.5%) and a strong Doppelbock called Optimator (6.8%). Its range of wheat beers under the Franziskaner label now accounts for more than half of all production.

Schöfferhofer

The range of Bavarian-style wheat beers from Binding of Frankfurt includes a tasty and lively Hefeweizen, a filtered golden, yeasty kristall and a dark dunkel (all around 5%).

Schultheiss Berliner Weisse

This is one of the most distinctive examples of the Berliner Weisse style, the pale, sourish, weak type of wheat beer that is favoured in the north. Major Berlin brewer Schultheiss blends fresh and more mature brews in order to create its bottle-conditioned Weisse (3%).

Schultheiss Pilsner

This hoppy Pilsner is the best-known brew in Germany from the Berlin Schultheiss brewery.

Starkbier

This strong, brown Starkbier (6.8%) has a dry, malty flavour. It is brewed by Irseer Klosterbräu just outside Munich.

Stauder TAG

This is a strong, dry, hoppy Pilsner (5.3%). The initials stand for Treffliches Altenessen Gold. It is brewed by a family brewery in Essen, which was founded in 1867. It also brews a soft standard Pilsner (4.6%).

Stephansquell

An amber, full-bodied Doppelbock (6.8%). This beer is brewed in Freising by the Weihenstephan brewery.

Triumphator

A seasonal, strong Doppelbock brewed by Löwenbräu of Munich.

Ureich Pils

This dry, gold Pilsner (4.8%) with a strong hop taste is the flagship brew from the Eichbaum brewery of Mannheim.

Urfrankisch Dunkel

This dark, malty Dunkel (4.4%) is bottled as Alt Franken. It is produced by the large Nuremberg Tucher brewery, which brews a wide range of traditional Bavarian beers.

Ur-Krostitzer

This crisp Pilsner (which should not be confused with Köstritzer Schwarzbier) comes from the former East German Krostitz brewery in the town of Krostitz near Leipzig.

Urstoff

This heavy, reddish-brown Doppelbock with a smooth, malt flavour, is produced by the Mönchshof Kloster brewery in Kulmbach.

Ur-Weisse

A wheat beer, Ur-Weisse (5.8%) uses 60% wheat in the mash and is bursting with flavour. It is slightly darker and more full-flavoured than the other wheat beers brewed by the Ayinger brewery.

Warsteiner

This bright, pale-gold Pilsner (4.8%) is the best-selling beer in Germany. The family brewery in Warstein has had to double its output over five years to six million hectolitres (1,319,814,000 gallons) in 1995, in order to keep up with demand.

Weizenhell

A slightly hazy, light-coloured wheat beer (4.9%) brewed by Schneider of Kelheim near Regensburg.

Witzgall Vollbier

A sweetish, copper-coloured lager from Schlammersdorf in Franconia.

Würzig

The name, meaning "spicy", is applied to two distinctive bottom-fermenting beers from the Hofmark brewery: Würzig Mild and Würzig Herb (meaning dry), both with a strength of 5.1%.

The former is a malty brew and the latter is sharply hoppy. Known for its distinctive swing-stoppered bottles, the traditional east Bavarian Hofmark brewery dates back to 1590. It still uses beechwood chips to clear its beers.

THE BREWERS

There are so many brewers in Germany that it is impossible even to list every German brewery of note. The following firms are worthy of honourable mention.

MAJOR BREWERIES

Augustiner

This is the least known brewery outside Munich, but possibly the most popular inside the town, probably because it produces lagers most faithful to the Bavarian city's malty tradition. This is especially true of its pale, smoothly soft hell (5.2%). It was once a monastic brewery dating back to 1328. Its connections with the holy order were broken in 1803. Its grand 19th-century brewhouse, built in 1885, is now a protected building. It has its own maltings in cellars beneath. Locally, some of its beers are still served from wooden casks.

Ayinger

"The most beautiful thing about Munich is the road to Aying", claims this well-respected country brewer, and it is not far wrong. This family brewery lies at the heart of a picturesque Bavarian village on the edge of the Alps, with its own guest house and beer garden. The beer matches the surroundings. The brewery produces a wide range of specialities: a Hell, an Altbairisch Dunkel, a Pilsner, three Bocks, a golden export-style beer called Jahrhundert-Bier, a Fest-Märzen, three Ayinger wheat beers, and a standard Hefe Weisse Bräu-Weisse (5%).

Binding

Binding is Germany's second-largest brewing group. The company is based in Frankfurt, where it celebrated its 125th anniversary in 1995.

The large brewing group includes DAB of Dortmund, Kindl of Berlin, and the Radeberg and Krostitz breweries in the former East Germany.

Binding has the distinction of having virtually created the alcohol-free beer market in Germany with its dominant Clausthaler brand, which it launched successfully in 1979. This now contains (0.45%) alcohol. German law specifies that non-alcoholic beer should not contain more than (0.5%) alcohol which is about the same percentage as apple juice.

The company also brews Romer Pilsner, two Binding Exports, a Doppelbock Carolus, a range of popular wheat beers under the Schöfferhofer brand name and Kutscher Alt.

PROTECTING THE CONSUMER

The German beer purity law, the Rheinheitsgebot, was first introduced in Bavaria in 1516 by Duke William IV, only gradually spreading to the rest of the country this century. The ruling – one of the world's first consumer protection laws – insisted that beer should only be made from malt, hops and water (yeast was not at first mentioned, as its working was not understood). It ensured that cheap adjuncts and sugars were not used, and that no beer was as wholesome as German beer. In 1987, the European Court ruled that the law was a trade barrier, preventing foreign beers being imported. Although the German government could not then stop beers which did not conform to the purity law crossing the border, German brewers resolved to stick to the ruling. It was a wise decision, as drinkers voted with their glasses to stay loyal to their pure beer. The Rheinheitsgebot is now seen as giving German beer a vital marketing edge in a competitive world.

Beck's

An innovative brewer, Beck's of Bremen has been brewing its famous Beck's Pilsner in the northern port since 1874. Early in the 20th century it was one of the first breweries to invest in ice machines and to cultivate a pure yeast culture. In 1917 it merged with its main export rival in Bremen, St Pauli. Between the wars the company also built two overseas breweries in Singapore and Djakarta in Malaya, these were lost in 1945 but Beck's licensed a brewery in China in 1992. Its sister company Haake-Beck brews a range of beers for the local market.

THE ROYAL BREWERS

World-famous for its beer hall in the heart of Munich, the Hofbräuhaus (HB) has the distinction of being the royal brewery. The royal connection dates back to 1589, when the Duke of Bavaria, Wilhelm V established the brewery.

Now owned by the state, it has only started to market its beers in recent years, cutting the number of brands down to two main ones – a wheat beer and its golden lager Hofbräuhaus Original München (4.9%), besides a number of seasonal specialities such as a maibock, marzen and Christmas Doppelbock called Delicator (7.5%).

Today, the HB brewing plant is located outside the city, next to the old airport. It is the smallest of the big six breweries in the beer capital.

Hofbräuhaus means "court brewhouse", and since Germany was once divided into many dukedoms and principalities, there are a number of royal breweries. The Hofbräuhaus Freising, originally owned by a bishop, is now run by Count von Moy. Located north of Munich, it claims to be the oldest brewery in Germany, dating back to 1160. It is best known for its wheat beers. Bavaria also boasts a Hofbräu Abensberg and a Hofbräu Berchtesgaden. Hofbräuhaus Wolters of Brunswick, now owned by the Lindener Gilde Brewery of Hannover, brews a hoppy Pilsner.

Brau und Brunnen
Germany's leading brewing group includes DUB of Dortmund, Küppers of Cologne, Bavaria St Pauli of Hamburg, and Einbecker and Schultheiss of Berlin.

DAB
Dortmunder Actien Brauerei, incorporated in 1868, is one of the north German city's three main breweries, all famous for their big, bold Export (or Dortmunder) beers. Dortmund is Germany's largest brewing centre and only beers brewed there are allowed to be called Dortmunder. DAB's Export is malty and dry, but the firm now concentrates more on its DAB Meister Pilsner. It also brews an altbier, a maibock and a DAB Tremanator Doppelbock. Local rival Hansa is now part of DAB.

DOM
One of the larger Kölschbier brewers in Cologne. The name of the brewery means "cathedral".

DUB
Dortmunder Union Brewery, the main rival to DAB with a towering brewhouse in the centre of the industrial city, was formed from the merger of a dozen breweries in the late 19th century. It brews a smooth, malty DUB Export but recently has concentrated on brewing Pilsner, notably Siegel Pilsner and the premium Brinkhoff's No.1.

Diebels
The largest brewer of Alt beers is based not in Düsseldorf but in the village of Issum near the Dutch border. Diebels is still a family firm. Founded in 1878, the brewery also produces light and low-alcohol versions of its well-known Diebels Alt.

Erdinger
Germany's biggest brewer of wheat beers was founded in 1886. The company buys much of the wheat it uses locally and even supplies local farmers with seed to ensure it receives the right kind of wheat. It brews a range of popular, light wheat beers, including Erdinger Kristall, Hefe and Dunkel (all 5.2%) and a stronger Weizenbock, Pikantus (7.3%).

Eichbaum
One of Germany's oldest brewers, established in Mannheim in the heart of the Rhineland in 1679, Eichbaum produces a wide range of beers, including a very dry Ureich Pilsner, Eichbaum Export Altgold (5.3%) and three wheat beers, and range in strength from a light, low-calorie Leichter Typ to a powerful dark Apostulator Doppelbock. Part of the third-largest brewing group led by Henninger, Eichbaum (the name means oak tree) also owns the Freiberger Brauhaus of Freiberg.

Hacker-Pschorr
Late in the 18th century, Joseph Pschorr built huge underground beer stores in Munich, making it possible for beer of consistent quality to be brewed all year round. The brewery was the first to export draught beer to the US in the 19th century. Since 1976, Hacker-Pschorr has been linked to Paulaner. The brewery brews a Hell (4.9%) and a Dunkel (5%).

Henninger

This Frankfurt brewery has an international reputation and its beers are sold in over 60 countries. It is the fifth-largest brewery in Germany. The brewery's 110-metre (361ft) high silo tower, containing 16,000 tonnes of barley, is one of Frankfurt's dominant landmarks.

Holsten

This internationally well-known Hamburg brewery was founded in 1879, and is famous for its dry, hoppy range of Pilsners, including Holsten Pils, the local Edel Pilsner and more widely available Premium Bier. Holsten also brews an export and a maibock (which is exported under the name Urbock).

The company owns a number of other German breweries, including Sächsische in Dresden. Holsten rivals Beck's as the leading beer exporter of Germany.

Above: Löwenbräu beer is famous the world over. The brewery produces wheat beers as well as Pilsners.

Klosterbräu

The name means "monastery brewery". Some German abbeys do still brew, such as the Benedictine Kloster brewery at Andechs in Bavaria, but they do not produce their own distinctive beers like the Trappists in Belgium. The Andechs abbey brews beers in the style of its home region, notably a pale Spezial and a Doppelbock. The Kloster title is also adapted by many commercial breweries with monastic connections, such as Irseer Klosterbräu and the Klosterbräu at Bamberg, which is the oldest producer of smoky Rauchbier.

Krombacher

This prominent specialist Pilsner brewer in Kreutzal-Krombach produces more than four million hectolitres (21,996,900 gallons) a year of its hoppy Krombacher Pils, one of the best-selling brand in Germany.

Löwenbräu

The Munich brewery with the highest international profile. Its beers are brewed around the world. In Bavaria, it brews malty lagers, from a Hell and a Dunkel to a hoppy Pilsner and strong Oktoberfest (6.1%). It also produces a range of wheat beers and runs the largest beer hall in Munich (the Mathäser holds 5,000 drinkers). Löwenbräu means "lion brew" and there are a number of other lesser-known Löwenbräu scattered around the country.

Paulaner

The largest brewery in Munich is also credited with having created the Doppelbock style. First established as an abbey

brewery in 1634 by the community of St Francis of Paula, it became known for its powerful Lenten beer. Commercial brewers took over in the early 1800s and developed this rich, ruby brew, calling it Salvator (saviour). Other brewers copied this Doppelbock, using similar names, and a new style was born. This complex dark beer became the standard-bearer of the brewery. Paulaner's firm, dry beers include Münchner Dunkel, an original hell, a pale Pilsner, and a Hefe Weissbier.

Schneider

The most celebrated specialist wheat beer brewers in Bavaria since 1872, Schneider offers the classic example of the cloudy, yeasty style in the spicy Schneider Original Hefe Weizenbier. There is also a sparkling kristall and a light (2.9%). Schneider is still a family-owned company, that brewed first in Munich and then in Kelheim, near Regensburg, from 1928.

Spaten-Franziskaner-Bräu

The famous brewery in Munich, founded in 1397, was originally named after the Späth family. In 1922 it merged with Franziskaner-Leistbräu.

OTHER OUTSTANDING BREWERS

Bavaria St Pauli

This brewery is in the St Pauli area of Hamburg in northern Germany. It brews mainly Astra Pilsner.

Bitburger

This Pilsner specialist was founded in the town of Bitburg in the Rhineland in 1817 and brewed one of the first Pilsners in 1883.

Einbecker

Part of the Brau and Brunnen group, the Einbecker Bräuhaus brews three malty Urbock-style beers – Hell, Dunkel and Maibock (all 6.5%). It also brews a Brauherren Pilsner (4.9%).

Above: The immaculate Schneider Weisse brewery in Kelheim near Regensburg. This family firm of specialist wheat brewers moved to Kelheim from Munich in 1928.

Below: The modern plant of Bitburger, the Pilsner specialist brewer. Bitburger Pils is exceptionally dry with a clean finish.

Füchschen

Im Füchschen (The Fox) is one of four home-brew pubs in Düsseldorf brewing its own malty Altbier.

Fürstenberg

The aristocratic family of the Fürstenbergs were first granted the right to brew by King Rudolf of Habsburg in 1283. Based in the Black Forest at Donaueschingen, their brewery uses water from a spring in the grounds of Fürstenberg Castle.

Gaffel

Founded, it is claimed, in 1302, this brewery in the centre of Cologne is known for its kölsch.

Garde

Some believe this brewery produces the definitive, fruity kölschbier at Dormagen-bei-Köln.

Hannen

Hannen, founded in 1725, is one of the leading brewers of Alt in Düsseldorf. It also brews Carlsberg in Germany.

Hansa

The light beers, including an export and Pilsner, of this famous Dortmund brewing name are now made mainly for supermarkets by DAB.

Herforder

Predominantly a Pilsner brewery in Herford near Hannover. As well as its full-bodied Pilsner (4.8%), it brews a malty export, a maibock and sommerbier.

Hopf

The family-owned brewery of Miesbach brews only wheat beers.

Irseer Klosterbräu

The village of Irseer, south-west of Munich, is dominated by the former monastery. Irseer Klosterbräu is a grand guest house with its own brewery, a small beer museum and vaulted Keller.

König

The name means "king". The large family-owned König brewery of Duisburg in the Rhineland hopes to be crowned king of the premium Pilsner. In 1995 its aromatic Pilsner (4.6%) was the fifth-best-selling brand in the country.

Above: The Pinkus Müller Altbierhaus in Munster in 1928.

Königsbacher

The brewery was founded in 1689 in the city of Koblenz where the Rhine and Moselle meet. It is best known for its hoppy Pilsner, but also produces an Alt and a powerful Urbock (7.3%).

Küppers

This is the largest brewer of kölschbier in Cologne. Besides a sweetish kölsch, it also brews an unfiltered version called Wiess.

Moravia

The name of this brewery in Lüneberg pays tribute to the Czech origins of the Pilsner style. It produces a hoppy, dry Pilsner.

Pinkus Müller

This historic home-brew pub has been brewing and serving beer in Münster since 1816. Pinkus Müller is now run by the fifth generation of the Müller family. Despite its small size, the brewery ships its beers around the world. Since 1990, all Pinkus beers have been produced organically.

The brews include an unusual pale alt beer (5%) brewed using wheat in the mash, which is matured for six months, developing a distinctive sourish, lactic taste. The brewery also produces a bottom-fermenting special (5%) and a golden Pilsner.

Rhenania

This independent family brewer in Krefeld, near Düsseldorf, was founded in 1838. It produces one of Germany's more widely available alts.

Ritter

This Dortmund brewery is now part of the larger Dortmund giant DUB. The brewery produces a good range of fruity beers, including a strong, flavoursome export and a golden-coloured, hoppy First Pilsner (4.8%).

Below: Brass bands, national costume and beer are essential parts of the Oktoberfest.

St Pauli Girl

The sister brewery to Beck's in Bremen, St Pauli Girl produces a similar beer. The odd name is derived from its Girl brand featuring a popular German barmaid. The beer is very popular in the US.

Spezial

The oldest Rauchbier (smoked beer) brewer in Bamberg, dating back to 1536, Spezial produces a lightly smoky brew called Lagerbier (4.9%) plus a more intense Märzen and a Bock at its home-brew pub.

Thurn und Taxis

An aristocratic Bavarian family brewery in Regensburg, Thurn und Taxis dates back to 1834. It produces a Pilsner (4.9%), a pale export (5.5%) and hell hefe weissbier (5.5%). The family still lives in the ornate Schloss St Emmeram in Regensburg. The brewery, which owns a number of other Bavarian breweries, was sold to Paulaner in 1997.

Uerige

The high altar of Alt. This rambling Düsseldorf tavern, Zum Uerige, has, since 1862, brewed the definitive version of this copper-coloured, top-fermenting beer, deep in flavour and bitterness. In the town it is known by the locals as "dat leckere Droppke" – that fine drop. The shining brewery can be seen from one of the many bars in the tavern.

Unertl

This tiny Bavarian brewery in Haag, east of Munich, has developed a big reputation for its delicious dark, organic wheat beers, notably its sourly fruity hefe weissbier (4.8%) and hefe weizenbock (6.2%).

Veltins

This specialist Rhineland Pilsner brewer led the fashion for premium brands with its sweetish Pilsner.

Weihenstephan

This brewery has long been a Bavarian institution. The former monastery brewery at Freising not only claims to be the oldest working brewery in the world, going back more than 950 years to 1040, it is also the home of Munich University's internationally famous Faculty of Brewing.

The modern hill-top brewery is now owned by the Bavarian Government, and sells its extensive range of excellent beers commercially. The brews include a malty hell, a dark, flavoursome dunkel, a hoppy, dry Edelpils and a range of deliciously fruity wheat beers.

Zum Schlüssel

The Schlüssel brewpub was the first Düsseldorf home of the Gatzweiler Alt brewery. Zum Schlüssel (the name means "The Key") still brews its own malty Schlüssel Alt.

Above: Serving beer in a hotel in Germany. The waitress appears to have four hands!

SMOKY SECRET

The Franconia region of Germany, in particular the small, beautiful medieval town of Bamberg, has maintained a smoky tradition. Here malt is produced for local brews over beech-wood fires, giving it and the final beer a lightly smoked taste.

Bamberg has nine breweries for only 70,000 people. The classic producer is probably the Brauerei Heller Trum, which makes Schlenkerla.

Right: The Schlenkerla Tavern is the main outlet for the Heller Trum brewery's smoked beers.

AUSTRIA

Pilsners may rule the world, but in the mountain fastness of Austria it is a different story. Most Austrian beer follows the style pioneered by Anton Dreher in 1841 – a darker, reddish-amber lager.

THE BULK OF AUSTRIAN BEER still draws on the original malty style, which was a halfway house between bottom-fermenting, brown beers of Munich and the golden Pilsners of the Czech Republic. This beer is known simply as lager or sometimes Märzen, indicating its darker origins in the old, dark lager styles, though it is now more like a deeper Bavarian Hell in colour. A fuller-bodied version is called Vollbier. Between them lager and Vollbier account for almost 80% of the Austrian beer market. The hoppier, drier Pilsner takes little more than 6%, while wheat beers, so popular in nearby Bavaria, manage just over 1%. Stronger lagers are referred to in ascending order of strength as Spezial, Bock and Starkbier. Weaker, low-alcohol styles are usually called Leichtbier or Radler.

Austrian beer is distinct from German brews. The country is not governed by a beer purity law, and allows the use of adjuncts (unmalted cereals) such as rice or corn in its brews, which tend to give Austrian beers a cleaner, less complex flavour. The structure of the Austrian brewing industry is much simpler than that of Germany. Although there are some 60 breweries, including a few new brewpubs and micro-breweries, two groups dominate: Brau AG in the west and north, and Steirische in the south. Schwechater, the brewery where Anton Dreher worked his magic, once controlled Vienna. Each of the two main groups courted this family firm with its aristocratic connections, and it was finally taken over by Brau AG in 1978. High society in the capital was shocked – the beer-brewing family of Mautner-Markhof had fallen.

Above: Austria is famed for its unique reddish-amber lagers, but Zipfer's pale lager appeals to more modern Austrian taste buds.

Since 1993, Brau AG and Steirische (made up of Gösser and Reininghaus) have combined with other Austrian breweries in a new Brau Union to expand into Eastern Europe, buying up breweries in Hungary and the Czech Republic.

THE BEERS

Adam Spezial
See Adambräu.

Adambräu
A refreshing alpine lager (5.2%) that is now brewed in Brau AG's Bürgurbräu brewery in Innsbruck. There is also a stronger Adam Spezial (5.7%), and a brown, malty festbier.

Columbus
A rich, malty, well-hopped lager (5.3%) from the Stiegl brewery.

Edelweiss
Austria's most popular range of wheat beers is produced for the Brau AG group by Hofbräu Kaltenhausen of Hallein near Salzburg. The beers tend to be lighter in flavour than their Bavarian counterparts and there is a full range: cloudy-gold Edelweiss Hefetrüb with a spicy, malt taste; filtered (and therefore clear), bright Edelweiss Kristallklar; and darker-amber Edelweiss Dunkel (all 5.5%). There is also a stronger Edelweiss Bock (7.1%).

Gold Fassl Pils
This crisp, dry, pale-gold, hoppy Pilsner (4.6%) is one of the range of beers produced by the Ottakringer brewery of Vienna, a local independent brewery.

Gold Fassl Spezial
A full-bodied, meaty, malty Spezial (5.6%) produced by the Ottakringer brewery.

Gösser
This is probably Austria's best-known international brand name. It is produced by the Gösser brewery in Leoben-Goss. The range includes a light lager Gösser-Gold, the gold, malty Gösser Märzen, a fruity, malty Gösser Spezial and a deep-brown, full-bodied, sweet Gösser Export.

Hirter
This is a range of beers from the brewery of the same name. The golden Export Pils (5.8%) is probably the best-known, but there is also a Märzen (5%), an unfiltered Zwickl (5.2%) and a hefty, strong Festbock (7%).

Hopfenperle
A hoppy premium Pilsner (5.4%) from the Schwechater brewery near Vienna. It should not be confused with the Swiss brewery of the same name.

Kaiser
Kaiser is Austria's leading beer brand. Besides a standard Kaiser draught, the range also includes a malty Vollbier called Kaiser Märzen (5.2%), a Spezial Kaiser Goldquell (5.6%), and a hoppier Pilsner called Kaiser Premium (5.4%). Other Kaiser beers include the dark Doppelmalz (4.7%) and the strong Kaiser Piccolo Bock (7.1%). The Kaiser beers come from the Brau AG group which is the leading brewing group in Austria.

Keller Bräu
This is a range of seven quality beers from the private Kellerbrauerei of Ried. It includes a Märzen, a Pils, a Spezial, a Dunkel and a Festbock.

MacQueen's Nessie
This strong brew (7.5%) claims to be a whisky-malt beer. Nessie does not contain any of the Highland spirit, however, but uses imported peaty Scottish whisky-malt in the mash in order to produce a smooth, smoky, reddish-coloured beer with a biscuity, malt character and a smoky finish. It is one of the speciality brews produced by the Eggenberg brewery.

Morchl
An unpasteurized, malty, dark lager (5%), produced by the Hirter brewery.

Naturtrub
This is the unfiltered version of Keller Bräu's Annen-Bräu.

Nussdorf Doppel Hopfen Hell
A top-fermenting, dry, hoppy brew (3.8%). Hopfen Hell is one of a range of brews from the Nussdorf castle brewery.

Old Whisky
This strong, seasonal (5.5%), top-fermented beer uses whisky malt and is produced by Nussdorf.

Ottakringer Helles
This brew is a distinctive light-gold-coloured lager (5.1%) with a malty flavour, produced by Ottakringer, Vienna's local independent brewery.

Paracelsus
This unfiltered Vollbier (4.9%) comes from the Stiegl brewery of Salzburg.

Privat Pils
A strong, dry, golden Pilsner (5.2%) with a malty flavour, brewed by Hirter.

Ratsherrn Trunk
This tasty Vollbier (5.3%), which is produced by the Bräucommune Freistadt brewery, won a gold medal at the International Monde Sélection competition in Rome in 1995.

St Thomas Bräu
This is a dry, fruity top-fermented Altbier (4.6%) from the Nussdorf castle brewery.

Schlank & Rank

This dry, hoppy, golden Pilsner (4.9%) is produced at Brau AG's Bürgurbräu brewery in Innsbruck under the Adambrau label. The name means "Slim & Trim".

Sigl

A standard bottled lager (4.9%) from the Sigl brewery. It is known for its unusual "beer bop" characters on the labels.

Sir Henry's Stout

This distinctive, hearty, chocolatey stout (5.2%) was the first beer produced by the Nussdorf brewery.

Steffl

This is a gold, malty premium lager (5.4%) from the Schwechater brewery near Vienna.

Vienna brewpubs

The Austrian capital has a number of cellar bars brewing their own tasty, unfiltered lagers, notably Salmbräu which produces a Hell, a Pilsner and a dark malty Bock.

Stiegl Goldbräu

This amber, malty Vollbier (4.9%) is the best-known brew from the Stiegl brewery.

Stiftsbräu

This malty, softly sweet, deep-brown, dark Stiftsbräu (3.6%) is produced by the Gösser brewery.

Trumer Märzen

This classic Vollbier (4.8%) is produced by the Josef Sigl brewery of Obertrum.

Trumer Pils

An excellent extra-dry Pilsner (4.9%), produced by the Josef Sigl brewery. It is traditionally served in a tall, narrow glass.

Urbock 23

This strong, creamy, golden, slightly oaky Bock (9.9%) with a rich malt and hops flavour is allowed to mature for a full nine months in the Eggenberg brewery.

Weihnachtsbock

A deep-gold, rich, malty winter Bock (7%) from the Stiegl brewery in Salzburg. A darker version is brewed as Freistadter.

Weizen Gold

This range of wheat beers produced by the Josef Sigl brewery of Obertrum includes an unfiltered, hazy, gold, spicy Weizen Gold Hefe Hell, a dark-amber-coloured, malty Dunkel and a sparkling malty, Weizen Gold Champagner (all 5.5%).

Wieselburger Stammbräu

A traditional, pale-gold malty Austrian lager (5.4%). This beer emphasizes its history – the Wieselburg brewery dates back to 1770 – both on the label, which shows old lagering casks, and through its use of old-fashioned traditional swing-stoppered bottles.

Wieselburger Spezial

This strong Austrian lager (5.7%) is produced by the Wieselburger brewery.

Zipfer Märzen

A pale-gold, hoppy marzen (5.2%) with a pronounced sour, malt flavour, produced by the Zipfer brewery, part of the Brau AG group.

Zipfer Urtyp

This hoppy, pale-gold Vollbier (5.4%) is produced by the Zipfer brewery in the town of that name.

THE BREWERS

Augustiner

This Salzburg brewery dates back to 1621. It is still owned by the monks of Kloster Mullen, although it is now run by a secular company. The monastery has its own large beer hall where Augustiner Bräu is served in large, stone steins.

Brau AG

The full name of Austria's leading brewing group is Österreichische Brau-Aktiengesellschaft (the Austrian Brewing Corporation). This large company is a major player in the Austrian market and brews every third glass of beer that is sold in the country. The company is based in Linz and has breweries at Schwechat, Wieselburg, Zipf, Hallein (Kaltenhausen) and Innsbruck (Bürgerbräu), which produces regional beers. Its main brand is Austria's most popular draught lager, the sweetish Kaiser Draught. It also sells a wide range of other beers under the Kaiser brand name.

Eggenberg

This small brewery in the town of the same name which lies halfway between Linz and Salzburg produces some rare Austrian speciality beers, most notably the monstrously named MacQueen's Nessie. made with imported Scottish whisky malt in the mash. It also brews one of the strongest beers in the country, the creamy, golden Urbock 23, (9.9%) and a popular gold lager Hopfenkönig (5.3%).

Freistadter

The independent brewery, based in Freistadt since 1777, brews according to the stricter German beer purity law. Best known for its award-winning Vollbier Ratsherrn Trunk (5.2%), it also produces a Freistadter Märzen (4.9%), a dark Freistadter Spezial Dunkel (5.1%), a Freistadter Pils (4.5%) and a Freistadter Weihnachtsbock, which is a robust, full-flavoured, dark winter Bock (6.6%).

Hirter

The independent brewery in Hirt, Karnten, claims to date back as far as 1270. It is best known for its Hirter Export Pils.

Hubertus

The family brewery at Laa an der Thaya, close to the Czech border, is now run by the sixth generation of the Kuhtreiber family. Its well-matured beers, which are brewed to the German beer purity law, include Hubertus Märzen, the dark Hubertus Dunkel, two Pilsners and a strong Hubertus Festbock.

Keller Bräu

The private Kellerbrauerei of Ried, Hochfeld, dates back to 1446. The brewery has been run by the Mitterbucher family since 1926.

Nussdorfer

Baron Henrik Bachofen von Echt established this brewery in the wine cellars of his grand castle at Nussdorf in Vienna in 1984.

Ottakringer

Vienna's local independent brewery is a family firm that dates from 1837. It produces one of the more distinctive Austrian lagers in its Ottakringer Helles. It also brews a speciality Bräune, a Dunkel and a Bock.

Puntigamer

The brewery, based in Graz, produces a range of soft, mild beers, besides two stronger bocks.

Reininghaus

This Graz brewery produces a range of fruity beers.

Schlägl

Abbey in Upper Austria which brews its own beers including a top-fermenting rye beer Goldroggen (4.9%).

Schwechater

Anton Dreher's original brewery on the edge of Vienna betrays its old aristocratic links through grand pavilions and tree-lined courtyards in the brewery grounds. Besides a soft lager, Schwechater Bier (5.2%), it also brews a Schwechater Pils (5.2%), a premium Pilsner Hopfenperle and a Schwechater Festbock (7.1%).

Sigl

There has been an independent Josef Sigl brewery at Obertrum near Salzburg since 1601. It produces probably the best Pilsner in Austria, the deliciously dry Trumer Pils. It also brews a pioneering range of wheat beers under the Weizen Gold brand, a Sigl Bockbier (7.3%) and a bottled lager (4.9%), famous for its odd labels that feature different trendy characters in a "beer bop collection".

Stiegl

Austria's biggest private brewery dates back to 1492. As well as Goldbräu and Pils, it also produces a quality spezial and a winter Bock. Stiegl also has a brewing museum, along with a Bräu Welt (Beer World) experience for visitors, showing how beer is brewed.

Steirische Bräuindustrie

The second largest brewer in Austria is based in Graz. Many of its beers are brewed uner the Gösser label.

Zipfer

This brewery in Zipf, founded in 1858, produces probably the hoppiest beers in the Brau AG group. It produces a range of beers, including a Pilsner and two strong, malty bocks.

Anton Dreher

In the 19th century Anton Dreher, a brewer in Vienna, worked with Sedlmayr in Munich to develop lager brewing. He was the father of Vienna-style lager – an amber-coloured, subtly malty, sweetish, bottom-fermented lager, which is made using "Vienna malt". The pioneering brew was introduced in 1841 (just before the first Pilsner Urquell was brewed). The style proved a popular export, and Dreher went on to found breweries throughout the Austrian Empire – Italy, Hungary, Mexico and Bohemia – and the popular style reached out across the globe. The beer's prominence faded almost in parallel with the decline of the Austrian Empire, and Dreher's Vienna company closed in the 1930s, Vienna-style lager is still brewed in parts of South America and Scandinavia as well as in Europe.

POLAND

Poles enjoy a glass of beer, but for many years small, unmodernized breweries have found it hard to match demand. In addition to this handicap, the hoppy drop has always struggled to fight the dominance of the national drink – vodka.

IN SHARP CONTRAST to its beer-loving neighbours to the west, Germany and the Czech Republic, Poland is a light imbiber, with Poles consuming less than 40 litres (70 pints) per head a year. This is partly because of a strong spirit-drinking tradition (especially in central and eastern areas), and partly because of the tax system that makes beer expensive compared to spirits.

At the turn of the century, Poland boasted more than 500 breweries. Lack of investment, however, meant that many closed. By the late 1980s a common sign in many shops and cafés was "Piwa Brak" – "no beer". Apart from a handful of larger companies like Okocim and the leading exporter Zywiec, most of the 80 or so breweries that remained were small and served a local area. Since the end of Communist rule, however, there have been fundamental changes in the Polish brewing industry. A growing number of breweries have been privatized, often linking up with western breweries to get funding for modernization. Most of the beer is still unpasteurized, although this is rapidly changing as modern processing techniques are introduced. By 1996, seven of the top 10 Polish breweries had some degree of foreign ownership, and the capital was bustling with many brands at higher prices. However, the government is trying to keep control of the industry in Polish hands by restricting foreign ownership of brewing companies to minority holdings.

A light, Pilsner-style of lager dominates, but there are also some fuller-bodied, export-style lagers and a few strong, bottom-fermenting dark brews called porters. These reflect the historical British influence throughout the Baltic. When the Napoleonic Wars stopped the export of British beers, local brewers responded to the existing demand by brewing their own dark beer.

Above: EB is one of the few Polish beers that is regularly exported. It is particularly popular in countries with large Polish communities.

THE BEERS

Dojlidy Porter
A strong, dark porter (9%) that is a typical example of the Polish porter style.

EB Specjal Pils
The mild, fresh, yellow-coloured lager (5.4%) from Elblag's brewery is triple-filtered. The liquor (water) with which it is made is drawn from the brewery's own deep wells.

Eurospecjal
This full-bodied, strong, golden lager (7.5%) is brewed by Zywiec in the city of Kracóv.

Gdańskie
This is one of the leading lagers (5.6%) from the Hevelius brewery which is situated in the shipbuilding city of Gdańsk.

Grodzisk
This rare, top-fermenting beer is said by the brewers to have been brewed since the 14th century in the town of Grodzisk Wielkopolski, near Poznań. It uses a high proportion of smoked wheat and is spontaneously fermented before being bottle-conditioned. The result is a tart, refreshingly sour, hazy golden ale with a heavy, smoky aroma. It is sold in a variety of strengths, the weakest of which is 5%.

Herbowe
A deep-gold, Pilsner-style lager (5.6%) from the Dojlidy brewery.

Hevelius
This super-premium, tasty lager (6.1%) is brewed by the firm of the same name in city of Gdańsk.

Kaper
A special, extra-powerful, malty, deep-gold lager (8.1%), which is brewed in Gdańsk by the Hevelius company.

BEER POWER

Poles undoubtedly love their beer. A political party, the Polish Beer Drinkers Party (PBP), which campaigned on a ticket of loving beer, holds several seats in the Polish parliament. The party, which started as a joke, now campaigns to deregulate the beer trade, and it publishes a weekly newspaper, *Kurier Piwny (The Beer Courier)*.

Karmelowe
A dark, low-gravity beer (3.5%) from the Okocim brewery.

Krakus
The soft, malty lager (5.4%) from the Zywiec brewery is named after the old name for the city of Kracóv.

Krolewskie
Krolewskie is brewed by the city of Warsaw's local Warszawski brewery. Before the end of Communist rule, this full-bodied lager (5.6%) was almost the only one that drinkers could find in the shops of Warsaw.

Lech Pils
A yellow-gold, hoppy, malty Pilsner (5.3%) from the Lech brewery.

Lech Porter
A strong, dark, cherry-coloured beer (7.4%) from the Lech brewery.

Lech Premium
This strong, malty, golden lager (5.4%) is one of Lech's leading brands.

Magnat
A full-bodied, strong golden lager (7.4%) from the Dojlidy brewery.

OK Jasne Pelne
Okocim's yellow-gold, malty "full light" lager has a strong, hoppy finish. It comes in various strengths.

Okocim Porter
A strong, dark, bottom-fermented porter (9%) from Okocim.

Warszawski Porter
A rich, dark, bottom-fermented porter (9%) from the Warsaw brewery.

Zywiec Full Light
This is a hoppy, fruity golden lager (5.6%), from Poland's famous Zywiec brewery, using fresh mountain water from Mount Skrzyczne.

Zywiec Porter
This rich, mahogany-coloured beer (9.2%) from Zywiec has heavy hints of roasted coffee and currants in the flavour.

THE BREWERS

Dojlidy

Located in Bialystok since 1891, this local brewery is typical of many of the smaller Polish breweries. It produced less than 200,000 litres (14,200 gallons) in 1992 while waiting to be privatized. Besides its main lagers, Zlote and Herbowe, it also produces Gotyckie, Magnat and Dojlidy Porter.

Hevelius

Founded in 1871 as the Danziger Aktien-Bierbrauerai-Kleinhammer in the port of Gdańsk, it was nationalized after the Second World War as Gdańskie Zaklady Piwowarskie. It was modernized in 1991 and renamed Hevelius that year, after the Polish astronomer. In 1996 the German brewers Binding took a 49% stake.

Above: The Old Town marketplace in Warsaw with open-air cafés and an old-fashioned horse and carriage designed for tourists.

Elbrewery

This is now the largest brewing company in Poland, and it controls nearly one fifth of the beer market. Elbrewery was founded in 1872 as the Brauerei Englisch Brunnen Elbing in the northern town of Elbing. The original name of the brewery demonstrates the early influence of English merchants in the Baltic beer trade.

The company, which also has a second modernized brewery in nearby Braniewo, really took off with the involvement of the Australian company Brewpole in 1991, followed by investment by the large Grolsch company of the Netherlands in 1995. Its flagship brew is the golden EB Specjal Pils.

Lech

Founded in 1951 in Poznań in west Poland, Lech also has a second brewery in Ostrow Wielkopolski and substantial maltings, making it the fifth largest brewer in the country. Following privatization in 1993, the firm is now owned by a Polish investor EAC, with a 15% share stake held by South African Breweries. It is best known for the golden lagers it produces – Lech Pils and Lech Premium – as well as the special, cherry-coloured Lech Porter.

Okocim

After Zywiec, this is the best-known Polish brewing company, with plants in Okocim, Kracóv and Jedrezejow. The brewery was founded by an Austrian, Jan Gotz, in 1845. Since privatization in 1992, when German giant Bräu und Brunnen gained a quarter share, Okocim has linked up with Danish brewer Carlsberg. Its OK Jasne Pelne (full light) lager appears in varying strengths. Dark beers include a low-gravity Karmelowe and a powerful Okocim Porter.

Warszawski

Founded in 1846, this is the leading brewer in the capital of Warsaw. Besides standard lagers under the names Krolewskie (5.6%) and Stoteczne (5.4%), it also brews Warszawski Porter. The bottles give a nod towards beer's Egyptian origins with a Sphinx on the label.

Zywiec

Poland's most famous brewery had noble origins. It was founded in 1856 in Zywiec near Kracóv, by Archduke Charles Olbracht Habsburg, adopting a crown as its emblem. It was owned by the Habsburg family until the Second World War. Under state control, it became Poland's leading beer exporter. On privatization in 1991, the Zywiec plant was extensively modernized. The company also runs smaller breweries in Cieszyn and Bielsko. In 1994, Heineken took a 25% stake in the company. Its main beer is Zywiec Full Light. There is also a softer Krakus and much more full-bodied Eurospecjal. Zywiec also brews one of Poland's most distinctive porters.

EASTERN EUROPE

*The common Communist heritage of Hungary, Bulgaria, Romania, Latvia,
Lithuania and Estonia has now been shaken off. The nationalized industries,
which for a long time struggled to meet even the modest demand from the region,
have been thrown open to investment from the West.*

THE FORMER COMMUNIST countries of Eastern Europe consume relatively little
beer, in part due to a strong spirit-imbibing tradition, but also because of
inadequate brewing capacity and a shortage of raw materials.

Although Hungary, Bulgaria and Romania are best known for their wine, they
have a healthy appetite for light lagers. Hungarians drink about 80 litres (17½
gallons) of beer per head a year. Foreign companies have shown great interest in
the region since the move away from Communism, and many countries have
been welcoming foreign investment with open arms. Hungary's brewing industry
is now almost entirely foreign-owned. In Bulgaria some 13 breweries were
struggling to keep up with demand, but now foreign investors have poured in,
and by 1996 western companies had an interest in more
than a third of the industry. In Romania too, a wide range
of companies from the West have obliged with
investment. In 1996, South African Breweries took a
major share of the Romanian market.

Since 1991, a joint company called Baltic Beverages
Holding (BBH), established by Scandinavian brewers, has
taken a major stake in the leading breweries of the three
small Baltic states of Estonia, Latvia and Lithuania. The
breweries have since been heavily modernized and the beer
ranges revamped to a more international style of Pilsners,
moving away from traditional beers.

In Russia and the Ukraine, at the start of the 20th century,
there were about 1,000 home-owned breweries producing a
range of German, Czech and even English-style beers. The
beer industry was severely damaged during the Revolution
and two world wars, and was slow to recover. It was then hit
by Gorbachev's drive against alcohol when breweries were mothballed or turned
into soft drinks factories, and the barley farming areas were badly hit by the
Chernobyl nuclear disaster. But despite acute beer shortages, the former USSR
has been wary of foreign involvement, and only 6% of production in 1995 was
foreign-controlled, though imports, especially from the Czech Republic, are
increasing and now account for about 10% of the market.

*Above: One of the yeasty lagers,
brewed by Aldaris, the biggest
brewer in Latvia. The brewery
was modernized in 1991 by the
BBH group.*

THE BEERS

Aldaris

This range of sweetish, yeasty lagers produced by Latvia's biggest brewery includes the light Aldaris Pilznes (4%), a hoppier Baltijas, a smoother Zelta (5%) and the more powerful Jubilejas and Latvijas (both 6%).

Amber Pilsner

This light, dry, unpasteurized Pilsner (4.5%) is brewed using rye and sugar in the mash as well as barley malt. It is produced by the Amber brewery in Nikolayev, in the Ukraine.

Astika Lager

This golden, soft, mild and refreshing lager (4.5%) is widely available in Bulgaria. It is produced by the country's best-known brewery, Astika of Haskovo.

Bak

Köbányai's Bak is Hungary's version of a German Bock. This beer is strong (7.5%), dark and sweet.

Baltijas

This hoppy, yeasty lager (4.5%) is produced by the Aldaris brewery in Latvia.

Bergenbier

This popular, standard, golden-coloured, Romanian lager has a refreshing alpine image, with a snowy mountain peak on the label. A deep-amber Bergenbier Bruna has also been added to Bergen's range.

Birziecie

This strong, malty, dark lager (6.1%) is brewed by Ragutu, Lithuania.

Burgasko Lager

This light lager comes from the Burgasko brewery at Burgas on the Black Sea coast of Bulgaria.

Dreher

The Austrian pioneer of Viennese red beers, Anton Dreher, bought the leading Budapest brewery Köbányai Serhaz in 1862 and so gave his name to Hungary's best-known beer brands.

After a gap of some 40 years during Communist rule from 1948, the Dreher name was revived for Köbányai's premium range of beers – including a refreshing, dry, hoppy Pilsner (5%), the fuller-bodied golden-coloured Export and a Bavarian-style bock called Bak.

Dvaro

This is a premium lager (5.2%) from Kalnapilis, Lithuania.

Ekstra

Like Dvaro, this is a premium lager (5.2%) produced by the Kalnapilis brewery, in Lithuania.

Gocseji Barna

This relatively dark lager, which is something like a German Dunkel, is produced by the Konizsai brewery in west Hungary.

Kamenitza Lager

Kamenitza is a regional lager brand produced by the Kamenitza brewery in Plovdiv, Bulgaria.

Kanizsai Korona

The Kanizsai brewery in Hungary brews this malty, export-style lager.

Lauku Tumsais

This hazy, amber brew (6%) has a warming, malty taste. It is produced by the Lacplesis brewery in Lielvarde, Latvia.

Moskovskoye

This fruity lager is the leading beer brand produced by the Moscow brewery.

Nikolaevskyi

An amber-coloured beer (5%) with a spicy hop character, brewed with rye and sugar as well as barley in the south Ukraine by the Amber brewery, built by the Czechs in 1973.

Palmse

A dark, malty lager brewed by Viru in Estonia.

Porteris

The ruby-black beer (7.4%), with a rich, liqueur-like texture from Aldaris, is reputedly the only porter brewed in Latvia.

Reval

A golden, all-malt, hoppy lager, produced by the Saku brewery of Estonia.

Ruutli Olu

A rich, dark, spicy bock (7.5%), which is lagered for 70 days. It is produced by the Estonian Tartu brewery. This strong, dark, cold-weather beer was introduced by the brewery in 1995. It is the strongest beer brewed in Estonia.

Below: A beer stall in Riga, Latvia, in summer.

Above and left: Pilsner-type lagers, typical of the Saku brewery in Estonia, which was founded in 1820.

THE BREWERS

Aldaris
Latvia's biggest brewery has been based in the capital Riga since 1865. It brews a range of sweetish, yeasty lagers. Aldaris controls more than half the country's beer market and has been owned by Baltic Beverages Holdings since 1992. In 1995, BBH introduced a cleaner-tasting Pilsner, Aldara Luksusa.

Amber
Like many regional breweries in the former Soviet Union, this is a fairly new Czech-built brewery. It was constructed in 1973 in Nikolayev in the southern Ukraine. It produces two main beers, Amber Pilsner and spicy, amber-coloured Nikolaevskyi. Hops are grown locally around Zhitomir, but a shortage of barley malt means rye and sugar are also used. Roasted malt particularly is in short supply, which limits the chance to brew darker beers. All production is bottled and unpasteurized, with a shelf-life of seven days.

Baltika
Work only began on this St Petersburg brewery in 1990 and had still not been completed in 1993 when the unfinished plant was taken over by Baltic Beverages Holding, a joint venture by Scandinavian brewers Pripps of Sweden and Hartwall of Finland. Baltika has since grown rapidly to become one of the largest brewers in Russia, selling 120 million litres (26 million gallons) in 1995, the bulk of it around St Petersburg where it controls two-thirds of the market. It

produces a range of light lagers, including the premium Parnas and Baltika Export on draught.

Bergenbier
The Romanian Bergenbier brewery is owned by Belgian giant Interbrew, which completed a new brewery at Blaj in 1995.

Borsodi
Part of the Belgian Interbrew empire since 1991, the Borsodi brewery in Bocs is the second largest in Hungary, controlling around a quarter of the market. Its main local lagers are Borsodi Vilagos and Rakoczi.

New brewpubs

Hungary's rapidly advancing economy has embraced the western trend for micro-breweries. Since 1989, the pioneer brewer, Zsolt Gyenge, has set up around 50 pub plants. Most of the micros brew all-malt beers according to the German beer purity law.

Saku Originaal
Smooth-tasting Originaal is the premium, all-malt lager from Saku, Estonia.

Saku Pilsner
This fresh-tasting, golden, all-malt Pilsner is the main lager from Saku of Estonia.

Siraly (Seagull)
Siraly is a light, malty lager brewed by Kanizsai, Hungary.

Sirvenos
The leading lager (4.2%) from the Lithuanian brewer Ragutis, which, unusually, uses local peas in the mash to help with head retention and to give the beer a more rounded, full-bodied flavour.

Talleros
This is the local lager brewed by the Heineken-owned Komaromi, Hungary.

Tartu Olu
This rich lager (6%) is one of the beers brewed by Tartu in Estonia.

Tume
A reddish-coloured, malty lager, Tume is brewed by Saku, Estonia.

Zagorka Lager
The light, golden Zagorka lager is produced by the Zagorka brewery, Bulgaria.

Zhigulevskoe (Ziguli)
One of the main Soviet lager brands, which, under Communist rule, was brewed right across the USSR from Moscow to the Far East. A premium version (4.4%), produced by the Obolon brewery of Kiev, uses a proportion of rice in the mash. This lager has sometimes been exported to the West.

FARMHOUSE BEER

The Baltic states still retain a local, farmhouse brewing tradition, producing rye and juniper beers similar to the Finnish sahti in the north, as well as other refreshing country brews. On a more commercial scale they produce a variety of lagers, some using unusual brewing materials such as peas, besides a few stronger porters.

Russia also has a tradition of producing its own country beer – a nourishing home-made rye brew called kvass, sometimes sweetened with local fruit juices, such as bilberries. Some breweries produce this relatively low-alcohol beer commercially.

Burgasko
This Bulgarian brewery was taken over by Belgian giant Interbrew in 1995.

Kalnapilis
This large brewery in Panevezys, Lithuania, complete with its own maltings, was founded in 1902 and was acquired by the huge Scandinavian conglomerate, BBH in 1994. Since then, the brewery has launched a new range of international-style lagers, led by the premium Dvaro and Ekstra brands.

Kamenitza
Interbrew's first grip on the Bulgarian market began when it took over this brewery early in 1995.

Kanizsai
The Kanizsai brewery in Nagykanizsa in western Hungary dates back to 1892. The German brewing giant Holsten of Hamburg has had an interest in the brewery since 1984. It is best known for its light Siraly (Seagull) lager and malty Korona (Crown), a common name for Hungarian beers. It also brews a darker lager, called Gocseji Barna.

Köbányai
First opened in 1855, this plant was bought by the Austrian brewer, Anton Dreher in 1862. Although he died the following year, his son made the Köbányai largest brewery in Hungary. After merging with its main local rivals Reszveny and Haggenmacher in 1933, and Fovarosi in 1934, Dreher controlled three-quarters of the beer market. With nationalization in 1948, the Dreher name disappeared, but it was revived some 40 years later after privatization. South African Breweries gained control of the brewery in 1993. The Dreher range of beers, based on old recipes, uses a high proportion of malt. Some lagers from the Communist period are still produced.

Komaromi
Heineken bought this modern brewery at Komarom in 1991, primarily to brew Amstel for the Hungarian market. Nevertheless, it also continues to brew a number of local lagers, such as Talleros.

Lacplesis
This small country brewery in Lielvarde, Latvia, brews on a former collective farm, where it grows its own grain.

Magadan
This brewery is located in the east in the Stalinist city of Magadan on the Sea of Okhotsk. It still produces the four standard brands once widespread across the former Soviet Union. These are Zhigulevskoe (Ziguli), Moscovskoe (Moscow), Russkoe (Russian) and Ukrainskoe (Ukrainian). All are similar, light, pale lagers that vary in recipe depending on the brewing materials available. The main difference is in their lagering times. Ziguli is lagered for 21 days, and Moscow for double that time, giving it a drier more acidic taste than the fresher Ziguli. This acidic flavour is not due to production problems in the run-down plant, but because many Russians like a sour edge to their beer. All brews add sugar to beef up the limited malt mash. Magadan also produces several commercial brands of kvass, the cloudy, unhopped rye country-beer, which is indigenous to Russia – one kvass is flavoured with lemon. In summer, this refreshing brew is sold unfiltered direct from tanker trucks in the streets.

Above: Shady outdoor tables in a Budapest café are a pleasant place to enjoy a relaxing beer in the heat of the summer months.

Moscow

The Moscow City Brewery, next door to Tolstoy's House, has been brewing since 1863 and was once the main testing plant for beer in the Soviet Union. Its leading lager is the fruity Moskovskoye (4.6%). An all-malt August (4.5%), named after the month of the failed army coup in 1991 that led to Boris Yeltsin's revolution, is exported.

Proberco

This brewery at Baia Mare in Romania is owned by Interbrew.

Ragutus

Like some other Lithuanian breweries, the Ragutus company in the major city of Kaunas uses a proportion of local peas in the mash for its main lager, Sirvenos, to help head-retention. It also brews a dark, malty Birziecie.

Saku

Estonia's leading brewery was founded in 1820 on a former nobleman's estate outside the capital Tallinn. It was taken

Above: Gleaming copper vats at the modernized plant of the Saku brewery in Estonia.

over by BBH in 1991. A new brewhouse was completed in 1992, and Saku now controls more than half of the Estonian beer market. Its main all-malt lagers are Saku Pilsner, a hoppier Reval, the premium Saku Originaal, and the reddish, malty Tume. Saku also brews a coffee-like porter each Christmas.

Tartu

This brewery in Tartu, Estonia, dating back to 1826 has impressive castellated, tower maltings. It was once famous for its Imperial Extra Double Stout, sold to the Russian court when the company was owned by the Belgian merchant Le Coq, who exported the stout for Barclay Perkins of London. It produces a range of lagers including a Pilsner, Rae, a firm-bodied, export-style

Alexander and the richer Tartu Olu, as well as a dark bock called Ruutli Olu.

Viru

The Viru brewery was built on a former collective farm in Estonia in 1975. It is now owned by the large Danish brewer, Harboe.

Zagorka

Heineken has a large interest in this brewery in Stara Zagora, Bulgaria.

Fragmented market

Altogether, there are about 250 breweries in Russia and the Ukraine. They mainly produce light lagers containing adjuncts, such as corn and rice, that are matured for little more than two to three weeks. Breweries primarily serve a local market, but there are some more widely available brands – Ziguli is probably the best example.

Above: A modern brewery in Russia that was built using Austrian investment.

THE CZECH REPUBLIC AND SLOVAKIA

The Czechs have a long and proud brewing tradition and are the biggest beer drinkers in the world. They were among the first to use hops, and their pioneering golden lager has become the most popular beer style in the world.

Above: Budweiser Budvar is an internationally known, classic example of the Czech all-malt lager style.

SINCE THE BREAK-UP of the old Czechoslovakia into the wine-drinking Slovakia and the beer-loving Czech Republic, the Czechs now officially drink more beer per head of population than any other country.

Czech beer sprang to international fame when the citizens' brewery in Plzen developed the first golden lager in 1842. The town – Pilsen in German – gave its name to what was to become the world's leading beer style, Pilsner or just pils – an aromatic, hoppy, bottom-fermented pale beer.

In 1938 Czechoslovakia still boasted more than 300 breweries. But, some 60 years later, the brewing craft is at a crossroads. During the long period of Communist rule, little changed in what had become a nationalized industry. Ironically, the lack of investment in new technology meant that the traditional brewing methods were preserved almost intact. Since the "Velvet Revolution" of 1989 there has been a rush to modernize, with tried and trusted traditional methods often replaced by gleaming new plants. Plzen's dark cellars of wooden conditioning casks, for instance, have been replaced by stainless-steel conical vessels. Character and quality are declining. There are still 70 breweries in the Czech Republic, plus a few brewpubs, but as the larger groups expand and smaller plants are expected to close.

Most Czech beers today are divided into Pilsners of differing strengths, usually indicated by the old degree method of measurement, with 8 indicating a weak brew, 10 an everyday beer and 12 a premium. Before 1989, 12-degree beer was the most popular, but since then, as prices have risen, drinkers have switched dramatically to the weaker 10-degree brews.

THE BEERS

Alt Brunner Gold
This is the malty premium 12 Pilsner (5.1%) brewed by Starobrno.

Bernard Granat
A full-bodied, 11-degree, dark beer (4.9%), produced using two different types of malt, by the family-run Bernard brewery at Humpolec (founded in 1597), which also brews a golden, dry 12% beer (5.1%). The brewery has been one of the leaders of the movement to gain tax concessions for small-scale breweries.

Bohemia Regent
This is a popular, fruity 12 (4.9%), produced by the Regent brewery.

Budweiser Budvar
This is the most famous of all Czech lagers internationally and perhaps now the classic example of its style. The all-malt Budvar (5%) still retains its soft fruitiness and heady aroma. The Budweiser brewery was founded in the town of Ceske Budejovice (Budweise in German) in 1895, using water from an underground lake. It rapidly became a major exporter, particularly to Germany and the US (where its beer was sold as Crystal). Since 1989 the company has doubled in size, with annual production

Black Regent
A full-bodied, ruby-red dark beer (4%) with a dark-malt and coffee flavour, produced by the historic Regent brewery.

THE BATTLE FOR BUDWEISER

Such is the fame of Budweiser Budvar that many of the leading breweries around the world have proposed mergers or other trading arrangements, but none have been as persistent as Anheuser-Busch of the United States, which sells its own leading beer under the Budweiser name. Over the last century, the two have frequently clashed in and out of court over the rights to the title. Anheuser-Busch argues that Budvar was not founded until 20 years after the American brewer launched his Bud, but the Czechs contend that, since the Samson brewery was operating in Budweis since 1795, this is irrelevant. Besides, any brewery in the town of Budweis should have the right to market its beers as Budweiser, as the word means "from Budweis". Nevertheless, Budweiser Budvar has been unable to market its beers under its own name in the United States (calling it Crystal instead), and Anheuser-Busch has to sell its flagship beer as Bud in countries like Spain, where the Czech company registered the Budweiser name first. The situation has intensified since the "Velvet Revolution", as exports were less of a priority under Communism. The American giant would like to resolve the long-running dispute by taking over the Czech brewery. However, the Czech Government, which owns the brewery, is wary of the overtures, not wanting to be accused of selling off the crown jewel of the nation's brewing industry.

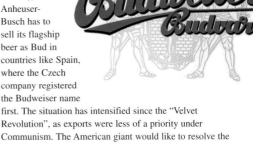

rising from 450,000 to 900,000 hectolitres (10 million to 22.5 million gallons). Traditional horizontal lagering tanks are still used, and the export beer is matured for more than 60 days. This export beer accounts for 60% of the brewery's export sales. New conical fermenters are used for producing a weaker 10-degree version (4%) with a blue label for consumption in the domestic market.

Cassovar
A rich, ruby-black, dark lager (5.5%) with a smooth cocoa and cream flavour, brewed in the Slovak town of Kosice.

Cernohorsky Granat
This dark, malty beer (3.5%) is brewed in Moravia by Cerna Hora.

Cernohorsky Lezak
An quality, golden Pilsner (3.5%) from Cerna Hora.

Chmelar
This pale, but relatively strong, hoppy beer (4.2%) is brewed by the small Zatec brewery. The name means hop-picker.

Crystal
Budweiser Budvar and Samson use this name for their premium beers when sold in the United States.

Drak
A rare, rich, dark, 14-degree Christmas brew (5.7%) from the Starobrno brewery. The name means dragon.

Dudak
A full-bodied premium pale 12 (5%) from the Stakonice brewery of South Bohemia.

Eggenberg
This is the name for a range of beers brewed at Cesky Crumlov in South Bohemia, which includes a pale and dark 10-degree (4%) and a full-bodied 12 (5%). The brewery, which dates back to 1560, is in an old armoury.

Gambrinus
The best-selling Czech beer is brewed by the brewery of the same name in Plzen. Gambrinus is restricted to domestic consumption, but still produces over 1.5 million hectolitres (33 million gallons) a year of a pale, aromatic 10-degree beer (4.1%) with a good,

hoppy character. A small amount of a stronger Gambrinus 12 (5.1%) is also brewed, mainly for export.

Granat
Granat is a popular name for a dark beer, which is used by a number of brewers including Olomouc, Cerna Hora and Hostan.

Herold Dark
A pitch-black, full-flavoured 13-degree brew (5.2%) which comes from the Herold brewery in Breznice. A pale 10-degree beer (3.8%) and stronger 12 (4.8%) are also available.

Holan 10
This hoppy, pale, unfiltered lager (3.5%) is brewed by Olomouc, for the local market.

Karamelové
The malty, dark, 10-degree lager (3.8%) comes from Starobrno of Brno.

Karel IV
A gold, fruity, pale 11-degree lager (4%) with a malty flavour. This is produced at the Karlovy Vary brewery in the famous spa town of that

name in western Bohemia, better known as Carlsbad. The beer is named after the king who founded the spa.

Konik
This best-selling, hoppy, pale-gold Pilsner beer (3.8%) is produced by the Ostravar brewery.

Kozel
This range of beers from the Velke Popovice brewery near Prague gained notoriety in the mid-1990s with their raunchy advertising. The name means goat. Its popular beers include a hoppy, pale-golden Kozel 10 (4.3%) with a fruity, sweet, malt flavour, a deep-golden, hoppy 12 (5%) and a dark, deep-brown 10 (4.3%) with a rich, malt flavour.

Krusovice
These include a dark, malty 10 (3.7%) with a very bitter flavour and a pale, thirst-quenching 12 (5.1%) with an aromatic, hoppy, sweet-malt flavour.

Lobkowicz
The pale, hoppy 12 (5%), from this family-run brewery is exported as Lobkov. A malty, dark 12 (4.6%) and a weaker, pale 10 are also available, and a 14 (5.5%) is occasionally produced.

Lucan
This pale, hoppy beer (3.6%) is brewed by the small Zatec brewery.

Martin Porter
This richly roasted, bitter-sweet porter (8%) is the strongest beer brewed in Slovakia. It is produced in the town of Martin, by the brewery of the same name.

Martinsky Lager
A malty, amber lager from the small Martin brewery in Slovakia.

Mestan Dark
This is the dark-amber, award-winning, malty beer (4.6%) produced by the Mestan brewery in the Prague suburb of Holesovice.

Nectar
This range of three fruity beers (10, 11 and a dark 10) comes from the Strakonice brewery of South Bohemia.

Novomestsky
This unfiltered, fruity, pale 11 (4%) is brewed in a rambling brewpub in the heart of Prague, established in 1993 in a shopping arcade.

Ondras
This premium, hoppy, pale, Pilsner beer (5%) is produced by the Ostravar brewery.

Osma
This weak, pale, 8 Pilsner (3.2%) is brewed by Starobrno.

Pilsner Urquell

The original flagship Pilsner of the Czech brewing industry. Its development in Plzen launched golden lager on the world for the first time in 1842. Pilsner Urquell (4.4%) is still a quality beer by any standards, particularly when fresh, with its delicate hop aroma and deep soft fruitiness. Urquell means original source.

Pivo Herold Hefe-Weizen

This spicy, fruity, top-fermented wheat beer (5.2%) is brewed in the Bavarian style by the Herold brewery. The style, long dead in the Czech Republic, has been revived by this brewery in Breznice.

Platan

Three pale beers are produced under this title – 10 (3.9%), 11 (4.4%) and 12 (5%), besides a dark beer (3.6%). All these beers are pasteurized.

Ponik

This is the weakest of the hoppy, pale Pilsners (3%) produced by the Ostravar brewer in Moravia.

Pragovar

A hoppy, premium, golden lager (4.9%) from the Mestan brewery of Prague.

Primator

This range of distinctive dry beers is brewed by the Nachod brewery in north-east Bohemia, which is owned by the town of Nachod. The Primator beers include a pale 10 and 12 and a chocolatey, dark 12 (5.1%).

Primus

A pale-gold, cut-price brew (3.8%) from Gambrinus.

Prior

An unfiltered, yeasty wheat beer (5%), introduced by Pilsner Urquell in 1995.

Purkmistr

One of the best Czech dark lagers (4.8%) from the Pilsner Urquell group, Purkmistr has a bitter-chocolate flavour balancing the initial malty sweetness. It is brewed at Domazlice.

Radegast

The range of beers from the Radegast brewery includes a popular, pale-gold 10 (3.8%) with a dry, hop flavour. The 12 (5.1%), which is sold as Premium light, has a golden hue and a dry hops and malt taste. The brown Premium Dark (3.6%) has a light, malt flavour.

Rezak

This is a half-and-half pale and dark lager, (4.1%), produced to satisfy the demands of drinkers who often mix their pale and dark lagers. It is brewed by Starobrno.

Samson

A range of crisp, dry, pale beers, produced by the brewery of the same name. The 10 (4%) has a bright-gold colour and a clean, crisp hops flavour. The 11 (4.6%) is a tawny-gold-coloured beer, with a creamier, sweeter hop flavour. A hoppier version of the 11 is sold in England under the name Zamec, and the sweet, ripe 12 (5%) is sold as Crystal in the US.

Starobrno 10

This deep-golden, hoppy 10 (4.3%) with a rich, bold flavour is a popular beer from the Starobrno brewery's range.

Staropramen 10

Besides a fresh and hoppy pale 10 (4.2%), this major Prague brewery produces a full-bodied 12 (5%) and a mellow dark (4.6%). The quality of the beers reflect the fact that the brewery has retained traditional methods of brewing.

Tas

A light, golden, tasty Pilsner (2.8%) brewed by the Cerna Hora brewery in Moravia.

Tatran

A range of lagers from the Vega brewery of Poprad in the Tatran mountains, Slovakia. It includes a Tatran export (8%) and a lighter Kamzik (4.1%).

Urpin Pils

The deep-gold, hoppy, Pilsner with a light, malt flavour from the Urpin brewery in Slovakia.

Vaclav 12

A hoppy, pale lager (5.6%), brewed by Olomouc.

Velke Popovice

See Kozel.

Vranik

A delicate, malty, dry, dark 10 (3.8%) from Ostravar.

Zamek

Export name for Samson 11.

Zatecka Desitka

A pale, hoppy beer (3.1%) from the Zatec brewery.

Zlaty Bazant

This gold-coloured, firm, dry Pilsner (4.4%) with a sweet, creamy, malt flavour is one of the popular lagers produced by the Slovakian Zlaty Bazant brewery.

THE BREWERS

Bernard

This family-owned brewery at Humpolec on the main road between Prague and Brno was founded in 1597.

Branik

Originally established by a group of innkeepers in 1900, Branik is now part of the Bass-owned Prague Breweries group led by Staropramen. The dramatic brewhouse and maltings lie among trees in the south of the city. Unfortunately, much of the traditional equipment inside was replaced with conical fermenters and a pasteurization plant in 1992 before Bass took over. Once famous for a strong 14-degree dark lager, it now brews a sweetish pale 10 and 12, and a dark 10.

Budweiser Budvar

The world-famous Budweiser brewery was founded in the town of Ceské Budejovice in 1895, using water from an underground lake. It rapidly became a major exporter, particularly to Germany and the US. Since 1989 the company has doubled in size, with annual production rising from 450,000 to 900,000 hectolitres ((10 million to 22.5 million gallons).

Cerna Hora

The small Moravian country brewery at Cerna Hora, north of Brno, built in 1896, produces a range of light but tasty Pilsners.

Chodovar

This small brewery with a long history dates back to 1573. It is located close to the Bavarian border at Chodova Plana, and brews three pale and one dark, nutty 10-degree beer.

HOPPING WITH HISTORY

The Czech Republic hop-growing tradition dates back to the 9th century, making it one of the longest-standing hop producers in the world. The area around the town of Zatec – better known under its German name of Saaz – became world-famous for the quality of its hops. One Bohemian king, Vaclav IV, even forbade growers from selling cuttings abroad on penalty of death to try to protect the green crop which was worth its weight in gold.

For much of the 19th century, Bohemian hops ruled the world, dictating quality, standards and prices. The town of Zatec was at the heart of a global business, only losing its dominant position after the First World War and the break-up of the Austro-Hungarian Empire.

Even today, major brewers like Anheuser-Busch of the United States still import large amounts of Czech hops. Their quality is so widely respected that the vast bulk of the crop is exported.

Gambrinus

This brewery, in Plzen, was once restricted to domestic production, but now produces over 1.5 million hectolitres (33 million gallons) a year of the best-selling Czech beer – a pale, 10-degree lager. It is part of the Pilsner Urquell group.

Herold

This ancient brewery in Breznice, south of Prague, came back from the dead and is now going strong. It was closed down by the Communist authorities in 1988, but brewer Stanislav Janostik rescued the baroque buildings that date back to 1720, and started up brewing operations there again in 1990. The traditional plant now produces a dark 13-degree, a pale 10-degree and a 12-degree, as well as a wheat beer.

Jihlava

The south-Moravian brewery in Jihlava dates back to 1860. In 1995 it was bought by the Austrian brewer Zwettl and it is now being modernized. However, it is uncertain whether its Jezek (hedgehog) beer brand will survive this restructuring.

Above: This promotional postcard from Ceske Budejovice acknowledges beer's Egyptian origins.

Krusovice

This historic brewery to the west of Prague in the Zatec hop-growing region was taken over by the German brewing group, Binding of Frankfurt, in 1994. The German giant has since invested heavily in modernizing the plant – and in the brewery's ancient heritage, calling its products the beers of King Rudolf II. Krusovice, dating back to 1581, was once part of the royal estate.

Lobkowicz

A family brewery south of Prague near Sedlcany.

Mestan

Part of the Bass-owned Prague Breweries group led by Staropramen, this plant in the suburb of Holesovice is best known for its award-winning, malty, dark 11.

Olomouc

The Moravian brewery, north-east of Brno, typifies the present contradictions in the Czech brewing industry. On the one hand it offers a tasty, unfiltered lager for Czech locals; on the other it now brews American beers under licence.

Ostravar

This substantial brewery in the mining town of Ostrava in northern Moravia was bought by Bass in 1995. The brewery, which dates back to 1897, received the last new brewhouse installed by the Communists in 1987. It produces a wide range of local beers, including three hoppy pale Pilsners called Ponik, Konik and the premium Ondras. It also brews Staropramen 10.

Pilsner Urquell

For 150 years Pilsner Urquell in Plzen has managed to maintain its traditional brewing methods, using huge wooden casks to mature each batch of its revered beer for three months. Watching these massive barrels being rolled out of the underground tunnels and into the brewery for repitching and repair was once one of the famous sights of the old brewing town, along with the grand gates to the brewery. Now only the triumphal arches remain, but behind, everything else has changed. Stacks of conical fermenters have replaced the old casks in a bid to increase the brewery's production and efficiency – and with them has gone a little of the complexity of the famous brew. Pilsner Urquell is the largest brewing group in the Czech Republic by far, producing 72.5 million gallons in 1994, almost double the output of its nearest rival. Pilsner Urquell accounts for about a fifth of the total Czech beer market and a large part of the country's exports. Besides the Urquell brewery itself, the brewing group also includes the neighbouring, larger plant of Gambrinus in Plzen, Domazlice and Karlovy Vary.

Platan

The Platan brewery is part of the South Bohemia breweries group along with Regent and Samson. Platan was originally developed by aristocratic landowners in Protivín, with records dating back to 1598. It takes its name from the local plane (platan) trees in its parkland home.

Radegast

Radegast has risen from being a distant local brewery in north-eastern Moravia, at Nosovice, to become the third largest national concern in the Czech Republic. Built in 1971, mainly to supply the Slovak and Polish markets, the privatized company markets its beers under the symbol of Nordic the god of hospitality, Radegast.

Regent

One of the oldest and most historic Czech breweries, Regent dates back to the 14th century in Trebon. Behind its fine facade, however, it is switching to conical fermenters.

Samson

This is probably the brewery in Ceské Budejovice (Budweis in German) that inspired Adolphus Busch to call his American beer Budweiser. Samson dates from 1795. Its heavily modernized brewery produces a wide range of crisp, dry, pale beers.

Starobrno

This is the major brewery in the Moravian city of Brno. It was founded in 1872 and brews a wide range of beers.

Staropramen

Staropramen – the name means "old spring" – has been brewing in the Smichov district of Prague since 1869. Taken over the the English brewers Bass in 1993, it has retained its open fermenting vessels and traditional lagering tanks.

U Fleku

Probably the most famous home-brew pub in the world, U Fleku also claims to be the oldest. U Fleku has been brewing in Prague since 1499 and its softly spicy, dark brew (5.5%) and wood-panelled rooms and courtyard are one of the taste-and-see attractions of the grand city.

Zlaty Bazant

This is Slovakia's best-known brewery. It produces the popular Golden Pheasant brand of lagers, in the southern town of Hurbanovo. The company is now controlled by the Dutch giant Heineken.

ITALY

The Mediterranean countries of Europe have traditionally been lands flowing with wine. At best, beer is viewed as a summer thirst-quencher. Italian consumption of beer might still be one of the lowest in Europe, but unlike most other markets it is expanding.

B REWING, IMPORTED FROM OVER THE ALPS, did not appear in Italy on any significant scale until the 19th century, and then it was limited mainly to the northern region. The Wuhrer brewery of Brescia, founded in 1828 by an Austrian, claims to be the first large commercial concern in the country. The number of breweries grew to about 100 by the end of the century, but then it rapidly declined as production was concentrated in the hands of a few leading companies such as Peroni and Moretti. Brewing – nearly all in a light Pilsner style – was still very small beer until the 1960s. Annual consumption in 1950 was no more than three litres (five pints) a head. However, in the next few decades demand surged, reaching 26 litres (46 pints) by 1995. Most of this (nearly 80%) is sold in bottles. Younger people began to regard beer as a fashionable drink; wine was for their parents or peasants. English-style pubs opened and imports from countries such as Germany and England rocketed, accounting for about one-fifth of all beer sales. Altogether there are about 20 breweries in Italy today, and many of the major brewers of northern Europe have stepped into this land of expanding opportunity, exporting enthusiastically and buying into the native breweries. Heineken, for example, now controls 40% of production since its purchase of Moretti and the Dreher Group. The French giant BSN (which produces Kronenbourg) has a stake in the country's top brewer Peroni, and through this accounts for 36% of the market. Carlsberg of Denmark also has an interest in the Poretti company.

Above: Italian beer may not have the cachet of the country's wine, but it is an increasingly popular drink. Peroni, the leading brewer, is making the most of the expanding market.

THE BEERS

Birra Moretti

A light, crisp, yellow-gold lager (4.6%) from Moretti.

Birra Peroni

A pale-gold lager with a malt and hop aroma and a hoppy taste, from Peroni.

Bruna

A reddish, all-malt, strong Munich-style lager (6.25%), with a smooth, spicy, roasted flavour. Brewed by Moretti.

Crystal

Peroni's range of draught premium lagers includes a Speciale and a darker, Viennese-style, malty Crystal Red (both 5.6%), plus an even stronger Crystal Gold (6.6%). Crystal Speciale is a clear, yellow-gold lager (5.6%) with a smooth, rich barley and malt flavour.

Forst Sixtus

This unusual, dark, abbey-style beer (6.5%) is brewed by the Forst family brewery in Lagundo.

Gran Riserva

Strong beers in Italy are known as double malts, and in 1996, to mark its 150th anniversary, Peroni introduced one in distinctive, tall, embossed bottles. Gran Riserva is a deep-gold, full-bodied lager (6.6%).

Italia Pilsner

This yellow-gold, light Italian Pilsner (4.7%) has a dry, bitter flavour. It is a leading brand in the north-west of the country. Itala Pilsen of Padua was taken over by Peroni in 1960.

Kronen

This bright-gold, export-style lager (5%) with a malty taste, from Forst, shows a Viennese influence.

McFarland

Despite its Irish image, this bottom-fermented red beer (5.5%) from Dreher is more a Viennese-style lager.

Nastro Azzuro

Peroni's pale-gold, clean, sweetish premium Pilsner (5.2%) was introduced in 1964. The name means "Blue Ribbon".

Raffo

A light, golden-yellow, dry, mildly bitter Pilsner (4.7%) from Peroni. Raffo is sold mainly around its home city of Taranto in southern Italy.

Rossa

This is probably the most characterful of Italy's red beers. The rosy-amber-coloured, richly flavoured, all-malt La Rossa (7.5%) from Moretti of Udine gives a robust reminder of northern Italy's former connections with Vienna and its Märzen-style brews.

Sans Souci

A pale-gold, malty export-style lager (5.6%) brewed by Moretti of Udine. It has a good hop balance.

Splügen

The brand name for this range of speciality lagers produced by the Poretti Brewery of Varese is taken from the name of a high mountain pass. The most celebrated of the beers is the deep-copper-coloured, faintly smoky Splügen Fumée, which is made with Franconian malt. There is also a coppery-red, robust, fruity Splügen Rossa (7%) and a German-style, black beer Scura (6%).

Werner Brau

A light Pilsner (4.5%) brewed by Poretti.

Wuhrer Pilsner

This pale Pilsner (4.7%) with a light, hoppy taste, is produced by the Wuhrer brewery in Brescia.

Right: A Roman relief of a tavern scene. The Romans preferred wine to beer.

THE BREWERS

Dreher

Italy was once part of a vast Austrian empire, and the celebrated brewer Anton Dreher of Vienna crossed the Alps to establish a brewery in Trieste in the 1860s. Today, the Dreher name lives on in a Milan-based group owned by Heineken. Besides a range of light lagers, its beers include a Vienna-style red lager called McFarland.

Forst

The medium-sized brewery in the mountains at Lagundo is owned by the Fuchs family. It brews beers that show an Austrian influence, notably in the export-style lager Kronen. Forst means "forest" in German.

Moretti

Founded in Udine in 1859, the Moretti brewery became well known on the international markets despite its relatively small size. This is helped by its appealing labels showing a moustachioed man blowing the froth off his glass of beer. Besides a light, crisp Birra Moretti there is also a more malty export Sans Souci and two more characterful, darker brews – an all-malt Moretti Bruna and the richly flavoured red Moretti Rossa. In recent years, the company has changed hands at a dizzy rate and is now owned by Dutch giant Heineken.

Peroni

Until Heineken combined Dreher with Moretti in 1996, Peroni was the leading Italian brewer. Founded in Vigevano in 1846, it soon concentrated its activities in Rome then spread out, taking over breweries throughout the peninsula. Since merging with Wuhrer in 1988, it has concentrated production at five plants. Its leading blue-ribbon brand is Nastro Azzurro, but it also brews a lighter Peroni Birra. Other similar regional brands include Itala Pilsen, Raffo and Wuhrer. There is also a "Crystal" range. In 1996, Peroni added a more full-bodied bottled Gran Riserva.

Poretti

The Poretti company was founded in 1877 in Varese, north of Milan. It now has a second brewery in Ceccano, south of Rome. Besides a light Pilsner – Werner Brau – it also produces a number of distinctive specialities under the Splügen brand name. Carlsberg has now bought the brewery.

Wunster

Wunster is another Italian brewery that has Germanic origins. The brewery was founded by the Bavarian Heinrich von Wunster and is based in Bergamo. For many years it was a family concern, but it is now part of the large Belgian Interbrew group.

MALTA AND THE ENGLISH CONNECTION

The tiny island country of Malta off the coast of Sicily has a distinctive brewing tradition and is something of an anomaly in the Mediterranean region.

The legacy of the British Empire still lingers over this independent Mediterranean island. Its one brewery, Simonds, Farsons, Cisk (which is now commonly known as Farsons) started up to brew beers for the sailors at the British naval base there, in the top-fermenting ale styles that they enjoyed back home. Simonds of Reading, England exported ale and stout to Malta in the 19th century, then helped to set up a brewery in cooperation with a local company Farrugian and Sons. Although the British are long gone, the brewery remains, still producing these English-style, top-fermenting ales and a range of lagers under the Cisk brand name.

The Farsons brewery now produces a darkish, soft, mild ale (3.6%) called Blue Label and a stronger ale (5%) called Brewer's Choice. It also brews a hoppy pale ale (4%), Hop Leaf and a creamy, milk stout (3.4%) with a dry finish,, Lacto, which is brewed using lactose (milk sugar) and claims to be "Milk Stout with Vitamin B for Extra Energy". The brewery at Mriehel also produces lagers under the Cisk label. As well as alcoholic drinks, Farsons is the island's main soft drink producer.

Water is a scarce resource on the rocky island of Malta so Farsons collects every spare drop of rainwater in huge rooftop reservoirs, to be stored in underground tanks.

GREECE AND TURKEY

Civilized chat over a drink is a key part of both Turkish and Greek social customs. But on these occasions beer has always come a rather ragged second to wine, or strong coffee and potent aniseed ouzo or raki.

Above: Keo, from Cyprus, won a Gold Medal for Excellence at the 1987 World Bottled Lager Competition.

CONTROL BY breweries from northern Europe has reached saturation point in Greece, virtually wiping out the local industry. The only large, Greek-owned brewery – Fix – closed in 1983, and foreign companies and brands now dominate the market. The country's Bavarian-influenced beer purity law (which insisted that beers were made using all-malt) has gone, under pressure from foreign brewers. However, the island of Cyprus has managed to maintain a popular local lager – Keo. Turkey, in contrast, has a thriving local producer in the shape of Efes, which worked hard to develop the market for international-style light lager after the state brewing monopoly, Tekel, was relaxed in 1955. The Danish-owned Turk Tuborg and state-run breweries in Istanbul, Ankara and Yozgat compete, but Efes dominates the Turkish market.

THE BEERS AND BREWERS

Aegean
This sweetish, malty Pilsner (5%) is produced in the north of Greece by Athenian Breweries, which is wholly owned by the Dutch giant Heineken. It has a hint of toffee and a slightly bittersweet edge.

Efes Pilsener
This golden, sweetish, full-bodied premium lager (5%), produced by Efes in Turkey, is widely exported. The company takes its name from the ancient Roman city of Ephesus, and its full title, Efes Pilsen Bira Fabrikasi, indicates an intention to brew a dry, hoppy Pilsner. The company also brews Efes Light, an Extra and an alcohol-free Alkolsuz

Efes. The Efes brewery has branched out in recent years and as well as running four breweries in its home country, it now also runs two malting plants and a brewery in Romania.

Keo
This sweetish, full-bodied, Pilsner-type lager (4.5%) is brewed in Lemesos, southern Cyprus, by the Keo brewery. It is bottled fresh and unpasteurized. Keo is one of the few remaining local brewers.

FRANCE

France is mainly associated with some of the great wines of the world, and French beer is rarely given a second thought. Beer in France is treated as a refreshment, not as a serious drink in its own right, and the industry is dominated by a few large companies.

D ROP INTO MOST FRENCH cafés and ask for *une bière* and you will be served a *pression* (draught) of light, refreshing but undemanding lager. Most of this beer is brewed in the Alsace region, close to the German border in the east of the country. The German influence is obvious in the place-names and the cuisine of the area, but most of the beer is a pale shadow of the better-quality brews across the border. The French do not have a beer purity law but use a variety of adjuncts, and have been the most vigorous campaigners against the German Rheinheitsgebot, claiming that it restrains trade. In addition, they allow their lagers much less time to mature than German brewers and they tend to use a relatively small quantity of hops.

The centre of the French lager brewing industry is Strasbourg and the major names are Kronenbourg and Kanterbräu, both owned by the same BSN conglomerate, which dominates about half the domestic beer market. The Dutch giant Heineken also has a major stake in the French market, owning the "33", Mutzig and Pelforth brands and controlling almost a quarter of the trade. In 1996, they added to this by taking over the sizeable Fischer group.

One region of France, the Nord-Pas de Calais in the north-east close to Belgium, does boast its own distinctive traditional beer style. A number of small breweries in this region, especially around Lille, brew "bières de garde" (keeping beers), which are strong, top-fermenting, bottle-conditioned ales. These were traditionally made in farmhouses in the winter and spring before the heat of summer made brewing too unpredictable. More commercial versions are now produced, some of which are bottom-fermented and filtered, but still retain an ale-like fruitiness through warm fermentation. They are often sold in champagne-style wired and corked bottles. The brewers who use barley and hops from the region are entitled to use the appellation "Pas de Calais/Région du Nord".

Above: Bière de garde from the rural north of France is still sold in large corked bottles. Jenlain is probably the most famous example of the type.

THE BEERS

Abbaye de Vaucelles

Not so much a Belgian abbey-style beer as a French bière de garde (7.5%), this amber-coloured, honey-like drink is brewed with herbs by the Choulette brewery for an abbey near Cambrai.

Ackerland

Two strong, malty lagers – the rich, malty, amber-coloured Ackerland Blonde (5.9%) and the dark Ackerland Brune (6.3%), which has a sweeter flavour – are sold under this brand name. Both are produced by the independent Meteor brewery of Hochfelden in Alsace. The name is taken from the agricultural area which lies around the village.

Adelscott

Labelled a "Bière au Malt à Whisky", this faintly smoky, amber-red, pale lager (6.4%) from the Adelschoffen brewery, is made using peaty Scottish malt. It created a niche market when it was launched in the early 1980s.

Adelscott Noir

This is another (6.6%) Bière au Malt à Whisky from Adelschoffen. It is almost black, with red highlights, and has an intense, peaty, slightly smoky flavour.

Amberley

Pelforth brewery of Lille introduced this whisky malt beer (7.3%) in 1993 as a rival to the popular brews produced by Adelscott.

Ambre de Flandres

A mellow, oaky, bottom-fermented bière de garde (6.4%) from the Jeanne d'Arc brewery at Ronchin, near Lille, sold under the Orpal brand name.

Ancre

A popular Alsace lager (4.8%), Ancre is brewed by Heineken at Schiltigheim.

Bière des Templiers

A dark, fruity, sedimented bière de garde (8.5%) from the Saint Sylvestre brewery.

Bière du Désert

This strong, pale-yellow-gold, fruity beer (7%) is brewed by Gayant.

Breug

See Terken.

Brune Spéciale

A deep, amber-brown dark lager (6.7%) with a roasted malt flavour, produced by the Terken brewery.

Certa

This alcohol-free beer was the first of its kind to be produced in France. Unusually, it is available on draught. Certa is brewed by Les Brasseurs de Gayant, a firm normally famous for its strong beers.

Ch'ti

The name is local Picardy patois for a French north-easterner and is the brand name for the bières de garde produced by the Castelain brewery of Bénifontaine, near Lens. The richly fruity beers from this coal-scarred region, featuring a rugged miner on the label, include a deep-gold, malty-fruity blonde and a darker brune version (both 6.5%) as well as a deep-amber-coloured Ch'ti Amber (5.9%).

Choulette Framboise

A seasonal, speciality, top-fermented, unpasteurized bière de garde (6%). It is flavoured with natural raspberry extract to produce a tart, fruity flavour and is brewed by La Choulette farmhouse brewery.

Cuivrée

Cuivrée is a powerfully smooth, Vienna-style reddish lager (8%) with a strong, fruity, malty flavour brewed by the independent Schutzenberger brewery of Schiltigheim.

Cuvée de Jonquilles

This is a golden-coloured, flowery, fruity, top-fermented, bottle-conditioned spring brew (7%) produced by the Bailleux family brewery in the Café Restaurant au Baron in Gussignies.

Démon

La Bière du Démon from Les Brasseurs de Gayant of Douai claims to be the strongest blonde beer in the world, with 12% alcohol. Brewed with extra malt and a special lager yeast, it has a fiery but rather heavy, honeyish character with a small head.

Fischer Gold

A strong lager (6.5%) with a perfumy aroma and a hoppy flavour from Fischer. It is sold in a distinctive swing-stoppered bottle.

Goldenberg

A strong, malty, golden beer (6.4%) from Gayant of Douai.

Goudale

Goudale is a pale top-fermented traditional bière de garde (7.2%) with a full, fruity flavour, from Les Brasseurs de Gayant. The beer is bottle-conditioned and wire-corked in the traditional manner.

Jubilator
Jubilator is a golden, aromatic, full-bodied, pale doppelbock (7%) in the German style, from the Schutzenberger brewery of Schiltigheim.

Killian
George Killian's Bière Rousse (6.5%), an Irish-style, strong, malty red ale, is brewed by Pelforth of Lille. The beer is sold in the Netherlands as Kylian.

Kronenbourg
The main Kronenbourg beer (5.2%) is a light-tasting lager and the stronger 1664 (5.9%), popularly known as "soixante-quatre", is smoother but a little more full-bodied. There is also a weaker Kronenbourg Légère (3.1%). A hoppier variant of the standard lager is called Kronenbourg Tradition Allemande, while Kronenbourg Tradition Anglaise is softer and deeper amber in colour. There is also a maltier, dark version of 1664 called Brune, and two seasonal brews, a rosy La Bière de Noël and a golden Kronenbourg Bière de Mars.

L'Angélus
The label for Annoeullin's hazy golden-bronze wheat bière de garde (7%) features J. F. Millet's painting of pious peasants at prayer in the fields. The beer has a very fresh, fruity, creamy flavour.

La Bière Amoureuse
This is a distinctly un-beerlike lager (4.9%). It is flavoured with ginseng and herbs. According to the brewers Fischer these "natural plant extracts" produce an aphrodisiac effect on the lucky drinker.

La Choulette
This is an amber-coloured, soft, fruity bière de garde (7.5%), produced by La Choulette farmhouse brewery using a blend of top and bottom-fermenting yeasts at warm temperatures. Local malts and Flemish and Hallertau hops are used in the brew, and the beers are roughly filtered in order to leave some yeast in the bottle. A blonde version is also available. Both are bottle-conditioned. The name comes from a traditional local game similar to golf.

Lutèce
This powerful, malty sourish bière de garde (6.4%) is produced by the Enfants de Gayant brewery in Douai.

Meteor
This light, hoppy, unpasteurized, Pilsner-style lager (4.6%) is produced by the Alsace brewery, Meteor.

Mortimer
Meteor's fruity, all-malt, copper-coloured, Vienna-style strong lager (8%) was first brewed in Hochfelden in 1993. It is bottled and packaged to look like a malt whisky.

Mutzig Old Lager
A strong, characterful, amber lager (7.3%), with a rich malt-and-hops flavour, produced by the Mutzig brewery in Alsace near the French-German border.

Jade
This is a *bière biologique* or organic beer. Jade is a refreshing, pale-yellow, fruity lager (4.6%) that is produced using only organically grown malt and hops by the Castelain brewery of Bénifontaine, near Lens. The unpasteurized, fresh, hoppy brew can be sold in a large, champagne-style bottle.

Jenlain
This strong, reddish-amber, all-malt bière de garde (6.5%) is the best-known of its type. It is a top-fermented brew, packed with spicy, fruity flavours. The Duyck brewery of Jenlain, near Valenciennes, still sells Jenlain in classic corked and wired bottles, but it is also available in smaller, capped bottles.

Mutzig Pilsner
A standard, golden, hoppy Pilsner (4.8%) brewed by the Mutzig brewery, Schiltingheim, Alsace.

Noordheim
A creamy, pale lager (4.7%) brewed by Terken of Roubaix for sale in supermarkets. It is sold in small 25 cl bottles.

Pastor Ale
Subtitled "C'est une symphonie", this all-malt, amber-coloured bière de garde (6.5%) hits all the right tart, fruity, hoppy notes. It is brewed using bottom-fermenting yeasts and Saaz and Flemish hops by one of the classic bière de garde producers, the Annoeullin farm brewery near Lille. It can be bought either unfiltered in tall, wire-corked bottles or in more conventional small capped bottles in packs. The name is a pun on Beethoven's *Pastorale Symphony*.

Patriator
Darker and fruitier than its sister beer Jubilator, Patriator (7%) is a doppelbock which is produced by the Schutzenberger brewery of Schiltigheim.

Pêcheur
See Fischer.

Pelforth Brune
A strong, sweetish, dark lager (6.5%) with a warm, rich, chocolatey-malt flavour, produced by the Pelforth brewery.

Pelforth Blonde
A light, fruity lager (5.8%) from the Pelforth brewery near Lille.

Pelican Lager
A standard, golden lager (4.8%) with a malty flavour, from the Pelforth brewery near Lille.

Porter 39
A rich, strong, roasted porter (6.9%), produced by the Pelforth brewery.

Saaz
A hoppy lager (5.2%) brewed by Gayant of Douai.

Saint Arnoldus
A fruity, abbey-style sediment beer (7.5%) from the Castelain brewery of Bénifontaine, near Lens. The beer is filtered, then yeast is added again before bottling.

Saint Landelin
A range of French top-fermenting abbey-style beers from Les Brasseurs de Gayant of Douai named after the founder of L'Abbaye de Crespin. The range includes: a sweet, creamy Blonde (5.9%), which has a rich-gold hue and a fruity flavour; a reddish-brown Saint Landelin Ambrée (6.1%), with a full, biscuity-malt

flavour; and a richer, dark Brune (6.2%), with a coffee-chocolatey flavour. All the beers are matured for two months before bottling.

Sans Culottes
There is nothing missing from this classic, golden bière de garde (6.5%) produced by La Choulette brewery of north-eastern France. Top-fermented and bottle-conditioned, it is full of yeasty character. The name, usually interpreted as meaning "without trousers", refers to the French revolutionary soldiers.

Schutz Deux Milles
This richly fruity, bottle-conditioned brew (6.5%) from Schutzenberger was originally brewed to mark the 2,000th anniversary of Strasbourg.

Sebourg
The blonde sister to Jenlain from the Duyck brewery of Valenciennes, this full-flavoured, aromatic bière de garde (6%) also comes in tall

corked and wired bottles. It is not brewed in Jenlain, but in the neighbouring village of Sebourg.

Septante Cinq
This powerful, reddish-amber-coloured lager (7.5%) is described as a bière de garde. It is the flagship brand of the Terken brewery.

Tourtel
This low-alcohol lager (1%) from Kanterbräu comes in blonde, amber or brown versions.

Trois Monts
This classic, harvest-gold, top-fermenting bière de garde (8%) is produced by the Saint Sylvestre brewery near the Belgian border. This complex, dry and winey brew is named after three local hills which stand out in the flat Flanders landscape.

Upstaal
A mild, pale lager (3%) with a sweet, appley taste, from Terken.

Wel Scotch
This dark-amber-coloured lager (6.2%) is produced by Kronenbourg, using Scottish whisky malt.

Willfort
A malty, dark lager (6.6%) from the Kronenbourg group.

"33"
Trente-trois is a popular number in France, south-east Asia and Africa, where this light export Pilsner (4.8%) with a malted cereal flavour has developed a large market in the old French empire. Originally brewed near Paris, it is now comes from Marseilles.

THE BREWERS

Adelschoffen

The Alsatian brewery in Schiltigheim, near Strasbourg, founded in 1864, has been described as a brewing laboratory. Its most famous creation is the Adelscott whisky malt beer.

Castelain

Specialist brewer of the Ch'ti bières de garde based at Bénifontaine near Lens.

La Choulette

La Choulette farmhouse brewery began to market the traditional, fruity La Choulette bière de garde in 1981. They are top-fermented and bottle-conditioned, and there are also seasonal specials. The brewery in Hordain, near Valenciennes, dates back to 1885.

Deux Rivières

Two Bretons set up this micro-brewery in 1985 in Morlaix in Brittany, inspired by tasting traditional Welsh

ales. Its two main bitters are Coreff Red Label (4.6%) and Black Label (6%).

Duyck

The family farmhouse brewery near Valenciennes, near the Belgian border, has brewed the best-known bière de garde, Jenlain, since 1922. Duyck kept the style alive when most other brewers in the region were abandoning these traditional beers. It also markets another golden country beer called Sebourg and two seasonal specialities, Duyck Bière de Noël (6.8%) and a refreshing pale Duyck Bière de Printemps.

Above: Bière du Démon.

Fischer

Founded in 1821, the brewery in Schiltigheim, near Strasbourg, also sells its beers under a French version of its name, Pêcheur. It brews a variety of lagers, such as Poussez, the cherry-flavoured Fischer Kriek and the so-called aphrodisiac lager – La Bière Amoureuse.

Gayant

Les Brasseurs de Gayant at Douai was formed in 1919 from a merger of four family breweries. Named after the two giants who traditionally protected this French Flanders town near Lille, the firm is famous for its strong beers. It produces a bière de garde, the top-fermented speciality of the region, called La Goudale (7.2%) but is better known for its devilishly powerful Bière du Démon (12%), which claims to be the strongest blonde beer in the world. It also brews a less strong, but far from arid, fruity Bière du Désert, and a rare abbey-style range of beers, Saint Landelin, and some more standard lagers which are marketed under the Saaz and Goldenberg brands.

Above: The handsome Duyck brewery in the hamlet of Jenlain.

Kanterbräu

Now seen as Kronenbourg's second-string brand, at one time Kanterbräu was the largest brewing group in France. Its main brewery at Champigneulles, near Nancy in Lorraine, dates back to 1887 and it also has a second smaller plant at Rennes in Brittany. Besides a light lager Kanterbrau (4.5%), it also brews a stronger Kanterbräu Gold and a low-alcohol lager called Tourtel. The brewery is named after a German brewmaster, Maître Kanter. In 1994 Kanterbräu formally combined with Kronenbourg under the name Les Brasseries Kronenbourg.

Kronenbourg

France's dominant beer brand takes its name from the Cronenbourg quarter of Strasbourg (the use of the K was felt to be more beerily Germanic). The company

grew after the Second World War by selling its premium Bière d'Alsace across France in small bottles, at a time when most take-home lagers were low in strength and sold in litre bottles. In 1952 a "super premium" Kronenbourg 1664, named after the firm's founding date, was added. In 1969 a vast brewery was opened at Obernai, and shortly afterwards the company became part of BSN.

Meteor

Probably the best of the Alsace lager brewers, this family company in Hochfelden, dating back to 1640, asked the Czechs if they could use the term Pilsner in 1927 and received a written agreement from Pilsner Urquell. Météor sells more than half its beers on draught in bars where it is unpasteurized. It also sells two strong lagers, Ackerland Blonde and Brune.

Mutzig

An Alsace brewery, that brews its beers at Schiltigheim.

Pelforth

This brewery near Lille, with its pelican trademark, has become famous for its strong speciality beers, notably its Pelforth Brune which was introduced in 1937. There's also a Pelforth Blonde and a standard Pelican lager. The name Pelforth is an anglicized abbreviation of "pelican" and "forte" (strong), which was adopted in 1972. It also brews George Killian's Bière Rousse, a porter, a whisky malt brew called Amberley, a rich bière de Noël (both 7.3%) and a seasonal spring bière de Mars (5.3%).

Saint Sylvestre

One of the classic country brewers of French Flanders, it has been brewing in the village of Saint Sylvestre Cappel near Hazebrouck for over a century. It produces a traditional bière de garde, Bock du Moulin, and the seasonal brews Bière de Mars and de Noël.

Schutzenberger

The only independent brewery left in the famous brewing town of Schiltigheim, near Strasbourg, was founded in 1740. It brews some of the most distinctive beers in Alsace, notably two French bockbiers, a pale Jubilator and the darker Patriator and a stronger-still Cuivrée (8%). Other beers include the bottle-conditioned Schutz Deux Milles and two seasonal brews for Christmas and spring.

Terken

Roubaix's independent brewery produces a wide range of beers under various brand names. It is best known for its flagship Septante Cinq, but it also brews Brune Spéciale, a blonde lager called Orland (5.9%), the festive Terken Bière de Noël (7%) and a low-alcohol brew called Elsoner. Its supermarket brands include Breug, Noordheim, Ubald, Überland and Upstaal.

BREWPUBS

Brasseurs

Les Brasseurs is a chain of home-brew pubs in northern France, which started with a palatial pub by the main railway station in Lille. The colourful, unpasteurized, all-malt beers include a Brasseurs ambre – blonde and brune – and a cloudy, fruity wheat beer, blanche.

Frog & Rosbif

The Paris home-brew pub in the Rue St Denis has been brewing English-style ales with Anglo-French punning names since 1993. The beers include a bitter Inseine, a stronger ale Parislytic and a stout Dark de Triomphe. In 1996 it opened a second brewpub, the Frog & Princess, across the Seine in St-Germain-des-Prés.

SWITZERLAND

Despite having one of the earliest-known, large-scale breweries in Europe – the Abbey of St Gallen, which dates back to the 9th century – the Swiss were predominantly wine drinkers until well into the 19th century.

SWISS BEERS tend to be as clean as the mountain air, but less breathtaking than the scenery. Little malting barley and few hops are grown in the rugged country. Led by the German-speaking areas of the north, however, in the mid-1800s the Swiss began to adopt the new bottom-fermenting lager beers from Bavaria. Some enterprising brewers in Zurich even chipped away their ice supplies from the Grindelwald glacier. Between 1850 and 1885 the number of breweries snowballed from 150 to 530. Since that date, much of the choice has melted away, leaving little more than 30 breweries remaining today. Once sales agreements helped to keep local breweries alive but now, like its alpine neighbour Austria, the country is dominated by two main groups – Feldschlösschen (which also controls Cardinal, Gurten, Valaisanne and Warteck) and the more internationally known Hürlimann (which includes Löwenbräu of Zurich). Heineken of the Netherlands also owns Haldengut and Calanda.

Like Austria, the main beer in Switzerland is a fresh, clean-tasting, malty lager. Although there is no complete beer purity law, most beers are all-malt and most brands are fairly similar in taste. Pilsners are barely mentioned. The Swiss prefer to ask for blonde lagers. Dark beers account for little more than 1% of sales. Most of the so-called specialities are just stronger, golden lagers, and only a few wheat beers are produced.

On international markets, Switzerland is probably best known for two distinctly different products. On the light side are low or no-alcohol brews, such as Birell, while at the heavyweight end of the market there is Samichlaus from Hürlimann, one of the strongest beers in the world. A recent innovation is the establishment of a chain of home-brew pubs, Back und Brau (Bake and Brew) which, as the name suggests, bakes baguettes and quiches while brewing fresh, unfiltered Huus (house) lagers and other beers, such as an Altbier.

Above: The Swiss beer market is dominated by two big names – Feldschlösschen and Hürlimann. Feldschlösschen's hoppy lager is a best-selling brew.

THE BEERS

Anker
A rare, dark, top-fermenting Altbier (5.8%) that was launched by the Cardinal brewery of Fribourg in 1980 in a bid to develop the limited speciality beer trade. It was marketed as a move back to tradition – "the way beer used to be".

Barbara
The patron saint of the artillery has given her name to this deep-golden-coloured "de luxe" strong lager (5.9%), produced by the Eichhof brewery in Luzern. It is a smooth, slightly sweet beer with a hint of malt.

Birell
Hürlimann of Zurich's golden, low-alcohol lager is now brewed around the world. Unlike many other near beers, the alcohol is not removed by distillation after fermentation, or by osmosis. Instead it uses a special yeast strain, which produces just 0.8% alcohol.

Braugold
This light, clear-gold premium lager beer (5.2%) is brewed to a special recipe using only the best ingredients. Eichhof claims that it is the best-selling premium brand beer in Switzerland.

Calanda Weizen
One of the few Swiss wheat beers, Calanda Weizen is a lightly fruity brew in the Bavarian style. It comes from the Calanda brewery, based in Chur in the eastern side of the country, and it was founded in 1780.

Cardinal Lager
A light, tawny-gold lager (4.9%), with a smooth, malt and hops flavour, produced at the Fribourg brewery.

Cardinal Rheingold
An amber, malty, strong lager (6.3%) with a gentle perfumed aroma, from the Fribourg brewery.

Castello
This strong, full-bodied, sweetish lager, has a malty flavour. It is brewed by Feldschlösschen.

Dreikönigs
Hürlimann's stark (strong), sweetish pale lager (6.5%) is brewed in Zurich. The name of this rich, malty beer means "Three Kings", from the coat of arms of a Zurich district.

Dunkle Perle
A dark, malty lager (5.2%) brewed by Feldschlösschen.

Eichhof Lager
This standard, refreshing, clear-gold lager (4.8%) is the flagship brew of the Eichhof brewery in Luzern. It is available on tap and in bottles and cans.

Hexen Bräu
A creamy, amber-brown Dunkel (5.4%) with a chocolatey flavour produced by Hürlimann. Its name means "witches' brew" and brewing coincides with the full moon. (See Swiss Moonshine panel.)

Hopfenperle
Feldschlösschen's hoppy lager (5.2%) from Rheinfelden is probably the most widely distributed beer in Switzerland.

Hubertus
This is a dark, strong, deep-amber-coloured, premium lager (5.7%) brewed by Eichhof in Luzern. The unusual colour comes from the roasted malts used in the mash. Its smooth, malty, slightly sweet flavour goes well with cold meats, especially game.

Hürlimann Lager Bier
This malty, golden, standard lager (4.8%) is the main brew from the Hürlimann brewery.

Löwenbräu
A malty, golden Pilsner-style lager (4.7%) with a light, hoppy flavour, from the Löwenbräu subsidiary of Hürlimann (no connection to the famous German, international brewing giant).

Moussy
A deep, bright-gold, alcohol-free beer with an intense malt flavour, from the Cardinal brewery, Fribourg.

Pony
This clear, sparkling deep-golden Pilsner-type beer (5.7%) with a strong, but well-balanced, bitter, hoppy flavour, is produced by the Eichhof brewery, Luzern.

Rheingold
This is a strong, full-bodied golden-coloured lager (6.3%). Rheingold is produced by the Cardinal brewery of Fribourg.

highly alcoholic cognac and cough-mixture character, it is a smooth beer to sip and savour before going to sleep.

Spiess Edelhell
This pale-gold lager (4.8%) is brewed to the original recipe of the Eichhof brewery's founder in 1834, and the label has changed little since then. The beer's smooth, well-rounded flavour is not too bitter, and the Eichhof brewery attributes this to the "secret" mix of cereals in the mash.

Sternbräu
A golden-amber, full-bodied Spezial (5.2%) with a malt and hops flavour, brewed by Hürlimann. The name means "star beer" and is inspired by the brewery's five-pointed star emblem.

Tambour
A strong, golden Starkbier (Starkbier means "strong beer") produced by the Wartek brewery.

Vollmond
See panel.

Wartek Lager
A hazy, golden lager, with a good malty flavour, produced by the Wartek brewery, Basel. There is also a malty Wartek Brune, and a fruity, copper-coloured, top-fermenting Wartek Alt.

Samichlaus
Classed as the world's strongest lager at a staggering 14%, Samichlaus (Santa Claus) is brewed just once a year at the beginning of December by Hürlimann of Zurich and then left to mature for 12 months before being ready to redden Father Christmas's nose the following festive season. This reddish-brown brew, first introduced in 1980, is testimony to the gutsy fighting qualities of Hürlimann's quality yeast strain, and a constant contender for the *Guinness Book of Records*. With its

THE BREWERS

Cardinal
The Fribourg brewery, founded in 1788, originally developed its Cardinal beers to celebrate the election of the bishop of Fribourg to the Papacy. It is one of the few national brands.

Eichhof
This is Switzerland's largest independent brewery, commanding a market share of 7%. The name Eichhof was born in 1937, but the company's origins can be traced back to a brewery set up by Traugott Spiess in Luzern in 1834.

Feldschlösschen
Switzerland's largest brewer, based at Rheinfelden, near Basel since 1874, merged with Cardinal of Fribourg, in 1992 and Hurlimann in 1996 to become Feldschlösschen-Hurlimann, the biggest brewer in the land by far.
The Feldschlösschen castle-like plant at Rheinfelden, set in grand grounds, looks a fitting home for the country's ruling beer dynasty. Its polished brewhouse even comes

complete with stained-glass windows and marble pillars.
Feldschlösschen's main lager is the hoppy Hopfenperle. There is also a darker Dunkle Perle, a stronger, sweeter Castello and an alcohol-free Ex-Bier.

Hürlimann
Hürlimann was founded in 1836 in Zurich, where it now dominates the market. It is Switzerland's best-known brewery abroad.

Löwenbräu
No relation to the Munich giant, this lion brewery is a subsidiary of Hürlimann, producing a range of similar lagers, as well as a Celtic Whisky Brew.

Ueli
This small brewery, established behind the Fischerstube café in Basle in 1974 was Switzerland's first micro-brewery. It brews a fruity Ueli Weizenbier, a malty Ueli Dunkel and a light Ueli Lager.

Wartek
This is the leading brewery in Basel, established in 1856.

SWISS MOONSHINE

The Swiss may have a rather conservative image, but one beer casts them in a totally different light. In 1992, the family-run Locher brewery of Appenzell, near St Gallen, revived an old tradition when it started brewing beers at the full moon, reflecting local beliefs about the effect of the moon's pull on earthly, particularly biological, events. Brewer Karl Locher claims that beer brewed at this time ferments more quickly. His golden Vollmond (full moon) lager, produced in two strengths (4.8% and 5.2%), caught the public's imagination – so much so that Hürlimann of Zurich began to brew its chocolatey, dark lager Hexen Bräu (5.4%) on the same monthly night shift when the full moon was peering through the clouds. The name means "witches' brew".

SPAIN

Recently, chilled, thirst-quenching, pale lager has taken a firm hold on the wine-drinking Spanish. Few other beers are now brewed or drunk there, and consumption has been rising rapidly over the last 20 years.

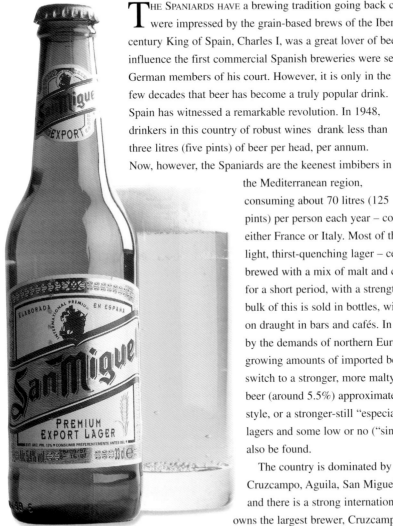

THE SPANIARDS HAVE a brewing tradition going back centuries. The Romans were impressed by the grain-based brews of the Iberian peninsula. The 16th-century King of Spain, Charles I, was a great lover of beer, and under his influence the first commercial Spanish breweries were set up by Flemish and German members of his court. However, it is only in the last few decades that beer has become a truly popular drink. Spain has witnessed a remarkable revolution. In 1948, drinkers in this country of robust wines drank less than three litres (five pints) of beer per head, per annum. Now, however, the Spaniards are the keenest imbibers in the Mediterranean region, consuming about 70 litres (125 pints) per person each year – considerably more than either France or Italy. Most of the beer that is drunk is a light, thirst-quenching lager – cerveza Pilsner that is brewed with a mix of malt and corn grits and matured for a short period, with a strength of about 4.5%. The bulk of this is sold in bottles, with a substantial amount on draught in bars and cafés. In recent years, influenced by the demands of northern European tourists and the growing amounts of imported beers, there has been a switch to a stronger, more malty, full-bodied "especial" beer (around 5.5%) approximately in the Dortmunder style, or a stronger-still "especial extra". A few dark lagers and some low or no ("sin") alcohol brews can also be found.

The country is dominated by five major breweries – Cruzcampo, Aguila, San Miguel, Damm and Mahou – and there is a strong international presence. Guinness owns the largest brewer, Cruzcampo, while Heineken controls its main rival, Aguila. Since Franco's demise in 1975 opened the door to foreign investors, international companies have been active in Spain, making the most of the boom in beer consumption.

Above: The best-known brand outside Spain, San Miguel, was originally brewed by a Filippino company.

THE BEERS

Adlerbräu

The copper-coloured, sweetish, fruity, malty cerveza especial (5.5%) with the German-sounding name is influenced by the style of Munich dunkels. It is brewed by Aguila (the Eagle).

Aguila Pilsner

Aguila's standard golden lager (4.5%) with a full-bodied, corn-sweet taste. It is allowed to mature for three weeks during its production.

Aguila Reserva Extra

At 6.5%, this is a powerful, malty "extra" from Aguila.

Alhambra

The refreshing Alhambra Pilsen (4.6%), which is also sold as "Star", the more malty Especial (5.4%), and dark Alhambra Negra (5.4%) all come from the brewery of the same name based in Granada.

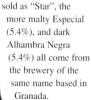

Ambar

A refreshing, golden lager (4.2%) and stronger deep-amber-coloured especial (5.2%) with a malty flavour, from La Zaragozana.

Bock-Damm

This is a deep, black-brown, malty, German-style bock beer (5.4%) with a thick, pale-cream head, produced by Damm. It is a specialist beer in Spanish terms, as well as a reminder of the Damm brewery's Germanic origins.

Cinco Estrellas

The name means "five stars" and this is the strong, darker, malty especial (5.5%) produced by the Mahou brewery of Madrid.

Cruzcampo

The Cruzcampo brewery is breaking out of its traditional market in Andalucía in the south of Spain, to launch national brands, including this pale-gold lager (4.7%) with a dry, sourish, citrus flavour.

Edel

This light-golden, all-malt, refreshing Pilsner (4.8%) is produced by Spain's pioneering lager producer, Damm. It is a premium product and is aimed at the quality end of the beer market.

Estrella Damm

This bright-gold, honeyish, premium-quality Pilsner (5.4%) is one of Damm's best-known beers. This "star" lager is a thirst-quencher, intended to be served cold on a hot day. A "light", low-calorie version is also available (3.2%).

Mahou Classic

This sweet, malty beer with a hoppy finish is the standard lager (4.8%) produced by Madrid's main brewery of the same name.

Marlen

A malty, Dortmunder-style lager (5.8%), Marlen is brewed by Zaragoza's La Zaragozana brewery.

Nostrum de San Miguel

This lager is smoother and richer than its stablemate San Miguel. It is an amber-gold-coloured, full-bodied, strong especial lager (6.2%).

San Miguel Premium

The malty, hoppy flagship lager of the San Miguel company is a relatively strong lager (5.4%) with light, citrus notes and good body. Like much of the company's output, it is aimed at the quality end of the market.

Estrella

Estrella, meaning "star", is a popular name for lagers, including Estrella del Sur from Cruzcampo, especials from Damm and Mahou (Cinco Estrellas) and an extra-powerful Estrella Extra from Coruna.

Voll-Damm

This tawny golden, full-bodied, robust, strong lager (7.2%) with a creamy, hop flavour is produced by Damm. It is much more similar to a Dortmunder Export lager than to the dark, Franconian Vollbier it is named after.

Xibeca

This popular, refreshing light-golden Pilsner (4.6%) is brewed by Damm of Barcelona. It is mainly produced and sold for home consumption in large 1-litre bottles as well as cans.

Zaragozana Export

This rich, reddish, extra-strong export lager (7%) is brewed by La Zaragozana brewery in the town of Zaragoza.

THE BREWERS

Aguila

A famous Spanish brewery dating back to 1900, Aguila (the Eagle) for many years flew high above the rest of the industry. Aguila had its roots in Madrid, but by 1980 the company was running eight breweries across the country and was half as big again as any of its rivals. By 1987, however, the rival Cruzcampo group was threatening to ease the eagle off the top perch, and Aguila came under the control of international giant Heineken. The number of plants was reduced from seven to four – in Madrid, Valencia, Córdoba and Zaragoza. Aguila, always well-known for its draught beer, brews a light Pilsner, a sweeter especial called Adlerbräu and more full-bodied Reserva Extra. Like many Spanish lagers, the beers are brewed with corn grits as well as barley malt and lagered for three weeks. Production is now concentrated in two large, modern breweries in Madrid and Valencia.

Alhambra

This is one of Spain's smaller breweries. It was founded in 1925 in the far south of the country in Granada. It has links with Damm in Barcelona.

Cruzcampo

Spain's largest brewing group was formed through the merger of a number of regional breweries in 1987. Since 1990, it has been owned by Irish stout brewers Guinness, who added Union Cervecera in 1991. The combine now controls about

Above: Cruzcampo is now owned by Guinness of Ireland.

a quarter of the market, with its traditional heartland in Andalucía in the south. It has five breweries in Seville, Jaen, Madrid, Valencia and Navarra. The group is building national brands, notably its main beer Cruzcampo. More local lagers include Keler, Alcázar, Victoria, Calatrava and Estrella del Sur.

Damm

The firm that pioneered lager-brewing in Spain was introduced by an Alsatian brewer Auguste Damm in 1876. The company later absorbed other breweries such as La Bohemia. Damm dominates Catalonia in north-eastern Spain and has breweries in Barcelona and nearby Llobregat, besides

plants in Murcia and at Palma on the island of Majorca. As well as a popular Pilsner Xibeca and especial Estrella, it brews a number of speciality beers, which reflect its Germanic roots, including an all-malt Edel, a dark Bock-Damm and a robust Voll-Damm. There is also a golden Estrella Light (3.2%) and a non-alcoholic Damm-Bier.

Mahou

The dominant brewer in the Spanish capital Madrid dates back to 1890. It has two breweries, one in Madrid and the other in Abrera.

San Miguel

The Asian brewing giant of the Philippines entered the Spanish market in 1956, building a plant in Lerida in Catalonia. From the start it concentrated on the premium end of the market and led the move to stronger especial beers. The company

also developed barley growing in Spain and the brewing of near all-malt beers. Its two main brews are the malty San Miguel and smoother, richer Nostrum de San Miguel. The Spanish San Miguel, with additional breweries in Burgos and Málaga, is now linked to Kronenbourg of France.

La Zaragozana

This small brewery has been operating in Zaragoza since 1900. Besides an Ambar lager (4.2%) and especial (5.2%), it also brews a German-style Dortmunder called Marlen (5.8%) and an extra-strong Export (7%).

Above: La Zaragozana uses horse-drawn drays to promote its beers.

PORTUGAL

Beer drinking has only become popular in Portugal in recent years, though breweries were founded on the Iberian peninsula in the 19th century. Golden lagers predominate, but there is an occasional native dark beer to be found.

Tʜᴇ Pᴏʀᴛᴜɢᴜᴇsᴇ ᴅɪᴄᴛᴀᴛᴏʀ Salazar kept the country in isolation for many years, shutting the local brewing industry off from foreign influence and investment. In 1889, seven small companies in Oporto combined, followed by another merger in 1934 based in Lisbon. These two groups dominated the country and survived nationalization (1977–1990) to form the basis of the modern industry.

Sociedad Central de Cervejas (Centralcer) and Uniao Cervejeira (Unicer) both run three breweries apiece and control about half the market each. Both concentrate on malty mild lagers. Portugal's beers tend to be good-quality interpretations of German styles and there are also a few dark lagers. Most beer is bottled. There are separate breweries on the islands of Madeira (Empresa) and the Azores (Melo Abreu).

Above: Portuguese brewers concentrate on stronger lagers, such as Sagres.

THE BEERS

Cergal
A mildly bitter, Pilsner-style lager (4.6%) with a light dry taste from Centralcer.

Coral
The main brand from Madeira's Empresa brewery is a light, golden lager with a light malt and hops flavour and a dry aftertaste.

Sagres

The Sagres brew from Central de Cervejas is named after the old, beautiful cape on the south-western tip of Portugal, where Prince Henry, the Navigator started his naval school in the 15th century.

Cristal
Unicer's deep-yellow-coloured, hoppy, sweetish lager (5.2%) also comes in a dark version, Cristal Brown.

Melo Abreu Especial
This orangey-coloured lager (5%) has a sweet, malt flavour. It is the main brand from the small Melo Abreu brewery in the Azores.

Onix
A mild, dark, Vienna-style lager (4.3%) with a medium body and pleasant caramel and hoppy flavour which comes from Centralcer.

Sagres
Central's best-selling fruity lager (5.1%) is sold in both popular, pale-yellow blonde (Sagres Pale) and rarer brown versions. The smoother, dark-brown-coloured, chocolatey, molasses-flavoured, dark

beer is in the style of a Munich Dunkel. There is also a premium Sagres Golden.

Super Bock
Unicer's pale, robust, malty, fruity lager (5.8%) is one of the most popular brands drunk in Portugal.

Topazio
A deep-gold, malty lager with a sweet aftertaste. It is a regional brand from Sociedad Central de Cervejas.

AFRICA

The Egyptians were the earliest recorded beer makers, and the tradition of brewing is widespread across the African continent. Local beers, made from fermented maize or millet, are still commonly brewed and enjoyed.

Drinking potent, cloudy home-brew has been a communal occasion for centuries across Africa. Thanksgivings, initiations, marriages and births have all long been celebrated around a pot or two of home-brewed beer. The enduring popularity of these native, top-fermented brews has meant that Africa is one of the areas of the world where the increasing dominance of bottom-fermented lagers has been kept partially at bay.

European settlers in Africa brought their own beer and brewing tradition to the continent. Africa's first commercial brewery was set up by a sailor from Antwerp, Pieter Visagie, in Rondebosch in the Cape of Good Hope as early as 1655. It took more than a century after that before local commercial production in southern Africa posed a challenge to imported beer but leading breweries, such as the Cape brewery and the Mariedahl brewery in Newlands, South Africa, were established in the early 1820s. European brews made their mark across the continent, and stouts from England remain an enduring favourite. However, once lager brewing arrived in the 1890s, pioneered by Castle Lager from South African Breweries, it rapidly replaced the earlier top-fermenting ales in the commercial market.

In the north of the continent, breweries tended to arrive later. More recent ventures have been set up by international groups such as Heineken and Interbrew, often as joint ventures with local companies. Carlsberg, for example, established Carlsberg Malawi Ltd in partnership with the Malawi Government in 1968. Virtually all these breweries produce local versions of international Pilsners, often made by mixing in local cereals such as maize, since little barley is grown in Africa.

Above: Tusker is a well-known, malty lager beer from Kenya, one of the few African countries where barley and hops are grown.

THE BEERS

Allsopp's White Cap

A sweetish, fruity, aromatic lager (4%) from Kenya Breweries. White Cap is named after the snowy peak of Mount Kenya. This lager was originally brewed by Allsopp, East Africa, but the company merged with Kenya Breweries in 1962.

Asmara Lager

The golden Asmara Lager, which is matured for more than four weeks, has a firm, malty flavour and excellent body. It is the only beer produced by the Asmara brewery in Eritrea.

Bière Bénin

This light, French-style lager comes from the Bénin brewery in Togo.

Bohlinger's

Bohlinger's is a dry, golden lager brewed by National Breweries of Zimbabwe, which was founded in 1911, and for many years was known as Rhodesian Breweries.

Bosun's

This light, fruity, golden bitter (4.5%) is brewed by the first European-style micro-brewery to be established in Africa – Mitchell's of Knysna in South Africa.

Camel Beer

This is the Blue Nile brewery's famous Sudanese lager brand. It was first launched in 1955. The recipe was originally based on an early English lager, brewed by the Barclay Perkins company, and was widely exported to Africa from London at the time.

Castle Golden Pilsner

This light lager from South African Breweries is brewed using barley malt and maize.

Castle Lager

This pale, lemony-tasting lager (5%) with a dry, hoppy finish is the leading beer brand from South African Breweries. It is brewed using barley malt, maize and sucrose. The name comes from the Castle brewery founded by Charles Glass in Johannesburg in 1884.

Castle Lager was the first bottom-fermenting beer produced in Africa, using plant bought by the South African Breweries pioneer, Frederick Mead, from the

Pfaudler Vacuum Company of the US. Once introduced in 1898, the lager proved to be such a popular refreshing drink in the hot African climate that South African Breweries decided to adopt the Castle name for all of its beers and breweries. Rival breweries, impressed by the success of the golden brew, rushed to imitate the trend and brew lager as well.

Castle Milk Stout

South African Breweries' full-bodied, dark, smooth milk stout (8%) is brewed using milk sugar (lactose), The range of Castle beers are also produced by National Breweries of Zimbabwe in which SAB has a stake.

Chibuku

A fast-fermenting, cloudy, traditional beer (3.5%) from Zimbabwe, with a chewy, cereal consistency. Chibuku has a refreshing, sour taste and a shelf-life of 3–4 days. It is sold as a value-for-money, low-cost product, particularly on draught in large, communal beer halls. In 1991 a premium version was introduced in a plastic bottle and because of its shape it was nicknamed "the Scud" after the missiles used in the Gulf War.

Club Pilsner

This light, refreshing Pilsner (4.5%) is lagered for an average of three weeks and uses cane sugar in the mash. It comes from Nile Breweries of Uganda.

ESB

One of the strongest beers in the whole of Africa. This smooth, golden, chill-filtered lager (7%) is produced by Nile Breweries of Uganda. It is made using cane sugar as well as barley malt in the mash. The beer's full name is Chairman's Extra Strong Brew.

Flag

This range of popular local light lagers is produced by Brasseries du Maroc (of Morocco). It includes Flag Pilsner, Flag Spéciale and a golden, hoppy, malty Flag Export.

Forester's

Following the world trend for real beers, this unfiltered and unpasteurized, full-bodied lager (5%) is brewed by the Mitchell's micro-brewery in Knysna, South Africa.

Gulder

A refreshing, slightly hoppy, dry lager (5%) that is the flagship brand of Nigerian Breweries. Gulder is also brewed in the company's plant in Ghana.

Hansa Urbock

The rich, reddish Urbock (6%) is brewed by the German-founded Hansa brewery in Swakopmund. Like all Namibian beers, it is brewed according to the German beer purity law. The warming winter brew provides Africa with a rare, German-style, dark lager.

Hunter's

A pale-gold, refreshing lager that is nevertheless full of flavour. Hunter's is brewed by a Czech brewmaster in accordance with the German beer purity law, using only malt, hops, barley and yeast. It is produced by the private Nesbitt brewery of Zimbabwe.

Legend Stout

A strong, rich stout (7%), with a roasted-chocolate flavour, produced by Nigerian Breweries. It is a rival to Guinness in the country that is the third largest market for stout in the world.

Lion Lager

Another leading lager (5%) from South African Breweries. It is slightly sweeter than SAB's other major brand, Castle. The Lion brand has been roaring since a Norwegian merchant Anders Ohlsson, who had been involved in beer brewing in Africa since 1862, established the Annaberg brewery in Cape Town in 1883.

Mamba Lager

This bright-gold, malty lager is probably the best-known beer from French West Africa. It has been brewed by Solibra in Abidjan in the Ivory Coast since 1960. The Solibra brewery also produces a Mamba Bock and a rich, tawny Mamba Brune.

Ngoma

A range of beers from Brasseries du Bénin of Lome, Togo. It includes a light, hazy-gold Pilsner with a well-balanced, hoppy flavour, and a darker, more malty, amber-coloured Special with a sourish malt flavour. The brand name Ngoma means "a drum".

Nile Special

This full-bodied lager (5.6%) is brewed by Nile Breweries, using cane sugar as well as barley malt. It is lagered for an average of three weeks.

Ohlsson's Lager

A golden lager (5%) named after the Ohlsson's brewery that is now owned by SAB.

Above: The Nile snakes through the African continent for over 4,000 miles (6,500 km). At its source in Uganda, Nile Breweries is now flourishing thanks to help from overseas. The great river slows as it nears the end of its course in Egypt, the country where the world's earliest brewers once produced their beer.

Raven Stout

This dark, rich, heavy stout (6%) is brewed by the Mitchell's micro-brewery of Knysna in South Africa.

Rex

A dry, golden lager produced by Nigerian Breweries.

Simba Lager

A popular golden lager in Zaire (formerly the Belgian Congo) Simba has been produced by the Brasimba brewery (in which the Belgian giant Interbrew has a stake) since 1923.

Tafel Lager

A refreshing, standard lager (4%) with a slightly bitter flavour, brewed according to the German beer purity law. Tafel is produced by the Hansa brewery in Swakopmund on the Namibian coast.

Windhoek

The Windhoek beers include a low-alcohol light (1.9%), a refreshing Windhoek lager (4%), a more hoppy export (4.5%) and a fuller-bodied, malty special (5.3%). The range of lagers, all brewed according to the German beer purity law, comes from Namibia Breweries' modern plant in Windhoek. The brewery opened in the outskirts of the town in 1986 when the old Garten Street premises were closed.

Zambezi

A pale-gold, light, refreshing lager (4.5%) with a sweet-sour flavour, from National Breweries, Zimbabwe.

DARKEST AFRICA

Some areas of Africa have a strong stout-drinking tradition. Nowhere is this more true than in Nigeria, the third-largest stout market in the world. Guinness Nigeria alone boasts four breweries in this heavily populated country. Local rivals to Guinness in Nigeria include Legend Stout by Nigerian Breweries, Power Stout by North brewery of Kano, Eagle Stout by Golden Guinea brewery of Umuahia, and Lion Stout by the Mopa brewery. The stouts produced by these breweries are much more than faint shadows left over from the British Empire. The Guinness sold here, for instance, is not the standard Guinness brewed in Ireland or even the more substantial Foreign Extra Stout sold elsewhere in Africa, but a stronger version still, weighing in at 8% alcohol by volume. This rich, bitter-sweet brew is a blend of a strong local pale beer and concentrated dark wort supplied from Dublin. It is sold as an energy-giving stimulant, "Guinness for Power", with potent properties. Advertising campaigns, free from the restrictions of Europe or America, once even suggested the possibility of "a baby in every bottle".

Star

A sweetish, hazy, golden, hoppy lager (5%). Star lager beer was first produced in 1949 in a Lagos brewery that is now owned by Nigerian Breweries. This most popular lager brand is now brewed and sold all the way across West Africa – from Sierra Leone to Ghana.

Tusker

Kenya Breweries' creamy, dry, golden lager appears in a variety of strengths. Tusker Premium, a strong, all-malt beer (5%), is brewed for international export. According to legend, it was named after the angry elephant which trampled to death one of the two brothers who founded the brewery.

THE BREWERS

Asmara

An Italian, Luigi Melotti, originally set up this company in Asmara, Eritrea, in 1939 to produce pure alcohol and spirits. It began to produce lager three years later. In 1984, it changed its name from Melotti to Asmara.

Blue Nile

This was the first brewery in the Sudan. It was built in the early 1950s and was established by the English brewing company Barclay Perkins. It brewed a little stout and brown ale (known as dark) when it opened in 1955. Today, however, production is mainly devoted to its main beer – a bottom-fermenting lager, Camel.

Brasseries du Bénin

Brasseries du Bénin of Togo in the former French West Africa produces a light, French-style, Bière Bénin lager and also markets beers under the Ngoma (Drum) brand name.

Brasseries du Maroc

Breweries of Morocco in north-western Africa is one of the few thriving brewing groups in a Muslim country. It runs three modern breweries in Casablanca, Tangier and Fès, alongside an extensive soft drinks operation. Brasseries du Maroc produces its own popular range of light lagers in bottles and cans, mainly

under the Flag brand name. These account for four-fifths of production and also include the Bock 49 and Stork brands, besides the non-alcoholic Crown.

Chibuku

Chibuku is the leading commercial producer of traditional native beer in Zimbabwe. It has 16 breweries scattered around the country in order to ensure fresh, live beer in each local market. It is sold mainly on draught in large, communal beer halls.

By 1995, a newly introduced take-home bottle accounted for 40% of the brewery's production.

East African Breweries

See Kenya Breweries.

Hansa

The Hansa brewery was founded in 1929 in the picturesque Namibian coastal town of Swakopmund. In 1968, it was taken over by South West (later Namibian) Breweries. As well as a refreshing Tafel Lager, it also produces a rich, reddish urbock and a refreshing golden Pilsner. Like all Namibian beers, these beers are brewed according to the German beer purity law Rheinheitsgetbot.

Kenya Breweries

Kenya Breweries was founded by two brothers in Nairobi in the early 1920s, using equipment from England. It was for many years known as East African Breweries. Some English-style ales and stouts were produced initially, using locally grown barley, but the company soon concentrated on a golden lager called Tusker. In 1952, the company opened a second brewery on the coast at Mombasa. It was bad timing, though, as the country exploded in the Mau Mau rebellion against British rule, and the African population boycotted European beers. As independence approached, the company merged in 1962 with its local rival, Allsopp, East Africa. Seven years later, the combine added another Nairobi brewery, City. In 1982, the group opened a new brewery in Kisumu near Lake Victoria. Today, the main lagers are Tusker and the more fruity White Cap (both around 4.2%), and a slightly more hoppy Pilsner. Unmalted barley is added as an adjunct to all three. Less full-bodied "export" versions are also produced using cane sugar, and a stronger, nearly all-malt, Tusker Premium (5%) for international sales.

Mitchell's

Africa's first micro-brewery was set up in 1984 by a former SAB brewer Lex Mitchell in Knysna on the southern coast of Cape Province, South Africa. His unfiltered and unpasteurized malty beers include a lightly fruity Bosun's Bitter (4.5%) and fuller-bodied Forester's.

Namibia

The Namibia Company was founded in 1920 as South West Breweries, when four German colonial breweries in the area amalgamated. In 1968, the Windhoek-based group absorbed its rival, Hansa of Swakopmund. When Namibia gained independence in 1990, the group was renamed Namibia Breweries. The company brews quality lagers such as Windhoek Export Lager following the beer purity law.

National

Founded in 1911 and known for many years as Rhodesian Breweries, National Breweries of Zimbabwe has two plants in Harare and Bulawayo.

Nesbitt

Zimbabwe's first independent brewery was founded at Chiredzi in 1990 and employs a Czech brewmaster, F. Mrazek, to brew its all-malt beers. Its main beer is the crisp Hunter's Lager.

Nigerian Breweries

The largest brewing company in Africa's leading brewing nation is Nigerian Breweries, with plants in Iganmu, Ibadan, Aba and Kaduna. Nigerian opened its first brewery in 1949 with the support of Heineken. It began by brewing a sweetish Star lager. Other lager brands have now been developed, notably the drier Gulder and Rex beers. The Nigerian Breweries group also produces a rich rival to Guinness – Legend Stout.

Nile Breweries

This Ugandan brewery was built with German investment and assistance in the town of Jinja in 1954, close to the source of the Nile. The brewery flourished until 1972, but it struggled in the years that followed. For 20 years, during and after Idi Amin's regime, the brewery was allowed to disintegrate.

The Nile brewery was revived in 1992 with help from the international giant Carlsberg. Three main lagers are produced: a light Club Pilsner, the fuller-bodied Nile Special and the extra-strong ESB. All of the brews use cane sugar as well as barley malt and are lagered for an average of three weeks. Nile Breweries controls more than 60% of the Ugandan beer market.

Solibra

This brewery was set up in the Ivory Coast in 1960. Its beers include the rich, the golden, malty Mamba, a bock and a brune. Mamba beer is now exported.

South African Breweries

This was the first brewing giant of the African continent. The company's roots lie in the Natal brewery of Pietermaritzburg, which was set up by Frederick Mead in 1891. In 1892 Natal took over Glass's Castle Brewery in Johannesburg to form South African United Breweries, which then became South African Breweries (SAB) in 1895.

SAB was not to dominate the country, however, until 1956 when it merged with its two main rivals, Ohlsson's (Lion), which controlled the Cape, and Union Breweries (Chandler's).

Today the main lagers that it produces – Castle and Lion – reflect this history. SAB also offers a wide range of other lager brands which includes Ohlsson's, Chandler's, Rogue and Old Dutch.

The company now holds substantial share stakes in many other African breweries and and has expanded into breweries in Eastern Europe.

Above: Even in bygone days, the need to supply beer to a thirsty nation meant that Namibia Breweries had to expand its brewery.

SOUTH AFRICAN SORGHUM BEERS

Beer brewing using sorghum and relying on spontaneous fermentation has long been a domestic industry in Africa, and it is not unusual to find women still selling home-brewed beers in the marketplaces. These thick, tawny brews or "porridge beers" are cheap and must be consumed within two or three days. They are generally regarded by African drinkers as more nutritious than pale European lagers.

Commercially brewed sorghum (millet) beers have been produced in South Africa from the early 20th century to meet the demands for beer from the black, urban population. They originated in Natal.

Their popularity, however, is partly due to the fact that until 1962 the majority of the black population was not allowed to buy European-style beers. Sorghum beers, which were called "Kaffir beers" by white South Africans, were sold in special bars reserved only for blacks, in open-air "beer gardens" or at roadside stalls.

Since the collapse of the apartheid regime, although the consumption of golden lagers has certainly soared, there has been no mass switch. In the late 1970s there were 32 commercial sorghum beer breweries in South Africa, and new ones are still being opened.

Above: Enjoying a sorghum beer in an open-air bar.

Above: A Zulu woman in South Africa prepares the mash for a sorghum brew. The thick, porridge-like mixture will be left open to the air and the action of wild yeasts for a few days in order to ferment, and will then be drunk within two or three days.

CHINA

Although the Chinese have been making alcoholic drinks for centuries, they have no real beer-brewing tradition. However, this is not going to stop China becoming the largest beer-brewing nation in the world by the year 2000.

OREIGN EXPERTISE played a great part in the initial development of the beer-brewing industry in China. The trend started at the beginning of this century – the Russians brewed in Harbin and the Germans in Tsingtao. Today, joint venture partners are bringing in new technology and capital to modernize the creaking Chinese industry. Some sources estimate that by the year 2000 China will be the world's largest beer producer in terms of volume. Official estimates of the number of breweries in China put it at approximately 850, though there are probably hundreds more "unregistered" breweries. No single brewer has a market share larger than 4%. The breweries fall into three main categories – joint-owned Chinese and foreign ventures, large national breweries and local breweries. They are owned and run in a bewildering diversity of ways – publicly quoted companies (such as Tsingtao), town breweries run by local entrepreneurs and state-owned concerns run by government agencies.

Although the current consumption of beer is relatively low, this seems set to change. Personal disposable income is rising steeply among some of the population, and at least some of this money seems to be being spent on beer.

Most beer is sold in the form of "value for money" brands. Large, returnable bottles of local brews make up the majority of sales. Most consumers are fiercely loyal to their local beer – seemingly no matter what the quality. Regional markets are often protected by official and unofficial restrictions – such as fines levied on "substandard" beers imported from other areas and charges to retailers for each crate of beer brought in from outside the region. In their protected markets, substandard local brewers have little incentive to improve.

Above: Germany leased the port of Tsingtao (now called Quingdao) and built a brewery there which still survives today, though it is now Chinese-owned.

THE BEERS

Baiyun Beer
A hazy-yellow lager beer from the Guangzhou brewery, Guangzhou City.

Canton Lager Beer
A gold-coloured, malty lager, from the Guangzhou brewery, Guangzhou City.

Chinese Ginseng Beer
A thin, pale lager (4.1%) brewed under licence in Britain using only natural ingredients and some Ginseng herbal seasoning.

Chu Sing
A pale-gold, malty lager from the Chu Jiang brewery, Guangzhou City.

Double Happiness Guangzhou Beer
A pale-gold, highly carbonated lager with a light, malt flavour. It is produced by Guangzhou brewery, Guangzhou City.

Emperor's Gold Beer
A gold lager with a slightly molasses aftertaste, produced by the Hangzhou brewery, Hangzhou City, using Zhejiang barley.

Five Star Beer
This golden lager has a mild, malty flavour. It is produced by the Shen Ho Shing brewery, Beijing.

Guangminpai
An unusual dark lager produced by the Shanghai brewery.

Hua Nan Beer
A pleasant, refreshing, yellow-gold lager beer, from the Guangzhou brewery, Guangzhou City.

Mon-Lei Beer
A reddish-coloured lager, brewed by the Beijing Wuxing and Shen Ho Shing breweries.

Nine Star Premium
This gold lager beer has a good malt and hop flavour. It is brewed by the Five Star brewery, Beijing.

Peking Beer
A pale-golden lager from the Feng Shon brewery, Beijing.

Shanghai (Swan) Lager
The popular name for lager which in this case comes from the emblem on the label of this malty, lightly hopped lager. It is brewed by the Shanghai brewery and is said to have once been the official drink served at Communist Party conferences.

Song Hay Double Happiness Beer
Gold, well-flavoured lager beer from the Guangzhou brewery, Guangzhou City.

Sun Lik
A traditional Chinese dragon decorates the label of this golden, malty lager (5%), brewed by the Hong Kong brewery.

Sweet China
A pineapple-flavoured, yellow-gold lager which comes from the Guangzhou brewery, Guangzhou City.

Tientan Beer
A hazy, yellow-gold lager from the Beijing brewery. The name means "Temple of Heaven".

Tsingtao Beer
A pale-gold, Pilsner-style lager (5%), with a malt and hops, vanilla flavour, brewed by the Tsingtao brewery in

Quingdao, Shandong province. Tsingtao is widely exported around the world in both bottles and cans, partly to fuel the thirst of Chinese populations in other countries. It is also popular among Westerners as an accompaniment to Chinese food. It is something of a cult beer in the US.
There is also a deep-amber Tsingtao Dark Beer.

West Lake Beer
A dark-gold-coloured, light lager beer (3.8%) which has a sweet, fruity flavour, and claims to contain no artificial ingredients – only hops, malt, rice and spring water from the West Lake region. It is brewed by the Hangzhou Zhongce Beer Co Ltd.

JAPAN

The first commercial brewery in Japan, Spring Valley in Yokohama, was started by an American, William Copeland, in 1869, when Japan opened up to trade with the West. At that time the beer was mainly for foreign traders and seamen.

Above: Japanese brewers have long been in the vanguard of technological innovation, producing high-tech beer styles such as dry beer.

BEER IS A RELATIVELY recent arrival in Japan. Gradually, the Japanese tried out the new drink and then embraced it with a passion, so that today the country is one of the leading beer-drinking nations in the world. As has been their way with many outside inventions they have adopted, the Japanese have refined and developed the product. Most of the lagers are ultra-clean, hi-tech versions of golden international Pilsners, using rice in the mash. The Japanese were pioneers in developing new styles, such as dry beers. There is a constant conveyor-belt of ingenious variations on a light lager, along with novelty presentations such as Sapporo's can that turns into a cup. Some dark beers are produced – a legacy from the early German influence.

Today, the brewing industry is dominated by four main groups: Kirin, Asahi, Sapporo and Suntory (with Orion on the island of Okinawa). A ruling that allowed only breweries producing a minimum of 450,000 gallons (two million litres) a year to operate froze small-scale, independent brewers out of the market. This ruling was repealed in 1994. The result was a flood of new micro-breweries and brewpubs producing fresh ji-biru (local beer). A number of these new ventures have been set up by established saké makers. The major brewers have responded to the rising popularity of more unusual brews by producing regional beers and opening their own brewpubs. At the same time, there has been growing demand for imported beers, which has encouraged the large groups to try out new beer styles, such as an alt-style beer produced by Kirin.

Most beer in Japan is sold in bottles or cans, with only a small amount available on draught. Bottled and canned beers marked "draft" are fine-filtered (in a process known as micro-filtration) but the majority are usually sold unpasteurized for the home market.

THE BEERS

Asahi Black Beer

Many Japanese like to blend this sweetish, red-brown, beer (5%) with a light lager.

Asahi Stout

This richly roasted, top-fermented stout is a potent brew (8%). It also has a hint of lactic sourness, like early English porters and stouts.

Kirin Beer

Japan's best-selling beer (4.9%) is a crisp, full-bodied, fresh-flavoured Pilsner brewed using Saaz and Hallertau hops. It is matured for up to two months before being sold unpasteurized.

Kirin Black Beer

This smoky, traditional, dark beer (5%) has a hint of roasted coffee and hops.

Kirin Ichiban Shibori

Kirin's second-best-selling beer was introduced in 1990. Brewed using just the first liquid run-off from the mash tun, Ichiban Shibori ("first wort") gives a smoother malt taste. It is sold in distinctive, tall bottles. This soft golden

lager (5.5%) has proved a major marketing success.

Kirin Stout

This marvellously rich, complex, bottom-fermenting stout (8%) has a hint of toffee.

Kuro-nama

This light, golden lager is marketed by Asahi as a late-night drink.

Kyoto Alt

See Kirin.

Malt's

Suntory's appropriately named malty, flagship lager is, unusually for a Japanese beer, brewed with 100% malt.

Sapporo Black Beer

Sapporo was the first Japanese brewery to brew a German-style, dark lager in 1892 and this classic, full-flavoured black beer (5%) is still brewed today, using crystal, chocolate and Munich malts as well as rice.

Sapporo Original Draft Black Label

The fourth-best-selling beer in Japan, this lively, light Pilsner (4.7%) was the first to use the micro-filtration technique instead of pasteurization to produce what is called a "draft" beer. It is sold abroad in stylish silver cans as Sapporo Draft.

Shirayuki

Two Belgian-style ales, a soft Shirayuki Blonde and a creamy Shirayuki Dark, are produced in the saké town of Itami, near Osaka, in a brewery restaurant run by the Shirayuki (White Snow) saké firm.

Shokusai Bakushu

Asahi launched this lager in 1996. It was designed to accompany meals and is sold under two different labels, pink and green. The pink version has a milder flavour.

Spring Valley

This hoppy, golden lager takes its name from Japan's first brewery, which was founded in Yokohama in 1869. It is brewed at a pub brewery in a tourist beer village close to Kirin's modern brewery in the port of Yokohama, near Tokyo.

Below: An old beer poster advertising Yebisu and Sapporo beer in the museum at the Sapporo brewery, Hokkaido.

Suntory Daichi

A smooth golden lager (4.8%) from Suntory which emphasizes its natural ingredients. It is brewed with 100% barley malts.

Super Dry

The original pioneer of the dry beer style, Super Dry became fashionable around the world for a brief time in the late 1980s and early 1990s. In the mid-1980s the Asahi brewery was in trouble, with falling sales and a reduced market share. A taste test on 5,000 consumers in 1985 found that people wanted a smooth, light-tasting beer. The resulting Asahi Super Dry was launched in 1987. This is a pale Pilsner, fermented for longer than normal. This reduces the body of the beer while increasing the alcohol content (to 5% from the then more usual 4.5%). The beer is less bitter than usual Pilsners, with virtually no aftertaste and a characteristic, dry, parching effect in the mouth. The intention was to create a thin, clean beer with little flavour, which would leave consumers in need of another drink. In both aims it succeeded beyond Asahi's most extravagant dreams. Since the early 1990s, while dry beers have fallen out of favour elsewhere, Super Dry has remained popular in Japan. In 1995, it was the country's second-best-selling beer after Kirin Lager, selling more than 121 million cases.

Right: The Asahi brewery in Tokyo, designed by Philippe Stark.

Yebisu

Sapporo's premium all-malt Dortmunder-style lager (5%) uses German aroma hops in order to produce one of the most fully flavoured mainstream beers brewed in Japan. It is named after a Tokyo brewery that was built at the turn of the century.

Z

Asahi brews this faintly fruity, top-fermenting light ale. The company claims that this unpasteurized brew is one of the "most technologically advanced beers" in Japan. In keeping with the Asahi company's policy of linking beers to different occasions, Z beer is marketed specifically as a holiday drink.

THE BREWERS

Asahi

Founded as the Osaka brewery in 1889, Asahi became part of the Dai Nippon brewing company in 1906. This was Japan's first beer giant. After the Second World War, Dai Nippon was split up into Nippon (later renamed Sapporo) and Asahi. The latter was the smaller of the two parts, but this changed dramatically in 1987 when Asahi launched Super Dry. The huge success of this brand rocketed Asahi's share of the market from 10% to 28% in 1995, making it Japan's second-largest brewing group. Other Asahi beers include Z, Double Yeasts and two more traditional brews, a sweetish red-brown, Asahi, Black Beer (5%), and a richly roasted, top-fermented Asahi Stout (8%). In 1996, Asahi launched a new marketing strategy linking such beers as Shokusai Bakushu and Kuro-nama to different occasions.

Kirin

Japan's largest brewer accounts for about half of the country's production, with 14 breweries. The company can trace its history back to Japan's first brewery, Spring Valley of Yokohama of 1869, and was foreign-owned until it was bought by Japanese interests, led by Mitsubishi, in 1970. It brews Japan's best-selling beer, Kirin Lager. Its other main beer is the more malty Ichiban. In 1995, Kirin Lager sold more than 151 million cases; Ichiban 76 million. In the search for a new sales success to equal Ichiban, the company has launched a wide range of local and speciality beers including a copper-coloured alt brewed from crystal malt in a micro-brewery in Kyoto. It also brews a slightly smoky Kirin Black Beer and a richer, more chewy bottom-fermenting Kirin Stout.

Sapporo

The oldest continuously operating brewery in Japan was founded in the town of Sapporo in 1876. It became part of Dai Nippon in 1906, before being split up again in 1949 and regaining its original name in 1964. This leading exporter of Japanese beer, has pioneered a number of beer styles and brewing techniques. It was the first Japanese brewery to brew a German-style dark lager in 1892. In 1971, it launched Japan's original all-malt premium beer, Yebisu, and was the first to introduce seasonal and regional beers.

It also pioneered the use of micro-filtration to produce unpasteurized "draft" beers. Today its best-selling beer is its Original Draft Black

Label, a lively dryish Pilsner, which is sold abroad as Sapporo Draft. There is also a low-priced, low-malt lager called Drafty.

The company runs a brewpub in Kawaguchi and popular German-style beer gardens alongside its breweries in Sapporo, Nagoya, Sendai and Shizuoka.

Suntory

The smallest of Japan's four main breweries, Suntory is primarily a wine-maker and distiller dating from 1899. It began brewing in 1963. Its flagship beer, the softly sweetish all-malt Malt's. A lighter brew named Super Hop's is also available. In addition there is a North American-style lager, Dynamic (brewed with Canadian yeast).

MICRO-BREWERIES AND BREWPUBS

Since 1994, Japan has seen a boom in micro-breweries and brewpubs. The result is more variety of beer styles.

Akasaka

A soft-drinks company set up this micro-brewery in a suburb of Tokyo. It brews a Pilsner and a dark Kuro Half.

Doppo

This micro was set up by the Miyashita saké company in Okayama. It brews German-style beers – Doppo Pilsner and a reddish Doppo Dunkel.

Gotenba Kohgen

The hot springs tourist town of Gotenba is home to a beer hall and brewery. It offers a light Pilsner, a malty Gotenba Dunkel and a fruity Weizen.

KIRIN

The Kirin is a legendary animal of ancient China – half dragon, half horse – which appeared to the mother of Confucius just before his birth 2,500 years ago. The sight of this benevolent creature was supposed to herald the arrival of great men, and it is regarded as a symbol of good luck, a harbinger of happy events to come. The name was first adopted by the Spring Valley Brewery for its beer in 1888, and the fabled animal still appears on Kirin's main brands today.

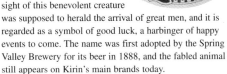

Kizakura Kappa

The Kappa saké company set up this brewpub in Kyoto. Its German-style ales include a Kappa Alt, a fruity kölsch and a sweeter Kölsch Mild, all brewed using saké yeast.

Kyoto

See Kirin.

Moku Moku

This rural micro-brewery in Nishiyubune, near Ueno, was set up by a farming co-operative. It brews a variety of country beers, including a Pilsner, a fruity amber ale, a peaty smoked ale and a tart Biscuit Weizen.

Okhotsk

This brewpub in Kitami on the island of Hokkaido is named after the nearby Sea of Okhotsk. Its wide range of beers includes a finely balanced Okhotsk Bitter.

Otaru

This brewpub in the port of Otaru, near Sapporo, produces German-style lagers, including a hoppy Otaru Helles and a malty, dark dunkel.

Sandaya

This brewpub near Osaka is run by a smoked meat company. The unfiltered beers include a yeasty Pilsner, a malty Festbier, a black beer and a well-roasted Sandaya Smoked Beer, which is served to accompany the smoked meat produced by the parent company.

Sankt Gallen

This small Tokyo brewpub was one of the first to open. It brews a range of seasonal, spiced ales including a hoppy Sankt Gallen Spring Ale and the sweeter St Valentine's.

Sumida River

Asahi's brewpub in its Tokyo office complex makes three German-style draught beers: a mild Altbier, a Kölsch called River Beer and a full-bodied, unfiltered Zwickelbier.

Uehara

One of Japan's first micro-breweries was set up in the Echigo pub in Makimachi. Its wide range of beers includes a fruity Uehara Pale Ale, a cloudy Uehara Weizen and a very powerful Old Ale.

Above: The beautiful stained-glass window in the Sapporo brewery.

THE REST OF ASIA

In the booming economies of the Far East, the beer market is expanding. There is a strong European influence on the industry in the shape of machinery and investment, and in the predominance of lagers.

ASIA'S BREWERIES are spread far and wide – from the far north of India, through Sri Lanka, Thailand, Malaysia and Vietnam, to Singapore and Indonesia. As a result, the influences are wide-ranging, and the brewers have to contend with a diversity of laws, even within some country boundaries. Some states of India, for example, are strictly prohibitionist, while others are very relaxed in their attitude to alcohol.

The colonial heritage has had a profound influence on beer drinking and brewing. Adventurers from Europe brought their technical brewing knowledge and their own particular tastes with them, and these in turn were adopted by the local drinkers. British ales have made their mark on the Indian subcontinent, particularly in the form of India Pale Ale and rich, dark stouts. Despite its distance, the Pilsner revolution in Europe, which has transformed the beer-drinking landscape into one of pale lagers, has taken a grip on Asia too.

Beer consumption per head is relatively low in the region. Singaporeans for example, who are believed to be among the highest consumers of beer in Asia, drink a meagre 25 litres (5½ gallons) per head per annum, compared to 130 litres (28½ gallons) in England. Nevertheless, the large population of the region means that there is still scope for the marketing muscle of international companies such as Heineken to be flexed, and for the development of large "local" brewers. San Miguel of the Philippines has been brewing for over 100 years and is one of the major players in the Asian market, with joint ventures throughout the region. Asian Pacific Breweries from Singapore is also a large-scale producer, with hundreds of breweries throughout Asia. The strong, golden lagers that the region's brewers tend to produce are now bouncing back across the globe on the coat-tails of Asian cuisine to become household names in the West.

Above: Indonesia's most famous brew is the award-winning Bintang. The Dutch influence is apparent both in its taste and in the squat bottle design.

THE BEERS

ABC Stout
This powerful, creamy bottom-fermenting stout (8.1%) is produced by Asia Pacific Breweries.

Amarit
A malty, sweet, pale-gold lager from Thailand, brewed by Thai Amarit Bangkok.

Anchor Beer
This dry, hoppy Pilsner was introduced by Asia Pacific Breweries in 1941.

BGI
A golden lager brewed in My Tho, Vietnam, by a joint venture between the French BGI group and the Vietnamese Government.

Bintang
A light, malty lager (5%) from Bintang in Indonesia.

Cerveza Negra
A black beer (5.2%) with a roasted malty taste, from San Miguel in the Philippines.

Cobra
One of the best-known lagers from India and a successful export to the West.

Flying Horse
A premium, golden lager beer (5%) from the Vinedale Breweries, Hyderabad, India.

Hite
A pale-gold, dry, hoppy Korean lager (4.5%).

Jubilee
A premium, amber-gold lager (5%) from the Vinedale Breweries, Hyderabad, India.

Kingfisher
This sweetish, malty draught lager (5%) from the Vinedale Breweries, Hyderabad, India, is brewed under licence in England. There is also a pleasant Kingfisher stout.

Lion Stout
A top-fermenting stout (7.5%) produced using Czech, British and Danish malt, Styrian hops and an English yeast strain. The ingredients are transported to the Ceylon brewery in Nuwara Eliya high in the tea-planting area of Sri Lanka. It is served by handpump in the Beer Shop in the town, and in UKD Silva in the holy city of Kandy.

Red Horse
A bock-style, pale-gold lager (6.8%) with a full-bodied flavour, from San Miguel in the Philippines.

Sando Stout
A rich, fruity, bottom-fermented stout (6%) from the Three Coins Brewery in Colombo, Sri Lanka. It is named after a Hungarian circus strongman.

San Miguel
This golden, Pilsner-style beer, made with 80% malt, is lagered for a month by the Filipino giant San Miguel.

Singha
A bright-gold lager (6%) with a hoppy flavour, brewed by the Boon Rawd Brewery in Thailand. It is named after the mythical half-lion creature shown on the label.

Tiger
This refreshing, gold-coloured lager (5.1%) is one of the best-known Asian beers. It is brewed in Singapore and Kuala Lumpur by Asia Pacific Breweries. Its marketing slogan, "Time for a Tiger", was even the title of a novel by the British writer Anthony Burgess.

Tiger Classic
A mellow, golden, seasonal beer, brewed by APB using crystal malt, in time for each New Year's festivities.

THE BREWERS

Asia Pacific Breweries
APB is a regional giant based in Singapore. It was formed in 1931 as a joint venture between Fraser & Neame and Heineken, and was originally called Malayan Breweries. It is involved in many joint ventures in the region.

Boon Rawd Brewery
This Thai brewery was set up in Bangkok in the 19th century using German technology.

Mohan Meakin
Edward Dyer established a brewery at Kasauli in 1855. In 1935 this company merged with the Meakin brewery, set up by Mr H.G. Meakin, to become Dyer Meakin Breweries Limited. The Mohan Meakin company's main brewery is the Solan Brewery in the Simla Hills.

San Miguel
This Filipino giant producer was the first brewery in South-east Asia. It was established as La Fabrica de Cerveza de San Miguel in a small brewery next to the colonial mansion of the Spanish governor-general in the heart of Manila in 1890. It is now responsible for 85% of the Filipino beer market and has many breweries in other countries in the region, including ventures in Guangzhou and Guangdong, China, and a brewery in Hong Kong. It has also set up joint ventures in Vietnam, Indonesia, Nepal and Cambodia. In total, San Miguel has over 250,000 retail outlets in Asia.

AUSTRALIA

*The image of beer drinking in Australia has often been ice-cold lager firmly
clenched in the fists of macho men. But, like the legendary six o'clock swill that
forced drinkers to knock back their beers in double-quick time, this hard-drinking
reputation is now gradually draining away.*

SINCE 1975, BEER DRINKING in Australia has remorselessly declined from
almost 140 litres (30¾ gallons) per head in 1975 to less than 100 litres (22
gallons) 20 years later. Sharp rises in excise duty, together with
the spectacular growth of an enterprising Australian wine
industry and increased consumption of wine, have
hastened this dramatic drop. The fall has had far-reaching
effects. Australia is a huge country with a relatively
small population of about 18 million. Once domestic
consumption started to slide, the large, well-developed
brewing industry had to look elsewhere for markets.

Two major Australian brewing groups led by Elders IXL
(Foster's) and the Bond Corporation
(Castlemaine and Swan) began to
scour the globe. Elders bought up breweries such as
Courage of England and Carling of Canada, making
Foster's an international brand. Bond moved into the
United States when it snapped up Heileman and
eventually claimed to be the fourth-largest brewing
company in the world. The two groups had
overreached themselves, however, and struggled under
heavy debt burdens. Elders was eventually
reconstructed as Foster's Brewing and sold off some of
its earlier acquisitions. Bond collapsed in a spectacular
fashion, and New Zealand's leading brewer, Lion
Nathan, then picked up the pieces of the brewing
business in Australia.

These two combines still completely dominate the
country. Foster's, which trades in Australia through its
subsidiary, Carlton and United Breweries (CUB), controls 54% of the beer
market, while Lion Nathan now controls almost 44%. This leaves little more than
2% for the two remaining independent breweries, Boag of Tasmania and Coopers
of Adelaide, plus a handful of new micro-breweries and brewpubs.

*Above: Most people equate
Australian beer with Foster's or
Castlemaine mass-market lagers,
but there are a number of
independent breweries, notably
Coopers of Adelaide.*

THE BEERS

Abbots Invalid Stout
CUB's strong stout (5.6%) is a rare reminder of Australia's early brewing links with England. Although now bottom-fermented, it still has a creamy, coffee character. Only found in Victoria, it is named after the co-operative Abbotsford brewery of Melbourne, which was taken over by CUB in 1925. The site now houses one of CUB's largest and most modern plants.

Black Crow
A fruity, all-malt dark ale (3.6%) from Coopers of Adelaide. Unlike the company's more celebrated brews, it is filtered before being bottled.

Blue Label
See Tooheys.

Broken Hill Draught
A dry, malty lager (4.9%) from the South Australian brewery of Adelaide, this beer is named after the famous mining town. It is one of Australia's truly regional brews and has been produced for the "Silver City" and surrounding areas for nearly 80 years. It is only available in kegs in the Broken Hill area.

Carbine Stout
Castlemaine's full-bodied dark beer (5.1%) from Brisbane was introduced in 1925. Despite the name, it is a bottom-fermented lager with a roasted-malt flavour.

Cascade
The Cascade range of bottom-fermented beers, produced at the Cascade brewery, includes a full-bodied Cascade Pale Ale (5.2%), a lighter Cascade Bitter (4.8%) and a pleasantly roasted Cascade Stout (5.8%). They also produce a crisp Cascade Lager (4.8%), a darker, Cascade Draught (4.7%) and the fuller-flavoured Cascade Premium (5.2%).

Castlemaine XXXX
Still described in Australia as a bitter ale, Castlemaine XXXX is a malty golden lager (4.8%), which uses whole hops rather than pellets or hop extracts. The brewery also brews an all-malt Castlemaine Malt 75 (4.8%), a Castlemaine Special Dry (5%), a low-carbohydrate Castlemaine DL (4.1%), XXXX Gold (3.5%), a low-alcohol Light (2.7%) and XL (2.3%).

Coopers Sparkling Ale
Coopers' best-known, yeasty, cloudy brew (5.8%) is a full-flavoured, bottle-conditioned strong pale ale. Coopers also brews two other bottle-conditioned beers – a richly roasted, robust Coopers Best Extra Stout (6.8%) and a fruity middle-strength Coopers Original Pale Ale (4.5%). The company also produces the filtered ale, Coopers Premium Clear (4.9%). All the beers are free of additives and preservatives.

Crown
This sweetish brew (4.9%) comes from Carlton.

D-Ale
See Diamond Draught.

Diamond Draught
A more fully fermented, low-carbohydrate beer (4.6%) than others from Carlton, this is also known as D-Ale.

Dogbolter
A powerful ale (7%), Dogbolter was initially brewed at the Sail and Anchor brewpub in Fremantle in 1983, but is now a bottom-fermenting, creamy, dark lager from the CUB-owned Matilda Bay Brewing Co. of Perth. The beer is cask-matured before bottling and takes twice as long to brew and ferment as most Australian beers.

Eagle Blue
This deep-amber-coloured low-alcohol beer (2.7%) is refreshingly bitter. The ice-brewing process has also been used to produce another low-alcohol alternative in the light-amber lager, Eagle Blue Ice (2.7%). Both are produced by the South Australian Brewing Company.

Eagle Super
This golden-amber, full-strength lager (5%) produced by the South Australian brewery, is available in bottles and cans.

Emu
Swan's Emu beers take their name from a Perth brewery taken over by Swan in 1928. The range includes four lagers, Emu Pilsner, Emu Export (4.9%), a hoppier Emu Bitter (4.6%) and the darker, more malty Emu Draft (3.5%).

Export Mongrel
This bronze-coloured wheat beer (5.1%), produced by the Traditional Brewing Company, is a variation on Yellow Mongrel, using a light crystal malt as well as wheat and barley malts.

Foster's Beer
This light, fruity lager (4%) has a worldwide reputation and is the beer most drinkers abroad associate with the Foster's name.

Foster's Light
A low-alcohol brew (2.5%) from Foster's.

Foster's Special
A bright-gold low-alcohol lager (2.8%) from Foster's.

Fremantle Bitter
This full-bodied, amber-coloured, bottom-fermenting beer (4.9%) is brewed by Matilda Bay.

Hahn Gold
A mid-strength lager (3.5%) with a smooth, hop and malt flavour and sweetish finish, from the Hahn Brewery.

Hahn Premium
A full-strength, straw-coloured, European-style lager (5%) with a balanced character and bitter taste, created by late-hopping with Tasmanian hops.

James Boag's Premium
The pale, full-flavoured premium lager, with a fresh, hayfield aroma, is lagered for more than 60 days. Like all Boag lagers, it is batch-brewed and made from Tasmanian malt and Pride of Ringwood hops. It was voted Australia's best beer in 1995.

Kent Old Brown
One of Australia's rare, top-fermented beers, this dark, fruity ale (4.9%) is one of the Tooth brewery's KB range.

Loaded Dog Steam Beer
A deep-copper, lager-style beer (4%) with a smooth, wheaty flavour and biscuity overtones. The "steam" style comes from the burst of gas released when the cask is tapped. The logo of a snarling dog comes from a short story, in which a mongrel wanders into a pub carrying a stick of dynamite. Brewed by the Traditional Brewing Company.

Longbrew
A speciality lager produced by Lion under the Hahn name, this is a more fully fermented beer (4.5%) than most Australian brews.

Matilda Bay Bitter
An amber, all-malt, bottom-fermenting, Australian-style bitter (3.5%) from the Matilda Bay brewery in Western Australia.

Melbourne Bitter
This dryish lager (4.9%) comes from CUB. It is quite similar to Victoria Bitter (Victoria's best-selling beer), also brewed by CUB.

Moonshine
The strong, spirited barley wine called Moonshine (8%) is produced by the small Grand Ridge brewery in rural Victoria.

COOPERS ORIGINAL

Thomas Cooper, a shoemaker, emigrated to Australia from Yorkshire in England in 1852 with his wife Alice. She was the daughter of a publican and when she fell ill, asked her husband to make her some beer as a tonic, giving him the recipe from her sickbed. According to family legend, this brew was so successful that Thomas Cooper went into brewing full-time in 1862. However, as a devout Wesleyan, he regarded pubs (but not beer) as evil, and so restricted his trade to direct deliveries to private houses. The brewery moved to its present site in Upper Kensington in 1880.

O'Flanagan's
The Swan brewery of Perth sells this draught stout (4.8%) as a rival to Guinness.

Old Southwark Stout
See Southwark Old Stout.

Original Chilli Beer
The Traditional Brewing Company in Melbourne brews this fiery chilli beer (4%). It is a smooth lager, but chilli is added at the second fermentation in the bottle to give an unmistakable bite.

Power's Bitter
A light-amber bitter (4.8%) with a dense, creamy head and a hoppy flavour.

Power's Gold
This light-gold, full-bodied, mid-strength lager (3.4%) from the Power brewery, has a hoppy aroma.

Power's Light
A pale-amber, low-alcohol lager (2.8%) with a full-bodied flavour and a clean, crisp aroma.

Razor Back
A creamy, roasted stout, named after a local pig, brewed by Traditional Brewing Company of Melbourne.

Red Ant
A hearty, robust red lager (4.5%) in the Australian style, produced by the Jerningham Street brewery.

Redback
Australia's first wheat beer (4.8%) was introduced by the pioneering Matilda Bay Brewing Co. of Perth. Named after a local spider, it is brewed using 65% wheat. Since being taken over by CUB, this filtered, fruity, golden brew is less spicy than before. Besides Redback Original, there is also now a lower-alcohol Redback Light. An associated brewpub in Melbourne, also called Redback, produces a more distinctive, unfiltered Redback Hefe-Weizen.

Red Bitter
Sometimes called Tooheys Red, this is a light-gold, dry lager (5%) that uses a high proportion of malt and hops in the brewing process.

Reschs DA

Dinner Ale is a deep-amber, full-strength lager (4.9%) with a robust, aromatic flavour and a sweet aftertaste, produced by the NSW brewery.

Reschs Draught

This fruity, golden lager (4.7%) is one of the distinctive range of lagers produced by the Resch brewery. There is also a lighter lager called Reschs Real Bitter.

Reschs Pilsner

A light, golden Pilsner (4.6%) with a distinct bitterness, from the Resch brewery in NSW.

Sheaf Stout

This dry, bitter, top-fermented stout (5.7%) from Tooth's brewery in Sydney is one of Australia's most distinctive beers.

Southwark Old Stout

This reminder of the English origins of many people in South Australia is a heavy, chocolatey brew (7.4%), reminiscent of a 19th-century London-style stout.

Southwark Premium

The South Australian brewery produces its sweeter beers under the Southwark label. These include Southwark Bitter (4.5%), the full-bodied, fruity Premium lager (5.2%) and Southwark Old Black Ale (4.4%).

Swan Draught

This crisp, gold, malty lager (4.9%) is the best-known beer produced by the Swan plant at Canning Vale. Others include Swan Export lager and Swan Gold (3.5%), for the low-calorie market.

Swan Lite

An ultra-low-alcohol, golden, lightly malted brew (0.9%) where the alcohol is removed by vacuum distillation.

Sydney Bitter

Despite its name, this is a pale, golden lager (4.9%) with a lightly hopped flavour and a light, bitter finish. It was one of the first speciality brews from Hahn.

Tooheys Draught

This pale, sweetish lager (4.6%) is one of Tooheys most popular brews.

Tooheys Old Black

A dark, fruity ale (4.4%) from Tooheys brewery. It is one of the few surviving "Old" top-fermenting beers produced by this concern.

Victoria Bitter

Despite the international reputation of Foster's Lager, this is the best-selling beer in Australia (4.9%). It accounts for a quarter of the total beer market and 60% of CUB's output. A similar brew is sold as Melbourne Bitter.

EARLY BREWS

Brewing arrived in Australia with the first European settlers. John Boston, who landed in Sydney in 1794, manufactured the first recorded beer. It would have been an interesting drink, as it was made from maize and flavoured with the leaves and stalks of the Cape Gooseberry. In 1804, the government set up the colony's first commercial brewery in Parramatta.

The early brews had a poor reputation. Good-quality ingredients were difficult to obtain, and fermentation of English-style, top-fermenting ales was difficult to control in the hot, harsh climate. Yeast deteriorated rapidly, and even if the brewing process could be controlled, the beer itself quickly went off once it was hauled away by bullock cart. The laxative effects of this warm, sour soup earned it the unsavoury nickname "swipes". Most drinkers preferred rum or strong imported beer.

The quality of the beer improved in the 1860s, with the founding of the Swan brewery in 1857 and Coopers brewery in 1862, but the real breakthrough came with the introduction of refrigeration in the 1880s. This allowed the controlled use of yeast, as well as bottom-fermentation, and meant that more reliable beers could be produced. In 1885, two German immigrants, Friedrich and Renne, set up the first lager brewery in Melbourne. Foster's was established nearby by the American Foster brothers in 1888. Although now famous throughout the world, the two brothers only stayed in Australia for 18 months, selling their Collingwood brewery within a year before returning to New York.

West End

South Australia's drier, slightly more hoppy lagers include West End Draught (4.5%), Export Bitter (4.9%) and West End Light (2.6%).

Yellow Mongrel

The rare, golden-straw-coloured, refreshingly fruity Australian wheat beer (3.5%) comes from Traditional

Brewing Company of Sydney. Green Bullet hops are used to offset the natural sweetness of the wheat, and give a characteristic bitter finish.

1857

These two lagers, the crisp 1857 Pilsner (4.8%) and more malty 1857 Bitter (3.5%) from Swan are named after the founding date of the brewery on the Swan River in Western Australia.

THE BREWERS

Boag's

Scottish immigrant James Boag and his son bought the Esk brewery on the island of Tasmania at Launceston in 1881. From 1922 until 1993, Boag's was linked with rival island brewers, Cascade of Hobart. This partnership was broken when CUB took over Cascade. Since then, Boag's has taken on new life as one of the few remaining independent breweries, and has revamped its range of beers with a Boag's Original Bitter (4.7%) and a cold-filtered Boag's Classic Bitter (4.9%). All use local Tasmanian malt and Pride of Ringwood hops. Unlike many Australian beers, the beers are batch-brewed in the traditional way. The company's lagers are also matured for 30 days instead of the more usual ten.

Carlton United Brewers

Victoria's leading brewery was founded in Melbourne in 1864 as Carlton and merged with five local rivals including Victoria and Foster's to form Carlton and

Above: Boag's advertising plays on the Australian image of hard drinking macho beer drinkers.

United Breweries in 1907. In 1990, the combine was renamed the Foster's Brewing Group, but the CUB subsidiary remained in charge of brewing in Australia. Today, it brews in five of the country's seven states, producing 950 million litres (209 million gallons) a year. Many of CUB's national brands are sold under the Carlton name, including the dryish Carlton Draught, Crown, the more fully fermented Diamond Draught or D-Ale, the extremely clean-tasting Carlton Cold Filtered Bitter (4.9%) and Carlton Light (3.3%).

Cascade

Founded by a Frenchman in 1824, Cascade is the oldest continuously operating brewery in Australia. It also has the grandest location. The fine front of the stone brewhouse in Hobart, Tasmania, is set against the soaring cliffs of the Cascade Mountains. Cascade was badly damaged by bush fires in 1967, but within 12 weeks was brewing again. In 1993, Cascade, then part of Tasmanian Breweries, was bought by CUB. It still produces Cascade beers.

Castlemaine

This Brisbane brewery began life many miles away in the town of Castlemaine in Victoria, where the Fitzgerald brothers had established a brewery in 1859. They set up another

Castlemaine brewery in Melbourne in 1871 and then expanded across the country to Brisbane, converting a distillery in Milton into a brewery in 1878. The Victoria interests were later sold to become part of CUB, but the Castlemaine brewery in Brisbane remained part of the rival group, merging with local brewers, Perkins, in 1928 to form Castlemaine Perkins. The main beer, Castlemaine XXXX, introduced in 1924, became Queensland's favourite beer and an international rival to Foster's. Castlemaine's other famous beer is the heavy, dark Carbine Stout. Castlemaine controls 65% of the Queensland market, but is now part of Lion Nathan.

Cooper's

When most other Australian brewers were switching wholesale to producing pasteurized, continuously brewed, pale mass-market lagers (even if some were called bitters), Coopers of

Adelaide stuck to its guns and continued to brew traditional, top-fermenting ales, which are still sold unfiltered, allowing the beer to mature in the bottle. The Cooper's brews remain the classics of the continent.

Founded in 1862 and still run by the Coopers family, the Upper Kensington brewery in the suburb of Leabrook still ferments its ales in open vats made of native jarrah wood using a distinctive yeast strain that is at least 85 years old. Extra wort is added to the beer on bottling in order to ensure a secondary fermentation of the beer in the bottle. Given the sediment that this process leaves in the bottle, it is surprising that Cooper's best-known yeasty, cloudy brew is called Sparkling Ale.

Coopers introduced their own lagers in 1969 and now use stainless-steel conical fermenters to produce a Draught Lager, a Dry Lager (both 4.5%), Coopers Light (2.9%) and the malty, dark Black Crow (3.6%).

The firm began exporting its ales in 1963 and now they are famous around the world. As a result, today less than a third of total production is sold in South Australia.

Foster's Brewing Group

The international name for Australian beer is also now the overall title of the country's leading combine. The Foster's Brewing Group includes Australia's leading brewer CUB as well as its international arms including Foster's Asia. Originally founded in Melbourne in 1888, Foster's was a lager pioneer, importing ice-making equipment from America. It was also a bottled-beer specialist and leader in the export field.

Grand Ridge

A small brewery in rural Victora at Mirboo North. It brews an Australian-style bitter ale (4.9%) – Gippsland Gold; a hoppy Pilsner (4.9%) – Brewer's Pilsner; an Irish-style stout (4.9%) – Hatlifter Stout; and a powerful extra-strong, pure-malt barley wine (8.5%) – Moonshine.

Hahn

Dr Charles Hahn founded a new brewery in Camperdown, Sydney, in 1988. Hahn had worked in New Zealand where he helped to develop Steinlager. His new brewery produced an all-malt Hahn Premium lager and a Sydney Bitter. It gained such a reputation it was bought by Lion Nathan

in 1993. Its name is still used for speciality lagers, including Hahn Dark Ice (5.2%) and a cold-filtered Hahn Gold (3.5%).

Lion Nathan

In 1992, New Zealand's leading brewery group bought up Bond Brewing in Australia (Castlemaine, Swan and Tooheys) and has since added South Australian and Hahn. It now dominates the Australian industry alongside Foster's CUB.

Matilda Bay

This pioneer of the new brewery and speciality beer movement was founded at Nedlands in Western Australia in the mid-1980s by Philip Sexton, a former brewer with Swan in Perth. Matilda Bay launched the country's first wheat beer called Redback and also a strong ale, Dogbolter. The company accepted substantial investment in 1988 from CUB, which acquired a controlling interest, to expand and build a new brewery in Perth. Matilda Bay still brews Redback and Dogbolter, Matilda Bay Bitter and a Fremantle Bitter.

Power

Hotel owner Bernard Power decided to challenge the might of the two big groups and set up his own large brewery at Yatala, near Brisbane, in 1988. However, after early success, his Power Brewing venture was taken over by CUB in 1992. The Queensland plant still brews Power's creamy, full-bodied Bitter, the weaker Power's Gold, and Light, and Brisbane Bitter and Pilsner.

Reschs

Edmund Resch bought the New South Wales Lager Company in Waverley, Sydney, in 1900 and soon established a sound reputation for his beers. The company merged with Sydney rivals Tooth's in 1920. Today, Resch beers are still brewed at Tooth's Kent brewery, now part of CUB.

South Australian

This major Adelaide brewery was founded in 1888 by the amalgamation of the city's Kent Town and West End breweries. In 1938 it bought the Southwark brewery and all production is now concentrated there in a modern brewery. The company controls almost 70% of the state market. The beers are sold under three main brands, Southwark, West End and Eagle.

Swan

Beer in Western Australia has traditionally been all about the birds. The Swan brewery was built in Perth by the Swan River in 1857 and in 1928 took over the rival Emu brewery. Now part of Lion Nathan, it controls almost three-quarters of the state market. In addition to the well-known Swan lagers, the company also markets a strong, top-fermenting dark Swan Stout (6.8%) and a smooth O'Flanagan's Cream Stout. Other lagers include 1857 Pilsner and 1857 Bitter, and a range of Emu lagers.

Tooheys

Sydney's Catholic Irish brewery was founded in 1869 when John Thomas and his brother James bought the Darling brewery. They moved to a new site to build the Standard brewery, used

until 1978 when production was moved to a modern site at Lidcombe in Sydney. It is now part of Lion Nathan. Tooheys' first beers were top-fermenting darkish ales. When the company started producing bottom-fermenting, golden lagers in the 1930s, it called these "new" beers as opposed to the "old" style ales. Lagers now dominate, notably Tooheys Draught (4.6%). Since 1985 Tooheys has pioneered the development of full-bodied, low-alcohol beers using crystal malt, through its Blue Label.

Below: Brisbane, home of Castlemaine brewery, showing the modern skyline and Brisbane River.

Tooth's

Merchant John Tooth founded the Sydney brewery in 1835. He called it the Kent brewery, after the English hop-growing county he came from. Its beers were sold under the KB brand. Tooth's absorbed its local rival, Reschs of Waverley, in 1929 but was taken over by CUB in 1983. Its beers are still brewed in NSW, including a soft malty KB Lager (4.7%) and two top-fermenting beers – a dark, rich Kent Old Brown and a full-bodied Sheaf Stout.

Traditional Brewing Company

This small brewery at the Geebung Polo Club pub in Hawthorn, Melbourne, has developed a reputation for brewing tasty, stylishly bottled ales. It started in 1985 and claims to be Melbourne's oldest established "boutique brewer".

ICE BEER

As the alcohol content rises in a brew, fermentation becomes more difficult because the action of the yeast is subdued by the alcohol it produces. One way around this difficulty is to freeze the brew. The water freezes before the alcohol and can then be removed to produce a concentrated, purified beer. However it is the effect of the freezing process on the flavour of the beer that has become popular, and few of the fashionable, ultra-smooth lagers weigh in at more than 5.5%. The ice beer craze has certainly arrived in Australia, with most of the main brewers introducing their own brands over the last couple of years.

BREWPUBS

Lion

This small brewery in North Adelaide was built in a pub complex in the mid 1980s. Its Old Lion beers include a hoppy Pilsner, a Sparkling Ale and a Porter.

Lord Nelson

Sydney's oldest hotel is home to a brewery which produces English-style ales, including Trafalgar Pale (4%), Victory Bitter (4.8%) and a rich, dark, malty Old Admiral (6.5%).

Port Dock

The Port Dock Hotel, a brewpub in Port Adelaide, was built in 1855. It uses malt extract to produce golden Lighthouse Ale (3.9%), creamy Black Diamond Bitter (4.9%) and strong Old Preacher (6%).

Pumphouse

A waterside brewpub in Sydney, Pumphouse's beers include the hoppy, English-style Bull's Head Bitter and the darker, more malty Federation.

Redback

This Melbourne brewpub is associated with the Matilda Bay Brewing Company and produces its own distinctive, unfiltered Redback Hefe-Weizen. It also offers Redback Original wheat beer (4.8%) and a lower-alcohol Redback Light.

Rifle Brigade

One of Australia's smallest breweries was installed in the Rifle Brigade pub in the central Victoria mining town of Bendigo in 1986. Its malt extract plant produces seven different beers, including the full-bodied Old Fashioned Bitter (5.3%), the richly roasted Iron Bark Dark (5.3%) and a wheat beer called Platman's (5%).

Sail and Anchor

Australia's first modern brewpub was set up in 1983 by Philip Sexton, a former brewer with the Swan brewery in Perth, when he bought the Freemason's Hotel in Fremantle, renamed it the Sail and Anchor, and installed a brewery on the premises. Later he went on to found the Matilda Bay

Above: An outback pub in Toncoola, South Australia. The rail was originally used for tethering horses.

Brewing Company in nearby Perth. The Sail and Anchor brews several top-fermenting ales served on a handpump, including a fruity English-style bitter called Seven Seas Real Ale (4.6%), a Brass Monkey Stout (6%) with a coffee character and a warming, rich, dark ale, Ironbrew (7%).

Scharer's

The small New South Wales brewery based at the George IV pub in Picton has been brewing German-style lagers since the mid-1980s, most notably a creamy, malty Burragarang Bock (6.4%), an amber Scharer's Lager (5%) and D'lite (3%).

The Inn, which is said to have been built in 1819, originally catered for "Officers and Gentlemen" passing through the town. Convicts, road gangs and future inmates of Berrima and Goulburn jails were often held in what are now the lagering cellars.

NEW ZEALAND

New Zealand has had a long love-hate relationship with beer. Although it is one of the world's top beer-drinking nations, the country has also been the home of a powerful temperance movement.

IN 1885, THE SCATTERED POPULATION of New Zealand boasted one brewery for every 6,000 people. These early breweries brewed British-style ales in a climate not far removed from that of northern Europe. Lager was not introduced until 1900, and then only in Auckland in the warmer north. This industry served hotels, which were more like American wild-west saloons than English pubs. Heavy drinking provoked a powerful temperance movement, which closed down hotels and introduced six o'clock closing during the First World War. This lasted for 50 years, and total Prohibition was narrowly avoided in a referendum in 1919.

Under pressure and struggling to survive, the New Zealand brewing industry concentrated at a much earlier stage than in most countries. The first national brewing company, New Zealand Breweries (later Lion Breweries), was formed in 1923 when ten of the largest breweries joined forces, thus controlling 40% of the trade. Seven years later, the rival Dominion Breweries group was formed. Today, the two combines, known as Lion Nathan and DB, dominate the beer market.

The early concentration of the brewing industry meant it invested heavily in research, influenced by the high standards of cleanliness in New Zealand's dairy industry. In the 1950s, Morton Coutts of Dominion developed continuous fermentation whereby beer is produced from a never-ending flow of wort and yeast through four aligned vessels. Rival New Zealand Breweries soon also adopted this cost-efficient system, replacing the traditional batch method. The result was that all beers were chilled, filtered and bottom-fermented. Most draught beers also abandoned the barrel in favour of large tankers that deliver beer direct to hotel cellar tanks. These mild, full-coloured lagers – often referred to as "brown" beers or ales – are sweet, most being primed with sugar and served very cold and highly carbonated.

With the removal of strict licensing restrictions in 1967, New Zealand has gradually adopted a more relaxed attitude to beer drinking. Since the 1980s, a few brewpubs and micro-breweries have appeared.

Above: New Zealand brewing is dominated by two groups. Many of the beers have their origins in Britain, and ale and stout are brewed as well as lager.

THE BEERS

Canterbury
A regional, amber-coloured "brown" beer (4%) with a malty, smooth flavour, barley overtones and a dry finish. It comes from Lion's Christchurch brewery on the South Island.

Coromandel Draught
A full-flavoured bitter beer (4%) is brewed by the Coromandel Brewing Company.

DB Export Dry
A pale-gold, hoppy, crisp beer (5%) from Dominion Breweries with a smooth, light, malt taste. It is lagered for longer than most New Zealand brews.

DB Natural
A fresh, unpasteurized, amber-coloured ale (4%) with a sweetish, roast-malt taste and a hoppy finish. It is bottom-fermented and micro-filtered by Dominion Breweries (DB).

Double Brown
A full-flavoured, amber-gold, bottom-fermented speciality beer (4%) with a fruity-malt flavour, brewed by Dominion.

Flame
This amber-gold lager with a smooth finish (5.2%) is produced by the Black Dog brewery in Auckland using the extreme brewing process. This first heats the malt and hops to 106°C (223°F) and then crash-cools the beer to emphasize the flavours.

Hawkes Bay Draught
This amber-coloured ale (4%) with a dry, malt taste, is a regional beer, brewed by Leopard in Hastings. Leopard, now part of Lion, was once New Zealand's third brewing force, behind Lion and Dominion.

Leopard Black Label
A golden-amber lager (4%) with a crisp, fruity flavour. It is brewed by Lion, using the traditional Leopard Brewery's batch-brewing process and a combination of New Zealand hops and a new, recently developed "black label" yeast.

Lion Brown
This amber-gold, sweet and fruity, malt-flavoured ale (4%) is one of Lion's best-selling brews.

Lion Ice
This light-golden-amber modern lager (4.7%) is a smooth, easy-drinking beer from Lion Breweries.

Lion Red
A deep-gold, malty, hoppy, sweetish beer (4%) with a good body. It is one of the leading brands in New Zealand produced by Lion Breweries.

Mainland Dark
Described as a dark ale, this is a richer lager (4%) than others from Dominion, brewed using a blend of roasted malts and barleys by DB's South Island brewery at Timaru.

Mako
This low-alcohol, light beer (2.5%) is brewed by Dominion. It is an authentic, bitter-style beer, brewed with extra hops.

Monteith's Black Beer
This black-coloured beer (5.2%) is stronger than an ale, yet it is lighter than a stout. It is produced by Monteith's using the traditional batch-brewing method and combining five crystal and chocolate malts in a special mash.

Monteith's Original Ale
The Monteith label is used for Dominion Breweries' new "boutique" range of beers, including the malty Monteith's Original Ale (4%), which is brewed from an original 1860s recipe.

Nugget Golden Lager
A crisp speciality lager (5%) from Monteith's.

Rheineck Lager
Relatively light, this golden lager (3.8%) is drier than most New Zealand brews.

Cook's special
Captain Cook, the English explorer who literally put New Zealand on the map, is credited with being the country's first beer brewer. Concerned about scurvy on his second visit in 1773, he brewed "beer" for the ship's crew by boiling up spruce and tea shrub leaves and twigs, mixed with molasses. The concoction was served to the sailors with a shot of rum and brown sugar stirred in, perhaps to help disguise the flavour!

Speight's Gold Medal Ale

A deep-gold, fruity, malt-and-hop-tasting ale (4%). It is still a major malty "brown" beer brand on the South Island. Speight's, established in Dunedin in 1876, was New Zealand's largest brewery before the First World War and the leading company in the merger that formed New Zealand Breweries (Lion) in 1923. The Lion group still brews in Dunedin.

Steinlager

Lion's premium, pale-gold, international lager (5%), much drier and more aromatic than its other beers, is mainly sold abroad. This sweetish, hoppy brew was originally introduced as Steinecker in 1958, named after the new, German-made, Steinecker continuous-fermentation brewing plant that had been installed in its Auckland brewery. After a legal challenge in the US from Dutch giant Heineken, the name was changed to Steinlager in 1962.

Steinlager Blue

Lion introduced this variant on its premium lager in 1993. It is a golden, medium-dry, malty lager with a light hop aroma.

Taranaki Draught

A dark, full-bodied, malty regional lager (4%) with a bitter flavour. It carries the name of the Taranaki brewery of New Plymouth, which was taken over and closed in the 1960s by Dominion Breweries (DB).

Trapper's Red Beer

Monteith's of Greymouth on the South Island produces this deep-red, speciality beer (4.4%), brewed with roasted crystal malt, using a batch-brewing method.

Tui

Although described as an East India Pale Ale, this is a sweet, golden-reddish lager (4%) with a clear, hoppy flavour and malty aftertaste from DB's Tui Brewery at Mangatainoka. The brewery itself dates back to 1889. It is most closely associated with the Hawke's Bay region on the North Island.

Vita Stout

The name of Dominion's smooth, sweet, dark-brown beer (4%) with a chocolate-malt and roasted-barley flavour hints at health-giving properties. Faced with a strong temperance movement in the early part of the 20th century, Kiwi breweries regularly claimed that their beer was full of health-giving properties and should be drunk regularly. Dominion's early Waitemata beer was sold as "The Secret of Good Health and Long Life" and "As Nourishing as Bread or Milk".

THE BREWERS

Dominion Breweries (DB)

Formed in 1930 in Auckland, Dominion Breweries has prided itself on its technological advances, notably the introduction of continuous fermentation in the 1950s. Besides its modern Waitemata brewery in Auckland, it also runs the Tui brewery at Manga-tainoka, Monteith's at Greymouth and the Mainland brewery at Timaru. The main beers are the best-selling, sweetish DB Draught, which uses the company's famous Clydesdale horses in its promotion, and the drier DB Bitter. Regional brands include Tui and Taranaki.

Although described as brown beers and ales, these are mid-strength, reddish-tinted and softly sweet lagers (all 4%). Paler lagers are led by DB Export Gold (4%) and the crisper Export Dry (5%). The company also produces a low-alcohol light beer, Mako (2.5%). Speciality brews, all bottom-fermented, include a fresher-flavoured, unpasteurized DB Natural, a fuller-flavoured Double Brown, a smoothly sweet Vita Stout and richer, more roasted Mainland Dark. DB have recently promoted a range of "boutique" beers, which are sold under the Monteith label in the speciality beer market.

Harrington

The Christchurch micro-brewery produces a rare New Zealand wheat beer and a tasty Dark Beer, besides more conventional lagers.

Lion

New Zealand's largest brewing company controls almost 60% of the domestic market. The overall group, which also owns substantial brewing interests in Australia, is called Lion Nathan. In New Zealand the company trades as Lion Breweries in the North Island and under its older name of New Zealand Breweries in the South Island. The group runs two breweries in the North Island, in Auckland and Hastings, and two in the South Island, in Dunedin and Christchurch. Its main brand is the best-selling, malty Lion Red and the sweeter, fruity Lion

Salvation

The birth of New Zealand's second-largest brewing group sums up the country's love-hate relationship with beer. When the Coutts family opened the Waitemata brewery in Auckland in 1929, the Women's Christian Temperance Movement marched to the site and prayed that the new brewery be turned into a food factory. In part their prayers were answered, for the new venture struggled to find a market and only survived by merging with a drinks wholesaler in 1930 to form Dominion.

Brown. There are also regional bottom-fermenting "brown" beers, including Hawkes Bay and Waikato Draught and, in the South Island, Speight's and Canterbury Draught. More golden, drier brews include a light Rheineck Lager and the company's international flagship brand, the crisp Steinlager (5%). In the 1980s, Lion abandoned the continuous fermentation system and reverted to more traditional batch methods to meet the demand for a wider variety of beers.

Mac's

When the Prime Minister Sir Robert Muldoon opened New Zealand's first micro-brewery in Stoke, in 1981, he described it as a David in an industry of two Goliaths. Nevertheless, the venture launched by former All-Black rugby player Terry McCashin has survived, and has even set up its own maltings to ensure supplies. The marketing for the all-malt beers, brewed to the German beer purity law using a bottom-fermenting lager yeast, emphasizes that no chemicals or preservatives are added. The main brews are a malty Mac's Ale, a hoppy Gold, a darker, fuller-bodied Black Mac (all 4%), a more powerful lager Extra (7%) and a Mac Special Light (1%).

Monteith

Dominion took over the Westland brewery in Greymouth in 1969, renamed it Monteith's Brewing Co. in 1995 and began to brew beers for the speciality market. These include the malty Monteith's Original Ale, a deeper-coloured Trapper's Red Beer and a crisp Nugget Golden Lager. The Westland brewery, established in 1858, retains open fermenting vessels, coal-fired boilers and traditional batch brewing. Greymouth, a mining area of the west coast of the South Island, has a large Irish population and prides itself on its pubs and beer.

Newbegin

Established in Onehunga near Auckland in 1987, this micro-brewery produces an all-malt lager, Silver Fern (4%) and a dark more robust Old Thumper.

New Zealand Breweries (NZB)

New Zealand's largest beer company, Lion, trades under its older name of New Zealand Breweries in the South Island. NZB was formed in 1923 when ten of the country's largest breweries merged, including Speight's of Dunedin, Staples in Wellington, Ward's of Christchurch and the Great Northern brewery (Lion) of Auckland.

Petone

Two former Lion employees set up this "boutique" brewery in Petone, near Wellington. They imported yeast from Britain to start fermenting the malty Strongcroft's Bitter.

Shakespeare

The country's first brewpub was founded in Auckland in 1986. Its beers include the soft, malty Macbeth's Red Ale, bitter Falstaff Real Ale, Barraclough Lager, pale gold with a light hop finish, and lightly bittered Willpower Stout, as well as the dramatically rich, hoppy King Lear Old Ale (7.5%).

Stockan

Henderson, near Auckland, is home to this brewery, which was partly financed by a vineyard. Set up in the mid-1980s on a larger scale than most micro-breweries, its beers include a spicy Stockan Ale and the chocolatey Dark Ale.

BREWING IN THE PACIFIC

The vast Pacific Ocean is peppered with hundreds of tiny islands, and on some of these there are brewers gallantly turning out brews for their small populations.

The South Pacific brewery in Papua New Guinea was set up in the 1940s by Australians who travelled to Papua New Guinea to work in the gold fields. They were frustrated by the lack of good quality beer, all of which was imported, so they built their own brewery in Port Moresby and used rain water collected in tanks to produce their own beers. Production started in 1952. Sales soared in the 1960s when Prohibition was ended for the islanders. The brewery is still going strong. It produces a malty, dry, golden lager (4.5%) called SP Lager and South Pacific Export Lager –a delicate malt lager (5.5%) that won the Brewex international gold medal award in 1980. There is also a deep-brown-black stout (8%) called Niugini Gold Extra Stout.

Western Samoa Breweries boasts Vailima, a smooth, refreshing lager (4.9%), which is actually brewed in Auckland, New Zealand, and the small Pacific islands of Tahiti and Fiji also have their own breweries. On Tahiti the Brasserie de Tahiti produces a pale-gold Hinano Tahiti lager (4.9%), which won a World Gold Medal for quality in 1990, as well as two local beers, Hei Lager Gold, a premium lager (5%), and Vaita, a virtually non-alcoholic lager (0.8%). The Calton brewery in Fiji makes a tawny brew with a malty flavour called Fiji Bitter Beer.

The Kona Brewing Company on Hawaii, the 52nd State of the US, brews Fire Rock Ale, a dark amber beer (4.1%), using pale and Munich malts and Cascade, Galena and Mount Hood hops, while the same company's Pacific Golden Ale (3.5%) is a golden-amber pale ale, created with a blend of pale and honey malts, hopped with Bullion and Willamette varieties.

CANADA

Prohibition hit Canada hard, and as a result the industry is dominated by the few big names that survived. The Canadians are not big beer drinkers, but the picture is now changing slowly and more small breweries are appearing.

B REWING IN CANADA has run parallel with its big neighbour south of the border, although technically Canada has often led the way. The first commercial brewery in Canada was set up in Montreal in 1786, by English immigrant John Molson, making it the oldest brewery in North America. He was followed by two other familiar names, Thomas Carling who started his brewery in London, Ontario, in 1840, and John Labatt who founded his brewery in the same town seven years later. Canada has had a love-hate relationship with alcohol, and, following the passing of the Scott Local Option Law in 1878, a nightmare cobweb of regulations ensnared the production and sale of beer. There was also the dry period of national Prohibition, which lasted from 1918 until 1932. When that ended, each province developed its own set of rigid rules – many of them are still in existence. In Ontario, for example, the Liquor Control Board is one of the biggest purchasers of alcohol in the world, and it has a monopoly on selling beer throughout its 585 stores. Also, taxes on alcohol in Canada are the highest of any nation, with tariffs making up 53% of the price in 1995. As a result of all this, beer in Canada is relatively expensive.

Local laws in Canada require beer to be brewed in the area where it is sold, so the three large groups which dominate brewing in Canada – Molson, Labatt and Carling – have breweries scattered across the provinces, often producing beers under a myriad of local labels. Originally the beer they produced was typical of the top-fermenting ales that reflected the English origins of the founding brewers, but they soon switched to bottom-fermenting lagers, and Labatt's pioneered the introduction of "ice beer" in 1993 which has proved so popular.

Since the early 1980s there has been a small-scale brewery revolution, particularly in British Columbia, Ontario and Quebec. By 1995, some 40 micro-breweries had been set up, bringing a new wave of beers to the bar. But many of these small breweries have had to struggle against stifling regulations.

Above: Molson is the oldest brewer on the North American continent. The company merged with Carling in 1989 to form a giant international company.

THE BEERS

Alpine Lager

This refreshing lager (5%) is produced locally by the independent Moosehead brewery for the Maritime provinces.

Anniversary Amber Ale

A red-amber, Bavarian-style, all-malt brew (5.5%) was created to celebrate 10 years of production at the Granville Island micro-brewery.

Arkell Best Bitter

Wellington County produces this light, bitter ale (4%) with a malt aroma in the brewing town of Guelph in the state of Ontario.

Big Rock Pale Ale

This quality pale ale (5%) is brewed at the Big Rock brewery in Calgary, which was founded by Ed McNally in 1985. Big Rock has created its own stampede, with demand rising for its tasty, all-malt, unpasteurized ales brewed by Bernd Pieper, who was formerly a head brewer with Löwenbräu in Zurich.

Black Amber

An extra-strong, amber ale (7%) from the small Big Rock brewery.

Blanche de Chambly

A cloudy, spicy, bottle-conditioned wheat beer (5%) from the Unibroue micro-brewery. This tart, refreshing brew won the Silver Medal in the 1995 World Beer Championship.

Brador

A rich, fruity, top-fermenting specialist ale (6.5%) from Molson.

Brasal Bock

An amber-brown, sweet-roasted, hoppy bock (7.8%), which is matured in oak barrels for three months.

Brasal Légère

The lightest lager brewed by the Brasal micro-brewery of LaSalle. The companion brew Brasal Hops Bräu (4.5%) is also quite light.

Brasal Special Amber

A malty, strong, German-style lager (6.1%).

Brick Bock

An unpasteurized German-style bock (6.5%) from the Brick micro-brewery.

Brick Premium Lager

This excellent, hoppy, golden lager (5%) is one of the award-winning brews from the Brick micro-brewery of Waterloo, Ontario.

Brick Red Baron

An unpasteurized ale (5%) produced by the Brick micro-brewery.

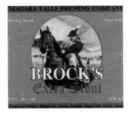

Brock's Extra Stout

Brock extra stout porter (5.8%) is one of the specialist beers brewed by the innovative Niagara micro-brewery.

Canadian Lager

An unexciting, but not unpleasant, standard lager (5%) produced by Moosehead.

Carling Black Label

A light-tasting, pale-gold, standard lager (5%) from Molson, which has proved to be a best-selling export to the UK.

Colonial Stout

This stout porter (4.8%) comes from the Upper Canada micro-brewery.

County Ale

This excellent, amber, malty, traditional ale (5%) with a hoppy aftertaste is a slightly stronger ale produced by the Wellington County micro-brewery.

Frontenac

This light ale (5%) comes from the popular small brewery, McAuslan, which is based in Ontario.

Granville Island Dark Bock

This delicious, amber bock (6.5%) brewed by Granville Island Brewing Company in Vancouver, British Columbia, is one of the finest beers in Canada. It has a rich, malt nose, a hearty, roasted-malt and hop flavour, good balance and an exceptionally long and well-balanced finish.

Grasshopper Wheat

This all-malt, unpasteurized wheat beer (5%) is produced by Big Rock of Calgary.

Griffon Brown Ale

A mahogany-brown, complex, full-bodied, slightly sweet, hoppy ale (4.5%) produced by Brasserie McAuslan.

Griffon Extra Pale Ale

This bright-gold, pale ale (5%) has a hoppy, fruity-malt flavour. It comes from the Brasserie McAuslan.

Gritstone Premium Ale

This strong ale (5.5%) is produced by the Niagara Falls Brewing Company.

Imperial Stout

This dark stout (5.5%) from Wellington County has a faint chocolate-malt nose, a light but complex malty flavour and a hoppy finish.

Island Lager

A full-bodied, hoppy, deep-gold lager (5%), from Granville Island Brewing.

John Labatt's Classic

This gold, highly carbonated lager (5%) from Labatt has a mild, hoppy aroma and a dull, malt and hop flavour.

La Fin du Monde

Unibroue produces this deep-yellow, fruity, spicy, extra-strong, triple-fermented ale (9%). It is conditioned in the bottle.

La Gaillarde

This unusual bottle-conditioned beer (5%) from Unibroue uses herbs and spices in place of hops.

Labatt Ice Beer

This pioneering ice beer, with a golden colour, malt and hop flavour and full body, weighs in at 5.6%.

Labatt's Blue

This grainy, deep-amber, slightly dry lager (5%) is Labatt's flagship brand.

Labatt's 50 Ale

This refreshing, bright-gold ale (5%) has a medium body, a light hop nose with fruity hints and a crisp, fresh flavour with a slightly sour malt finish.

Lord Granville Pale Ale

This all-malt, copper-red, fruity pale ale (5%) from the Granville Island brewery is brewed in accordance with the German beer purity law, using only barley malt, hops, water and yeast in the brew.

McAuslan Pale Ale

This zesty pale ale (5%) from Brasserie McAuslan has a smooth, well-balanced hop and malt flavour.

McNally's Extra Pure Malt Irish Style Ale

This deep-amber, extra-strong, unpasteurized, all-malt beer (7%) from Big Rock brewery has a powerful, roasted-malt nose, a rich malt flavour, and a hop and malt aftertaste with hints of caramel.

Magpie Rye

This is an unpasteurized, tart-flavoured rye beer (5%), which comes from the Big Rock brewery in Calgary.

Maple Wheat Beer

A strong, syrupy beer (8.5%) from the Niagara Falls Brewing Company.

Maudite

A warming, mellow, bottle-conditioned red ale (8%), from the Unibroue micro-brewery.

Mitchell's ESB

A copper-coloured, English-style ale (5.5%) from the Spinnakers brewpub.

Molson Canadian Lager

The most famous of Molson's products (5%) is pale gold with a dry malt nose and hints of hops. Its flavour is smooth and well-balanced with malt and hops and a long, dry finish.

Molson Export Ale

This light, brownish-gold ale (5%) is a little fuller than the lager, with a crisp, hoppy taste, good body and a long malt and hop aftertaste.

Molson Special Dry

A slightly stronger lager (5.5%) from Molson.

Moosehead Lager

This is the popular, mild, pale-malt lager (5%) that gave its name to the brewery.

Moosehead Pale Ale

This pale-gold ale (5%) has a yeasty, malt-hop nose, a well-hopped, slightly sweet malt flavour, and a dry malt-hop finish. It is brewed at the Moosehead brewery.

Mount Tolmie

This dark ale (4.2%) is brewed by the Spinnakers brewpub, using four malt types and Mount Hood hops.

Ogden Porter

This strong porter (6.2%) comes from the Spinnakers brewpub in Victoria, British Columbia.

Okanagan Spring Brown Ale

A deep-brown, top-fermented ale (5.6%), brewed with two-row barley malt and Hallertauer hops by the Okanagan Spring brewery, British Columbia.

Okanagan Spring Pilsner

A light, golden, hoppy Pilsner (4.5%) from the Okanagan Spring brewery, British Columbia.

Pacific Real Draft

This light, pleasant lager (5%) is the best-known brew from the Pacific Western brewery.

Publican's Special Bitter

The Upper Canada micro-brewery produces this special top-fermented, amber-brown, English-style bitter (4.8%).

Raftman

This gold, smoky, bottle-conditioned beer (5.5%) is brewed using peat-smoked whiskey malt by the Unibroue micro-brewery.

Rebellion Malt Liquor

This deep-gold, malt liquor (6%) has a sweet, full, honey taste with a malty hop finish. It is a very pleasant, well-rounded beer from the Upper Canada Brewing Company.

Red Baron

This pale-gold lager (5%), brewed by the Brick Brewing Company, has a light hop and malt aroma, a mild malt flavour and a hoppy finish.

Red Cap Ale

The Brick Brewing Company produces this classic beer (5%) using the original Carling recipe.

Red Dog

A golden, German-style ale (5.5%) with a faint malt and hop nose and a dry, malty flavour.

St-Ambroise Framboise

A Belgian-style, light, pink-red, raspberry fruit beer (5%), from the Brasserie McAuslan.

St-Ambroise Oatmeal Stout

A black, chocolatey, malt and roasted barley, traditional, dry stout (5.5%), brewed using oatmeal in the mash by McAuslan Brasserie, St Ambroise, Quebec.

St-Ambroise Pale Ale

A reddish-gold, robust, malty ale with a clean taste – a characteristic of the Cascade hops used in the brew by Brasserie McAuslan.

Signature Amber Lager

This amber, all-malt lager is brewed under the Signature label by Molson.

Signature Cream Ale

A characterful, all-malt ale. It is one of Molson's prestige Signature brews.

Sleeman Cream Ale

As with all Sleeman brews, this tawny-gold, malty cream ale (5%) is sold in a distinctive embossed bottle.

Sleeman Original Dark

This dark-amber ale (5.5%) has a malty aroma and is lightly hopped. It comes from the Sleeman brewery.

Spinnaker Ale

An amber, English-style ale (4.2%) from Canada's first brewpub, Spinnaker.

Spinnaker Hefe-Weizen

This spicy, cloudy beer is a speciality brew from the Spinnaker bewpub.

Trapper Lager

A deep-gold lager with a grapey nose and a thin, sweet taste from the Niagara Falls Brewing Company.

True Bock

This is a red-amber German-style bock beer (6.5%) with a complex, warm, soft malty flavour and a pleasant hop nose. It is the most interesting beer from the Upper Canada micro-brewery in Toronto. The brewery also produces a light wheat beer (4.3%) with a tart, fruity aroma, a standard lager (5%) and an English-style IPA (4.8%).

Warthog Ale

The Big Rock Brewery in Calgary produces this all-malt, unpasteurized ale (4.5%).

Waterloo Dark

An unpasteurized dark draft ale (5.5%) from the Brick Brewing Company.

Wellington Imperial Stout

A rich, brown-black, top-fermented stout (5.5%) brewed using speciality malts by the Wellington County Brewery.

Legal restrictions

The legal restrictions on the Canadian brewing industry stem from the Prohibition of the 1920s and rigid state laws. Micro-breweries have had to struggle against these barriers. In spite of this, Canada has always been at the forefront of brewing developments.

THE BREWERS

Big Rock

Founded by Ed McNally in 1985, the Big Rock brewery is dedicated to the batch-brewing of premium beers following the German beer purity law. It uses a cold multi-microfiltration system rather than pasteurization. Among its best-known brews are Buzzard Breath Ale, a light to medium-bodied ale, McNally's Extra Pure Irish-style Ale, Warthog Ale, which is copper-coloured and nutty, Magpie Rye Ale and Grasshopper Wheat Ale.

Brasal Brasserie Allemande

This is Quebec's largest micro-brewery. It was founded in the city of LaSalle, Montreal in 1989, by the Jagerman family to brew German-style lagers according to the German beer purity law.

Brick

The Brick Brewing Company was established in 1984 in Waterloo, Ontario. Brick laid the foundations for the new brewery movement in eastern Canada. Its unpasteurized beers, many of them award-winners, are mainly European-style lagers developed by founder Jim Brickman.

Carling

One of Canada's leading international brewing names, Carling was founded in Ontario in 1840 by Sir Thomas Carling. Later in the 19th century Carling merged with the rival brewery O'Keefe, founded by Eugene O'Keefe in 1862, forming Carling O'Keefe. The company was taken over by the Australian giant, Foster's, in 1987, but that company overreached itself and Carling was merged with Molson in 1989. They then formed the largest brewing group in Canada, with vast overseas interests. The flagship brew, Carling Black Label, is one of the best-selling lagers in the UK. Because of the state laws in Canada that stipulate that beer must be brewed within the state boundaries, the company runs a large number of breweries, which produce local beers under various labels.

Granville Island Brewing

Businessman Mitch Taylor set up Canada's first micro-brewery in Vancouver's waterfront crafts area in 1984. It brews Bavarian-style all-malt lagers, notably Island Lager.

Labatt

One of Canada's two brewing giants, Labatt was taken over by the Belgian brewing company Interbrew in 1995. It also owns Latrobe (Rolling Rock) in the US.

The brewery was founded in London, Ontario, in 1847 by John Labatt. Despite the brewery being burned down twice in the 19th century, the company persevered, surviving Prohibition to take over many rival regional brewers after the Second World War.

Today it runs seven breweries across Canada, and at one time it marketed almost 50 brands. Its main lager is Labatt's Blue (5%). Local beer brands include

Kokanee and Kootenay in the West and Schooner and Keith's IPA in the East, besides Blue Star in Newfoundland.

Labatt pioneered ice beer (introduced in 1993). During the brewing process the beer is chilled to 4°C (39.2°F) to form ice crystals, which are then removed leaving a stronger (5.6%) but rather bland brew behind.

McAuslan

After two years preparation this small brewery in Montreal began brewing in 1989. The famous British brewer Alan Pugsley helped to formulate the recipe for its first brew – St-Ambroise Pale Ale. The brewery has since gone from strength to strength, and in the seven years since launching, it has introduced four new beers, St-Ambroise Oatmeal Stout, Griffon Extra Pale Ale, Griffon Brown Ale and Frontenac, a golden, lightly hopped extra pale ale.

Molson

The oldest brewer in North America dates back to 1786 when English immigrant John Molson set up the Molson brewery in Montreal. Now based in Toronto, it is the rival giant to Labatt, with nine breweries and about 50 brands. Molson merged with Carling O'Keefe in 1989 to make it the largest Canadian brewer,

Oland was killed in an explosion in 1917 when two ships collided in Halifax harbour – the company moved to St John's, New Brunswick. In 1931 George Oland renamed his main beer Moosehead and this proved to be such a successful innovation that the company name was changed to Moosehead in 1947.

The beer is enormously popular in the US. It also brews local Alpine Lager (5%) for the Maritime Provinces, and a dry Moosehead Pale Ale.

with 53% of the market. Best known for its Molson Canadian Lager (5%) and Molson Special Dry (5.5%), it introduced a new range of all-malt beers in 1993, which are marketed under the Signature brand name. These brews have found a ready acceptance in the home market.

Moosehead

Moosehead, Canada's oldest and largest independent brewery, was founded by Susannah Oland in Halifax, Nova Scotia, in 1867. The company used old family recipes from Britain and then won the contract to supply beer to the Canadian forces. It became known as the Army and Navy brewery.

After a troubled history – the brewmaster Conrad

Niagara Falls

This innovative micro-brewery on the Canadian side of the Niagara falls produced the first North American ice beer, the smoothly malty Niagara Eisbock (8%) in 1989. It was inspired by the local Eiswein.

Niagara was set up by the Criveller brothers, Mario and Bruno, after their Ethiopian brewery in Addis Ababa was nationalized. Since then the brewery has added an Apple Ale and a Kriek (both 6.5%) made with cherries.

Okanagan Spring Brewery

A small, specialist brewery established in Vernon, British Columbia. Their most prestigious brew is the Old English Porter, full-bodied and rummy (8.5%), but the company also produces a golden, malty Premium Lager, a Pale Ale and an Old Munich Wheat Beer that has a dry cider aroma and roasted-malt flavour.

Sleeman

The fourth-largest brewer in Canada (behind Molson, Labatt and Moosehead), Sleeman was first founded in Guelph, Ontario, in 1834, but closed in 1939. In 1985, John Sleeman decided to resurrect the family brewing business, opening a new plant in Guelph in 1988. Its beers are sold in distinctive embossed bottles.

Spinnakers

Canada's first brewpub had to overcome several legal hurdles before opening in Victoria, British Columbia, in 1984.

Permission to brew and sell beer on the same premises required a change to federal law and a local referendum. Spinnakers had to make the bar into a restaurant and build another storey to house the bar. Paul Hadfield brews mainly English-style ales and some lambic-style brews.

Unibroue

Quebec's largest micro-brewery was founded in 1991 in Chambly, Montreal, by Belgian beer enthusiast André Dion. It produces a range of characterful beers, such as Eau Bénite, that are even exported to France.

Upper Canada

Frank Heaps founded this Ontario micro-brewery in 1985 in a Toronto warehouse. It is now one of the largest new breweries in North America, and exports its beers to Europe. It uses water from the Caledon Hills 48 km (30 miles) away, trucking it in daily to ensure the purity of its beers.

Wellington County

The small Wellington County plant was set up in the Ontario brewing town of Guelph in 1985 to brew English-style ales, including some of the first cask-conditioned beers in North America to come from a commercial brewery, besides an Imperial Stout (5.5%) and Iron Duke strong ale (6.5%).

UNITED STATES OF AMERICA

The United States is the largest brewer in the world and its big-name lagers are famous the world over. Recently it has become the land of the born-again brewer, as micro-breweries spring up to meet the growing demand for variety.

ONCE THE US heaved with Europe's best beers – from English ales and Irish stouts to Czech Pilsners. Many of the leading brewers were German immigrants and brought with them that country's rich range of styles. Then came Prohibition. The Volstead Act of 1919 destroyed a thriving and colourful brewing industry by outlawing the manufacture and sale of alcohol. By the time Prohibition was repealed 14 years later in 1933, most of the original companies had vanished. The way was open for a few combines to dominate the trade – with a much-reduced range of beers.

When most Americans asked for a beer in the 1970s, they expected to receive a chilled pale lager, low in hops and light in flavour. Nothing much else was produced. This bland lager was increasingly sold in cans through supermarkets and stores. With little to distinguish between beers in taste, the emphasis was on marketing. The brand image became bigger than the beer, and the big brands gradually squeezed out those with less marketing muscle.

America is the home of light beer, a low-calorie lager launched by Miller in 1975. By 1995, three of the top four best-selling beers were light beers.

At the end of the 1970s, new small-scale breweries began to appear. Some, like New Amsterdam, used the spare capacity at established breweries to brew their beer. This contract brewing system helped struggling regional breweries to survive, while launching colourful new beers. By the 1990s new brewery business was booming. Some micro-breweries produced draft and bottled beers for local bars and stores, while others set up brewpubs to serve their beers direct to the customers. There are now about 1,000 new ventures with 92 micro-breweries and 138 brewpubs opening in 1995 alone. This speciality market is relatively small, but it is growing all the time.

Above: Anchor Steam Beer, brewed in San Francisco, was one of the pioneering brews of America's modern beer renaissance.

THE BEERS

Abita Amber

This light-amber, sweetish, malty European-style beer (3.8%) is brewed by Abita Brewing Co. Inc., Louisiana's first micro-brewery. Abita also brews a Golden Lager, a brilliant-amber, hoppy Fall Fest, an amber Bock Beer and Purple Haze Raspberry Wheat Ale.

Acme Pale Ale

This famous Californian brand was revived in 1996 by North Coast, the award-winning Californian brewery in Fort Bragg, which began as a brewpub in 1988. Other beers include Scrimshaw Pilsner (4.5%) and Blue Star Wheat (4.8%). It also brews a rich, intense Old Rasputin Russian Imperial Stout.

Adirondack Amber

This amber-coloured, Bavarian-style lager (5%), with a classic Pilsner flavour, is part of the Saranac range from FX Matt.

Alimony Ale

This famous nut-brown, orange-tinged ale ("the bitterest beer in America") is brewed by beer enthusiast Bill Owens. Alimony's bitter finish is complemented by a sweet-malt entry. Owens originally brewed the beer in honour of an employee who was going through a divorce. Bill Owens opened America's third brewpub, Buffalo Bill's, in Hayward, California, in 1983.

Amber

This unpasteurized, golden, smooth, malty lager (4.5%) is brewed by the Thomas Kemper Brewing Company.

American Originals

Anheuser-Busch sells its speciality beers, based on turn-of-the-century recipes, under the American Originals name. Beers include Muenchener Amber and Black and Tan Porter.

Anchor Steam Beer

A bright, copper-coloured cross between an ale and a lager (5%) with a well-rounded, malty taste and a crisp finish. Fritz Maytag's brewery revived this gold-rush-era beer, produced using a shallow-fermenter brewing method, perfected by forty-niners when no refrigeration was available.

Apricot Ale

This mild ale (3.5%) has a subtle apricot taste from start to finish. It is made with real apricots by Hart Brewing.

Auburn Ale

This ale is brewed by the family-run Leinenkugel lager brewery in Chippewa Falls, Wisconsin.

Augsburger

This is the brand name for speciality German-style beers from the US's fourth largest brewer, Stroh. Augsburger beers were originally developed by the Wisconsin brewer, Huber.

Bachelor Bitter

This copper-coloured, cold-conditioned, English-style ale (5%) with hints of grapefruit and evergreen is brewed by Deschute's brewery in Bend, Oregon. This Pacific Northwest brewery began life in 1988 as a brewpub but has expanded rapidly to meet demand.

Baderbräu

These German-style lagers from Chicago's Pavichevich brewery (set up in 1989 in Elmhurst, Illinois) comply with the German Reinheitsgebot beer purity law. The beers included a hoppy, bronze-coloured Pilsner (4.8%) and a light-brown, malty bock (5.4%).

America's Largest Selling Ale

Ballantine's Ale

Once one of the best-selling ales in America, Ballantine's was originally brewed in Albany, New York, in the 1830s before moving to Newark, New Jersey. In the 20th century, the beers have been brewed by a variety of companies, but are now produced by Pabst in Milwaukee. The best-known Ballantine beer is the copper-coloured hoppy IPA, but there is also a lighter Ballantine Ale.

Ballard Bitter

This strong, caramel-coloured bitter (5.9%), brewed by Redhook, is aggressively hopped, but offers some maltiness and a dry finish.

Banquet Beer
This pale-gold lager put
Coors on the map when it
was launched in the 1960s.

Bert Grant's
A range of "real ales" from
the Yakima Brewing and
Malting Co. brewpub in
Yakima, WA. The brews
include an English-style IPA
(4.2%), a fruity, malty
Scottish Ale (4.7%), a
chocolatey Imperial Stout
(6%), a hoppy Hefe Weizen
(4.2%), a rich Perfect Porter
(4%) and the flowery Amber
Ale (5.5%).

Big Butt Doppelbock
A German-style doppelbock
from Leinenkugel, Wisconsin.

Big Shoulders Porter
This chocolate-brown porter
has a slightly roasted taste
with a good hops balance. It
is produced by the family-
run Chicago brewery, the
only commercial brewery left
in the "windy city".

Bigfoot Barley Wine
This powerful, bottle-
conditioned, russet barley
wine (10.6%), brewed by
Sierra Nevada, has a fruity,
bittersweet taste.

Black and Tan
A dark-brown mix of a
specially made stout and
Saranac Adirondack Lager.
The Black and Tan has a
chocolate-malt nose, a
medium body and roasted
barley flavour with hints of
fruity hops.

Black and Tan Porter
This dark-amber-coloured
speciality beer by Anheuser-
Busch has a toasted-malt
aroma, a smooth, dry malt
flavour and a dry malt finish.

Black Butte Porter
A dark-reddish-brown, cold-
conditioned, unfiltered porter
(5.5%), with a tan head and a
rich, roasted-malt taste with
a touch of chocolate, was a
surprise success for
Deschute's in Bend, Oregon.

Black Chocolate Stout
This potent stout (8.3%),
produced annually by the
Brooklyn brewery, is a
classic imperial stout with a
rich, creamy texture and a
deep-malt, burnt-coffee taste.

Black Hawk Stout
This light-bodied stout,
brewed by Mendocino –
California's first micro-
brewery – is fruitier than
either Irish or English stout,
with a flavour of chocolate,
caramel and coffee.

Blackened Voodoo
This dark, ruby-brown beer
(5%) with a light, malt
aroma and slightly sour tang,
brewed by Dixie, caused
some outrage and was
banned in Texas when
launched in 1992, with
allegations that it was the
devil's brew.

Blackhook Porter
This dark-chestnut porter
(4.9%) has a robust malt and
coffee nose and a bitter,
roasty finish with hints of
coffee. It is brewed by the
Redhook Ale brewery in
Woodinville, WA.

Blue Fin Stout
This ebony stout (5%) has a
roasted malt nose with hints
of molasses. It has a medium
body and a bitter coffee
finish. It is brewed by
Shipyard in Portland, Maine.

**Blue Heron Pale Ale
(Bridgeport)**
This attractive, copper-
coloured, malty American
pale ale (5.8%) with a white
head has a sweet malt and
complex, bitter flavour and a
dry finish. It is available in
cask-conditioned form in the
brewery bar of Oregon's
oldest micro-brewery,
Bridgeport.

**Blue Heron Pale Ale
(Mendocino)**
This excellent, hazy-gold,
English-style pale ale (5.9%)
from Mendocino Brewing
has a dry, hoppy character
and a touch of fruit and
sweet maltiness.

Blue Moon
In 1995, the brewing giant
Coors launched this range of
speciality beers with a
Belgian White, Nut Brown
and Honey Blonde Ale. They
were developed in its Sandlot
micro-brewery in Denver,
Colorado. The beers are
brewed under licence
by F.X. Matt of Utica,
New York.

Blue Star Wheat Beer
A good version of American
wheat beer (4.8%) brewed by
North Coast. It is a pale,
clean, dry brew with a soft,
refreshing flavour.

Bohemian Dunkel
This rich, well-rounded,
unpasteurized, dark lager
(5.6%) is brewed by Kemper,
using chocolate-malt and
Styrian hops.

Boulder Amber Ale
A robust, bright-amber ale
(4.5%) with a yeasty, malty
nose and a well-balanced
malt and hop taste. It is
brewed by Rockies Brewing
in Boulder, Colorado.

Brooklyn Lager
Dubbed the pre-Prohibition
beer, the dry-hopped
Brooklyn Lager (4.5%) was
launched in 1987 in New
York. Originally all the beer
was contract-brewed upstate
by F.X. Matt of Utica, but in
1996 the company opened its
own brewery in Brooklyn,
reviving the area's brewing
traditions. Once Brooklyn
was one of the country's top
beer towns with breweries
like Piels, Shaefer and
Rheingold. It also brews a

strong Brooklyn Brown Ale (5.5%), a dry Brooklyn IPA (7.4%) and an annual Black Chocolate Stout (8.3%).

Budweiser

The world's leading beer brand from Anheuser-Busch of St Louis was first launched in 1876 and named after the famous brewing town in the Czech Republic. Budweiser is the epitome of a light American lager, using rice in the mash to give a crisp, clean taste that belies its alcohol content of 4.7%. Despite using eight hop varieties, it is very lightly hopped. Anheuser-Busch also takes pride in maturing the "King of Beers" in tanks containing beechwood chips to smooth out the flavour. In 1995, about one in four beers sold in America was a Budweiser.

Cascade Golden Ale

Another unfiltered, cold-conditioned, English-style ale (4.1%) from Deschute's.

Celebration Ale

This is one of the best of the American IPAs. It is a copper-coloured ale (5.1%), brewed by Sierra Nevada Brewing. It has a pungent,

floral nose with hints of caramel malt and a roasted malt and earthy hops flavour and a long, full-bodied finish. This is a real gem.

Celis White

This is a Belgian-style wheat beer (5%), flavoured with coriander and orange peel, from the Celis brewery in Austin, Texas.

Cerveza Rosanna Red Chili Ale

This odd, slow-burning speciality beer, flavoured with red chillies, is occasionally produced by the Pike Place brewery of Seattle. It goes well with Mexican food.

Chesterfield Ale

A golden, bottom-fermented ale with a flowery hop aroma, from Yuengling, America's oldest brewery.

Christian Moerlein

A malty lager brewed by Hudepohl-Schoenling of Cincinatti, named after an early brewer in the city. A Reinheitsgebot brew with plenty of body and a full, smooth finish.

Cold Spring Export Lager

This mild, crisp, gold lager, brewed by Cold Spring Brewing Company in Cold Spring, Minnesota, has a crisp, malty flavour and a dry, hoppy finish.

Coors

A range of lagers from this American giant. There is a full-bodied Original, a refreshing clean-flavoured Extra Gold, a Light, and a variety of Winterfest beers.

Crazy Ed's Cave Creek Chili Beer

This golden, hot-pepper specialty beer has a nose, taste and finish dominated by jalapeño peppers. It is brewed by Evansville Brewing Company in Evansville, Indiana, for the Black Mountain brewery of Cave Creek, Arizona.

Cream City Pale Ale

This top-fermented amber ale (4.2%) has a complex, hoppy nose with woody and citrus hints, a spicy hop taste and a long, dry hop finish. Brewed by the Lakefront micro-brewery.

Dortmunder Gold

This is a malty, dry, full-bodied, strong, export-style lager (5.4%) in the Dortmunder style. It is brewed by Great Lakes.

Dundee's Honey Brown Lager

A tasty brown lager from Genesee in New York.

East Side Dark

A deep-chestnut bock (6.5%) with a brown head, from Lakefront Brewery in Milwaukee, Wisconsin. This medium-bodied beer is sweet, with a deeply roasted malt flavour and a velvety smooth finish.

Eliot Ness

This amber-red, Vienna-style lager (5.4%) with a roasted-malt, buttery, fruity taste, is named after the man who jailed the notorious 1920s Chicago bootlegger Al Capone, and is brewed by Great Lakes.

Elk Mountain Amber Ale

Made with 100% barley malt, whole cone hops and English sale yeast, this amber ale (4.1%) has a malt and hops nose, a hoppy flavour with touches of sweet malt, and a dry hop and malt aftertaste. Brewed by Anheuser-Busch.

Espresso Stout

In keeping with its name, this deep-brown stout with a dark-brown, creamy head boasts a long coffee-like aftertaste. It has a good thick body, a rich chocolate and charcoal nose and a powerful roasted-malt flavour. It is made by Hart Brewing Company in Kalama, Washington, the makers of the Pyramid line of brews.

Esquire Extra Dry

A deep-gold, rich, malt-flavoured lager from the small regional Jones Brewing in Smithton, Pennsylvania.

Esquire Premium Pale Ale

This straw-coloured pale ale from Jones Brewing in Smithton, Pennsylvania, is hoppy from nose to finish.

Eye of the Hawk

A well-balanced, strong, amber ale (7.6%), brewed by Mendocino. It has a fruity nose, followed by a malty taste with assertive hopping.

Fall Fest

This sweetish, malty, European-style beer (4.9%) is brewed by Abita in Louisiana.

AMERICAN BEERS OVERSEAS

The major American brewers have been relatively slow in going international, mainly due to the attraction of the massive domestic market on their doorstep. This insular attitude is in sharp contrast to the soft drinks industry in which American brands like Coca-Cola dominate the world. The world's largest brewer, Anheuser-Busch of St Louis, only established Anheuser-Busch International in 1981. Its top beer, Budweiser, is now brewed in eight overseas countries and sold in 70 others. Second-placed Miller of Milwaukee only seriously developed overseas interests in the early 1990s, spurred by the realization that, while the beer market has peaked in the United States, it is still growing abroad. The company is now making a major push to double its foreign business by the year 2000.

Full Sail Nut Brown Ale

This English-style brown ale (5.4%) has an auburn colour, a nutty nose and a rich, roasted-malt flavour with hints of fruit and smoke. It is brewed by Full Sail in Hood River, Oregon.

Frontier

A cloudy, dark-amber American pale ale (4.2%) with a spicy, hoppy nose and a big, complex, highly carbonated flavour with a dry finish. An award-winning beer from Alaskan Brewing in Juneau, Alaska.

Genny Bock

An occasional deep-amber, malty bock, brewed by Genesee in Rochester, New York.

George Killian's Red Ale

This pale, copper-red ale from Coors (3.9%) has a light body, a toasted-malt nose and a fresh hop and malt flavour.

Gerst Amber

This malty beer is brewed by Evansville, a small former Heileman brewery in Indiana, which was bought out by its employees.

Grant's Scottish Ale

This reddish-amber American ESB (5%) with an off-white head, a hoppy, fruity aroma, a roasted-malt entry and an earthy hop finish, is brewed by Bert Grant of Grant's Yakima Brewing in Yakima, WA.

Great Northern Porter

A dark, reddish-brown porter (5.4%), brewed by Summit Brewing in Minneapolis, MN, with a rich, dark aroma and a big, fruity, roasted-malt and chocolate flavour, and hints of liquorice.

Growlin Gator Lager

A yellow-gold, light, refreshing lager (3.7%), brewed with pale malt and Yakima and Saaz hops by the August Schell Brewing Company.

Hampshire Special Ale

A strong, intensely malty winter ale (7%) with an earthy nose and a bitter-sweet finish, from Geary's Brewing in Portland, Maine.

Heartland Weiss

This hazy-gold, refreshing white wheat beer with a spicy, malt flavour is produced by the Chicago brewery.

Hefeweizen

This pale-yellow, hazy, unfiltered, unpasteurized, wheat beer (5%) is brewed by Thomas Kemper. It has a crisp, refreshing flavour.

Heimertingen Maibock

This powerfully pale German-style spring beer (7.5%) is brewed by Summit.

Helenbock 1992 Oktoberfest

This amber-coloured, German-style beer (4.2%) is made with Hallertau and Saaz hops and Munich malts. It has good body with a light head, a hearty hop aroma, a powerful malty flavour with a hop bite and a dry finish. It is contract-brewed by August Schell Brewing in New Ulm, MN, for Friends B.C. in Helen, Georgia.

Hell Doppel Bock

This rich and warming Bavarian-style beer (7.2%) comes from Heckler, a Californian venture set up in Tahoe City in 1993 by Keith Hilken after he had trained at a number of German breweries. Heckler produces only Bavarian-style lagers with German ingredients, brewed according to the Reinheitsgebot beer purity law. Hell Doppel Bock, like all Heckler beers, is currently contract-brewed by the Schell Brewery in New Ulm, Minnesota.

Hell Lager

This Bavarian-style lager (4.9%) comes from Heckler of Tahoe City. Made with German ingredients, it complies with the Reinheitsgebot beer purity law.

Helles Gold

This German-style lager (4.5%) is one of a range of German-style beers brewed by Pennsylvania, a pioneer of craft brewing on the East Coast. Set up in 1988 by Thomas Pastorius in the former Eberhardt and Ober brewery in the Deutschtown area of Pittsburgh, the brewery uses imported German plant.

Henry Weinhard's Private Reserve

This medium-gold beer (3.75%) is brewed by the G. Heileman Brewing Company, using Cascade hops. It has a medium body, an inviting hop nose and a well-balanced malt and hop flavour with a light hop finish. Each bottling is numerically identified on the neck of the bottle.

Hickory Switch Smoked Amber Ale

This ale (4.4%) is brewed using cold-smoked malt by Otter Creek in Middlebury, Vermont. It has a beautiful chestnut colour, a delicate smoky aroma and smoked-malt taste.

Honey Double Mai Bock

A golden, refreshing, strong German-style bock (7%) with a tall white head and a blend of sweet malt and tangy hops. It is traditionally brewed to be served in May, hence the name, but Stoudt's Brewing makes it available year-round.

Honeyweizen

Brewed with local honey in Washington State, this unpasteurized beer (5%) is produced by Kemper.

Hudy

This range of beers is produced by the Hudepohl-Schoenling brewery, formed in 1986 by the merger of Cincinnati's last two breweries in a city once famous for its brewers.

Iron City Lager

This lager from the Pittsburgh Brewing Company in Pennsylvania attracts strong local loyalty, despite the fact that it is a very bland American-style lager, in the same vein as Budweiser.

Jax Lager

This golden lager is produced by the Pearl brewery, the Texas rival to Lone Star, based in San Antonio.

Jax Pilsner

This light, refreshing yellow-gold Pilsner is a good thirst-quenching hot-weather drink. It has a pleasant malt nose, a mild but slightly sweet malt and hop flavour and a lot of carbonation. It is brewed by Pearl in San Antonio, Texas – now part of the S & P Company Brewing Group.

Jazz Amber Light

This amber-coloured, light beer (3.2%) is brewed in New Orleans by Dixie.

Jubelale

A mahogany, strong ale (6%) with a tan head, a fruity malt aroma and a roasted-malt, fruit and hops flavour. It is brewed by Deschute's, using an unfiltered, cold-conditioned technique.

Kilsch Lager

A striking German-style Pilsner (6.5%) with a cloudy-gold-coloured body, and a white head. It has a hoppy aroma and a sweet, malt entry followed by a long crisp finish. It is brewed by Lakefront brewery.

Latrobe

See Rolling Rock.

Legacy Lager

A bottom-fermented, German-style Pilsner (4.8%) with a deep-gold body, a tall white head, and a malty taste with a hint of butterscotch. It is brewed by Chicago Brewing, the only commercial brewery apart from Miller that is left in the "Windy City".

Legacy Red Ale

A bright, copper-coloured Irish-style red ale (4.9%) from the Chicago Brewing Company. It has a roasted-malt nose, a full-bodied malty entry and a tangy bitter finish.

Leinenkugel

This light, flowery premium beer is popular in Wisconsin where it is brewed by the family-run Leinenkugel Brewery in Chippewa Falls.

Liberty Ale

A strong, hazy bronze American IPA (6%) with a big malty hop nose, a powerful malt flavour with spicy hops, and a grapefruity finish. This is the first American beer to be dry-hopped in modern times. It is one of the best IPAs available.

Little Kings Cream Ale

This cream ale (5.5%) is brewed by Hudenpohl-Schoenling of Cincinnati.

Lone Star

This gold, crisp, light malt lager (3.5%) from the famous Texas brewery (part of Heileman) is regarded as the state's national beer.

Mactarnahan's Scottish Ale

This bright-copper-coloured, malty American pale ale (4.8%) has a fruity flavour with hints of caramel. Brewed by Portland Brewing.

Meister Bräu

A low-budget beer brewed by Miller. It used to sell itself by saying it tasted like Bud, but cost less.

Michelob

Made with a high percentage of two-row barley malt and imported hops, this gold lager has a balanced hop and dry malt flavour, and a medium long finish with a slight hop character. It is named after a town in Czechoslovakia.

Milwaukee's Best

Another cut-rate beer brewed by Miller. Just like Meister Bräu but with different packaging.

Mirror Pond Pale Ale

A deep-gold, unfiltered, cold-conditioned American-style pale ale (5.3%) with a creamy head and a flowery flavour with earthy hints, from Deschute's.

Moondog Ale

A pale-copper-coloured English-bitter-style ale (5%) with a dry, well-hopped flavour. Brewed by the Great Lakes Brewing Company in Cleveland, Ohio.

Moose Brown Ale

Brewed by Shipyard in Portland, Maine, and available on tap at the Great Lost Bear in Portland, this brown ale has a faint hop and malt nose, and a strong malt flavour balanced with a dry hop aftertaste.

Muenchener Amber

This ale, based on a turn-of-the-century recipe, is one of Anheuser-Busch's speciality American Originals beers.

Mystic Seaport Pale

This English-style pale ale (4.8%) from the Shipyard brewery in Portland, Maine, is bright-amber with a beige head. It has a perfumey, earthy nose, a fruity entry and a dry finish.

Northwoods Lager

This Germanic lager is brewed by the family-run Leinenkugel lager brewery in Wisconsin.

Obsidian Stout

This dark-brown, ruby-tinted, potent stout (6.9%) is brewed by Deschute's using an unfiltered, cold-conditioning method. It has a fresh, full-bodied malty flavour with a dry, roasty finish.

Oktoberfest

This strong, Bavarian-style lager (6%) comes from Heckler of Tahoe City. It is brewed with German ingredients and complies with the beer purity law.

Old Bawdy Barley Wine

A golden, oak-aged barley wine (9.9%) brewed by Pike Place brewery using peated distillers malt, which gives a smoky edge to the taste.

Old Crustacean

A cloudy, copper-coloured, strong, hoppy beer (10.2%) with a creamy head. It has a rich malt and apricot nose, a sweet caramel and roasted-malt entry, followed by fruit and scorched malt. It is one of the most complex and interesting beers available and is brewed by the Rogue micro-brewery, founded in Newport, Oregon, in 1988.

Old Foghorn

A deep-copper barley-wine-style ale (8.7%) with a creamy tan head, a hoppy, malty nose and a taste of fruit, hops and roasted malt. It is Anchor's strongest beer.

Old Knucklehead

A dark-copper ale with a sweet, roasted-malt nose, a malty, bitter-sweet taste and a long warm finish. This ale is produced by the Oregon micro-brewery Bridgeport, and is served in cask-conditioned form in the brewery bar.

Old Milwaukee

A range of lagers from the Stroh Brewery, Detroit. It includes a standard pale-gold Old Milwaukee Beer with a good malt flavour (3.6%), a pale, yellow-gold, clean-tasting Premium Light Beer, the highly carbonated, golden Genuine Draft and a deep-gold, strong Ice Beer.

Old No. 38 Stout

This award-winning stout (5.6%), named after a steam engine, is brewed by North Coast. It is very dark black, with a ruby hue and a dense brown head. The nose is of roasted malt and barley, and it has a rich barley flavour with a bitter, burnt, malt flavour.

Old Rasputin Russian Imperial Stout

A dark, reddish-brown, rich, intense stout (7.8%) with a hoppy roasted malt nose, a roasty flavour and a bitter finish. It is brewed by North Coast.

Old Thumper

This is an American version of the English ale (5.7%), brewed in Portland, Maine, by Shipyard.

Oregon Honey Beer

A pale-gold honey beer (4%) with a gentle, earthy aroma of hops and a malty flavour, from the Portland brewery.

Pearl Lager

This golden lager is produced by the Pearl brewery, the Texas rival to Lone Star, based in San Antonio.

Pennsylvania Dark

This German-style, deep-ruby-brown lager (5%) has a delicious roasted taste with hoppy notes.

Pennsylvania Oktoberfest

A German-style lager (6%) brewed by Pennsylvania.

Pennsylvania Pilsner

This clear-gold, sweet, malty, lightly-hopped German-style lager (5%) is one of a range of German-style beers brewed by Pennsylvania in the Deutschtown area of Pittsburgh, using imported German plant.

Perfect Porter

This rich, dark Scottish-style porter (4%) is brewed by Bert Grant of Yakima.

Pete's Wicked Winter Brew
A delicious, red-amber ale (4.2%) with hints of nutmeg and raspberry in its flavour. It is one of the wide range of speciality brews from Pete's Brewing Company.

Pike Pale Ale

The bold Pale Ale (4.5%) is the best-known brew from the Seattle Pike brewery founded by famous "Marchand du Vin" beer importer Charles Finkel in 1989. Pike also brews a 5X Stout, an IPA and a lusty, oak-aged Old Bawdy Barley Wine. In 1996, Pike opened a new brewery with a pub attached.

Pike XXX

A dense, black stout (6.2%) with a creamy dark-brown head and a malt and coffee nose. The flavour starts off sweet and is then followed by a strong coffee flavour and a bitter, burnt, hoppy finish. This excellent stout has a rich, creamy body and texture.

Pintail

This ale is produced by the Oregon micro-brewery in Bridgeport, and is available in cask-conditioned form in the brewery bar.

Point Special

This better-than-average American lager is brewed at the Wisconsin Point brewery founded in 1857 at Stevens Point.

Portland Ale

This malty ale (5%) was the first beer to be produced by the Portland brewery when it opened in Oregon in 1986. The brewery has two pubs in Portland.

Pottsville Porter

This bottom-fermented, dark porter is produced by America's oldest brewery, Yuengling.

Premium Verum

This malty lager is the most notable beer brewed by the Kentucky brewery, Oldenburg. The Fort Mitchell brewery is famed for its occasional weekend beer camps, when visitors taste the brews, tour the brewery and visit the neighbouring American Museum of Brewing History.

Pullman Pale Ale

This pale ale (5.9%) comes from the Californian Riverside brewery set up in Riverside in 1993.

Pumpkin Ale

This beer is made using huge, home-grown pumpkins and is spiced with cinnamon, nutmeg and cloves. It is another delicious and interesting beer from Bill Owens.

Raincross Cream Ale

This mellow pale ale (5.9%) is produced by the Californian Riverside brewery, which was set up in Riverside in 1993.

Rainier Ale

The fruity Rainier Ale was a much sought-after beer in the years before the micro-brewery revolution hit the north-west.

The ale was known as "The Green Death" owing to the colour of its label and high alcohol strength. It is produced by the Rainier brewery.

Red Bull

A strong, golden, malt-liquor brand (7.1%) produced by Stroh in Detroit for the Canadian market.

Red Hook ESB

This deep-amber, strong extra-special bitter (5.4%) comes from the ground-breaking Red Hook brewery founded in 1981 by Paul Shipman and Gordon Bowker in the Ballard area of Seattle.

Red Hook Rye

This golden, unfiltered beer (5%) with a dry grainy flavour is brewed by Red Hook. Red Hook has embarked on a series of expansions and is rapidly becoming a national brewer.

Red Sky Ale

This amber-coloured, complex, strong ale (5.6%) is produced by St Stan's brewery, whose other beers tend to be German-style alts.

AN AMERICAN CLASSIC

Red Tail Ale

This hazy, copper-coloured, strong English-style ale (6.5%) is brewed by Mendocino.

Riverwest Stein Beer

A striking, bright-copper Märzenbier (6.5%) with a delicate beige head, a buttery caramel nose and a caramel flavour with hints of scorched smoke.

Roggen Rye

This golden, unfiltered, unpasteurized rye beer (5%) is brewed by Thomas Kemper, using flaked grain and pale barley malt.

Rogue-n-Berry

Marionberries are used to flavour this beer from the Rogue micro-brewery.

Rolling Rock

This lager brand revived the fortunes of the Latrobe brewery of Pennsylvania, founded in 1893. The light lager stands out from the crowd due to the fired-on label on its green bottles.

Ruedrich's Red Seal Ale

This rich, amber-coloured, award-winning beer, brewed by North Coast Brewing Company, is the epitome of a good American ale. It is a pleasant combination of hoppy dryness and malty flavours with fruity notes.

Samuel Adams Boston Lager

This bright-amber Pilsner has a fresh, hoppy nose, a sweet-malt entry, a caramel flavour and a dry, malty finish. It is brewed by Boston Beer Company,

Samuel Adams Boston Stock Ale

This bright-amber ale (5%) has a complex, earthy nose and a hoppy, off-dry palate. It is brewed by Boston Beer Company.

Schaefer Beer

A light-gold lager, produced by the Schaefer Brewing company in Detroit and promoted as the US's oldest lager beer.

Schlitz

A range of beers from the Stroh brewing company. Schlitz beer is the standard pale-gold lager; there is also a Light Beer, a Malt Liquor, a Draught and an Ice Beer.

Schmaltz's Alt

This strong, dark alt (6%) is brewed by the family-owned Schell brewery in New Ulm, Minnesota.

Scrimshaw Pilsner

Brewed by North Coast, this well-balanced lager (4.4%) has a sweet, malty entry and a crisp finish.

1994 SMOKED PORTER

Seasonal Smoked Porter

The distinctive, intense taste of Alaskan's award-winning annual porter (6.4%) comes from using malt kilned over alder wood in the local fish smokehouse.

Shakespeare's Stout

An ebony-coloured export stout (6.1%) with a creamy, dark-brown head. Shakespeare has a complex hoppy, chocolatey, smoky, malt nose and a bittersweet, fruity flavour with a dry, burnt, bitter finish.

Shea's Irish Amber

This traditional East-Coast ale is brewed by Genesee in Rochester, New York.

Shiner Bock

This dark, amber bock (4.4%) is brewed by a small local brewery in Shiner, Texas, called Spoetzl, founded in 1909.

Shipyard Export

This export beer (5.1%) comes from Portland's Shipyard brewery.

Signature

See Stroh's.

Snow Goose

This complex old ale (6.4%) is brewed by the Wild Goose micro-brewery in Maryland. It has a beautiful dark-copper, orangey colour, a pungent, hoppy nose and a caramelized malt flavour, followed by a long, bitter, malty finish.

Stegmaier

Stegmaier lager and porter are the best-known brews from the Lion brewery in Wilkes-Barre, Pennsylvania.

Stoney's Lager

This light lager is produced by the small regional Jones Brewing in Smithton, Pennsylvania.

Stoudt's Festbier

A copper-coloured Märzenbier (5.1%) from the Stoudt brewery in Adamstown, Pennsylvania, which complies with the German Reinheitsgebot beer purity law. Festbier has a beautiful head, a roasted malt nose and a caramel finish.

Stroh's

This lager is one of the ranges of beers from the Stroh brewing company. It includes a copper-amber bock, a Light Beer (3.1%), a standard American Beer and Signature lager.

Tabernash

This small Denver micro-brewery produces a range of four beers. The golden Weiss is a top-fermenting German-style wheat beer with a spicy, fruity flavour. It is bottle-conditioned. Golden is a light-gold, hoppy Pilsner.

Munich is a deep-brown, rich, malty, Bavarian-style dunkel, brewed using six different malts in the mash. Amber claims to be a traditional ale brewed according to 19th-century methods to produce a deep-amber ale with a light, crisp lager finish.

Triple Bock

This heavyweight beer (17.5%) is brewed at the Bronco Winery in Ceres, California, using a champagne yeast, primed with maple syrup and matured for three months in former Tennessee whisky casks. It is the most powerful of the contract beers from the Boston Beer Company.

Turbo Dog

This is Abita's deep, ruby-amber, strong, darkish, dry-hopped beer (4.9%) with a roasted-malt flavour and long, dry aftertaste.

Twelve Horse Ale

This bright-gold, refreshing lager (3.8%) with a dry hops finish, is brewed by Genesee in Rochester, New York.

Victoria Avenue Amber Ale

A dark, scarlet-amber ale (5.8%) with a tan-coloured head, from Riverside. It has a malty nose with hints of fruit, a sweet malt and caramel palate and a slightly bitter, malty finish.

Wassail Winter Ale

Brewed by Full Sail, this strong winter warmer (6.5%) is a hazy, dark-amber ale with a fruity nose and a complex malt flavour with a bitter, tangy finish.

Weizen Berry

This rosy-gold, unfiltered, unpasteurized fruit and wheat beer (5%) has a raspberry nose and a malty raspberry flavour. It is brewed by the Thomas Kemper Brewing company in Poulsbo, Washington.

Wheat Berry Brew

This malty beer (4.5%) is made from local Oregon marionberries. It is brewed by Portland.

7th Street Stout

This potent, ruby-black, rich stout (6%) is brewed by Riverside Brewing in Riverside, California. It has a rich, malty aroma and a burnt, bitter, malt, full-bodied flavour.

Above: Customers outside the Second Class Saloon in Alaska, 1899, which was owned by Wyatt Earp during the Gold Rush.

THE BREWERS

Abita

Set up in 1986 at Abita Springs near New Orleans, Louisiana's first new brewery produces sweetish, malty European-style beers.

Alaskan

This highly regarded brewery was established in the Alaskan capital of Juneau in 1986. Its rich beers have won many awards.

Anchor

See panel right.

Anderson Valley

The Californian brewery at the Buckhorn Saloon in Boonville has been famous for its richly flavoured beers since 1987.

Anheuser-Busch

The undisputed giant of the American brewing industry has 12 breweries and 44% of the US beer market. In 1995 it sold 87.5 million barrels, nearly double that of its nearest rival, Miller. Its leading brand Budweiser is the biggest-selling beer in the world, brewed in eight overseas countries and exported to more than 70.

Anheuser-Busch is a family company. The story started in 1860 when German immigrant Eberhard Anheuser (1805-80) bought a failed brewery in St Louis, Missouri. His energetic son-in-law Adolphus Busch (1839–1913) turned it into a national success. Busch used the new rail system to introduce the first fleet of refrigerated wagons, he pioneered the use of pasteurization and in 1876 launched the first national beer brand, Budweiser. Twenty years later he added a premium brew, Michelob. Sales reached a million barrels by 1901.

During Prohibition the company brewed the non-alcoholic Bevo. After the Second World War, sales soared, with eight regional breweries built to meet demand.

The original brewery in St Louis is now a tourist attraction and houses the company's Clydesdale horses.

Besides Budweiser and Michelob, the company brews about 30 beers. In response to the micro-brewery movement Anheuser-Busch has introduced its own speciality beers.

Boston Beer Company

The Boston Beer Company has its beers produced to order by other breweries in Pennsylvania, New York and Oregon. Formed in 1985, ten years later the company was the ninth-largest US brewer, with sales of a million barrels per year. The brews are named after Samuel Adams, one of the organizers of the Boston Tea Party of 1773. Jim Koch revived his ancestors' brewing recipes with his Boston Lager and now produces a wide range of beers. The Boston Beer Company also has its own small brewery.

Catamount

A small brewery started in White River Junction, Vermont, in 1985 by Steve Mason, who had trained in England. He named his new enterprise after the cougar or mountain cat – catamount.

Celis

See panel opposite.

ANCHOR

Anchor is the guiding light of the new brewery revolution in North America. When Fritz Maytag, the heir to a washing-machine empire, bought a bankrupt brewery in San Francisco in 1965, his main aim was to preserve a piece of Californian history. The Anchor brewery, founded in 1896, used a unique American method of brewing perfected in the California Gold Rush days when no refrigeration was available. Very shallow fermenters cooled the brew, producing a cross between a lager and an ale. Maytag maintained this tradition and his Anchor Steam Beer (5%) gained a national reputation. It helped inspire the new brewery movement by showing that quality beers of character had a market in America. Maytag has since added a range of other brews, including Liberty Ale (6.1%), Anchor Porter (6.3%) and Old Foghorn (8.7%).

In 1989, Maytag extended his exploration into beers from the past by making a brew using an ancient Sumerian recipe.

CELIS

The Celis story is one of the most remarkable in the world of beer. Pierre Celis started not one but two pioneering breweries – each on a different continent.

Born in Belgium, Celis grew up next to a brewery. When the local "white" wheat-beer style disappeared, he decided to revive it, setting up the De Kluis (the Cloister) brewery in Hoegaarden in 1966. Its refreshing, spicy Hoegaarden beer proved so popular that, after expanding the brewery a number of times, he sold up to Belgium's largest brewer Interbrew in 1989. He had revived a beer style that was widely copied in his home country.

Hoegaarden had also been successful as an export to the United States. Celis decided to cross the Atlantic, and in 1992, he opened the Celis Brewery in Austin, Texas, to brew his Belgian-style wheat beer now called Celis White. It too proved a huge success and was soon copied by others.

History also repeated itself in another way. In 1995, Celis sold a controlling interest to American brewing giant Miller. In 1996 the company doubled capacity. The Celis brewery also brews other Belgian-style beers, including Celis Raspberry (5%), a richer Grand Cru (8.7%), a Pilsner Celis Golden (5%) and a Pale Bock (5%).

Coors

Coors boasts the biggest single brewery in the world, filling the town of Golden, near Denver, Colorado. The plant is capable of brewing 20 million barrels a year. The US's third-largest brewing company has just one other brewery at Memphis, Tennessee.

A family firm founded by Adolph Coors in 1873, Coors was an unremarkable regional brewery until its Banquet Beer developed a cult following in the 1960s, spurred on by its fresh Rocky Mountain water image. Now Coors Light is its flagship brand. A slightly more malty Extra Gold is brewed under licence by Scottish Courage in England. Coors is noted for its refusal to pasteurize its beers, only chilling and micro-filtering them. Its most distinctive beer is its annual Winterfest. Coors also pioneered the first red ale, George Killian's, which was introduced back in 1978. The brewery launched a range of speciality beers under the Blue Moon name in 1995.

Dixie

This legendary New Orleans brewery was founded in 1907. It still ages its "slow-brewed" beers in cypress wood vessels. Its main beers are the malty Dixie (4.5%) and Jazz Amber Light. It also brews the notorious dark beer, Blackened Voodoo.

Dock Street

An innovative restaurant brewery in Philadelphia, which produces a wide range of beers such as a ginger wheat and a juniper rye. Its bottled beers – notably Dock Street Amber (5.3%), Dock Street Bohemian Pilsner (5.3%) and Dock Street Illuminator (7.5%) – are contract-brewed by F.X. Matt of Utica, New York, for the Dock Street restaurant in Philadelphia.

Frankenmuth

The Michigan town of Frankenmuth was founded in 1845 by Bavarian immigrants from Franconia, in Germany, the world's most brewery-packed region. Inevitably, the town built its own brewery, dating back to 1862. In 1987, the Frankenmuth brewery was rebuilt. Its German-style beers include Frankenmuth Dark (5.2%), Pilsner (5.2%), Old Detroit Amber (5.9%) and Bock (6.4%).

Full Sail

Founded in 1987 at the windsurfing centre of Hood River, Oregon, this brewery's fruity ales have grown in popularity on the West Coast. Bottled beers include Golden (4.4%), Amber (5.9%) and Nut Brown, as well as a range of seasonal beers.

Geary's

New England's first micro-brewery opened in Portland, Maine, in 1986. Its founder David Geary had worked in various Scottish and English breweries and the influence is obvious in the beers.

The flagship beer is Geary's Pale Ale (4.5%), but the brewery also produces a dark Geary's London Porter (4.2%), Geary's American Ale (4.8%) and a warming winter Hampshire Special.

Genesee

The largest independent regional brewery in the US was founded in Rochester, New York, in 1878. It still follows the north-eastern tradition of ale brewing, notably with the soft, sweetish Twelve Horse Ale, Cream Ale and Shea's Irish Amber. It also produces an occasional Genny Bock and other speciality beers such as Dundee's Honey Brown Lager.

Great Lakes

This extensive range of widely acclaimed beers has poured from Cleveland's first micro-brewery, which was set up in an old saloon in Ohio in 1988. The range of beers includes Moon Dog Ale, Dortmunder Gold, a Vienna-style lager Eliot Ness, a Porter (5.9%) and a Great Lakes' IPA (6.9%).

Harpoon

The Mass Bay brewery has been brewing Harpoon ales in Boston since 1987, notably a Harpoon Ale, Light, Pilsner, IPA and Stout. Its bottled beers are contract brewed by F.X. Matt of Utica, New York.

Heileman

The fifth-largest brewing company in the US is based in La Crosse, Wisconsin, where it is known for its Heileman Old Style and Special Export lagers. This brewpub in Davis, California, has been operating close to the university brewing school since 1990. It is known for its extensive range of German-style lagers, including a Hübsch Hefe-Weizen (5%), Märzen (5.5%) and Doppelbock (7.5%).

Matt

F.X. Matt has been brewing in Utica in upstate New York since 1888, originally as the West End brewery. Now it mainly contract-brews speciality beers for other companies. The first was New Amsterdam in 1982. In 1985, the firm also introduced its own successful Saranac range of beers including Adirondack Amber, Pale Ale, Golden (5.2%) and Black and Tan.

Mendocino

Mendocino is one of the standard-bearers of the new brewery revolution in the United States. In 1983 it was California's first brewpub, opened in an old saloon. The brewery in Mendocino County now brews a wide range of excellent English-style ales.

Miller

The second-largest brewer in the United States, Miller has more than a fifth of the beer market and runs the five main brewing plants. Founded in 1855 when German immigrant Frederick Miller bought a small brewery in Milwaukee, the company was taken over by tobacco giant Philip Morris in 1970. Miller Lite, which was launched in 1975, created a huge new market for low-calorie beers. In little more than ten years, production soared from around five million barrels to more than 40 million per year.

Its other high-profile brand is bottled Genuine Draft, launched in 1986 using a special cold-filtered process, which means that the beer does not need to be pasteurized. The oldest brand Miller High Life, is now part of Miller's popularly priced range, which also includes Miller Meister Bräu and Milwaukee's Best. In addition, Miller brews a non-alcoholic beer called Sharp's and a Magnum Malt Liquor.

The Miller company has responded to competition from the fast-growing speciality beer market in a number of ways. In 1990 it introduced a range of all-barley beers under the Miller Reserve brand name, including an Amber Ale. It also markets various brands under the company's original name, Plank Road Brewery. In addition, Miller has also directly taken over smaller breweries. In 1988, for example, it bought the old Leinenkugel brewery of Wisconsin, which still sells its lager under the Leinenkugel name. In 1995 Miller bought a majority interest in the successful Celis Brewery of Texas and Shipyard of Maine.

New Amsterdam

The original contract brewer, New Amsterdam was founded in New York in 1982 by Matthew Reich. He contracted established brewer F.X. Matt of Utica to brew his New Amsterdam beers, selling them as if from a micro. New Amsterdam's best-known beers are its Ale and Amber.

New Glarus

This Wisconsin village brewery was set up in 1993 by a former Budweiser brewer who trained in Germany. In 1996 it revived a famous old Californian brand – Acme Pale Ale. It specializes in European lagers, notably Edel-Pils, Wisconsin Bock and Weiss.

Pabst

The US's sixth largest brewery, Pabst, is best-known for Pabst Blue Ribbon lager, "the working man's beer". Founded in Milwaukee in 1844 as Best Brewing, Frederick Pabst married into the Best family, rapidly expanded sales and in 1889 the company's name was changed to Pabst. After being recognized as America's Best Lager at the World Exposition in 1893, Pabst began fixing blue ribbons to its bottles, giving their flagship beer its name.

Below: A gleaming copper in the modern Pyramid micro-brewery.

Pete's

Home-brew enthusiast Pete Slosberg has been marketing his Pete's Wicked Ale with wicked success since 1986. Contract brewed in St Paul, Minnesota, nine other speciality beers have since joined the original chestnut ale (5.1%) including Pete's Bohemian Pilsner and Pete's Amber (both 4.9%) and summer and winter brews.

TOP TEN BREWERS

This table shows the largest brewers, with their market share and number of barrels sold in 1995. Although the top three brewers account for 77% of the market, their grip is slipping – the previous year they controlled 81%. The new speciality brewers are creating a more diverse market, with one of them, the Boston Beer Company (Samuel Adams) becoming the ninth-largest US brewer.

BREWER	MARKET SHARE	NO. OF BARRELS
1 Anheuser-Busch	44.1%	87.5 million
2 Miller	22.7%	45.0 million
3 Coors	10.2%	20.3 million
4 Stroh's	5.4%	10.8 million
5 Heileman	4.0%	7.9 million
6 Pabst	3.2%	6.3 million
7 Genesee	0.9%	1.8 million
8 Latrobe	0.6%	1.2 million
9 Boston	0.5%	1.0 million
10 Pittsburgh	0.5%	0.9 million

Plank Road Brewery

This was the original name of the Miller brewing giant. It now markets various beers under this brand name, including Icehouse and Red Dog.

Pyramid

One of the success stories of the craft brewery movement, the Pyramid brewery was set up as Hart Brewing in 1984 in the small logging town of Kalama in Washington State, brewing Pyramid Pale Ale. Since then, Pyramid has grown into the third-largest

new venture in the United States. Pyramid ales include Pyramid Pale Ale, Pyramid Wheaten Ale, Pyramid Best Brown and Pyramid Rye (all 5.1%). It also brews a range of seasonal brews including Porter (5.4%) and Snow Cap (6.9%).

St Stan's

Inspired by visits to Germany, Garith Helm built a brewery in Modesto, California. St Stan's is best-known for its original unpasteurized Amber Alt.

Schell

This rare midwest regional brewery was founded in 1858 by German immigrant August Schell in New Ulm, Minnesota, and it is still family-owned. It produces pre-Prohibition-quality lagers. The family's elaborate 1858 mansion and beer garden are now a site of national historic importance. Its lagers include an all-malt Schell Pilsner (5.3%), a Schell Weizen (4.4%) using 60% wheat and an Oktoberfest (5.3%).

Schlitz

Once one of the best-known breweries – and brands – in the US, "The Beer that made Milwaukee Famous" is no longer brewed in the city since the brewery was taken over by Stroh's in 1982.

Sierra Nevada

One of the leaders of the craft brewery revolution, Sierra Nevada has grown to be the largest in the west. It was founded by keen home-brewers Ken Grossman and Paul Camusi in Chico, California, in 1981. Its flagship beer is the highly acclaimed Sierra Nevada Pale Ale (5.5%). It also brews a Sierra Nevada Porter (5.9%) and Sierra Nevada Stout (6%).

Sprecher

The former Pabst brewer Randall Sprecher revived the German brewing arts that Milwaukee had largely forgotten when he set up his own brewery in the town in 1985. His robust beers include an all-malt Sprecher Special Amber, Sprecher Black Bavarian (6%) and an unfiltered Sprecher Hefe-Weiss. He also brews an occasional Sprecher Irish Stout (6%).

Stoudt's

The first American micro-brewery to be designed and developed by a woman, Carol Stoudt's German-style beers have won about 20 medals at the Great American Beer Festival since she set up her brewery in Adamstown, Pennsylvania, in 1987. Her beers, brewed to the Reinheitsgebot beer purity law, include Stoudt's Gold Dortmunder (5%). In addition, she brews two Belgian Abbey ales, plus English-style ales and stout.

Straub

This small, long-established, family-owned brewery in rural Pennsylvania at St Mary's produces a light Straub Beer.

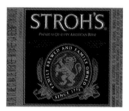

Stroh's

The US's fourth-largest brewing company was originally founded in 1850 in Detroit. Bernhard Stroh emigrated to America from Germany in 1849 where his family had started brewing in the late 1700s at Kirn. The next year he started a small brewhouse in Detroit, and five generations of the Stroh family have run the brewery ever since. During Prohibition, the company continued to operate producing "near" beers and

alternative products made from brewing ingredients, including a popular malt extract that was a favourite of local home-brewers. Recently the company has expanded with a series of acquisitions, culminating in the takeover of the Heileman Brewing Company of Wisconsin in 1996. A number of the Stroh beers are advertised as being "fire-brewed", meaning that direct heat on the coppers is used to boil the wort, a process that was started by Julius Stroh in the early 1900s. The best-known brands are Stroh's Lager and Signature. The company also produces maltier German-style beers under the Augsburger name and has recently developed a number of low-alcohol beers, especially Stroh's Non-Alcoholic beer.

Summit

This midwest brewery was opened by Mark Stutrud in 1986 in St Paul, Minnesota, and has steadily grown in size and reputation. Best known for its Extra Pale Ale and IPA, it also brews seasonal German-style beers including a Hefe Weizen and a Düsseldorfer Alt (4.9%).

Tabernash

This micro-brewery in Denver, Colorado, concentrates on brewing German-style beers, such as its malt-accented dark Munich lager and an unfiltered Bavarian-style wheat beer, Tabernash Weiss.

Thomas Kemper

Thomas Kemper was founded in Washington State in 1985 specifically to brew German-style lagers, soon establishing itself near the coastal town of Poulsbo. In 1992 it merged with another north-west brewer, Pyramid Ales. It produces a range of unpasteurized beers. Seasonals include a Belgian White (4.4%) and Maibock (6.5%). See also Pyramid.

Twenty Tank

The Twenty Tank brewpub opened in a former sheet metal shop in 1990 in the heart of San Francisco's SOMA club district. The brew-kettle and mash vessels are in plain view for customers in the bar and restaurant. It offers a wide variety of house-brewed ales.

Widmer

North America's first modern Hefeweizen, a cloudy draught beer, surprised drinkers when it was launched by the Widmer brothers, Kurt and Rob, in Portland, Oregon, in 1986. The Widmer brewery uses a top-fermenting German alt yeast, and its original beer was a rich-copper-coloured alt. There is an unfiltered Hefeweizen available, and the brothers also brew an Amber, Blackbier and a fruity Widberry.

Wild Goose

One of the first micro-breweries in the mid-Atlantic states was founded in Cambridge, Maryland, in 1989. It brews a range of English-style ales, including Wild Goose Amber (5%) and IPA (5.3%).

Yakima

The Yakima Brewing Company was set up in 1982 in the heart of the hop-growing area in Washington State by Bert Grant, an engaging ale pioneer who opened the first modern brewpub in the US. Grant was an experienced brewing chemist. In 1982 he branched out on his own to brew better-quality beers, starting with the Yakima brewpub. He built a larger commercial brewery in 1991. Many of the beers produced by Yakima reflect his Scottish ancestry.

Yuengling

The oldest brewery still operating in the United States was founded in 1829 in Pottsville, Pennsylvania, where deep cellars were dug into the hillside to keep the beer cool during maturation. Still family-run, it is best known for its bottom-fermented Pottsville Porter and Chesterfield Ale, which are now enjoying renewed sales with the revival of interest in specialist beers. Yuengling also brews a Premium and Traditional Lager and a blended lager-porter called Black and Tan.

Zip City

This sophisticated New York brewpub and restaurant was established in the former headquarters of the National Temperance Society in Manhattan. It brews mainly unfiltered German-style lagers, including a Märzen and a Dunkel, to accompany its gourmet food.

Below: At the beginning of Prohibition in the US government agents closed down hundred of saloons.

LATIN AMERICA

Now best known for light, thin lager drunk straight from the bottle with a wedge of lime, Central and South American beer has a much richer tradition than is widely appreciated.

Above: Dos Equis, "Two Crosses", is a rich, dark, high-quality lager brewed in Mexico which has proved popular in many export markets.

THE MAYANS were brewing beer from fermented corn stalks long before Spanish conquistadors made their mark. Meanwhile, in northern Mexico, the Aztecs enjoyed a fermented drink made with sprouted maize. Even after the conquest, peasants in isolated areas remained loyal to pulque, a drink brewed with the juice of the agave plant. It keeps for just a day or two (the name means "decomposed") and can still be found today, along with other indigenous drinks. An Inca legend claims that specially chosen maidens would chew cooked maize to a pulp to prepare it for brewing – their beauty and the purity of saliva were considered an aid to fermentation.

The Spanish conquistadors set up small breweries – cervecería – across the continent from the 16th century onwards. Beer came a poor second to distilled spirits, such as mescal or tequila, however, until Bavarian, Swiss and Austrian brewers introduced lager to Mexico in the 19th century, and ice-making machines arrived on the continent.

During Prohibition, which devastated the North American brewing industry from 1919 to 1933, the sleepy Mexican town of Tijuana became an outpost of alcohol tourism for thirsty Americans. As a result, at one point there were 75 bars on its 200m (600ft) main street.

Mexico remains the leading beer producer in Latin America. Its two biggest breweries, Cervecería Modelo and Cervecería Moctezuma, dominate the home market. Brazil, which was colonized by the Portuguese rather than the Spanish, and has a brewing tradition that looks to Germany, is the second-largest producer. Brazil also produces a traditional black (negra) beer. Lagers are the popular drink of choice in Latin America, with most brewers offering a Pilsner. Light, cheap and cheerful lagers made using rice, corn or other adjuncts in the mash are widely available, although other, more eclectic and traditional brews can also be found.

THE BEERS

Africana

This rich, dark lager (5.5%) is a cross between a Munich-style dunkel and a Vienna Red, brewed with hops, rice and maize. It has an aroma of roast malt, a smooth chocolate taste and a hoppy aftertaste. It is brewed by Argentina's Bieckhart brewery in Buenos Aires.

Ancla

Columbia's Ancla brewery offers a range of all-malt beers. These include Cerveza Ancla which is made with German and Canadian hops and matured for four weeks, Ancla Premium (4.8%) and the amber-coloured Ancla Roja (4.1%). Ancla also offers the all-malt Naval Super Premium (4.8%) and an all-malt, alcohol-free beer.

Antarctica Pilsen

This Brazilian beer, the eighth most popular beer in the region, is gold-coloured and highly carbonated, with a strong hop aftertaste.

Bavaria Gold Beer

Golden-coloured and unremarkable, this fruity, slightly malty lager-style beer (3.5–5%) is brewed by Cervecería Costa Rica S.A.

Belikin Beer

The malty, golden, dryish lager (3.5–5%), from the Belize Brewing Company in Ladyville, is a pleasant, fizzy beer, best served cold.

Belikin Stout

A strong, dark-brown, faintly hoppy, rich stout (6–7.5%) with a sweet, malty aroma from the Belize Brewing Company.

Biekhart Cerveza Pilsen

A malty Pilsner-style lager (4.8%), made using pale malt from Argentinian barley, rice, maize and American Cascade hops. It is brewed by the Argentinian Biekhart brewery.

Biekhart Especial

This golden premium lager (5%) is more aromatic and fully flavoured than its sister brand, Cerveza Pilsen, from the Biekhart brewery.

Bohemia

This superior, strong lager (5.4%) from Cuauhtémoc in Mexico is made with Saaz hops, to give it a malty, full-bodied taste with a hint of vanilla. In 1995, Bohemia was the most popular beer in Mexico.

Brahma Chopp Export

From Brazil's Companhia Cervejaría, this yellow-gold, malty, slightly sour beer was the fourth-best-selling beer in South America in 1996.

Brahma Pilsner

This quality, hoppy Pilsner (5%) from Brazil's Companhia Cervejaría, based in Rio de Janeiro, has a rich malty, bittersweet taste with a hint of vanilla.

Corona Extra

Corona Extra (4.6%) is a lager made with about 40% rice and a relatively low proportion of hops. Cheap to make and refreshing when served very cold, this beer was designed for the taste-buds of the Mexican working man, and is served in a distinctive clear bottle. It was taken up eagerly by American tourists, who took to drinking it with lime, much to the amusement of the Mexicans, although the lime and lager fashion is now taking off in Mexico as well.
Corona is the best-known brew from the Modelo brewery of Mexico City, one of the country's two major brewing companies. It is now widely exported and is a familiar designer beer which can be found in the bars of many of the European capital cities.

Cuzco

This very pale, yellow-gold, fizzy, malty, Pilsner-style lager (5%) is brewed using 100% barley by the Compañia del Sur del Perú S.A. It takes its name from the ancient Inca city in the high Andes of Peru.

Mexico's malty legacy

One of the few legacies of the Austrian Emperor Maximilian's short and inglorious reign over Mexico between 1864 and 1867 is a strongly Germanic influence on that country's brewing industry. The malty, dark-amber beers of Vienna may be hard to find in Austria today, but the old style is still very popular in the former colony.

Naval Superpremium
A Brazilian all-malt beer
(4.8%) from Ancla.

Negra León
Brown rather than black,
León is made by the Yucatán
brewery (owned by Modelo)
in Mexico. It is chocolatey in
taste and quite similar to its
sister brew, Negra Modelo.

Dos Equis
Dos Equis ("Two Crosses")
is a rich, dark-red, high-
quality, Vienna-style lager
(4.8%) with a fruity,
chocolatey taste. Brewed in
Mexico by Moctezuma, it
has also proved popular in
export markets.

Kaiser Bock
Introduced by Cervejarías
Kaiser in 1994 as a cold-
weather drink, this amber-
coloured, pasteurized beer
was the first bock to be
produced in Brazil.

Kaiser Gold
This premium pasteurized
Pilsner was initially launched
as Kaiser Copa 94, to mark
Brazil's entry in soccer's
World Cup. Due to their
success, it was renamed
Kaiser Gold in 1995.

Negra Modelo
Despite its name, Negra
Modelo (Black Model)
(5.3%) is more of a deep
amber-brown colour. It is a
cross between a spicy Vienna
red and a softer Munich
dunkel, with a chocolate
aroma, a hint of fruit and
spices, and a hop finish.
This classic, first-rate
Mexican beer enjoys a
justified reputation among
beer connoisseurs both at
home and abroad.

BLACK BREW

Black beer was first produced in the parts of the Upper
Amazon Basin in the 15th century, using roasted barley
and dark-pigmented grains to give its distinctive colour,
and lupins for flavour (the lupin is a distant relative of the
hop). A modern version, Xingu, is brewed commercially
by Cervejaría Cacador in Brazil.

Peru Gold
A dry, tart and refreshing
lager (5%), Peru Gold has a
rich corn-and-vanilla aroma.
It is brewed by Peru's
Cervesur. The bottle label
features a memorable
Peruvian Indian face mask.

Polar Lager
Venezuela's leading brand is
a light, thin lager (5%) that
takes the style of Sol and
Corona to an extreme.
Despite this, it is the second-
best-selling beer in South
America, where the Polar
Brewing Company sells over
12 million hectolitres (264
million gallons) of it each year.

Porter
A rich, top-fermenting,
dark beer (8%) from the
Companhia Cevejaría of
Brazil. Some say it takes its
name from Portugal, the
country that colonized
Brazil, rather than from the
beer style.

Sol
In the 1980s, the
Moctezuma
brewery's Sol
succeeded Corona
Extra as the
fashionable Mexican
beer to drink. Sol
(4.6%) is a thin, light
lager with a high
proportion of
adjuncts. Like its
arch-rival, it is
sold in a
distinctive,
embossed bottle.

Superior
This pale lager
(4.5%) from
Moctezuma has
more hop
character than its
stablemate Sol.

Tecate
Launched in the 1950s by
Cuauhtémoc of Mexico, this
pale, light ("clara") lager
(4.5%) is low in flavour, but
good for satisfying thirst in a
hot climate. It was originally
served with salt and fresh
lemons – a custom that
probably inspired the
recent craze for drinking
Mexican lagers with a
slice of lime.

Xingu
This Brazilian black
beer (5%) is a modern
version of the historic
Amazonian drink. It
is brewed
commercially by
Cervejaría Cacador,
using hops rather
than lupins to add
flavour and act as a
preservative. Sweet
and malty, Xingu,
named after a
tributary of the
Amazon River, is
the fourth-best-
selling beer in
South America.

THE BREWERS

Ancla
Cervecería Ancla S.A. in Columbia produces a range of quality beers made with 100% pure malt, which come in amber glass bottles as well as in cans. The company has positioned itself at the top end of the domestic market and uses the marketing slogan "Por cultura es colombiana". A modernized plant opened in 1996, with a capacity of 1.2 million hectolitres (26 million gallons) per year.

Bieckhart
Cervecería Bieckhart has a range of German-influenced beers, even though its home is in the capital city of the former Spanish colony Argentina, Buenos Aires. It brews a golden lager and the rich, dark lager Africana.

Cardenal
Venezuela's second beer company after Polar is home to a typical Latin American light, thin lager called Andes, as well as a range of interesting Germanic beers,

among them the golden, malty beer, Tipo Munich (in the Munich style) and an authentic-tasting Nacional "Cerveza Tipo Pilsen" (in the Pilsen style).

Cervecería La Constancia
The San Salvador brewery in El Salvador offers a range of bottom-fermented lager beers: Pilsener of El Salvador Export Beer, Suprema Special Beer, Regla Extra, Noche Buena Special Dark Lager and Cabro Extra.

Cervesur (Compañia Cervecera del Sur del Perú S.A.)
Based in southern Peru, Cervesur has been brewing since 1898, when it was founded in Arequipa under the name Sociedad Industrial Ernesto Günther & Francisco Rehder. It adopted its present title in 1926. It brews using Andes water, barley from its malting plant in Cuzco as well as imported barley, malt and hops. Unusually for Latin America, it concentrates on 100% barley beers and does not use adjuncts. Brews include both

Pilsners and dark beers. Export brews are Cusqueña Pilsner and Cuzco Beer, Cusqueña Dark and Cuzco Dark (both 5.6%), as well as Peru Gold. In 1996, it was the first brewery in Latin America to be awarded a quality certificate by TUV Bayern. Cervesur first began exporting beer to Chile in 1978. By 1995, it controlled 17.5% of the beer market in Lima and accounted for 69% of Peru's beer exports.

Companhia Cervejaría
This Brazilian group brews a quality malty Brahma Pilsner, Brahma Chopp, as well as a top-fermenting, extra-strong porter (8%). The company produces more than 31 hectolitres (660 gallons) of beer annually.

Cuauhtémoc
Now merged with Moctezuma, this brewery offers a pale ("clara") lager called Chihuahua (named for the Mexican state) similar to Corona or Sol, as well as Tecate, another "clara" lager, the best-selling beer in Mexico, and the fuller-bodied, malty Bohemia, brewed with Saaz hops.

Kaiser
Kaiser, Brazil's third-largest brewery, was set up in 1983. The first plant was opened in Divinópolis in Minas Gerais State. Today, it has six plants across the country. The brewery is run by specialist technicians, trained by master brewers in Belgium. Beers, available both bottled and on draught, include Kaiser Cerveja and Premium Pilsner. It was the first Brazilian company to develop a bock, in 1994. In

Beer and chilli

Light, cheap lagers like Sol and Corona are reputed to go well with spicy Mexican food, but Mexico's dark and amber lagers are a better match for hot, robust flavours.

1995, it changed its name to KAC (Kaiser Consumer Relations). The company's marketing strategy has fixed it firmly in the minds of Brazilian beer drinkers in just ten years, partly due to the company's distinctive spokesman, "Shorty".

Moctezuma
Since merging with Cuauhtémoc, the Cervecería Moctezuma of Monterey has since overtaken Modelo and has become Mexico's largest brewery. The merged group, which controls seven breweries in the country, is owned by a large holding company called Valores. Moctezuma was founded in 1894 in Orizaba, Veracruz.

Modelo
The Cervecería Modelo of Mexico City is one of Mexico's two brewing giants. Modelo produces its beers at the single largest brewing plant in the country. Beers include the cheap, refreshing Corona Extra and tasty, Vienna-style dark lagers, Dos Equis and Negra Modelo.

Polar Brewing Company
This Venezuelan company is best known for the extremely light and thin Polar lager which is the country's leading lager brand.

Above: Bars in Mexico tend to be an all-male preserve – a place for a quiet drink after a hard day's work.

THE CARIBBEAN

Rum, fermented from locally grown cane sugar, is the region's favourite tipple but, perhaps surprisingly for an area with a warm climate that grows little grain, there is also a strong beer culture, and drinkers show a marked preference for dark stouts and strong lagers.

INHABITANTS OF THE CARIBBEAN islands have been producing beer for centuries, using maize to brew a kind of porridge, which was then left to ferment. The recipe and name may vary from island to island (*chicha, izquiate* and *sendecho,* to name a few), but the technique remains the same.

The arrival of European brews and brewers in the 19th century had a great impact on the drinking and brewing habits of the region. Today in the Caribbean, lager is a popular drink and international giants, such as Heineken, brew many conventional Pilsner-style beers. They are often served ice-cold as a thirst-quencher for the beach, as an alternative to rum and coke, or sipped in relaxed island bars, as an accompaniment to seafood. There are also many strong, relatively sweet, full-flavoured lagers available. Jamaica's most popular exported beer, Red Stripe, which is now a familiar sight in the US and the UK, is a classic example of this Caribbean-style golden brew. Another European beer style that has been wholeheartedly taken into the bosom of the Islands is rich, strong, dark stout. Many in these exotic climes believe dark beers to possess aphrodisiac or virility-enhancing qualities. Guinness Stout, the classic of this type, has been brewed here for over 150 years and is now produced under licence at the Central Village Brewery in Spanish Town, Jamaica. Other breweries in Trinidad, Granada and St Vincent produce similar dark brews. These "exotic stouts", as they are often known, are usually brewed with a higher alcohol content than stouts produced in England or Ireland.

At the other end of the scale, but continuing the theme of rich, dark brews, another popular product from many breweries in the Caribbean is a dark drink made from malt extract. It is more of a soft drink than an alcohol-free beer.

Above: Carib is a relatively dry lager from Trinidad that bucks the trend for sweet, strong lagers and dark, heavy stouts throughout the Caribbean.

THE BEER

Banks Lager Beer

A pale-gold, sweet, malty lager (4.5%) from the Banks brewery in Bridgetown Barbados.

Bohemia Cerveza

A hazy, pale, amber-gold standard lager (5%) brewed in Ciudad Trujillo, Dominican Republic, by the Cervecería Bohemia.

Caribe

A dry, light-flavoured, pale-yellow lager (4.5%) from the Caribe Development Company, Port of Spain, Trinidad.

Corona

A pale, golden-yellow lager (4.5%) from the Cervecería Corona in Puerto Rico.

Dragon Stout

A deep-brown, sweetish, rich, malty stout (7.5%). It is brewed in Kingston, Jamaica, by Desnoes & Geddes. This potent brew is believed by some to aid virility.

Ebony Super Strength

A deep-brown ale (8%) with a high alcohol content that gives it an almost port-like quality, from the Banks brewery in Barbados.

Kalik Gold

A golden, rich, malty lager which is high in alcohol, from the Commonwealth Brewery in the Bahamas.

Red Stripe

A pale-gold, lightly hopped, strong lager (4.7%) with a full flavour, from the family-run Desnoes & Geddes in Kingston, Jamaica. It is now brewed under licence in the UK, where it is a particular favourite with the West Indian population.

Royal Extra Stout

A deep-brown, classic stout with a malty flavour. Brewed by the Caribe Development Company in Port of Spain, Trinidad.

THE BREWERS

Banks (Barbados) Breweries Ltd

This major player in the Caribbean market is also a familiar name on the South American mainland, where it has a brewery in Guyana.

Desnoes & Geddes Ltd

A family-owned firm set up in 1918 in Kingston, Jamaica, by Eugene Desnoes and Thomas Geddes. Heineken now has a small shareholding.

Granada Breweries Limited

This bright idea by the Caribbean Development Company was first registered as a company in 1960, but it wasn't until the 1970s that it really began to thrive.

St Vincent Brewery Ltd

Set up in 1985 on the island of St Vincent, this small brewery produces its own-brand, Hairoun Lager, as well as brewing Guinness and EKU Bavaria under licence.

Salty liquor

In 1994 Granada Breweries unveiled the solution to its problem of water shortages during the dry season. It had drilled its own borehole to tap underground water and installed a desalination plant.

Left: Enjoying a beer and chewing the fat is part of the relaxed Caribbean way of life. Red Stripe is the region's leading lager.

SPIRITS

AQUAVIT

Germany: Schnapps Denmark: schnaps
Sweden/Norway/Netherlands: snaps

FLAVOURINGS

Aniseed
Fennel seeds
Dill
Cumin seeds
Caraway seeds
Bitter oranges

A**MONG THE VARIOUS** spirits whose collective
names are derived from the phrase "water
of life", Scandinavian aquavit or akvavit has a
particularly ancient history. It is known to have
been distilled in northern Europe since
medieval times, and its use as a drink – as
distinct from its purely medical application –
dates back at least to the 15th century.

Production of aquavit is very similar to that of
flavoured vodkas. Its base is a neutral grain
and/or potato spirit, which is rectified to a high
degree of purity and then aromatized, usually
with fragrant spices. The Scandinavian
countries and Germany are the production
centres of true aquavit. Its
alternative name, schnapps,
derives from an old Nordic
verb snappen, meaning to
snatch or seize. It denotes the
way in which it is traditionally drunk, snatched down the
throat in a single gulp.

HOW IT IS MADE

Potatoes are boiled in a con-
traption rather like a huge
pressure-cooker, and the
resulting starchy mass
is then mixed with
malted grains. After
fermentation with
yeasts, it is double-
distilled to obtain
a neutral spirit.
Dilution brings it
down to a drinkable
strength, and contact
with charcoal – as
well as the accepted
flavouring elements
– gives it its final
character.

TASTES GOOD WITH

Despite its cinematic association with reckless
drinking sessions, aquavit has a genuine gastronomic history. It formed an integral part of the
original Swedish smörgåsbord, which was a
more modest feast than the lavish spreads of
today. It consisted of just bread,
fish (generally herring) and
perhaps cheese, washed
down with aquavit. The dry
savouriness of the spirit complemented the appetizing role
of the salty food. Divorced
from its edible accompaniments, aquavit lives on
today as an aperitif,
knocked back in one
and followed by a
chaser of local beer.

HOW TO SERVE

Aquavit should be
served like good vodka
– that is, ice-cold and
neat from a receptacle
no bigger than a shot-
glass. The bottle
should be kept in the
freezer prior to
serving. It makes a
superb wintertime
aperitif, especially for
guests who have just
come in from the cold.

MIXING

Try substituting aquavit
for the vodka in an
otherwise textbook
Bloody Mary.

AALBORG
A premium high-
strength aquavit from
Denmark

PEACH COUNTY
SCHNAPPS
A mild
fruit-flavoured
commercial
schnapps

ARAK

ALTHOUGH THE DISCOVERY of distillation is still hotly disputed, it is just possible that some form of arak, or raki, was the very first spirit. There are claims that it was made in India around 800 BC, and certainly the production of a fiery, clear spirit on the sub-continent, and down in the South Pacific too, goes back many centuries.

Arak is not really one drink, but a generic name for a group of clear distillates, for which the base material and method of production vary according to the region of origin. In Java, Sumatra and Borneo, the fermented juice of sugar-cane provides the base, but there are also rice versions. The sap of palm trees, which ferments very readily in sultry temperatures, is popular as a source of arak in India.

The drink came to the Middle East and the Mediterranean with the

OTHER NAMES
Arrack, arraki, racki, raki, rakija

HOW TO SERVE
Like aquavit, arak or raki should be drunk in fairly abstemious measures. Owing to its rough potency, arak is not generally served chilled, and it is safer to sip it appreciatively rather than down it in one.

FLAVOURINGS
Figs, dates, grapes, raisins and plums

early Arab spice trade; its common name is derived from the Arabic word for juice or sap, arak. Other easily fermentable products such as dates and figs gradually infiltrated the making of arak, and are still used in parts of North Africa and the Middle East. Finally, grape wine came to play its part in the old wine-making cultures of Greece and Cyprus, including that made from raisins.

In the West today, arak is most commonly encountered in the form of raki, the aniseed-tinged spirit of Greece and Turkey. Some coloured raki is very fine, and is based on old cask-aged brandies, but most is a colourless and pretty raw-tasting spirit that can be anything up to 50% alcohol by volume (ABV). Raki is made throughout the Balkan countries of south-east Europe, sometimes from figs or plums rather than grapes.

MIXING
If drunk as an appetizer, the more basic grade of raki may well be taken with ice in Greece and Cyprus.

TASTES GOOD WITH
Around the Mediterranean region, raki is nearly always drunk as an aperitif, but if you are lucky enough to find a particularly mellow example, it may be better drunk at the latter end of the meal, after coffee.

RAKI
Simple Turkish raki that has not been cask-aged

BITTERS

FLAVOURINGS

Numerous herbs and roots impart greater or lesser degrees of bitterness to all of these drinks.

Gentian is quite common. It is a flowering alpine plant, the root of which is rendered down to a bright yellow essence that has been used as a tonic and anti-fever remedy in folk medicine for centuries.

Quinine was the New World alternative to gentian. It is an extract of the bark of the cinchona tree, a native of South America.

Seville oranges The dried peel of this bitter variety is essential in Campari.

THE TERM "BITTERS" refers to any one of a number of spirits flavoured with bitter herbs or roots, which are generally held to have medicinal properties. They range from products such as Campari, which can be drunk in whole measures like any other spirit, to those that are so bitter that they are only added in drops to season another drink.

Bitterness is the last of the four main taste sensations (the others being sweetness, saltiness and sourness) that developing tastebuds learn to appreciate. A fondness for bitter flavours is often thought to be a sign of the palate having reached its true maturity.

The link between bitterness and health is evident in the fact that tonic water was originally conceived as an all-purpose pick-me-up containing the stimulant

quinine, rather than as a mixer for gin, although these days its flavour tends to be drowned with artificial sweetening. The other unquestionably effective medicinal role of bitters is as an aid to digestion.

The origins of bitters lie in the flavouring elements that were commonly added to the very earliest spirits. These elixirs were taken as restoratives and remedies for any number of conditions, ranging from poor digestion to painful joints. The apothecaries who concocted them drew on the collected wisdom of herbal medicine, and added extracts of bark, roots, fruit peels, herbs and spices to enhance the healing powers of the drink.

Bitters are made all over the world. Perhaps the most famous of all is Angostura. An infusion of gentian root with herbs on a strong rum base, Angostura was invented in the 19th century by a German medic who was personal doctor to the South American revolutionary hero Simón Bolívar. He named it after a town in Venezuela, although today it is made exclusively in Trinidad, albeit still by the company founded by its inventor. Angostura is one of the few such medicinal drinks that can lay claim to actually having been formulated by a doctor.

In Europe the two major centres of production

UNDERBERG
An intensely pungent
digestive bitter from
Germany

CAMPARI
Italy's most famous
bitter aperitif also
comes in a ready-
mixed bottle with a
crown cap

MIXING

Negroni: Thoroughly mix equal measures of gin, Campari and sweet red vermouth with ice in a tumbler and add a squirt of soda.

Americano: As for Negroni, but leave out the gin and add a few drops of Angostura.

Pink gin (below): Sprinkle about half-a-dozen drops of Angostura into a goblet-shaped glass, roll it around to coat the inner surfaces, then dash it out. Add ice-cold gin, which will then take on the faintest pink tint.

of bitters are Italy and France. Italy has Campari – a bright red aperitif of uncompromising bitterness, which is made in Milan – and also Fernet-Branca. Like Germany's Underberg, it is sold in little bottles and is often recommended as a hangover cure. France's famous bitters include Amer Picon (which was invented as an anti-malarial remedy by an army officer serving in Algeria), Toni-Kola and Secrestat.

English fruit bitters, such as orange and peach, were widely used in the cocktail era of the 1920s. Hungary's runner is Unicum, which balances its bitterness with a slight sweetness, while the Latvians add their own treacle-dark dry tonic, Melnais Balzams (Black Balsam), to their coffee.

FERNET-BRANCA
The Italian bitter much prized as a hangover cure

HOW TO SERVE

Campari is classically served with soda water and a twist of lemon peel, but don't drown it. Amer Picon may be served the same way, or perhaps as a bittering element with gin for those whose need to be picked up requires more than a straight dry Martini. Underberg and Fernet-Branca can be quaffed straight as stomach-settlers or just to aid digestion, while Angostura is essential in a pink gin – the drink of officers and gentlemen.

UNICUM
A deeply coloured bitter speciality of Hungary

ANGOSTURA
The most widely used bitter in the cocktail repertoire

BRANDY

STRICTLY SPEAKING, the term brandy applies to any grape-based spirit distilled from wine. There are "brandies" made from other fruits – such as Normandy's calvados, made from apples – but we shall deal with these under their own headings. The English name is a corruption of the Dutch *brandewijn*, in turn derived from the German *Gebranntwein*, meaning burnt wine, which is an apt term for the product of distillation.

The most famous of all true brandies is cognac, named after a town in the Charente region of western France. It was to here that traders from northern Europe, particularly the Netherlands, came in the 17th century, putting in at the port of La Rochelle to take delivery of consignments of salt. They inevitably took some of the region's thin, acidic wine with them as well. Because of tax regulations, and to save space in the ships' holds – always a major consideration – the wines were boiled to reduce their volume by evaporation. On arrival at their destination, they would be reconstituted with water. However, it came to be noticed that the Charente wines positively benefited from the reduction process. It was but a short step from there to actual distillation.

HOW TO SERVE

The finest and oldest brandies should not be mixed. Younger products mix reasonably well with soda; the vogue for brandy-and-tonic being assiduously promoted in Cognac, of all places, is not one that finds favour with the author. In the Far East, brandy is mixed with plenty of iced water as a very long drink, and consumed with food.

MARTELL
The oldest house in Cognac is still a brand leader

HOW TO SERVE

Fine cognac should be drunk just as it comes, without mixers and certainly without ice. It is traditionally served in balloon glasses that allow room for swirling. Tradition is not often a reliable guide, and the aromas are much better appreciated in something resembling a large liqueur glass, which mutes the prickle of the spirit. The bouquet is also encouraged by a gentle warming of the glass in the hand (for which the balloon was indisputably better designed), but recourse to those lovely, old, silver brandy-warmers, which allowed you to barbecue the tilted glass over a little petrol flame, is not recommended.

Such was the fame and the premium paid for the distilled wines of the Charente that they came to have many imitators. None, however, could match the precise local conditions in which cognac is made. Its chalky soils, the maritime climate and the ageing in barrels fashioned from Limousin oak were the indispensable features that gave cognac the pre-eminent reputation that it enjoys to this day.

France's other brandy of note, armagnac, is made in the southwest of the country. Armagnac is based on a wider range of grape varieties and made using a slightly different method to cognac. Although not as widely known as cognac, it has its own special cachet in the spirits market and is preferred by many as the better digestif.

There are grape brandies produced all over Europe and the Americas, as we shall see in the succeeding pages. The best are generally made by the pot-still method of distillation. Some inferior spirit, artificially coloured and flavoured, used also to be known as brandy, but has been banned from using the term within the European Union following the introduction of a new law in 1989.

COGNAC

The Cognac region covers two *départements* on the western side of France near the Bay of Biscay: inland Charente, and Charente-Maritime on the coast. Cognac is a small town close to the border between the two. The vineyards are sub-divided into six growing areas, the most notable of which are Grande Champagne and Petite Champagne, just south of Cognac itself.

As we have seen, the fame of cognac had been well and truly established in the Dutch and British markets by the end of

HENNESSY X.O
Premium cognac
in a singularly
shaped decorative
bottle

the 17th century. The industry's first great entrepreneur was Jean Martell, a Jersey-born opportunist who, in 1715, turned away from a life of crime (smuggling) in order to found the house that still bears his name. Cognac's other leading brands are Hennessy, Courvoisier and Rémy Martin. Smaller but no less distinguished companies include Hine and Otard.

The relative qualities of different cognacs depend almost entirely on the length of time they have been aged and the cognacs are classified accordingly. No brandy that has earned the right to the Cognac *appellation contrôlée* (AC) status may be blended from spirits that are less than two years old. At the bottom rung of the quality classification for the British and Irish markets is VS (historically known as three-star, and still designated by a row of three stars on the label). VS may contain brandies as young as three years old, but the basic products of most of the leading companies will contain some significantly older reserves.

The next stage up is VSOP, Very Special (or Superior) Old Pale, an old British term that arose in London in the 19th century to denote a particularly fine – but paradoxically light-coloured – batch of cognac. (Although cognac derives most of its colour from wood-ageing, caramel can also be added to influence the colour, provided it does not affect the taste. Any slight sweetness in the spirit derives from correction with sugar solution just before bottling.) VSOP is the five-star stuff because the youngest spirit it contains must have spent at least five years in wood.

Those blended from minimum six-year-old cognacs may be entitled XO, or given any one of a number of names the houses invent for themselves, such as Reserve, Extra, Cordon Bleu, Paradis or classically Napoléon – so named because the bottles supposedly contain brandies aged since the time of the *Empéreur*.

The prices that the oldest cognacs command are breathtaking, yet the enjoyment can never be proportionately greater than that to be had from good VSOP. In many cases, you may be paying for something that looks like a giant perfume

COURVOISIER
Along with Martell, this is
one of the most widely
drunk cognacs in the
world.

REMY MARTIN
The basic Rémy is a VSOP
grade of cognac.

NAMING

"Brandy" is just a generic term for any distilled grape spirit. They get very upset in Cognac and Armagnac these days, and perhaps understandably, if you refer to their products unceremoniously as brandy. It is happily used by quality producers in Spain, California and elsewhere. Note that none of these products contains any added flavouring element. If they do, they cease to be "brandy", at least in terms of the European Union definition of 1989.

bottle fashioned in cut crystal and presented in a silk-lined box. If you really want to try one of these luxury products, it makes sense to wait until your next trip through duty-free.

It is often thought that the optimum age for the best cognacs is about 40 years old, but it must always be borne in mind with any spirit that it can only age in cask. Once it is bottled, no further development takes place.

ARMAGNAC

Armagnac, which was thought of until about the middle of the 19th century merely as France's "other brandy", is made in the Pays de Gascogne in the far southwest of the country. There are three sub-regions – Bas-Armagnac, Ténarèze and Haut-Armagnac – of which the first is usually

ARMAGNAC
"Hors d'Age" on
an armagnac
label denotes very
long cask-ageing

considered the best. Despite its lesser renown, armagnac has a legitimate claim to be considered the more venerable product, distillation in the region having been reliably dated back to the 1400s. Its chief distinguishing characteristics compared to cognac are these: while cognac is made largely from the Ugni Blanc grape, armagnac's base wine is made from a blend of several varieties; a local black oak (as distinct from Limousin) is used for the maturation; and the continuous still (invented by Edouard Adam) is widely used to distil the spirit.

So inextricably bound up with armagnac production was Adam's patent still that, for a long period this century, it was the only authorized apparatus for producing armagnac. Continuous distillation yields a spirit rich in the aroma-containing impurities that give any brandy its character, which is why armagnac is noticeably more fragrant than cognac. Many tasters describe it as having a "biscuity" aroma, while others – by no means fancifully – detect a floral topnote like violets. The flavour tends to be drier because it isn't adjusted with sugar, and the absence of caramel as a colouring matter makes it generally paler than a cognac of the same age.

The labelling system is comparable to that of cognac. The exception is that the youngest armagnacs may be released in the British market after two years in cask rather than three. The designations VS, VSOP and XO are defined in exactly the same way. Vintage-dated armagnac – the unblended produce of a single year's harvest – has always been a peculiarity of the region (although vintage labelling has just been relegalized in Cognac). If the label on, say, a 1959 armagnac looks suspiciously new, remember that it is because it has probably only recently been bottled. The ageing can only take place in wood, not glass.

Part of the charm of the Armagnac region is that many of the producers are still rural artisans, rather than globally important companies catering to the luxury market, as in Cognac. Their brandies are often distilled in shared portable stills that are driven around the countryside at production time. As a result, prices for even the top armagnacs are considerably gentler.

OTHER EUROPEAN BRANDIES

Spain The most significant producer of grape brandy, in terms of both quantity and quality, outside France is Spain. The premium products are accorded the same attention to detail at every stage of their manufacture as the finest in Cognac and Armagnac and, as a result, are fully capable of withstanding comparison with their French counterparts.

Spanish brandy production is concentrated in the sherry region of Jerez, in the south of the country. Indeed, most of it is distilled by the sherry houses, such as Gonzalez Byass, Domecq and Osborne. The grapes from which the base wine is made generally come from La Mancha, the huge central plain that represents the grape basket of Spanish viticulture, but the wines are distilled and aged in sherry country. This entitles them to the designation of Brandy de Jerez – a dependable indicator of quality.

Maturation is by a process known as fractional blending, or the *solera* system, which is also used for the finest sherries. A *solera* consists of a stack of barrels piled up in rows. The new spirit enters the top row and, at intervals of several months, a quantity of it is drawn off and added to the next row down, where it displaces a similar quantity into the row below, and so on. The bottom row contains the oldest brandies which are drawn off in fractions for bottling.

The brandy gains greater age characteristics by this process than it would if it were left to mature undisturbed in the same barrel, as in France, for a similar period.

Top brands include Lepanto, made by Gonzalez Byass, Sanchez Romate's Cardinal Mendoza and Osborne's Conde d'Osborne, which comes in an idiosyncratically shaped bottle designed by the mad genius of 20th-century Spanish art, Salvador Dali. The brand leader, though, is Fundador, a Domecq product, and one that deserves a much better reputation. In Catalonia, the pace-setting Torres winery makes its own very drinkable brandy.

Germany The best German offering seen on export markets is Uralt, an aged product made by a distiller in the Rheingau called Asbach. It receives a maturation period of around 18 months. Like the country's less good sparkling wines, most German brandy is made from imported French or Italian base wine, and so it has no particular indigenous character.

Others Italy's brandies are fairly basic commercial spirits, most coming from the volume producer Stock. Portugal makes a handful of good brandies, but its industry is heavily geared to supplying grape spirit for the port shippers. In southeast Europe, Cyprus makes brandies of about the same level of sophistication as the fortified wines it once called "sherry", while Bulgaria still produces a decent aged brandy from base wine principally derived from the Ugni Blanc grape of Cognac.

LEPANTO
Spain's leading brandy, made by Gonzalez Byass of sherry fame

MIXING

Alexander: Shake equal measures of VSOP cognac, dark brown crème de cacao and thick cream with ice and strain into a cocktail glass. Sprinkle the surface with nutmeg or powdered chocolate for the most comforting cocktail in the repertoire.

B & B (Bénédictine and brandy): The traditional mix is half-and-half with good cognac, stirred not shaken, and not usually iced.

METAXA

Among the brandies produced on the mainland of Greece (and to some extent on the island of Samos), the abidingly popular Metaxa deserves a special mention. Despite the brouhaha with which it is treated in Greece itself, and a distinctly specious system of age-labelling, it is a fairly basic industrial product.

Greek brandy isn't ever going to fare well against aged cognac for the simple reason that the grape varieties that go into it are not generally of sufficiently high acidity to produce a suitable base wine. The mainstays are Savatiano (widely used in retsina) and the Muscat grape that produces the golden dessert wines of Samos and other islands, and the distillers are not above using base wines that contain some red grapes.

There are three grades of Metaxa, ascending in quality from three stars to

five and seven. The last is sometimes said to have been cask-aged for around half a century, a claim we can confidently take with a cask of salt. It is relatively pale in colour (which fact alone makes the age claim suspicious) and much sweeter on the palate than cognac, with a highly moreish toffee or caramel quality.

AMERICAN BRANDIES

USA Brandy has been made in the United States since the days of the pioneers, most of it in what is now the premier wine-growing state of California. At one time, brandy production was simply a convenient means of using up sub-standard grapes that were considered unfit for quality wine production, as it still is in many of Europe's viticultural regions. In the last 30 years or so, however, a turn towards producing finer aged spirits has been made, and a number of these American products are capable of giving some of the famous VSOP cognacs a run for their money.

Not all are made in the image of cognac; some are discernibly more orientated towards the Spanish style. The brandies are habitually matured in barrels of home-grown American oak,

MIXING
Never on Sunday
(from Michael Walker's *Cinzano Cocktail Book*): Stir a measure of Metaxa with half a measure of ouzo, a splash of lemon juice and a dash of Angostura over ice. Strain into a tall glass and top with equal quantities of champagne and ginger beer.

METAXA
The holiday maker's favourite

CARNEROS ALAMBIC
Brandy from the Napa Valley, California

MIXING

Brandy Blazer: Put two measures of cognac in a saucepan with one sugar cube and the thinly pared rind from half an orange and one lemon. Heat gently, then remove from the heat and light the surface of the liquid. The alcohol will burn with a low, blue flame for about one minute. Blow out the flame. Add half a measure of Kahlúa and strain into a heat-resistant liqueur glass. Decorate with a cocktail stick threaded with a twist of orange rind.

which gives a more pronounced aroma to the spirit, accentuated by the heavily charred inner surfaces of the barrels. These conditions result in brandies of great richness and complexity. Names to look out for include Germain-Robin and RMS (the latter brand owned by Cognac star Rémy Martin). Some of the top California wineries have also turned out some impressive efforts, while bulk producer Gallo in Modesto make a passable version intended for mixing.

Latin America There is a long tradition of drinking fiery spirits all over Central and South America, in which grape brandy plays its part – particularly in the areas where the early Spanish colonists first planted vines. Mexico is the most important producer. Its flagship is a big-selling global brand called Presidente, made in the light, simple style of a rough-and-ready Spanish brandy.

The peculiarly South American offering, however, is pisco. There is still much dispute over whether it originated in Peru or Chile, the two centres of production (with a modest

contribution from Bolivia). I shall forbear to come down on either side of the fence, except to point out that the Pisco valley and the seaport of the same name are in Peru, but the Chileans simply insist that that was one of the principal export destinations for their indigenous spirit, and the name just stuck.

Despite receiving some cask-ageing, pisco is always colourless because the barrels it matures in are so ancient that they have no colour left to give to the spirit. In Chile, the longer the maturation, the lower the dilution before bottling, so the finer grades (Gran Pisco is the best) are the strongest. Owing to widespread use of members of the Muscat grape family in the base wine, nearly all types and nationalities of pisco are marked by an unabashed fruitiness on the nose and palate.

The myth that pisco is a throat-searing firewater strictly for the peasants is probably based on the exposure of delicate European sensibilities to the lower grades. Top pisco has every right to be considered a world-class spirit.

PISCO
A top-quality pisco from Peru

MIXING

Pisco Sour: Half-fill a small tumbler with smashed ice. Put in two measures of freshly squeezed lime juice and sweeten to taste with icing sugar. Stir well to dissolve the sugar. Add a measure of pisco, and give the drink a final stir.

CALVADOS

IN AREAS WHERE wine grapes could not be grown with success, other fruits came to supplement grains in making fermented and distilled drinks. The most important fruit, after grapes, to act as a source of alcohol is the apple. Apple trees are capable of fruiting in much more wintry conditions than the vine, and since many varieties of apple are too tart or bitter to give much pleasure as eating apples, cider became the obvious alternative to beer in the cooler northern climates.

The distillation of cider is probably quite as old as the practice of distilling wine for grape brandy. In its heartland – the Normandy region of northern France – the earliest reference to an apple distillate dates from 1553, but we have no means of knowing how long, prior to the mid-1500s, it had already been going on.

If the name of the Normans' apple brandy, *calvados*, sounds more Spanish than French, that is because it derives from a story that tells of a ship, the *El Salvador*, from the mighty Spanish armada, which was dashed to smithereens off the Norman coast. The *département* came to be known as Calvados, and its traditional spirit was named after it. There is no historical corroboration of the story, and no one in Normandy seemingly expects you to believe it.

Like cognac and armagnac, calvados received its *appellation contrôlée* status quite soon after the introduction of the AC system: 1942. At the heart of the region is one particularly fine area called the Pays d'Auge, prized for its soils and the lie of its land, which has its own designation. (The rest is straight appellation Calvados.) Both the pot-still double distillation and the continuous method are used, although the calvados of the Pays d'Auge area may only use the former.

There are hundreds of different varieties of cider apple, classified into four broad taste groups: sweet, bitter-sweet, bitter and acid. The bitter-sweet ones make up the lion's share of the blend in a typical calvados. After distillation, the spirit goes into variously sized barrels of French oak for maturation. Supposedly, the younger a calvados is, the more likely it is to smell and

OTHER NAMES
USA: applejack
UK: apple brandy/cider brandy

HOW TO SERVE

Younger calvados works surprisingly well with tonic, as long as you don't drown it. (I prefer half-and-half to one third-two thirds.) Hors d'Age, etc., must be drunk unmixed.

CALVADOS
The best calvados comes from the Pays d'Auge

APPLE BRANDY
A fine, powerful apple spirit from Somerset, England

MIXING

Depth Charge: Shake equal measures of calvados and cognac with half a measure of fresh lemon juice, a dash of grenadine and ice. Strain into a cocktail glass.

taste of apples; the older ones take on the vanilla and spice tones of the wood.

Age indications are not dissimilar to those of cognac and armagnac. Three-star (or three-apple) calvados spends a minimum of two years in cask, Vieux or Réserve three years, and Vieille Réserve or VSOP four years. Those aged for six or more years may be labelled Hors d'Age or Age Inconnu ("age unknown"!). If a calvados is labelled with a period of ageing, such as 8-year-old, then the age specified refers to the youngest spirit in it, not the average. Should you come across any of the small amount of vintage-dated calvados, note that the date refers to the year of distillation – the year *after* harvest.

In the United States, an apple spirit has been made ever since the first British settlers found that the apple trees they planted in New England proved hardier than grain crops. Applejack, as it is most commonly known, is made in much the same way as calvados, starting with good cider and distilling it twice in a pot still. The spirit is then aged in oak for anything up to about five years. The younger stuff is pretty abrasive, but on the eastern seaboard – as in Normandy – they like it that way. Laird's is one of the bigger-selling brands.

The alternative way of making applejack, now officially frowned on, was to freeze the cider. Water freezes before alcohol, so if the first slush to form was skimmed away, what was left would be virtually pure alcohol. (A derivative of this technique is used today in the making of both ice beers and ice ciders in order to strengthen them.)

Apple brandy, or cider brandy, is now being revived in the west of England. Somerset is, after all, considered by many to be capable of producing the world's best ciders. When properly aged, it can be quite impressive, although devotees of calvados are unlikely to be fooled by it in a blind tasting.

HOW IT IS MADE

Apples are harvested from September through to December, depending on the variety. A precise blend of juices from the four types is fermented into cider at about 5–6% alcohol. This is subjected to a double distillation (or continuous distillation, except in the Pays d'Auge region of Calvados). The spirit is then aged in cask for anything up to 40 years, and bottled at 40–45% ABV.

APPLEJACK
America's answer
to calvados

HOW TO SERVE

In Normandy, there is a gastronomic tradition called the *trou normand* (literally "Norman hole"). A shot of neat calvados is drunk in place of a sorbet before the main course of a meal. The idea is that the spirit punches a hole through the food already consumed and allows you to go on eating in comfort.

EAU DE VIE

E AU DE VIE IS the French phrase for the Latin *aqua vitae*, water of life. Strictly speaking, the term refers to all spirits distilled from fermented fruits, starting with wine-based cognac and armagnac. By the same token, calvados could therefore be considered an eau de vie of cider. Since the names of these individual spirits are legally protected by France's geographical *appellation contrôlée* regulations, they have come to be known by those names instead of being referred to as eaux de vie.

Spirits can be produced from many other fruits as well as grapes or apples, though, and these are

much less precisely defined. The term eau de vie, therefore, tends now to be reserved for these other fruit brandies. Apart from their basic ingredients, the main attribute that distinguishes eaux de vie from cognac and armagnac is that they are colourless because they haven't been aged in wood like their more famous cousins. The theory is

LA VIELLE PRUNE
Pascall makes this celebrated plum eau de vie

POIRE-WILLIAMS
Eau de vie flavoured with William pears

that they develop in glass, which rather flies in the face of what is scientifically known about spirits – namely, that development stops once they are in the bottle.

Of the variety of fruits used, the most often encountered – and those producing the most delicious eaux de vie – are the various soft summer berries. Alsace, a wine region of north-east France that has lurched from French to German domination and back again since the late 19th century, is a particularly rich source of these spirits. Some of them are made by winemakers, others by specialist distillers. What they have

in common is high alcohol (sometimes around 45% ABV), absence of colour and a clear, pure scent and flavour of their founding fruit. They are not sweetened, and should not be confused with the syrupy liqueurs of the same flavours, which tend to be coloured anyway.

Eau de vie of this kind is also made in Switzerland and Germany.

TASTES GOOD WITH

Served very cold in small measures, they can work well with certain desserts, particularly frangipane-based tarts topped with the same fruit as that used to make the eau de vie.

FRAMBOISE SAUVAGE
Eau de vie flavoured with wild raspberries

FRAISE
A popular eau de vie from strawberries

EAUX DE VIE
Three of the not-so-common types – mirabelle, fleur de bière and kirsch – are available in miniature bottles

GIN

OF THE FIVE essential spirits (brandy, whisky, rum, vodka and gin), gin is the only one that really has a reputation to live down. Down the years it has been the calamitous curse of the urban poor, the Mother's Ruin by which young girls in trouble tried to inflict miscarriages upon themselves, the bathtub brew that rotted guts during American Prohibition, and the first resort of the miserable as the storm-clouds of depression gathered. It was all so different in the beginning.

Although the English often claim to be the true progenitors of gin (as well as, more convincingly, of port and champagne), its origins in fact go back to 16th-century Holland. Like many other distilled drinks, the first inspiration behind the creation of gin was medicinal. The blend of herbs and aromatics used in it were believed to guard against all the ills that flesh was heir to. Principal among the elements of these concoctions was juniper, the Dutch word

OTHER NAMES

Holland: genever *France*: genièvre (although almost everybody in France now calls it "gin")

for which – genever – is the linguistic root of the English word "gin".

The dark little berries of the juniper tree contribute to the characteristic strong perfume of gin. They are prized medicinally as a diuretic, to counteract water retention. Despite the predominance of juniper in the aroma and flavour of gin, however, it is not the only added ingredient. Precise recipes vary according to the individual distiller – they each have their own secret formulae – but other common components include angelica, liquorice, orris root, dried citrus peel, and caraway and coriander seeds.

HOW TO SERVE

The age-old mixer for gin is of course Schweppes tonic, the production of which is almost exclusively sustained by gin-drinkers. A gin and tonic is usually offered as a long drink with a slice of lemon and plenty of ice, but equal measures is a more sensitive way of treating the gin. Gin rubs along with any old mixer, though: orange juice, bitter lemon, ginger beer, whatever. (It isn't very nice with cola perhaps, but then few things are.)

BOMBAY SAPPHIRE
More delicately aromatic gin than the commercial norm

GORDON'S
This is the brand leader among London gins

MIXING

The number of gin-based cocktails is legion, but here are a few of the more durable ones:

Gin Fizz: Shake a good measure of gin with a teaspoon of caster sugar and the juice of half a lemon. Pour into a tall glass and top with fresh soda water. (This is not noticeably different to a **Tom Collins**, except that the latter may have a little less soda added. Then again, leave out the soda altogether, stir it in a tumbler rather than shaking it and call it a **Gin Sour**.)

Gimlet (below): Stir equal measures of Plymouth gin and Rose's lime cordial in a tumbler with a couple of ice cubes.

It may well have been British soldiers returning home from the Thirty Years' War who first brought the taste for Dutch genever across the North Sea. Then again, it may simply have been travellers to the continent starting or ending their journeys in Amsterdam. However that may be, a form of gin was being distilled in London in the 17th century, using the basic beer ingredients – hops and barley – and the essential juniper berries.

The meteoric rise in gin's popularity in Britain had two main causes. Firstly, periodic hostilities with the French led to the application of punitive tariffs to their exports and, just as port came to be the wine of patriotic choice among the elite, so gin replaced cognac. To compound that,

reform of the excise system then produced an anomaly whereby beer was suddenly subjected to a much stricter levy than before, so that gin was actually cheaper. Not surprisingly, it became the staple drink of the poorest classes, who consumed it in much the same quantities as they had beer. The gin shops were born, and public drunkenness and alcohol-related illnesses soared.

For the great mass of the London poor, getting "blotto" was the only way of escaping grim reality. So began gin's long association with gloom and despond (which still persists today in the enduring myth that gin is more of a depressant than the other spirits). The purveyors of gin sold their wares in terms that no

BELGRAVIA LONDON DRY GIN
One of the lesser-known London brands

MIXING

Gin Rickey: Half-fill a tall glass with ice. Add two measures of gin, the juice of half a lime or a quarter of a lemon and a generous dash of grenadine. Stir vigorously, then top with fresh soda.

White Lady: Shake a measure of gin with half a measure of Cointreau and half a measure of fresh lemon juice, with ice, and strain into a cocktail glass. (Some recipes also add a teaspoon of egg white. My bible, the *Savoy Cocktail Book*, clearly indicates the White Lady to be innocent of such a substance. It simply gives the drink a frothier texture, if that's what you like.)

FLAVOURINGS

Juniper berries
(essential)
Coriander seeds
Caraway seeds
Orris root
Dried orange and lemon
peel
Angelica
Liquorice, fennel or
anise
Almonds
Cardamom pods

MIXING

Gin Smash: Dissolve a tablespoon of caster sugar in a little water, in a cocktail shaker. Add four large fresh mint sprigs and bruise, using a muddler to press the juices out of the mint. Half-fill the shaker with cracked ice and add two measures dry gin.
Shake the cocktail vigorously for 20 seconds, then strain into a small glass filled with crushed ice and a little finely chopped mint.

advertiser today could get away with; the wording on one signboard famously ran: *"Drunk for a penny. Dead drunk for tuppence. Clean straw for nothing"*. Such was the addiction of the masses to gin that it was actually made illegal by an Act of Parliament in 1736, but the law was hastily reversed six years later after it was predictably discovered that the contraband stuff that was now being drunk was considerably more toxic than the official spirit had been.

In 1750, the great social satirist William Hogarth produced his famous engraving *Gin Lane*. It depicted in minute detail the degradation and squalor that was being wrought by widespread consumption of gin. A century later, gin was still being blamed by critical commentators such as the author Charles Dickens as the corrosive solace of the destitute, although Dickens was more concerned to blame social inequity for the condition of the poor, rather than to see drink in itself as an evil. It was in this period, however, that the great Temperance movements took root, and the poor were encouraged to fear drink as the devil's potion.

It was only in the late Victorian period that gin began to reassume a more dignified apparel. Because of its colourlessness and its absence of wood-derived richness, it was seen as a usefully ladylike alternative to Scotch whisky and cognac. The all-too-recent association with the sordid doings of the idle poor meant that some euphemism had to be found for it – a facility Victorian society was supremely practised in. For a while, it was improbably referred to as "white wine". Finally, the gin and tonic, the world's favourite aperitif, was born, and a new era in gin's fortunes was ushered in.

During the period of Prohibition in the United States (1919–33), gin became one of the more readily available sources of illicit hooch, largely because it was so

BEEFEATER
*One of the
most famous
London gins*

MIXING

Dry Martini: No cocktail recipe is more energetically argued over than the classic dry Martini. It is basically a generous measure of virtually neat stone-cold gin with a dash of dry white vermouth in it. But how much is a dash? Purists insist on no more than a single drop, or the residue left after briefly flushing the glass out with a splash of vermouth and then pouring it away. (They puzzlingly refer to such a Martini as "very dry", as if adding more vermouth would sweeten it. In fact, the terminology harks back to the original recipe, when the vermouth used was the sweet red variety.) Some go for as much as half a measure of vermouth, and I have at hand a book that suggests a two-to-one ratio of gin to vermouth – guaranteed to send the purist into paroxysms of horror. I have to admit I incline more to the purist philosophy, though: the vermouth should be added as if it were the last bottle in existence. The drink should properly be mixed gently in a separate jug, with ice, and then strained into the traditional cocktail glass (the real name of which is a martini glass). A twist of lemon peel should be squeezed delicately over the surface, so that the essential oil floats in globules on top of the drink, but *don't* put the lemon twist in the glass. And hold the olive. (Add a cocktail onion, however, and the drink becomes a **Gibson**.)

easy for amateur distillers to make. All that was needed was to add whatever flavourings you could lay your hands on to a basic grain spirit, and then bottle it as soon as you liked. It is sometimes said that a lot of the more outlandish cocktails of the Jazz Era owed their inspiration to the need to disguise the disgusting taste of home-made gin.

The reason that gin continues to provide the base for so many cocktails is that it is such a good mixer. Its lack of colour means that it doesn't turn an off-putting muddy hue when blended with fruit juices, as the brown spirits do, while its aromatic quality gives it something for the mixers to mingle with, as distinct from the absolute neutrality of vodka. Gin has inevitably lost a lot of ground to vodka in the more recent youth market, as its peculiar

PLYMOUTH GIN
Coates is the only producer of Plymouth gin.

BOOTH'S
FINEST
Note that the company was established during the ban on gin in the UK

perfume is something of an acquired taste to untutored palates. In the 1990s, however, it suddenly found itself gaining new cachet among certain American rap artists, becoming the preferred tipple enthusiastically celebrated in their lyrics as "juice and gin" (in other words gin and orange, known to the Scott Fitzgerald set in the 1920s as Orange Blossom).

TYPES OF GIN

English Gin There are two types. London dry gin is by far the more commonly known, although it doesn't necessarily have to be distilled in the capital. It is an intensely perfumed spirit, and varies greatly in quality between producers. Gordon's, Booth's and Beefeater are the most famous names, but some speciality products have established a conspicuous presence on the market in recent years, notably Bombay Sapphire in the pale blue, tinted bottle.

MIXING

Gin Swizzle: Beat together (as if you were preparing eggs for an omelette) a double measure of gin, a teaspoon of gomme (sugar syrup), the juice of a lime and a couple of firm dashes of Angostura in a large jug, with ice. When the drink is good and foaming, strain it into a tall glass. Alternatively, make the drink in the tall glass and stir it up with an old-fashioned swizzle stick.

The other type is Plymouth gin, of which there is only one distiller, Coates, at the Blackfriars distillery in the centre of the city, not far from the waterfront. Plymouth is a distinctly drier gin than the big London brands, its spirit is impressively rounded and the range of aromatics used in it somehow give it a subtler bouquet than most gin-drinkers may be used to. It makes an incomparable Pink Gin.

A very small amount of gin is cask-aged and referred to as golden gin after the colour it leaches out of the wood.

Dutch Genever This is quite a different drink to English gin, owing to the more pungently flavoured grain mash on which it is based. The mixture of barley, rye and corn is often quite heavily malted, giving the older spirits a lightly beery tinge in the colour. There are basically two grades, labelled either Oude (old) or Jonge (young), the latter looking more like the English article. They frequently come in an opaque "stone" bottle.

HOW TO SERVE

Speciality gins can be served neat. Chill the bottle in the freezer, and serve the measures in small glasses. A taller, narrow-sided, stemmed glass – rather like a short champagne flute – is traditional in the Netherlands.

DUTCH GENEVER

The prototype
for London Gin

KIRSCH

KIRSCH IS THE ORIGINAL cherry spirit. It is a colourless pure distillate – a true brandy or eau de vie, in other words – made from cherries. It is included separately because it has traditionally been seen as a distinctive product from the other fruit brandies. A fair amount is made in the Alsace and Franche-Comté regions of eastern France, where they know a thing or two about such matters. It is also a particular speciality of the Schwarzwald, the Black Forest region of Bavaria in western Germany – hence its German name, which simply means "cherry". (Confusingly, Kirsch is not related to cherry brandy.)

When the cherry juice is pressed for the initial fermentation, the stones are ground up too and left to infuse in it. The stones impart a characteristic slightly bitter note to the spirit, and bequeath a minute and harmless amount of cyanide to it in the process. It is generally given a short period of ageing, but in large earthenware vats rather than barrels, so that it remains colourless. The true Kirsch cherry is the black Morello (the type that crops up in the Black Forest gâteau, Bavaria's gift to the world's

KIRSCH
A cherry eau de vie with an identity all of its own

OTHER NAMES
Germany: Kirschwasser, or Schwarzwalder

MIXING
Rose: Shake equal measures of Kirsch and dry vermouth with a dash of grenadine and plenty of ice. Strain into a cocktail glass.

dessert trolleys), but these days, red varieties are often used instead.

Kirsch is also made in Switzerland and Austria.

TASTES GOOD WITH
Use Kirsch to add a touch of alcoholic richness to desserts, whether for soaking the sponge base for a mousse, or moistening fresh fruit such as pineapple. Indeed, its flavour blends unexpectedly well with all sorts of fruits. Beware any bottle labelled "Kirsch de Cuisine". It is an inferior product, smelling more like candle-wax than cherries, whose roughness is supposedly disguised when used in cooking. And if you believe that…

HOW TO SERVE
Lightly chilled in small glasses, Kirsch makes a refreshing after-dinner tipple.

MARC

IN THE VINEYARDS of Europe, winemakers have long had to accustom themselves to the precarious existence that reliance on nature forces on them. A bumper harvest of ripe, healthy grapes means plenty of good wine and a healthy income. But what if frost decimates your crop in the spring and the sun doesn't shine when you most need it? In the lean years, you may well be grateful for a by-product you can fall back on to ease the financial squeeze.

For many thrifty wine producers, marc has traditionally been the answer. After the grape juice has been pressed for fermentation, a mass of smashed skins and pips, or pomace, is left, itself capable of fermentation. Marc is the distillate of this residue. In France, the most celebrated Marc is made in Burgundy and Champagne, frequently by producers enthusiastic enough to buy other growers' leftovers, but there is also some made in Alsace, Provence and the isolated eastern region of the Jura.

In Italy, Marc is known as grappa, and such is the connoisseurship surrounding it that varietal grappa, made from the skins of single grape varieties, has become

HOW TO SERVE
Their strong tannins make marcs unsuitable for mixing. They are intended for drinking neat, though their profoundly earthy flavour may come as a shock to the uninitiated. On the calvados principle that a strong spirit aids digestion, the Burgundians in particular value them as after-dinner drinks.

OTHER NAMES
Italy: grappa (also used in California)
Portugal: bagaceira
Spain: aguardiente (but that term may also be applied to any fiery grape spirit, including brandy)

something of a fad. An indication of its potential trendiness is that several producers in California (where the climate is sufficiently benign not to need such a stand-by) are making versions of grappa too. In all regions, the finer spirits may be treated to maturation in oak, resulting in a burnished golden colour, but most of it is clear.

TASTES GOOD WITH
I once ate a sorbet in Reims that had been made with Marc de Champagne, and anointed with yet more of it. It was acutely horrible, but in a somehow intriguing way. More beguiling is the use of Marc de Bourgogne for marinating the rind of the powerful local soft cheese of Chambertin.

GRAPPA
A varietal grappa made from Moscatel grapes

MARC DE CHAMPAGNE
Made by the champagne giants Moët & Chandon

MESCAL

ESCAL, OR MEZCAL, is one of Mexico's indigenous drinks. It is a pale yellowish spirit made from the juice of a species of cactus called the agave. The pressed juice is fermented to make pulque, a kind of beer of around 5–6% alcohol, which is known to have been consumed in Aztec times. It is then distilled once by the continuous method to produce mescal. (A second distillation removes more of the off-putting impurities in the spirit and results in the more highly prized tequila.)

It would be fair to say that mescal doesn't have a particularly illustrious image. It is the rapacious firewater that contributes to the downfall of the dissolute British

HOW TO SERVE

If the idea of chewing the worm as it is doesn't appeal, try liquidizing it in a cocktail. I have swallowed it in sections like aspirins, but the promised heroism – not surprisingly – failed to appear.

Consul in Malcolm Lowry's celebrated novel of alcoholism, *Under the Volcano*. In the past, it was considered to be capable of inducing gruesome hallucinations, a feature Lowry's novel reports, but it is hard to account for this since the agave cactus – or American aloe, as it is sometimes known – is not one of the hallucinogenic species.

Mescal is often sold with a pickled white agave worm in the bottle. It is genuine, and is intended to be eaten as the last of the drink is poured out. Supposedly, ingestion of the worm encourages great heroism in those already brave enough to swallow it. Again, the myth persists that the worm, which feeds on the agave plant, contains hallucinogenic properties. If that is likely to be your only motivation for trying it, don't bother. (The psychedelic drug, mescaline, was derived from the peyote cactus, not the agave.)

HOW IT IS MADE

The unlovely agave plant has an enormous core, the shape of a pine-cone, which is surrounded by great, spiny fat leaves. This core, or heart, is hacked away and the expressed juice – which is milky-white and extremely bitter – is fermented into pulque. Mescal is the first rough distillation of the pulque. It may be given a short period of ageing in wood, but it is not intended to be a sophisticated product.

TASTES GOOD WITH

Agave worm.

MESCAL
A little white worm
lurks at the bottom
of every bottle

HOW TO SERVE

If you want to tame its fire, try mixing mescal with a little freshly squeezed lime juice and topping it up with soda or tonic water. In Mexico, inevitably, they just knock it back as it is, like schnapps. It is hard to find a mescal, even commercially bottled, that doesn't smell dirty, an aroma that does tend to pierce through whatever it's mixed with.

RUM

RUM IS PROBABLY the least understood of the five main spirits, despite the fact that, in its white version, it is one of the biggest-selling of them all. Indeed, it is debatable whether many of those knocking back Bacardi-and-Cokes in bars around the world realize they are drinking some form of rum at all. In the popular mind, the drink is inextricably associated with a rather antiquated pantomime idea of "Jolly Jack Tars" and a life on the ocean wave.

There is some uncertainty over the origin of the spirit's name, but the favourite theory is that it is a shortening of a rather marvellous old West Country English word "rumbullion", itself of unknown origin, but generally denoting any hard liquor.

The invention of rum probably dates from not long after the foundation of the sugar plantations in the West Indies, in the early 16th century. Until the voyages of Christopher Columbus, sugar was a luxury product, and much sought after in southern Europe, having originally been brought from India into Venice

OTHER NAMES
France: rhum
Spain: ron

by Persians and then by Arabs. When the Spanish explorers landed in Hispaniola (modern-day Haiti and the Dominican Republic) and the neighbouring Caribbean islands, they saw in them promising environments for cultivating sugar cane and thereby breaking the stranglehold on the market that the Arabs had.

If yeasts need sugar to feed on in order to produce alcohol, then the sugar plant was always going to be an obvious source for some kind of distillate. When first pressed,

HOW TO SERVE
The best dark rums, and aged rums in particular, should be served straight, unchilled, as digestifs. They make stimulating alternatives to malt whisky or cognac. Premium white rums from the independent producers are also best enjoyed neat, but they should be served cold.

NOTABLE PRODUCERS
Appleton, Myers (Jamaica);
CSR (St Kitts);
Green Island (Mauritius);
Clément, Rhum St James, La Mauny (Martinique);
Havana Club (Cuba);
El Dorado (Guyana);
Cockspur, Mount Gay (Barbados);
Barbancourt (Haiti);
Pusser's (British Virgin Islands)

CAPTAIN MORGAN
The leading brand dark rum

MIXING

Rum is the base for many of the more way-out cocktail concoctions on offer today, its heady richness contributing to the explosive power required. Here are two classics:

Bacardi Cocktail: The original, after which the brand is named. Shake a double measure of white rum with the juice of half a lime, a teaspoon of grenadine, and ice. Strain it into a cocktail glass.

Cuba Libre (below): Mix a generous measure of light or golden rum with a tablespoon or so of freshly squeezed lime juice, pour over ice, and top up with cola.

cane juice is a murky, greenish colour and full of impurities. Boiled down, it eventually crystallizes into sucrose and a sticky, brown by-product, molasses, that would readily have fermented in the tropical conditions. Rum is the spirit derived from distilling the fermented molasses.

Sugar soon became a widespread everyday product in Europe. The astronomical demand for it was serviced by one of the most notorious manifestations of European colonial history – the slave trade – and rum played a crucial part in the circular trade that came to be established. Settlers in New England financed their trips to West Africa by selling rum. A consignment of African slaves would be delivered to the West

Indies and sold for molasses, which would then be shipped back to New England to be turned into more rum.

The association of rum with the British Navy in particular derives from the fact that rum was provided to the ratings as a standard daily ration in the 18th century. The tradition continued throughout the most glorious period of Britain's maritime history, basically because rum could withstand hot weather more sturdily than beer could. The initial allowance was a fairly rollicking half-pint a day, which eventually was watered down into the despised

WOOD'S 100
A particularly rich naval-strength dark rum

MIXING

Petite Fleur: (from Michael Walker's *Cinzano Cocktail Book*): Shake equal measures of white rum, Cointreau and freshly squeezed grapefruit juice with ice and strain into a cocktail glass.

Mai Tai (below): Blend a measure each of dark rum and light rum with half-measures of tequila, Cointreau and apricot brandy, a measure of freshly squeezed orange juice, a splash of grenadine and a few drops of Angostura and ice cubes in a liquidizer. Decant into a very large wine glass. Approach with trepidation.

MIXING

Planter's Punch: Shake a double measure each of light rum and fresh orange juice with a couple of teaspoons of fresh lemon juice and ice, and strain into a large glass. (Some authorities insist on a dash of grenadine just for good measure.)

Ti Punch (below): Stir a generous measure of good white rum with a splash of cane syrup and the pounded zest and juice of a lime in a large tumbler with plenty of crushed ice. (Not to be confused with tea punch, which is actually based on tea.)

growing sugar cane specifically for distillation.

Some rum is made from the pressed cane juice itself, but most is made from the fermented molasses. In the former French colonies in particular, there is a distinguished tradition of *rhum agricole*, speciality products made on small sugar farms, in which rums are produced with different strains of yeast. They are individually appreciated in the same way that a wine drinker appreciates wines made from single grape varieties.

Both methods of distillation are practised for rum

HOW TO SERVE

Of the commercial products, white rum mixes famously well with cola, but also with orange juice or more tropical flavours such as pineapple or mango. Dark rum has traditionally been seen as compatible with blackcurrant or peppermint cordials, as well as the ubiquitous cola (below).

"grog" and then mixed with lemon juice as an anti-scorbutic (but it was still not much less than a third of a pint of spirit). It was only as recently as 1970 that it was decided that perhaps encouraging the lads to drink around eight measures of spirit every day might not be the best guarantee of military efficiency.

Rum is today produced all over the West Indies and eastern South America, to a lesser extent in the Indian Ocean area – the Philippines and Mauritius – and in smaller quantities still in the United States and even in Australia. A lot of it is inevitably a by-product of the sugar-refining industry, but the best grades are made by smaller, independent companies

BACARDI
The world's favourite white spirit brand

MIXING

Hot Buttered Rum: In a tall glass, mix a teaspoon of demerara sugar in a good double measure of strong black rum. Add half a teaspoon of ground cinnamon and a knob of unsalted butter and fill with hot water. (Remember to stand a spoon in the glass to conduct the heat if the water has just boiled.) Stir well to dissolve the butter and sugar.

Pina Colada (below): Whizz up two measures each of white rum and pineapple juice, with a couple of teaspoons of shredded fresh coconut and ice, in a liquidizer. (For that tropical touch, the drink should ideally be poured into a pineapple shell with a good lining of fruit left in it and drunk through straws.)

and, as with other spirits, the premium versions are double-distilled in a copper pot still. Continuous distillation and thorough rectification are used mainly by the bulk producers, particularly for the relatively neutral-tasting white rums that lead the market. Freshly distilled spirit from the pot still method is very high in impurities and must be allowed to mellow through a period of cask-ageing, which in turn gives colour to the darker rums. Some companies adjust the final colour with caramel, but not to a degree that would affect the flavour.

After white rums, dark rum is the next most important category commercially, and it is certainly where the superior products are found. Leading brands are Captain Morgan and Lamb's, but there are many others. Some of them are bottled at the original naval strength of more than 50% ABV (Wood's Navy Rum, for example, is 57%), the traditional name for which was "overproof". The everyday dark rums are a more standard 40%, while Bacardi is adjusted down to 37.5% to put it on a level with the other commercial white spirits.

In between the two styles is the increasingly

MOUNT GAY BARBADOS
A major Caribbean brand of golden rum

MIXING

Daiquiri: Shake a double measure of white rum with the juice of half a lime or a quarter of a lemon, a teaspoon of caster sugar and ice. Strain into a cocktail glass. (Adding half a measure of some fruit liqueur, together with 50g/2oz of the equivalent fresh fruit, puréed, is a popular spin on the original Daiquiri. A strawberry version made with fraise liqueur is especially enticing.)

FLAVOURINGS

A small amount of rum is aromatized with mixed spices and fruits such as raisins and plums. Some of Guyana's Demerara rums are flavoured in this way

MIXING

Zombie: Blend a measure each of dark rum, light rum and apricot brandy with half-measures of pineapple juice and freshly squeezed lemon and orange juices in a liquidizer, with ice, and pour into a large goblet.

of the residue of the first distillation – known as dunder – may be added to the molasses during fermentation. Commercial white rums are rectified and bottled immediately. Coloured rums are cask-aged, sometimes for decades, before they are bottled.

TASTES GOOD WITH

More than any other basic spirit, rum makes an excellent accompaniment to fruits of all kinds. A "salad" of orange segments in golden rum was already a traditional dish in the 18th century. Rum can be added to the syrup for all fruit salads, though, and works particularly well with pineapple and banana. It is excellent for adding an enriching note to sponge-based desserts such as charlottes. Rum baba – the soft sponge filled with raisins and soaked in light rum – would, of course, be nothing without it.

popular golden or light rum, which is a particular speciality of Cuba and Puerto Rico aged for less time in barrel. The darkest and heaviest rums, some not far from the colour of thick black treacle, traditionally come from Jamaica. Good white rum, such as the white Rhum St James from Martinique, is full of burnt-sugar richness, a world away from the blandness of commercial white. Some exporters make a virtue of selling rums with 30 or 40 years of cask age, and there is even a tiny production of vintage-dated rum for the true connoisseur.

HOW IT IS MADE

Juice from the sugar cane is pressed and either fermented straight, or else boiled down to extract the molasses, which itself forms the basis of the ferment. It is either continuously distilled or, for speciality products, double-distilled in a pot still. For a headier product, some

LAMB'S
One of the
leading brands
of dark rum

SLIVOVITZ

TRUE SLIVOVITZ IS, or was, the local fruit brandy, or eau de vie, of Serbia and Bosnia-Herzegovina. I say "was" because the ravages of the war in the early 1990s in the former Yugoslavia, of which those countries were once part, put paid to a lot of the production capacity of the distilleries. Indeed it put paid to whole distilleries in some cases. A little did continue to be made, however (its rarity value leading one London retailer at the time to triple the price of its remaining stocks), and with peace production may rise once more.

It is to be hoped so because, at its best, slivovitz is one of the most distinguished and delicious eaux de vie made anywhere in Europe. The base fruit is a particular variety of black plum called Madjarka, which imparts a richly heady scent to the spirit. For the best grades, the spirit is cask-aged, and steeped in yet more whole fresh fruit during maturation to emphasize the flavour. It comes in a variety of weirdly shaped bottles, some tall and thin, some round and flask-shaped, still others of faceted glass.

Slivovitz has always been made and drunk elsewhere in eastern and central Europe, notably Bulgaria, Hungary, Germany, Austria and Italy. In the Balkans, it may also go by its other name of *rakija*. This name denotes its origin as one of the European fruit versions of the arak that came from the Far East.

HOW IT IS MADE

Black plums are crushed along with their stones and fermented very slowly over a period of around three months. A double distillation is carried out, and then the new spirit is aged in great casks of Slovenian oak. Sometimes, whole plums are thrown in to macerate the spirit while it ages. It is generally bottled at about five years old and at 35–40% ABV.

TASTES GOOD WITH

A little slivovitz added to stewed plums, or even to a traditional Christmas pudding, will enrich the dish no end.

SLIVOVITZ
is heady with the scent of ripe black plums

OTHER NAMES

Bosnia, Croatia, Serbia: sljivovica. Also rakija/prakija/slivovka

SLJIVOVICA
A Croatian slivovitz in a flask-shaped bottle

HOW TO SERVE

As with all such spirits, slivovitz is most commonly drunk unchilled, as a digestif.

TEQUILA

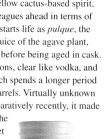

TEQUILA IS THE NATIONAL spirit of Mexico. It is one stage further down the road to refinement than its fellow cactus-based spirit, mescal, but several leagues ahead in terms of drinking pleasure. It starts life as *pulque*, the fermented beer-like juice of the agave plant, and is distilled twice before being aged in cask. It comes in two versions, clear like vodka, and golden (or Oro), which spends a longer period in contact with the barrels. Virtually unknown in Europe until comparatively recently, it made its first inroads into the world's drinks cabinet by travelling northwards to the USA, and it is now something of a cult drink in the youth market.

The name, tequila, is echoed in the full botanical name of the

HOW TO SERVE

The correct way of drinking tequila: your drink is served to you cold and straight in a small shot-glass. You then season your tongue with citrus and salt, by first squeezing a wedge of lime (lemon for the wimps) and then pouring salt on to the back of the hand and licking at each in turn. To be anatomically precise, the hand should be held at a 45° angle away from the body, with the thumb extended downwards, and the juice and salt deposited along the groove between the bases of the thumb and forefinger. (Some make things easier by just sucking on the piece of lime.) The tequila is then thrown back in one gulp like schnapps, carrying the seasonings with it. The process is repeated ad infinitum.

Believe it or not, this really is how tequila is widely drunk on its native territory. If it sounds like a fiddly and indescribably messy procedure, the answer is that it is, but long practice induces a sort of head-tossing, devil-may-care sanguinity in experienced users.

MIXING
Tequila and Orange: Have done with the fuss, and drink it on the rocks with fresh orange juice. It makes an enlivening change for those grown weary of vodka-and-orange.

CUERVO TEQUILA
The white version of Mexico's national spirit

MIXING

Margarita: Shake equal measures of tequila and Cointreau with the juice of half a lime and plenty of ice. Dip a finger in and run it around the rim of a cocktail glass. Up-end the glass briefly in a saucerful of coarse-ground salt, then strain the drink into it. (This is the classic tequila cocktail, but it is just a customized way of getting round the tradi-tional salt-licking routine – with a slug of Cointreau for sweetly counteracting the salt. Some recipes add egg white too. No accounting for taste.)

plant from which it is sourced: *Agave tequilana.* Perhaps what put everybody else off trying it for so long was the thought of a spirit made from cacti, and indeed even the finest grades don't actually smell particularly inviting. It has a sweaty, slightly muggy quality that must have come as something of a jolt at first to tastebuds honed on squeaky-clean vodka.

In recognition of its cultural importance, the production of tequila has been strictly delimited within Mexico. It may be distilled in only a handful of towns, including Tequila itself, and in the area immediately surrounding Guadala-jara. Two of the brands most commonly encountered on the export markets are Cuervo and Montezuma, the latter usually in an engraved bottle.

HOW IT IS MADE

Like mescal, tequila is distilled from the chopped, pressed and fermented hearts of agave plants. The juice is quite high in acidity, which lends even the refined spirit a certain piquancy. It is distilled a second time in a pot still, and then matured in wooden casks, briefly for the white version, and up to five years for the Oro.

GOLDEN MONTEZUMA
Gold tequila has aged in cask for longer than white

MIXING

Tequila Sunrise: Half-fill a tall glass with crushed ice. Put in a goodly measure of tequila and top up with fresh orange juice. Quickly dollop a tea-spoon of grenadine into the centre of the drink. (The bright red grena-dine sinks to the bottom and then blends upwards into the orange in a very becoming way, hence the drink's name.)

VODKA

IN ONE SENSE, vodka is the closest thing to perfection ever conceived in the long history of spirits. Had it been invented in the 1990s, in the era of alco-pops and ice beers, it would be hailed as a supremely adept piece of marketing wizardry. Nobody, other than a confirmed teetotaller, could possibly dislike it, for the simple reason that it tastes of nothing whatsoever. It is pure, unadulterated, uncomplicated alcohol. At least, most of it is.

The word "vodka" is a Russian endearment meaning "little water", from their word for water, *voda*. It doesn't denote the flavourlessness of the spirit, however, but derives from the widespread linguistic practice in Europe of referring to all distillates originally as a form of water (as in the Latin *aqua vitae* and French *eau de vie*).

Precisely because it is such a simple drink, it is almost impossible to pinpoint the origins of vodka historically. A potent spirit distilled from various grains, and

OTHER NAMES
Poland: wodka

indeed potatoes – still wrongly believed in the popular imagination to be its main ingredient – has been made in Poland, Russia and the Baltic states of Latvia, Lithuania and Estonia since the very early days of distillation in Europe.

But as to where a drink specifically recognizable as vodka first arose is a matter for the Poles and the Russians to sort out between themselves. (Most outsiders, it should be said, tend to come down on the Polish side of the fence these days.) What is certain is that, by the time home distillation had become a favoured way of passing the long, grim northern winters in Poland, peasant families were producing their own vodkas on an extensive scale.

The discovery of rectification

HOW TO SERVE

Everything should be almost painfully cold. The bottle should be kept in the freezer and the glasses too should be iced. If there isn't a heavy mist of condensation on the outside of the glass, it isn't cold enough.

Some shots are thrown back like schnapps, owing to an old folk belief that if you inhale the fumes for more than a split second, you will get too drunk too quickly. The aged vodkas, and specialities such as Zubrowka, are more often sipped appreciatively. A little shot-glass is traditional, but in some homes, a rather larger, narrow tumbler, or even something like a goblet wine glass is used.

SMIRNOFF
The basic red label brand is the market leader

ABSOLUT
Blue label Absolut is the unflavoured version

techniques did not take place until the beginning of the 19th century, and so these early distillates would have tasted pretty unclean, to say the least. Any herbs, seeds or berries that were to hand would be steeped in the spirit to mask its rankness. So the first vodkas were not the anonymous products preferred today, but the true ancestors of the flavoured vodkas that are sometimes greeted as nothing more than novelty items by modern drinkers.

Nonetheless, it was the neutral, ultra-purified grain vodka – made from wheat or rye – that came to commercial prominence in the West. So prevalent is it now, particularly among younger drinkers who have yet to discover and appreciate the taste of unrectified, cask-matured spirits such as good whisky and cognac, that it is hard to believe that hardly anyone in western Europe or America had heard of it until the late 1940s.

BLACK LABEL SMIRNOFF
A softer, mellower product

BLUE LABEL SMIRNOFF
The strongest at 45%

MIXING

Basic vodka has no scent or flavour, meaning it is not the most inspiring ingredient in the cocktail repertoire. All it can really do is confer an extra slug of alcohol for those hell-bent on the short-cut to oblivion. As a result, the sky's the limit.

Black Russian: The true Black Russian is simply equal measures of vodka and Tia Maria, or Kahlúa, mixed with ice cubes in a tumbler. However, the fashion in recent years has been to serve it as a long drink in a big glass, topped up with cola. Alternatively, leave out the cola, add a measure of single cream, shake it up and it becomes a **White Russian**: Then again, substitute dark brown crème de cacao for the Tia Maria and create a **Piranha**.

Black Cossack (below): Add a good slug of vodka to a half-pint of Guinness.

It all changed with the first stirrings of interest in California during the period of the Beat Generation.

Not only did vodka possess the aforementioned neutrality that made it such an obvious beginner's spirit, but it was also seen as a provocatively dissident thing to drink in the era of the onset of the Cold War. Vodka was the favoured "hooch" of the Soviet bloc, and in the witch-hunting atmosphere of 50s America, nothing was more guaranteed to inflame bourbon-drinking patriots than to see young folks imbibing the spirit of Communism with such evident glee. The late Alexis Lichine,

FLAVOURINGS

Vodka will happily take up whatever flavouring a producer decides to give it, including:
Lemon peel
Bison grass
Red chilli peppers
Cherries
Rowanberries
Blackcurrants
Apples
Sloes
Saffron
Tarragon
Walnuts
Honey
Liquorice
Rose petals

LIMONNAYA

A leading lemon-flavoured vodka

MIXING

Screwdriver: That nightclub favourite, vodka and orange. The name, according to one theory, originated among workers on American oil-rigs who – finding themselves short of swizzle-sticks – resourcefully used their screwdrivers to stir the drink. In the Baltic states, the freshly squeezed orange juice is served to you in a separate little jug and you mix to taste. Even here the cocktail name is in use, although, as I discovered in Riga, to make yourself perfectly clear, you must ask the barman for a "skrew". When first marketed on the west coast of the USA, it was suggested that it be drunk with ginger beer. Thus did the first **Moscow Mule** come to light.

drink historian, attributes the start of vodka's meteoric rise in the West to the purchase of a recipe for rectified vodka from a Russian refugee called Smirnoff by an American company, on the eve of the Second World War. The rest is history.

Vodka is still very much the drink of gastro-nomic choice in its native lands, drunk as aperitif, digestif and even as an accompaniment to food. It is nearly always taken icy-cold, preceded in Polish homes by the ritual wishing of good health – *na zdrowie* – to one's family and friends. The quantities consumed may raise eyebrows in our Western unit-counting culture, but a vodka hangover is very rare, owing to the relentless clean-up job the drink is given during distillation. This removes nearly all of its con-geners, the substances that impart character to the dark spirits.

Fruit flavourings are very common, and make a drier, more bracing alternative to the equiva-lent liqueurs. Perhaps the most celebrated flavoured product is Zubrowka, bison-grass vodka, which is generally sold with a

ABSOLUT *Kurant is solidly fruity and flavoured with black-currants*

MIXING

Bloody Mary: Everyone has his or her own proprietary recipe for the next best hangover cure after aspirin. Some strange people even put tomato ketchup into it. Others round out the alcohol with a splash of dry sherry. Here is my own formula.

Put a slice of lemon and two or three ice-cubes in a tall glass, add a teaspoon of Lea & Perrin's Worcestershire sauce, a teaspoon of freshly squeezed lemon juice, a pinch of celery salt, a generous dash of Tabasco and about half-a-dozen twists of the black pepper mill, and stir to coat the ice. Fill the glass to about an inch-and-a-half from the top with tomato juice and pour on a generous measure of vodka. Stir well to combine the alcohol.

blade of grass in the bottle. Bison grass is the gourmet preference of the wild bison that roam the forests of eastern Poland, and the beast is usually depicted on the label.

Wisniowka (cherries), Limonnaya (lemon) and the Swedish Absolut company's Kurant (blackcurrant) are all appetizing drinks. Pieprzowka, which is infused with chilli peppers, is a variety for real aficionados: the spirit is emphasized by the hot spice burn of its flavouring component. Russia's Okhotnichya – "Hunter's Vodka" – is impregnated with orange peel, ginger root, coffee beans, juniper berries and even a drop of white port.

Neutral vodkas are produced all over the

world now, although most grades are only intended to be served in mixed drinks. Russian Stolichnaya, particularly the Cristall bottling, is an honourable, silky-smooth exception. Smirnoff makes three types, in red, blue and black labels to denote varying strength, and there are brands with such names as Black Death and Jazz Jamboree. Scandinavian vodkas such as Finlandia and Absolut have their deserved followings, while most British vodka tends to be little more than patent alcohol. At one time, vodka production had even travelled south from Russia into Iran, but the coming of Islamic rule brought that to a halt.

Also seen on the export markets is Polish Pure Spirit, bottled at around 70% ABV, and much beloved by reckless students as a dare.

How It is Made

Although potatoes and other vegetables, and even molasses, have been used to make vodka at various times in its history, commercial vodka is nowadays virtually exclusively made from grains, the principal one of which is rye. A basic mash is made in the usual way by malting the grains and encouraging them to ferment with cultured yeasts. The resulting brew is then continuously

PIEPRZOWKA
This vodka has been coloured and flavoured with chillies

distilled in a column still apparatus to higher and higher degrees of alcoholic strength, thus driving off nearly all of the higher alcohols or fusel oil. As a final insurance policy against flavour, the finished spirit is then filtered through a layer of charcoal, which strips it of any remaining character. It is then bottled at around 37.5% for commercial strength and released without further ado.

In the case of flavoured vodkas, the aromatizing elements are added to the new spirit after rectification, and left to infuse in it over long periods – sometimes three years or more. Occasionally, a speciality vodka will be aged in cask and take on a tinge of colour; others derive their exotic hues from the addition of spices, flowers or nuts.

Tastes Good With

Ice-cold vodka is the classic accompaniment to finest Russian caviare, itself served on heaps of ice. In the Scandinavian countries, it is also drunk, like aquavit, with marinated and smoked fish such as herring, mackerel and even salmon. Superchef Martin Blunos at Restaurant Lettonie, near Bristol in England, has created a sumptuously theatrical dish of scrambled duck egg served in the shell amid a slick of flaming Latvian vodka, topped with sevruga caviare and with blinis and a shot of freezing vodka on the side.

STOLICHNAYA
This smooth vodka should be sipped appreciatively

Mixing

Balalaika: Shake a measure each of vodka and Cointreau with half a measure of lemon juice and plenty of ice, and strain into a cocktail glass.

Barbara: Shake a measure of vodka with half-measures of crème de cacao and single cream, with ice, and strain into a cocktail glass. (This is essentially a vodka-based **Alexander**.)
Katinka (from Michael Walker's *Cinzano Cocktail Book*): Shake a measure-and-a-half of vodka with a measure of apricot brandy and half a measure of fresh lime juice with ice, and pour over a heap of slivered ice in a cocktail glass.
Vodkatini: Basically a classic Martini, but with vodka replacing the gin.
Czarina: Stir a measure of vodka with half-measures of apricot brandy and dry vermouth and a dash of Angostura with ice in a mixing jug. Strain into a cocktail glass.

WHISKY

WHISKY (OR WHISKEY, depending on where it hails from) is one of the world's leading spirits. Its history is every bit as distinguished as that of cognac and, like the classic brandies of France, its spread around the world from its first home – the Scottish Highlands, in whisky's case – has been a true testament to the genius of its conception. Tennessee sour mash may bear about as much relation in taste to single malt Scotch as Spanish brandy does to cognac, but the fact that they are all great products demonstrates the versatility of each basic formula.

Whiskies are produced all over the world now. As the name is not a geographically specific one, they may all legitimately call themselves whisk(e)y. In Australia and India, the Czech Republic and Germany, they make grain spirits from barley or rye that proudly bear the name. The five major whisky-producing countries are Scotland, the United States, Ireland, Canada and Japan, which are covered in this chapter.

The name "whisky" itself is yet another variant on the phrase "water of life" that we have become familiar with in the world of spirits. In translation, the Latin *aqua vitae* became *uisge* beatha in the Scots branch of Gaelic and *usquebaugh* in the Irish; it eventually was mangled into the half-Anglicized "whisky"

and was in official use by the mid-18th century.

In countries that lacked the warm climate for producing fermented drinks from grapes, beer was always the staple brew and, just as brandy was the obvious first distillate in southern Europe, so malted grains provided the starting-point for domestic production further north. Unlike brandy, however, which starts life as wine, whisky doesn't have to be made from something that would be recognizable as beer. The grains are malted by allowing them to germinate in water and then lightly cooking them to encourage the formation of sugars. It is these sugars on which the yeasts then feed to produce the first ferment. A double distillation by the pot still method results in a congener-rich

HOW TO SERVE

The finest whiskies are not necessarily drunk neat. It is widely believed that taming some of the spirit's fire helps to bring up the array of complicated scents and flavours in good whisky. To that end, it is normally drunk with a dose of water, ideally the same spring water that goes into the whisky itself, otherwise any pure, non-chlorinated water. Half-and-half are the preferred proportions in Scotland and Ireland, while in Tennessee and Kentucky they add a little less than half.

LAPHROAIG
One of the richest of the peaty styles of Scotch produced in Islay

MACALLAN
This 18-year-old whisky is one of the best-loved Highland malts

spirit that can then be matured – often for decades for the finer whiskies – in oak barrels.

Just as with other spirits that haven't had the life rectified out of them, whisky is nearly always truly expressive of its regional origins and the raw materials that went into it. For that reason, a passionate connoisseurship of this spirit has arisen over the generations, similar to that which surrounds wine. Even more than brandy, whisky handsomely rewards those who set out with a conscientious approach to the tasting and appreciation of the spirit.

SCOTLAND

Home distillation in Scotland can be traced back to the 15th century, when the practice of distilling surplus grain to make a potent drink for clan chieftains was established. Initially, the drink was – like all spirits – primarily valued

for its medicinal powers, and early examples were no doubt infusions of herbs and berries rather than the pure grain product we know today. Although other cereals would at first have been used, the pre-eminence of malted barley was acknowledged relatively early on in the development of Scotch.

Before the Act of Union that brought England and Scotland together politically in 1707, Scotch was hardly known in England. Gin was the national drink south of the border. Once the English laid their administrative hands on Scotland, they did their level best to bring whisky distillation under statutory control, but with only very partial success. Those whisky-makers within striking distance of the border fled northwards with their stills into the Highlands, and the production of Scotch continued unabated as an almost wholly illicit activity.

Eventually, by a combination of threats and bribes, the authorities managed to place the whole enterprise under licence so that, by the 1870s, there

GLENLIVET
A 10-year-old Spey-
side malt from the
Scottish Highlands

TASTES GOOD WITH

Scotch is naturally the only accompaniment to the ceremonial haggis on Burns Night (January 25). Whether it is a precise gastro-nomic match may be open to question, but to order a bottle of Rioja would be missing the point somewhat. Un-iced Scotch is also great with hearty soups: thick, barley-based Scotch broth or cock-a-leekie should ideally have a fair amount of whisky in them anyway.

TALISKER

Talisker whisky is the only malt whisky produced on the island of Skye.

AUCHENTOSHAN

A Lowland malt distilled not far from Glasgow.

MIXING

Rusty Nail: Equal measures of Scotch and Drambuie mixed with ice and strained into a small glass, or poured over crushed ice.
Whisky Mac (below): The classic cold remedy is half and half good Scotch and green ginger wine (preferably Crabbie's) with no ice.

were just half-a-dozen arraignments in Scotland for illegal distilling (as against nearly 700 only 40 years earlier).

The advent of continuous distillation came to Scotland courtesy of Robert Stein, who invented a rudimentary version of the column still in 1826. Although Scotch had traditionally been characterized by the richness and depth of flavour that marks all pot-still products, the development of the new method allowed a lighter spirit of more obvious commercial appeal to be produced. By the late 19th century, the habit of blending true malt whisky with straight grain spirit made by continuous distillation from unmalted barley (and maize, or corn) was widespread. These were the types of Scotch that were introduced to cautious English palates.

In the early years of this century, a Royal Commission was set up to determine the parameters for Scotch whisky production, i.e. the methods of distillation, rules on blending, minimum maturation times and, of course, the salient geographical point – that Scotch could only be distilled and aged in Scotland. The Commission reported in 1909, its conclusions were refined slightly in 1915, and it remains in force today as the legal textbook for an industry of worldwide importance that is also a central support of the Scottish economy.

THE FAMOUS GROUSE
One of the leading brands of blended Scotch

TYPES OF SCOTCH

The most highly prized of Scotch whiskies are the single malts. These are whiskies that are produced entirely from malted barley, double-distilled, and made exclusively at a single one (hence the terminology) of Scotland's 100 or so working distilleries. Some of these products are aged for many years. Twenty-five-year-old Scotch will be shot through with all sorts of profoundly complex flavours and perfumes picked up from the wood in which it has matured and perhaps, according to some, from the sea air that wafts around the coastal distilleries. Remember that – as with other spirits – aged malt can't continue to develop once bottled.

Some malts are the blended produce of several single malts, in which case they are known as vatted malts. They are often assembled from several distilleries within a particular region in order to illustrate the local style comparable to specific regional subdivisions in a *vin de pays* wine area.

Whiskies made from corn or unmalted barley are known as grain whiskies and are always considerably

WHYTE & MACKAY
This whisky is re-blended for a second period of maturation

lighter in style than the malts. They could be described as beginner's Scotch since they have far fewer of the aromatic components that account for the pedigree of great malt, but they should by no means be seen as worthless imitations. They have their role to play.

The greater part of that role is in the production of blended Scotch, whisky made from a mixture of malt and grain spirits. This is the market-leading category, occupied by virtually all of the big brand names, such as Bell's, J&B, Johnnie Walker, Ballantine's, Whyte & Mackay, The Famous Grouse, White Horse and Teacher's. Most of these have fairly low concentrations of malt in the blend, although Teacher's and Johnnie Walker's Black Label

J&B
This blended whisky is popular in the American market; J&B stands for Justerini & Brooks

bottling are notable exceptions.

Scotch whisky is mostly retailed at the standard dark spirit strength of 40% ABV, or perhaps slightly above (avoid any that are below). A small proportion of the best grades are bottled from the barrel undiluted. These are known as "cask-strength" whiskies. You are not intended to drink them as they come, but the distiller is inviting you to dilute them with water yourself and find the precise level of potency that suits you.

AREAS OF PRODUCTION

For the purposes of whisky production, Scotland is divided up into four broad regions: the Lowlands, south of Stirling; the tiny Campbeltown, on a narrow peninsula west of Ayr; Islay and the Western

GLENMORANGIE
One of the most celebrated Northern Highland malts.

TEACHERS
One of the maltier blended whiskies.

GIFT WRAPPING
Malt whiskies are often sold in elegant presentation cartons.

Isles, comprising Jura, Mull and Skye; and the Highlands. The Highlands can be further sub-divided into the Midlands, the Western, Northern and Eastern Highlands and Speyside.

As a (very) rough guide to the regional styles, Lowland whiskies are the gentlest and sweetest styles of Scotch, while Campbeltown's are fresh and ozoney. Islay produces an instantly recognizable pungent spirit, full of seaweed aromas, and particularly marked by the influence of the peat that fires the drying kilns for the grain, while many Highland malts have a soft smoki-ness to them. There are numerous distilleries, though, and each has evolved its own style.

HOW IT IS MADE

In the case of the malts, the grains of barley are soaked in water to encour-age them to germinate. Soon after they have begun sprouting, the process is arrested by heating them in a kiln, in which variable quantities of peat will be added to the fuel, depending on

the intended final flavour of the whisky. After kilning, the grain is mashed and drained and then poured into large tanks to begin fermenta-tion, either with natural or cultured yeasts. (Yeast strains have a pronounced effect on the flavour, too.) The resulting brew is then double-distilled in the traditional copper pot still.

The other factor of huge significance in deter-mining the character of a whisky is the type of maturation vessel. Scotch was traditionally aged in casks that had previously been used for shipping sherry, and some still is, but used bourbon casks from Kentucky are now quite common. In both cases, the wood is American oak, capable of imparting great richness to a whisky. (There is at least one product on the market that has been aged in old port casks.) Whiskies aged for long periods will derive a certain char-acter from the action of oxygen seeping through the pores of the wood.

WHITE HORSE
A pronounced
peatiness marks
the flavour of
this blended
whisky

JOHNNIE WALKER
Red Label is the
biggest selling
whisky of all.

JOHNNIE
WALKER
The Black Label
has a higher
malt content
than the red

MIXING

Manhattan: The favourite Manhattan has come to be equal measures of American or Canadian whiskey and sweet red Italian vermouth, mixed over ice in a large glass, with perhaps a dash of Angostura but certainly with that indispensable cocktail cherry popped in. A dry Manhattan uses dry French vermouth instead of sweet. The accepted compromise is to make up the vermouth quotient with 50% of each.

UNITED STATES

In North America, where whiskey is mostly spelled with an "e" as it is in Ireland, production of the drink goes back only as far as the 18th century. Its roots are embedded in the era leading up to Independence. Before that, the staple spirit in America was dark rum, made from molasses transported from the West Indies by the slave ships. It was British and Irish settlers, bringing their own whisky with them from the old countries, who provided the impetus for the development of what is today America's national spirit.

The first American whiskeys were made with malted barley and rye, in vague imitation of the European archetypes. Soon, however, a group of distillers in Bourbon County, Kentucky, began producing pure corn whiskey. By happy chance, their little communities were descended upon from 1794 onwards by droves of tax refugees who were fleeing from revenue officers in Pennsylvania, after staging an armed uprising against the new State excises on liquor. Suddenly, the Kentuckians had a ready-made new market for their own product and, before

too long, Kentucky bourbon was well on its way to assuming a place in the ranks of the world's fine spirits.

Rye whiskey is still made in the eastern states of Pennsylvania, Maryland and Virginia, but seemingly in ever-decreasing quantities. It is the whiskeys of Kentucky and Tennessee that represent the cognac and armagnac, if you will, of American spirit production.

BOURBON

Nowadays, most bourbon distilleries are concentrated not in Bourbon County, but around the towns of Louisville, Bardstown and Frankfort. Nonetheless, only whiskeys from the state of Kentucky are entitled to be called bourbons. Bourbon is not a straight corn whiskey, but one made from a mixture of not less than 51% corn with malted barley, like a blended Scotch. Some may contain a little rye. The chief distinguishing taste characteristic of bourbon, however, derives from the barrels in which it matures. They are made of American oak, as one would expect; unlike the barrels used for Scotch, however, they are always brand new. Furthermore, they are heavily charred, or toasted, on the insides to a depth of about

WILD TURKEY BOURBON comes from Lawrenceburg, Kentucky

TASTES GOOD WITH

Somehow, there is a distinct cultural affinity between bourbon and Tennessee whiskeys and huge flame-grilled carpetbag steaks, at least if you're in Bardstown or Nashville.

HOW TO SERVE

The Americans call their spring waters branchwater or "branch". A Scots drinker normally eschews ice; in the States they cram the tumbler full. "On the rocks" means ice but no water.

FLAVOURINGS

Discounting the whisky-based liqueurs, the only case of a straight whisky being flavoured is that of certain Canadian products that have minute amounts of other drinks added to them: grape wine, wines from other fruits (prunes are a favourite), unfermented fruit juices, even sherry

MIXING
Old-Fashioned:

Grind up a sugar lump with a good shake from the Angostura bottle in the squat tumbler that is named after this drink. Add plenty of ice and a cheering quantity of Canadian or straight rye whisky. Throw in a twist of lemon peel, a slice of orange and a cocktail cherry, and serve with a stirring implement in it.

5mm/¼ in, which allows the spirit freer access to the vanillin and tannins in the wood. Nobody quite knows where the charring tradition came from, but it seems quite likely that it was the result of a happy accident.

There are two distinct styles of bourbon, sweet mash and sour mash, the differences arising at the fermentation stage of the grains. For sweet mash, the yeasts are allowed to perform their work quite quickly over a couple of days, while for sour mash, some yeast from the preceding batch augments the brew. This doubles the length of the fermentation and ensures that more of the sugars in the grain are consumed.

Most bourbon is labelled "Kentucky Straight Bourbon", which means it is made from at least 51% corn, is aged for a minimum of two years in charred new barrels and has been made and matured within the prescribed areas. It is the equivalent category to single malt Scotch. Some, sold as "Blended Straight", is made from more than one lot of straight bourbon, and corresponds to vatted malt. Most bourbon is bottled at a slightly higher strength than standard Scotch – about 43–45% ABV.

The leading brand by a long chalk is Jim Beam, made at Bardstown and virtually synonymous with

bourbon on the export markets. Other brands include Wild Turkey, Evan Williams, Early Times, Old Grand-Dad and the pace-setting Maker's Mark (the one with the top dipped in red sealing-wax).

TENNESSEE

South of the bourbon state of Kentucky, in neighbouring Tennessee, an entirely different but equally distinctive style of whiskey is made. Tennessee sour mash is represented by just two distilleries – Jack Daniel's in Lynchburg, and George Dickel in Tullahoma. Their various bottlings represent some of the richest and smoothest whiskeys made.

Whereas bourbon is matured in charred barrels, Tennessee takes the principle a stage further by actually filtering the newly made spirit through a mass of charcoal. In the yards behind the distilleries, they burn great stacks of sugar maple down to ash and then grind it all into a rough black powder. This is

JACK DANIEL'S
By far the bigger
brand of the two
Tennessee whiskeys

MAKER'S
MARK
Small-volume
production allied
to top quality

piled to a depth of around 3 metres/10 feet into so-called mellowing vats, all sitting on a fleecy woollen blanket. The whiskey drips at a painfully slow rate from holes in a gridwork of copper pipes above the vats, and filters gradually through the charcoal bed, before being cask-matured in the usual way.

Jack Daniel's is one of the world's best-loved whiskey brands. Its market-leading Old No. 7, in the famous square bottle, first established the kudos of JD by winning a Gold Medal at the 1904 World's Fair in St Louis. Its great rival, Dickel (which spells its product "whisky" in the Scottish way), matures its No. 12 brand for several years longer, and the results are evident in a more discreet and mellower nose and deeper colour. It is bottled at 45% ABV.

One of the great ironies of Tennessee whiskey is that both producers have their distilleries in "dry" counties where it is forbidden to sell alcohol, which means that they may not avail themselves of

the doorstep custom they could enjoy from public visits. A glass of soul-saving spring water is offered instead.

IRELAND

The origins of distillation in the Emerald Isle are lost in swathes of Irish mist, but are certainly of great antiquity, at least as old as those of Scotch. There are those who have claimed that it was Irish missionaries who first brought the knowledge of distilling to France, and thus made brandy possible. Whether that is true or not, Irish whiskey once enjoyed an unrivalled reputation as a more approachable style of spirit than Scotch malt. It was only when blended Scotch began to be made on any significant scale towards the end of the 19th century that Irish whiskey was nudged out of the frame.

The reasons for the greater accessibility of Irish whiskey lie in its production process. No peat is used in the kilns, so that there is none of the smoky pungency that is present in some degree in most Scotch. Secondly, punitive taxes on malted barley in the mid-19th century meant that the Irish distillers began to use a mixture of malted and unmalted grain in their mash, making it traditionally a blended product long before the recipes for today's

JAMESON

The brand leader on the export market

JIM BEAM
A particularly
popular bourbon

PADDY
This whiskey is
distilled at
Midleton, just
outside the city
of Cork

MIXING

Whisky Sour: Mix the juice of half a lemon with a level teaspoon of icing sugar in a tumbler with two or three cubes of ice. When the sugar is dissolved, add a generous measure of whisky and stir again – American whiskeys are best for this preparation. (Some add a brief squirt of soda. If you find this formula a little *too* sour, add a little more sugar, but this is the way I like it.)

CANADIAN CLUB

The leading brand of Canadian whisky.

standard Scotch brands had even been dreamed about.

Most famously of all, Irish whiskey is subjected to a triple distillation by the copper pot still method. The third passage of the spirit through the stills results in a product with a softer, ultra-refined palate profile while still retaining all of its complexity. By law, the whiskey must then be cask-aged for a minimum of three years, although in practice most are aged for two to three times that period. It is usually bottled at 40% ABV.

The brand leader on the export markets is Jameson's. Other notable names include Bushmills, John Power, Murphy's, Paddy, Dunphy's and Tullamore Dew. All but one are made in the Republic, mostly in the environs of Dublin or Cork. The exception is Bushmills, which is located in County Antrim in Northern Ireland.

(There is another Irish "whiskey" of course, made on illegal travelling stills that the authorities have always found notoriously difficult to track down. Perhaps they have more constructive things to do. For all its reputation as toxic brain-scrambler, poteen – pronounced "pocheen" – is an unassailable part of Ireland's folk history, and will continue to be so for as long as taxation rates on the official stuff are as rapacious as they are.)

CANADA

Canada's whiskies are made from blends of different grains, the greater proportion of each brand based on an original mash that combines rye, corn and malted barley. They nearly always contain some spirit, however, that is produced entirely from the heavier-tasting rye, but it usually accounts for less than a tenth of the final blend. As a result, they have the reputation of being among the lightest classic whiskies of all, even more so than the triple-distilled Irish.

The whisky industry in Canada dates back only to the last century, when it arose as an offshoot of the agricultural production of grain. It was quite common at one time to pay the millers in kind with some of the grain, and distillation has long been a traditional way of using up surpluses the world over. The earliest

producers – and, despite the country's size, there are still only a handful – were Hiram Walker, Seagram's and Corby's, all in the province of Ontario.

Distillation is by the continuous process, in gigantic column stills. Different spirits produced from different mashes, or fermented from different yeast strains, are painstakingly blended by the distiller – before the maturation in some cases, afterwards in others. All whiskies must spend at least three years in the barrels, which are of new wood, but there is a noble tradition of aged products in Canada for whiskies that are 10, 12, even 18 years old on release. As elsewhere, the standard blends are sold at 40% ABV, but speciality aged bottlings may be somewhat stronger.

A curiosity of Canadian whisky is that the regulations permit the addition of a tiny quantity of other drink products, such as sherry or wine made from grapes or other fruits. While this may account for no more than a hundredth part of the finished product, it makes its presence felt in the fleeting suggestion of fruitiness in the flavours of some whiskies.

CROWN ROYAL
A Canadian brand
owned by
Seagram's

Most of the distilleries are situated in the eastern provinces of Ontario and Quebec. The leading label is Hiram Walker's Canadian Club, first blended in the 1880s, and is supported by the Burke's and Wiser's ranges from Corby's, McGuinness's Silk Tassel, Alberta Springs and Seagram's Crown Royal.

JAPAN

Of the countries under consideration here, Japan has by far the youngest whisky industry – of even more recent provenance than its efforts at wine making. The first distillery was established only in 1923, and it is only in the last 30 years or so that its products have come to the attention of whisky-drinkers other than the Japanese themselves.

The model for Japan's whiskies is single malt Scotch, but there are equally successful spirits made in the idiom of blended Scotch. The base is a mash of malted barley, dried in kilns fired with a little peat (though considerably less than is the case in Scotland, and so yielding a less aromatically defined product). Distillation is by the pot still method. Some of the brands are aged in used sherry or bourbon casks, as for Scotch, others in heavily charred new American oak barrels, as for bourbon itself. Some distilleries buy in a proportion of unused Scottish spirit for blending in with the home-grown whisky. The premium brands

SUNTORY
The 12-year-old Yamazaki is a kind of Japanese single malt

are generally bottled at around 43% ABV.

The giant drinks company Suntory, which has a finger in all sorts of pies from classed-growth Bordeaux to the green melon liqueur Midori, is also the biggest producer of Japanese whisky, accounting for virtually three-quarters of the industry's annual output. Behind Suntory comes the Nikka company, and then the smaller producers Sanraku Ocean and Seagram's, which is anything but small everywhere else.

In Japan, whisky is nearly always taken heavily watered. Whereas in Scotland, the mix is usually half-and-half, the Japanese prefer to take it as a long pale-yellowish drink in tall glasses filled to the top with spring water and with plenty of ice – about the most denatured form in which fine whisky is commonly drunk anywhere in the world. It is drunk both as an aperitif and as an accompaniment to food.

Among the more illustrious products are Suntory's 12-year-old Pure Malt from its Yamazaki distillery on Honshu, the principal island; Nikka Memorial 50, Sanraku Ocean's single malt Karuizawa (also from Honshu); and Seagram's top labels Crescent and Emblem.

HOW TO SERVE
Whiskies go well with soda for those who prefer a friskier drink, and to some extent with ginger ale (especially those fruity Canadian spirits). They should then be iced.

LIQUEURS

ADVOCAAT

FLAVOURINGS
Oranges
Lemons
Cherries
Vanilla

A DVOCAAT IS A Dutch speciality. It is essentially a customized version of the humble egg nog, without the milk: a mixture of simple grape brandy with egg yolks and sugar, as thick and as yellow as tinned custard. Most of it is sold in this natural form, although it is possible in the Netherlands to buy vanilla- and fruit-flavoured versions. As a result of its velvety texture and bland wholesomeness, advocaat is often thought of as a drink for the elderly, and is commonly added to mugs of hot chocolate or strong coffee.

There are a few widely available brands of advocaat on the market: the red-labelled Warninks is probably the most familiar, but Fockinks, and the liqueur specialists, Bols and De Kuypers, also make it. The standard bottled strength is quite low for a liqueur – around 17% ABV, which is about the same strength as the average fortified wine.

HOW TO SERVE
In the Netherlands, advocaat is drunk both as aperitif and digestif. Unmixed, its texture is such that it is often consumed with a teaspoon. Taken in a hot beverage, it makes a comforting bedtime drink.

WARNINKS
Probably the
most famous
advocaat brand

MIXING
Snowball: Put a generous measure (a couple of fluid ounces) of advocaat in a tall glass and top up with ice-cold sparkling lemonade. If you require a bit more of a kick, add a dessertspoon of sweet brown sherry to it as well. (This is the kind of "cocktail" generally considered safe to give to minors, since it resembles nothing so much as a particularly rich milkshake.)

HOW IT IS MADE
Commercial grape spirit is bought in and sweetened with sugar syrup. Only the yolks of the eggs are added, along with an emulsifying agent to prevent the mixture from separating.

TASTES GOOD WITH
As the ready-made basis of an egg nog, it can be made into a long drink by topping it up with whole milk and a sprinkling of nutmeg.

ADVOCAAT
This is the only manufactured drink in this book to contain egg yolk.

AMARETTO

O F ALL THE LIQUEURS that rely on almonds for their principal flavouring, amaretto is the most famous. It has become widely associated in people's minds with one particular Italian brand, Disaronno Amaretto, made by a company called Illva, although there are other liqueurs that may properly be called amarettos. The famous amaretto comes in a rectangular bottle, with a label in the form of an old scroll and a disproportionately large, square screw-top. The flavour is not entirely derived from almonds but from the stones of apricots too. Resembling a kind of liquid marzipan, the taste is strong and sweet and is quite assertive even when mixed in a cocktail.

Legend has it that the recipe was given to an Italian painter, Bernardino Luini, in the 16th century by an innkeeper who was the model for the Virgin Mary in his wall-painting of the Nativity at Saronno. Whether or not there is much truth in the tale, the original domestic concoction was probably grape brandy in which apricot kernels – with their strongly almondy flavour – had been steeped.

HOW IT IS MADE
Almond extracts, along with apricot kernels and seeds, are steeped in brandy, and the resulting drink is sweetened with sugar syrup and coloured to a deep brown

DISARONNO
AMARETTO
The most famous brand of Italian amaretto

MIXING
Godmother: Mix Disaronno Amaretto with an equal measure of vodka in a tumbler full of ice.
Godfather (below): As above, but substitute Scotch for the vodka.

TASTES GOOD WITH
Just as a frangipane mixture, full of ground almonds, makes a good base for almost any fruit tart, so amaretto works well in the syrup for a fruit salad, or added to whipped cream or ice cream for most fruit-based desserts. It also marries deliciously with chocolate in super-rich *pot au chocolat*, and is excellent in a liqueur coffee, and perhaps with cognac too.

CASONI
AMARETTO
Amaretto's flavour is like marzipan in a bottle

OTHER NAMES
France: crème d'amandes

FLAVOURINGS
Almonds
Apricots

HOW TO SERVE
Although sweet, the flavour of Disaronno Amaretto is quite complex enough for it to be enjoyable on its own, but it works better chilled. Serving it *frappé* (poured over crushed ice) is highly refreshing.

ANIS

CONFUSION REIGNS as to the precise differences between anis and pastis, and indeed whether there are any meaningful differences at all. They are both flavoured with the berries of the aniseed plant, originally native to North Africa, and are popular all around the Mediterranean. They both turn cloudy when watered, and are both claimed as the respectable successor to the outlawed absinthe.

One august authority claims that pastis should be flavoured with liquorice rather than aniseed, although the two are very close in taste. Another claims that anis is simply one of the types of pastis. Still another claims that, whereas anis is a product of the maceration of aniseed or liquorice in spirit, pastis should properly be seen as a distillation from either of the two ingredients themselves.

They can't all be right of course, but for what it's worth, I incline to accept the last definition. For one thing, anis tends to be lower in alcohol than pastis – liqueur strength rather than spirit strength. The one thing we can be sure of

FLAVOURINGS
Anise berries (aniseed). Sometimes the seeds of star anise – an oriental shrub that bears a fruit in the shape of an eight-pointed star – may be used. The flavour is fairly similar, though by no means identical

HOW TO SERVE
The only true way to serve anis is to take it ice-cold in a little thick-bottomed tumbler. The addition of a small amount of water – usually about as much again – turns it milky but with a faint greenish tinge. It is considered a great appetite-whetter.

OTHER NAMES
France: Anise *Spain*: Anís

is that pastis is always French (the word is old southern French dialect), whereas anis – particularly with that spelling – can also be Spanish. In Spain, there are sweet and dry varieties, whereas French anise tends mainly to be dry.

Ever since the days of the medical school of Salerno, and probably earlier, extract of anis has been seen as a valuable weapon in the apothecary's armoury. It is thought to be especially good for ailments of the stomach.

ANISETTE
Anisette is quite definitely a liqueur. It is French, sweetened, and usually somewhat stronger than anis. The most famous brand is Marie Brizard, from the firm named after the Bordelaise who, in the mid-18th century, was given the recipe by a West Indian acquaintance.

ANIS
This liqueur is made in Spain as well as France

ANISETTE
The sweet liqueur form of anis, typified by this Marie Brizard anisette

AURUM

IF THE NAME of Argentarium evokes silver, that of Aurum hints at gold. One glance at its colour will explain why. Made in the Abruzzi mountains, on the Adriatic coast of Italy, Aurum is a brandy-based proprietary liqueur in which a mixture of orange peel and whole oranges is infused, and the lustrous golden intensity of its appearance enhanced by saffron. It is claimed that the basic formula is of great antiquity. Aurum was given its Latin name by the celebrated Italian writer Gabriele d'Annunzio. The name hints that it may at one time have contained particles of genuine gold, harking back to the alchemical origins of distillation, and it has logically been argued that Aurum was the true forerunner of Goldwasser.

HOW IT IS MADE
No mere industrial spirit is used in Aurum. The brandy in it is distilled by the makers from vintage Italian wines, and the distillate is cask-aged for around four years to take up wood colour. The oranges (and other citrus fruits) are infused separately in more brandy, and then the infusion is triple-distilled. This, and the first brandy, are then blended and allowed another period of oak maturation.

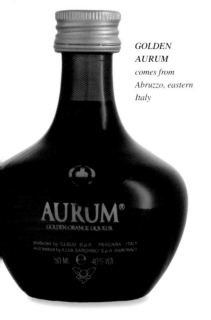

GOLDEN AURUM comes from Abruzzo, eastern Italy

ARGENTARIUM
One of a handful of liqueurs that are still produced by religious orders, Argentarium is made in a monastery in the Lazio region of Italy, north of Rome. It is based on grape brandy, flavoured with a collection of herbs that grow wild on the surrounding hillsides, some of which are gathered by the monks themselves. Most of it is consumed locally.

BENEDICTINE

"DEO OPTIMO MAXIMO" (Praise be to God, most good, most great), exclaimed the Benedictine monk, who formulated the liqueur that now bears his order's name, on first tasting the results. Or so the story goes. It was reputedly in 1510, so it isn't easy to verify. What is certain is that his monastery at Fécamp, in the Normandy region of northern France, produced this cognac-based herbal liqueur until the time of the French Revolution in 1789, when the monasteries were forcibly closed and production banned.

Bénédictine was officially extinct until the 1860s, when it was revived by a descendent of the monastery's lawyers, Alexandre Le Grand. On finding the secret recipe among a bundle of yellowing papers, he was inspired to build an extraordinary new distillery in the high Gothic style at Fécamp, and the now secularized liqueur – first christened Bénédictine by Le Grand – lived to fight another day.

Bénédictine is a bright golden potion of honeyed sweetness, containing a herbalist's pantheon of medicinal plants and spices. The exact formula is known only to three people at any given time, but it is thought to contain as many as 75 aromatizing ingredients.

HOW TO SERVE
It is imperative to serve a speciality product such as **Aurum** (below) by itself as a digestif. It should not be chilled but rather warmed in the hand like fine cognac, and served in the same sort of glass to appreciate its aromas.

Bénédictine should ideally be served straight in a large liqueur glass at the end of a meal, but its makers clearly have no qualms about its use as a mixing ingredient by those who find the sweetness of classic liqueurs too much to take *au naturel*.

BENEDICTINE One of the old monastic liqueurs

CHARTREUSE

U NLIKE BENEDICTINE, CHARTREUSE really is still made by monks – of the Carthusian order – at Voiron, near Grenoble, not far from the site of their monastery, La Grande Chartreuse. Expelled from France at the time of the French Revolution, the order was allowed back into the mother country after the defeat of Napoleon, only to be kicked out again in 1903. It was then that a second branch of the operation was founded at Tarragona, in eastern Spain, and it continued as Chartreuse's second address until 1991, long after the production was finally re-established in France in 1932.

The Carthusians are a silent order, which has no doubt helped to keep the recipe a secret; like its Norman counterpart, it is known only to a lucky trio. Proceeds from the worldwide sales of Chartreuse are ploughed back into the order's funds, from where it goes to pay for all kinds of charitable works.

There is a premium version of Chartreuse (the original recipe is said to date from 1605) called Elixir, which is sold in miniature bottles at a fearsome 71% ABV, but it is principally sold in two incarnations today, green (55%) and yellow (40%). The latter is a deep greenish-yellow hue, sweet, honeyed and slightly minty in flavour; while the green Chartreuse is a pale, leafy colour, has a less pungent herbal scent and is distinctly less viscous.

Additionally, the order produces a rare higher grade of each colour, labelled VEP, for *vieillissement exceptionnellement prolongé* (exceptionally long ageing).

GREEN CHARTREUSE
Intensely powerful and aromatic.

YELLOW CHARTREUSE
Sweeter than green Chartreuse and of normal spirit strength.

MIXING

Alaska: Shake three-quarters gin to one-quarter yellow Chartreuse with ice and strain into a cocktail glass.

Bijou: Stir equal measures of Plymouth gin, green Chartreuse and sweet red vermouth with ice and a dash of orange bitters in a mixing jug. Strain into a cocktail glass. Add a cherry and a twist of lemon.

HOW IT IS MADE

By varying processes of distillation, infusion and maceration, over 130 herbs and plants are used to flavour a base of grape brandy. They were all once gathered from the mountains surrounding the monastery, but some are now imported from Italy and Switzerland. It is aged in casks for up to five years, except for the VEP, which receives twice that long.

TASTES GOOD WITH

The French sometimes fortify their hot chocolate with a reviving splash of the green Chartreuse. The yellow is thought more suitable for coffee.

HOW TO SERVE

If you find Chartreuse overwhelming on its own, do as the French do and serve it mixed as a long drink with tonic or soda and plenty of ice.

ELIXIR VEGETAL

This is the original Carthusian elixir, bottled at very high strength

COINTREAU

ONE OF THE MOST POPULAR branded liqueurs of all, Cointreau is, properly speaking, a variety of Curaçao. This means it is a brandy-based spirit that has been flavoured with the peel of bitter oranges. When it was launched in 1849 by the Cointreau brothers, Edouard and Adolphe, it was sold under the brand name Triple Sec White Curaçao, but so many other proprietary Curaçaos began to be sold as Triple Sec that the family decided to give it their own name instead.

The centre of operations, as well as a distillery, are located in Angers, in the Loire valley, but it is also made in the Americas. A variety of different bottlings is made at different strengths, including a cream version, but the best-loved Cointreau is the one that comes in a square dark-brown bottle at 40% ABV.

COINTREAU
One of the best-loved liqueurs of them all

Despite its spirit strength, Cointreau tastes deliciously innocuous. It is sugar-sweet and colourless, but has a powerful fume of fresh oranges, with an underlying vaguely herbal note too. The oranges used in it are a clever blend of bitter green Seville-style varieties from the Caribbean (the island of Curaçao itself is close to Venezuela) and sweeter types from the south of France.

HOW IT IS MADE

Cointreau is a double distillation of grape brandy, infused with orange peel, sweetened and further aromatized with other secret plant ingredients.

TASTES GOOD WITH

If the balance of other seasonings is right, it works admirably in the orange sauce classically served with duck. It is excellent in a range of desserts, particularly so in rich chocolate mousse.

HOW TO SERVE

Absolutely everybody's favourite way of serving Cointreau is either on the rocks or *frappé*, depending on whether you like your ice in chunks or crystals. The cold then mitigates some of the sweetness of the liqueur, while the pure citrus flavour is exquisitely refreshing.

CREAM LIQUEURS

CREAM LIQUEURS ARE an ever-expanding category in the contemporary market. Whether the makers acknowledge it or not, cream liqueurs all owe something of their inspiration and appeal to the archetypal brand, Bailey's Irish Cream. The manufacturers tend to push them particularly at Christmas, where they occupy a niche as the soft option for those who feel they need a spoonful of sugar and a dollop of cream to help the alcohol go down.

Bailey's itself is a blend of Irish whiskey and cream flavoured with coffee. It became suddenly chic in the 1970s, but was quickly saddled with the image of the kind of soft, svelte drink that unscrupulous boys plied unsuspecting girls with in nightclubs. Since then, cream liqueurs have gone on multiplying.

Coffee and chocolate flavourings are particularly common, and indeed some cream liqueurs are made by confectionery companies, such as Cadbury's and Terry's. Then again, some of the more reputable liqueur-makers have produced cream versions of their own top products (for example, Crème de Grand Marnier) in order to grab a share of this evidently lucrative market.

I have to say I decline to take these products seriously. At best, they are substitutes for real cream cocktails, but they are always sweeter and less powerful than the genuine home-made article, and many of them contain an artificial stabilizer to stop the cream from separating. In any case, why rely on somebody else's formula when you can follow your own specifications? Once you have made your own brandy Alexanders, you won't want chocolate cream liqueur.

The extreme was reached when another Irish drinks company of some repute launched a product called Sheridan's in the early 1990s. It came in a bifurcated bottle with two tops, one half filled with a black liquid that was coffee-flavoured Irish whiskey, the other with thick white cream. The idea was that you poured first from one side of the bottle and then from the other – remembering to screw the top back on to the first half – in order to simulate the appearance of a liqueur coffee. (Little matter that Irish coffee is supposed to be served hot.) I am told the product has not so far proved conspicuously successful, perhaps because it involves such a fandango when it comes to serving it in bars.

BAILEY'S
The daddy
of all cream
liqueurs

CADBURY'S
CREAM
LIQUEUR
A ready-made
brandy
Alexander at
a pinch

CREME LIQUEURS

A WHOLE RANGE OF liqueurs that use the prefix "*crème de*" may be bracketed together here. They are nothing at all to do with cream liqueurs, despite the terminology. They nearly always consist of one dominant flavour indicated in the name, often but not always a fruit, and are usually appropriately coloured. In the main, they are bottled at 25–30% ABV, and may be considered among the more useful building-blocks of the cocktail-mixer's repertoire.

Originally, the term "crème" was used to indicate that these were sweetened liqueurs, as distinct from dry spirits such as cognac or calvados. They were mainly French in origin – the Marie Brizard

FRAISE DES BOIS
This version of crème de fraise uses wild strawberries

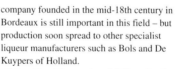

MIXING

The use of these liqueurs in cocktail-making is as limitless as the flavours themselves. Sometimes they work well with each other (try brown cacao and fraise, or banane and noyau, for example) but they will need a very dry base to counteract the cumulative impact of the sweetness. They all work well in cream cocktails, but one flavour is usually quite sufficient. Let your imagination off the leash.

Fruit Daiquiri: The original Daiquiri recipe of white rum shaken with the juice of half a lemon and a pinch of sugar can be adapted by adding a measure of any of the fruit liqueurs to it (and perhaps some puréed fruit as well), but you may then want to leave out the sugar.

Stinger: The adaptable Stinger is simply a half-and-half mixture of any spirit with white crème de menthe, shaken with ice and served over smashed ice in a cocktail glass. The prototype version is probably with cognac.

Alexander: The recipe for this given in the brandy chapter can be adapted with other spirits too – gin is particularly successful – but it is always the brown crème de cacao that must be used.

FLAVOURINGS

The flavours of such liqueurs are numerous, and the following list does not pretend to be exhaustive. The French names are given first, since that is how they are labelled.

Most commonly seen are: crème de banane (banana), cacao (cocoa or chocolate – comes in dark brown and white versions), cassis (blackcurrant), fraise (strawberry), framboise (raspberry) and menthe (mint – comes in bright green and white versions).

company founded in the mid-18th century in Bordeaux is still important in this field – but production soon spread to other specialist liqueur manufacturers such as Bols and De Kuypers of Holland.

Before the widespread availability of such products, the sweetening element in a cocktail used to be sugar, pure and simple, or perhaps a sugar syrup. The crème liqueurs had the advantage of not only providing that sweetness, but also of introducing another flavour into the drinks they were added to. They have since become indispensable in extending the horizons of both the professional and amateur bartender, and are usually a recommended purchase in any guide giving advice on starting your own cocktail bar at home.

Most of these products will be based on a neutral-tasting, un-aged grape brandy, with the various flavouring ingredients either infused or

CRÈME DE FRAISE

A basic strawberry liqueur from Marie Brizard of Bordeaux.

HOW TO SERVE

If these drinks are to be taken as befitted their original purpose, as pleasant aids to digestion at the end of a grand dinner, they are best served *frappé* – i.e. poured over shaved ice – rather than neat. In that way, some of their sugary sweetness is mitigated.

MIXING

Oracabessa: Shake a measure of dark rum with a measure of crème de banane and the juice of half a lemon with ice and strain into a tall glass. Float some thin slices of banana on the surface of the drink and top it up with sparkling lemonade. Garnish lavishly with fruits.

Silver Jubilee: Shake equal measures of gin, crème de banane and cream with ice and strain into a cocktail glass.

Blackout (from Lucius Beebe's *Stork Club Bar Book*): Shake a measure and three-quarters of gin and three-quarters of a measure of crème de mûre with the juice of half a lime and plenty of ice and strain into a cocktail glass.

Stratosphere: A few dashes of crème de violette are added to a glass of champagne until a mauve colour is obtained. The scent-edness is then enhanced by adding a whole clove to the glass. (An American violet liqueur, Crème Yvette, was at one time the only correct product to use in this very ladylike aperitif.)

English Rose: Shake a measure and a half of London gin with three-quarters of a measure of crème de roses, the juice of half a lemon, half a teaspoon of caster sugar and half an egg-white, with ice, and strain into a wine glass. (Alternatively, you can make this in an electric blender for that extra frothiness.)

CRÈME DE CACAO

Cacao – cocoa or chocolate – is available in two versions, dark and white, to please the chocoholics.

macerated in the spirit rather than being subject to distillation themselves. The difference, essentially, between infusion and maceration is that the former involves some gentle heating action, while the latter is just a cold soaking of the flavouring element in the spirit until it has been broken down and has imparted its aromatic compounds. Maceration is obviously a considerably slower process than infusion. In both cases, the ingredient has to be rendered water-soluble, in the case of maceration particularly so.

Since these are intended to be rich but simple products, with one overriding flavour, the crème liqueurs are not generally treated to

CREME DE BANANE
Banana is one of the more versatile flavours

ageing in wood. Oak maturation would interfere anyway with the often bold primary colours of the drinks, as well as obscuring the tastes.

They are more often than not sold in 50cl bottles. You will find as you use them that a certain amount of powdery sugar deposit builds up underneath the screw tops; simply give them a good wipe down every now and then.

HOW THEY ARE MADE

After the infusion or maceration, during which take-up of flavour is obtained, the aromatized spirit may then have to be strained to remove any solid particles caused by making the

CREME DE CASSIS
Cassis is also a speciality of Burgundy

MIXING

Kir: The world-famous aperitif created in Burgundy, and originally named after a mayor of Dijon, consists of a glass of light, dry, acidic white wine with a teaspoon or two (depending on taste) of crème de cassis. The classic wine to use is a Bourgogne Aligoté of the most recent vintage, but any fairly neutral-tasting but *sharp* white wine will do. Add the cassis to a glass of non-vintage Brut champagne and the drink becomes a **Kir Royale** (below).

CRÈME DE FRAMBOISE

Red fruit liqueurs, such as framboise, are very good if added by the teaspoon to a glass of basic champagne or sparkling wine.

FLAVOURINGS

More obscure flavours include: crème d'ananas (pineapple), café (coffee), mandarine (tangerine), mûre (blackberry), myrtille (bilberry), noyau (almond), roses (rose-petal), thé (tea), vanille (vanilla), violette (violet)

flavouring agent water-soluble. It is then sweetened, usually by means of the addition of sugar solution, or sometimes with a sugar and glucose mix. Unless it is possible to achieve a striking colour naturally (which is in fact quite rare), the colour is then created by the addition of vegetable-based colouring matter such as carotene or beetroot. Red colourings are often created by adding cochineal. These colourings do not affect the flavour. The liqueur is then subjected to a heavy filtration to ensure a bright, crystal-clear product. It is transferred into neutral, stainless steel tanks to await bottling.

CREME DE MURE

A richly flavoured blackberry liqueur.

CREME DE MENTHE

Green crème de menthe is sweet and spearminty

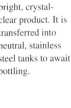

CREME DE PECHE

Peach is an unusual flavour to find in a crème liqueur.

MIXING

Grasshopper: Shake equal measures of green crème de menthe, white crème de cacao and thick cream with ice and strain into a cocktail glass.

TASTES GOOD WITH

The most obvious way to use these liqueurs is as boosting ingredients in desserts that are themselves flavoured with the same principal ingredient, especially in the case of the fruit ones. Enliven your strawberry mousse with crème de fraise, your blackberry cheesecake with crème de mûre, and so forth. (On the other hand, a richly gooey *pot au chocolat* can get along quite well without crème de cacao if you have used top-quality chocolate.) The flowery crème liqueurs make exotic additions to the syrup for a simple fruit salad.

BRAMBLE

Fruit liqueurs are also made in the UK.

CURACAO

First invented by the Dutch, Curaçao was a white rum-based liqueur flavoured with the peel of bitter green oranges found by the settlers on the Caribbean island of the same name, not far off the coast of Venezuela. Desipte its geographically specific name, the liqueur has never been subject to anything like appellation regulations. It is made by many different companies in a number of countries, where brandy is used as the starter spirit.

A variant name in common use was Triple Sec,

ORANGE
CURACAO
All Curaçao is
flavoured with
bitter oranges

MIXING

Olympic: Shake equal measures of cognac, orange Curaçao and freshly squeezed orange juice with ice and strain into a cocktail glass. Decorate with a twist of orange peel.

Oasis: Pour a double measure of gin over ice-cubes in a tall glass. Add half a measure of blue Curaçao. Top up with tonic water and stir well. Garnish with a slice of lemon and sprig of mint.

the most famous example being Cointreau, although confusingly Curaçao is not at all *sec* but always sweet. The bitterness of the oranges – which are green simply because they are not quite ripe, not because they are some notably exotic variety – balances the sweetness, however, to the extent that drinkers may have been prepared to consider it dry.

Curaçao comes in a range of colours in addition to the clear version. The orange Curaçao, especially from companies like Bols, is often particularly bitter, its colour a deep, burnished tawny orange. Curaçao also comes in bright blue, dark green, red and yellow versions for novelty value, but the flavour is always of orange. The strength is generally somewhere between 25–30% ABV.

The name of the island is not, of course, Dutch but Portuguese, after the original discoverers. More perplexity is occasioned over the correct way to pronounce "Curaçao" than over the name of any other liqueur. It should properly be "curashow" (to rhyme with "miaow"), but it is corrupted by English speakers into something like "cura-say-oh".

FLAVOURING
Bitter oranges

HOW TO SERVE
The bitterness of the fruit mixes well with other bitter flavours, so orange Curaçao and tonic makes a particularly appetizing long drink. Alternatively, use a not-too-sweet sparkling lemonade, if you can find one. It also goes well in equal measures with either dry or sweet vermouth. Curaçao is not especially pleasant taken neat.

OTHER NAMES

Triple Sec (only for the colourless version, strictly speaking)

HOW IT IS MADE

The blossom and dried peel of wild oranges are steeped in grape brandy or even neutral spirit; the resulting infusion is then sweetened, clarified and coloured according to style.

CURACAO

Blue Curaçao enjoyed something of a vogue in the cocktail renaissance of the early 1980s, though its colour makes it hard to mix with.

TRIPLE SEC
The term tends to be used for the colourless Curaçao

MIXING

Whip: Shake equal measures of cognac, dry vermouth and white Curaçao with a dash of pastis (e.g. Pernod) and plenty of ice and strain into a cocktail glass. (It should be noted that this lethal cocktail contains no non-alcoholic ingredient. Caution is advised.)
Rite of Spring (below): Mix a double measure of vodka and a measure of green Curaçao with ice in a mixing-jug. Decant into a tall glass and top up with clear lemonade. Dangle a long twist of lemon peel in the drink.

TASTES GOOD WITH

Indispensable in the classic crêpe Suzette. In the recipe given by the great French chef Auguste Escoffier, the pancake batter is flavoured with tangerine juice and Curaçao and the cooked crêpe sauced with butter, sugar and tangerine zests. These days, it is generally Cointreau that is used in this ever-popular dessert.

CUARANTA Y TRES

Cuaranta is a sweet liqueur made in the Cartagena region of eastern Spain, based on a recipe that supposedly dates from classical times when the Phoenicians founded Carthage, in North Africa, and introduced viticulture. It is concocted from a brandy base with infusions of herbs, but has a noticeably predominant flavour of vanilla, which rather torpedoes the Carthaginian theory since vanilla was only discovered in the 16th century by Spanish explorers in Mexico. Not much seen outside its region of production, it is nonetheless held in high regard locally.

DRAMBUIE

D RAMBUIE IS SCOTLAND'S (and, for that matter, Britain's) pre-eminent contribution to the world's classic liqueurs. Hugely popular in the United States, it is a unique and inimitable concoction of Scotch whisky, heather honey and herbs. The story goes that the recipe was given as a reward to one Captain Mackinnon in 1745, after the defeat at Culloden by Charles Edward Stuart – or Bonnie Prince Charlie, as the pretender to the English throne has ever since been better known. The lad that was born to be king was of course ferried to Skye, and from thence to France, away from the clutches of the nefarious English. Captain Mackinnon was his protector.

That story has inevitably since been debunked by meticulous historians. The truth is almost certainly the other way round. It was the Mackinnons who revived the spirits of the fugitive Prince with their own Scotch-based home concoction, which was very much a typical blend of the period, an unrefined spirit disguised with sweet and herbal additives.

Today, the spirit is anything but unrefined, being a mixture of fine malt and straight grain whiskies, to which the flavourings are added. The Mackinnon family still makes it, though near Edinburgh now rather than on Skye. They registered its name (from the Gaelic *an dram buidheach*, "the drink that satisfies") in 1892. It has been in private production since the time of the Bonnie Prince, but was only launched commercially in 1906 – with spectacular success.

TASTES GOOD WITH
A hunk of rich Dundee cake doused in Drambuie is a sumptuous cold-weather treat.

DRAMBUIE
Perhaps
Britain's
greatest
contribution to
the liqueur
world

CYNAR
Cynar is a liqueur for the very brave. It is a soupy, dark-brown potion made in Italy, which is flavoured with artichoke hearts (its name derives from the Latin for artichoke, *cynarum*). All of the savoury bitterness of the globe artichoke, boldly illustrated on its label, is in it, and if that sounds like fun, go ahead and try it. I once swallowed a modest measure of it in a little backstreet bar in Venice, and of all my shimmering memories of the watery city, Cynar is not, I have to say, the loveliest.

HOW TO SERVE
Serve Drambuie as it comes, over ice, or with an equal measure of Scotch as a **Rusty Nail**.

GALLIANO

ANOTHER OF ITALY'S liqueur specialities, golden-yellow Galliano is chiefly known on the international cocktail scene for its matchless role of livening up a vodka-and-orange in the Harvey Wallbanger cocktail, and for its tall conical bottle. It was invented by one Arturo Vaccari, a Tuscan distiller who named his new creation in honour of an Italian soldier, Major Giuseppe Galliano. In 1895 Galliano held out under siege at Enda Jesus in Ethiopia for 44 days against the vastly superior Abyssinian forces under the command of Haile Selassie's nephew.

The formula, as we are accustomed to hear in the world of liqueurs, is a jealously guarded secret, but it is said to be based on up to 80 herbs, roots,

MIXING
Harvey Wallbanger:
Pour a generous measure of vodka over ice in a highball glass, top up with fresh orange juice and float a measure of Galliano on top.

GALLIANO
This Italian classic comes in a distinctive conical bottle

MIXING
Milano: Shake equal measures of gin and Galliano with the juice of half a lemon and ice, and strain into a cocktail glass.

berries and flowers from the alpine slopes to the north of Italy. Among its flavours is a strong presence of anise or liquorice, and there is a pronounced scent of vanilla. It is also naturally very sweet. Despite the complexity of its tastes, it is a valuable addition to the bartender's battery.

HOW IT IS MADE
The various flavouring ingredients are steeped in a mixture of neutral spirit and water and then distilled; the resulting potion is then blended with refined spirits. It is bottled at 35% ABV.

FIOR D'ALPI
No liqueur makes more of a show of itself than Fior d'Alpi. Made in northern Italy, its name means "Alpine flowers", and those – along with a fistful of wild herbs – are its principal flavourings. It is a delicate primrose hue and comes in a tall narrow bottle. What catches the eye in the shop window, though, is the gnarled little tree that sits inside every bottle. If you leave the bottle undisturbed for a while, the sugar in the drink will form a crystallized frosting on the twigs that can look touchingly Christmassy. That, coupled with the agreeable sweetness of the liqueur itself, is what keeps it popular – at least in Italy. Similar products are sold as Millefiori and – what else? – Edelweiss.

GLAYVA

Like Drambuie, Glayva is a Scotch whisky-based liqueur made near Edinburgh, but it is of much more recent provenance. The drink was first formulated just after the Second World War. Its aromatizers are quite similar to those of Drambuie, although its flavour is intriguingly different. Heather honey and various herbs are used, and so is a quantity of orange peel, resulting in a noticeably fruitier attack on the palate.

The noble Scot commemorated in the case of Glayva is one Master Borthwick, the phlegmatic 16-year-old credited with carrying Robert the Bruce's heart back to Scotland after the King's defeat at the hands of the Saracens. Not content

GLAYVA

The original formula for Glayva is much older than the product itself

MIXING

Saracen: Shake a measure of Scotch whisky, half a measure each of Glayva and dry sherry and a dash of orange bitters with ice. Pour into a tumbler and add a splash of soda. Decorate with a piece of orange rind.

with rescuing the regal heart, the indomitable lad cut off the head of a Saracen chieftain he had killed, impaled it on a spear, and brought that back too just to keep his spirits up. All of those pubs named the Saracen's Head recall the event, as did the Moorish head once depicted on the Glayva label.

TASTES GOOD WITH

Like the other Scotch-based liqueurs, Glayva is particularly good added to an ice cream, perhaps one flavoured with honey and/or orange, like the drink itself.

FLAVOURINGS

Heather honey
Orange peel
Various herbs

HOW TO SERVE

Glayva should be served just as it is, in a standard whisky tumbler. Its fruitiness makes it slightly better for chilling than Drambuie, but don't overdo it.

GOLDWASSER

Goldwasser, or Danziger Goldwasser to give it its archetypal name, recalls the great Catalan physician Arnaldo de Villanova who, in the 13th century, is reputed to have cured the Pope of a dangerous illness by giving him a herbal elixir containing specks of gold. In so doing, he also saved his own skin from the Inquisition. Since the search for the elixir of life was intimately bound up with alchemy's project of turning base metals into gold, it was only natural that gold itself should be seen as being beneficial to health.

FLAVOURINGS
Aniseed
Caraway seeds
Citrus fruits

GOLDWASSER
All Goldwasser came originally from Gdansk, like this one

HOW TO SERVE
The prettiness can be enhanced by serving Goldwasser in a little cut-crystal liqueur glass.

OTHER NAMES
France: Liqueur d'Or or eau d'or

MIXING
Generally, there is no point in mixing Goldwasser because you then bury the gold flakes. However, I am indebted to Lucius Beebe's 1946 *Stork Club Bar Book* for the following recipe for a layered cocktail (to be used only if you are sure your eggs are free of salmonella):

Golden Slipper: A measure of yellow Chartreuse is poured into a *copita* or sherry glass. A separated egg yolk is then dropped whole on to the surface of it, and a measure of Goldwasser carefully poured on top of that. (I haven't tried this. I suspect it may look rather prettier than it tastes.)

The commercial prototype of the drink was first made in the Baltic port city of Danzig (now Gdansk in Poland). Based on the drink kümmel, it is flavoured with both aniseed and caraway seeds and is colourless, less sweet than many liqueurs, and it really does have a shower of real golden particles added to it, in memory of Arnaldo. When the bottle was poured, the gold specks flurried up to general approbation like the flakes in a snowstorm toy. (There was also for a time a silver version, Silberwasser.) Liqueur d'Or was a now-extinct French version of the same thing. Some brands also had a citric fruit flavour – sometimes lemon, sometimes orange.

TASTES GOOD WITH
Soufflé Rothschild is a very classical, hot dessert soufflé made from crème patissière and crystallized fruits that have been macerated in Danziger Goldwasser. It is served in individual soufflé dishes surrounded by strawberries.

GRAND MARNIER

GRAND MARNIER IS ONE of the best-loved of all the world's orange-flavoured liqueurs. The original product is a little younger than Cointreau, its big French rival, but the style is quite different. In the sense that the oranges used in it are bitter varieties from the Caribbean, it may be classed as another type of Curaçao, but it is a distinctly finer product than most ordinary Curaçao.

The house that owns it was founded in 1827 by a family called Lapostolle. Louis-Alexandre Marnier later married into the family business and it was he who, in 1880, first conceived the liqueur that bears his name. Encountering the bitter oranges of Haiti on a grand tour, he hit upon the idea of blending their flavour with that of finest cognac, and then giving it a period of barrel-ageing that basic Curaçao never receives.

Today, the production of the liqueur is split between two centres, one at Château de

GRAND MARNIER
Fully the equal of the higher grades of cognac

Bourg in the Cognac region, the other at Neauphle-le-Château, near Paris. The initial blending is carried out at the former site, the ageing at the latter. What results is a highly refined, mellow full-strength spirit that has a warm amber colour and an intense, festive scent of ripe oranges. It is sweet, but the distinction of the Fine Champagne cognac on which it is based prevents it from being in any way cloying when served straight.

The Marnier-Lapostolle company also decided to try cashing in on the mania for cream liqueurs that has arisen in the last 20 years or so by launching a Crème de Grand Marnier at much lower strength, which I can't find it in my heart to recommend.

HOW IT IS MADE

The juice of Caribbean oranges is blended with top-quality cognac. After full amalgamation of the flavours, it is then re-distilled, sweetened and given a period of cask-ageing.

TASTES GOOD WITH

It is the classic ingredient in duck à l'orange, and may also be used in a whole range of desserts, particularly flamed crêpes and anything made with strong chocolate.

FLAVOURING
Oranges

HOW TO SERVE
As reverently as best cognac.

KAHLUA

KAHLÚA IS THE only liqueur of any note to
have been conceived in Mexico. It is a
dark brown coffee-flavoured essence packaged
in a round-shouldered, opaque bottle with a
colourful label. Although some of it is still
made in Mexico using home-grown coffee
beans, it is also made under licence in Europe
by the Danish company Peter Heering. It is
inevitably often compared to the other, more
famous coffee liqueur, Tia Maria, but it is
slightly thicker in texture and somewhat less
sweet than its Jamaican counterpart.

FLAVOURING
Coffee

KAHLUA
A liqueur with the
stimulant properties
of strong coffee

TASTES GOOD WITH

To enhance the flavour of a coffee dessert such
as a soufflé or ice cream, Kahlúa somehow
gives a smoother result than the more
commonly used Tia Maria.

MIXING

Black Russian: Certain
aficionados insist on
Kahlúa rather than Tia
Maria with the vodka.
Either way, it is as well
not to adulterate the
drink with cola.
Alexander the Great:
Shake a measure-and-a-
half of vodka with half
a measure each of
Kahlúa, crème de cacao
and thick cream and
plenty of ice. Strain into
a cocktail glass. (This
drink is reputed to have
been invented by the
great Nelson Eddy.)

IZARRA

Izarra is a sort of Basque version of
Chartreuse, made in Bayonne in southwest
France. It is flatteringly imitative to the
extent that it comes in two colours – yellow
and green – both full of aromatic herbs gathered wild in the Pyrenees. Green Izarra is
higher in alcoholic strength. (It is in fact, at
55%, exactly the same strength as green
Chartreuse, but doesn't really have the same
complexity of flavour.) The name means
"star" in the local dialect. Izarra is based on
armagnac, which is given a redistillation
with the aromatizing ingredients, followed
by a period of cask-ageing. Not surprisingly,
it is not much seen outside its native region.

KUMMEL

KUMMEL IS ONE of the more ancient liqueurs. All we know is that it originated somewhere in northern Europe, although we do not know exactly where. The best guess is Holland, but the Germans have a respectable enough claim on the patent as well (its name is, of course, German). Certainly, it was being made in Holland in the 1500s, and it very much fits the image of such drinks of the time, in that it would have been an unrefined grain spirit masked by an aromatic ingredient.

The ingredient in this case is caraway seeds. A certain amount of needless confusion is created by the fact that the name looks as though it has something to do with the more pungent cumin. This is only because, in certain European languages, caraway is often referred to as a sort of cumin. They have nothing to do with each other, the misleading nomenclature only arising because the seeds are supposed to look vaguely similar.

MIXING
Tovarich: Shake a measure and a half of vodka, a measure of kümmel and the juice of half a lime with ice, and strain into a cocktail glass.

FLAVOURING
Caraway seeds

A key episode in kümmel's history occurred at the end of the 17th century, during Peter the Great's sojourn in Holland. He took the formula for the drink, to which he had grown rather partial, back to Russia with him, and kümmel came to be thought of as a Russian product, or at least as a Baltic one. The Baltic port of Riga, now capital of Latvia, was its chief centre of production throughout the 19th century, and some was also made in Danzig (now Gdansk), where they eventually came to add flecks of gold to it and call it Goldwasser.

Versions of kümmel are today made not just in Latvia but also in Poland, Germany, Holland, Denmark and even the United States. Not the least valued property of caraway, valued since Egyptian times, is its ability to counteract flatulence, which is why it was one of the traditional ingredients of gripe water for babies.

HOW IT IS MADE
The base is a pure grain distillate, effectively a type of vodka, in which the seeds are infused. Most brands are fairly heavily sweetened but they are always left colourless.

TASTES GOOD WITH
Try adding it to the mixture for old English seed cake, which is made with caraway seeds.

KUMMEL
Wolfschmidt is the leading brand of kümmel

39%vol KUMMEL 50cl
WOLFSCHMIDT

HOW TO SERVE
Kümmel is nearly always served on the rocks in its countries of origin.

LIQUEUR BRANDIES

S OME FRUIT LIQUEURS have traditionally been referred to as "brandies", even though they are properly nothing of the sort in the sense that we now understand that term. There are essentially three fruit brandies – cherry, apricot and peach – and, although they are occasionally known by other names, it is as cherry brandy, etc. that drinkers know them best.

Strictly speaking, these products belong to the same large category as those liqueurs prefixed with the phrase "crème de", in that they are sweetened, coloured drinks, based on simple grape brandy that has been flavoured with the relevant fruits, as opposed to being

FLAVOURINGS
Apricots
Cherries
Peaches

CHERRY BRANDY
Indispensable in the making of a Singapore Sling

OTHER NAMES
France: Apricot brandy is sometimes known as Apry or Abricotine.
Liqueur brandies may eventually come to be known as apricot liqueur, etc. if the term "brandy" is enforced for grape distillates only. (The alternatives could well be crème d'abricot, de cerise and de pêche.)

MIXING
Paradise: Shake a measure of gin with half a measure each of apricot brandy and fresh orange juice and ice, and strain into a flared wine glass.

HOW TO SERVE
The best of these liqueur brandies make wonderful digestifs served in small quantities, provided they are not the very sweetest styles.

primary distillates of those fruits themselves. The maceration of the fruit usually includes the stones or pips as well, for the bitter flavour they impart and – in the case of apricot kernels especially – the distinctive flavour of almond.

Of the three, the apricot variant has probably travelled the furthest. There are true apricot distillates made in eastern Europe, of which the Hungarian Barak Pálinka is the most renowned, but they are dry like the fruit brandies of France. Good examples of sweet apricot liqueurs are Bols Apricot Brandy, Cusenier and Apry made by the Marie Brizard company.

Cherry brandy is one of the few liqueurs that may just have been invented by the English, the role of creator being claimed by one Thomas Grant of Kent. The original version was made with black morellos, although other cherry varieties may be used in modern products, depending on what is locally available. English

MIXING

Angel Face: Shake equal measures of gin, apricot brandy and calvados with ice and strain into a cocktail glass.

Singapore Sling: Shake a measure of gin, a measure of cherry brandy and the juice of half a lemon with ice and a pinch of caster sugar. Strain into a tall glass and top with soda. (Some like to put in a splash of Cointreau too, but that may be over-egging the pudding.)

Pick-Me-Up: Mix a measure each of dry French vermouth and cherry brandy with a couple of dashes of gin and a shovelful of ice in a tumbler and knock back. (This is but one of the many recipes for pick-me-ups. As with all of them, it is intended to be drunk PDQ or, as Harry Craddock – Cocktail King of the Savoy Hotel in the 1920s – used to put it, "while it's laughing at you".)

Wally (from the *Stork Club Bar Book*): Shake equal measures of calvados (or apple-jack), peach brandy and fresh lime juice with ice, and strain into a cocktail glass.

cherry brandy contributed to the downfall of the dissolute King George IV, who consumed it in ruinous quantities, perhaps to get over the memory of his doomed affair with Mrs Fitzherbert in Brighton.

Among the more famous cherry liqueur brands are Cherry Heering, now properly known as Peter Heering Cherry Liqueur, which was first formulated in the mid-19th century by a Danish distiller of that name. The Heering company grows its own cherries to make this product, which is cask-aged. Others include Cherry Rocher, de Kuyper, Garnier, and Bols, and there are brands produced in Germany and Switzerland.

Peach brandy is the one least frequently seen, its most famous manifestation probably being the one marketed by Bols.

HOW THEY ARE MADE

The pressed juice and stones of the respective fruits are generally mixed with a neutral grape spirit (more rarely a grain spirit), sweetened with sugar syrup and macerated until take-up of flavour is complete. If the fruit juice itself has fairly high natural sweetness, correspondingly less syrup will be added. In some cases, the liqueurs may be treated to a period of cask-ageing, followed by adjustment of the colour with vegetable dyes.

TASTES GOOD WITH

They all work well in fruit-based desserts that use the same fruits, for example hot soufflés, tarts and charlottes.

APRICOT BRANDY
Cusenier's liqueurs all come in these distinctive bottles

HEERING
Named after a Danish distiller in the last century.

MALIBU

WITH THE GROWTH of tourism in the Caribbean islands, it was only a matter of time before liqueurs flavoured with coconut began to make their presence felt on the international market. Of these, the most famous is Malibu. Presented in an opaque white bottle, with a depiction of a tropical sunset on the front, it is a relatively low-strength blend of rectified Caribbean white rum with coconut extracts. The flavour is pleasingly not too sweet. Malibu was a better product than most of the range of liqueur concoctions with totally tropical names that bombarded the market during the cocktail renaissance of the early 1980s.

Another reasonably good product was Batida de Coco, a coconut-flavoured neutral spirit made in Brazil that was also exported in quantity to the holiday islands of the Caribbean. Cocoribe was similar.

They are all colourless products, with an alcohol level slightly higher than that of fortified wine. Since the success of these proprietary products, some of the famous Dutch and French liqueur manufacturers have got in on the act and also marketed variants of crème de coco.

HOW TO SERVE
These drinks are not great on their own, but make excellent mixes with ice and fruit juices, which is how they were intended to be served in the first place.

MALIBU
Perhaps the best
of the coconut
liqueurs

MIXING
Pina Colada: A sort of cheat's version can be made using Malibu instead of real coconut milk. Mix in equal measures with white rum and plenty of ice. Top up with pineapple juice.

Batida Banana: Mix equal measures of Batida de Coco with crème de banane and several ice-cubes in a tall glass. Top up with whole milk. (This is a dangerously moreish drink, effectively little more than a grown-up milkshake.)

HOW THEY ARE MADE
Most of the coconut liqueurs are based on ultra-refined white rum, although one or two are made with a neutral grain alcohol. The dried pulp and milk of the coconut are used to flavour the spirit, which is then sweetened and filtered.

TASTES GOOD WITH
A splash of coconut liqueur may productively be added to the sauces in Cajun or Far Eastern dishes, particularly those of Thai or Indonesian cuisine where coconut itself figures strongly. Otherwise, it is splendid as a flavouring in a richly creamy ice cream.

BATIDA DE COCO
Brazil's contribution to the coconut collection.

MANDARINE NAPOLEON

MANDARINE IS ANOTHER TYPE of Curaçao, this time made with the skins of tangerines as opposed to bitter Caribbean oranges. By far the most famous brand is Mandarine Napoléon, the origins of which really do derive from the drinking preferences of the Emperor Napoleon I. The key figure in its history is a French chemist, one Antoine-François de Fourcroy, who rose to prominence in France as a key figure in public administration after the Revolution.

Following the demise of the Jacobin regime, de Fourcroy found favour with Napoleon Bonaparte to the extent that he was made a member of his Imperial State Council. When the tangerine first arrived in Europe from China (hence its synonym, mandarine) at the end of the 18th century, there was something of a craze for it. The fashion was to steep the peel in cognac after eating the fruit, and Antoine-François records in his diary that many was the night he was called on to share in the Emperor's indulgence.

Mandarine Napoléon was launched in 1892 by a Belgian distiller, Louis Schmidt, who stumbled on the recipe in de Fourcroy's correspondence while pursuing some chemical

MANDARINE NAPOLEON
A French invention now made in Belgium

HOW TO SERVE
Despite its sweetness, it does work well as an after-dinner drink taken straight or *frappé* in a traditional brandy balloon.

FLAVOURING
Tangerines

researches. It was only after the Second World War, when the distillery was relocated from Belgium to France, that the Fourcroy family once again became involved, eventually taking on the worldwide distribution of Schmidt's liqueur. As it became ever more successful, they moved the production back to Brussels, where it remains.

The tangerines used in Mandarine come exclusively from Sicily. Other companies make versions of tangerine liqueurs – the Italians themselves of course make one from their Sicilian crop – but Mandarine Napoléon remains justifiably the pre-eminent example, a thoroughly individual product that has deservedly won international awards.

HOW IT IS MADE
For Mandarine Napoléon, tangerine skins are steeped in cognac and other French brandies. The spirit is then re-distilled, sweetened, coloured with carotene to a vivid yellowy-orange and matured for several months. It is bottled at 38% ABV.

TASTES GOOD WITH
Add it to tangerine-flavoured mousses or use it as the fuel to flame sweet pancakes.

MIXING
Titanic: Mix equal measures of vodka and Mandarine Napoléon over ice in a tumbler, and top up with soda water.

MARASCHINO

THE ORIGINAL MARASCHINO (which should be pronounced with a "sk" sound in the middle, not "sh") was a distilled liquor of some antiquity made from a sour red cherry variety. The Italian name for the cherry was Marasca, which grew only on the Dalmatian coast. When the Italian-speaking enclave of Dalmatia was incorporated into the then Yugoslavia, Italian production of maraschino was continued in the Veneto, where plantings of the Marasca cherry were established from cuttings.

Maraschino is a clear liqueur derived from an infusion of pressed cherry skins in a cherry-stone distil-

FLAVOURING
Marasca cherries

MARASCHINO
The traditional
straw-covered
bottle of Luxardo

HOW TO SERVE
The best grades of maraschino should be smooth enough to drink on their own, but the sweeter it is, the more recourse to the ice-bucket you may feel is necessary.

MIXING
Tropical Cocktail: Shake equal measures of dry French vermouth, maraschino and white crème de cacao with a dash each of Angostura and orange bitters and plenty of ice. Strain into a wine glass.

late. (This secondary infusion is why maraschino should technically be considered a liqueur rather than a spirit, as distinct from Kirsch.) After further distillation to obtain a pure, clear spirit, it is aged, ideally for several years. It always remains colourless, and should have a pronounced bitter cherry aroma, backed up by the nuttiness of the cherry stones.

A number of Italian firms are especially associated with the production of maraschino, notably Luxardo (which traditionally sells its product in straw-covered flasks at a knee-trembling 50% ABV), the venerable Drioli company and Stock.

HOW IT IS MADE

The pomace of pressed cherries is infused over gentle heat in a cherry distillate for several months. It is then rectified and transferred to neutral maturation vessels, made either from a light wood such as ash or from glass. It is sweetened with sugar syrup and left to age for several years.

TASTES GOOD WITH

It is incomparable for soaking the sponge in a layered cake, or poured over fresh cherries and many other fruits, such as peaches or apricots.

MIDORI

AN INSTANT HIT when it was launched in the early 1980s, Midori was another stroke of marketing genius from the giant Japanese drinks group, Suntory. Not content with its range of fine Scotch-style whiskies and classed-growth Bordeaux property, Château Lagrange, Suntory aimed for a slice of the cocktail action with this bright green liqueur in an idiosyncratic little bottle of textured glass.

The flavouring agent is melons,

MIDORI
Cornering the market in melon liqueurs

not a particularly common one in the liqueur world, but its vivid green colour is achieved by means of a dye. Indeed, its greenness is its principal sales pitch, since *midori* is the Japanese word for green. The colour is perhaps intended to evoke the skins of certain melon varieties, as opposed to the flesh that is actually used to flavour it. Having said that, Midori doesn't especially recall any melon variety; it is actually much closer to banana, in both aroma and taste. It is sweet and syrupy, and at the lower end of standard alcoholic strength for liqueurs.

TASTES GOOD WITH
It was seized on by chefs in some of the more adventurous restaurants for use in desserts that involve tropical fruit. Salads of mango, pineapple, melon, passion-fruit and so forth are perfect choices, although again, there is that unapologetic colour to contend with.

MERSIN
Mersin is a Turkish version of Curaçao, a colourless liqueur based on grape spirit and flavoured with oranges and herbs. It is commonly taken with a chaser of the fierce black coffee of Turkey.

FLAVOURING
Melon

HOW TO SERVE
Midori is much better mixed than served straight, when its flavour quickly cloys. It blends beautifully with iced fruit juices, notably orange, except that the resulting colour is horribly lurid. Lemonade may make a more visually appealing marriage, but a sweet mixer with a sweet liqueur is never a brilliant idea.

NUT LIQUEURS

THE NUT-FLAVOURED liqueurs deserve to be considered separately since they form quite a large sub-group. Drinks relying on coconut for their principal taste are dealt with elsewhere (see Malibu); the flavourings here are those of hazelnut, walnut and almond.

In their French manifestations, the first two of those are straightforward enough. They are named noisette and crème de noix, after the French words for hazelnut and walnut respectively. In the case of almonds, it all becomes a little more complicated, basically because certain fruit stones, such as those of apricots and cherries, have an almond-like taste. A liqueur that contains almonds themselves is called crème d'amandes. However, a liqueur called crème de noyau – "noyau" being the French for the stone in which the almond-like kernel of a fruit is encased – will contain no actual almonds, only an approximation of the flavour.

These are all brandy-based drinks in which the chopped nuts are steeped in a clear grape spirit

OTHER NAMES

Almond liqueurs: Amaretto (Italian), Crème d'amandes (French)
Hazelnut liqueurs: Noisette (French)
Walnut liqueurs: Crème de noix (French), Nocino (Italian)

FRANGELICO
A branded liqueur
done up to look like
a monk

NOCINO
A strong walnut
liqueur from Italy

HOW TO SERVE

These drinks are quite commonly taken with crushed ice as a digestif in France. Alternatively, they may be iced, slightly watered – about the same amount of water as liqueur – and drunk as aperitifs. The tradition in France is for a sweet appetizer (with the obvious exception of champagne), as distinct from the drier British taste.

and the resulting liqueur is clarified and bottled in a colourless state. The exception is crème de noyau, which more often than not has a faint pinkish hue if it has been made from cherry stones. They are all sweet, with fairly syrupy textures, and make invaluable additions to the cocktail repertoire.

Italy produces a range of nut-based liqueurs, too. There is the distinctive almond-flavoured Disaronno Amaretto, and also a walnut liqueur called Nocino. In the 1980s, a product called Frangelico was released. It was a delicate straw-coloured liqueur flavoured with hazelnuts and herbs, then dressed up in a faintly ridicu-lous dark brown bottle designed to look like a monk. The large brown plastic top represented his cowl, and around the gathered-in waist, a length of white cord was knotted. It looked like a particularly embarrass-ing tourist souvenir, but the liqueur itself turned out to be delicious, not too sweet, and with an intriguing range of flavours.

EAU DE NOIX
A rare French
walnut liqueur

MIXING

Pink Almond: Shake a measure of Scotch with half a measure each of crème de noyau, Kirsch, fresh lemon juice and orgeat (a non-alcoholic almond syrup) with ice, and strain into a cocktail glass. (If you can't get orgeat, double the quantity of noyau.)

Walnut Whip: Shake equal measures of cognac, crème de noix and thick cream with ice and strain into a cocktail glass.

Mad Monk (below): Shake a measure each of gin and Frangelico with the juice of half a lemon and ice. Strain into a wine glass and add a squirt of soda.

HOW THEY ARE MADE

The nuts are crumbled up and left to infuse with the base spirit before sweetening and fil-tration. They are bottled at the average liqueur strength, around 25%. In the case of the crème de noix of Gascony, the walnuts are beaten off the trees while still green, the spirit is sweet-ened with honey and subjected to a further distillation. For crème de noyau, fruit stones are the infusion agent. They are usually either cherry or apricot, but peach and even plum may also be used.

TASTE GOOD WITH

They work well with nutty desserts – anything using almond paste or praline – but also in a chocolate mousse, or drunk alongside a piece of rich, dark fruitcake. Frangelico served chilled makes an unlikely table-fellow for a piece of mature Stilton.

FLAVOURINGS
Almonds
Walnuts
Hazelnuts
Fruit stones
Honey (in the case of some crème de noix)

PARFAIT AMOUR

THE LONG ASSOCIATION of drinking with seduction is celebrated in the name of purple Parfait Amour, "perfect love". In the 18th century particularly, the use of alcohol in amorous pursuits had less to do with getting your intended too stupefied to know what they were doing, than with stimulating the erotic impulses with artful concoctions of spices and flowers mixed with the alcohol.

Parfait Amour liqueur is really the only surviving link to that noble tradition. It is almost certainly Dutch in origin; its name, as with all such potions,

FLAVOURINGS

Lemons or other citrus fruits (such as the larger, shapeless citron of Corsica)
Cloves
Cinnamon
Coriander seeds
Violets

HOW TO SERVE

It is best to serve Parfait Amour unmixed, or else blended with something colourless such as lemonade, in order not to interfere with your beloved's enjoyment of the colour. It tastes better chilled, although you may feel that an excessively cold drink may numb the erogenous zones, which wouldn't do at all.

MIXING

Eagle's Dream: Whizz up a measure and a half of gin, a measure of Parfait Amour, the juice of half a lemon, half a teaspoon of caster sugar and the white of an egg with smashed ice in a liquidizer, and strain into a large wine glass.

is French because that was considered the romantic language par excellence. As its (added) colour would lead you to expect, it is subtly scented with violets, but the flavour owes more to fruits and spices than flowers, which marks it out quite distinctly from the colourless crème de violette. The main components are citrus fruits – usually lemons – and a mixture of cloves and other spices.

The drink enjoyed great popularity during the cocktail boom in the 1920s. Apart from anything else, no other liqueur is quite the same colour. There was once a red version of it too, but somehow purple has come to be more inextricably associated with passion. Today, Parfait Amour is made not only by the Dutch liqueur specialists Bols, but by certain French companies as well.

HOW IT IS MADE
The various aromatizing elements are macerated in grape spirit, which may then be re-distilled, and the purple colour is achieved by means of a vegetable dye.

TASTES GOOD WITH
What else but a box of violet creams?

PASTIS

Pastis is one of the most important traditional drinks of Europe, despite having
only minority status in Britain and the other
northern countries. Around the Mediterranean
fringe of Europe, from southeast France to the
Greek islands, in its various derivatives, pastis
functions in the same thirst-quenching way as
beer does further north. It is important in terms
of the quantity consumed locally, and is of
great cultural signifi-
cance too. It is an
in-between-times
drink rather than just
an aperitif; it's a drink
for lazy afternoons
watching *boules* being
played in the village
square. There is also
the tradition of illicit
home distillation.

Drinkers the world

OTHER NAMES
France: pastis *Greece*: ouzo *Spain*: ojen

MIXING
Monkey Gland: Shake two measures
of gin with a measure of fresh orange juice
and three dashes each of pastis and
grenadine and plenty of ice, and strain into
a large wine glass.

over have, on first contact with pastis, usually
been fascinated by its most famous property –
namely, that it clouds up when mixed with
water. This attribute, indeed, is what gives the
drink its name, *pastis* being an old southern
French dialect word meaning muddled, hazy
or unclear.

PERNOD AND ABSINTHE
The very close similarities of pastis to anis have
been noted elsewhere (see Anis). Depending on
which authority you consult, the principal
flavouring element in pastis is either liquorice
or aniseed – perhaps more often the former –
but there are other herbal ingredients in it as
well. A neutral, highly rectified alcohol base,
generally of vegetable origin, provides the
background for the aromatizing agents, which
are steeped in it before essence of liquorice or
anise is added and the whole mélange is sweetened and diluted.

Aniseed has been known as a digestive aid in
medicine since the time of the Egyptians, which
is why, to this day, many over-the-counter

RICARD
The famous
pastis
of southern
France

stomach-settling remedies contain a hint of its flavour. (Oxyboldene, a popular French brand, is a case in point.) The history of pastis is somewhat entangled, however, with a similar type of drink that came to be seen as anything but health-giving. By the beginning of the 20th century, the name of absinthe was mud.

Apart from home distillates, and excepting individual brands, the only category of drink that has ever become extinct is absinthe. It was considerably stronger than much of today's commercial pastis, but what really doomed it was that it contained wormwood in concentrations that were held responsible for poisoning the brains of those who habitually drank it. During the late 19th century, absinthe became known as the house drink of decadent Parisian artists, Symbolist poets and others, many of whom died the kinds of squalid deaths associated with laudanum use during the English Romantic period 60 and 70 years earlier.

When absinthe was given its marching orders in France by a governmental decree of 1915, other countries soon followed suit. One of its chief manufacturers – the firm of Henri Pernod, which had been making it for over a century – then turned to making a similar product without wormwood at lower alcoholic strength, and using anise as its main flavouring agent. In effect, Pernod was the sanitized version of absinthe. The reissued edition of that great reference work, *The Savoy Cocktail Book*,

MIXING
Yellow Parrot: Shake equal measure of pastis, yellow Chartreuse and apricot brandy with ice, and strain into a cocktail glass over crushed ice.

PERNOD
Ricard's
northern
French
counterpart

HOW TO SERVE
Pastis should ideally be served in a small, thick-bottomed glass with about the equivalent amount of water. The water should be very cold, so as to obviate the need for ice. Those with slightly sweeter tastes may add sugar to it. The best way to do this is to balance a perforated spoon or metal tea-strainer with a sugar-cube on it across the top of the glass and then pour the water over it. (This was the traditional way to sweeten absinthe.)

specifically recommends using Pernod as a substitute in those of its recipes that originally called for absinthe.

Pernod is perhaps the most familiar pastis on the market today. The other main French brand, Ricard, is now part of the same group, although they are made at opposite ends of France. Berger is the other company of note making this sort of product. In northern European countries, where there is often an ambivalence about the flavour of aniseed or liquorice in a drink, Pernod and Ricard have been much favoured as bases for a fruit-juice mixer, but the only unimpeachably authentic way to drink them in their native regions, particularly around the town of Marseilles, is diluted with a small quantity of water.

Somewhat unexpectedly, absinthe has made a cautious comeback in certain European countries, notably Switzerland and Portugal. Presumably it contains considerably less wormwood and therefore is only vaguely comparable to the real thing. A theory has gained currency that it was really only banned because it was

highly alcoholic (in which case the hallowed Chartreuse might have been expected to find itself in more difficulties than it has). A scientific writer, Harold McGee, points out that wormwood contains a toxic oil called thujone, which was almost certainly linked to the formation of lesions on the cerebral cortex of the recklessly heavy user. You pays your money…

SPAIN

The Spanish equivalent is *ojen* (pronounced "oh-hen"). It is named after the town where it is made and is sold in two versions: sweet and dry.

GREECE

After pastis, the most familiar relative of this family of drinks is Greek ouzo, much beloved of holidaymakers on the Peloponnese and the islands, perhaps even more so than retsina. The flavouring agent is anise and, like pastis, the drink turns milky-white when water is added. It is drunk in much the same way, except perhaps with somewhat more water than is common in France, and generally as an aperitif. The bottled strength is around 35–40% ABV, again similar to pastis.

FLAVOURINGS

Herbs – possibly including coriander, camomile, parsley, veronica (which was once used in France as a substitute for tea), even spinach!

HOW TO SERVE

Ouzo should be served cold in a small, thick-bottomed glass, either on its own, with about the equivalent amount of water, or with an ice cube or two.

OUZO
The drink of the sunny Greek islands.

MIXING

Cocktails that include pastis tend to be among the most dramatic in the repertoire. Many of these contain no non-alcoholic ingredients. That is because a relatively small amount of pastis will have plenty to say for itself in even the most ferocious of mixes, concoctions that would drown the presence of many of the more delicate liqueurs.

Block and Fall: Stir together a measure each of cognac and Cointreau with half a measure each of pastis and calvados, over ice, in a tumbler.

Hurricane: Shake a measure and a half of cognac with half a measure each of pastis and vodka and ice, then strain into a cocktail glass.

Ojen Cocktail: Shake a double measure of dry ojen with a teaspoon of sugar, half a measure of water, a dash of orange bitters and ice, and strain into a small tumbler.

HOW THEY ARE MADE

The various herbs and plants are usually infused in a straight, highly purified vegetable spirit base and essence of anise or liquorice added. Further blending with rectified alcohol is followed by sweetening, and the drink is bottled at an average 35% ABV.

TASTES GOOD WITH

The combination of aromatizers in pastis is a particularly successful one with fish, either for marinating or adding to a sauce. Try marinating chunks of tuna in olive oil, pastis and dill and then grilling them on skewers.

PIMM'S

FOREVER ASSOCIATED with the English summer, Pimm's No. 1 Cup is a proprietary version of a fruit cup created by the eponymous Mr Pimm in the 1820s. James Pimm originally devised his recipe in order to mark out his own establishment in the City of London from the run of common-or-garden oyster bars – oysters being not much more than ten a penny in those days – which traditionally served stout ale to wash the bivalves down.

He did such a roaring trade with his fruit cup that Pimm began to market it ready-mixed in 1859, the asking price for a bottle being a stiffish three shillings. Since that time, Pimm's has gone through a number of owners, including – at the turn of the century – the then Lord Mayor of London, Sir Horatio Davies. Popular throughout the British Empire during colonial times, it came to enjoy a sudden vogue in France and Italy after the war.

In the early years of the 20th century, Pimm's was elaborated into six different versions, each based on a different spirit. The market has since whittled these down to just two, Pimm's Vodka Cup and the original – still sold as No. 1 Cup, and based on London gin, with an unmixed strength of 25% ABV. Pimm's has suffered somewhat from being seen as too fiddly to prepare. Its present owner, one of Britain's biggest drinks companies, has tried to combat that by launching little cans of pre-mixed Pimm's.

TASTES GOOD WITH
Classic English picnic foods – cucumber sandwiches, hard-boiled quail's eggs, crackers with cream cheese and crudités – are all made the more splendid with plenty of Pimm's. Take a big jug and throw in half a bottle of Pimm's and a litre of lemonade.

FLAVOURINGS
All highly secret of course, but it contains fruit extracts – notably orange – and at least one other alcoholic ingredient, perhaps Curaçao. Who knows?

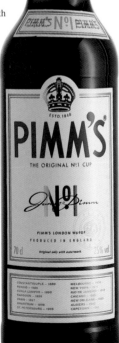

PIMM'S
The quintessential flavour of an English summer

POIRE WILLIAM

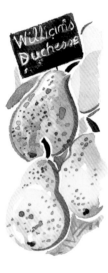

POIRE WILLIAM IS NOT to be confused with true pear brandy, which is a colourless spirit, eau de vie de poire, made in Alsace and Switzerland. The big liqueur companies nearly all make a sweet pear-flavoured liqueur, traditionally lightly coloured and made by the usual method of infusing crushed fruit in neutral grape spirit. Some may have a brief period of cask-ageing, but most don't.

One of the curiosities of Poire William – which is so named after the particular variety of pear used – is that, while its aroma is very strong and evocative, the flavour is often disappointingly mild. This is true of pears generally. The Williams is a gorgeously aromatic fruit when fully ripe but, used in cooking, its flavour often all but vanishes, which isn't at all true of the best apple varieties. As such, I find the liqueur has to be used in fairly enthusiastic quantities in a cocktail in order to get the best out of it.

Pear-flavoured liqueurs are made in France (about the best brand is Marie Brizard), Italy (which has Pera Segnana), Germany and Switzerland. A novelty product is Poire Prisonnière, which comes with a whole pear in the bottle. I remember as a student seeing one in a shop window in Venice and debating with a friend how on earth they managed to get the pear in. We eventually concluded they must somehow hand-blow the bottle around the fruit. So much for

MIXING

Old William (from G. Marcialis and F. Zingales's *Cocktail Book*): Pour a double measure of Poire William over ice in a tumbler. Add a half-measure each of maraschino and fresh orange and lemon juices, and mix thoroughly. Decorate with orange and lemon slices.

youthful ingenuity. The pears are in fact *grown* in the bottles, which are attached to the tree, so that each fruit has its own private greenhouse. Before the bottles are filled with the liqueur, the pears are pricked in order to release their juices.

TASTES GOOD WITH

Poire William is excellent poured over certain fresh fruits, notably pink grapefruit segments, pineapple or, of course, pear.

*POIRE WILLIAM
Delicately flavoured French pear liqueur*

*POIRE PRISONNIERE
The pear is painstakingly grown in the bottle*

PUNSCH

PUNSCH IS MORE FAMILIARLY known in English-speaking countries as Swedish punch, although even then it isn't a drink many people have come across. Its lineage can be traced back to the 18th century, when Sweden's ocean-going trading vessels began doing business in the East Indies. Among the commodities they brought back was some of the arak that is the traditional spirit of those regions. Some arak is rice-based, some a distillate of sugar-cane, and therefore more like rum.

In its raw state, it wasn't much to northern European tastes, and so a few drink companies took to blending it with grape brandy and various wines and cordials, in effect creating a kind of powerful punch in the process. Like a traditional punch, the mixture is also highly spiced – just what the doctor ordered in the depths of the grim Scandinavian winter.

The original punch was a British colonial invention, but by the 18th century, a vogue for it had spread not only to

PUNSCH
The real thing
– a cask-aged
punch from
Sweden

OTHER NAMES
Britain: Swedish punch

MIXING
Diki-Diki: Shake a double measure of calvados, half a measure each of punsch and grapefruit juice, with ice, and strain into a cocktail glass.
Grand Slam (below): Mix a double measure of punsch with a measure each of dry white and sweet red vermouth, with ice, in a jug, and then strain over crushed ice in a wine glass.

Scandinavia but into France as well. Rum was a favoured base ingredient, variously boosted with hot tea, lemon juice and sweet spices such as cinnamon. Punch was, in every way, the grand-daddy of the cocktail.

In an echo of the British habit, Swedish punch was usually served hot, at least until the end of the last century. Since that time, the universal fashion for alcoholic drinks to be served cold has meant it is now drunk straight or even iced.

HOW IT IS MADE
These days, punsch is exclusively a rum-based drink, to which other forms of alcohol – including wine – are added, together with a quantity of fragrant spices, such as cinnamon and cloves. It is sweetened and then aged for several months in cask.

TASTES GOOD WITH
Punsch works reasonably well with little salty nibbles made with strong cheese.

FLAVOURINGS
Sweet spices, such as cinnamon and cloves

HOW TO SERVE
To relive the old days, warm the punsch gently (without letting it boil) in a small saucepan and serve it in big, heat-proof, wine glasses.

RATAFIA

OTHER NAMES

France: Pineau des Charentes (Cognac), Floc de Gascogne (Armagnac), Pommeau (Calvados)

Rᴀᴛᴀꜰɪᴀ ᴡᴀꜱ, ᴄᴇɴᴛᴜʀɪᴇꜱ ᴀɢᴏ, a forerunner of the liqueur, in that it involved steeping fruits or nuts in a sweetened spirit base. That wouldn't in itself earn it a separate entry in this guide, were it not for the fact that the term ratafia has come to be applied mainly now to a type of aperitif made in the brandy-producing areas of France. The brandy is mixed with fresh fruit juice.

Ratafia is not a geographical name. It derives from the old French practice of concluding any formal agreement, such a legal contract or business transaction, with a shared drink – a "ratifier", if you like. The original phrase is Latin: *rata fiat* ("let the deal be settled").

There are also ratafias made in wine areas – particularly Burgundy and Champagne – in which the naturally sweet grape juice is mixed in with some of the regional wine. The most celebrated ratafia, however, is Pineau des Charentes, made in the Cognac region from grape juice fortified with cognac. It can't be considered a fortified wine, though, for

the very good reason that the grape juice has not undergone fermentation. It comes in white and rosé versions, and always has the sweetness of ripe grape juice about it.

In Armagnac, not to be outdone, they make their own version of this drink by exactly the same method. Called Floc de Gascogne, its production – like that of armagnac itself – is on a much more modest commercial footing than its Charentais counterpart.

There is also a variant of this type of ratafia made in the Calvados region of Normandy, in which fresh apple juice is fortified with apple brandy. It is called pommeau, and is a considerably more palatable proposition (to the author's taste at least) than either Pineau or Floc.

HOW IT IS MADE

By adding grape brandy to unfermented grape juice, or conversely apple brandy to apple juice, in each case to an average bottled strength of around 17% ABV.

TASTES GOOD WITH

Ratafia works quite well as an accompaniment to a slice of aromatic melon – better than most wine, at any rate.

HOW TO SERVE

These drinks should be served, vigorously chilled, in wine-glass quantities as aperitifs. In Armagnac, they mix the Floc with sparkling wine and call it a *pousse-rapière* (literally "rapier-pusher").

PINEAU DES CHARENTES
The ratafia of the Cognac region

POMMEAU
An apple ratafia from Normandy

SAMBUCA

AN ITALIAN LIQUEUR that became quite fashionable beyond its home region of Rome in the 1970s and 80s, Sambuca Romana is a clear, moderately sweet, quite fiery drink, flavoured with elderberries and aniseed. Its name is derived from the botanical name for elderberry, *Sambucus nigra.* There are other herbs and roots in it too, but these are the two predominant flavours.

In the days when every drink had to be dignified with its own particular serving ritual, it was decreed that Sambuca was to be garnished with coffee beans and set alight. Aficionados of the custom differed quite sharply as to whether the correct number of beans was two or three. Such detail scarcely mattered since what mostly preoccupied the drinker was how to swallow it without singeing the nose.

To earn your Sambuca stripes, you have to blow out the flame on a glassful and then swallow the drink in one, like an oyster. In Rome, they will ask you whether you want it *con la mosca,* literally "with a fly" (i.e. with the coffee beans). There, they are not merely for garnish. If you say *si,* you will be expected to crunch the beans up as you drink.

MIXING

Matinée (from Michael Walker's *Cinzano Cocktail Book*): Shake a measure of gin, half a measure each of Sambuca and thick cream, half an egg white and a dash of fresh lime juice with plenty of ice, and strain into a cocktail glass. Sprinkle with finely grated nutmeg.

TASTES GOOD WITH

A chilled glass of Sambuca makes a good accompaniment to a genuine Italian *torta*, one of those heavenly sticky cakes of dried fruits, almonds and lemon zest.

FLAVOURINGS
Elderberries
Aniseed

SABRA

This is Israel's entry in the spirits and liqueurs stakes – a svelte concoction flavoured with a clever mélange of Jaffa orange and chocolate. Despite the bitterness contributed by the orange peels, the resulting drink is exceptionally sweet. Try mixing it with cognac and ice to throw it into relief.

SAMBUCA
A fiery liqueur
in more ways
than one

HOW TO SERVE
If you are going to try the flaming Sambuca trick, it helps to serve the liqueur in a narrow glass like an old-fashioned sherry schooner, because the flame will take more easily on a smaller surface.

SLOE GIN

SLOE GIN, AND its French equivalent *prunelle*, rely for their flavour and colour on a type of small bitter-tasting plum, the fruit of a shrub called the blackthorn. English sloe gin, as marketed by companies such as Hawker's, is nothing more than sweetened gin in which sloes have been steeped and then strained out once they have stained the spirit a deep red. The fruits contribute a strong, rather medicinal taste to the drink.

Prunelle, from the French word for the fruit, is not red but green, and is made by macerating the fruit kernels in a grape spirit base. Although the colour may be added, it does reflect the greenish flesh of the fruit. Liqueur companies such as Garnier and Cusenier (theirs is called Prunellia) make it, and it is especially popular in Anjou, in the western

part of the Loire valley. They also make eau de vie from sloes in Burgundy and Alsace.

The plant itself is a wild shrub that grows quite plentifully throughout Europe, its little sour fruits only ripening properly in early winter. Sloe gin is still quite widely made at home in country areas of England, but only with commercial gin, of course.

HOW IT IS MADE

Sloe gin is easy to knock up at home if you have access to the fruits. The best ratio is about half-a-pound of sugar to a pound of the fruit, but if the fruit is very sour, you may want to increase the sweetening by a couple of ounces. The fruit should be partly squashed or pierced to encourage absorption of the flavour. Top up your bottle with gin (or vodka, if you prefer, but gin makes a more interesting marriage of flavours). Leave it sealed for at least three months, shaking it up from time to time, and then strain the spirit off the solids.

TASTES GOOD WITH

Like cranberries or rowanberries, sloes make a good, tart jelly for garnishing strong gamey meats. Perhaps a slug of sloe gin in the sauce or gravy would help matters along.

FLAVOURING
The fruit of the wild blackthorn bush

OTHER NAMES
France: Prunelle/Prunellia

HOW TO SERVE
Sloe gin is best served as it comes and at room temperature. A marketing push for a brand of sloe gin a few years ago suggested adding a teaspoon or two of it to a glass of sparkling wine, which isn't a bad idea – especially if the sparkling wine is a bit rough.

SLOE GIN
A sloe gin from one of the big names in gin

SOUTHERN COMFORT

THE FOREMOST AMERICAN liqueur is Southern Comfort, a fruitier counterpart to the Scotch-based liqueurs. Naturally American whiskey is used as its starting point. As so often in the world of proprietary liqueurs, the exact composition of Southern Comfort is a closely guarded commercial secret, but what we do know is that the fruit flavouring it contains is peach.

Its origins probably lie in the mixing of bourbon with peach juice as a traditional cocktail in the southern states. Back in Mississippi, down in New Orleans (as the song goes), there was once a mixed drink called Sazerac. A recipe for it is given in the *Savoy Cocktail Book*. It consists of a shot of rye

SOUTHERN COMFORT
A fruity whiskey liqueur of the Deep South

MIXING
Southern Peach: Shake a measure each of Southern Comfort, peach brandy and thick cream with a dash of Angostura and plenty of ice, and strain into a tumbler. Decorate with a wedge of peach.

FLAVOURING
Peaches

whiskey, with a sprinkling of peach bitters, a lump of sugar and a dash of absinthe. So traditional is it that a New Orleans company has been producing a pre-mixed version of it since around the middle of the 19th century.

Peaches themselves are grown in great quantities in the southern states; the Georgia peach is one of America's proudest agricultural products. The practice of blending the peach juice with whiskey in the bars of New Orleans undoubtedly also played its part in influencing the creation of Southern Comfort.

Today, the company that owns the brand is the same one that has the leading Tennessee whiskey brand, Jack Daniel's. The Southern Comfort distillery is located in St Louis, in the state of Missouri. The bottled strength is high – 40% ABV – which is perhaps one of the reasons it appealed so much to the late great rock legend Janis Joplin.

TASTES GOOD WITH
Southern Comfort makes a good substitute for bourbon poured over the traditional light fruitcake at Thanksgiving or Christmas. Quantities should be extremely generous, though: a whole bottleful is not unknown.

HOW TO SERVE
Southern Comfort is intended to be meditatively sipped, like other fine American whiskeys, but you could try taming its fire and emphasizing its fruitiness with a mixer of peach nectar. It's also fine with orange juice on the rocks.

STREGA

THE NAME STREGA, a popular proprietary liqueur produced in Italy, is Italian for "witch". It is so called because it is supposedly based on a witches' brew, an aphrodisiac love-potion guaranteed to unite any pair of lovers who drink it in eternal togetherness. You have been warned.

It is a bright yellow concoction full of all sorts of complex flavours. The fruit base is a citrus blend and it reputedly also contains around six dozen different botanical herbs, making it not dissimilar in style to the yellow version of Chartreuse. It has

STREGA
This Italian liqueur is full of complex flavours

the same kind of syrupy texture, too, and is considered an especially good digestif.

Although the colour resembles that other Italian liqueur speciality, Galliano, Strega's flavour is quite different, more obviously herbal and with a stronger citrus element.

TASTES GOOD WITH

As an accompaniment to freshly cracked nuts at the end of a meal, Strega works particularly well.

HOW TO SERVE
Strega is more appealing served *frappé*, on crushed ice, which takes the edge off its sweetness, than served on its own.

SUZE

IF I HAD TO NOMINATE one other product to make up a perfect trinity of aperitifs with champagne and pale dry sherry, it would unhesitatingly be Suze. Some may consider that Suze, and the various related Swiss and German products, should technically be considered under "Bitters", but they are not always direct distillates; some are actually wine-based. What they do all have in common is that they rely for their impact on gentian.

Gentian is a wild mountain plant found in the Alps and the mountains of the Jura, in France. It has large yellow flowers, but it is principally valued for its roots, which can grow up to a yard long and have one of the most uncompromisingly bitter flavours found anywhere in the plant world. It was once the quinine of its day, before that plant was brought back from the Americas in the 17th century. Like quinine, gentian has had a distinguished history in the pharmacist's repertoire; it was thought to be particularly good for ailments of the liver.

The Suze brand is owned by pastis manufacturers Pernod-Ricard, and it has a very

SUZE
Well worth a journey to France to taste

OTHER NAMES
France: Gentiane *Germany*: Enzian

MIXING
Drought: Shake equal measures of gin and Suze with a small splash of fresh orange juice, and strain into a cocktail glass. (This is an unimaginably dry mixture, and a particular energizer to the appetite.)

FLAVOURING
Gentian root

delicate primrose colour. It is based on wine, and its flavour is so dry and bitter, even when mixed with a little water or served on ice, that it acts as an extraordinarily powerful appetite-rouser.

Other similar products may be labelled Gentiane in France and Switzerland, or Enzian in Germany. The German products tend to be direct distillates of the gentian root, though, rather than wine-based.

HOW IT IS MADE
In the case of Suze and similar products, an extract of gentian is steeped in a white wine base, which imparts a little faint colour to the liquid. It is then clarified and bottled at fortified wine strength.

TASTES GOOD WITH
Suze is great served with any bitter nibbles, and is extremely appetizing with the more pungent varieties of green olive.

HOW TO SERVE
Pour a measure of Suze into a tumbler with either the merest splash of very cold water or a single cube of ice just to freshen it up.

GENTIANE
An alternative French brand of gentian aperitif.

TIA MARIA

JAMAICA'S CONTRIBUTION to the world of liqueurs, Tia Maria, has turned into one of the best-loved of all such products in both America and Europe. It is a suave, deep brown coffee-flavoured drink that proves itself highly versatile on the cocktail circuit as well as for after-dinner sipping.

It is based, not surprisingly, on good dark Jamaican rum of at least five-year-old standard and flavoured with the beans of the highly prized coffee variety, Blue Mountain. In addition to the coffee, the palate is further deepened by the addition of local spices too. Although the liqueur is sweet, noticeably sweeter than its Mexican counterpart Kahlúa, for example, the aromatic components in it prevent it from being cloying. This makes it one of the few such drinks that is actually quite acceptable to savour on its own.

Not the least reason for its popularity in Europe was the craze for the cocktail Black Russian, usually taken with Coca-Cola, in

TIA MARIA
The world's most
famous coffee liqueur

MIXING

Sunburn: Shake equal measures of cognac and Tia Maria, half a measure each of fresh orange and lemon juices and ice, and strain into a cocktail glass.
Proportions of the classic **Black Russian** (below) vary according to taste. Two parts vodka to one part Tia Maria on ice, with no mixer, makes a very adult drink.

which it provides a luxurious note of richness to what is otherwise a fairly prosaic mix.

HOW IT IS MADE

Coffee beans and spices are infused in a base of cask-aged rum, which is then lightly sweetened. It is bottled at just under 27% ABV.

TASTES GOOD WITH

Tia Maria is brilliant for lacing chocolate desserts, and of course makes a good liqueur coffee – particularly when the coffee used is Blue Mountain.

TRAPPISTINE

Another of the few remaining liqueurs made by religious orders, Trappistine is made at the convent of the Abbaye de Grâce de Dieu in the eastern French *département* of Doubs, not far from the Swiss border. A naturally pallid, yellow-green colour, it is based on armagnac and contains macerations of many wild herbs.

VAN *der* HUM

VAN DER HUM IS SOUTH AFRICA'S equivalent of Curaçao, made by several producers in the Cape, including the giant national wine consortium KWV. The whimsical name literally translates as "What's-his-Name". Its base is Cape brandy, of which there is a large annual production, and the citrus fruit used is a tangerine-like orange variety locally known as *naartjies*. Much in the way of Curaçao, the peels of the orange are infused in the brandy and supplemented with a herb or spice element. The precise formula may vary from one producer to the next, but nutmeg is a favoured addition.

Rather like Mandarine Napoléon, the drink derives from the practice of steeping citrus peels in the local brandy. Such a concoction would have been widely produced domestically by early Cape settlers, and the formula came to be replicated on a commercial scale. It is a reliable and attractive liqueur, its pale gold colour and pronounced bitter orange scent adding to its appeal. The bottled strength is generally 25%-plus.

VAN DER HUM
South Africa's
answer to orange
Curaçao

MIXING

Sundowner: Shake a measure and a half of South African brandy or cognac and a measure of Van der Hum with half a measure each of fresh orange and lemon juices and ice. Strain into a cocktail glass.

LA VIEILLE CURE

The correct translation of this liqueur's name is "The Old Rectory", not – as it would seem – "The Old Cure". The mistranslation would be right on at least one score, though. It was once a golden potion made by the monastic order at the abbey of Cenons, near Bordeaux. It used over 50 different curative wild herbs macerated in blended brandies, and was very much a typical medieval alcohol remedy, first conceived in the days when distillation went hand in hand with the pharmacist's art. The flavour has been compared to that of Bénédictine. To enjoy it to the full, La Vieille Cure should be served neat and un-iced in small liqueur glasses. In the 1980s, the production passed into the hands of one of the large French drinks companies of the region, but the liqueur's manufacture should not be confused with the wine-producing château of the same name in Bordeaux.

VERVEINE

Verveine du Vélay, to give it its full title, is another of those liqueurs that models itself stylistically on Chartreuse, to the extent that it comes in green and yellow, with the green the stronger. It is a brandy-based herbal concoction made near Puy, in the Auvergne region of central France. Verveine is the French for verbena, a flowering herb whose leaves have been used in folk medicine for centuries as a restorative for the liver and also for neuro-logical complaints. Its bitter flavour is apparent in the liqueur named after it (though there are other herbs in it too), the sharpness gentled with a little honey.

FLAVOURINGS
Naartjie peels
Nutmeg and other spice
and herb aromatizers

HOW TO SERVE
Traditionally, Van der Hum is quite heavily sweetened by the manufacturer. For those who prefer a drier drink, the customary thing is to mix it half-and-half with brandy. Some companies bottle it ready-mixed as Brandy-Hum – the Cape equivalent of B & B.

FORTIFIED WINES

MADEIRA

OF ALL THE CLASSIC fortified wines of southern Europe, Madeira is the one with the most singular history. It comes from the island of the same name in the Atlantic Ocean; a volcanic outcrop, Madeira is actually slightly nearer to the coast of North Africa than it is to Portugal of which it is an autonomously governed region.

The evolution of this wine belongs to the days of the trading ships that plied the East India routes in the late 1600s. Madeira's geographical position made it a natural port of call for north European vessels on their way to Africa and the East Indies, and so they would load up with wine at the port of Funchal, the island capital. It gradually came to be noticed that, whereas many table wines would be badly spoiled by the combination of violent

shaking and the torrid heat in which they travelled the oceans, Madeiras were eerily improved by the experience.

The shippers were so sure of the benefits the sea voyage conferred on the wine that they began to send wines that were only destined for the European markets all the way to Indonesia and back. Some went the other way, and a great connoisseurship of Madeira grew up in the newly independent United States. Until virtually the end of the 19th century, this is how the most highly prized Madeiras were all made.

Eventually, it simply wasn't financially practical to keep treating Madeira to a round-the-world cruise, and so the conditions it endured at sea – the tortuous heat, especially – were recreated in the wineries or "lodges" where the wines originated. Some Madeira is heated simply

HOW TO SERVE
Serve Madeira in a good-sized sherry glass or small wine glass. The drier styles may benefit from a little light chilling, but the richer, darker styles, with their overtones of treacle toffee and Christmas cake, should be served at room temperature.

RICH MALMSEY
This is the sweetest style of Madeira

VERDELHO
The second driest style – this 5-year-old Madeira is only very slightly sweet

MIXING

It was common in America once to substitute sweet Madeira for the brandy in a **Prairie Oyster**, that most challenging of hangover cures, involving a raw egg yolk, salt and cayenne pepper and a dash of Worcestershire sauce.

Boston (below): Shake equal measures of dry Madeira and bourbon with half a teaspoon of caster sugar and yet another egg yolk. Strain into a small wine glass and sprinkle with grated nutmeg.

by being left under the roof of the lodge to bake in the heat of the tropical sun. Some is stored in rooms where fat central heating pipes run around the walls throughout the summer swelter, and even the lowest grades are matured in vats that have hot-water pipes running through them.

There are four basic styles of Madeira, named after the grape varieties that go into them. The palest and driest style is Sercial. Then comes Verdelho, a little sweeter and darker, then Bual, and finally Malmsey (the last is an English corruption of the Portuguese name Malvasia). The wines are also graded according to how long they have been aged. This may be given as a minimum age on the label (5-year-old, 10-year-old and so on), or one of the accepted descriptive terms may be used. "Reserve" equates roughly to 5-year-old, "Special Reserve" to 10, "Extra Reserve" to 15. Some Madeira is vintage-dated, meaning it is the unblended produce of the stated year's harvest.

HOW IT IS MADE

A light, white base wine is made from any of the four main varieties, perhaps supplemented with some juice from the local red grape Tinta Negra Mole (though it is theoretically of declining importance). For the sweeter styles, Bual and Malmsey, the fermentation may be interrupted early on by the addition of grape spirit, meaning that some natural sugar remains in them, while the drier wines (Sercial and Verdelho) are fermented until more of the sugar has been consumed before being fortified. The wines are then subjected to heat during the cask-ageing, either by one of the heating systems known as an *estufa* (stove), or else by just being left in the hottest part of the lodge, in which case it may be known as a *vinho canteiro*.

SERCIAL
The palest and driest style of Madeira

TASTES GOOD WITH

The driest styles present the answer to that age-old problem of what to drink with soup. They are particularly good with clear, meaty consommé. As you proceed to the richer end of the scale, drink them with mince pies, Christmas cake and other dense fruitcake mixes or, of course, Madeira cake.

MARSALA

Sicily's very own fortified wine is named after the town of Marsala, in the province of Trapani at the western end of the island. Like many of the fortified wines of southern Europe, it has an English connection. It was effectively invented by a wine merchant, John Woodhouse, in 1773, in direct imitation of the sherry and Madeira in which he was something of a specialist. In the rough-and-ready way of the time, he simply added a quantity of ordinary brandy to the traditional white wines of western Sicily, and found on shipping them that the result was a reasonably close approximation of the already established fortified wines.

Woodhouse founded a commercial operation on the island at the end of the 18th century, and won valuable orders

TERRE ARSE
A vintage-dated
Marsala from
Florio

from the Royal Navy among others. Marsala was carried on Nelson's ships during the hostilities with France, and the wine's reputation quickly spread. Although the early trade was dominated by English merchants, Italians themselves eventually got in on the act. The first significant house of Italian origin was Florio, founded by an entrepreneur from the mainland in 1832.

It is fair to say that Marsala's development since that period has been one of slow decline as a result of conflicting theories about how it should be made, and the widespread use of irrigation in the vineyards where it is grown. Irrigation can result in grapes of lower sugar concentration, which means that alternative methods of sweetening the wine have had to be found.

The rules and regulations governing the production of Marsala

SECCO
The driest style
of Marsala

HOW TO SERVE
Dry and medium-dry Marsala, of which there is a regrettably small amount, should be served chilled in generously sized sherry glasses as an aperitif. The sweetest styles should be served at room temperature as digestifs or with certain types of old, dry cheese.

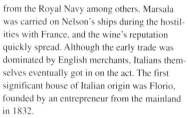

MIXING

Casanova: Shake a measure of bourbon with half a measure each of sweet Marsala and Kahlúa, a measure of thick cream and plenty of ice. Strain into a cocktail glass.

Inigo Jones (from Michael Walker's *Cinzano Cocktail Book*): In a mixing-jug, stir together a measure of cognac, a measure of sweet Marsala, a measure of dry rosé wine and a dash each of fresh orange and lemon juices with plenty of ice. Strain into a tumbler half-filled with crushed ice.

were only finally codified in 1969, and are considerably more flexible than those controlling the manufacture of the other famous fortified wines. Perhaps the least satisfactory aspect of them is the nature of the sweetening agents that may be added. It can be either a fortified grape juice, or just grape juice whose sweetness has been concentrated by cooking. This latter ingredient, known in Italian as *mosto cotto*, is not in itself alcoholic. The best Marsalas have natural sweetness from ripe grapes, which is retained through interrupted fermentation.

Marsala is classified by age – Fine is one year old, Superiore two, Superiore Riserva four, Vergine five, Stravecchio ten – and by sweetness. Dry is labelled "secco", medium-dry "semisecco" and the sweetest "dolce". It also comes in three colours. The better grades are both shades of tawny, either amber (*ambra*) or golden (*oro*), but there is a red version too (*rubino*). Producers of note include de Bartoli, Pellegrino and Rallo.

HOW IT IS MADE

Light white wines from local grape varieties Grillo, Inzolia and Catarratto are turned into Marsala by one of three methods. They can be fortified with grape spirit in the traditional way, or sweetened and strengthened with either alcohol-boosted juice from ultra-sweet, late-ripened grapes or with cooked grape juice concentrate. Concentrate is only permitted in the Ambra Marsala. The wines are then cask-aged for varying periods.

TASTES GOOD WITH

Marsala has come to be seen as even more of a kitchen ingredient than Madeira. It is indispensable as the alcohol element in both zabaglione and tiramisù, while the scallopini of veal, beloved of Italian trattorias the world over, are often sauced with a sticky brown reduction of Marsala.

DOLCE
This is best suited for classic Italian desserts

FINE

Fine Marsala is the youngest style

RISERVA

Superiore Riserva Marsala is four years old

MUSCAT *and* MOSCATEL

SWEET FORTIFIED WINES are made from Muscat all over the world. It is easy to think Muscat is a single grape variety, but it is in fact a grape family. Some of its offshoots are of the highest pedigree, notably a type the French call Muscat Blanc à Petits Grains. Others, such as Muscat of Alexandria and Muscat Ottonel, are of humbler extraction, and give correspondingly less exciting wines. Moscatel is the name the family assumes on the Iberian peninsula.

This is a quick global tour of the styles of sweet wine the Muscat relatives make. All should be served chilled as dessert wines or on their own. They tend to be in the range of 15–18% ABV, except for the first category, Australian Muscats, which reach up to 20%.

AUSTRALIAN LIQUEUR MUSCATS

These are hugely rich, strong, fortified Muscats made in and around the town of Rutherglen, in the north-western corner of the Australian state of Victoria. They are produced by a method that seems to combine a little of all the ways of making fortified wine. The grapes are left to overripen and shrivel on the vine, so that they are halfway to becoming raisins. After pressing, they ferment part-way, but the fermentation is arrested by fortification with grape spirit, keeping massive quantities of natural sugar in the wine. The cask-ageing they then receive combines elements of the *solera* system used in Spanish brandy and sherry, and the action of searing sunshine, as in *canteiro* Madeiras. Among the more notable producers are Stanton & Killeen, Mick Morris and Chambers.

VIN DOUX NATUREL MUSCATS

A group of Muscat wines made in southern France are made by virtually the same method as port. Their collective name, *vins doux naturels*, means "naturally sweet wines". The grapes are picked very ripe and the normal process of fermentation is stopped by adding a powerful grape spirit, so the natural grapey sweetness of Muscat is retained. There are six appellations for this type of wine, the most famous of which comes from the southern Rhône valley – Muscat de Beaumes de Venise. Best producers are Domaine Durban and Domaine de Coyeux.

Four of the others are located down in the Languedoc. They are Muscat de Frontignan, de Lunel, de Mireval and de St Jean de Minervois. The sixth, Muscat de Rivesaltes, is grown even further south, in Roussillon, near the Spanish border. De Rivesaltes does not have to be made from the noblest Muscat, though, and the quality varies hugely between producers.

SETUBAL MOSCATEL

This is a highly traditional fortified wine based on the Muscat of Alexandria grape, together with a couple of its more obscure cousins. It is made on the Setúbal peninsula in western Portugal, southeast of Lisbon, and was recognized

MUSCAT DE BEAUMES DE VENISE Domaine de Coyeux is one of the best producers of Muscat

as a regionally demarcated wine in the first decade of the 20th century. The process is the same as for the French *vins doux naturels*, except that after fortification, the grape skins are allowed to macerate in the finished wine for several months. Some Setúbal Moscatel is released after five years or so when its colour is already a vivid orange from the wood. Other wines are aged for a couple of decades, deepening to burnished mahogany until they are a treacle-thick essence of pure Muscat flavour. The most significant producer is José Maria da Fonseca.

MOSCATEL DE VALENCIA

Around Valencia, on the eastern coast of Spain, they make what the French would call a *vin de liqueur*, that is, a wine that hasn't

SETUBAL MOSCATEL
A 20-year-old Moscatel from Portugal's Setúbal

really fermented as such but for which the grapes have merely been pressed and then fortified with grape spirit. (In that respect, they could be considered similar to the ratafias made in the brandy regions of France.) Moscatels de Valencia are not made from the most distinguished Muscat variety and are more often than not seen in screw-top bottles. When very fresh and very well chilled, these can be pretty refreshing drinks, particularly in the stunning heat of a Spanish summer.

JEREPIGO

Jerepigo is the South African version of Moscatel de Valencia, except that it most emphatically does use the aristocratic Muscat Blanc à Petits Grains variety, here known – just to confuse everybody – as Muscadel or Muskadel. Otherwise, the production is the same, with grape spirit being added to the very sweet, freshly pressed grape juice. Vintages of Jerepigo (the name is Portuguese in origin) are occasionally released at around 15 years old, and are found to retain much of their initial freshness.

JEREPIGO
An old vintage of South Africa's answer to fortified Moscatel.

MOSCATEL DE VALENCIA
A highly ornate bottle for what is in fact a very simple drink

PORT

PORT IS THE ONLY one of the major fortified wines to be based on a red wine. True, there is such a thing as white port, but it only accounts for a fraction of the production. Port hails from only one delimited area, the Douro valley in northern Portugal. So popular has it traditionally been as a style of wine that many non-European wine-making countries have been trying their hands at port lookalikes since the 19th century. The difference today is that, in the countries of the European Union at least, they are no longer allowed to be called port.

The drink originated during one of the frequent periods of hostilities between the English and the French in the 1600s, as a consequence of which the English authorities declared a punitive tax levy on goods imported from

COCKBURN'S
1991
A vintage port from one of the English shippers

France. This hit the wine trade hard. Wine shippers had to look to Portugal, England's oldest European ally, with whom there were preferential trade tariffs, to supply their customers. Journeying inland along the river Douro, the English merchants happened upon the fierce red wines of the region and found them pretty much to the domestic taste. As was common practice at the time, they fortified them with a little brandy for the sea voyage.

Thus was port born. Originally, it was of course a dry wine, since these were fully fermented wines that were being augmented with brandy. However, it only took the chance discovery of the effects of fortification

GRAHAM'S
1989 LBV
Port from a single year matured in the shipper's cellars

on an extremely ripe, sweet wine to remodel port in the image with which we are familiar today. To preserve that sweetness, the wines would have their normal fermentation interrupted (or "muted") with brandy, so that some of the grape sugars would remain unconsumed by the yeasts.

Eventually, it was considered that using a simple local grape spirit was cheaper than buying fine cognac for the fortification. Also, port was coming to be seen as a fine wine in its own right, and so it was desirable that the fortifying agent should be as neutral as possible, in order to allow the characteristics of the underlying wine to be shown off.

Port styles have since multiplied almost *ad infinitum*. At the top of the quality tree are the vintage ports, wines of a single year that must be bottled within two years of the harvest and are intended for long ageing. Late-bottled vintage (LBV) is also the product of a single year, but, one that has been kept in cask in the shipper's premises for longer – around six years usually – in order to be more mature on bottling, and readier to drink on purchase. Vintage Character port is an everyday blended product and nothing special, while the fine old tawny ports are often aged for many years in barrel so that their initial full-blooded red fades to an autumnal brown.

Other countries producing good port-style fortified wines are Australia (where the favoured grape variety is the spicy Shiraz), South Africa and the United States. There is a very good Greek fortified red called Mavrodaphne that makes an agreeable alternative to the more basic offerings of the Douro.

HOW IT IS MADE

The fermentation of Douro wines is stopped part-way through by the addition of grape spirit, to produce a sweet, strong, liquorous wine. Various periods of cask-ageing are given to the various grades. The bottled strength is in the region of 18-20%, but can be as high as 22%.

TASTES GOOD WITH

Port is excellent with nuts and with mature, strong hard cheeses, such as Cheddar, but less good with its traditional partner, Stilton.

TAYLOR'S 20 YEARS OLD
Twenty years is the average age of the blend

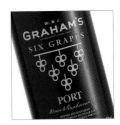

GRAHAM'S SIX GRAPES
A fairly basic ruby port

COCKBURN'S FINE RUBY
This is the lowest port designation

QUINTA DO CRASTO
An LBV from a small Portuguese producer

QUADY'S
A port-style fortified wine from the USA

SHERRY

ALTHOUGH FORTIFIED WINES bearing the name of sherry have been produced around the world for well over a century, true sherry comes only from a demarcated region in the southern Spanish province of Andalucía. There are three main centres of production – Jerez de la Frontera, Puerto de Santa María and Sanlúcar de Barrameda. The last is the traditional home of a type of pale, delicate dry sherry called manzanilla.

The production process for sherry is one of the most complicated of any fortified wine. When the new white wine is made, it

is fermented until fully dry, and then transferred into large butts. Some sherries, the ones that are destined to end up as the pale dry style known as fino (or manzanilla), develop a film of yeast culture called *flor* on the surface of the wine. In some barrels, the layer of *flor* dies out because it has consumed all the remaining nutrients in the wine, whereupon it breaks up and sinks to the bottom of the butt.

HOW TO SERVE

Fino and manzanilla, and the sweetened pale sherries, should be served very well chilled, preferably from a freshly opened bottle. In Spain, they think nothing of drinking a bottle of dry sherry as we would a table wine. The other styles should be served at room temperature. Finos are brilliant aperitifs, old olorosos best at the other end of the meal.

TIO PEPE
Muy Seco is the
very driest style
of sherry

HARVEYS
BRISTOL CREAM
A big-selling brown
cream sherry

Parkeroo (from Lucius Beebe's *Stork Club Bar Book*): Mix a double measure of pale dry sherry and a measure of tequila in a jug with ice. Decant into a champagne flute filled with shaved ice and add a twist of lemon peel.

With the subsequent greater exposure to the air, the colour of the wine deepens through oxidation, and the style known as amontillado results.

Some wines develop no *flor* at all and go on to turn a deep, woody brown colour. These are oloroso sherries. The fortification of the wine varies according to the style. Fino may be fortified to only 15% ABV, whereas oloroso is generally bottled at around 20%. At this stage, all of the wines are naturally dry, and some – the true connoisseur's sherries – will be bottled in that condition after ageing in cask.

Many commercial sherries, however, are made sweet by the addition of a quantity of *mistela*, the juice of raisined grapes to which grape spirit has been added. The best sweet sherries are sweetened with PX, which stands for Pedro Ximénez, the name of a grape variety whose berries are left to dry in the sun until loss of moisture has concentrated their sugars to an almost unbelievable degree. Some houses bottle some of their PX separately as a speciality product.

Other countries that produce sherry-style wines are Australia (which makes about the best outside Jerez), the United States, South Africa and Cyprus. Within Spain itself, there are two other regions near Jerez that produce similar fortified wines in the same range of styles, but they are not as distinguished as sherry. One is Montilla-Morilés, the other the virtually forgotten Condado de Huelva.

Spain's other great, now sadly nearly extinct, fortified wine is Málaga, made around the Mediterranean port of that name. Its finest wines are deep brown, caramel-sweet creations of great power, once hugely popular in Britain, now forsaken by fashion.

TASTES GOOD WITH

Dry sherries are good with salted nuts such as almonds, with piquant nibbles such as olives and salty fish like anchovies, and with Serrano ham or its Mediterranean equivalents. The sweet old olorosos are wonderful with rich, dark fruitcake and hard Spanish sheep's milk cheeses such as Manchego.

Adonis: Mix a double measure of pale dry sherry, a measure of sweet red vermouth and a dash or two of Angostura in a jug with ice, and strain into a wine glass.

Sherry Flip: Shake a double measure of brown cream sherry, half a teaspoon of caster sugar and a whole egg, with ice, and strain into a wine glass. Sprinkle grated nutmeg on top. (Alternatively, whizz this up in a liquidizer.)

Sherry Cocktail (below): A good double measure of pale dry sherry is mixed with three dashes each of dry vermouth and orange bitters, and plenty of ice, and strained into a large wine glass.

EMVA CREAM
A Cypriot wine, no longer labelled as "sherry"

VERMOUTH

ERMOUTH IS AS FAR removed from the natural produce of the vine as it is possible for a fortified wine to get. Not only is it strengthened with spirit, but it is also heavily aromatized with herbs and botanical ingredients in order to make a distinctive type of drink that is usually intended for drinking – either mixed or unmixed – as an aperitif. There is no particular connoisseurship of vermouth, as there is for aged sherries and vintage ports. This is an everyday product made to a consistent and unchanging recipe by each manufacturer.

The presence in vermouth of that cocktail of herbs

HOW TO SERVE

A drop or two only of dry French vermouth is needed for the perfect dry Martini or Vodkatini.

All these drinks should be served as aperitifs or at the cocktail hour. Vermouth is not as fragile once opened as pale dry sherry tends to be. It doesn't have to be drunk up within a few days, and is able to withstand extremes of temperature far more hardily than the other light fortified wines.

MARTINI EXTRA DRY
The top brand of vermouth internationally

and roots alerts us to the fact that this was originally a medicinal drink. That said, the practice of adding herbs to wine goes back to ancient Greek times, when the extra ingredients may have been put in as much to disguise the taste of spoiled wine as for their curative powers. A popular early additive was wormwood, villain of the piece when absinthe was outlawed, yet much prized as a tonic for the stomach from classical antiquity through to medieval times and the beginnings of distillation in Europe.

As far as a drink identifiable as the precursor of modern vermouth is concerned, we have to travel back to the 1500s in order to find a merchant called d'Alessio selling a wormwood wine in Piedmont (now in northwest Italy). The inspiration had come from similar German products, probably produced on a domestic scale, and it is from the German word for wormwood, *Wermuth*, that the modern English word is derived. It was already popular in England by the middle years of the following century.

Two centres of vermouth production came to be established. One was in d'Alessio's part of Italy, close to the alpine hills that were a handy wild source of the various botanical ingredients that went into the wine, and the other over the border in eastern and southeastern France. As the big commercial companies were founded, two distinct styles of vermouth emerged, one pale and dry with pronounced bitterness, the other red and sweet and not quite so bitter. The former was the style associated with France, the latter with Italy. So ingrained did these

NOILLY PRAT
A bone-dry
vermouth
produced in
the south of
France

MIXING

Lily: Shake equal measures of gin, Lillet and crème de noyau with a dash of fresh lemon juice and ice, and strain into a wine glass.

Perfect Cocktail (below): Shake exactly equal measures of gin, dry vermouth and sweet vermouth with ice, and strain into a cocktail glass. (Substitute Pernod for the gin and you have a **Duchess**.)

definitions become that, even now, drinkers still refer to "French" and "Italian" to mean dry and sweet respectively, when these may not necessarily be the geographical origins.

In fact, sweet and dry vermouths are made in both countries, and indeed elsewhere, including the United States. Brands vary according to the number and type of the herbal ingredients added, but the basic style remains the same from one batch to the next. Cloves, cinnamon, quinine, citrus peels, ginger, perhaps a touch of wormwood still (although the banning of absinthe sharply decreased the amount of wormwood that was considered acceptable in other drinks) are typical elements in the pot-pourri of aromatizers that go into the modern vermouths.

FLAVOURINGS

May include quinine, coriander seeds, cloves, juniper, ginger, dried orange and lemon peel, hyssop, camomile, raspberries, rose-petals, and so on.

As with many of the traditional liqueurs, the medicinal image of vermouth was – by the onset of the 20th century – something of an albatross around its neck, rather than a marketing opportunity. It was once again the cocktail era that rode to its rescue, finding multifarious uses for both styles of vermouth. After all, if the traditional dry Martini was destined to be the only use to which dry vermouth could be put behind the bar – one drop at a time – then not a great deal of it was ever going to be sold. Because it is quite as perfumed, in its way, as gin, vermouth proved hugely versatile in mixed drinks, and the demand for it

today – thanks in part to the big proprietary brands – remains reasonably steady.

The bulk-producing Italian firm of Martini e Rossi, based at Turin, is still the vermouth name that springs most readily to mind for consumers today. Other Italian producers are Riccadonna, Cinzano and Gancia. In France, the Marseillan producer Noilly Prat makes one of the more highly regarded dry vermouths, but also has a sweeter style. The region of Chambéry in eastern France has been awarded the *appellation contrôlée* for its vermouths, which include a strawberry-flavoured fruit version called Chambéryzette. As

CINZANO
BIANCO
Hugely
popular
brand of
sweet white
vermouth

CARPANO
PUNT E MES
A deep red
vermouth
produced at
Turin

MIXING
Bronx: Shake a measure of gin, half a measure each of dry and sweet red vermouth and the juice of no more than a quarter of an orange with ice, and strain into a cocktail glass.

well as red and white styles of vermouth, there is a golden or amber variant, and a rosé.

Other similar branded products include Lillet of Bordeaux, owned by one of the classed-growth claret châteaux, which blends a proportion of fruit juice in with the wine base along with the customary herbs; the French Dubonnet, a red or white sweet vermouth also full of highly appe-tizing quinine bitterness; and Punt e Mes, a similar but dark-coloured Italian product that combines sweeten-ing and bittering elements in intriguing balance.

DUBONNET
The red version
mixes well with
lemonade

MIXING

Bamboo: Shake two measures of dry sherry and three-quarters of a measure of sweet red vermouth with a dash of orange bitters and ice, pour into a large cocktail glass. Add one or two ice cubes if you like.

HOW IT IS MADE

A low-alcohol, mostly white wine is produced and may be allowed a short period of ageing. For the sweeter styles of vermouth, it then has a quantity of sugar syrup added to it before the fortification with spirit. This is usually grape spirit but may occasionally also be derived from vegetable sources such as sugar beet. The wine is then transferred into large barrels or tanks to which the dried aromatising ingredients have already been added. From time to time, the mixture is stirred up manually with wooden paddles. After absorption of the flavourings, the vermouth will be bottled at around 17% ABV. Some producers insist their vermouths will con-tinue to age in the bottle for a couple of years if kept. There are no vintage vermouths.

TASTES GOOD WITH

Dry vermouths are particularly useful in the kitchen for adding to sauces to accompany fish. The herbal ingredients in the vermouth add an attractive savoury note to the dish. A seasoned reduction of Noilly Prat, lemon juice and single cream is a fine way to treat good white fish such as sole or turbot.

MIXING

Bentley: Shake generous equal measures of calvados and red Dubonnet with plenty of ice, and strain into a cocktail glass.
Midsummer Night: Shake equal measures of gin and Punt e Mes with a half-measure of cassis and ice. Strain into a cocktail glass.

NON-ALCOHOLIC MIXERS

ALTHOUGH MANY of the drinks talked about in this book are commonly drunk unmixed, such as single malt whiskies, aged brandies and rums, and the fortified wines, the great majority of them would not be consumed at all were it not for non-alcoholic mixers. Some of these are so familiar as to need no explanation; others may be more rarely used, but nonetheless constitute an important element in the mixed drink and cocktail repertoire.

FRUIT JUICES

Of all the fruit juices, orange is probably the most important for mixing with single spirit shots, most notably with the white spirits that don't muddy its colour. To the cocktail-maker, freshly squeezed lemon juice is undoubtedly the most versatile ingredient. The juice of lemons has the uncanny ability to accentuate the flavours of other fruits, almost in the manner of a seasoning (try tasting a fresh fruit purée with and without lemon juice to demonstrate this point), and so it complements the fruit-flavoured liqueurs very well. Additionally, its sourness mitigates the syrupy sweetness of many of the classic liqueurs. Lime juice is yet more sour and is used in drinks that should have a particularly biting tang. Pineapple makes a sweetly exotic element in some rum-based mixtures.

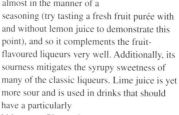

ORANGE JUICE

WATER

The simplest of all mixers is the one that dilutes the strength of ardent spirits without altering the character of their basic flavour. Water is indispensable to whisky drinkers, who claim that it enhances rather than mutes the aromatic personalities of their favoured spirit. Water softens the olfactory impact of the alcohol while allowing the complexities of grain, peat and wood to announce themselves.

Pastis drinkers use plain water, too, for the cloudiness that gives the drinks their collective name can only be obtained by mixing. In all cases, good spring water or mineral water is preferable to heavily chlorinated tap – especially so in the case of Highland and Lowland malts.

SPARKLING BEVERAGES

To achieve the diluting effects of water without changing flavour, and add a refreshing sparkle to a mixture, soda water is the required ingredi-ent. At one time, no bar (or home for that matter) was complete without a soda-siphon. They were charged with tablets of sodium bicarbonate and dispensed a stream of bubbling water through a pressurized nozzle. Nowadays, there is effectively no difference between bottled or canned soda and carbonated mineral water.

TONIC WATER

Tonic water and gin go together like Fred Astaire and Ginger Rogers. A sweetened fizzy water flavoured with the bittering component, quinine, tonic is medicinally named for the anti-malarial properties it demonstrated in tropical climes. It is useful not just with gin, but with vodka and even calvados –

SODA-SIPHON

FRESHLY SQUEEZED LEMON JUICE

wherever the dryness of a drink can be made the more appetizing with bitterness.

Lemonade should not be thought of solely as a children's drink, as it provides a useful way of administering citric sourness and fizz to a long drink. The best lemonades for bar use are not as sweet as the kids may like them, and some are actually still, in which case you may just as well use lemon juice and a pinch of sugar.

LEMONADE

All cola is derived from the invention of Coca-Cola in the United States in the late 19th century by one John Pemberton. It was originally intended as a stimulating tonic drink, and included the ground nuts of the cola tree, along with crushed coca leaves. The latter are also the source of the drug cocaine, which came to be frowned on in the early years of this century, and so Coca-Cola removed them from the recipe. Rum and neutral vodka seem to be the main spirits with which cola mixes most happily, coffee-flavoured Kahlúa and Tia Maria its closest liqueur companions.

COCA-COLA

Ginger ale or ginger beer also has its uses, with Scotch for example, but perhaps most famously with vodka as a Moscow Mule. Vodka-maker Smirnoff now makes a pre-mixed version of this drink.

SYRUPS

Cocktail-making would not be quite what it is without the availability of a range of flavoured non-alcoholic syrups to add complexity and interest to a drink. Of these, the most famous is grenadine, used to give a strong red colouring to otherwise clear mixtures, and to create the red-orange-yellow colour spectrum in the classic

Tequila Sunrise. Grenadine is made principally from the juice of the pomegranate, the peculiar Asiatic fruit that looks like a thick-skinned onion but, when cut, reveals a mass of jewel-like seeds within. It is thick, ruby-coloured and intensely sweet; some brands are made with a small alcohol quotient, but no more than about 3% ABV.

Orgeat is another little-seen syrup that was once used very widely in cocktails. Its flavouring element was almonds and it added that telltale taste of marzipan to a drink, even when used in very sparing quantities. Its name derives from the French word *orge*, meaning barley, which was once one of its ingredients.

Other syrups, flavoured with a whole greengrocer's shop of exotic ingredients, are now available. Pineapple, apricot, strawberry, banana, even kiwi-fruit are produced, and can add an appetizing dash of fruit flavour to a mixed drink, without the extra alcohol that liqueurs bring.

In addition to the flavoured syrups, it is also possible to buy a bottled neutral sugar syrup called gomme, but as it consists only of sugar and water, you may as well make your own.

GRENADINE
The principal
flavour of this
red syrup is
pomegranate

GOMME
This is simply a straight
sugar and water syrup

ORGEAT
An almond-flavoured syrup
once widely used

GINGER BEER

A traditional English summer concoction, ginger beer works well as a mixer for basic Scotch, and with vodka for a Moscow Mule.

INDEX

(g) = grape

A

A Pint-a Bitter 227
Aass brewery, Norway 257
Abbaye d'Aulne 265
Abbaye d'Orval brewery, Belgium 270, 273
Abbaye de Bonne Espérance 265
Abbaye de Notre-Dame de Scourmont brewery, Belgium 266, 274
Abbaye de Vaucelles 325
Abbaye des Rocs brewery, Belgium 265, 273
Abbey St Gallen 330
Abbot Ale 227
Abbots Invalid Stout 353
Abbotsford brewery, Australia 353
ABC Stout 351
Abita brewery, US 371, 374, 379, 380
Abouriou (g) 74
Abro brewery, Sweden 259
Abruzzi 91
absinthe 442, 470–1
  Absinthe Cocktail 472
Absolut 426, 427
Abstrunk 287
Achd Bambarcha Schwarzla 287
Achouffe brewery, Belgium 270, 273
Ackerland 325
Acme Pale Ale 371, 383
Aconcagua 154
Adam, Edouard 400
Adam Spezial 303
Adambräu 303
Adelaide Hills 165, 172
Adelschoffen brewery, France 325, 328
Adelscott 325
Adirondack Amber 371
Adler 265
Adlerbräu 334, 335
Adnams brewery, England 227, 229, 238, 241
Adonis 495
Advocaat 440
  Snowball 440
Aecht Schlenkerla Rauchbier 287
Aegean 323
Aerts 270
Affligem 265
Africa: North 131
  see also South Africa
Africana 387
agave plant: mescal 415
  tequila 422, 423
Agiorgitiko (g) 125
Aglianico (g) 92
Aglianico del Vulture 92
Agnus Dei 265
Aguila brewery, Spain 333, 334, 335
Ahr 114
Airén (g) 100
Aix-en-Provence, Coteaux de 68
Ajaccio 69
AK 227
Akasaka Micro-brewery, Japan 349
Akershus brewery, Norway 257
Alameda 141
Alaska 444
Alaskan brewery, US 374, 380
Albana di Romagna 89
Albani brewery, Denmark 253, 254
Albariño (g) 96
Albillo (g) 97
Alcañón (g) 98
Alcazar 335
Alcolsuz Efes 323
Aldaris brewery, Latvia 310, 311
Aldchlappie Hotel brewpub, Scotland 251

Ale of Atholl 247
Alella 100
Alentejo 107
Alexander 401, 447
Alexander the Great 458
Alfa brewery, Netherlands 279, 281
Algarve 107
Algeria 131
Alhambra brewery, Spain 334, 335
Alicante 101
Aligoté (g) 57, 59, 67
Alimony Ale 371
Alken-Maes brewery, Belgium 267, 270
Alko 260
Allbright 220, 221
Alloa brewery, Scotland 247, 248, 249, 250
Allsopp brewery, England 206, 227
Allsopp's White Cap 338
Almansa 101
almonds: amaretto 441
  nut liqueurs 466–7
Aloxe-Corton 57, 59
Alpes-Maritime 78
Alpine Lager 365
Alsace 50–3, 112, 407, 413, 414
  Gewürztraminer 51
  Pinot Noir 52
  Riesling 51
Alt Brunner Gold 315
  Franken 287
  Weltzlar 287
Altenmünster 285, 289
Altmünster Abbey 284
Alto Adige 87
amaretto 441
  Godfather 441
  Godmother 441
Amarit 351
Amazon Bitter 227
Ambar 334
  Lager 335
Amber Ale 279
Amber brewery, Ukraine 311
Amber Lager 371
Amber Pilsner 310, 311
Amberley 325
Ambre de Flandres 325
Amer Picon 397
American Museum of Brewing History 377
  Originals 371
Americano 397
Amersfoorts Wit 279
Ammeroois 279
amontillado sherry 102, 103
Ampurdan-Costa Brava 100
Amstel brewery, Netherlands 279, 281
Anatolia 127
Anchor Steam brewery, San Francisco, US 210, 380
  Beer 351
  Steam Beer 371, 380
Ancla 387
Ancre 325
Andalucía 102
Anderson Valley brewery, US 380
Andes 389
Angel Face 461
Angelus 325
Angostura Bitters 396
Anheuser, Eberhard 380
Anheuser-Busch brewery, US 200, 204, 315, 318, 371, 372, 373, 376, 380
Animator 287
Anis 442, 469
Anisette 442
Anjou 40, 41
Anker brewery, Belgium 268
  Ale 331
Ankhíalos 125

Anniversary Amber Ale 365
Annoeullin brewery, France 327
Ansells brewery, England 227, 241
Antarctica Pilsen 387
aperitifs 21
Apollo Brewpub, Denmark 254
Apostulator 287
Apple Ale 369
Applejack 405
apples, calvados 404–5
Apricot Ale 371
apricot brandy 460, 461
  Angel Face 461
  Paradise 460
  Yellow Parrot 470
Apry 460
aqua vitae 428
Aquavit 394
Aqui mineral water 187
Arak 395, 475
Arbois 76
Arcen brewery, Netherlands 280, 281
Arcener 279
Archdruid 221
Archers brewery, England 227, 228, 231, 241
Arcobräu 287
Arctic Pils 257
Ardèche, Coteaux de l' 67, 78
Argentarium 443
Argentina 148–9, 150–1
  Cabernet Sauvignon 150, 151
  Chardonnay 151
Arinto (g) 107, 109
Arkell Best Bitter 365
  Kingsdown Bitter, England 233, 234, 236, 240, 241
Armagnac 398, 400
Arneis 85
Arrabida 107
Arrols 80/- 247
Arthur Pendragon 227
Artois brewery, Belgium 273
Arundel brewery, England 227, 235
Asahi brewery, Japan 204, 346, 347, 348
  Super Dry 348
Ash Vine brewery, England 233
Asia Pacific Breweries 350, 351
Asmara brewery, Eritrea, Africa 338, 341
  Lager 338
Asti 85
Astika Lager 310
Astra 287
  Pilsner 298
Athenian Breweries, Greece 323
Athiri (g) 126

Aubance, Coteaux de l' 41
Aube valley 47, 48
Auburn Ale 371
Auckland 181
Augsberger 371
August 313
  Schell brewery, US 374
Augustijn 265
Augustiner Bräu 304
  brewery, Austria 295, 304
  brewery, Germany 295
Auld Alliance 247
Aurum 443
Australia 134, 135, 164–77
  Cabernet Sauvignon 134, 164
  Chardonnay 134, 164
  Chenin Blanc 167
  Gewürztraminer 167
  Grenache 172
  liqueur Muscats 490
  Marsanne 167, 175
  Merlot 167
  Muscat 165, 167, 169, 177
  Pinot Noir 167
  Riesling 166, 168
  Sauvignon Blanc 167
  Sémillon 166
  Shiraz 167
Austria 120–1
  see also Alto Adige
Autumn Frenzy 193
Auxerrois (g) 52
Auxerrois (Malbec) (g) 74
Auxey-Duresses 58
Avec les Bons Voeux de la Brasseries 265
Aventinus 287
Ayinger brewery, Germany 287, 288, 289, 294, 295
  beers 287

B

B & B (Bénédictine and brandy) 401
B&T brewery, England 230, 237, 240
Babadag 119
Bacardi 419
  Bacardi Cocktail 417
Bacchus (g) 116, 119
Bachelor Bitter 371
Back und Brau 330
Backdykes brewery, Scotland 248
Baco Noir (g) 147
Baden 116–17
Baderbräu 371
Badger brewery, England 241
Badgers Beers 227
Baga (g) 106
Bailey's Irish Cream 446
Bailleux brewery, France 325
Bairrada 106
Baiyun Beer 345
Baja California 155
Bak 310
Balalaika 427, 445
Balearic Islands 101
Balifico 93
Ballantine's 431
Ballantine's Ale 371
Ballard Bitter 371
Ballard's brewery, England 227, 239, 241, 371
Balloon glasses 398
Baltic Beverages Holdings (BBH) 309
Baltijas 310
Baltika brewery, Russia 310, 311
Bamboo 499
Bandol 69
Banks Breweries Ltd, Barbados 391
Banks brewery, England 227, 235, 245
Banner Bitter 227
Banquet Beer 372, 381
Banyuls 72

Barak Pálinka 460
Barbara 331, 427
Barbaresco 85
Barbera (g) 83, 89, 92, 135
Barbera d'Alba 85
Barbera d'Asti 85
Barbera del Monferrato 85
Barclay Perkins 313, 338, 341
Bardolino 62, 88
Barn Owl Bitter 227
Barolo 82, 85
Baroque (g) 75
Barossa Valley 135, 165, 167, 170–1
Barraclough Lager 363
Barsac 38
Basilicata 92
Bass brewery, England 206, 241
Bateman brewery, England 237, 239, 240, 241
Batham's brewery, England 227, 241
Batida Banana 462
Batida de Coco 462
Battin brewery, Luxembourg 285
Battleaxe 227
Baux de Provence, Les 68–9
Bavaria 226, 279
  brewery, Netherlands 279, 281
  St Pauli brewery, Germany 287, 298
Bavarian Gold Beer 387
Bavik brewery, Belgium 271, 273
BBH 309, 311
Beacon Bitter 227
Beam, Jim 434
Beamish and Crawford brewery, Ireland 217
  Red Ale 215
  Stout 215
Bear Ale 247
Béarn 75
Beast 227
Beaujolais 29, 62–3
Beaujolais Nouveau 63
Beaujolais-Villages 63
Beaumanor Bitter 227
Beaune 58, 59
Beaune, Côte de 55, 57–9
Beck's brewery, Germany 287, 295
Beechwood 227
Beefeater 412
beer: adjuncts 200
  adulterants 201
  flavour enhancers 201
  ingredients 187, 192, 200–1
  styles 202–3
Beijing brewery, China 345
Bekaa Valley 130
Bel Pils 265
Belarus 129
Belhaven brewery, Scotland 248, 250
Belikin Beer 387
Belle-Vue brewery, Belgium 265, 273
Bellegems Bruin 273
Bellet 69
Bell's 431
Benchmark 227
Bénédictine 443
  B & B 401
Benefontaine brewery, France 325, 326
Bentley 499
Bergenbier brewery, Romania 310, 311
Berger 471
Bergerac 73
Bergkelder (g) 163
Bering 253
Berliner Burgerbräu, Germany 287
  Weisse 213
Bernard brewery, Czech Republic 315, 318

Bernauer Schwarzbier 287
Bernkastel 114
Berrow brewery, England 239
Bert Grant's beers 372
    Yakima Brewing Company
        206, 372
Bethanian 279
BGI 351
Bianco di Custoza 88
Biekhart Cerveza Pilsen 387
    Especial 387
Bière Bénin 338
Bière de Mont St Aubert 274
Bière des Ours 273
Bière des Templiers 325
Bière du Démon 328
Bière du Désert 325, 328
Bierzo, El 96
Biferno 92
Big Butt Doppelbock 372
Big Rock brewery, Canada 365,
    366, 367, 368
Big Shoulders Porter 372
Bigfoot Barley Wine 372
Bijou 444
Binchoise brewery, Belgium 273
Binding Brewing Group,
    Germany 288, 291, 292,
    294, 295
Binissalem 101
Bintang brewery, Indonesia
    350, 351
Bio-Bio 154
Birell 208, 330, 331
Birburger 209
Birra Moretti 321
Birziecie 310, 313
Bishop's Ale 227
Bishop's Finger 227
Bishop's Tipple 228
Bitburger brewery, Germany
    287, 298
Bitters 396–7
Bjørne Bryg 253
Black Adder 228
Black Amber 365
Black & Tan Porter 372
Black Biddy 215
Black Bitter 359
Black Butte Porter 372
Black Cat Mild 228
Black Chocolate Stout 372
Black Cossack 427
Black Crow 353, 357
Black Diamond 228
Black Douglas 247
Black Forest 413
Black Hawk Stout 372
Black Jack Porter 228
Black Mac 363
Black Magic 228
Black malt 193
Black Mountain brewery, US 373
Black Regent 315
Black Rock 228
Black Russian 425, 458, 482
Black Sheep brewery, England
    228, 236, 241
Blackawton brewery, England
    230, 242
Blackened Voodoo 372, 381
Blackhook Porter 372
Blackout 448
Blagny 58
Blanc de Blancs 48
Blanc de Noirs 48
Blanche de Chambly 365
Blanche de Charleroi 274
Blanche de Namur 213, 265
Blanche des Bruges 265
Blanche des Honnelles 265
Blanquette de Limoux 72
Blauburgunder (g) 114
Blauer Wildbacher (g) 121
Blaufränkisch (g) 114, 120, 121,
    122, 123
Blaye, Côtes de 34
Block brewery, Belgium 265,
    271, 273
Block and Fall 472
Blue Fin Stout 372

Blue Heron Pale Ale 372
Blue Label 322, 353
Blue Moon 372
Blue Nile brewery, Africa
    338, 341
Blue Star Wheat Beer 368, 372
Blunderbus 228
Blunos, Martin 427
Boag's Classic Bitter 356
Bobal (g) 100
Bock-Damm 334
Bock de Moulin 329
Bockor brewery, Belgium
    269, 273
Boddingtons brewery, England
    228, 241
Bodgers 228
Bofferding brewery,
    Luxembourg 285
Bohemia 387
    Cerveza 391
    Regent 315
Bohemian Dunkel 372
Bohlingers 338
Bokkereyer 265
Bolgheri 89, 93
Bolivia 155
Bols 440, 447, 451, 460, 461, 468
Bombardier 228
Bombay Sapphire 412
Bombino (g) 91, 92
Bommes 38
Bond Corporation 352
Bonnezeaux 41
Boon brewery, Belgium 274
Boon Rawd brewery,
    Thailand 351
Booth's 412
Bor Best 228
Bordeaux 30–9, 54
    Cabernet Sauvignon 30–5
    Merlot 30–5
    Sauvignon Blanc 36–9
    Sémillon 36–9
Borsodi brewery, Hungary 311
    Vilagos 310, 311
Borthwick, Master 455
Borve Brewpub, Scotland
    247, 250
Bosco (g) 86
Boskeun 206
Bosnia-Herzegovina,
    slivovitz 421
Bosteels brewery, Belgium 274
Boston 487
Boston, John 355
Boston Beer Company, US 211,
    378, 379, 380
Bosun Bitter, Poole, England 228
Bosun's Bitter, Africa 338, 342
    St Austell, England 228
Botrytis cinerea 38
Boulder Amber Ale 372
Bourbon 433–4
    Boston 487
    Casanova 489
Bourboncuis (g) 66, 71
Bourg, Côtes de 34
Bourgogne see Burgundy
Bourgogne des Flanders 265
Bourgogne Grand Ordinaire 60
Bourgogne Passetoutgrains 60–1
Bourgueil 42
Bouzeron, Bourgogne Aligoté
    de 59
Bouzy 48
Brabantine 274
Brachetto (g) 69
Brachetto d'Acqui 86
Brador 365
Bragot (Bragawd) 222
Brahma Chopp 389
    Export 387
    Pilsner 387
Brains Old brewery, Wales 220,
    221, 223
Brakspear brewery, England
    235, 241
    Bitter 228
    Special 228
Brand brewery, Netherlands 279,

280, 281, 282
    Oak Bitter 228
Brandy 398–403
    Alexander 401, 447
    Aurum 443
    B & B (Bénédictine and
        brandy) 401
    brandy blazer 403
    eaux-de-vie 406–7
    liqueur 460–1
    ratafia 476
    Sidecar 445
    Sundowner 483
    see also Calvados
Branik brewery, Czech
    Republic 318
Branoc 228
Branscombe Vale brewery,
    England 228, 236, 238
Braquet (g) 69
Brasal Brasserie Allemande,
    Canada 368
    Bock 365
    Légère 365
    Special Amber 365
Brasimba brewery, Africa 340
Brass Monkey Stout 359
Brasserie de Tahiti 363
Brasserie du Bénin, Togo, Africa
    338, 339, 341
Brasserie du Maroc, Africa
    338, 341
Brasserie McAuslan, Canada 365,
    366, 367, 368
Brasserie Nationale 284, 285
Brasseries Réunies de
    Luxembourg Mousel et
    Clausen 284, 285
Brasseurs beers 329
Bräu AG 304
Bräu AG brewery, Austria
    303, 304
Bräu und Brunnen 308
Bräu und Brunnen Group,
    Germany 296
Braugold 331
Brauhernen Pilsner 287
Brauherren Pilsner 298
Braumeister 287
Brazil 148, 149, 152
    breathing (of wine) 15
Breganze 88
Bremer Weisse 287
Brenin 221
Breug 325
Brew 228, 237
Brew 97 228
Brew XI 228
Brewer's Choice 322
Brewer's Droop 229
Brewer's Pilsner 357
Brewer's Pride 229
Brewery-on-Sea, Lancing,
    England 228, 229, 231,
    236, 237

Brick Brewing Company, Canada
    365, 367–8
Bridge Bitter 229
Brigand 265
Briljant 279, 282
Brindisi 92
Brindle 221, 223
Brinkhoff's No. 1 287
Brisbane Bitter 358
    Pilsner 358
Bristol Stout 229
Britain see United Kingdom
British Columbia 147
Brizard, Marie 442, 447, 460, 474
Brno 318
Broadside Ale 229
Broadsword 247
Brock Extra Stout 365
Broken Hill Draught 353
Bronx 497
Brooklyn brewery, US 372
Broughton brewery, Scotland 247,
    248, 249, 250
Brouilly 63
Broyhan Alt 288
Brugs Straffe Hendrick 265
Brugs Tarwebier (Blanches de
    Bruges) 213, 265
Brugse Tripel 265
Bruna 321
Brune Spéciale 325
Brunehaut brewery, Belgium 274
Brunello di Montalcino 89
BSN (Kronenbourg) 320
Bual 111, 487
Buccaneer 229
Bucelas 107
Buchan Bronco 247
Buckley's Best Bitter 221, 223
Bud Dry 204
    Ice 206
Budel brewery, Netherlands 279,
    281, 282
Budweiser 200, 315, 373
Budweiser Budvar brewery, Czech
    Republic 315, 318
Bugey 76, 77
    wine 83, 124, 127–8
Bulgaria: brandy 401
    wine 310, 312
Bull's Head Bitter 359
Bulldog Pale Ale 229
Bullion 229
Bullmastiff brewery, Wales 220,
    221, 223
Bunces brewery, England 227,
    229, 235, 238, 239
Bunny Hug 471
Buorren 279
Burgasko brewery, Bulgaria
    310, 312
Burgenland 121
Burgerbräu brewery,
    Germany 290
Burgundy 30, 54–61, 414
    Chardonnay 55
    Pinot Noir 56
Burragarang Bock 359
Burton Bridge brewery, England
    229, 231, 235, 239
Burtonwood brewery, England
    229, 239, 241
Busch, Adolphus 380
    Golden Pilsner 288
Bush 266
Bushmills 436
Butcombe brewery, England 229,
    240, 241
Butterknowle brewery, England
    227, 228, 229, 232, 233, 235
Buur 253
Buzet 74
Buzz 229
Buzzard Breath Ale 368

C
Cabardès 71
Cabernet d'Anjou 41
Cabernet Franc 30, 32, 33, 34, 42,
    43, 73, 87, 147
Cabernet Sauvignon 30, 68, 70,
    73, 88, 90, 93, 99, 120, 128,

130, 134, 138, 141–5, 150,
    151, 153, 154, 164–5, 167,
    171–6, 179
Cadbury's 446
Cadillac 39
Caffrey's Irish Ale 215
Cahors 74
Cains brewery, England 229,
    231, 242
Calabria 92
Calanda brewery, Switzerland 331
Calatayud 98
Calatrava 335
Calder's 247
Caledonian brewery, Scotland
    205, 247, 248, 250
California 29, 83, 134, 135,
    136–7, 138–42
    brandy 402–3
    Cabernet Sauvignon 138
    grappa 414
    Merlot 138
    Pinot Noir 138
    Sauvignon Blanc 138
    Shiraz 142
Calton brewery, Fiji 363
Caluso Passito 86
Calvados 404–5
    Angel Face 461
    Bentley 499
    Depth Charge 405
    Diki-Diki 475
    Wally 461
Calvi 69
Cambrian brewery, Wales
    220, 223
Cambridge Bitter 229
Camel Beer 338
Cameron brewery, England 229,
    238, 242
Campania 84, 92
Campari 396, 397
Campo de Borja 98
CAMRA 226
Canada: whisky 436–7
    wine 146–7
Canadian Lager 365
Canaiolo (g) 90
Cannonau (g) 93
Canon-Fronsac 33
Canterbury 361
Canterbury (NZ) 183
Cantillon brewery, Belgium 271,
    272, 274
Canton Lager Beer 345
Cap Corse, Coteaux du 69
Cape brewery, Africa 337
Cape Riesling (g) 158
Captain Morgan 419
Capucijn 279
Caracole brewery, Belgium 274
    caraway seeds, kümmel 459
Carbine Stout 353, 356
    carbonic maceration 72
Carcavelos 111
Cardenal brewery, Venezuela 389
Cardinal brewery, Switzerland
    331, 332
Carema 86
Carib 390
Caribbean 416, 462
Caribe Development Company,
    Trinidad 391
Carignan (g) 66, 68, 71, 98
Cariñena 98
Carling Black Label 229, 365
Carling brewery, Canada 368
Carling O'Keefe brewery,
    Canada 368
Carlsberg brewery, Denmark 252,
    253, 254, 255, 308, 320, 337
    Carlsberg Foundation 255
    Carlsberg Let 253
    Carlsberg Malawi Ltd 337
Carlton United Brewers, Australia
    353, 356
Carmignano 90
Carnegie Porter 259
Carnelian (g) 145
Carneros 140, 141
Carolus 288

Carpinteria 155
Carthusians 444
Casablanca (Chile) 153, 154
Casanova 489
Cascade 188, 353
Cascade brewery, Tasmania 356
Cascade Golden Ale 373
Casper's Max 279
Cassis 69
Cassovar 315
Castel del Monte 92
Castelain brewery, France 328
Castello 331, 332
Castillon 34
Castle Ale 229
Castle Eden brewery, England
  229, 230, 231, 242
Castle Golden Pilsner 338
Castle Lager 200, 337, 338
Castle Milk Stout 338
Castle Special Pale Ale 229
Castlemaine brewery, Australia
  353, 356
Castlemaine Perkins, brewery,
  Australia 356
Castlemaine XXXX 353, 356
Catamount brewery, US 372, 380
Catarratto (g) 93, 489
cava 98, 99
CD 288
Celebration Ale 373
Celebrator 288
Celis brewery, US 373, 380, 381
  Pieter 213, 266, 269
  White 266, 373
Cencibel (g) 100
Central Village brewery,
  Jamaica 390
Central Vineyards see
  Loire, Upper
Cephalonia 126
Cepparello 93
Ceres brewery, Denmark 253, 254
Cereza (g) 150
Cergal 336
Cerna Horna brewery, Czech
  Republic 315, 316, 317, 318
Cernohorsky Granat 315
  Lezak 315
Cérons 39
Cerro Chapeu 155
Certa 325
Cervecería Ancla S.A., Colombia
  387, 389
Cervecería Bieckhert, Argentina
  387, 389
Cervecería Corona, Puerto
  Rico 391
Cervecería Costa Rica S.A. 387
Cervecería La Constancia 389
Cervecería Moctezuma, Mexico
  386, 388, 389
Cervecería Modelo, Mexico 386,
  387, 389
Cervejaría Cacador, Brazil 388
Cervesur (Compañia Cervecera
  Del Sur Del Peru S.A.) 388–9
Cerveza 387
Cerveza Negra 351
Cerveza Rosanna Red Chilli Ale
  204, 373
Cerveza Tipo Pilsen 389
César (g) 60
Ceske Budejovice 318
Cesky Crumlov brewery, Czech
  Republic 316
Ceylon brewery, Sri Lanka 351
Chablis 55–6, 82
Chacoli di Guetaria 98
Chairman's Extra Strong
  Brew 338
Challenger 229
Chalonnaise, Côte 55, 59–60
Chambers 490
Chambéryzette 498
Chambolle-Musigny 56
Champagne 44–9
  Kir Royale 449
  Marc de Champagne 414
  Stratosphere 448
Champenois, Coteaux 48
Chapeau 266, 275

Chardonnay 42, 43, 47, 55–61,
  63, 70, 76, 79, 99, 121, 128,
  134, 138–45, 147, 150–4, 157,
  158, 160, 161, 162, 164–6,
  168–76, 178, 180–3
Charentais, Vin de Pays 79
Charente 398
Charles Quint 266
Charlie, Bonnie Prince 453
Chartreuse 444
  Alaska 444
  Bijou 444
  Golden Slipper 456
  Yellow Parrot 470
Chassagne-Montrachet 58–9
Chasselas (g) 43, 52, 77
Château-Chalon 76–7
Château-Grillet 65
Château Neubourg 279
Châteauneuf-du-Pape 64, 66
Châtillon-en-Diois 67
Cheers 261
Chénas 62
Chenin Blanc (g) 41, 42, 43, 144
  see also Steen
cherries: Kirsch 413
  maraschino 464
cherry brandy 460–1
  Pick-Me-Up 461
  Singapore Sling 461
Cherry Heering 461
Chesterfield Ale 373, 385
Cheverny 43
Chianti 82, 89, 90
Chiaretto 88
Chibuku 338
Chibuku Breweries, Zimbabwe,
  Africa 341
Chicago brewery, US 375
Chihuahua 389
Chile 136, 148, 152–4
  brandy 403
  Cabernet Sauvignon 152–4
  Chardonnay 152–4
  Sauvignon Blanc 153, 154
  Sémillon 153
Chiltern brewery, England 227,
  228, 229
Chimay brewery, Belgium 212,
  266, 274
  ales 266
China 131
Chinese Ginseng Beer 345
Chinon 42
Chiroubles 63
Chitry 60
Chmelar 316
chocolate malt 193
Chodovar brewery, Czech
  Republic 318
Chorey-lès-Beaune 58
Choulette brewery, France 325,
  326, 327, 328
Christian Moerlein 373
Christmas Juleol 257
Christoffel brewery, Netherlands
  279, 282
Ch'ti 325
Chu Jiang brewery, China 345
Chu Sing 345
cider 404
Cigales 97
Cinco Estrellas 334
Cinquempre 86
Cinsaut (g) 66, 68, 130, 131,
  157, 159
Cinzano 498
Cirò 92
Clairette de Die 67
Clairette du Languedoc 71
Clairette (g) 66, 67, 71
Clare Valley 166, 169
clarets 30
Clark brewery, England 232, 234
Clarysse brewery, Belgium 268,
  270, 274
Clausthaler 208, 288
Clevner 52
Club Pilsner 338, 342
Cluss Bock 288
Cnudde 204

Coach House brewery, England
  228, 229, 232, 233
Coachman's Best 229
Coates 412
Cobra 351
Coca-Cola 501
Cochonne 266
Cocker Hoop 229
Coconut, Malibu 462
Cocoribe 462
coffee: Kahlúa 458
  Sambuca 477
  Tia Maria 482
cognac 398, 399–400
  Alexander 401
  Block and Fall 472
  brandy blazer 403
  Depth Charge 405
  Hurricane 472
  Inigo Jones 489
  Olympic 451
  Sunburn 482
  Walnut Whip 467
  Whip 452
Cointreau 445
  Balalaika 427, 445
  Block and Fall 472
  Margarita 423, 445
  Petite Fleur 417
  Sidecar 445
Cola 501
Colares 107
Cold Spring Export Lager 373
  colheita port 109
College Ale 229
Colli dell'Etruria Centrale 90
Colli Orientali 88
Colli Piacentini 89
Collio 88
Collioure 72
Colombard (g) 158, 167
Colombus 279, 283, 303
Commandaria 127
Companhia Cervejaría, Brazil
  387, 388, 389
Conca di Barbera 99
Conciliation Ale 229
Concord (g) 145
Condado de Huelva 103
Condado de Tea 96
Condrieu 64–5
Conero, Rosso 90–1
Constantia 156, 159, 161
Coonawarra 169, 173
Cooper's brewery, Australia 353,
  356–7
  beers 353–4
Coopers WPA 229
Coors 373
  brewery, US 188, 206, 372, 373,
  374, 381

Copertino 92
Coral 336
Corbières 72
Corby's 436, 437
Corcoués/Logne 40
Coreff 328
Cornas 65
Coromandel Brewing Co.,
  NZ 361
Corona 391
Corona Extra 387
Corse, Vin de 69
Corsendonck 267
Corsica 69, 78
Cortese (g) 86
Cortese di Gavi 86
Corton, Le 57
Corton-Charlemagne 57
Costers del Segre 98–9
Costières de Nîmes 67
Côte de Nuits 55, 56–7
Côte de Nuits-Villages 57
Côte des Blancs 47
Côte d'Or 54, 55
  see also Beaune, Côte de; Côte
  de Nuits
Côte-Rôtie 64
Cotleigh brewery, England 227,
  232, 235
Cotnari 129
Coulée de Serrant 41
Country Best Bitter 230
Country Stile 230
County Ale 365
Cour-Cheverny 43
Courage brewery, England 212,
  229, 230, 231, 233, 242
Courvoisier 398
Coutts, Morton 360
Cowra 176
CPA (Crown Pale Ale) 221
Craftsman 230
Crazy Ed's Cave Creek Chilli
  Beer 204, 373
Cream City Pale Ale 373
cream liqueurs 446
Creemore Springs brewery,
  Canada 368
Crémant d'Alsace 52–3
Crémant de Bourgogne 61
Crémant de Limoux 72
Crémant de Luxembourg 122
Crème d'amandes 466
Crème de banane: Batida
  Banana 462
  Oracabessa 448
  Silver Jubilee 448
Crème de cacao 448
  Alexander the Great 458
  Grasshopper 450
Crème de cassis: Kir 449
Crème de framboise 449
Crème de menthe:
  Grasshopper 450
  Stinger 447
Crème de mûre 450
  Blackout 448
Crème de noix 466, 467
  Walnut Whip 467
Crème de noyau 466, 467
  Pink Almond 467
Crème de pêche 450
Crème de roses: English Rose 448
Crème de violette:
  Stratosphere 448
Crème liqueurs 447–50
Crépy 77
Crete 126
Crimea 129
Criolla (g) 150
Cristal 336
Cristal Alken 267
Cristal Brown 336
Croatina (g) 89
Crombe brewery, Belgium
  270, 274
Cromwell Bitter 230
Crouch Vale brewery, England
  234, 237, 240
Crouchen (g) 158
Crown 353

Crown Buckley brewery, Wales
  220, 221, 223
Crozes-Hermitage 65
Cruzcampo brewery, Spain 333,
  334, 335
Crystal 316, 321
  malt 193
Cuaranta y Tres 452
Cuauhtémoc brewery, Mexico
  387, 388, 389
Cuba Libre 417
Cuervo 423
Cuillin 247
Cuivrée 325
Cumberland Ale 230
Cumières 48
Curaçao 445, 451–2
  Gloom Chaser 457
  Mandarine Napoléon 463
  Oasis 451
  Olympic 451
  Rite of Spring 452
  Whip 452
Cusenier 460, 478
Cusquena 389
Cuvée d'Aristées 267
Cuvée de Jonquilles 325
Cuvée de Koninck 267
Cuvée de l'An Neuf 274
Cuvée de l'Hermitage 267
Cuvée René 276
Cuzco 387, 389
Cwrw Castell 221
  Tudno 221
Cyclades, the 126
Cynar 453
Cyprus: brandy 401
  wine 126–7
Czarina 427
Czech Republic 83, 122–3

D

D-Ale 353
DAB (Dortmunder Actien
  Brauerei), Germany 204, 288,
  289, 291, 296
Daiquiri 419, 447
Daleside brewery, England
  230, 234
Dali, Salvador 401
Damm brewery, Spain 333,
  334, 335
Dampfbier 288
D'Annunzio, Gabriele 443
Dansk Dortmunder 253
  LA 253
Danziger Goldwasser 456, 459
Dão 105
Daredevil Winter Warmer 230
Dark de Triomphe 329
  Island 247
Dart 259
Davies, Sir Horatio 473
De Bartoli 489
De Dolle brewery 206, 270, 274
De Keersmaeker brewery,
  Belgium 270, 274
De Kluis brewery, Belgium 269
De Koninck brewery, Belgium
  267, 274
De Kroon brewery,
  Netherlands 282
De Kuypers 440, 447, 461
De Smedt brewery, Belgium 265,
  266, 270, 275
De Troch brewery, Belgium
  266, 275
Deacon 230
Dealul Mare 129
decanting wine 17
Deep Ender's 373
Deep Shaft Stout 230
Deidesheim 116
Delerium Tremens 267
Delicator 288
Dent brewery, England 236, 239
Dentergems Wit 213, 267
Depth Charge 405
Deschute brewery, US 371, 372,
  373, 375, 376
Desnoes & Geddes brewery,
  Jamaica 391

Deuchars IPA 247, 250
Deux Rivières brewery,
    France 328
Devil Gold 230
Devon Gold 230
Diamond Draught 353, 356
Diano d'Alba 86
Dickel, George 434, 435
Dickens, Charles 410
Diebels brewery, Germany 202,
    288, 296
Diekirch brewery,
    Luxembourg 285
Diki-Diki 475
Dimiat (g) 128
Dinkelacker brewery, Germany
    288, 292
Director's 230
Disaronno Amaretto 441
Dixie brewery, US 372, 375, 381
D'lite 359
Dock Street brewery, US 381
Dr Johnson's Draught 221
Dogbolter 353, 357
Dogliani 86
Dojlidy brewery, Poland 307, 308
Dokkur 263
Dolceacqua 86
Dolcetto (g) 29, 83, 86
Dolcetto d'Acqui 86
Dolcetto d'Alba 86
Dôle 122
Dolphin Best 230
DOM brewery, Germany 296
    Kölsch 288
    Pilsner 288
Domaine de Coyeux 490
Domaine Durban 490
Domecq 401
Dominator 279
Dominion Breweries (DB), N.Z.
    360, 361, 362
    beers 361–2
Dommelsch brewery, Netherlands
    279, 282
Domus brewery, Belgium 267
Donnington brewery, England
    227, 240, 242
Doppelbock Bugel 267
Doppo Micro-brewery, Japan 389
Dornfelder (g) 114, 115, 116
Dorset Best 230
Dort Maltezer, Ridder 283
Dortmunder Gold 373, 382
Dos Equis (Two Crosses) 386,
    388, 389
Double Brown 361
Double Chance 230
Double Diamond 230
Double Dragon 221
Double Enghein Brune 268
Double Happiness Guangzhou
    Beer 345
Double Maxim 230
Double Stout 230
Douglas 247
Douro 105
Dragon Stout 211, 391
Dragonhead Stout 247
Dragon's Breath 221
Dragonslayer 230
Drak 316
Drambuie 453
    Rusty Nail 453
Draught Bass 230
    Burton Ale 230
Drava 123
Drawwell Bitter 230
Dreher, Anton 213, 305, 312
Dreher Bak 310
Dreher brewery, Italy 321, 322
    Export 310
    Pilsner 310
Dreikönigs 331
Drie Hoefijzers brewery,
    Netherlands 281, 283
Drie Ringen brewery, Netherlands
    279, 282
Drioli 464
Drôme, the 67
Drought 481
Drumborg 174

dry beer 346
Dry Martini 411
Du Bocq brewery, Belgium 210,
    213, 265, 269, 271, 275
DUB (Dortmunder Union
    brewery), Germany 204, 287,
    288, 296
Dubonnet 499
    Bentley 499
Dubuisson brewery, Belgium 266
Duckstein 288
Dudak 316
Duffy's 365
Duivelsbier 268
Dundee's Honey Brown Lager
    373, 382
Dunkle Perle 331
Dunphy's 436
Dupont brewery, Belgium 210,
    265, 270, 272, 275
Duras, Côtes de 74
Durbanville 161
Dutch genever 412
Duvel 268
Duyck brewery, France 326,
    327, 328
Dvaro 310, 312
Dyffryn Clwyd brewery, Wales
    220, 224

E
Eagle Blue 353
Eagle Blue Ice 353
Eagle IPA 230
Eagle Stout 340
Eagle Super 353
Eagle's Dream 468
Early Times 434
East African Breweries,
    Africa 341
East Side Dark 373
Easy Street Wheat 373
Eau-de-vie 406–7
    slivovitz 421
EB Specjal Pils 307
Ebony Dark 221, 223
    Super Strength 391
Echt Kölsch 288
Ecuador 155
Edel 314
Edel Pils 297
Edelweiss 303
Edelwicker (g) 52
Eden Bitter 230
Eden Valley 166, 171–2
Edinburgh Strong Ale 247
Edmund II Ironside 230
Efes brewery, Turkey 323
Egelantier 279
Eggenberg 316
Eggenberg brewery, Austria
    303, 304
Egill brewery, Iceland 263
Eichbaum brewery, Germany 287,
    291, 294, 296
Eichhoff brewery, Switzerland
    331, 332
Einbeck 203
Einbecker brewery, Germany 287,
    288, 298
Eisbock 203
Eiswein 113, 121
Ekstra 310, 312
EKU brewery, Germany 289
Elbling (g) 122
Elbrewery brewery, Poland 308
Elbschloss brewery, Germany 292
Elders IXL 352
Eldridge Pope (Hardys) brewery,
    England 237
Elegantier 279, 282
Elephant 253
Elgin 162
Elgood brewery, England 229,
    231, 235, 242
Eliot Ness 373, 382
Elizabethan 230
Elk Mountain Amber Ale 373
Emilia-Romagna 89
Emperor's Gold Beer 345
Empresa brewery, Portugal 336
Emu 353

Ename 275
English gin 412
English Rose 448
Enkel 279
Entre-Deux-Mers 34, 37
Enville Farm brewery, England
    206, 230, 231
Enzian 481
Epernay 46
Epineuil 60
Epirus 125
Erbaluce di Caluso 86
Erdinger brewery, Germany 213,
    289, 291, 296
ESB 230
ESB Africa 338, 342
Esgana (g) 107
Espresso Stout 373
Esquire Extra Dry 374
Esquire Premium Pale Ale 374
Est! Est!! Est!!! di
    Montefiascone 91
Estrella del Sur 334, 335
ESX Best 230
Etoile, L' 76
Euler brewery, Germany 287, 289
Eupener brewery, Belgium 275
Europa 336
Eurospecjal 307
Evansville brewery, US 374
Everard brewery, England 227,
    230, 235, 239
Exmoor brewery, England 227,
    231, 237, 242
Export Mongrel 353
Eye of the Hawk 374
Ezerjó (g) 123

F
Facon brewery, Belgium 275
Fakir 273
Falcon brewery, Sweden 259
Falerno del Massico 92
Fall Fest 374
Falstaff Real Ale 363
Famous Grouse 431
Fargo 231
Fargues 38
Farmer's Glory 231
Farsons Brewers, Malta 322
Faugères 71
Favorita 86
Faxe brewery, Denmark
    253, 254
Fed Special 231
Federation Ale 359
Federation brewery, England 231,
    232, 242
Feldschlösschen brewery,
    Germany 288, 289
Feldschlösschen Breweries,
    Switzerland 330, 331
Feldschlösschen Ex-Bier 332
Felinfoel brewery, Wales 220,

221, 224
Felix Kriekbier 268
Felix Oud Bruin 268
Fendant (g) 122
Feng Shon brewery, China 345
Fer Servadou (g) 74, 75
Fernão Pires (g) 106
Fernet Branca 397
Fest-Märzen 289
Festive 231
Fetească (g) 129
Feuerfest 289
Fiano d'Avellino 92
Figari 69
Fiji Bitter Beer 363
Finlandia 427
fino sherry 102, 103
Fior d'Alpi 454
Fire Rock Ale 363
First 289
Fischer brewery, France 325,
    327, 328
Fitou 72
Fitzgerald, F. Scott 411
Five Star brewery, Beijing,
    China 345
Fixin 56
Flaccianello della Pieve 93
Flag 338
Flagey-Echézeaux 56
Flame 361
Fleurie 62–3
Floc de Gascogne 476
Floreffe brewery, Belgium 265,
    268, 269
Florio 488
Flowers brewery, England
    231, 242
Flying Herbert 231
Flying Horse 351
Fockinks 440
Folle Blanche (g) 40
Fondillon 101
Fonseca, José Maria da 491
Forester's 339, 342
Formidable Ale 231
Forschungs brewery, Germany
    291, 292
Forst brewery, Italy 321, 322
Fort Mitchell brewery, US 377
Fortunator 289
Fortyniner 231
Foster's Brewing Group,
    Australia 353, 354, 355,
    356, 357
Founders 231
Fourcroy, Antoine-François
    de 463
Frambozen 201
France: Anis 442
    Bénédictine 443
    brandy 398–400
    calvados 404–5
    Chartreuse 444
    Cointreau 445
    Mandarine Napoléon 463
    Muscat 490
    nut liqueurs 466–7
    pastis 469–71
    ratafia 476
    vermouth 497
    Verveine du Vélay 483
    La Vieille Curé 483
    wine 28–9
    see also Alsace; Beaujolais;
        Bordeaux; Bugey; Burgundy;
        Champagne; Corsica; Gascony;
        Jura; Languedoc-Roussillon;
        Loire; Médoc; Provence;
        Rhône; Savoie
Franche-Comté 413
Franciacorta 89
Francs, Côtes de 34
Frangelico 467
    Mad Monk 467
Franken (Franconia) 116
Frankenmuth brewery, US 381
Franklin's Bitter 231
Frankovka (g) 122
Franschhoek 160, 163

Franz Inselkammer brewery,
    Germany 287
Franz Joseph Jubelbier 289
Franz Sailer brewery, Germany
    291
Franziskaner 289
Fraoch 247
Frascati 91
Freedom Pilsner 231
Freeminer Bitter 231
Freiberger Brauhaus,
    Germany 289
Freidrich and Renne 355
Fréijoers 285
Freisa d'Asti 86
Freisa di Chieri 86
Freistadter brewery,
    Austria 304–5
Fremantle Bitter 354
Friart brewery, Belgium 275
Friuli 88–9
Frog & Rosbif brewery,
    France 329
Frog Island brewery, England 234
Fronsac 33
Frontenac 365, 368
Frontier 374
Frontignan 72
Frontonnais, Côtes du 75
Fruit Daiquiri 447
Fruit juices 500
Frydenlund Pilsener 257
Frysk Bier 279
Füchschen brewery, Germany 298
Fuggles Imperial 231
Full Sail brewery, US 374,
    379, 381
Fuller's brewery, England 229,
    230, 233, 242
Funck, Henri 284
Fundador 401
Furmint (g) 123
Fürstenberg brewery, Germany
    289, 298
F.X. Matt brewery, US 371–2, 382

G
Gaffel brewery, Germany 298
Gaglioppo (g) 92
Gaillac 74–5
Gales brewery, England 233, 236
Galestro 90
Galliano 454
    Harvey Wallbanger 454
    Milano 454
Gallo 403
Gamay (g) 43, 60, 62, 67, 77
Gambellara 88
Gambrinus brewery, Czech
    Republic 316, 317, 318
Gamla Stans brewery,
    Sweden 259
Gamle Special Dark 253
Gammel Porter 253
Gamza (g) 128
Gancia 498
Garde brewery, Germany 298
Gargoyle 231
Garnacha (Grenache) (g) 95, 96,
    98, 101
Garnier 478
Gascogne, Côtes de 75, 79
Gascony 73–5
Gattinara 86
Gatz Alt 289
Gatzweiler brewery, Germany 289
Gavi 86
Gayant brewery, France 325, 326,
    327, 328
GB Mild 231
Gdanskie 307
Geary's Micro-brewery, US 381
Geelong 231
Geisenheim 116
Genesee brewery, US 373, 378,
    379, 382
Genny Bock 374, 382
Gentian: bitters 396
    Suze 481
Gentiane 481
George IV, King of
    England 460–1

George Killian's Irish Red
206, 374
Georges Bitter Ale 231
Georgia (CIS) 129
Gereons brewery, Germany 298
Germain-Robin 403
German Purity Law see
Rheinheitsgebot
Germany: brandy 401
Gewürztraminer 113, 116, 117
Kirsch 413
kümmel 459
Pinot Noir 113, 115
Riesling 112 , 123
wine 83, 112–17
Gers 78
Gerst Amber 374
Gevrey-Chambertin 56
Gewürztraminer (g) 51, 53, 113,
116, 117, 119, 120, 139,
160, 167
Gibbs Mew brewery, England
228, 230, 237, 240
Gibson 411
Gigi brewery, Belgium 272, 275
Gigondas 66
Gilde Pils 289
Gildenbier 268
Gillespie's 247
Gimlet 409
gin 408–12
Angel Face 461
Blackout 448
Bronx 497
Bunny Hug 471
Drought 481
Dry Martini 411
Eagle's Dream 468
English Rose 448
Gibson 411
Gimlet 409
Gin Fizz 409
Gin Rickey 409
Gin Smash 410
Gin Swizzle 412
Lily 497
Mad Monk 467
Matinée 477
Merry Widow 496
Midsummer Night 499
Milano 454
Monkey Gland 469
Oasis 451
Paradise 460
Perfect Cocktail 497
pink gin 397
Silver Jubilee 448
Singapore Sling 461
sloe gin 478
White Lady 409, 445
ginger ale 501
Ginger Tom 231
Gingersnap 205, 231
Gippsland Gold 357
Giraf 253
Girardin brewery, Belgium 275
Gisborne 181
Givry 60
Gladiator 279
Gladstone 231
glasses: balloon 398
wine 18–19
Glass's Castle brewery, Africa 342
Glayva 455
Glenrowan-Milawa 175, 177
Gloom Chaser 457
Gocseji Barna 310, 312
Godello (g) 96
Godfather 441
Godmother 441
Golan Heights 130
Gold Brew 221, 223
Gold Fassl 303
Gold Label 231
Golden Amber 247
Golden Best 231
Golden Bitter 231
Golden Brew 221
Golden Gate 374
Golden Guinea brewery,
Africa 340

Golden Label 231
Golden Mead Ale 206
Golden Pale 247
Golden Promise 205, 247
Golden Slipper 456
Golden Tang 480
Goldenberg 325
Goldwasser 443, 456, 459
Golden Slipper 456
Gomme 501
Gonzalez Byass 401
Gordon's 412
Gordon's Ales 247
Gorilla 259
Gosser 303
Gotenba Kohgen Brewpub,
Japan 349
Gothic Ale 231
Gotlands brewery, Sweden 259
Gotyckie Magnat 308
Gotz, Jan 308
Goudale 325
Gouden Boom brewery, Belgium
213, 265, 272
Carolus 268
Goudenband 268
Goulburn Valley 175
Goumenissa 125
Gouveio (g) 109
Gouverneur 280, 283
Governor 231
Graduate 231
Gran Riserva 321
Granada brewery, Granada,
W.I. 391
Granary Bitter 231
Granat 316
Grand Marnier 457
Gloom Chaser 457
Grand Prestige 278
Grand Ridge brewery,
Australia 357
Grand Slam 475
Granite Belt 166, 177
Granite brewery, Canada 368
Grant, Thomas 460
Grant's Scottish Ale 374
Granville Island Brewing
Company, Canada 365,
366, 368
Grappa 414
Grasă (g) 129
Grasshopper 450
Grasshopper Wheat 366
Grauburgunder (g) 113, 116
Grave del Friuli 88
Graves 31, 32, 35, 36, 37, 38
Great Lakes brewery, US 373,
376, 382
Great Northern brewery, N.Z. 363
Porter, Ireland 215
Porter, US 374
Great Western 174
Grechetto (g) 91
Greco di Bianco (g) 92
Greco di Tufo 92
Greece: brandy 402
Mavrodaphne 493
ouzo 472
wine 83, 124–6
Green Caribbean 465
Greene King brewery, England
227, 238, 242
Greenmantle 248
Grenache (g) 66, 68, 71, 72,
135, 142, 167
see also Garnacha
Grenadine 501
Grion Brown Ale 366, 368
Extra Pale Ale 366, 368
Grifi 93
Grignolino 86
Grillo (g) 489
Grimbergen 268
Gritstone Premium Ale 366
Grodzisk 307
Grolleau (g) 41
Grolsch brewery, Netherlands
280, 282, 308
Grøn 253
Gros Manseng (g) 75
Gros Plant (g) 40

Gros Plant du Pays Nantais 41
Groslot (g) 41
Growlin Gator Lager 374
Grozet 248
Grüner Veltliner (g) 120, 121
GSB 231
Guangminpai 345
Guangzhou brewery, China 345
Guinness, Black Cossack 427
Guinness brewery, St James's
Gate, Dublin, Ireland 188,
209, 211, 215, 217, 218–19,
335, 340
Draught 215
Extra Stout 214
Foreign Extra Stout 215
Special Export 215
Stout 390
Gulder 339, 342
Gull 263
Gulpener brewery, Netherlands
279, 280, 281, 283
Gulpener Dort 280, 283
Gumpoldskirchner 120
Gunpowder 232
Gutturnio 89
Gyenge, Zsolt 311

H

Haacht brewery, Belgium 265,
266, 267, 271, 276
Haake-Beck brewery, Germany
287, 290, 295
Hacker-Pschorr brewery,
Germany 205, 287, 289, 296
Hahn brewery, Australia 354, 357
Hall & Woodhouse brewery,
England 227, 230, 238, 241
Hambleton brewery, England 234
Hammerhead 232
Hampshire brewery, England 227,
230, 233, 240
Hampshire Special Ale 374, 381
Hanby brewery, England 230, 237
Hancock's brewery, Wales
220, 224
HB 221
Hangzhou brewery, China 345
Hannen brewery, Germany 298
Hansa brewery, Germany 298
Hansa brewery, Namibia, Africa
339, 340, 341
Hansa brewery, Norway 257
Hansen, Emil 199, 255
Hapkin 268
Harboe 313
Harboe brewery, Denmark
253, 254
Harbour Bar brewpub,
Scotland 251
Hardington brewery, England 235
Hardy brewery, England 243
Hardys & Hansons brewery,
England 233, 242
Harp Export 215
Lager 215

Harpoon brewery, US 382
Harrier SPA 232
Harrington Micro-brewery,
N.Z. 362
Hárslevelü (g) 123
Hart brewery, US 371, 373
Hartwall brewery, Finland 260,
261, 262
Harvest Ale 232
Harvey Wallbanger 454
Harveys brewery, England 230,
232, 238, 239, 243
beers 232
Harviestoun brewery, Scotland
248, 249, 250
Hatlifter Stout 357
Hatters 232
Hausbeier 285
Haut-Brion 36, 37
Haut-Médoc 31–2, 33
Haut-Montravel 73
Haut-Poitou 43
Haute-Savoie 77
Hautes-Côtes-de-Beaune 59
Hautes-Côtes-de-Nuits 57
Hawker's 478
Hawkes Bay 181
Hawkes Bay Draught 361
hazelnuts, nut liqueurs 466–7
HB Hofbräuhaus München 289
Headstrong 232
Heartland Weiss 374
Heather Ale 247
Heckler brewery, US 375, 376
Heering, Peter 458, 461
Hefeweizen 374
Hei Lager Gold 363
Heileman brewery, US 375,
376, 382
Heimertingen Maibock 374
Heineken brewery, Netherlands
278, 280, 281, 282, 308, 312,
313, 319, 320, 330, 335,
337, 390
Helenbock 1992 Oktoberfest 374
Hell Doppel Bock 375
Lager 375
Heller brewery, Germany 287
Helles Gold 375
Hennessy 398
Henninger brewery, Germany 297
Henri Funck Lager Beer 285
Henry Weinhard's Private
Reserve 375
Hérault, l' 70, 71, 78, 79
Herbewe 307, 308
herbs, bitters 396
Herforder brewery, Germany
209, 298
Heritage 232
Herman Joseph's 375
Hermitage 64, 65
Herold brewery, Czech Republic
316, 317, 318
Herrtua 261
Hersbrucker Weizenbier 232
Hertog Jan Pilsner 282
Hessische Bergstrasse 116
Het Kapittel 268
Hevelius brewery, Poland
307, 308
Hexen Bräu 331, 332
Hickory Switch Smoked Amber
Ale 375
Hick's Special Draught 232
High Force 232
High Level 232
Highgate brewery, England
232, 243
Highland Hammer 248
Hilden brewery, Ireland 215,
216, 217
Hinano Tahiti Lager 363
Hine 398
Hirter brewery, Austria 303, 305
Hispaniola 416
Hite 351
Hobgoblin 232
Hochheim 115
Hoegaardens brewery, Belgium
201, 213, 268, 272
Grand Cru 269

Hof 253
Hofbräu Abensberg 296
Hofbräuhaus (The Royal brew-
ery), Germany 288, 289, 296
Hofbräuhaus Freising 296
Oktoberfest 208
Original Munchen 296
Wolters, Brunswick 296
Hoffmans Lager 216
Hofmark brewery, Germany 294
Hogarth, William 410
Hogs Back brewery, England 194,
227, 239
Holan 316
Holden brewery, England 232,
240, 243
Holsten brewery, Germany 289,
297, 312
Holt brewery, England 232, 243
Honey Double Mai Bock 375
Honeyweizen 375
Hong Kong brewery, Hong
Kong 345
Hook Norton brewery, England
230, 233, 235, 243
Hop and Glory 233
Hope & Anchor Breweries,
Sheffield 206
Hopf brewery, Germany 289, 298
Hopfenperle (Austria) 303
Hopfenperle (Switzerland)
331, 332
hops 187, 194–7
Horse-Ale 269
Hoskins & Oldfield brewery,
England 231, 240
Hoskins brewery, England
227, 236
Hostan brewery, Czech
Republic 316
HSB 233
Hua Nan Beer 345
Hubertus 331
Hubertus brewery, Austria
289, 305
Hubsch Hefe-Weizen 382
Hudenpohl-Schoenling brewery,
US 373, 375, 376
Hudy 375
Hull brewery, England 231, 243
Hungary 83, 123
Hunter Valley 165, 166, 176
Hunter's 339, 341
Hürlimann brewery, Switzerland
188, 330, 331, 332
Hurricane 472
Huyghe brewery, Belgium
267, 270
Hydes brewery, England 240, 243

I

ice beer 356
Ice Wine: Canadian 146–7
see also Eiswein
Icehouse 375
Ichiban 348
Shibori 347
Ichtegems Oud Bruin 269
Idaho 144
Illva 441
Imperator 280
Imperial Extra Double Stout 313
Imperial Russian Stout 233
Imperial Stout, Canada 366
Imperial Stout, Denmark 253
Ind Coope brewery, England 227,
230, 243
India 131
Indiana's Bones 233
Inigo Jones 489
Innkeeper's Special 233
Inseine, Frog & Rosbif 329
Inspired 233
Interbrew, Belgium 269, 272, 276,
311, 312, 337, 368
Inzolia (g) 93, 489
Irancy 60
Irish Festival Ale 216
Irish whiskey 435–6
Iron City Lager 375
Iron Duke 366

Iron Strong Ale 369
Ironback Dark 359
Ironbrew 359
Ironbridge Stout 233
Irouléguy 75
Irsay Oliver (g) 123
Irseer Klosterbräu, Germany 289, 290, 298
Island Lager 366
Isle of Skye brewery, Scotland 247
Isonzo 89
Israel: Sabra 477
    wine 130
Istria 129
Italia Pilsner 321, 322
Italy: Aurum 443
    brandy 401
    Cynar 453
    Fior d'Alpi 454
    Galliano 454
    grappa 414
    maraschino 464
    nut liqueurs 467
    Sambuca 477
    Strega 480
    vermouth 496–7
    wine 82, 83, 84–93
Izarra 458

J
J & B 431
Jack Daniel's 434, 435, 479
Jacobins 269
Jacobite Ale 248
Jacquère (g) 77
Jade 326
Jahrhundert 289
Jamaica: Tia Maria 482
James Boag brewery, Australia 354, 356
Jameson's 436
Japan: whisky 437
    wine 131
Jax Pilsner 375
Jazz Amber Light 375, 381
Jenkins, D.T., brewery, Wales 223
Jenlain 326
Jennings brewery, England 229, 230, 233, 237, 243
Jerepigo 491
Jerez 401
Jerez de la Frontera 102
Jerningham Street brewery, Australia 354
Jever brewery, Germany 290
Jihlava brewery, Czech Republic 318
John Labatt's Classic 366
John Smith's brewery, England 233, 234
Johnnie Walker 431
Joiners Arms Brewpub, Wales 224
Jolly Jack Tar Porter 221
Jones brewery, US 374, 378
Jouloulot Christmas Beer 261
ju-biru 346
Jubelale 375
Jubilator 326
Jubilee 351
Jubileeuw 280, 283
Juliénas 62
Jumilla 101
juniper berries, gin 408
Jupiler 269
Jura 76–7, 414
Jura, Côtes du 76
Jurançon 75
J.W. Lees 243

K
Kadarka (g) 123, 128
kaffir beer 343
Kahlúa 458
    Alexander the Great 458
    Black Russian 458
Kaiser Bock 388
Kaiser brewery, Brazil 389
Kaiser Cerveja 389
Kaiser Doppelmalz 303
Kaiser Draught 303, 304
Kaiser Gold 388

Kaiser Goldquell 303
Kaiser Märzen 303
Kaiser Piccolo Bock 303
Kaiser Pilsner 290
Kaiser Premium 303
Kaiserdom 290
Kaliber 216
Kalik Gold 391
Kalnapilis, brewery, Lithuania 312
Kaltenberg brewery, Germany 290, 292
Kamenitza brewery, Bulgaria 310, 312
Kamptau-Donauland 121
Kane's Amber Ale 248
Kanizsai brewery, Hungary 312
Kanterbräu brewery, France 327, 329
Kaper 307
Kappeli Brasserie, Finland 262
Kapuziner 290
Karamelové 316
Karel IV 316
Karhu 3 261
Karjala 261
Karlovy Vary brewery, Czech Republic 316
Karmelowe 307
Katinka 427
Keersmaekers, Josef 267
Keith's IPA 368
Kékfrankos (g) 123
Keler 335
Keller Bräu brewery, Austria 303, 305
Kelts, König 299
Kent Old Brown 354
Kenya Breweries, Africa 338, 340, 341
Keo brewery, Cyprus 323
Kerner (g) 113, 116
Kilkenny Irish Beer 216
Killian 326
Killian's Irish Red 206
Kilsch Lager 375
Kimberley Best Mild 233
Kimberley Classic 233
Kindl brewery, Germany 290, 295
King Alfred's 248
King & Barnes brewery, England 233, 238, 243
King Lear Old Ale 363
Kingfisher 351
Kingsdown Ale 233
Kir 21, 59, 449
Kir Royale 449
Kirin brewery, Japan 346, 347, 348, 349
    beers 347
Kirsch 413
    Rose 413
Kizakura Kappa Brewpub, Japan 349
Klein Karoo 162
Klevner (g) 52
Klisch Lager 375
Kloster-Urtrunk 290
Kloster Urweisse 290
Klosterbräu brewery, Germany 287, 297
Köbanyéi brewery, Hungary 312
Koch, Jim 380
Koff 261
    Porter 261
Kokanee 368
Komaromi brewery, Hungary 312
Kona Brewing Company, Hawaii 363
Kongens Bryg 253
König, Ludwig 290
König brewery, Germany 290, 299
König Pilsner 290, 299
Königsbacher brewery, Germany 299
Konik 316
Koningshoeven 280 brewery, Netherlands 283
Konizsai Korona 310
Kootenay 368
Korbinian 290

Korenwolf 280
Kostritz brewery, Germany 290
Köstritzer Schwarzbier 290
Kozel 316
Krakus 307
Kräusen 290
Kriek, traditional Belgian beer 200, 201, 264, 369
Krolewskie 307
Krombacher brewery, Germany 297
Kronen, Italy 321
Kronen brewery, Germany 204, 290, 291
Kronenbourg brewery, France 326, 327, 329
    beers 326
Kronenburg brewery, Denmark 188
Kroon brewery, Netherlands 279
Krostitz brewery, Germany 294, 295
Krusovice brewery, Czech Republic 316, 319
Kulbacher Eisbock 205
Kulminator 186, 291
kümmel 456, 459
    Tovarich 459
Küppers brewery, Germany 206, 291, 299
Kurant 426
Kuro-nama 347, 348
Kutscher Alt 291, 295
kvass 312
KWV 483
Kylian 280
Kyoto Alt 347

L
La Bière Amoureuse 326
La Bière de Noël, Kronenbourg 326
La Bière du Démon 325
La Chouffe 269
La Choulette 326
La Divine 269
La Fin du Monde 366
La Gaillarde 366
La Gauloise 269
La Goudale 328
La Meilleure 269
La Montagnarde 273
La Rochelle 398
La Rossa 321
La Trappe 280
Labatt, John 364, 368
Labatt brewery, Canada 206, 276, 366, 368
labels, wine 24–5
Lacplesis brewery, Latvia 312
Lacryma Christi del Vesuvio 92
Lacto Milk Stout 322

Ladoix 57
Lagoa 107
Lagos 107
Lagrein 87
Laird's Ale 248
Lake County 139
Lakefront brewery, US 373, 375
Lalande-de-Pomerol 33
Lambrusco 62, 89
Lamb's 419
Lammin Sahti 261
Lammsbräu Pils 291
Lancaster Bomber 233
Landlord 233
Langhe Monregalesi 86
Langhorne Creek 172
Languedoc, Coteaux du 71
Languedoc (-Roussillon) 67, 70–2
Lapin Kulta 261
Lapostolle family 457
Larkins Best Bitter 233
Larkins brewery, England 239
Latin America, brandy 403
Latrobe brewery, US 375
Lauku Tumsais 310
Lauritz 257
Layon, Coteaux du 41
Lazio 84, 91
Le Grand, Alexandre 443
Lebanon 130
Lech brewery, Poland 307, 308
Lees brewery, England 231, 232, 234, 243
Leeuw brewery, Netherlands 280, 281, 283
Lefebvre brewery, Belgium 268, 276
Leffe 269
Leffe Abbey 269
Legacy Lager 375
Legacy Red Ale 375
Legend Stout 339, 340, 342
Leichter Typ 291
Leinenkugel brewery, US 371, 372, 375, 376
Lembeek 274
Lemnos 310
lemon juice 500
lemonade 501
Len de l'El (g) 74
Leningrad Cowboy 261
Lente Bok 280
Leopard brewery, N.Z. 361
Lerida 98
Leroy brewery, Belgium 272
Les Brasseurs, France 329
Letts brewery, Ireland 217
Liatiko (g) 126
Liberty Ale 375, 380
Lichfield brewery, England 231, 233, 238
Lichine, Alexis 425–6
Liebfraumilch 96, 112, 115
Liefmans brewery, Belgium 204, 269, 276
    beers 269
Lighthouse Ale 359
Liguria 86
Lillet 499
Lily 497
Limberger (g) 114
Limburgse Witte 270, 276
lime 500
    Margarita 423, 445
Limonnaya 426
Limoux 71
Lindeboom brewery, Netherlands 283
Lindemans brewery, Belgium 276
Linder Gilde brewery, Germany 288, 289, 292
Lingen's Blond 280
Lion Breweries (Lion Nathan), N.Z. 360, 361, 362
Lion Brewpub, Australia 359
Lion Ice 361
Lion Lager, Africa 339
Lion Nathan brewery, Australia 352, 356, 357
Lion Stout (Africa) 340

Lion Stout (Asia) 351
Lion's Pride 366
liqueur brandies 460–1
Liqueur d'Or 456
Liqueur Muscat 177
Liqueur Tokay 177
liqueurs 440–83
Lirac 66
Little Kings Cream Ale 376
Livermore Valley 141
Loaded Dog Steam Beer 354
Lobkowicz brewery, Czech Republic 316, 319
Locher brewery, St Gallen, Switzerland 332
Loire 40–3, 79
    Chenin Blanc 41, 42–3
    Gamay 43
    Sauvignon Blanc 43
Loire, Upper 40, 43
Lombardy 86–7
London dry gin 412
London Pride 233
Lone Star 375
Longbrew 354
Lord Granville Pale Ale 366
Lord Nelson Brewpub, Australia 359
Loupiac 39
Loureiro (g) 105
Louwaege brewery, Belgium 268
Löwenbräu brewery, Germany 291, 294, 297
    beers 291
Löwenbräu of Zurich, Switzerland 331, 332
Lower Great Southern 168
Lowry, Malcolm 415
Lubéron, Côtes du 67
Lucan 316
Lucifer 270
Ludwig Pils 257
Lugana 87
Lugton Inn Brewpub, Scotland 251
Luini, Bernardino 441
Lussac 33
Lutèce 326
Luxardo 464
Luxembourg 122
Luxembourg Export 285
Luxembourg Export Lager 285
Lynesack Porter 233
Lysholmer 257

M
M&B 234
Maasland brewery, Netherlands 281, 283
Mac's Micro-brewery, N.Z. 363
Macabeo (g) 99
MacAndrews 248
Macardles Ale 216
McAuslan Brasserie, Canada 366, 368
Macbeth's Red Ale 363
Maccabéo (g) 71
McChouffe 270
Macedonia 125
McEwan's brewery, Scotland 248, 250
McFarland 321
McGee, Harold 471
McGregor 270
McGuinness 437
Mack brewery, Norway 257
Mackeson brewery, England 233
Mackinnon, Captain 453
McLaren Vale 172
Maclay's brewery, Scotland 248, 249, 251
McMullen brewery, England 227, 229, 230, 231, 238, 243
McNally's Extra Pure Malt Irish Style Ale 366, 368
Mâcon 60
Mâcon-Villages 60
Mâconnais, the 55, 60
MacQueen's Nessie 303
Mactarnahan's Scottish Ale 376
Mad Monk 467

Madeira 110–11, 486–7
Boston 487
Prairie Oyster 487
Madiran 75
Macs Pils 270
Magnat 307
Magnet 234
Magnum Malt Liquor 382
Magpie Rye 366, 368
Mahou brewery, Spain 333, 334, 335
Mai Tai 417
Main Street Bitter 221
Mainland Dark 361, 362
Maipo 154
Maisel brewery, Germany 288, 291
Majorca 101
Maker's Mark 434
Mako 361
Málaga 95, 103, 495
Malbec (g) 30, 74, 149, 150, 151
Malcolm's 248
Malepère, Côtes de la 71
Malibu 462
Pina Colada 462
Malmsey 111, 487
malt 187, 190–1, 193
Malt and Hops 234
Malta 322
Maltezer 280
malting 190–1
Malton brewery, England 230
Malt's 347
Malvasia (g) 90, 91, 92, 95, 109
Mamba Lager 339
Mancha, La 100
Mandarine Napoleon 463
Mandelaria (g) 126
Manhattan 433
Mann's brewery, England 234, 243
Manseng 75
Mansfeld 285
Mansfield Arms Brewpub, Scotland 251
Mansfield brewery, England 234, 235, 243
Mantinia 125
manzanilla sherry 103
Maple Wheat Beer 366
Maranges 59
Maraschino 464
Old William 474
Tropical Cocktail 464
marc 414
Marches, the (Italy) 90–1
Marches de Bretagne, Vin de Pays des 79
Marckloff 270
Maréchal Foch (g) 147
Maredsous 270
Margaret River 166, 168
Margarita 423, 445
Margaux 31-2, 33
Maria Gomes (g) 106
Mariage Parfait beers 274
Mariedahl brewery, Africa 337
Marlborough (NZ) 178, 179, 180, 182–3
Marlen 334, 335
Marmandais, Côtes du 74
Marnier, Louis-Alexandre 457
Marsala 92–3, 488–9
Casanova 489
Inigo Jones 489
Marsannay 56
Marsanne (g) 65, 66, 69, 79, 135, 142, 175
Marston Moor brewery, England 229, 230
Marston's brewery, England 188, 212, 234, 236, 243
Martell, Jean 398
Martens brewery, Belgium 210, 270, 271, 276
Martin brewery, Slovakia. 316
Martini, Dry 411
Martini e Rossi 498
Martinsky Lager 316
Maryland 145
Marzemino 87

Mascara, Coteaux de 131
Matakana 181
Mataro (g) 167
Matilda Bay Brewing Company, Australia 353, 354, 357
Matinée 477
Maudite 366
Mauldon brewery, England 228, 234, 243
Maule 154
Maury 72
Mautner-Markhof 302
Mauzac (g) 71, 72, 74
Mavro (g) 126, 127
Mavrodaphne 125, 493
Mavrud (g) 128
Maximator 280
Maximilaan Brewpub, Netherlands 279, 280
Mazuelo (g) 98
Mechelsen Brune 268
Médoc 30, 32, 33, 35
Meister Brau 376
Meister Pils 291
Melbourn brewery, England 243
Melbourne Bitter 354
Meliton, Côtes de 125
Melnais Balzams 397
Melnik (g) 128
Melo Abreu Especial 336
melon: Midori 465
Melon de Bourgogne (g) 29, 40
Mencía (g) 96
Mendocino brewery, US 372, 374, 378, 382
Mendocino County 138, 139
Mendoza 149, 150-1
Ménétou-Salon 43
Méntrida 100
Mercurey 59-60
Merlin's 248
Merlot 30, 35, 70, 73, 74, 87, 88, 122, 138, 141, 143, 145, 153, 154, 161, 167, 180
Merman 248
Meroué (g) 130
Merry Widow 496
Merseguera (g) 100
Mersin 465
Mescal 415
Mestan brewery, Czech Republic 316, 317, 318
Mestreechs Aajt 280
Metaxa 402
Meteor brewery, France 325, 326, 329
Meursault 58
Mexico: brandy 403
Kahlúa 458
mescal 415
tequila 422–3
wine 149, 155
MIA see Murrumbidgee Irrigation Area
Michelob 376
Midi see Languedoc
Midori 465
Green Caribbean 465
Midsummer Night 499
Mikro brewery, Norway 257
Milano 454
Milawa 175
Millennium Gold 234
Miller brewery, US 376, 382
Miller High Life 382
Miller Icehouse 206
Miller Lite 208, 382
Milwaukee's Best 376, 382
Minervois 73
Ministerley Ale 234
Mirror Pond Pale Ale 376
Misket (g) 128
Mission (g) 136, 150, 155
Missouri 145
mistela 101
Mitchells & Butlers brewery, England 228, 234, 240–1, 243
Mitchell's brewery, England 233, 234, 237, 243
Mitchell's ESB 366
Mitchell's Micro-brewery, South Africa 338, 340, 342

Mittelrhein 114
mixers, non-alcoholic 500–1
Mohan Meakin, India 351
Moinette 270
Moku Moku Micro-brewery, Japan 349
Moldova 83, 129
Moles brewery, England 228, 234
Molette (g) 77
Molise 92
Molson brewery, Montreal 206, 368–9
Canadian Lager 366, 369
Export Ale 366
Special Dry 366, 369
Mon-Lei Beer 345
Monastrell (g) 101
Monbazillac 74
Mönchshof Kloster brewery, Germany 290, 291, 294
Mondeuse (g) 77
Monferrato 86
Monica (g) 93
Monkey Gland 469
Monkey Wrench 234
Montagne de Reims 47
Montagny 60
Montalcino, Rosso di 89
Montefalco 91
Montepulciano (g) 90, 92
Montepulciano, Vino Nobile di 90
Montepulciano d'Abruzzo 91
Monterey County 142
Montezuma 423
Monthélie 58
Montilla 95
Montilla-Moriles 103
Montlouis 43
Montravel 73
Montrose 248
Moondog Ale 376, 382
Moonlight brewery, N.Z. 363
Black Beer 361
Original Ale 361
Moonraker 234
Moonshine 354, 357
Moorhouse brewery, England 228, 236
Moortgat brewery, Belgium 265, 268, 270, 276
Moose Brown Ale 376
Moosehead brewery, Canada 365, 367, 369
Lager 366
Mopa brewery, Africa 340
Moravia 122
Moravia brewery, Germany 299
Morchl 303
Moretti brewery, Udine, Italy 321, 322
Morey-St-Denis 56
Morgon 63
Morillon (g) 121
Moristel (g) 98

Morland brewery, England 235, 244
Mornington Peninsula 175
Morocco 131
Morocco Ale 234
Morrells brewery, England 229, 231, 234, 239, 244
Morris, Mick 490
Mort Subite 270
Mortimer 326
Moscatel 490–1
Setubal 111
Moscatel de Valencia 100–1, 491
Moscato (g) 85, 86
Moscato d'Asti 86
Moscato di Pantelleria 93
Moscophilero (g) 125
Moscovskoye 312
Moscow brewery, Russia 313
Moscow Mule 426
Mosel-Saar-Ruwer 112, 114–15
Moselle Luxembourgeoise 122
Moskovskoye 310, 313
Moss Bay Extra 376
Mossel Bay 162
Moulin-à-Vent 62
Moulin Hotel Brewpub, Scotland 251
Moulis 33
Mount Tolmie 366
Mourvèdre (g) 66, 68, 69, 71, 72, 142, 167
Mousel brewery, Lux 285
Moussy 331
Mudgee 176
Muenchener Amber 376
Mug Bitter 280, 283
Müller-Thurgau (g) 113, 114, 115, 116, 117, 119, 120, 180, 181
Münchner Dunkel 297
Munich Oktoberfest 293
Murfatlar 129
Murphy's 248
Murphy's brewery, Ireland 216, 217
Murray River 167, 169
Murray's Heavy 248
Murrumbidgee Irrigation Area 176
Muscadelle (g) 36, 38, 74, 177
Muscadet (g) 29, 40–1
Muscadet Côtes de Grandlieu 40
Muscadet de Sèvre-et-Maine 40
Muscadet des Coteaux de la Loire 40
Muscat 52, 158, 162, 165, 402, 403, 490–1
see also Moscato
Muscat Blanc à Petits Grains (g) 72, 121, 123, 177
Muscat d'Alexandrie (of Alexandria) (g) 72, 111, 150, 167
Muscat d'Alsace (g) 52, 53
Muscat de Beaumes-de-Venise 67, 490
Muscat de Berkane 131
Muscat de Frontignan 490
Muscat de Lunel 72, 490
Muscat de Mireval 72, 490
Muscat de Rivesaltes 72, 490
Muscat de St-Jean-de-Minervois 72, 490
Muscat Gordo Blanco (g) 167
Muscat Ottonel (g) 52
Muscat of Patras 125
Muscat of Samos 126
Muscatel 162
Mutiny 234
Mutzig brewery, France 326, 327, 329
My Tho, Vietnam 351
Mystic Seaport Pale 376

Napa Valley 135, 138, 140–1
Napoleon I, Emperor 398, 463
Nastro Azzurro 321, 322
Natal brewery, Africa 342
National Breweries of Zimbabwe, Africa 338, 340, 341
Natte 280
Natterjack 234
Naturtrub 303
Naval Super Premium 387, 388
Navarra 83, 96
Nebbiolo (g) 29, 83, 85, 86
Nectar 316
Neer brewery, Netherlands 280
Negra León 388
Negra Modelo 388, 389
Négrette (g) 73, 75
Negroamaro (g) 92
Negroni 397
Negru de Purkar 129
Nelson 182
Nemea 125
Nero d'Avola (g) 93
Nesbitt brewery, Zimbabwe, Africa 339, 341
Nethergate brewery, England 235, 239
Netherlands: advocaat 440
gin 408–9, 412
kümmel 459
Neuchâtel 122
Neusiedlersee 121
New Amsterdam brewery, US 382
New Glarus brewery, US 383
New Mexico 136
New South Wales 166, 176
New South Wales Lager Company, Australia 358
New York State 145
New Zealand 178-83
Cabernet Sauvignon 180
Chardonnay 178, 180, 181
Merlot 180
Pinot Noir 179
Riesling 178, 180
Sauvignon Blanc 178, 180, 181
New Zealand Breweries (NZB), N.Z. 360, 362, 363
Newbegin brewery, N.Z. 363
Newcastle Amber 234
Newcastle Brown Ale 204, 234
Ngoma 339
Niagara Falls Brewing Company, Canada 365, 366, 369
Niederösterreich 121
Nielluccio (g) 69
Nigerian Breweries, Africa 339, 340, 342
Nightmare Porter 234
Nikka 437
Nikolaevskyi 310, 311
Nile Breweries, Uganda, Africa 338, 339, 342
Nine Star Premium 345
Nitra 123
noble rot 38
Noel Ale 234
Noilly Prat 498
Noisette 466
non-alcoholic mixers 500–1
Noordender 327, 329
Norfolk Nog 234
Norman's Conquest 235
North brewery, Africa 340
North Brink Porter 235
North Coast brewery, US 371, 372, 376, 378
North Yorkshire brewery, England 228, 231
Northwoods Lager 376
Nostrum de San Miguel 334
Nova Scotia 147
Novomestsky 316
Nugget Golden Lager 361
Nuigini Gold Extra Stout 363
Nuits-St-Georges 56–7
Nuragus (g) 93
Nuremburger Tucher brewery, Germany 294
Nussdorf brewery, Austria 303, 304, 305
Nut Brown Ale 235

N

Nachod brewery, Czech Republic 317
Nag's Head Brewpub, Wales 224
Nahe, the 115
Namibia Breweries, Africa 340, 341
Nantes see Pays Nantais
Náoussa 125

nut liqueurs 466–7

O

O Rosal 96
Oakhill brewery, England 244
Oasis 451
Oberdorfer 291
OBJ 235
Obsidian Stout 376
Oeil-de-Perdrix 122
Oerbier 270
Oeste 106
Off the Rails 221
O'Flanagan's 354
Ogden Porter 367
Ohlsson's Lager 339
Ojen 471
  Ojen Cocktail 472
OK Jasne Pelne 307
Okanagan Spring brewery, B.C.,
  Canada 367, 369
Okanagan Valley 147
Okhotnichya 426
Okhotsk Brewpub, Japan 349
Okocim brewery, Poland 307, 308
Oktoberfest 376
Old Admiral 359
Old Baily 235
Old Bawdy Barley Wine 377
Old Bircham 235
Old Bob 235
Old Brewery Bitter 235
Old Buzzard 235
Old Crustacean 376
Old Detroit Amber 381
Old Ebenezer 235
Old English Porter 369
Old Expensive 235
Old-Fashioned 434
Old Fashioned Bitter 359
Old Foghorn 376, 380
Old Grand-Dad 434
Old Growler 235
Old Hooky 235
Old Jock 248
Old Knucker 235
Old Knucklehead 376
Old Lion Pilsner 359
Old Manor 248
Old Masters 235
Old Mill brewery, England
  229, 235
Old Milwaukee 376
Old Munich Wheat Beer 369
Old Nick 235
Old No. 38 Stout 376
Old Nobbie Stout 221
Old Original 235
Old Peculier 235
Old Preacher 359
Old Rasputin Russian Imperial
  Stout 376
Old Smokey 235
Old Southwark Stout 354
Old Speckled Hen 235
Old Spot Prize Ale 235
Old Stockport Bitter 235
Old Thumper 236, 363, 377
Old Tom 236
Old Vienna 367
Old Whisky 303
Old William 474
Olde Merryford Ale 236
Olde Stoker 236
Olifants River 160
Olomouc brewery, Czech
  Republic 316, 319
oloroso sherry 102
Oltrepò Pavese 86
Olvi brewery, Finland 260,
  261, 262
Olympic 451
Ondenc (g) 74
Ondras 316
Onix 336
Ontario 147
Op-Ale 270
Optimator 291
Optimo Bruno 270
Oracabessa 448
orange 500
  Cointreau 445

curaçao 451–2
  Grand Marnier 457
  Harvey Wallbanger 454
  Screwdriver 426
  Tequila and Orange 422
  Tequila Sunrise 423
Orange River 162
Oranjeboom brewery, Netherlands
  281, 283
Oregon 135, 143
Oregon Honey Beer 377
Orgeat 501
Original Chilli Beer 354
Original Porter 236
Orkney brewery, Scotland 247,
  248, 249, 251
Orland, Terken 329
Ormeasco 86
Ornellaia 93
Ortega (g) 119
Orval 212, 270
Orvieto 91
Osborne 401
Osma 316
Ostravar brewery, Czech Republic
  316, 317, 319
Otago 180, 183
Otard 398
Otaru Brewpub, Japan 349
Ottakringer brewery, Austria
  303, 305
Otter Creek brewery, US 375
Oud Beersel 270
Oud Kriekenbier 270, 274
Oudaen brewery, Netherlands 283
Oudenaards Wit Tarbebier
  270, 274
Ouzo 472
Ovada 86
Owd Roger 236
Oyster Stout, Porter House 216
  Marston's 236

P

Paarl 158, 160–1
Pabst brewery, US 383
Pacherenc du Vic-Bilh 75
Pacific Golden Ale 363
Pacific Real Draft 367
Paddy 436
Padthaway 172–3
País (g) 136, 153, 155
Palatinate *see* Pfalz
Palette 69
Palm brewery, Belgium 270
Palmela 107
Palmer brewery, England 238, 244
Palmse 310
Palomino (g) 96, 102
Pantelleria 93
Paracelsus 303
Paradise 460
Parel 281
Parellada (g) 98, 99
Parfait amour 468
  Eagle's Dream 468
Parislytic 329
Parkeroo 495
Parnas 311
Paros 125
Pasteur, Louis 198–9
Pastis 442, 469–72
  Block and Fall 472
  Bunny Hug 471
  Hurricane 472
  Monkey Gland 469
  Yellow Parrot 470
Pastor Ale 327
Pater Noster 270
Patras 125
Patriator 327
Patrimonio 69
Pauillac 31–2
Paulaner brewery, Germany
  292, 297
Pauls and Sandars 192
Pauwels Kwak 271, 274, 276
Pavichevich brewery, US 371
Pays Nantais 40–1
peach brandy 460, 461
  Southern Peach 479
  Wally 461

peaches: Southern Comfort 479
Pearl brewery, US 375, 377
pears: Poire William 474
Pécharmant 74
Pécheur 327
Pêcheur 327
Pedigree 236
Pedro Giménez (g) 150
Pedro Ximénez (g) 102, 495
Pedwar Bawd 221
Peking Beer 345
Pelforth brewery, France 206, 325,
  326, 329
  beers 216
Pelican Lager 327
Pellegrino 489
Peloponnese, the 125
Pembroke Docks brewery,
  Wales 224
Pendle Witches Brew 236
Penedés 99
Penn's Bitter 236
Pennsylvania 145
Pennsylvania brewery, US
  375, 377
Pera Segnana 474
Perfect Cocktail 497
Perfect Porter 377
Periquita (g) 106, 107
Pernand-Vergelesses 57
Pernod 470–1
  Red Witch 471
Pernod-Ricard 481
Peroni brewery, Italy 321, 322
Peru: brandy 403
  wine 155
Peru Gold 388, 389
Pessac-Léognan 31–2, 37
Pete's brewery, US 383
Pete's Wicked Winter Brew 377
Peter the Great 459
Peter's Porter 236
Petit Chablis 55, 56
Petit Courbu (g) 75
Petit Manseng (g) 73, 75
Petit Verdot (g) 30
Petite Fleur 417
Petite Sirah (g) 155
Petone brewery, N.Z. 363
Petrus 210, 271
Peza 126
Pfalz 112, 116
Pfaudler Vacuum Company 338
Phoenix 216
Phoenix brewery, England
  236, 240
Piave 88
Piceno, Rosso 90–1
Pick-Me-Up 461
Picpoul (g) 66, 71, 89
Pictish Ale 247
Piedirosso (g) 92
Piedmont 85–6

Pieper, Bernd 365
Pieprzowka 426
Pikantus 291, 296
Pike Place brewery, US 204, 373,
  376, 377
Pilgrim brewery, England 236
Pilsener Mack-Oil 257
Pilsener Xibeca 335
Pilsissimus 291
Pilsner Celis Golden 381
Pilsner Hopfenperle 303, 305
Pilsner Jubileeuw 283
Pilsner Nikolai 261
Pilsner Urquell 209, 314, 317
Pilsner Urquell brewery, Czech
  Republic 319
Pimm's 473
Pina Colada 419, 462
pineapple 500
  Pina Colada 419, 462
Pineau des Charentes 476
Pink Almond 467
pink gin 397
Pinkus Hefe Weizen 292
Pinkus Müller brewery, Germany
  292, 299–300
Pinot Blanc (g) 52, 87, 121
Pinot Gris (Grigio) (g) 51, 53, 87,
  88, 120, 123, 135, 143
Pinot Meunier (g) 47
Pinot Noir 43, 47, 52, 56–1, 77,
  87, 112, 119, 120, 122, 129,
  141, 143, 147, 153, 154, 162,
  167, 175, 179
  see also Spätburgunder
Pinotage (g) 159, 160
Pintail 377
Piranha 425
Pisco 403
Pisco sour 403
Pittsburgh brewery, US 375
Pivo Herold Hefe-Weizen 317
Plain Porter 216
Plank Road brewery, US 383
Planter's Punch 418
Plassey brewery, Wales 220, 221
Platan brewery, Czech Republic
  317, 319
Platman's 359
plums, slivovitz 421
Plymouth gin 412
Plzen (Pilsen), Czech
  Republic 319
Point Special 377
Poire Prisonnière 474
Poire William 474
  Old William 474
Poland, vodka 424–5, 426
Polar Brewing Company,
  Venezuela 388, 389
Polish Pure Spirit 427
Pomerol 31, 33, 34, 35
Pommard 57
Pommeau 476
Ponik 317
Pontac (g) 159
Pony 331
Poole brewery, England 228
Poperings Hommelbier 271
Poretti brewery, Italy 321
port 108–9, 492–3
  Port in a Storm 493
Port Dock Brewpub, Australia 359
Port of Spain brewery,
  Trinidad 391
Porter 197, 327, 388
Porter House Brewpub, Ireland
  216, 217
Porteris 317
Portimão 107
Portland Ale 377
Porto Vecchio 69
Portugal: brandy 401
  port 492–3
  Setúbal Moscatel 490–1
  wine 82, 83, 104–11
Portugieser (g) 114, 120
Postin brewery 261
Poteen 436
Pottsville Porter 377, 385
Pouilly-Fuissé 60
Pouilly-Fumé 43

Pouilly-Loché 60
Pouilly-sur-Loire 43
Pouilly-Vinzelles 60
Poulsard (g) 76
Poverty Bay 181
Power, John 436
Power Brewing Company,
  Australia 354, 357, 358
  Stout 340
Pragovar 317
Prague Breweries Group 318, 319
Prairie Oyster 487
Preignac 38
Premières Côtes de Bordeaux
  34, 39
Premium Verum 377
Primator 317
Primitivo (g) 83, 92
Primitivo di Manduria 92
Primorska 123
Primus 317
Primus Pils 271
Prinzregent 292
Prior 317
Priorato 99
Pripps brewery, Sweden 212,
  258, 259
Privat Pils 303
Privatbräuerei Diebel,
  Germany 288
Prize Old Ale 236
Proberco brewery, Romania 313
Progress 236
Prohibition 410–11
Prosecco di Conegliano 88
Prosecco di Valdobbiadene 88
Prosit Pils 274
Provence 68–9, 414
Prunelle 478
Ptarmigan 248
Publican's Special Bitter 367
Puerto de Santa María 102
Puglia 92
Puisseguin 33
Puligny-Montrachet 29, 58
Pullman Pale Ale 377
Pumphouse Brewpub,
  Australia 359
Pumpkin Ale 377
Punsch 475
  Diki-Diki 475
  Grand Slam 475
Punt e Mes 499
  Midsummer Night 499
Puntigamer brewery, Austria 305
Purkmistr 317
Pyramid brewery, US 383

Q

Quarts de Chaume 41
Quebec 147
Queensland 166, 177
Quincy 43
quinine, bitters 396
Quintus 281

R

Raaf brewery, Netherlands
  281, 283
Radeburger Pilsner 292
Radegast brewery, Czech
  Republic 317, 319
Radius 269
Raffo 321
Raftman 367
Ragutus brewery, Lithuania 313
Rain Dance 377
Raincross Cream Ale 377
Rainier Ale 377
Raki 395
Rakoczi 311
Rallo 489
Ram Rod 236
Ramisco (g) 107
Ramsbottom Strong 236
Rapel 152, 154
Rapier Pale Ale 236
Rapsani 125
Rasteau 67
Ratafia 476
Ratsherr 292
Trunk 303, 304, 305

Ratskeller Edel-Pils 292
Rauchenfels brewery,
    Germany 210
Raven Ale 248
    Stout 340
Razor Back 354
Rebellion brewery, England 234,
    236, 237
Rebellion Malt Liquor 367
Red Ant 354
Red Baron 367
Red Bitter 354
Red Bull 377
Red Cap Ale 367
Red Dog 367
Red Erik 253
Red Hook brewery, US 378
Red House 351
Red Lion Brewpub, Wales 224
Red MacGregor 248
Red Sky Ale 378
Red Stripe 390, 391
Red Tail Ale 378
Red Witch 471
Redback Brewpub, Australia
    354, 359
Redhook Ale brewery, US
    371, 372
Reepham brewery, England 231,
    235, 236
Refosco (g) 88
Régal 285
Regent brewery, Czech Republic
    315, 319
Reichelbräu Eisbock 292
    of Kulmbach 203
Reichensteiner (g) 119
Reininghaus brewery, Austria 305
remuage 46
Rémy Martin 398, 403
Reschs brewery, Australia
    355, 358
Reserva Extra 335
Retsina 126
Reuilly 43
Reval 310, 313
Reverend James 222
Rex 340, 342
Rezak 317
Rheineck Lager 361
Rheingau 115
Rheingold 331
Rheinheitsgebot (German Purity
    Law) 286, 295
Rheinhessen 115
Rheinpfalz see Pfalz
Rhenania brewery, Germany 300
Rhodes 126
Rhoditis (g) 125
Rhône 64–7
Rhône, Côtes du 67
Rhône-Villages, Côtes du 66
Rias Baixas 96
Ribatejo 106
Ribeiro 96
Ribera del Duero 83, 97
Ricard 471
Riccadonna 498
Ridder brewery, Netherlands 280,
    281, 283
Ridleys brewery, England 227,
    229, 235, 236, 237, 244
Rieslaner (g) 113
Riesling 51, 53, 112, 113, 114,
    115, 116, 117, 119, 120, 121,
    128, 144, 145, 146, 147, 153,
    154, 158, 166, 169, 170,
    180, 182
    Cape 158
    sparkling 117
Riesling Italico 86
Rifle Brigade Brewpub,
    Australia 359
Riggwelter 236
Ringnes brewery, Norway
    256, 257
Ringwood brewery, England 231,
    236, 244
Rio Negro 151
Rioja, La (Argentina) 151
Rioja (Spain) 82, 83, 94, 95

Rioja Alavesa 95
Rioja Alta 95
Rioja Baja 95
Rite of Spring 452
Ritter brewery, Germany 289, 300
Riva brewery, Belgium 270, 276
Riverland 169
Riverside brewery, US 378, 379
Riverwest Stein Beer 378
Rivesaltes 72
Rkatsiteli (g) 129
RMS 403
Roaring Meg 237
Robertson Valley 162, 163
Robertus 281
Robinson's brewery, England 236,
    237, 244
Robola (g) 126
Roche-aux-Moines, La 41
Rochefort brewery, Belgium
    212, 276
Rockies brewery, US 372
Rocky Cellar Beer 312
Rodenbach brewery, Belgium 188,
    271, 277
Rodenbach brewery of
    Roeselare 210
Roggen Rye 378
Rogue-n-Berry 378
Rolle (g) 69, 71, 86
Rolling Rock 378
Roman brewery, Belgium 277
Romania 83, 124, 128–9
Romer Pilsner 292
Romorantin 43
Rooster's 237
rosado wines 95, 96
Rose 413
Rose de Gambrinus 271
Rose Street Brewpub,
    Scotland 251
rosé wines 41, 43, 48, 61, 106
    see also rosado wines
Rosette 74
Roshu de Purkar 129
Rossa 321
Rossese (g) 86
Rosso di Montepulciano 90
Rotgipfler (g) 120
Roupeiro (g) 107
Roussanne (g) 65, 66, 77, 142
Roussette (g) 65, 77
Roussette de Savoie 77
Roussillon see Languedoc
Roussillon, Côtes du 70, 72
Royal Extra Stout 391
Royal Navy 417–18, 488
Royal Oak 237
Royal Pilsner 259
Ruby Ale 206
Ruchè 86
Ruddles brewery, England
    237, 244
Rüdesheim 115
Rudgate brewery, England
    227, 239
Rueda 97
Ruedrich's Red Seal Ale 378
Ruffiac (g) 75
Ruländer (g) 113, 117
Rully 59
rum 416–20
    Bacardi cocktail 417
    Cuba Libre 417
    Daiquiri 419
    Fruit Daiquiri 447
    Green Caribbean 465
    Hot Buttered Rum 419
    Mai Tai 417
    Malibu 462
    Oracabessa 448
    Petite Fleur 417
    Pina Colada 419, 462
    Planter's Punch 418
    punsch 475
    Ti Punch 418
    Tia Maria 482
    Zombie 420
Rumpus 237
Ruppertsberg 116
Russia 129
    vodka 424–7

Russkoe (Russian) 310, 312
Rusty Nail 430, 453
Rutherglen 175, 177
Ruutli Olu 310, 313
Ruwer see Mosel-Saar-Ruwer
Ryburn brewery, England 237
Rye whiskey 433
Ryedale 237

S
S-A 222
Saale/Unstrut 117
Saar see Mosel-Saar-Ruwer
Saaz 327
    hops 318, 389
Sabra 477
Saccharomyces Carlsbergensis
    199, 252, 255
Sachsen (Saxony) 117
Sachsische brewery, Germany 297
Sagrantino (g) 91
Sagrantino di Montefalco 91
sahti 260, 261, 262
Sail and Anchor Brewpub,
    Australia 353, 359
St-Ambroise beers 367
St-Amour 62
St Andrews 248
St Arnoldus 327
St-Aubin 58
St Austell brewery, England 232,
    239, 240, 244
St Benoît 271
St Bernardus brewery,
    Belgium 277
St-Chinian 71
Ste-Croix-du-Mont 39
St-Emilion 31, 32–3, 34, 35
St-Estèphe 31-2, 33
St Feuillen brewery, Belgium
    275, 277
St-Fiacre 40
St Francis of Paula 297
St Georgen brewery,
    Germany 292
St-Georges 33
St Idesbald 271
St Jakobus 292
St-Joseph 65
St Jozef brewery, Belgium 277
St-Julien 31–2
St Landelin 327
St Laurent (g) 120, 122
St Louis 271
St-Mont, Côtes de 75
St-Nicolas-de-Bourgueil 42
St Pauli Girl brewery,
    Germany 300
St-Péray 65
St-Philbert de Bouaine 40
St-Romain 58
St Sebastiaan 271
St Sixtus 271

St Stan's brewery, US 383
St Sylvestre brewery, France
    327, 329
St-Véran 60
St Vincent brewery Ltd, St
    Vincent 391
Saison de Pipaix 271
Saison de Silly 271
Saison Régal 210, 271
Saku brewery, Estonia 310,
    311, 313
Salem Porter 237
Salento 92
Salice Salentino 92
Salisbury Best 237
Salmbräu Brewpub, Austria 304
Salopian brewery, England 205,
    231, 233, 234, 237
Salta 151
Salvator 292, 297
Sambuca 477
    Matinée 477
Samichlaus 330, 332
Sammarco 93
Samos 126
Samson 317
Samson brewery, Czech
    Republic 319
Samuel Adams Cream Stout 211
    Boston Lager 378
    Boston Stock Ale 378
Samuel Smith's brewery, England
    235, 237, 238, 244
San Benito 142
San Juan 151
San Luis Obispo 142
San Miguel brewery, Philippines
    350, 351
San Miguel brewery, Spain 333,
    334, 335
San Miguel Nostrum 334
San Miguel Premium 334, 335
Sancerre 43
Sanchez Romate 401
Sandaya Brewpub, Japan 349
Sandels 261
Sando Stout 351
Sandy Hunter's 248
Sangiovese (g) 29, 83, 89, 90,
    91, 93
Sangiovese di Romagna 89
Sankt Gallen Brewpub, Japan 349
Sanlúcar de Barrameda 102, 103
Sanraku Ocean 437
Sans culottes 327
Sans Souci 321, 322
Santa Barbara County 142
Santa Clara Valley 142
Santa Cruz 142
Santenay 59
Santenots 58
Santorini 126
Sanwald 292
Saperavi (g) 129
Sapporo brewery, Japan 346,
    348–9
    beers 347, 349
Saracen 455
Saranac 382
Sardinia 93
Sartène 59
SAS 237
Sassicaia 89, 93
Satan 271
Saumur 40, 42
Saumur-Champigny 42
Saussignac 74
Sauternes 37, 38–9
Sauternes-Barsac 38, 39
Sauvignon Blanc 36, 37, 38, 42,
    43, 69, 70, 73, 74, 89, 128,
    134, 153, 154, 158, 160, 161,
    167, 178, 180–2
Sauvignon Vert (Sauvignonasse)
    (g) 153
Savagnin (g) 76, 122
Savatiano (g) 125, 402
Savennières 41
Savigny-lès-Beaune 58
Savoie 76, 77
SBA 237
SBB 222

Scaldis 266
Scandinavia: aquavit 394
    vodka 427
Schaefer brewery, US 378
Schaffbräu brewery, Germany 289
Scharer's Brewpub, Australia 359
Schaumwein 117
Schele Os 281
Schell brewery, US 378, 384
Scheurebe (g) 113, 116, 119
Schiehallion Lager 248
Schierlinger Roggen 292
Schilcher 121
Schiopettino (g) 88
Schläql 305
Schlank & Rank 303
Schlenkerla 209, 292
Schlitz brewery, US 378, 384
Schlosser 202
Schlüssel Alt 301
Schmaltz's Alt 378
Schmidt, Louis 463
Schnapps 394
Schneider brewery, Germany 213,
    287, 292, 294, 297
Schöfferhofer 294
Schönburger (g) 119
Schooner 368
Schultheiss brewery,
    Germany 294
Schutz Deux Milles 327, 329
Schutzenberger brewery, France
    325, 326, 327, 329
Schwechater brewery, Austria 305
Sciacarello (g) 69
Scotland: Drambuie 453
    Glayva 455
    whisky 429–32
Scottish & Newcastle brewery,
    England 234
    Courage brewery, Scotland 251
Screwdriver 426
Scrimshaw Pilsner 378
Seagram's 436, 437
Seasonal Smoked Porter 378
Seattle Pike brewery, US 377
Sebourg 327, 328
Secrestat 397
Sedlmayer, Gabriel 255, 294
Sekt 116, 117
Sémillon 36, 38, 73, 74, 143, 150,
    153, 166, 176
Septante Cinq 327, 329
Serbia, slivovitz 421
Sercial 107, 111, 487
serving wine 15
Setúbal Moscatel 111, 490–1
Setúbal Peninsula 111
Seven Seas Real Ale 359
Seville oranges, bitters 396
Seyssel 77
Seyval Blanc (g) 119, 145, 147
Sezuens 271
Shakemantle Ginger 237
Shakespeare brewery, N.Z. 363
Shakespeare Stout 378
Shanghai (Swan) Lager 345
Sharp's 382
Shea's Irish Amber 378, 382
Sheaf Stout 355
Shefford Bitter 237
Shen Ho Sing brewery,
    China 345
Shepherd Neame brewery,
    England 227, 236, 237, 244
Sheridan's 446
sherry 95, 102-3, 494–5
    Adonis 499
    Bamboo 499
    Parkeroo 495
    Saracen 455
    Sherry Cocktail 495
    Sherry Flip 495
sherry-style wine 127, 129,
    160–1, 177
Shipyard brewery, Portland, US
    372, 376, 377, 378, 379
Shirayuki 347
Shiraz 159, 164, 167–74
    see also Syrah
Shokusai Bakushu 347, 348
Shropshire 237

Sicily 92–3
  marsala 488–9
Sidecar 445
Sierra Foothills 141
Sierra Nevada brewery, US 372,
  373, 384
Sigl brewery, Austria 304, 305
Signature Amber Lager 367
  Cream Ale 367
Silberwasser 456
Silly brewery, Belgium 210, 268,
  269, 271, 277
Silly Brug-Ale 272
Silvaner (g) 52, 113, 115, 116,
  117, 122
Silver Fern 363
Silver Pilsner 253
Silver Jubilee 448
Simba Lager 340
Simon Noël 285
Simonds, Farsons, Cisk, (Farsons)
  Brewers, Malta 322
Sinebrychoff brewery, Finland
  260, 261, 262
Singapore Sling 461
Singha 351
Single Malt 237
Sipon (g) 123
Sir Henry's Stout 304
Siraly (Seagull) 310
Sirvenos 311, 313
Sjoes 281
Skull Splitter 249
Slaghmuylder brewery,
  Belgium 272
Slaughter Porter 237
Sleeman brewery, Canada
  367, 369
  Cream Ale 367
  Original Dark 367
Slivovitz 421
Sloe gin 478
Sloeber 272
Slovakia 122-3
Slovenia 123
Smiles brewery, England 231,
  232, 237
Smirnoff 426, 427
Smith, John, brewery,
  England 244
Smith, Samuel, brewery,
  England 244
Smithwick's brewery, Ireland 206,
  216, 217
smoked beer 301
Smuggler 237
Sneck Lifter 237
Snow Goose 378
Snowball 440
Soave 87, 88
Sociedad Central de Cervejas
  (Centralcer), Portugal 336
Soda water 500
Sol 388
Solaia 93
solera system 103, 401
Solibra brewery, Africa 339, 342
Somontano 98
Son of a Bitch 222, 223
Song Hay Double Happiness
  Beer 345
Sonoma Valley 140
Sonora 155
sorghum beer 343
Sort Guld 253
SOS 237
South Africa 156–62
  Cabernet Sauvignon 161
  Chardonnay 158, 160
  Gewürztraminer 160
  Jerepigo 491
  Pinot Noir 159, 162
  Sauvignon Blanc 158, 160
  Shiraz 159
  sparkling wine 163
  Steen (Chenin Blanc) 157, 158
  Van der Hum 483
South African Breweries, Africa
  309, 337, 338, 342
South America, rum 418
South Australian brewery,
  Australia 353, 355, 358

South Pacific brewery, Port
  Moresby 363
Southern Comfort 479
Southern Peach 479
Southwark beers 355
SP Lager 363
Spain: brandy 401
  Cuaranta y Tres 452
  Izarra 458
  Moscatel de Valencia 491
  ojen 471
  sherry 494–5
  wine 82, 83, 94–103
Spanish conquistadores 386
Spanna 86
sparkling beverages 500–1
sparkling wines 42, 52–3, 61,
  72, 85, 116, 117, 122, 129,
  163, 183
  opening 17
Spätburgunder (g) 114–17
Spaten brewery (Spaten-
  Franziskaner-Bräu),
  Germany 289, 291, 294, 298
Special Oudenaards 268
Speciale 338
Speight's brewery, N.Z. 362, 363
Spendrup's brewery, Sweden 259
Spezial brewery, Germany 300
Spiess Edelhell 332
Spinnakers Brewpub, Canada
  367, 369
  Bitter 237
spirits 394–437
Spitfire 237
Splügen 321
Spoetzle brewery, US 378
Sprecher brewery, US 384
Spring Valley 347
Springhead brewery, England
  232, 237
Squinzano 92
Stag 237, 238
Stakonice brewery, Czech
  Republic 316
Stan Smith's Oatmeal Stout 211
Stanton & Killeen 490
Staples brewery, N.Z. 363
Star 340, 342
Starkbier 294
Starobrno brewery, Czech
  Republic 315, 316, 317, 319
Staropramen brewery, Czech
  Republic 317, 319
Stauder TAG 294
Steen (Chenin Blanc) (g) 157, 158
Steenbrugge Dubbel 272
  Tripel 272
Steendonck 270
Steeplejack 238
Steerkens brewery, Belgium 271
Steffl 304
Stegmaier 378
Steiermark 121
Stein, Robert 430
Steinlager 362
Steinlager Blue 362
Steirische Bräuindustrie brewery,
  Austria 305
Stella Artois 272
Stellenbosch 161, 163
Stephansquell 294
Sternbräu 332
Stiegl brewery, Austria 303,
  304, 305
Stiftsbräu 304
Stig Swig 238
Stille Nacht 272
Stillman's 80/- 249
Stinger 447
Stingo 203
Stock 401, 464
Stockan brewery, N.Z. 363
Stolnichaya 427
Stones brewery, England 238, 244
Stoney's Lager 378
storing wine 14–15
Stoteczne 308
Stoudt's Micro-brewery, US 375,
  379, 384
Straffe Hendrick brewery,
  Belgium 272, 277

Stratosphere 448
Straub brewery, US 384
Strega 480
  Golden Tang 480
Stroh's brewery, US 371, 376,
  377, 378, 379, 384
Strohwein 121
Strong Suffolk 238
Strongarm 238
Strongcroft's Bitter 363
Stronghart 238
Struis 281, 283
Styria 121
sugar, rum 416–17, 420
Sultana (g) 167, 169
Sumida River Brewpub,
  Japan 349
Summer Lightning 238
Summerskill's brewery, England
  233, 240
  Best Bitter 238
Summit brewery, US 374, 384
Sun Lik 345
Sunburn 482
Sundowner 483
Suntory 437, 465
Suntory brewery, Japan 346, 347,
  348, 349
Super Bock 336
Super Dortmunder 281
Super Dry 348
Super Ice 206
Superior 388
Superleeuw 281, 283
Sussex Bitter 238
Sussex Mild 238
Suze 481
Suze Drought 481
Swan brewery, Australia 355, 358
Swan Valley 168
Swartland 160
Sweden, punsch 475
Sweet China 345
Sweetheart Stout 249
Switzerland 122
Sydney Bitter 355, 357
Sylvester 281
Syrah 64, 66, 68-9, 70, 71, 142,
  150, 153
  see also Shiraz
syrups 501
Szekszárd 123

T
Tabernash brewery, US 379, 385
Taddy Porter 238
Tafel Lager 340
Tall Ships 250
Talleros 311, 312
Tally Ho 238
Tāmalioasă (g) 129
Tambour 332
tangerines: Mandarine
  Napoléon 463
Tanglefoot 238

Tannat (g) 74, 75, 155
tannin 13
Taranaki Draught 362
Tarragona 99
Tarrango (g) 167
Tartu brewery, Estonia 313
  Olu 311, 313
Tarwebok 281
Tas 317
Tasmania 166, 177
tasting wine 12–13
Tatran 317
Taurasi 92
Tavel 66
Tavira 107
Taylor brewery, England 231, 244
Teacher's 431
Tecate 388, 389
Temperance movement 410
Tempranillo (g) 95, 98–101, 150
Tennent's brewery, Scotland 206,
  249, 251
Tennessee whiskey 434–5
Tequila 422–3
  Margarita 423, 445
  Parkeroo 495
  Tequila and Orange 422
  Tequila Sunrise 423
Terken brewery, France 325,
  327, 329
Teroldego 87
Terra Alta 98
Terry's 446
Tetley brewery, England 238, 244
Texas 145
Thai Amarit, Bangkok 351
The Ghillie 249
Theakston brewery, England 235,
  238, 244
Thessaly 125
Thomas Hardy brewery,
  England 244
Thomas Hardy's Ale 238
Thomas Kemper brewery, US 371,
  374, 378, 379, 385
Thongue, Côtes de 78–9
Thrace 125
Three Coins brewery, Colombo,
  Sri Lanka 351
Three Sieges 239
Thurn and Taxis brewery,
  Germany 300
Thwaites brewery, England 230,
  239, 244
Ti Punch 418
Tia Maria 458, 482
  Black Russian 482
  Sunburn 482
Tibouren (g) 68
Ticino 122
Tientan Beer 345
Tiger Best Bitter 239
Tiger Classic 351
Tignanello 93
Timmermans brewery, Belgium
  265, 277
Timothy Taylor's brewery,
  England 233
Tinners Ale 239
Tinta Barocca (g) 160
Tinta Negra Mole (g) 110, 487
Tinto de Toro (g) 97
Tinto Fino (g) 97
Tipo Munich 389
Tirol Export Lager 304
Titje 272
Toby 239
Tocai Friulano 88
Tokaji (Tokay) 123
Tokay-Pinot Gris (g) 51
Tolly Cobbold brewery, England
  239, 245
Tolly's Strong Ale 239
Tom Hoskins Porter 239
Tom Kelley 259
Tomintoul brewery, Scotland
  249, 251
Tomlinson brewery, England 239
Tomos Watkin brewery, Wales
  220, 222, 224

Tongerlo 272
Toni-Kola 397
tonic water 500–1
Tooheys brewery, Australia 354,
  355, 358
Tooth's brewery, Australia 354,
  355, 358
Top Dog Stout 239
Top Hat 239
Topazio 336
Topsy-Turvy 239
Torgiano 91
Toro 96–7
Torres winery 401
Torrontés (g) 96, 149, 150, 151
Touraine 40, 42-3
Tourtel 327, 329
Tovarich 459
T'owd Tup 239
Traditional Ale 239
Traditional Bitter 239
Traditional Brewing Company,
  Australia 353, 354, 358
Traditional English Ale 194, 239
Traditional Welsh Ale 222
Trafalgar Pale Ale 359
Trajadura (g) 105
Trapper Lager 367
Trapper's Red Beer 362
Trappistine 482
Traquair House brewery, Scotland
  247, 248, 249, 251
Trebbiano (g) 83, 87, 90, 91, 92
Trebbiano d'Abruzzo 91
Treixadura (g) 96
Trelawny's Pride 239
Trentino-Aldo Adige 87
Tressot (g) 60
Tricastin, Coteaux de 67
Triple Bock 379
Triple Diamond 249
Triumphator 294
Trois Monts 327
Trollinger (g) 113, 116
Tropical Cocktail 464
Troublette 274
Trousseau (g) 76
True Bock 367
Trumer 304, 305
Tsingtao brewery, China 344, 345
Tuborg brewery, Denmark
  253, 254
Tui 362
Tulbagh 162
Tullamore Dew 436
Tume 311, 313
Tunisia 131
Turbo Dog 379
Turkey: Mersin 465
  wine 29, 127
Tursan 75
Tuscany 84, 89–90
Tusker 340
Twelve Horse Ale 379, 382
Twenty Tank Brewpub, US 385
Tynllidiart Arms Brewpub,
  Wales 224

U
U Fleku brewery, Czech
  Republic 319
Uehara Micro-brewery, Japan 349
Ueli Micro-brewery,
  Switzerland 332
Uerige brewery, Germany 300
Ugni Blanc (g) 75, 158, 400, 401
Ukraine 129
Ukrainskoe (Ukrainian) 311, 312
Uley brewery, England 235
Ulster brewery, Ireland
  215, 217
Umbel Ale 239
Umbria 91
Underberg 397
Unertl brewery, Germany 301
Uniao Cervejeira (Unicer),
  Portugal 336
Unibroue Micro-brewery, Canada
  365, 366, 367, 369
Unic Bier 272
Unicorn brewery, England
  232, 235

Union brewery, Belgium 267
Cervecera 335
United Kingdom: gin 409–10
wine 118–19
United States: applejack 405
beer 370–85
brandy 402–3
Southern Comfort 479
whisky 433–5
wine 136–7
see also California; New York;
Oregon; Texas; Washington
Unstrut 117
Upper Canada Brewing Company,
Canada 367, 369
Upstaal 327, 329
Ur-Krostitzer 294
Ur-Weisse 294
Uralt 401
Uran Pils 317
Urbock 304
Ureich Pils 294
Urfrankisch Dunkel 294
Urpin brewery, Slovakia 317
Urstoff 294
Urtyp Pilsner 281
Uruguay 155
Us Heit brewery, Netherlands
279, 283
Ushers brewery, England 231,
234, 239, 245
Utiel-Requena 100
Uva di Troia (g) 92

V
Vaakuna 261
Vaccari, Arturo 454
Vaclav 317
Vacqueyras 66
Vaita 363
Val d'Arbia 90
Val de Salnes 96
Valais, the 122
Valdeorras 96
Valdepeñas 100
Valencia 100–1
Valiant 239
Valkenburgs Wits 281
Valle d'Aosta 86
Vallée de la Marne 47
Vallet 40
Valpolicella 82, 87, 88
Valtellina 86
Van der Hum 483
Sundowner 483
Van Ecke brewery, Belgium
268, 271
Van Honsebrouck brewery,
Belgium 265, 269
Van Steenberge brewery, Belgium
265, 270
Van Vollenhoven Stout 281
Vander Linden brewery, Belgium
268, 277
Vandervelden brewery,
Belgium 270
Vapeur brewery, Belgium
266, 271
Varois, Coteaux 69
Varsity 239
Vaud, the 122
Vaux brewery, England 230, 245
Veltins brewery, Germany 301
Veneto 87–8
Venezuela 148, 155
Venloosch Alt 281
Ventoux, Côtes du 67
Verboden Vrucht 269, 272
Verdejo (g) 97
Verdelho 111, 487
Verdicchio (g) 91
Verdicchio dei Castelli di Jesi 91
Verdicchio di Matelica 91
Vermentino (g) 69, 86
Vermouth 496–9
Adonis 495
Bamboo 499
Bronx 497
Dry Martini 411
Grand Slam 475
Manhattan 433
Merry Widow 496

Perfect Cocktail 497
Pick-Me-Up 461
Rose 413
Sherry Cocktail 495
Tropical Cocktail 464
Whip 452
Vernaccia di Oristano 93
Vernaccia di San Gimignano 90
Verveine du Vélay 483
Vice Beer 239
Victoria 135, 165, 166, 174–5,
177, 335
Victoria Avenue Amber Ale 379
Victoria Bitter 355
Victory Ale 239
Victory Bitter 359
Vidal (g) 146
Vieille Curé, La, 483
Vieille Cuvée 269
Vieille Provision 272, 274, 275
Vienna (Wien) 121
Vieux Temps 272
Vigneronne 272
Viking 239
Viking brewery, Iceland 263
Bjor 263
Vilana (g) 126
Vilanova, Arnaldo de 456
Village Bitter 239
Villány 123
vin de paille 76
vin jaune 76
Vin de Pays d'Oc 70, 78, 79
Vin de Pays du Jardin de la France
43, 78
vin jaune 76
Vin Santo 90
Vinedale Breweries, Hyderabad,
India 351
Vinho Verde 82, 104–5
Vins doux naturels Muscats 490
Viognier (g) 64, 70, 79, 139, 142
Viosinho (g) 109
Virginia 145
Viru brewery, Estonia 313
Vita Stout 362
Viura (g) 95, 96, 97
Vivarais, Côtes du 67
vodka 424–7
Alexander the Great 458
Balalaika 427, 445
Barbara 427
Black Cossack 427
Black Russian 425, 458, 482
Bloody Mary 426
Czarina 427
Golden Tang 480
Harvey Wallbanger 454
Katinka 427
Moscow Mule 426
Piranha 425
Rite of Spring 452
Screwdriver 426
Tovarich 459
Vodkatini 425
White Russian 425
Volkoren Kerst 281
Voll-Damm 334
Vollmond 332
Volnay 58, 59
Vosne-Romanée 56
Vougeot 56
Vouvray 42–3
Vranik 317

W
Wachau 121
Wachenheim 116
Wadworth brewery, England 231,
234, 240, 245
Waggle Dance 206, 239
Waiheke Island 181
Waikato Draught 363
Wairarapa 182
Wales 119
Walker, Hiram 436, 437
Walker Bay 162
Wallace IPA 249
Wallop 239
Wally 461
Walnut Whip 467
walnuts, nut liqueurs 466–7

Ward's brewery, England 206,
239, 245
Ward's brewery, N.Z. 363
Warninks 440
Warstein brewery, Germany 294
Warsteiner 209, 294
Warszawski brewery, Poland
307, 308
Wartek brewery, Switzerland 332
Warthog Ale 367
Washington State 143–4
Wassaill 239
Wassaill Winter Ale 379
Water 500
Waterloo Dark 367
Watneys brewery, England 245
Waverley 70/- 249
Weihenstephan brewery, Germany
290, 301
Weihnachtsbock 304
Weiselburger 304
Weissburgunder (g) 113, 117
Weitzen's Feast 261
Weizen Gold 304
Weizenberry 379
Weizenhell 294
Wel Scotch 327
Wellington County brewery,
Canada 365, 367, 369
Wells brewery, England 228, 230,
231, 245
Welschriesling (g) 120,
121, 123
Welsh Bitter 220, 222
Welsh Brewers, Wales 224
Werner Brau. 321, 322
West End 355
West Flanders brewery 188
West Indies 418
West Lake Beer 345
Western Samoa Breweries 363
Westmalle brewery, Belgium 212,
272, 277
Westvleteren brewery, Belgium
212, 272, 277
Wetzlar brewery, Germany 288
Wheat Berry Row 379
Wherry Best Bitter 240
Whip 452
whisky 428–37
Bunny Hug 471
Manhattan 433
Old-Fashioned 434
Pink Almond 467
Rusty Nail 430, 453
Saracen 455
Southern Comfort 479
Whisky Mac 430
Whisky Sour 436
see also Bourbon
Whistle Belly Vengeance 240
Whitbread brewery, England 231,
240, 245
Whitbread brewery, Wales 224

Whitbread Mackeson 211
Whitby brewery, England
235, 239
White Dolphin 240
White Horse 431
White Lady 409, 445
White Russian 425
Whitewater brewery, Ireland
216, 217
Whyte & Mackay 431
Wickwar brewery, England 228,
229, 236
Widmer brewery, US 385
Wiecske Witte 281, 283
Wien see Vienna
Wieselburg brewery, Austria 304
Wild Cat 249
Wild Goose Micro-brewery, US
378, 385
Wild Turkey 434
Willfort 327
Williams, Evan 434
Willie Warmer 240
Willpower Stout 363
Wilmot's Premium 240
Wiltshire Traditional Bitter 240
Wiltz brewery, Lux. 285
Windhoek 340
Wine, Kir 449
Winter Royal 240
Winter Warmer 240
Wisconsin 383
Wisniowka 426
Witkap 272
Witte Raaf 281
Witzgal Vollbier 294
Wobbly Bob 240
Wolverhampton & Dudley
Breweries, England 245
Wood brewery, England
237, 245
Wood's Navy Rum 419
Woodeforde's brewery, England
234, 240, 245
Woodhouse, John 488
Worcester (SA) 162
wormwood: absinthe 470–1
vermouth 496
Worthington brewery,
England 245
beers 222, 240
Wrasslers XXXX Stout 216
Wrexham Lager Beer Company,
Wales 225
Wuhrer brewery, Italy 320, 321
Wunster brewery, Italy 322
Württemberg 116
Würzig 294
Wuxing brewery, China 345
Wychwood brewery, England 232
Wye Valley brewery, England 240

X
Xarel-lo (g) 99, 100
Xibeca 334
Xingu 388
XL Old Ale 240
XXX 240
XXXB Ale 240
XXXX Mild 240
Xynisteri (g) 126, 127
Xynomavro (g) 125

Y
Yakima brewery, US 372, 374,
377, 385
Yarra Valley 175
Yates Bitter 240
yeast 187, 198-9
Yebisu 348, 349
Yecla 101
Yellow Mongrel 355
Yellow Parrot 470
Young Pretender 249
Young's brewery, England 235,
236, 240, 245
Younger's brewery, Scotland
249, 251
Yperman 272
Yucatan brewery, Mexico 388
Yuengling brewery, US
373, 385

Z
Z 348
Zagorka brewery, Bulgaria 313
Zambesi 340
Zamek 317
Zaragozana brewery, Spain
334, 335
Zatec brewery, Czech Republic
316, 317, 318
Zatecka Desitka 317
Zatte 281
Zhigulevskoe (Zhiguli) 311, 312
Zierfandler (g) 120
Zinfandel (g) 83, 138, 139, 141,
142, 154, 161
Zip City Brewpub, US 385
Zipfer brewery, Austria
304, 305
Zlaty Bazant brewery, Slovakia
317, 319
Zombie 420
Zubrowka 426
Zum Schlüssel brewery, Germany
289, 301
Zweigelt (g) 120, 121
Zwettl Brewers 318
Zywiec brewery, Poland 307, 308

2XS 240
3B 240
4X 240
4X Stout 215
6X 240
7th Street Stout 379
"33" 327
1066 240
1857 Bitter 355
1857 Pilsner 355

Acknowledgements
With the exception of sources noted,
all photographs for pp 6–9 and
28–183 by Mick Rock/Cephas
Picture Library. Other Cephas
photographs: Aviemore Photography:
pp6, 9; Kevin Argue: p146; Nigel
Blythe: pp37t, 54b, 79b,113,114,
115b, 131b; Andy Christodolo:
pp125t, 135b, 149t, 150, 151, 166,
176, 169, 171, 175, 179b, 180, 182;
David Copeman: pp110, 111; Jeff
Drewitz: p176; Rick England: pp153,
154; Juan Espi: pp157, 160, 161r;
Andrew Jefford: p130; Kevin Judd:
pp179r, 183; MJ Kielty: p53b; Lars-
Olof Nilsson: p123t; Alain Proust:
pp158, 159, 16l, 162, 163t; John
Rizzop: p147; Ted Stefanski: pp134t,
135t, 140b; Peter Stowell: p88; Helen
Stylianou: p126; Mike Taylor: p131t.
The publishers would also like to
thank Brian Glover for images from
his archive; Axiom Photographic
Agency: pp187bl, 347br; The Beer
Cellar and Co. Ltd: p272b; Bruce
Coleman Picture Library: p300tr;
Eddie Parker:p152; Edifice: pp196b,
348b, 359t; ET Archive: pp198b,
321b; Greg Evans Photo Library:
pp188b, 312, 391b; Mary Evans
Picture Library: pp187t, 195t, 199b;
John Freeman: pp 197t, 241b;
German Wine Information Service:
p116; Guinness Archives: pp218tr,
219tr; Jane Hughes: pp28t, 34b, 109b,
137b, 139, 141, 142; Jayawardene
Travel Photography Library: pp308t,
339, 358b; Morris & Verdin p210t
(Robert Wheatcroft); Patrick Eager:
p163b; Peter Newark's Historical
Pictures: pp219tl and tc, 243t, 244bl,
245br, 293tr; Peter Newark's Western
Americana: pp379b, 385br; Ann
Ronan: p201b; Sopexa (UK) Ltd:
p62t; South American Pictures: p 155;
Wines of Chile: p149; Trip Photographic Library: pp194t (C. Treppe),
255br (R. Powers), 310, 311, 313t (T.
Noorits), 313b (I. Burgandinov), 343
(D. Saunders), 389b (R. Belbin); Zefa
Pictures: pp186, 189t and b, 196tl,
199t, 200, 293tl and b.